ROMANCE TODAY

In loving memory of our friend,
Natalie Abbott

Contents

Library of Congress Cataloging-in-Publication Data

Romance today: an A-to-Z guide to contemporary American romance writers/edited by John
Charles and Shelley Mosley; Joanne Hamilton-Selway and Sandra Van Winkle, associate editors;
foreword by Kristin Ramsdell.
     p. cm.
  Includes bibliographical references and index.
  ISBN 0–313–32841–2 (alk. paper)
  1. Love stories, American—Bio-bibliography. 2. Authors, American—20th century—
Biography—Dictionaries. I. Charles, John, 1962- II. Mosley, Shelley, 1950- III. Hamilton-Selway,
Joanne. IV. Van Winkle, Sandra.
  PS374.L6R66   2007
  813'.08509—dc22
  [B]   2006027918

British Library Cataloguing in Publication Data is available.

Library of Congress Catalog Card Number: 2006027918
ISBN: 0–313–32841–2

First published in 2007

Greenwood Press, 88 Post Road West, Westport, CT 06881
An imprint of Greenwood Publishing Group, Inc.
www.greenwood.com

Printed in the United States of America

The paper used in this book complies with the
Permanent Paper Standard issued by the National
Information Standards Organization (Z39.48–1984).

10   9   8   7   6   5   4   3   2   1

ROMANCE TODAY

An A-to-Z Guide to
Contemporary American Romance Writers

Edited by John Charles and Shelley Mosley

Joanne Hamilton-Selway and Sandra Van Winkle, Associate Editors

Foreword by Kristin Ramsdell

GREENWOOD PUBLISHERS

Westport, Connecticut • London

FOREWORD

Despite the persistent, unparalleled popularity of the romance fiction genre, good biographical information for its authors is neither abundant nor easily accessible. To be sure, there is plenty of such information available for writers of historical significance (e.g., Jane Austen, the Brontës, and more recently, Daphne du Maurier and Georgette Heyer); however, similar information for current or lesser-known romance authors is much more limited. General sources such as *Contemporary Authors* include biobibliographical information on some of the more prominent romance authors; however, the few available sources that specifically target romance authors are either dated or limited in their coverage. For example, *Twentieth Century Romance and Historical Writers,* 3rd ed., is more than a decade old and focuses primarily on British writers. *North American Romance Writers, 1985–1995,* edited by Kay Mussell and Johanna Tunon, though more current, includes essays from only 50 writers.

Fortunately, *Romance Today: An A-to-Z Guide to Contemporary American Romance Writers* goes a long way toward remedying this situation. Picking up where *Twentieth Century Romance and Historical Writers* leaves off, this source combines features of both books mentioned above, providing both biographical and up-to-date bibliographical information for more than 100 American romance writers. Carefully chosen for both the quality of their work and their prominence in the field, the authors included, as a whole, write across the full spectrum of the romance genre, ensuring that the rich and endless variety of romance fiction is well represented. The informative biobibliographic essays included are not only insightful but also distinctively unique in that they are based on statements provided by the romance authors, who then recheck the finished essays for accuracy. Current, well researched, comprehensive, and diverse, this much-needed reference source will be welcomed by readers, writers, librarians, and researchers alike.

Kristin Ramsdell

PREFACE

PURPOSE

Nathaniel Hawthorne once said, "Easy reading is damned hard writing." For anyone who believes that penning a romance is easy or that anyone can do it, think again. One of the things we hope to do with the publication of *Romance Today: An A-to-Z Guide to Contemporary American Romance Writers* is to dispel the numerous misperceptions that continue to plague the romance genre, including the myth that all romance writers are alike. Many people still think of Dame Barbara Cartland, with her pink, fluffy fashion sense, or Meryl Streep's frilly, frothy character in *She Devil* as the "typical" romance novelist, and with models like this, it is easy for critics to dismiss the entire genre. But in reality, all romance novelists are not alike, as readers of this reference source will quickly discover. Among the authors featured in this book are a retired colonel, a physician, a UNESCO artist, librarians, college professors, a translator for the Chinese government, a demographer for the United Nations, and even a former nun—strong, accomplished women (and a few men) who write romance fiction because of their love of the genre.

Romance Today is meant to serve as a resource for researchers, librarians, and readers who want to know more about a particular author. While it is true that the Internet has brought new opportunities for romance authors to connect with their readers through the creation of their own Web pages—and thus for readers to learn more about their favorite authors—the ephemeral nature of these very Web pages means that information about many of these authors is lost when the Web pages no longer exist. *Romance Today* is our humble attempt to preserve the significant literary contributions of some of today's outstanding romance authors for posterity.

SCOPE

In 2005, more than 2,000 romances were published, and there are currently more than 1,600 published romance authors in the United States. Narrowing down the field of authors to consider for this reference book to a select few proved to be quite a challenge. Librarians with expertise in the romance genre were asked whom they would feature in a biocritical dictionary of romance authors. A final list, which had 250 names on it, was assembled from this individually compiled effort. A realistic word count limit for the book prohibited us from including all the names selected by the genre experts, so from this master roster, a little more than 100 authors were invited to participate in this project. A few authors declined to take part—the main reason being fear of identity theft. For this same reason, a handful of authors asked that we use only their pseudonyms, but that was the exception rather than the rule. Since the authors included in this resource are still living, the amount of personal information they chose to share was left entirely to their discretion. Thus, some essays contain more biographical details than others.

The authors chosen for this book reflect the diversity of the romance genre itself and had to meet several criteria, including the following:

- The author was still living at the time her or his essay was written.
- The author is a citizen or long-term resident of the United States.
- The author has written at least five romance novels, the last of which was published no earlier than 2002.
- At least one of the author's books was nominated for, was a finalist in, or won awards within the genre (such as the Romance Writers of America's RITA); has appeared on national best seller lists (such as the *New York Times* or *USA Today*); or has made a significant contribution to the field.

Most of this book is based on primary-source information—the authors themselves. The authors answered a lengthy questionnaire, which served as the basis of each essay. Follow-up correspondence or interviews with the authors themselves produced more information. Their books were read and analyzed. After each essay was written, it was sent to the author to verify its accuracy. No essay has been included in this work without author approval. A small, select number of secondary sources, such as authors' Web sites and other critical sources, were also consulted to add additional depth to individual essays.

ORGANIZATION OF THE BOOK AND HOW TO USE IT

- The essays are arranged alphabetically by author's name or pseudonym.
- Works are listed chronologically by date of publication under the author's name or pseudonym and then by format (books, novellas, genre-related essays). Lists are separated by pseudonym or name, with the author's most famous appellation appearing first.
- Reprints and reissues are not included.
- Because of space considerations, series titles are not included in the lists of works cited but may be mentioned within the essays.
- Each essay includes an analysis of several of the author's significant works as well as an overall view of the style and theme prevalent in his or her oeuvre.
- While each entry is signed by its principal essayist(s), this was truly a collaborative effort, and *all* the essays have had input in one form or another from *multiple* members of the team.

So, with all of that being said, *Romance Today* offers only a sampling of the literary riches contained within the wonderful world of the romance genre. Our hope is that this work will serve as an inspiration for further exploration of this long-neglected area of popular American fiction.

ACKNOWLEDGMENTS

First and foremost, the authors would like to thank the ever gracious Jayne Ann Krentz, not only for her support of this project, but also for her lasting, ongoing contributions to the romance genre. In addition, the following have our undying gratitude:

The multitalented Kristin Ramsdell, for sharing her extraordinary knowledge of the genre with us.

The hard-working, tireless staff of Romance Writers of America, for their wonderful assistance.

The talented and versatile authors represented in this work, for their willingness to share both their lives and their insights about the romance genre.

The visionary Lynn Araujo, the editor who proposed this project in the first place.

The incredibly patient George Butler, the editor who guided this book to its completion.

Donna Seaman, *Booklist* editor extraordinaire, who in her own quiet and generous way, has provided much encouragement.

The incomparable Jennie Burrell, for the many hours she devoted to this project.

Our individual families, who tolerated this interruption in our lives together with grace and a good sense of humor. Thank you, David, Jessica, Andy, Jennifer, Vicki, Ida, Bill, Ryan, Monica, Cody, and Peter.

Our spoiled cats, Ada, Pascal, Oreo, Blackberry, Peppermint, eBay, Toast, and Speedy, who refused any interruption.

And of course, Mr. Big, not a cat, but almost as small and demanding.

SHANA ABÉ

Shana Abé. Courtesy of Shana Abé.

For RITA finalist Shana Abé, it's all about connection. She believes the reason romance has been civilization's most enduring theme of artistic expression is "because everyone, either openly or secretly, in their heart of hearts, craves that ultimate connection to another soul." Abé's richly detailed, emotionally engrossing novels definitely play a part in keeping her readers well connected.

Abé hadn't always aspired to become a writer. Growing up in rural Texas in the late 1960s and early 1970s, when the space program was in the forefront of national attention, Abé decided to become an astronaut. She soon discovered that the required math "spoiled the fun," and she turned her attention to the arts. Her family moved to Colorado when she was 12, and she later attended the University of Southern California in Los Angeles, earning a bachelor's degree in fine arts. Abé's father, who is now retired, worked in sales. Her mother is one of the top public school administrators in the country.

Abé worked at a number of jobs, including stints as a hot dog vendor and cocktail waitress. For her, the most interesting position she held was that of professional model. She was able to travel extensively for 11 years, and for some of that time she lived and modeled in Japan.

Abé always enjoyed reading romances, so that genre seemed to be the natural choice when deciding where to apply her writing talent. She describes her style as "a little dark," but more importantly, "deeply emotional." To Abé, "the emotional connection of the characters is always paramount. If the reader isn't fully able to empathize with the hero/heroine, the story is a failure."

Abé enjoys the creative process of writing: "tapping into something bigger than I, a universal consciousness." She believes that writers are conduits for that process. Her advice for writer's block, or those times when the motivation to write isn't there, is to simply play hooky for a while. Abé follows her own advice, "but eventually I get back to work." Abé adds, "You have to, as a writer. No one else is going to finish that book for you."

Abé prefers not to dwell very long on the source of her inspiration: "I'm afraid to think about it too much." Her story ideas seem to "materialize from different directions every time," although rarely does a single character inspire the story. Sometimes, one sentence or an entire situation comes to mind that grows into a plot idea. "It's always changing," Abé observes. One of her story ideas, which would later develop into *The Truelove Bride* (1999), arose from a Scottish legend in which a man's clan would be cursed if he didn't marry a warrior maiden.

For her books, Abé's favorite locale is the lush landscape of Great Britain. She has even conjured some remote and mysterious islands of her own around Scotland. Abé uses a number of different settings in her novels, beginning with her medievals, but she admits that she is particularly fascinated with eighteenth-century Scotland and enjoys doing the research necessary to make the descriptions of her settings as accurate as possible. Her 2004 novel *The Last Mermaid* employs three linked stories that take place in different time periods—the Dark Ages, the eighteenth century, and present day—and in two very different locales—Scotland and Los Angeles. As a result, Abé cites this novel as her most "challenging undertaking."

Abé's heroes and heroines are all basically honorable characters, even though it may not always be evident in their behavior. No clinging females for this author—her heroines are resourceful, independent, daring, and intelligent. Abé writes many of her own personality traits into her characters, even the villains, to give them an "emotional sincerity" that can only stem from the writer. "If you don't truly understand the characters you create, you're just cheating," she says.

Abé considers her 2000 novel *A Kiss at Midnight,* part of the Meet Me at Midnight series, her most difficult to write because it needed to be completed in only six months. This unique take on Y2K paranoia moves the action to Y1K, the year 1000, where a certain Doomsday is also feared. Salvation will only come, according to ancient divination, if Rafael of Leonhart takes Alderich from the Rune family. Rafael kidnaps Serath Rune, the granddaughter of the Lord of Alderich, thinking that the old man will gladly exchange his lands for the return of Serath. Rafael couldn't be more wrong. The Lord of Alderich not only doesn't care for Serath but also had her mother burned as a witch. Eventually, Rafael comes to realize that although Serath is useless as a bargaining chip, she's his true soul mate, worth more to him than any piece of land. Full of action and textured, multilayered characters, this beguiling book keeps the reader guessing until the very end.

According to Abé, the easiest novel for her to write was 1999's *The Truelove Bride,* which she started while on tour in Scotland. Abé recalls, "The whole story just flowed through me like a dream." Lady Avalon d'Farouche, the heroine of this book, is psychic. She knows what everyone around her is thinking. In fact, she can even feel what they feel. Her gift isn't limited to humans—it extends to animals. Lady Avalon has more than extrasensory powers to make her special. She's also a brave warrior maiden, willing to put her life on the line for what she believes. Sir Marcus Kincardine, a courageous veteran of the Crusades, feels that he is obligated to marry Avalon to fulfill a prophecy born of an old family legend.

Unfortunately, the villain of the piece, Bryce d'Farouche, Avalon's guardian, has nefarious plans for his ward and her psychic powers. This bewitching tale of twelfth-century England showcases Abé's ability to create unforgettable characters and place them in a setting so finely detailed that it, too, almost becomes a character in its own right.

While Abé describes each of the novels she has written as having a "special, memorable quality of its own," *A Rose in Winter* (1998) is her "sentimental favorite" because it was her first published book, loosely based on her own love story with her husband. In this novel, Damon Wolf and Lady Solange pledge themselves to one another at a young age. However, in order to please King Edward, Solange's wealthy father expects her to wed the ruthless, cold-blooded alchemist, Lord Redmond, and threatens to kill Damon if she refuses. After eight years in a brutal, unbearable marriage, Solange is visited by Damon, who tells her that her father has died. When she convinces Damon to help her escape, the book morphs into a compelling adventure, full of twists and turns. This stunning, sensual debut novel set the standard for Abé's next medieval historicals.

Intimate Enemies (2000) is Abé's tale of Romeo and Juliet: "bittersweet but, of course, with a more gratifying ending." Both the heroine of the story, Lauren MacRae, and the hero, Arion du Morgan, are brave warriors, evenly matched in intelligence and courage. Lauren, as acting laird of her clan, forms a tentative alliance with Arion, a British earl, in order to keep the Viking invaders at bay. Even though she has developed feelings for Arion, Lauren's clan is forcing her to marry an abusive ogre of a man. Lauren finds herself not only fighting for her land but also for the man she has come to love. *Intimate Enemies* is an excellent example of Abé's brand of literary magic.

Abé and her husband, Darren, a physician of oriental medicine, live in Los Angeles. When she isn't writing romances, she enjoys other creative outlets, such as drawing and painting and tending to Banzai and Honey Belle, their pet house rabbits. Abé has also written and illustrated several children's stories for family and friends. Although none of these interests appear in her novels, she has used her rabbits' names as characters in her books.

A recurrent theme in Abé's compelling novels is "the triumph of love." She adds, "There is something fundamentally appealing in knowing that however deeply the plot twists, this man and this woman will end up together, and in love, no matter what." Abé feels that the appeal of the genre is the assurance of a happy ending and the uplifting hope the stories contain. Romance readers appreciate, understand, and celebrate it. "There's nothing wrong with hope," says Abé.

BIBLIOGRAPHY

Books: *The Promise of Rain.* New York: Bantam, 1998; *A Rose in Winter.* New York: Bantam, 1998; *The Truelove Bride.* New York: Bantam, 1999; *Intimate Enemies.* New York: Bantam, 2000; *A Kiss at Midnight.* New York: Bantam, 2000; *The Secret Swan.* New York: Bantam, 2001; *The Last Mermaid.* New York: Bantam, 2004; *The Smoke Thief.* New York: Bantam, 2005.

SHELLEY MOSLEY AND SANDRA VAN WINKLE

CHERRY ADAIR

One thing readers can count on in Cherry Adair's books is that strong, sexy, and honorable men will meet their match and find romance with strong, sexy, and determined women. Whether she is writing sizzling adventure novels or contemporary romances, Adair knows that there is nothing more appealing than watching a so-called alpha male being tamed by a woman who is his equal.

Adair was born in Cape Town, South Africa, to English parents who came to South Africa as teenagers and stayed. Eventually, the family settled in Cape Town near its prestigious university, which housed one of the finest music schools in South Africa. Adair's mother became a well-known opera singer, performing at both Covent Garden and La Scala. She met Adair's father, a magician, while rehearsing for the role of Mimi in *La Boheme* in Johannesburg. It was love at first sight, and they were married soon afterward. Four years and two children later, Adair's parents divorced. Eventually, Adair's mother found a new "happily ever after" ending with the man who would become Adair's stepfather.

Cherry Adair. Courtesy of Cherry Adair.

Adair attended the University of Cape Town, where she received a double degree in business administration and interior design. Living in South Africa during the apartheid years presented unique challenges for Adair, who was once suspected of subversive activities by the South African government. While in her twenties, Adair moved from South Africa to the United States. She worked as an interior designer in San Francisco and eventually opened her own design business in the Bay area. She met her husband in 1977, when he walked into her store looking for some wallpaper. It took just two weeks for her to realize that he was the only man for her. They married, and Adair became the proud stepmother of two new daughters.

Adair wanted to be a writer before she could even speak: "In fact, I would make stories, which I would tell my mother in enthusiastic gibberish. She would nod and smile, not understanding a word. But, bless her heart, she did understand *me* and always encouraged me to follow my heart." Adair wrote 17 full manuscripts before her dream of becoming a published author finally came true in 1994 when Harlequin bought Adair's book *The Mercenary* for their Temptation line. In *The Mercenary,* when T-FLAC (Terrorist Force Logistical Assault Command) operative Marc Savin's partner disappears while on a dangerous mission, Marc finds he must work with his partner's telepathic twin sister, Victoria "Tory" Jones, to find him. *The Mercenary* not only introduced readers to Adair's fictional antiterrorist agency, T-FLAC—which would play a role in her future romantic suspense novels and earn her a nomination for a Romance Writers of America RITA award—but also gave readers a wonderful taste of her distinctive blend of passion and danger.

With her next book, *Kiss and Tell* (2000), Adair built on the foundation she had established with *The Mercenary* as she fashioned another addictive tale of intrigue and romance. When the book's heroine, Marnie Wright, retreats to her beloved grandmother's cabin in the California woods to do a bit of quiet thinking about her future, she becomes tangled up in a dangerous, high-stakes game of espionage. Caught trespassing on property belonging to her neighbor, reclusive mountain man Jake Dolan, Marnie finds herself being whisked away for her own good into Jake's high-tech, state-of-the-art, security-protected cabin after she stumbles into the middle of a plot by men from Jake's past who are out to eliminate him. *Kiss and Tell,* a fast-paced tale of romantic suspense, expertly seasoned with a dash of Adair's sharp sense of humor, garnered her a second RITA nomination in 2001.

More literary adventures with the men of T-FLAC followed, as Adair detailed the sizzlingly sexy stories of Marnie Wright's four brothers, all T-FLAC operatives, in *Hide and Seek* (2001), *In Too Deep* (2002), *Out of Sight* (2003), and *On Thin Ice* (2004). Whether set in a remote corner of South America *(Hide and Seek),* a South Pacific island paradise *(In Too Deep),* the deserts of the Middle East *(Out of Sight),* or the frozen tundra of Alaska *(On Thin Ice),* each of these books features a refreshingly exotic locale. "My attention to detail and diligent research for just the right thing to use in my house has carried over into my writing," says Adair, who successfully translated her skills as an interior designer into her books through her vivid, realistically detailed settings.

Adair often spends a considerable amount of time researching the background and location of her books to get this wonderful sense of place. For her book *In Too Deep,* Adair created her own fictitious South Pacific locale, Paradise Island, but she used the extensive information she had gathered on Tahitian flora and fauna to give her island a vibrant sense of verisimilitude. In *On Thin Ice,* Adair's expertly evoked Alaskan setting and the grueling Iditarod race become integral parts of the story. Adair drew on her personal knowledge of South Africa to give her book *Hot Ice* (2005) its colorful locale, which, in its own way, becomes as much a character as the protagonists themselves. Even when she is creating a fictional setting, such as the villain's hideout in *Hot Ice,* which she cleverly based on Dante's seven circles of hell, Adair's attention to detail and dramatic imagination are evident.

Adair is known and loved by readers for her sexy, adrenaline-drenched novels of romantic adventure, but she also has a gift for writing laughter-laced, contemporary romance, such as her two books *Seducing Mr. Right* (2001) and *Take Me* (2002). In *Seducing Mr. Right,* the book's heroine, Catherine Harris, hopes to convince Luke Van Buren, the man she has had a crush on since they were both teenagers, to finally start noticing her as a woman and not a just a friend by asking him to give her some lessons on how to seduce Mr. Right. In *Take Me,* interior decorator Jessie Adams agrees to a marriage of convenience with business executive Joshua Falcon, but the one thing she has always wanted is a baby. Joshua refuses to consider her written requests for a child, so when Jessie tries meeting with him in person, she uses the fact that her husband doesn't recognize her as a means of trying to seduce him into giving her the baby she wants. With both of these books, Adair cleverly translates two of the romance genre's most popular themes—the childhood crush that blossoms into romance and the marriage of convenience that becomes a love match—into two sparkling and deeply emotional love stories, both of which were nominated for RITA awards.

"I'm a reader first and a writer second—I love seeing how the romance genre grows and changes with its readers. Women are standing up for themselves and getting voices— heroines reflect that pattern. It's a joy to read, and write, about strong women partnered with strong men," says Adair. For Adair's many fans, it's a match made in heaven.

BIBLIOGRAPHY

Books: *The Mercenary.* Toronto: Harlequin, 1994; *Kiss and Tell.* New York: Ballantine, 2000; *Seducing Mr. Right.* Toronto: Harlequin, 2001; *Hide and Seek.* New York: Ballantine, 2001; *Take Me.* Toronto: Harlequin, 2002; *In Too Deep.* New York: Ballantine, 2002; *Out of Sight.* New York: Ballantine, 2003; *On Thin Ice.* New York: Ballantine, 2004; *Hot Ice.* New York: Ballantine, 2005; *Edge of Danger.* New York: Ballantine, 2006; *Edge of Fear.* New York: Ballantine, 2006; *Edge of Darkness.* New York: Ballantine, 2006.

Novellas: "Dance with the Devil" in *Date with the Devil.* Toronto: Harlequin, 2004; "Playing for Keeps" in *Dare Me.* New York: Signet, 2005; "Snowball's Chance" in *Red Hot Santa.* New York: Ballantine, 2006.

JOHN CHARLES

REGAN ALLEN. *See* Regina Scott

CATHERINE ANDERSON

Deafness, spousal abuse, and divorce—these are subjects many romance writers would not even consider using in a book. Author Catherine Anderson is different. She has not only dealt with these subjects in her historical and contemporary romances, but has also done so in an emotionally eloquent, impressively honest way that has earned her the admiration and love of millions of readers.

Anderson was born and raised in Grants Pass, Oregon, and the desire to write was a part of her life from early on. Anderson's mother was a writer, giving her love of the written word and storytelling to her daughter, who grew up listening to the sound of her mother typing away on an Underwood typewriter. This inspired Anderson to write her own stories for her dolls, and she later began putting her thoughts into words on whatever source of paper might be nearby.

Although Anderson married young, she always found time for her writing, even if no one else saw her finished work. Even when she was writing solely for her own pleasure, Anderson dreamed of someday becoming a published author, but realistically, she knew how difficult the process could be. So putting her hopes for a career as a writer on hold, Anderson pursued a more practical path when she decided to attend college in her early thirties. Anderson initially chose to major in accounting, believing it would provide her with skills that would be useful to her husband's business career. While she excelled at the uncreative subject of math, she found no joy in it. When a professor asked her to use some examples of her creative writing in class, Anderson was inspired to rethink her career path. Anderson nervously asked her husband if he would mind her dropping her accounting classes and leaving college to pursue her desire to become a writer. Her always-supportive husband immediately bought Anderson an electric typewriter of her own.

For Anderson, the path to her first published book was not quick or easy, but her perseverance eventually paid off. At that time Harlequin was looking for new writers for its Intrigue line, so she submitted a manuscript. Her first book, *Reasonable Doubt,* was published by Harlequin as part of its Intrigue series in 1989. *Reasonable Doubt* was followed by three more books for the Intrigue series—*Without a Trace* (1989), *Switchback* (1990), and *Cry of the Wild* (1992)—which helped give Anderson a track record as a published author in the romance genre. Even though her first four books were written within the structure of the Intrigue line, they bear the marks of Anderson's own style and interests. *Switchback* and *Without a Trace* take place in the Pacific Northwest, a setting that is special to the author, while the Alaskan wilderness setting of *Cry of the Wild* reflects Anderson's love of wild places.

After writing four contemporary novels in a series, Anderson felt the need to branch out to longer, single-title romances. After studying the romance market at that time, she found that Native American romances were very popular with readers. Because Anderson had never come across a romance featuring Comanche characters, she decided to use this Native American tribe as inspiration for her first historical romance. A scarcity of materials on the subject meant that Anderson would spend four years researching the Comanches before she had enough information to write convincingly about the subject. Anderson fell in love with her subject while doing the background research for *Comanche Moon,* and in a twist of fate, she would discover years later that she had her own connection with the Comanches: Anderson is part Shoshone, the tribe from which the Comanches first broke away.

Comanche Moon, published in 1991, is the story of Hunter, a Comanche warrior who travels across the western wilderness seeking the "honey-haired woman" who will fulfill his tribe's sacred prophecy. Loretta Simpson, the woman Hunter seeks, wants nothing to do with the Comanches, a tribe that had brutally murdered her parents. When Loretta is taken prisoner by Hunter, she tries to resist her captor, only to find that her destiny is with him. *Comanche Moon* led to four more historicals focused on the Comanches—*Comanche Heart* (1991), *Indigo Blue* (1992), *Comanche Magic* (1994), and *Cheyenne Amber* (1994)—all of which feature a Native American hero or heroine.

Anderson's book *Coming Up Roses* (1993) was another historical romance, but it signaled another change for the author since this book had no Native American connections. In this award-winning romance, the author deals beautifully and sensitively with the topic of spousal abuse, as an abused wife, with the help of the hero, regains her sense of worth and value. *Coming Up Roses* would be followed by three more historicals: *Annie's Song* (1996), *Keegan's Lady* (1996), and *Simply Love* (1997).

Annie's Song is one of the author's most popular books, but it was one of the most difficult for her to write. The heroine, Annie Trimble, is deaf and misunderstood by the people in her town, who think of her as the "idiot girl." When Alex Montgomery discovers that his younger brother forced his attentions on Annie, Montgomery offers to marry her out of guilt and to give the child she carries his name, only to find that he falls in love with the beautiful, innocent woman once they are married. Until she began writing a book with a deaf heroine, Anderson says she never realized how much she "used the sense of hearing to enhance descriptions and flesh out scenes." According to Anderson, "It was like trying to write a book with one hand tied behind my back."

With nine historical romances to her credit, Anderson needed a change, so she wrote her first single-title contemporary romance, *Forever After* (1998). The switch to a contemporary time frame provided a new challenge for Anderson, who subsequently returned to historical romances with *Cherish* (1998). Her next book, *Baby Love* (1999), another contemporary romance, introduced the Kendrick family to her readers. While writing Rafe Kendrick's story in *Baby Love,* Anderson became attached to the idea of writing about the character's younger brother, Ryan. After writing her next contemporary novel, *Seventh Heaven* (2000), Anderson convinced her editor to let her write *Phantom Waltz* (2001) so that she could focus on writing about the Kendrick family, and eventually, the Colter family.

Phantom Waltz once again proved Anderson's ability to deal sensitively with topics most writers would not dream of using in a romance. In *Phantom Waltz*, the heroine, Bethany Colter, is wheelchair bound after a barrel-racing accident. When her first lover abandons her after the accident, Bethany's family tries to protect her by keeping men away from her. When Ryan Kendrick first meets Bethany, he has no idea she uses a wheelchair and falls in love with her. Bethany and Ryan must deal with some difficult challenges as their romance develops, but the love they have for each other keeps them together.

All of Anderson's books, including her three contemporary romances *Sweet Nothings* (2002), *Always in My Heart* (2002), and *Only by Your Touch* (2003), reflect her interest in reading about genuine, hard-working people who have been battered and bruised by life, but who still search for love and happiness. Molly Wells, the heroine of *Sweet Nothings,* flees an abusive husband and finds a new life and new resources on Jake Coulter's ranch. The divorced husband and wife, Tucker and Ellie Grant, in *Always in My Heart* must put aside their differences when their two young boys run away into the wilderness. In *Only by Your Touch,* Chloe Evans bears the scars from a brutal divorce but tries to build a new life for herself and her son Jeremy, with the help of Ben Longtree.

Anderson is an author who loves to write. This comes across in her emotionally nourishing and poignant romances. Her ability to deftly blend sweetness and sensuality makes her stories worth treasuring.

BIBLIOGRAPHY

Books: *Reasonable Doubt.* Toronto: Harlequin, 1988; *Without a Trace.* Toronto: Harlequin, 1989; *Switchback.* Toronto: Harlequin, 1990; *Comanche Moon.* New York: Harper, 1991; *Comanche Heart.* New York: Harper, 1991; *Cry of the Wild.* Toronto: Harlequin, 1992; *Indigo Blue.* New York: Harper, 1992; *Coming Up Roses.* New York: Harper, 1993; *Comanche Magic.* New York: Harper, 1994; *Cheyenne Amber.* New York: Harper, 1994; *Annie's Song.* New York: Avon, 1996; *Keegan's Lady.* New York: Avon, 1996; *Simply Love.* New York: Avon, 1997; *Forever After.* New York: Avon, 1998; *Cherish.* New York: Avon, 1998; *Baby Love.* New York: Avon, 1999; *Seventh Heaven.* New York: Avon, 2000; *Phantom Waltz.* New York: Onyx, 2001; *Sweet Nothings.* New York: Onyx, 2002; *Always in My Heart.* New York: Signet, 2002; *Only by Your Touch.* New York: Signet, 2003; *Blue Skies.* New York: Signet, 2003; *Bright Eyes.* New York: Signet, 2004; *My Sunshine.* New York: Signet, 2005; *Summer Breeze.* New York: Signet, 2005; *Sun Kissed.* New York: Signet, 2005.
Novellas: "Shotgun Bride" in *Tall, Dark, and Dangerous.* New York: Harper, 1994; "Fancy Free" in *Three Weddings and a Kiss.* New York: Avon, 1995; "Beautiful Gifts" in *True Love Wedding Dress.* New York: Onyx, 2005.

JOHN CHARLES

JANE ANDERSON. *See* Jane Toombs

MARTHE ARENDS. *See* Katie MacAlister

JUDITH ARNOLD

Judith Arnold. Courtesy of Judith Arnold.

F rom the very beginning of her career, Judith Arnold has created characters who are survivors. Her heroes and heroines are not only single fathers and busy mothers, businesswomen and reporters, musicians and waitresses, but also a rape survivor, a cancer patient, and a traumatized Vietnam veteran—people who have experienced the trials and tribulations of the real world. At their core, her sharply defined characters are people who believe in a message of hope and optimism and refuse to accept defeat. They fight for what is good and right, and they triumph in the end.

Arnold was born in Brooklyn, New York, in 1953. Her father, an immigrant from Germany, arrived in the United States when he was seven years old. He served in World War II and later became a businessman. Arnold's mother was born in the United States and taught first grade. Arnold always wanted to be a writer, and before she could write, she would make up stories. While growing up on Long Island, New York, Arnold's sister taught her to read and write, and by the time Arnold was four, the world of books had opened up to her: "I can't remember a time when I wasn't creating stories and putting them into words."

Arnold attended Smith College, where she majored in music and graduated Phi Beta Kappa. While a sophomore, Arnold took a playwriting class and won a five-college playwriting

also writing as Ariel Berk
also writing as Thea Frederick

contest. The contest came with a sizable monetary prize, and Arnold thought, "Hey, I can make money writing plays." She continued her education at Brown University, where she received a master's degree in creative writing. After receiving her degree, she became an assistant professor of English and writing at California State University at Chico.

She spent the next decade pursuing a career as a playwright, while writing prose fiction on the side. Arnold's plays have been staged at the Eugene O'Neill Memorial Theater Center in Connecticut; the American Conservatory Theater in San Francisco; the New Playwrights Theater of Washington in Washington, D.C.; and various off-Broadway venues.

While working in the theater, Arnold learned that earning money as a playwright was not an easy thing: "By the time I reached my late twenties, I was burned out on the theater. Having to travel at my own expense to theaters around the country to work on scripts that might ultimately not receive full productions drained me. Even worse was having directors, actors, and producers all meddling with my words." She also became disenchanted with teaching: "I was tired of teaching 'bonehead English' (remedial freshman composition courses), rather than the literature and creative writing courses I had been trained to teach. I just wanted to burrow down in my office to write." In 1978, she was awarded a National Endowment for the Arts grant and quit teaching to write full-time. Arnold was unable to sell the three literary novels she had written during this time, so she "decided to try writing something more commercial."

In 1982, while Arnold was teaching at Sacred Heart University and Quinnipiac College, both in Connecticut, she read her first romance book. Arnold recalls the following:

> I'd read the novel as research—I was trying to find a commercial fiction genre I might be able to write—but loved the book and quickly read several more. Then I wrote two complete manuscripts, which I sent to two publishers. Both were rejected within three weeks (rejections used to come much more quickly in the early days!). I had met a literary agent through my playwriting agent, and he'd read the literary novels I had written and taken an interest in me. So, after receiving these quick rejections, I phoned him and asked if he'd have a look at the manuscripts. He considered one "promising" and sent it to Leslie Wainger at Silhouette. She said she couldn't buy it (it was too short, for one thing, and it contained elements that weren't considered suitable for romance fiction) but she sent me the four launch books for a new imprint called Desire, which Silhouette was about to introduce. I read those four Desires, wrote a book, and had my agent send it to Leslie in October of 1982. On February 7, 1983, (yes, I remember the date), she bought the book.

This book, the story of a single father of a handicapped child who willingly restructures his whole life around his daughter, was *Silent Beginnings,* and it was published under the pseudonym Ariel Berk by Silhouette.

Arnold's experience as a playwright proved to be indispensable to her new career as a romance novelist: "I'm often complimented on the realism and flow of my dialogue. Also, playwriting demands that the writer frames scenes and creates action, something the audience can see and hear." Her skill in creating believable characters and realistic dialogue in her first novel was evident, and it became obvious that the success of *Silent Beginnings* was no fluke. Arnold continued writing under the pseudonym of Ariel Berk and wrote 13 titles for Silhouette, including *Remedies of the Heart,* which was a finalist for the Romance Writers of America Golden Medallion Award (now the RITA) in 1985. In 1984, Arnold wrote one novel, *Beloved Adversary,* for Berkley under the name Thea Frederick. Arnold began writing as Judith Arnold for the first time for Harlequin with her book *Come Home to Love* (1985). By the 1990s, she used the Arnold name for all of her books, including *Safe Harbor,* a 1992 RITA finalist.

For Arnold, very few of her books came easily to her; she says most are a "real struggle" to write. Two titles, *Cry Uncle* (1995) and *The Wrong Bride* (1999) were particularly difficult, because, despite the fact that they were comedies, Arnold wrote them at especially dark times in her life: "*Cry Uncle* was written during a very strenuous period in my sister's battle with cancer, and *The Wrong Bride* was the first thing I wrote after she died. Needless to say, I was not in the mood to write comedies during those painful times, but somehow, I wrote the books. *The Wrong Bride* is one of my best-selling titles, and *Cry Uncle,* which also sold well, is often mentioned as a favorite by fans. I can barely bring myself to look at these books, though, because they remind me of what I was going through when I wrote them." Despite the personal traumas she endured while writing these books, Arnold managed to show her comedic side, beginning with the witty and wisecracking *The Wrong Bride.* In this sparkling contemporary romance, Phillip Keene and Cassie Webber talk about getting married, but Phillip leaves town and literally drops out of sight. When Cassie finds out that her former lover is engaged to someone else, she figures out a way to attend his wedding—with a camera crew. Revenge was never so sweet, or so funny.

Arnold doesn't have a favorite among her books: "I love them all, even the most difficult ones. I will say, however, that the book I wrote that seems to have touched readers the most profoundly is *Barefoot in the Grass,* in which a breast cancer survivor learns to adjust to her new body and take a chance on love again, and the hero learns that a woman doesn't have to be a 'perfect 10' to be beautiful. That book came out in 1997, and I still receive mail from readers who tell me *Barefoot in the Grass* changed their lives or helped them to face their own challenges." In Arnold's poignant tale, a breast cancer survivor who is also a lawyer wonders if she can ever find romantic love again after having a mastectomy. She moves to a small town and finds the perfect hero but hesitates to add a physical element to their relationship, fearing that he will find her scarred body repulsive. The hero's reaction to the love of his life and the moral of this emotion-filled and sensitively written story have given other women in the same situation hope and confidence.

Arnold's love of New York and her gift for creating a vivid sense of place reach full bloom with *Love In Bloom's* (2002) and *Blooming All Over* (2004)—two connected novels that feature the world-famous Bloom's kosher delicatessen, which is loosely based on Zabar's, a New York City landmark. Julia Bloom is a lawyer who is not entirely satisfied with her life as it is. When Julia's grandmother Ida, matriarch of the Bloom family, taps her to be the new owner of the family's delicatessen, Julia's world is turned upside down, especially once she becomes involved with reporter Ron Joffe, who is investigating a possible financial scandal at Bloom's. *Love In Bloom's* is more than just the story of the romance between Julia and Ron; it is the tale of two sisters—one conventionally successful and one bohemian—and their relationship with the rest of their eccentric family. *Love In Bloom's* is a bright, funny, and appealing comedy with such a strong sense of place that it becomes a paean to New York City. Not only was the book a RITA finalist in 2003, but it also proved to be such a success for Arnold that it inspired a sequel, *Blooming All Over,* which features the romantic adventures of the free-spirited sister, Susie, and her love, Casey Gordon, a bagel maker at Bloom's.

When describing the heroes of her novels, Anderson says, "My heroes tend to be 'guys.' They aren't perfect; they aren't cruel; they aren't power-mad. They're down to earth, occasionally clueless, and usually funny. They love women but don't really understand them.

They enjoy sex and have a healthy attitude about it, seeing it not as a tool of conquest or domination, but as a really fun activity to share with a woman." Ned Donovan, the hero of *The Fixer Upper* (2005), embodies all of these qualities. The recently widowed parent of a young son, Eric, Ned has moved from Vermont to New York City. When Eric applies to the Hudson School, one of Manhattan's most prestigious private academies, without Ned's knowledge, Ned ends up meeting the head of admissions, Libby Kimmelman, and becomes smitten. *The Fixer Upper* refers both to the renovation of Libby's brownstone, which is going co-op, and also to Libby's life, which has been in a holding pattern ever since her divorce. In this book, Arnold delivers a strong and compelling love story, and her sharp sense of humor especially shines in her depictions of teens and children, whom she succeeds in making individuals rather than just the typical stereotypes found in many novels.

According to Arnold, "All romance fiction is really about hope—the hope that things can work out well in the end, that two people, sometimes working at cross-purposes, can find common ground and forge a union. I like to think of my stories as parables of peace; a man and a woman are in conflict, and somehow they figure out a happy, loving solution to that conflict." Arnold imbues her rich cast of characters with that same sense of hope and optimism, which is one reason why her emotionally appealing and beautifully written books are so well loved.

BIBLIOGRAPHY

Writing as Judith Arnold

Books: *Come Home to Love.* Toronto: Harlequin, 1985; *Modern Man.* Toronto: Harlequin, 1985; *Flowing to the Sky.* Toronto: Harlequin, 1985; *Jackpot.* Toronto: Harlequin, 1986; *Special Delivery.* Toronto: Harlequin, 1986; *Man and Wife.* Toronto: Harlequin, 1986; *On Love's Trail.* Toronto: Harlequin, 1986; *Best Friends.* Toronto: Harlequin, 1987; *Promises.* Toronto: Harlequin, 1987; *Commitments.* Toronto: Harlequin, 1987; *Dreams.* Toronto: Harlequin, 1987; *Comfort and Joy.* Toronto: Harlequin, 1987; *Twilight.* Toronto: Harlequin, 1988; *Going Back.* Toronto: Harlequin, 1988; *Harvest of the Sun.* Toronto: Harlequin, 1988; *One Whiff of Scandal.* Toronto: Harlequin, 1989; *Turning Tables.* Toronto: Harlequin, 1989; *Survivors.* Toronto: Harlequin, 1990; *Lucky Penny.* Toronto: Harlequin, 1990; *Change of Life.* Toronto: Harlequin, 1990; *One Good Turn.* Toronto: Harlequin, 1991; *Loverboy.* Toronto: Harlequin, 1991; *Raising the Stakes.* Toronto: Harlequin, 1991; *Safe Harbor.* Toronto: Harlequin, 1991; *Trust Me.* Toronto: Harlequin, 1992; *The Woman Downstairs.* Toronto: Harlequin, 1992; *Opposing Camps.* Toronto: Harlequin, 1992; *Sweet Light.* Toronto: Harlequin, 1992; *Just Like Romeo and Juliet.* Toronto: Harlequin, 1993; *Oh, You Beautiful Doll!* Toronto: Harlequin, 1993; *Flashfire.* Toronto: Harlequin, 1993; *The Parent Plan.* Toronto: Harlequin, 1994; *Private Lies.* Toronto: Harlequin, 1994; *Alessandra and the Archangel.* Toronto: Harlequin, 1994; *The Marrying Type.* Toronto: Harlequin, 1994; *Cry Uncle.* Toronto: Harlequin, 1995; *The Lady in the Mirror.* Toronto: Harlequin, 1995; *Timeless Love.* Toronto: Harlequin, 1995; *Married to the Man.* Toronto: Harlequin, 1996; *A Stranger's Baby.* Toronto: Harlequin, 1996; *Barefoot in the Grass.* Toronto: Harlequin, 1996; *Courting Trouble.* Toronto: Harlequin, 1997; *Father Found.* Toronto: Harlequin, 1997; *Father Christmas.* Toronto: Harlequin, 1997; *Father of Two.* Toronto: Harlequin, 1998; *Legacy of Secrets.* Toronto: Harlequin, 1998; *Found: One Wife.* Toronto: Harlequin, 1998; *The Wrong Bride.* Toronto: Harlequin, 1999; *Found: One Son.* Toronto: Harlequin, 1999; *Her Secret Lover.* Toronto: Harlequin, 1999; *Doctor Dad.* Toronto: Harlequin, 2000; *Birthright.* Toronto: Harlequin, 2000; *'Tis the Season.* Toronto: Harlequin, 2000; *Hush Little Baby.* Toronto: Harlequin, 2001; *Looking for Laura.* Toronto: MIRA, 2001; *Somebody's Dad.* Toronto: Harlequin, 2002; *Love In Bloom's.* Toronto: MIRA, 2002; *Hidden Treasures.* Toronto: Harlequin, 2003; *Right Place, Wrong Time.* Toronto: Harlequin, 2003; *Heart on the Line.* Toronto: MIRA,

2003; *Blooming All Over.* Toronto: MIRA, 2004; *The Fixer Upper.* Toronto: MIRA, 2005; *In the Dark.* Toronto: Harlequin, 2006.

Novellas: "Chocolate Kisses" in *My Valentine.* Toronto: Harlequin, 1993; "Rich Man, Poor Man" in *How to Marry a Millionaire.* Toronto: Harlequin, 1996; "Baby Jane Doe" in *Millennium Baby.* Toronto: Harlequin, 2000; "Daddy's Girl" in *All Summer Long.* Toronto: Harlequin, 2001; "In the Stars" in *Written in the Stars.* Toronto: Harlequin, 2001; "Fools Rush In" in *Fool for Love.* Toronto: Harlequin, 2004; "One for Each Night" in *Burning Bright.* Toronto: Harlequin, 2004.

Genre-Related Essays: "Women Do" in *Dangerous Men and Adventurous Women: Romance Writers on the Appeal of the Romance.* Philadelphia: University of Pennsylvania Press, 1992; "This I Do for Me" in *North American Romance Writers.* Lanham, MD: Scarecrow Press, 1999.

Writing as Ariel Berk

Books: *Silent Beginnings.* New York: Silhouette, 1983; *Promise of Love.* New York: Silhouette, 1984; *Remedies of the Heart.* New York: Silhouette, 1984; *Hungry for Love.* New York: Silhouette, 1985; *Breaking the Ice.* New York: Silhouette, 1985; *False Impressions.* New York: Silhouette, 1985; *Teacher's Pet.* New York: Silhouette, 1985; *No Plan for Love.* New York: Silhouette, 1986; *Game, Set, Match.* New York: Silhouette, 1987; *Playing with Matches.* New York: Silhouette, 1987; *Together Again.* New York: Silhouette, 1988; *Peace of Mind.* New York: Silhouette, 1989; *A Package Deal.* New York: Silhouette, 1989.

Writing as Thea Frederick

Book: *Beloved Adversary.* New York: Berkley, 1984.

JOANNE HAMILTON-SELWAY, JOHN CHARLES, AND MARION EKHOLM

ADELE ASHWORTH

Adele Ashworth writes about intelligent women getting what they want and the
men who learn to understand what makes them tick. She writes of heroes who
need the heroine's love, though they rarely know it at the time, in the fascinating
historical time period of the nineteenth century. Inspired by these brilliantly complicated
characters, Ashworth has created emotionally rich, wonderfully imaginative stories of love
and passion.

Ashworth was born in Cape May Courthouse, New Jersey, in 1963. Her mother grew
up near Carlsbad, New Mexico, and received a music scholarship to the University of New
Mexico, but dropped out of school because she didn't want to major in music. After raising
three children, Ashworth's mother returned to college and earned a PhD in speech pathol-
ogy, eventually becoming a leading expert on speech in relation to brain damage. Her father
was originally from South Dakota and has a PhD in engineering. Ashworth's parents met
while her father was working as a scientist on Kirkland Air Force Base in Albuquerque.
Ashworth grew up in Albuquerque and lived there until she began her junior year of high
school. In 1979, her family moved to Salt Lake City, where they lived until Ashworth's
graduation from college.

Ashworth spent two years at Utah State University before transferring to the University
of Utah, where she earned her degree in mass communication/broadcast journalism. After
graduating, Ashworth worked in a variety of jobs, including a position as a customer service
representative for America West Airlines for over seven years: "In those days, a customer
service representative meant that I worked as a flight attendant, gate agent, reservation
agent, ticket agent, baggage claim agent, [and so forth]. I really enjoyed that job and can
still carry four cups of coffee in turbulence without spilling a drop."

Ashworth remembers always being interested in writing: "I never really thought about
becoming a writer: I simply *was* a writer, or thought of myself as one." As early as the sixth
grade, Ashworth was writing: "I wrote nine one-page chapters for a class project. That was
a sci-fi adventures series with three orphans—a brother and two sisters—who lived

underwater in a futuristic dome world. I called the story "Plastic City," and each chapter had the orphans saving people from giant ocean snakes or dangerous air leaks. I had a very vivid imagination."

Always a fan of the romance genre, Ashworth decided to try her hand at writing a novel, and in 1990, she started her first book. In 1993, Ashworth resigned from her job at America West Airlines, determined to pursue a writing career full-time. Though it took her three years to decide to write full-time, it only took her three months to finish what would be her first published book. Ashworth completed *My Darling Caroline* in 1995, and two years later, her agent sold it to Berkley/Jove. *My Darling Caroline* was published in 1998, winning the Romance Writers of America's RITA award for best first novel, and Ashworth's career took off.

My Darling Caroline features a wonderfully appealing, unconventional heroine in Lady Caroline Grayson, a young woman whose dream is to become a botanist. Caroline has a brilliant mind and is able to do impressive mathematical problems in her head, but she is bound by the conventions of the Regency era, a time when women were not permitted to study at universities. Nevertheless, Caroline's plans to attend New York University in disguise to study botany are shattered when her father arranges a marriage with the handsome, sullen Earl of Weymerth, who is forced into the marriage for business reasons. Skillfully incorporating a wealth of information about botany, Ashworth takes the classic marriage-of-convenience plot and breathes new life into it, with her tender and poignant tale of two people who gradually discover their love for each other.

Winter Garden, published in 2000, proved to be the easiest of Ashworth's books to write. She says, "Though at the time I thought it was the most difficult. But the book just seemed to flow from my brain to my fingertips. It is also the only book I had absolutely no revisions on at all. My publishers printed it just as I wrote it." The book's heroine, Madeleine DuMas, is a French spy working for the English government, when she arrives in the small English village of Winter Garden with the objective of discovering who is behind an opium smuggling ring. As her cover, Madeleine accepts the position of translator for scholar Thomas Blackwood, who, unbeknownst to Madeleine, is also employed by the English government. In *Winter Garden,* Ashworth delightfully explores the popular theme of "Beauty and the Beast" with her deeply emotional romance between reclusive Thomas and confident Madeleine. Ashworth also cleverly reverses the traditional roles of the hero and heroine, not only making Madeleine the experienced one and Thomas the hesitant one in their personal relationship, but also making Madeleine the veteran spy and Thomas the novice in their professional relationship.

Winter Garden was followed by *Someone Irresistible* in 2001, in which Ashworth uses both the famous Crystal Palace and the Victorian dinosaur craze as inspirations for her story of the romance between scientist Nathan Prince and dinosaur sculptor Mimi Sinclair. Nathan is dishonored when proof of his career-making find of the bones of a Megalosaurus disappears, and he suspects Mimi's father of being involved in the theft. Nathan reluctantly needs Mimi's artistic skills to help him regain his name and reputation. Ashworth loved writing *Someone Irresistible:* "I truly had a blast, partly because the research was just too much fun for me! As a lover of history, I had a wonderful time exploring the dynamics of popular culture and dinosaur history, study and exploration during the nineteenth century." In Nathan, Ashworth has created a deliciously complex hero, battling between reason and emotion, who ultimately meets his match—personally and professionally—in the smart and rebellious Mimi.

In 2004, Ashworth began a trilogy with *Duke of Sin,* another of her irresistibly intricate and subtle Victorian historicals. Floral designer Vivian Rael-Lamont is a woman with secrets. Someone discovers those secrets and threatens to ruin the reputation she has painstakingly cultivated, unless Vivian can acquire an original Shakespearean sonnet from the reclusive William Raleigh, Duke of Trent. Having supplied flowers for some time to the Duke's household, Vivian knows all about William, including the scandalous rumors that he murdered his first wife. When Vivian attempts to purchase the manuscript, the duke proposes another kind of payment: her companionship. Secrets abound in *Duke of Sin,* with Vivian's personal secrets, the death of William's first wife, and a blackmailer who will stop at nothing. Ashworth brilliantly combines all of her favorite traits in William, a dark, brooding, and mysterious hero who meets his match in Vivian, who is beautiful, independent, and intelligent. Ashworth also gives readers a refreshingly mature couple whose touching romance gradually develops into a passionate, physical relationship.

For Ashworth the appeal of writing romances is all about the characters: "I much prefer writing character-driven books. Romance is about people in larger-than-life situations who conquer all negatives to be together. It's about beauty, goodness, and ultimate love prevailing between two individuals. It's about the triumph of hope. There's nothing more enjoyable to create than a story where happiness wins in the end." Readers have come to expect the kinds of complicated, unique, and subtly nuanced characters that the talented Ashworth delivers in her lushly sensual and elegantly written love stories.

BIBLIOGRAPHY

Books: *My Darling Caroline.* New York: Jove, 1998; *Stolen Charms.* New York: Jove, 1999; *Winter Garden.* New York: Jove, 2000; *Someone Irresistible.* New York: Avon, 2001; *When It's Perfect.* New York: Avon, 2002; *Duke of Sin.* New York: Avon, 2004; *Duke of Scandal.* New York: Avon, 2006.

JOHN CHARLES AND JOANNE HAMILTON-SELWAY

STEPHANIE BANCROFT. *See* Stephanie Bond

JILL BARKIN. *See* Susan Johnson

VICTORIA BARRETT. *See* Vicki Hinze

JAYNE BENTLEY. *See* Jayne Ann Krentz

PATTI BERG

With vulnerable but plucky heroines and some of the hunkiest heroes in romance fiction, Patti Berg has crafted entertaining tales of love and romance, filled with wit and passion. Readers have come to rely on Berg for her light touch with contemporary romances, her feisty heroines with the men to match, and a guarantee of plenty of sexy sparks and humor that have won her more and more fans with each book she publishes.

Berg was born in El Monte, California, in 1950. Her father was born and raised in Idaho, the youngest of 14 children. He underwent several surgeries after serious burns at 18 months of age nearly destroyed his hands. While he was not able to serve in World War II, he was able to lead a normal life and worked as a forklift operator for most of his adult life. He died in 1994. Berg's mother, who was proud of working as a heavy-equipment operator during World War II, was a skilled seamstress. As Berg remembers, "There's not much my mom couldn't do."

Like most authors, Berg was creative at a young age, as early as elementary school, and wrote short stories and plays. However, Berg says that she was not an enthusiastic student in grade school, excelling only in history and English. As a senior in high school, she decided to get serious about her studies and was proud to make all As and one B. She also became more outgoing, attending ball games and dances. Her writing progressed from romances featuring The Beatles' Paul McCartney as the hero and Berg herself as the leading lady to "deep, dark poems" about Vietnam and love lost and found. After high school, she had no desire to go to college but attended a business school for a year.

Berg held several secretarial jobs from 1969 until 1986, when she started writing marketing and advertising literature for a software company. After unfulfilling jobs selling real estate and even cosmetics, she returned to secretarial work in 1989 and in 1995 went back to writing marketing literature.

Berg says she "decided to get serious" about her writing in 1992. Her goal was to complete a book, and she finished it in time to enter it in the 1993 Romance Writers of

America Golden Heart contest, an award designed to honor the manuscripts of RWA's unpublished members. The contest brought their work to the attention of the publishing community. Berg sent this same story to Bantam, who loved it but couldn't buy it because of a surplus of inventory. However, the editor at Bantam recommended it to another publishing house, who did buy the story, titled *Enchanted*. To complete her good fortune, Berg was informed that she was a finalist for the Golden Heart award.

In 2000, Berg retired from her job as an energy analyst for the California Energy Commission to write full-time from her northern California home. She says that old movies help fire her imagination, especially those with dashing heroes like Errol Flynn, Tyrone Power, and Cary Grant. Her heroes are strong and handsome and have a powerful sense of family. Her heroines are plucky go-getters who share the hero's love of family.

Berg's first book, *Enchanted* (1994), is named by many of her fans as their favorite of her books. *Enchanted* features a light paranormal/fantasy premise, which Berg also uses in her next four books and an appealing matchmaker named Merry Nicholas, who appears in Berg's second novel, *Wishes Come True* (1996).

If I Can't Have You (1998) is the romantic story of 1930s matinee idol Trevor Montgomery, a cross between Tyrone Power and Cary Grant. When Trevor wakes up next to the bloody body of his costar, hungover and fearing he may have committed murder, he decides to end his life. But when his efforts to drown himself in a swimming pool fail, he resurfaces and finds himself propelled forward into the 1990s. With the help of Hollywood memorabilia collector Adriana Howard, he must discover who killed his costar. And, if they can change the past, perhaps he and Adriana can end up together, as they were meant to.

Looking for a Hero (1998) is Berg's favorite of her books. It features another hero from the past who is magically transported into the twentieth century, a hero "full of love and devotion and haunted by revenge." Morgan "Black Heart" Farrell is thrown from his seventeenth-century pirate ship onto a beach in present-day St. Augustine, Florida, where he meets Kate Cameron, a young widow with a precocious daughter. As their attraction grows, Morgan learns that his enemies have followed him and will continue their vendetta.

Berg can say that she lives the happy endings of her books. She has been married to the same man since 1976; they married after knowing each other for only two months. She has one daughter. When asked what about the romance genre appeals to her, Berg says it is "the 'happily ever after' endings, the growing relationships." Her books echo these sentiments and leave her fans wanting more.

BIBLIOGRAPHY

Books: *Enchanted.* New York: Jove, 1994; *Wishes Come True.* New York: Avon, 1996; *Till the End of Time.* New York: Avon, 1997; *If I Can't Have You.* New York: Avon, 1998; *Looking for a Hero.* New York: Avon, 1998; *Wife for a Day.* New York: Avon, 1999; *Bride for a Night.* New York: Avon, 2000; *Born to Be Wild.* New York: Avon, 2001; *Something Wild.* New York: Avon, 2002; *Stuck On You.* New York: Avon, 2003; *And Then He Kissed Me.* New York: Avon, 2003; *I'm No Angel.* New York: Avon, 2004.
Novella: "Sinfully Scottish" in *My Scottish Summer.* New York: Warner, 2001.

JOANNE HAMILTON-SELWAY

ARIEL BERK. *See* Judith Arnold

ELIZABETH BEVARLY

Elizabeth Bevarly. Courtesy of Elizabeth Bevarly.

Reality has no place in the contemporary romance novels of Elizabeth Bevarly. What is particularly refreshing about this fact is that the author herself is the first to admit it. Bevarly's sparkling contemporary romances were never intended to provide readers with a dose of reality. Instead, what they do offer is a brilliant blend of delightful characters, deliciously sexy romance, and a quirky sense of humor that many readers find utterly irresistible.

Bevarly was born in 1961 in Louisville, Kentucky. The youngest of three children in her family, Bevarly grew up in a firmly middle-class household in Louisville with a father who worked for an insurance company and a mother who stayed at home with her kids. Bevarly was one of those people who knew early on that she wanted to be a writer. As a child of 12, Bevarly was determined to become a novelist, and by the time she was 16, Bevarly, inspired by her own appetite for reading romances, decided she would concentrate on writing love stories. Bevarly even went as far as picking out a pen name for herself—Rachel Tyrone—but Bevarly's path to publication would take a few detours along the way.

Bevarly attended the University of Louisville, where she received her bachelor of arts degree in English, with honors, in 1983. While in college, Bevarly worked as an editorial assistant for a medical journal, a job that provided invaluable training in the spelling of obscure phrases. Bevarly was halfway through her master's degree when she decided to take a break from her academic studies. A few years later, she tried graduate school again, this time applying and being accepted at George Washington University in Washington, D.C., where she studied international affairs for one semester before deciding that politics was just not her thing.

Bevarly then returned to Louisville, where she put her English degree to good use in such varied work experiences as bartender, movie-theater cashier, sales clerk for Crabtree and Evelyn and The Limited, and a bridal registry consultant for a department store. As Bevarly herself says, "English degrees are a lot more versatile than people think." In 1986, Bevarly married her high school sweetheart, who was in the Coast Guard at the time, and the two spent the next few years moving around a lot.

Bevarly was living in New Jersey, working for The Limited, when she began writing her first romance in January of 1988. Every day, Bevarly's husband would drop her off early at the mall, and she would spend a couple of hours before the store opened writing in the food court. On her breaks and at lunchtime, Bevarly would take a notebook into the storeroom and write behind racks of pants. She wrote at night and on her days off. Six months later, when she was done, Bevarly bought a typewriter at Sears and took another month to type the manuscript. Finally, her first romance novel was finished.

Bevarly turned down a promotion at work, positive that she would be able to sell her book and begin a new career as an author: "Part of this was simply naiveté on my part, because I simply didn't know anything about the romance business, save what I read in Kathryn Falk's *How to Write a Romance and Get It Published*. Part was also my confidence in my work and my belief that the writing was good." Bevarly targeted Silhouette as the publisher she wanted to sell her first book to and sent off her manuscript.

Bevarly recalls, "I was almost immediately rejected by a form letter that pretty much let me know that no one had even read my book." Not someone to take defeat lightly, Bevarly decided that if she found an agent, he or she might be able to get the manuscript in front of someone who would read it and possibly publish it. Bevarly went through *Writer's Market,* compiling a list of all the new or newly formed agencies, thinking they might be willing to take on a newcomer. She started querying agents. Thirteen rejections later, Bevarly found an agent interested in representing her work. She mailed the agent her book, thinking it would be at least weeks before she heard anything. A week later, returning home from an anniversary trip with her husband, Bevarly answered a call from her agent, who had already sent the manuscript to Silhouette. Within a few weeks, an editor at Silhouette made an offer to buy the book, which was published less than a year later as *Destinations South* (1989).

For *Destinations South,* Bevarly used one of her favorite locales, the Caribbean. Having once briefly lived in and fallen in love with the area, the exotic Caribbean was a natural choice for one of the settings in the book. The heroine, Hester Somerset, flees the rat race in the big city for a new life on a beautiful island in the tropics. When workaholic executive Silas Duran arrives and is temporarily stuck staying with Hester, he finds himself not only seduced by the colorful locale but also by Hester. Bevarly found her first book to be the easiest to write, perhaps because there was none of the pressure that would come later as a published author having to meet deadlines and make best-seller lists. *Destinations South* proved to be the beginning of a bright new career for Bevarly, who would form a long-lasting writing relationship with Silhouette.

While many authors tend to pick one particular theme for their books, Bevarly has found that over the years "different things have become more important to me, so different themes have been present in my books. Right now, I find that the concept of family has a strong presence in my books, because there has been a lot going on in my own family for the past several years." This theme of family is particularly strong in some of her more recent romances, such as *He Could Be the One* (2001); *Take Me, I'm Yours* (2002); *The Ring on Her Finger* (2003); and *The Thing about Men* (2004). "Before that, babies and pregnancy were recurrent themes because I and both of my sisters-in-law were getting pregnant and having babies at the same time," says Bevarly. This is reflected in the From Here to Maternity and From Here to Paternity series romances that Bevarly wrote for Silhouette. "Even before that" Bevarly says "my characters tended to wander a lot, probably because I was at a point where I was kind of wandering, figuratively speaking." Some of the exotic settings of Bevarly's first books, such as *Up Close* (1992) and *The Honeymoon* (1995), best reflect this particular time in the author's own life.

The glittering, glamorous world of the wealthy is the background for many of Bevarly's romances. For example, in *Take Me, I'm Yours,* the heroine, Ruby Runyan, takes refuge in a nearby yacht after discovering that her new boyfriend is connected to the mob. There she stumbles into hero Keaton Hamilton Danning III, who, once he gets to know Ruby better, discovers just how meaningless and empty his life has been taking care of a deposed royal. In *Her Man Friday* (1999), private investigator Leo Friday thinks social secretary Lily Rigby is the logical suspect when it comes to embezzling millions from her wealthy employer. However, after spending time with Lily on her employer's palatial estate, Leo discovers Lily has secrets he never would have suspected and learns that the rich aren't necessarily that different from the rest of us.

While Bevarly may use the lifestyles of the wealthy and powerful for many of her stories, she wisely understands that money doesn't always buy happiness. All the money in the world doesn't mean much to Lucinda Hollander, heroine of *The Ring on Her Finger*. What she really wants is the love and acceptance of family members, whose comments about her "different learning style" are their way of not acknowledging Lucinda's dyslexia. It is only later in the book, after Lucinda meets her employer's young daughter who shares the same problem, that Lucinda realizes her worth shouldn't depend on meeting some unrealistic standard set by the people she thought loved her. In a nicely developed secondary romance in this same book, Nathaniel, a wealthy horse breeder, accepts a bet from Lucinda's employer that he can successfully seduce the family's innocent nanny, Rosemary. As Nathaniel spends time with Rosemary, he realizes that he is tired of his endless, emotionally empty flings with beautiful socialites and that what he wants is a permanent relationship with someone like kind, sweet Rosemary.

Louisville, Kentucky, frequently plays a role as the setting for many of Bevarly's books, a logical choice since she grew up there and is quite familiar with the region. This knowledge of the area gives books of hers like *My Man Pendleton* (1998) and *The Ring on Her Finger* their wonderfully vivid sense of place. Bevarly particularly enjoyed writing *My Man Pendleton* since it not only allowed her to write about one of her favorite cities, but also because Pendleton, the hero of the book, became a very special character to her. Bevarly even managed to use her own love of old movies to give *My Man Pendleton* the feel of a classic film.

Bevarly has proved she is one of those rare writers who is equally as gifted at writing stand-alone titles as she is at writing category romances. Even when she uses a common or old-fashioned device, such as the secretary in love with her boss—which is the basis of *That Boss of Mine* (1999)—or the marriage of convenience that sets her book *When Jayne Met Erik* (2001) into motion, Bevarly manages to come up with a story that is not only believable but also entertaining. What is particularly impressive about *When Jayne Met Erik* is that not only did Bevarly have to devise a convincing reason for her modern-day heroine to accept an offer of marriage from a complete stranger, but she also had to incorporate characters from three other books being written by other authors for the Amber Court continuity series, of which *When Jayne Met Erik* was a part. The resulting romance is sexy, clever, and fun—in other words, classic Bevarly.

In addition to contributing titles to continuity series involving other authors, Bevarly has created her own series of connected books. A few examples include Bevarly's loosely linked series featuring different members of the same family, such as Family McCormick and Monahan books. One of Bevarly's most inventive series is Blame it on Bob, a trio of three romances—*The Virgin and the Vagabond* (1998); *Beauty and the Brain* (1998); and *Bride of the Bad Boy* (1998)—all set in the small town of Endicott, Indiana. Bevarly uses the quirky premise that when someone in Endicott is born in the year that Comet Bob appears and then makes a wish the next time the comet is seen, whatever that person wishes for will come true. With the Blame it on Bob series, Bevarly crafted three different, yet equally enjoyable romances.

From her series romances to her contemporary comedies, the one thing that unites all of Bevarly's superbly crafted love stories is her distinctive brand of humor. Bevarly knows just how sexy a sense of humor can be, and fortunately for readers, almost all of her heroes and heroines come fully equipped with this important feature. An excellent example of this is *Undercover with the Mob* (2004), in which Natalie Dorset at first scoffs at her landlady's suggestion that their new tenant, Jack Miller, is "connected." Later, Natalie begins to wonder if her new, and quite sexy, neighbor really does whack people for a living. Bevarly gives Natalie a deliciously dry sense of humor that is not only wonderfully appealing to Jack but also to readers.

If there is one thing that Bevarly finds to be true about all of her books it is "that falling in love makes all the difference." Bevarly explains, "Don't get me wrong. I think you can be very happy without falling in love. And I think you can have a wonderful life without ever being in love. But I don't think you can be completely happy until you fall in love. And I think human beings just do not feel whole unless they're in love. It's such a fundamental part of our psyche that needs to be in a committed relationship with another person. All of us look for that. And when we find it, we just feel happier. So maybe that's what is at the crux of all my books. That you can be happy regardless of what you are doing and who you are. But if you fall in love, then you're even happier!"

BIBLIOGRAPHY

Books: *Destinations South,* New York: Silhouette, 1989; *Close Range.* New York: Silhouette, 1990; *Donovan's Chance.* New York: Silhouette, 1990; *Moriah's Mutiny.* New York: Silhouette, 1991; *Up Close.* New York: Silhouette, 1992; *An Unsuitable Man for the Job.* New York: Silhouette, 1992; *Jake's Christmas.* New York: Silhouette, 1992; *Hired Hand.* New York: Silhouette, 1993; *Return Engagement.* New York: Silhouette, 1993; *The Wedding.* New York: Harper, 1993; *A Lawless Man.* New York: Silhouette, 1994; *The Honeymoon.* New York: Harper, 1995; *A Dad Like Daniel.* New York: Silhouette, 1995; *The Perfect Father.* New York: Silhouette, 1995; *Dr. Daddy.* New York: Silhouette, 1995; *Father of the Brat.* New York: Silhouette, 1996; *Father of the Brood.* New York: Silhouette, 1996; *Father on the Brink.* New York: Silhouette, 1996; *Roxy and the Rich Man.* New York: Silhouette, 1997; *Lucy and the Loner.* New York: Silhouette, 1997; *Georgia Meets Her Groom.* New York: Silhouette, 1997; *Bride of the Bad Boy.* New York: Silhouette, 1998; *Beauty and the Brain.* New York: Silhouette, 1998; *The Virgin and the Vagabond.* New York: Silhouette, 1998; *The Sheriff and the Imposter Bride.* New York: Silhouette, 1998; *My Man Pendleton.* New York: Avon, 1998; *Society Bride.* New York: Silhouette, 1999; *That Boss of Mine.* New York: Silhouette, 1999; *A Doctor in Her Stocking.* New York: Silhouette, 1999; *Her Man Friday.* New York: Avon, 1999;

Dr. Mommy. New York: Silhouette, 2000; *Dr. Irresistible.* New York: Silhouette, 2000; *First Comes Love.* New York: Silhouette, 2000; *Monahan's Gamble.* New York: Silhouette, 2000; *How to Trap a Tycoon.* New York: Avon, 2000; *The Temptation of Rory Monahan.* New York: Silhouette, 2001; *The Secret Life of Connor Monahan.* New York: Silhouette, 2001; *When Jayne Met Erik.* New York: Silhouette, 2001; *He Could Be the One.* New York: Avon, 2001; *Taming the Prince.* New York: Silhouette, 2002; *Take Me, I'm Yours.* New York: Avon, 2002; *The Ring on Her Finger.* New York: Avon, 2003; *Taming the Beastly MD.* New York: Silhouette, 2003; *The Thing about Men.* New York: Avon, 2004; *Undercover with the Mob.* Toronto: Harlequin, 2004; *Just Like a Man.* New York: Avon, 2005; *The Newlyweds.* New York: Silhouette, 2005; *Indecent Suggestion.* Toronto: Harlequin, 2005; *You've Got Male.* Toronto: HQN, 2005; *Express Male.* Toronto: HQN, 2006.

Novellas: "Ever True" in *A Sprinkle of Fairy Dust.* New York: St. Martin's Press, 1996; "Just Desserts" in *Love by Chocolate.* New York: Jove, 1997; "Only Fifteen Shopping Days Left ..." in *Christmas Spirits.* New York: Jove, 1997; "Top Cat and Tales" in *A Message from Cupid.* New York: St. Martin's Press, 1998; "The Wedding Wager" in *Do You Take This Man.* New York: Silhouette, 1999; "The Short, Hot Summer" in *Opposites Attract.* New York: Jove, 2000; "A Daddy for Her Daughters" in *A Mother's Day.* New York: Harlequin, 2002; "Rapid Transit" in *Write It Up.* Toronto: HQN, 2006.

JOHN CHARLES

ROSANNE BITTNER

For RITA finalist Rosanne Bittner, the historical setting of her novels is as important as the relationship between her heroes and heroines: "When I'm writing, I never think to myself that I am writing a romance. I'm simply telling a story that involves America's history." Her strong sense of history flavors everything Bittner writes.

Bittner was born in January 1945, in LaPorte, Indiana. Her parents, Frank Reris and Ardella Williams, moved to southwestern Michigan when Bittner was one year old. Her father was employed in a bomb-manufacturing plant in LaPorte, and her mother was a housewife. Bittner married her husband, Larry, nearly forty-one years ago, and together they have two sons, Brock and Brian, as well as several grandchildren. Now semiretired, Larry still helps with the family business, of which Bittner herself is secretary/director.

Throughout her adolescence, Bittner read voraciously and wrote volumes of poetry but "lacked the courage" to tackle novel writing. At the age of 34, she made her first attempt at penning a book and realized immediately that writing was more than a hobby—it was how she wanted to make her living. In 1984, Bittner began writing full-time, delighted to be realizing her dream.

The heroes in Bittner's books are courageous men who are fierce in battle but gentle with their women. They tend to hide their vulnerabilities and emotional pain from others. Noah Wilde, also known as Noah Barnes, from *Into the Wilderness: The Longhunters* (2002), the first book in Bittner's Westward America! series (*Into the Valley: The Settlers,* 2003; *Into the Prairie: The Pioneers,* 2004), is a case in point. Although Noah's father is French, Noah himself is a spy for the British. Noah is badly injured when defending the heroine, Jessica Matthews, in an Indian raid during the French and Indian War. Jessica nurses him back to health, and he goes to the governor's mansion to report the attack. Once there, however, he is imprisoned, making it impossible for him to save Jessica's family from a massacre. The violence and brutality of the attack are vividly detailed, as is the guilt Noah carries for not being there to save them.

Bittner says her heroines are "very strong women of conviction and courage, and usually women of faith." Bittner sees a lot of her own personality in her heroines. An excellent example of this is Addy Kane, the heroine of *Until Tomorrow* (1995) who has accepted a teaching job in a Colorado mining town. Anxious to leave her small Illinois hometown for the wild Colorado Territory, Addy is caught in the middle of a bank robbery and taken hostage while she's withdrawing her savings. Parker Cole, an ex-Confederate soldier and one of the robbers, is impressed with Addy's bravery and spunkiness and protects her from the other outlaws. Time passes, but Parker is unable to forget Addy. He follows her to Central City, Colorado, determined to win her love, despite the fact that Addy has rich and powerful suitors. In the story's final irony, a good "bad guy" instead of a bad "good guy" wins the heart of the heroine.

Colorado and Wyoming are Bittner's two favorite settings for her Old West romances because of their mountains, deserts, and so-called big sky qualities. Using actual places for her settings lends tremendous realism to Bittner's stories. She prefers to rely on dialogue and action to propel her plots, instead of "lifeless narration." Her only recurrent theme is American history, and several of her novels record the struggles of Native Americans during the settlement of the western territories.

Bittner's early inspiration came from writers Louis L'Amour and Celeste de Blasis. She doesn't have a novel that she considers her most difficult to write and enjoys the whole process of creating each one of them. Bittner names her 1996 novel *Eagle's Song* as the easiest for her to write because she was so familiar with all of the characters. *Eagle's Song* is the seventh book in Bittner's Savage Destiny series, which chronicles the Monroe family. The other six titles—*Sweet Prairie Passion* (1983), *Ride the Free Wind* (1984), *River of Love* (1984), *Embrace the Wild Land* (1984), *Climb the Highest Mountain* (1985), and *Meet the New Dawn* (1986)—were written in a three-year period. *Eagle's Song* was written after a 10-year hiatus, Bittner says, because she "was overwhelmed with emotion" and "needed a break from the Monroe family." However, the story of Abbie Monroe and her grandchildren was waiting to be told until this book, which finally brings closure to the saga.

In 2004, Bittner turned her talents to the inspirational market. Her first faith-based effort, *Where Heaven Begins* (2004), a story set in Alaska during the 1890s gold rush, was a finalist for the 2005 Willa, awarded by Women Writing the West. *Where Heaven Begins* was followed by *Walk by Faith* (2005) and *Follow Your Heart* (2005). Currently, Bittner is working on a love story set during World War II, under the pseudonym Frances Rose.

To the prolific Bittner, her favorite novel is whichever one she's currently working on, and when that one is completed, she's excited about the next novel. Writer's block is never a problem. Bittner finds that her plot ideas always precede her characters. While developing a story, she enjoys living with her characters, getting to know them well, and watching them grow and evolve as the story unfolds. As evinced by Bittner's large oeuvre and number of books in print, so do her readers.

BIBLIOGRAPHY

Books: *Sweet Prairie Passion.* New York: Kensington, 1983; *Savage Destiny.* New York: Kensington, 1983; *Ride the Free Wind.* New York: Kensington, 1984; *Embrace the Wild Land.* New York: Kensington, 1984; *River of Love.* New York: Kensington, 1984; *Climb the Highest Mountain.* New York: Kensington, 1985; *Lawless Love.* New York: Kensington, 1985; *Arizona Bride.* New York: Kensington, 1985; *Meet the New Dawn.* New York: Kensington, 1986; *Tame the Wild Wind.* New York: Bantam, 1986; *Rapture's Gold.* New York: Kensington, 1986; *Prairie Embrace.* New York:

Kensington, 1987; *Savage Horizons*. New York: Warner, 1987; *Destiny's Dawn*. New York: Popular Press, 1987; *Frontier Fires*. New York: Warner, 1987; *Tennessee Bride*. New York: Warner, 1988; *Texas Bride*. New York: Warner, 1988; *Ecstasy's Chains*. New York: Kensington, 1989; *This Time Forever*. New York: Warner, 1989; *Arizona Ecstasy*. New York: Kensington, 1989; *Embrace the Wild Land*. New York: Kensington, 1989; *Sioux Splendor*. New York: Kensington, 1990; *Montana Woman*. New York: Bantam, 1990; *Sweet Mountain Magic*. New York: Kensington, 1990; *Embers of the Heart*. New York: Bantam, 1990; *Oregon Bride*. New York: Warner, 1990; *In the Shadow of the Mountains*. New York: Bantam, 1991; *Comanche Sunset*. New York: Kensington, 1991; *Song of the Wolf*. New York: Bantam, 1992; *Thunder on the Plains*. New York: Doubleday, 1992; *Caress*. New York: Kensington, 1992; *Outlaw Hearts*. New York: Bantam, 1993; *Tender Betrayal*. New York: Bantam, 1993; *Unforgettable*. New York: Kensington, 1993; *Wildest Dreams*. New York: Bantam, 1994; *Full Circle*. New York: Kensington, 1994; *The Forever Tree*. New York: Bantam, 1995; *Until Tomorrow*. New York: Kensington, 1995; *Sioux Splendor*. New York: Kensington, 1995; *Chase the Sun*. New York: Bantam, 1995; *Eagle's Song*. New York: Kensington, 1996; *Texas Embrace*. New York: Kensington, 1997; *Shameless*. New York: Kensington, 1998; *Love Me Tomorrow*. New York: Kensington, 1998; *Texas Passions*. New York: Kensington, 1999; *Mystic Dreamers*. New York: Tor, 1999; *Mystic Visions*. New York: Tor, 2000; *Love's Bounty*. New York: Kensington, 2000; *Mystic Warriors*. New York: Forge, 2001; *Into the Wilderness: The Longhunters*. New York: Forge, 2002; *Into the Valley: The Settlers*. New York: Forge, 2003; *Into the Prairie: The Pioneers*. New York: St. Martin Press, 2004; *Where Heaven Begins*. New York: Steeple Hill, 2004; *The Pioneers*. New York: Forge, 2004; *Walk by Faith*. New York: Steeple Hill, 2005; *Follow Your Heart*. New York: Steeple Hill, 2005.

Anthologies: "Indian Summer" in *Cherished Moments*. New York: St. Martin's Press, 1995; "For the Sake of Love" in *Cherished Love*. New York: St. Martin's Press, 1997; "Miss Chocolate and the Law" in *Love by Chocolate*. New York: Jove, 1997.

SANDRA VAN WINKLE

STEPHANIE BOND

Humor, romance, and suspense. From these three ingredients, Stephanie Bond has crafted a marvelous list of romances. She proves just how entertaining love, laughter, and a bit of danger can be.

Born in Kentucky, Bond grew up on a farm in the small town of Olive Hill. Bond's parents were great at nurturing her different interests, including gardening, sewing, painting, and of course reading. An insatiable bookworm, Bond quickly exhausted the resources of her small school library, so she looked forward to annual visits from her aunt, who would bring books to share, including many Harlequin romances and romantic suspense novels.

Bond was not someone who always dreamed of becoming a writer. In high school, she focused more on business classes, and as a senior got a part-time job in a local shoe store. The whole process involved in running a small business fascinated Bond, and it seemed like she was most destined for a career in business. Bond attended Morehead State University on an academic scholarship, where she studied computer programming. While in college, Bond bought out the local shoe store and spent her college years studying and managing her new business.

After graduating from Morehead State University in 1987, Bond accepted a position as a computer programmer for a petroleum company in Lexington. Two years later, with the intention of rising through the corporate ranks, Bond began studying for her MBA. In 1990, Bond married Christopher Hauck. Five years later, while finishing up her last graduate class, one of Bond's instructors told her she had a flair for writing and might want to consider submitting her work academically.

After graduating with her MBA, Bond took her instructor's advice, but instead of writing for professional journals, she decided to try writing a romance novel. Initially, Bond intended to write a historical romance, but she quickly discovered she was spending more time researching her book than writing it, so she switched to a contemporary romance.

---

also writing as Stephanie Bancroft

Two years later, in 1995, after writing her book on weekends, in the evenings, and on lunch hours, Bond sold her contemporary romance to Harlequin for their new Love and Laughter line. Still working for the petroleum company but living in Atlanta, Bond would write four more books for Harlequin and Bantam before she changed to part-time employment. Five books later, in 1997, Bond finally left the corporate world to write fulltime.

Bond's first book, *Irresistible?* (1997), shows her flair for being able to neatly integrate romance and comedy. In the book, the heroine, Ellie Sutherland, agrees to participate in a clinical study involving a pill that supposedly will make the user irresistible to the opposite sex. While Ellie is initially doubtful of the study's claims, she soon finds herself changing her mind when men, including sexy lawyer Mark Blackwell, suddenly seem to find her irresistible.

Bond quickly became a favorite with category romance readers, and she went on to write more titles for a variety of different series for Harlequin, including their Love and Laughter, Temptation, and Blaze lines. In addition to writing for Harlequin, Bond adopted the pseudonym Stephanie Bancroft and wrote three contemporary romances for Bantam's Loveswept line in 1997 and 1998, including *Almost a Family,* her only book which doesn't contain some measure of comedy.

When it comes to her heroes and heroines, Bond is particularly fond of using the initial idea that opposites attract, which she incorporates in her 2000 title *It Takes a Rebel.* The book's hero, Jack Stillman, relies on his charm and college athletic record to get away with doing the least amount of work possible, but when Jack mistakes Alexandra Tremont for the IRS auditor he's expecting, he initially ruins any chance he might have of landing the advertising campaign for Tremont Department Stores. Jack convinces Alexandra's father to give him another chance, but Alexandra isn't about to let Jack get the account or tempt her with his sexy charm. Bond beautifully manipulates the chemistry between carefree Jack and businesslike Alexandra into a deliciously sexy, lightly humorous romance, which was voted one of Top Ten Favorite Books for the year 2000 by the members of the Romance Writers of America and won Bond her first RITA.

Seeking Single Male, another of Bond's 2000 titles, is also a great example of her gift for romantically pairing up two completely different kinds of people. Lana Martina thought she was meeting someone who was interested in her ad for a gay roommate. Greg Healy thought he was answering a single's ad for his shy brother. From this misunderstanding, a comically clever romance is brewed as the two of them are forced into working together on a town renovation project and gradually find themselves falling in love.

With her first book for St. Martin's Press, *Our Husband,* published in 2000, Bond demonstrated that in addition to knowing how to mix humor and romance, she also knew a thing or two about suspense. With each subsequent book that she wrote for St. Martin's, and later for Avon, Bond continued to refine her always-enjoyable blend of passion and danger. Women's relationships also play a big part in these books as Bond explores the ties that connect sisters, friends, and even carpooling gal pals. For example, in her book *I Think I Love You* (2002), Regina Metcalf tries to reconnect with her two sisters while they all deal with a dangerous secret from their past. In *Kill the Competition* (2003), Bond's heroine, Belinda Hennessey, finds support and some much-needed help from her three friends, all of whom share a ride into work. When Belinda's nasty boss is found murdered, Belinda becomes the police's prime suspect.

Whether humorous romantic suspense novels or sexy romantic comedies, Bond's books are the perfect choice for any reader who appreciates love stories laced with laughter.

BIBLIOGRAPHY

Writing as Stephanie Bond

Books: *Irresistible?* Toronto: Harlequin, 1997; *KIDS Is a 4-Letter Word.* Toronto: Harlequin, 1998; *WIFE Is a 4-Letter Word.* Toronto: Harlequin, 1998; *Manhunting in Mississippi.* Toronto: Harlequin, 1998; *Naughty or Nice?* Toronto: Harlequin, 1998; *Club Cupid.* Toronto: Harlequin, 1999; *About Last Night …* Toronto: Harlequin, 1999; *It Takes a Rebel.* Toronto: Harlequin, 2000; *Too Hot to Sleep.* Toronto: Harlequin, 2000; *Our Husband.* New York: St. Martin's Press, 2000; *Seeking Single Male.* Toronto: Harlequin, 2000; *Two Sexy.* Toronto: Harlequin, 2001; *Got Your Number.* New York: St. Martin's Press, 2001; *I Think I Love You.* New York: St. Martin's Press, 2002; *Kill the Competition.* New York: Avon, 2003; *Cover Me.* Toronto: Harlequin, 2004; *Party Crashers.* New York: Avon, 2004; *Whole Lotta Trouble.* New York: Avon, 2004; *My Favorite Mistake.* Toronto: Harlequin, 2005; *In Deep Voodoo.* New York: Avon, 2005; *Body Movers.* Toronto: Harlequin, 2006; *Finding Your Mojo.* New York: Avon, 2006; *Just Dare Me.* Toronto: Harlequin, 2006.

Novellas: "After Hours" in *Midnight Fantasies.* Toronto: Harlequin, 2001; "Door #2 Diamond Mine" in *Behind the Red Doors.* Toronto: Harlequin, 2003; "Nobody's Fool" in *Fool for Love.* Toronto: Harlequin, 2004; "Taking Care of Business" in *Love So Tender.* Toronto: Harlequin, 2005.

Writing as Stephanie Bancroft

Books: *Almost a Family.* New York: Bantam, 1997; *License to Thrill.* New York: Bantam, 1997; *Your Wish Is My Command.* New York: Bantam, 1998.

JOHN CHARLES

ELIZABETH BOYLE

Passion and humor with a generous dash of intrigue and danger are the main ingredients in Elizabeth Boyle's sensual historicals set in the Regency era.

Born outside of Seattle, Washington, Boyle's parents imbued her with a love of reading and an interest in storytelling that would eventually influence Boyle's decision as an adult to become an author. As a child, Boyle developed quite a family reputation for her stories, especially those featuring an imaginary cow named John Clapper. Boyle attended Seattle University where she majored in English and history, thus combining her two favorite interests and preparing her for her eventual career as a historical romance writer.

While it isn't surprising that someone with Boyle's interests and talent for crafting stories would become a writer, her path to best-selling and award-winning historical romance author took a few detours along the way. After graduating from college, Boyle realized she needed a job that paid a salary, so she worked as a paralegal for 12 years, becoming involved in cases of insurance fraud and police misconduct. Her work with a software firm introduced Boyle to the FBI, U.S. Customs, and the Royal Canadian Mounted Police as she pursued software pirates and provided her with plenty of inspiration as she began writing her own adventure-filled historical romances.

Boyle began writing seriously in 1990. By 1995 she had completed three manuscripts and had started writing a book that took a somewhat unusual path to publication. Instead of submitting it to publishers and hoping that her work, which would eventually be called *Brazen Angel* (1997), might be chosen from a slush pile of incoming unpublished manuscripts, Boyle submitted the first three chapters to the Diamond Dell contest sponsored by Dell Publishing. When Boyle was chosen as one of the contest's five finalists, the publisher asked her to send the complete book for final judging. What the publisher didn't know at the time was that Boyle didn't have a completed manuscript.

Over the next five weeks, Boyle worked very hard to finish her book, writing early in the morning before going to work and late at night so that she would have a completed manuscript to send to Dell. Boyle ended up writing and polishing her book right up until the last two days before it was due at the publisher's offices in New York. When Boyle missed the last Federal Express deadline on Saturday, her wonderfully supportive husband, Terry (the model for all her fictional heroes), booked a Sunday flight and carried the book to New York himself, arriving on time to deliver it to Dell on Monday.

All of Boyle's hard work and dedication paid off when *Brazen Angel* won the Diamond Dell award in 1996. It would go onto be nominated for two RITA awards: Best First Book and Best Long Historical. *Brazen Angel* won the RITA for Best First Book.

Brazen Heiress (1998) and *Brazen Temptress* (1999), both featuring D'Artier family members as either the hero or heroine, would follow *Brazen Angel,* as Boyle continued to explore the dangerous and intrigue-filled world of espionage during the Regency era.

Published in 2000, *No Marriage of Convenience* is the only one of Boyle's books that is not connected in some fashion to her other romances. It was originally intended to be the second book she wrote, but Boyle's publisher asked her to write *Brazen Heiress* instead. When Boyle moved from Dell to Avon and her new publisher asked for a book idea from her, she was able to offer them, with a few small changes, *No Marriage of Convenience*—a book she had been waiting three years to finish.

In *No Marriage of Convenience,* the hero, Oxford professor Mason St. Clair, inherits the title Earl of Ashlin along with three hoydenish nieces. Needing a lady to help launch his nieces into society, Mason accepts the beautiful and popular actress Riley Fontaine's offer to chaperone the girls and tutor them in the womanly arts in order to pay off the debt she owed the former Earl of Ashlin. Love, laughter, and danger all play a part in the story as Riley tries to reign in the girls, Mason tries to fight his attraction to Riley, and both search for the identity of the person trying to kill Riley.

While she didn't know it at the time, Boyle's next romance, *Once Tempted* (2001), would become the first in a new series of linked books. Having been inspired by an exhibition of Spanish art and interested in writing a treasure hunt romance, Boyle came up with idea of the legendary king's ransom. The book's hero, Major Robert Danvers, desperately seeks the ransom, the key to which is held by the romance's heroine, linguist Olivia Sutton. In addition to being the first of her romances to feature a Danvers hero, *Once Tempted* introduces several secondary characters, such as the spymaster Mr. Pymm, who will go onto play other small roles in future books. Another Danvers hero, Robert's older brother Colin, gets a chance at romance in *One Night of Passion* (2002), which actually takes place before *Once Tempted* and details how Colin met his future wife, Georgianna Escott, at a Cyprian's Ball.

Clever readers can discern the influence of one of Boyle's favorite movies, *It Happened One Night,* in her next book, *Stealing the Bride,* which was published in 2003. The hero, Temple, who is Colin Danver's cousin, is coerced into retrieving runaway heiress and friend Diana Fordham, who is being pursued by a number of suitors intent on finding and wedding the wealthy lady. For several reasons, Temple must find Diana first and see her wed to a suitable husband, but he never imagines he will end up being the one to marry the exasperating hoyden. *Stealing the Bride* offers a wonderful example of Boyle's ability to brilliantly balance humor, passion, and danger in a story.

The theme of hidden identities is one that readers frequently encounter in Boyle's romances. All three of Boyle's Brazen romances feature at least one person whose real identity is masked by another personality. Whether it is pirate captain Maureen Hawthorne, who is turned into a lady by the British admiralty in an attempt to trap the hero Julien D'Artier in *Brazen Temptress;* Lily D'Artier, who disguises herself as an heiress to keep

Napoleon from using important documents about the British espionage network in *Brazen Heiress;* or Sophie D'Artier, the elusive lady bandit sought after by Giles Corliss in *Brazen Angel,* Boyle loves writing books in which the main characters are not quite the people they first appear to be. Exploring the real person behind the mask is infinitely appealing to Boyle, who believes that all of us in some way or another must discover who the people in our own lives really are.

While some authors say that either characters or plot ideas come to them first, for Boyle it is really a question of both playing a part. For some books, such as *Brazen Angel* and *No Marriage of Convenience,* the idea for a plot came first. For other books, Boyle enjoys digging around to discover more about the characters, which in turn inspires an idea for their story. In some cases, secondary characters such as Colin Danvers or Temple simply demand to have their own book.

Even though a plot idea might inspire one book while a particular character may prompt another story, one thing does remain constant in all of Boyle's romances: Regency England is her preferred time period. This fascinating era—with the turmoil of the French Revolution, the beginnings of the Industrial Revolution, the warfare between England and France, and the elegant, splendid world of the *ton*—provides a wealth of material from which the gifted and inventive Boyle fashions her literary magic. Married for over a decade to her own hero, Boyle considers her primary job being a stay-at-home mother to her two young sons. But she's all too happy to have her other job, which allows her to escape toddler-dom and enter the enchanting and always exciting world of historical romantic fiction.

BIBLIOGRAPHY

Books: *Brazen Angel.* New York: Dell, 1997; *Brazen Heiress.* New York: Dell, 1998; *Brazen Temptress.* New York: Dell, 1999; *No Marriage of Convenience.* New York: Avon, 2000; *Once Tempted.* New York: Avon, 2001; *One Night of Passion.* New York: Avon, 2002; *Stealing the Bride.* New York: Avon, 2003; *It Takes a Hero.* New York: Avon, 2004; *Something about Emmaline.* New York: Avon, 2005; *This Rake of Mine.* New York: Avon, 2006; *His Mistress by Morning.* New York: Avon, 2006.

JOHN CHARLES

EMILY BRADSHAW. *See* Emily Carmichael

PAMELA BRITTON

Pamela Britton. Photo by Rae Monet, photographer. Courtesy of Pamela Britton.

A trick-riding, circus-performing nanny; a monkey with an attitude; a guardian angel in love with his charge; and a computer wizard who wants to be a cowboy—these are just a few of the characters from the vivid imagination of award-winning author Pamela Britton. She delights her readers with her wit and humor, passionate love scenes, and ingenious plots.

Britton was born in Bellflower, California, to Dr. Jack S. Leib, a graduate of UCLA with a degree in optometry, and Anita Leib, who served as his office manager throughout his career. Britton grew up in San Jose, California, where she received her high school diploma. She and her husband, Michael S. Baer, a contractor, have one daughter, Codi.

Part of Britton's résumé is traditional. She worked for several years for a real-estate developer, and then switched to managing group health-insurance plans. The rest of her employment history isn't quite as conventional: Britton found work being a model; drawing horses; and working for race teams, including NASCAR's Winston Cup. Many of the experiences from Britton's colorful career become part of her books.

Britton didn't always want to be a writer. One day, after reading a novel that pushed all of her hot buttons, Britton threw down the volume in disgust and said that she could "write a better book." Her husband said, "So then, why don't you?" and a writer was born. Britton says that her first book "stank." Set on improving, she worked with a retired schoolteacher who taught her grammar, and joined a critique group whose members taught her story, pacing, and plot. Britton's second book, *My Fallen Angel* (2000), a sequel to her first book, eventually sold to HarperCollins.

When developing characters, Britton says she uses a so-called Heinz 57 method. She feels there's a little part of her as well a bit of her friends in all her characters. Britton's favorite book *Tempted* (2004), was the easiest for her to write because the heroine is so much like her. Mary Brown Callahan doesn't want to be a spy, but her smuggler father insists she work as a nanny for Revenue Commander George Alexander Essex Drummond, the "Devil Marquis" of Warrick. Falling in love with the spunky nanny isn't hard, but because of his disreputable family tree, George cares too much about what society thinks. In light of Mary's station in life, he offers her a position not as his wife, but as his mistress. Mary doesn't care for George's proposition, and she lets him know in no uncertain terms. Mary, one of Britton's typical can-do heroines, plays Henry Higgins to George's Eliza Doolittle, and she is more than up to the challenge of turning her stuffy employer from elitist to egalitarian. As in her other books, Britton makes ample use of humor to enrich the story.

The Pygmalion theme is also present in Britton's book *Scandal* (2004). Charles Reinleigh Drummond Montgomery, sixth Earl of Sherborne, first appeared as the rakish cousin of the Devil Marquis in *Tempted*. Charles, or "Rein," falls out of favor with his uncle when he accidentally runs over the old man's vicious, obnoxious, but beloved dog. When his uncle dies, Rein is heir to the family fortune. However, the uncle gets back at his nephew from the grave by putting a strict condition on the inheritance—Rein must live anonymously among the common people of London for one month without any resources except the clothes on his back. Anna Rose Brooks lives with her grandfather, an eccentric, poverty-stricken inventor. Rein suffers a head wound when Anna's kite falls on his head, and she tends to him, giving him shelter in their shabby rooms. As a penniless man, Rein has to join Anna when she sells her wares on the mean streets of London. This humbling experience transforms the self-indulgent, stubborn nobleman into a genuine human being. In *Tempted,* as in many of her other books, Britton delightfully explores the transforming strength of love.

Another recurrent theme in Britton's books is the Cinderella story. Britton states, "My heroines are almost always down-on-their-luck women who find their Prince Charming." However, the difference between the title character of the classical fairy tale and Britton's heroines is their spunk and resourcefulness. Her Cinderellas always have to overcome obstacles in order to succeed. The heroine in *Seduced* (2003), Elizabeth Montclair, is only a member of society because crazy King George liked the shoes her cobbler grandfather created for him so much that the king made her grandfather an earl. A social outcast, no one in his right mind would marry her. Lucien St. Aubyn has earned the title "The Duke of Death" because everyone associated with him meets an untimely demise. When Elizabeth is found alone with Lucien, a notorious rogue, at an event, the *ton* brands her compromised, so Lucien offers for her hand. Lucien shares the one trait found in all Britton's heroes: they're never afraid to show their emotions to the heroine. Because of this, Elizabeth quickly realizes that Lucien's licentious behavior is a facade, and she falls in love with him. Just as they settle into their new life together, charges carrying the death penalty are brought against Lucien for the murder of his brother. In this particular story, Britton twists the Cinderella tale by having the heroine save the hero. *Seduced* showcases Britton's talent for characterization. The pages are filled with a whole cast of colorful characters: hard-to-forget servants, three-dimensional villains, a long-suffering pariah of a heroine, and an intensely guilt-ridden hero.

According to Britton, the hardest book for her to write was her first contemporary single title, *Dangerous Curves* (2005), the first book in her NASCAR series (*In the Groove,* 2006; *On the Edge,* 2006). She adds, "It had a lot of suspense in it, and I had a hard time balancing that with the romance." But balance them she did, and quite nicely. Fast-paced and filled with action and suspense, *Dangerous Curves* is the story of Blain Sanders, who never did forgive Cece Blackwell for building a better and faster car than he did when they were teenagers. Now a NASCAR star and owner of his own racing team, Blain is forced to turn to Cece, an FBI agent with an expertise in explosives, when someone kills his best friend during a race. Part of Blain's ego is still smarting from Cece's high school triumph, but even he has to admit she's the best person for the job. Soon, the persistent but elusive killer targets Blain, and, in a refreshing role reversal, Cece becomes his protector. Elements such as an unexpected villain, NASCAR information woven cleverly throughout the story, and a setting so real the reader can almost smell the exhaust fumes help make Britton's foray into contemporary romantic suspense a successful one.

Britton says her muse strikes without warning, whether she is "watching TV or eating mashed potatoes." Britton claims she doesn't have time for writer's block. She writes at least six hours a day, and can usually produce 10 pages, if not more. Usually, plot ideas come to her before the characters do.

According to Britton, romances are what she'll "always write." She says the genre appeals to her as a writer because she likes to "give readers happily ever afters." Britton loves the ability to create her own world, one in which love conquers all. Because of her husband's dare and that one poorly written book, readers, too, can visit the wonderful world of Britton's vivid imagination.

BIBLIOGRAPHY

Books: *My Fallen Angel.* New York: HarperCollins, 2000; *Enchanted by Your Kisses.* New York: HarperCollins, 2001; *Seduced.* New York: Warner, 2003; *Cowboy Lessons.* Toronto: Harlequin, 2003; *Tempted.* New York: Warner, 2004; *Scandal.* New York: Warner, 2004; *Cowboy Trouble.* Toronto: Harlequin, 2004; *Dangerous Curves.* Toronto: Harlequin, 2005; *In the Groove.* Toronto: Harlequin, 2006; *Cowboy M.D.* Toronto: Harlequin, 2006; *Lord Shameless.* Toronto: Harlequin, 2006; *On the Edge.* Toronto: Harlequin, 2006; *Cowboy D.V.M.* Toronto: Harlequin, 2006.
Novellas: "Wanted: One Hot-Blooded Man" in *Honk if You Love Real Men.* New York: St. Martin's Press, 2005; "Big, Bad Santa" in *Red Hot Santa.* New York: Ballantine, 2005.

SHELLEY MOSLEY

ANNE BROCK. *See* Suzanne Brockmann

SUZANNE BROCKMANN

Suzanne Brockman. Courtesy of Suzanne Brockman.

New York Times best-selling and RITA award-winning author Suzanne Brockmann did not originate the concept of a military hero, but more so than any other author, she is responsible for popularizing this kind of romantic hero with readers. With her Troubleshooter series featuring Navy SEAL Team Sixteen, and her "Tall, Dark, and Dangerous" series featuring Navy SEAL Team Ten, Brockmann not only introduced millions of readers to the fascinating world of the United States Navy SEAL program, but also enlightened them about the dangers these brave men face in the defense of their country.

Brockmann was born in 1960 in Englewood, New Jersey, to Elise-Marie and Frederick J. Brockmann. Her mother was an English teacher who later became a stay-at-home mom, and her father was a teacher; university professor; and later, superintendent of public schools in Guilford, Connecticut, and Farmingdale, New York. Brockmann grew up in a house "filled with books," and her childhood years were spent living in both New York and Connecticut. As a child, Brockmann did not dream of becoming a writer. Instead, her youthful career goals initially centered on becoming an Air Force pilot, and then later, a rock star.

---

also writing as Anne Brock

Brockmann first dabbled in the literary arts during her high school years when she wrote a *Star Trek* novel to entertain one of her friends in chemistry class. After graduating from Farmingdale High School in 1978, Brockmann attended Boston University School of Public Communication for several years before leaving college to become a songwriter and the lead singer in a local rock band. In addition to her career in music, Brockmann also worked as a word processor operator, ice-cream truck driver, aerobics instructor, and office/administrative temp.

When she did finally embrace the idea of writing for a living, Brockmann started out writing screenplays and TV scripts. She eventually wound up writing scripts on spec for such TV shows as *Star Trek: The Next Generation* and *Quantum Leap,* though none were ever produced. It was at this time that Brockmann set a goal for herself of being able to write a script from initial pitch to finished draft in 48 hours. Brockmann later found that her ability to write quickly and her structured work habits would come in quite handy when she began to write category romances.

Earning a living as a screenwriter was not easy, and the competition was fierce. Brockmann believed one way to distinguish herself from the crowd of other television film writers was to become published in genre fiction. After seriously studying the market, Brockmann decided the romance genre offered the most potential for new authors, and she set out to write her first love story in June of 1992. As it turned out, the romance genre proved to be the perfect choice for Brockmann.

Brockmann's first romance, *Future Perfect,* the story of an author struggling with writer's block and his romance with a bed-and-breakfast owner, was published in August, 1993, by Meteor Kismet. Brockmann's next book, *Hero Under Cover,* was published by Silhouette as part of their Intimate Moments line in 1994. Brockmann quickly developed a reputation with editors as an author who could be counted on to consistently deliver high-quality books within a short deadline. Soon, Brockmann was publishing up to seven romances a year, primarily for Silhouette and for Bantam's Loveswept line.

It was while brainstorming ideas for some kind of new hook for a trilogy of books that Brockmann came up with the idea of a series of romances featuring U.S. Navy SEALs. A friend had recently read something on SEAL training in *Newsweek* magazine and encouraged Brockmann to take a look at the article. Once she had read about the SEALs and the demanding course of training they had to endure, Brockmann knew she had the seed of an idea for her next series of books. In June 1996, *Prince Joe,* in which media consultant Veronica St. John gives Lt. Joe "Cat" Catalanotto lessons in etiquette so that he can impersonate a visiting European prince, became the first in her Tall, Dark, and Dangerous series published by Silhouette. The trilogy soon became an ongoing series featuring the men of SEAL Team Sixteen.

Not only did Brockmann's Tall, Dark, and Dangerous series become a favorite with readers, but it also received its share of critical acclaim. *Everyday, Average Jones* (1998) and *The Admiral's Bride* (1999), both part of the series, became RITA finalists. In addition, *The Admiral's Bride* was voted one of the Romance Writers of America's Top Ten Favorite Books for 1999. *Taylor's Temptation* (2001), another Tall, Dark, and Dangerous book, was chosen as one of the Romance Writers of America's Top Ten books for 2002. Even though the Tall, Dark, and Dangerous books quickly went out of print after their initial publication (like many series romances), they had became so popular with readers that Harlequin, the publisher, eventually began reissuing individual titles through their MIRA imprint.

Heart Throb, the story of fallen actor Jericho Beaumont, who struggles to rebuild his career, and movie producer Kate O'Laughlin, who isn't sure she is willing to take a chance on him, was published in 1999. It became Brockmann's first mainstream contemporary romance title. *Bodyguard* (1999), another compelling, fast-paced tale of romance and suspense, in which Brockmann pairs up a former mob wife and an FBI agent, soon followed and won a RITA in 2000 for Best Contemporary Single Title Romance.

The Unsung Hero, published in 2000, became the first book in Brockmann's Troubleshooters series. With each book in the series, a different SEAL is brought forward to act as the protagonist, but other members of the group frequently surface to play secondary roles in the story. Brockmann's Troubleshooters series, featuring both the large and small acts of heroism of a remarkable group of men and women, immediately found favor with readers. *The Unsung Hero* was the number-one choice on Romance Writers of America's Top Ten List of Favorite Romances for 2000, and *Over the Edge* (2001) became RWA's number-one Top Ten Favorite Book for the year 2001.

As a young girl, Brockmann became fascinated with World War II, and she read everything she could on the subject. Growing up during the Vietnam War era, it is easy to understand why Brockmann might be drawn to World War II, since it was a war in which it was much easier to distinguish the good guys from the bad guys. Brockmann's interest in World War II resurfaced when she began writing *The Unsung Hero.* In the book, the main focus is on Navy SEAL Lt. Tom Paoletti, who returns to his small New England hometown and thinks he spots a terrorist who is supposed to have died several years earlier. Another portion of the story deals with Tom's uncle Joe and his uncle's good friend and next-door neighbor Charles Ashton, both of whom served in World War II and seem to be struggling with a secret they share. Brockmann began including a secondary story line set during World War II as part of the plot of the books that followed in the Troubleshooters series. *The Defiant Hero* (2001) includes flashbacks of the World War II–era romance of the heroine's grandmother, Eve, as well as heroic events at Dunkirk. In *Over the Edge,* Brockmann pairs the story of the Danes' selfless efforts to save their Jewish citizens during the German invasion with a contemporary story of the rescue mission of a kidnap victim who happens to be an American senator's daughter.

Brockmann is an author who likes to set challenges for herself. A good example of this is the relationship she created between Lt. Sam Starrett and FBI agent Alyssa Locke. Brockmann wanted their romantic relationship to realistically unfold over a series of books in the Troubleshooters series. Readers are introduced to the two as secondary characters beginning with *The Unsung Hero,* in which Sam and Alyssa first meet and clash professionally. The two meet up again in *The Defiant Hero* and not only butt heads again professionally, but also indulge in a memorable night of passion. In *Over the Edge,* neither one can forget the night they shared. But just as Sam and Alyssa seem ready to pick up where they left off, Sam's former girlfriend, a very pregnant Mary Lou, shows up, forcing the ever-honorable Sam to marry her. In *Out of Control* (2002), readers experience the effect of this event from Alyssa's point of view, while in *Into the Night* (2002), Sam finally has the chance of a future with Alyssa after his wife, Mary Lou, asks for a divorce. Finally, in *Gone Too Far* (2003), Alyssa and Sam take center stage, but just as they seem poised to start over romantically, their relationship becomes even more complicated when Sam is accused of murdering his ex-wife and Alyssa is one of the agents investigating the case. Building and sustaining readers' interest in Alyssa and Sam's relationship through all of these books took a great deal of skill on Brockmann's part. However, she succeeded brilliantly in not only integrating the romance into the plotlines of Troubleshooters novels, but also in delivering an intensely suspenseful and sizzlingly sexy conclusion to Sam and Alyssa's love story in *Gone Too Far.*

Brockmann says she truly believes that "people are people and a love story is a love story," and this is reflected in her books, which celebrate the richness and diversity of America itself. For example, Brockmann's *Harvard's Education* (1998), the story of U.S. Navy SEAL Daryl "Harvard" Becker and FinCOM agent P. J. Richards, was only the second out of more than 800 Intimate Moments romances published by Silhouette to feature both an African American hero and heroine. *Gone Too Far* includes a secondary interracial romance between a black World War II pilot and a white woman, who is also a pilot. Then there's FBI agent Jules Cassidy, who just happens to be gay. Jules plays secondary roles in several of Brockmann's Troubleshooters books and, eventually, is given his own romantic story in *Hot Target* (2005). The need to love and be loved is a common thread that connects human beings, and few authors work with this theme as expertly and powerfully as the superbly talented Brockmann.

BIBLIOGRAPHY

Writing as Suzanne Brockmann

Books: *Future Perfect.* New York: Meteor Kismet, 1993; *Hero Under Cover.* New York: Silhouette, 1994; *Embraced by Love.* New York: Pinnacle, 1995; *Not Without Risk.* New York: Silhouette, 1995; *A Man to Die For.* New York: Silhouette, 1995; *No Ordinary Man.* Toronto: Harlequin, 1996; *Kiss and Tell.* New York: Bantam, 1996; *Prince Joe.* New York: Silhouette, 1996; *Forever Blue.* New York: Silhouette, 1996; *The Kissing Game.* New York: Bantam, 1996; *Frisco's Kid.* New York: Silhouette, 1997; *Otherwise Engaged.* New York: Bantam, 1997; *Forbidden.* New York: Bantam, 1997; *Stand-in Groom.* New York: Bantam, 1997; *Ladies' Man.* New York: Bantam, 1997; *Time Enough for Love.* New York: Bantam, 1997; *Love with the Proper Stranger.* New York: Silhouette, 1998; *Freedom's Price.* New York: Bantam, 1998; *Body Language.* New York: Bantam, 1998; *Everyday, Average Jones.* New York: Silhouette, 1998; *Harvard's Education.* New York: Silhouette, 1998; *It Came Upon a Midnight Clear.* New York: Silhouette, 1998; *Heart Throb.* New York: Fawcett, 1999; *The Admiral's Bride.* New York: Silhouette, 1999; *Undercover Princess.* New York: Silhouette, 1999; *Bodyguard.* New York: Fawcett, 1999; *Identity: Unknown.* New York: Silhouette, 2000; *Get Lucky.* New York: Silhouette, 2000; *The Unsung Hero.* New York: Ballantine, 2000; *The Defiant Hero.* New York: Ballantine, 2001; *Taylor's Temptation:* New York: Silhouette, 2001; *Over the Edge.* New York: Ballantine, 2001; *Out of Control.* New York: Ballantine, 2002; *Into the Night.* New York: Ballantine, 2002; *Letters to Kelly.* New York: Silhouette, 2003; *Gone Too Far.* New York: Ballantine, 2003; *Scenes of Passion.* New York: Silhouette, 2003; *Night Watch.* New York: Silhouette, 2003; *Flashpoint.* New York: Ballantine, 2004; *Hot Target.* New York: Ballantine, 2005; *Into the Storm.* New York: Random House, 2006; *Breaking Point.* New York: Random House, 2006.

Writing as Anne Brock

Book: *Give Me Liberty.* New York: Kensington, 1997.

JOHN CHARLES

CONNIE BROCKWAY

Connie Brockway. Photo by Heidi Eckhalt, photographer. Courtesy of Connie Brockway.

In the publishing world, conventional wisdom holds that once an author has written a particular story that has found favor with readers, the author should continue to write that same kind of book over and over again. Award-winning, best-selling author Constance "Connie" Brockway has spent most of her writing career breaking that particular rule. Since Brockway has the rare ability to be able to write not only light, witty historical romances but also dark, brooding, and emotionally intense love stories, each new book she writes tends to be quite different from the one before it. Therefore, while readers might not always be sure which kind of Connie Brockway they're getting with her latest novel, one thing they can count on is that it's bound to be a rare literary treat.

Brockway, who comes from a family of state-champion female swimmers, was born in Minneapolis, Minnesota. Her father was the president of International Multifoods, a Minnesota-based milling company, and her mother was the consummate executive wife and loving mother, who liked nothing better than reading to Brockway and her brother and playing catch with them in between cooking up gourmet meals. Though her family did spend some time during her grade school years in a small town in New York, Brockway spent most of her childhood growing up in the suburbs of Minneapolis.

Brockway attended Macalester College in St. Paul, where she graduated magna cum laude with a double major in art and English. During her college years, Brockway won several awards for both her art and her writing, and after graduating from Macalester in 1976, she was accepted into the creative writing program at the University of Minnesota. That same year, Brockway married medical student David Brockway. While attending graduate school, Brockway used her art skills to work as a graphic artist for the School of Medicine. Brockway also received training as a certified master gardener by the University of Minnesota Extension Office, and she spent two years working as a horticultural expert for a garden center in Minneapolis, in addition to working as a graphic illustrator.

When her daughter was born, Brockway opted to give up her job as a graphic illustrator and her career in horticulture to become a stay-at-home mother. After her daughter entered kindergarten, Brockway decided to give herself one year to try to write a book before "dusting off her pens and pencils" and "looking for another illustrator's job." Brockway briefly flirted with the idea of writing the next great American novel before she remembered the old writing adage, "Write what you know." Ultimately, Brockway decided to write the kind of book she herself enjoyed reading: one rich in history and filled with centuries-old gossip about lords and ladies, exotic locales, and lives transformed by passion and love.

Brockway was a complete novice when it came to the practical details of how a book gets published, but she saw something called the Romance Writers of America mentioned in a newspaper article she was reading. She called the number in the contact information for the article, went to a workshop given by the local RWA chapter, and began writing her first historical romance. In 1994, Brockway's first book became a finalist for the RWA's Golden Heart awards and was bought by Avon, who published the book that year as *Promise Me Heaven.*

In *Promise Me Heaven,* when Lady Catherine "Cat" Sinclair discovers she must wed a wealthy man, she sets out to find a rake to tutor her in the art of seduction. Cat picks Thomas Montrose as her teacher, even though Thomas is officially retired from the seduction business. Thomas agrees to give Cat the benefit of his vast experience in the sensual arts but never expects that she will become an expert so quickly! Readers immediately fell in love with Brockway's gift for blending wit and sensuality. *Anything for Love,* also published in 1994, followed *Promise Me Heaven* and has the distinction of being the only one of Brockway's historical romances to be set entirely in the United States.

A Dangerous Man (1996), Brockway's third historical romance, opens with a bang when the hero, gunslinger-for-hire Hart "Duke" Moreland, shoots the heroine, Mercy Coltrane, to save her from a kidnapper. Six years later, when her brother disappears, Mercy comes to England looking for Duke, the man who once shot her, to get his help. After being introduced to the Earl of Perth, Mercy realizes the Earl is none other than Duke, and she sets out to blackmail him into helping her locate her brother. Since he has inherited a title and is trying to arrange suitable matches for his sisters, the last thing Duke wants is the truth about his past getting out. When danger threatens Mercy, though, Duke is forced to choose between honor and love. Darker in tone than her previous two books, *A Dangerous Man* beautifully explores the themes of obligation, choices and their consequences, and the redeeming power of love.

As You Desire, published in 1997, proved to be the complete opposite of the dark, emotionally intense *A Dangerous Man.* Light in tone and brimming with Brockway's insouciant charm, *As You Desire* proved to be a "gift book" for the author. "I supposed because the characters were completely clear to me from the outset, I never had to go searching for them in the writing," she recalls. Set in exotic Egypt in the late nineteenth century, the romance that blossoms between fortune-hunting rogue Harry Braxton and linguist/Egyptologist Desdemona Carlisle is pure literary magic. The wonderfully witty *As You Desire* earned Brockway her first RITA nomination.

With *All Through the Night* (1997), Brockway once again turned to the dark side of romance for the story of Colonel Jack Seward, who played a small role in Brockway's first romance, *Promise Me Heaven,* and widow Ann Wilder, who turns out to be the notorious cat burglar known as "Wrexhall's Wraith." While Brockway finds each book challenging in its own way, she believes that *All Through the Night,* with its complex characters and sensually explicit plot dealing with the themes of erotic obsession, guilt and compulsion, and betrayal and redemption, was perhaps harder for her to write than any other book. Brockway says, "It is a dark, edgier book. It really had little humor, and subsequently, writing the characters, their conflict, and that conflict's resolution—as well as the whole darn plot—was like trying to play an orchestral piece with a limited number of notes."

Inspired by the sparkling, romantic 1940s cinematic comedies of Tracy and Hepburn, *My Dearest Enemy,* which appeared in 1998, is another of Brockway's light historical romances. In the book, independent-minded, fervent feminist Lily Bede and Avery Thorne, a 98-pound weakling turned muscular world adventurer, find themselves matching wits when they must compete for the same estate. Lily is given five years to run the estate, during which time Avery stays away, traveling the globe. But he falls in love with Lily through the letters she includes when she sends him his allowance. Lily is an excellent example of Brockway's brand of pragmatic and practical heroines, and honorable, humorous Avery proves to be more than a match for her. Women's issues and women's relationships also play an essential part in *My Dearest Enemy.* Brockway wanted to show how friendships between women, in this case Lily and Evelyn, a cousin of Avery's who lives at the estate, are important and can continue to flourish even after one or both fall in love. *My Dearest Enemy* won Brockway her first Romance Writers of America's RITA award in 1999.

Brockway's next three books were the McClairen's Isle trilogy. Including *The Passionate One* (1999), *The Reckless One* (2000), and *The Ravishing One* (2001), this was her first series of connected romances. The idea of writing a trilogy actually came from Brockway's editor, who suggested that if Brockway wanted to build an audience for her writing, she might want to consider the idea of a series of connected novels. Brockway, inspired by tales she heard about castles while traveling in Scotland, came up with the idea of a trilogy revolving around a dispossessed Scottish clan and the English family who is deeded the confiscated estates. Each book in the trilogy features a different Merrick sibling—Ash, Raine, and Fia— three children of the nefarious Earl of Carr, an English nobleman banished to the Scottish Highlands for his societal sins.

Brockway found herself presented with several challenges in creating her McClairen's Isle books. The first came from having to retell the story of Ronald Merrick, the infamous Earl of Carr, and all of his children in each book of the trilogy. Once Brockway found a way around this obstacle, she concentrated on developing the stories of each of the Merrick siblings. One of the most interesting elements about the McClairen's Isle books is how the reader's perceptions of a character, such as Fia, change as different details and subtle nuances of the characters are revealed with each book in the trilogy. Featuring Brockway's lush, lyrical writing style, the McClairen's Isle books are emotionally intense and at times quite dark, but a good dose of the author's wonderfully acerbic sense of wit helps to lighten the brooding tone of this truly magnificent trilogy.

The Bridal Season (2001), the first of two loosely connected historical romances set in Victorian England, marked Brockway's return to the lighter side of romance. The book's heroine, music-hall performer Letty Potts, while trying to escape from her occasional partner in crime, assumes the identity of wedding coordinator Lady Agatha Whyte. Initially, Letty has no intention of continuing to masquerade as Lady Agatha, but she finds she just can't leave the Bigglesworth family, who hired the celebrated wedding coordinator, in the lurch. So Letty ends up in the village of Little Bidewell, where she meets the irresistibly handsome local magistrate, Sir Elliot March. Sir Elliot, however, proves to be a threat to her future in more ways than one. Letty is another of Brockway's quick-witted and sensible heroines, and while she is basically an unrepentant thief (which annoyed some of Brockway's readers to no end), Letty isn't anyone's victim. One of Letty's most appealing qualities is that she refuses to let her past mistakes define her future, and in doing so, the all-too-human Letty gives herself permission to have a happily ever after ending of her own. The frothy and witty *The Bridal Season* was not only chosen as one of the Romance Writers of America's Top Ten Favorite Books of the year in 2002, but it also won Brockway her much deserved second RITA award.

For *Once Upon a Pillow*, published in 2002, Brockway collaborated with longtime friend and fellow romance writer, Christina Dodd. The idea for the book came from Dodd's husband, who suggested the two write a romance about a bed. Given this kernel of inspiration, Brockway and Dodd developed the story of the Masterson bed and its owners through the centuries. Living approximately 1,500 miles away from each other in different states proved to be no obstacle for Brockway and Dodd, who each wrote separate stories about a couple whose romance had ties to the bed. The two then coauthored the writing that connected the stories together. Brockway especially enjoyed writing her two romances for *Once Upon a Pillow*, since it allowed her the opportunity to write a romance set in the medieval era, a time period she had not had the chance to explore as an author.

A soldier, a swordsman, and a scoundrel—these are the three heroes of Brockway's next trilogy, The Rose Hunters. Set in Regency England and Scotland, the books center around three childhood friends: Christian "Kit" MacNeill, Ramsey Munro, and Hunter Dand. Known collectively as The Rose Hunters, the three become entangled with the Nash sisters—Kate, Helena, and Charlotte—after the sisters' father saves their lives in France. Kit, Ramsey, and Hunter have all sworn to protect and serve the Nash sisters. And each of the Rose Hunters finds himself having to honor his promise to a different Nash lady, beginning with 2004's *My Pleasure* (Kit and Kate's story); followed by 2004's *My Seduction* (Helena and Ramsey's story); and culminating in 2005's *My Surrender* (Hunter and Charlotte's story), which brings the trilogy to its triumphant conclusion.

While each of The Rose Hunters books stands as a complete story in and of itself, Brockway skillfully builds the overall story arc of the trilogy through a connecting story line involving the identity of the traitor who betrayed Kit, Ramsey, and Hunter while they were imprisoned in France. Imbued with a rich sense of history, including some fascinating details about roses, swordsmanship, and espionage, The Rose Hunters books explore such themes as obligation, sacrifice, trust, friendship, revenge, and honor—all within a trio of superbly sensual, thoroughly romantic love stories. The Rose Hunters books also earned Brockway the rare distinction of having two books nominated for a RITA award in the same year, when *My Pleasure* and *My Seduction* were both selected as finalists for this award in 2005.

Whether light and sparkling, dark and edgy, or somewhere in between, Brockway's superb novels have the one thing that matters most to readers: a happy ending. Brockway puts it best when she says, "I think, at heart, romance writers (and readers) are optimists. We like to believe that lessons learned provide illumination and not darkness, that struggle is rewarded, and that the past does not irrevocably blight the future. The romance between hero and heroine is a demonstration of, perhaps even an allegory for, that optimism." In a time when these qualities seem to be in short supply, Brockway, in her unique and inimitable way, gives readers what they and the world need most: hope and love.

BIBLIOGRAPHY

Books: *Promise Me Heaven.* New York: Avon, 1994; *Anything for Love.* New York: Avon, 1994; *A Dangerous Man.* New York: Dell, 1996; *As You Desire.* New York: Dell, 1997; *All Through the Night.* New York: Dell, 1997; *My Dearest Enemy.* New York: Dell, 1998; *McClairen's Isle: The Passionate One.* New York: Dell, 1999; *McClairen's Isle: The Reckless One.* New York: Dell, 2000; *McClairen's Isle: The Ravishing One.* New York: Dell, 2001; *The Bridal Season.* New York: Dell, 2001; *Once Upon a Pillow* (coauthored with Christina Dodd). New York: Pocket, 2002; *Bridal Favors.* New York: Dell, 2002; *My Seduction.* New York: Pocket, 2004; *My Pleasure.* New York: Pocket, 2004; *My Surrender.* New York: Pocket, 2005; *Hot Dish.* New York: Signet, 2006.

Novellas: "Heaven with a Gun" in *Outlaw Love.* New York: Dell, 1997; "Lassie Go Home" in *My Scottish Summer.* New York: Warner, 2001; "Glad Rags" in *True Love Wedding Dress.* New York: Onyx, 2005.

JOHN CHARLES

JO ANN BROWN. *See* Jo Ann Ferguson

LISA CACH

Originality is perhaps the best word to describe romance author Lisa Cach's books. From contemporary chick lit to historical paranormals, this talented author mixes love and laughter together with highly entertaining results.

Lisa Cach lives in Seattle, Washington. Perhaps the first evidence of Cach's highly original writing skills appeared during high school when she submitted a paper for her high school biology class, in which she created her own fictional animal—a "frat," half frog, half bat. Before turning to romance writing, Cach accepted a job as an English conversation teacher in Japan. Then, after earning a master's degree in psychology, she worked the graveyard shift at a crisis hotline for three years, writing her romance novels during the quiet spells between calls.

Cach began seriously writing romances in 1989 but was dissatisfied with her first attempt (a book that involved an amnesia plot). After taking a break from writing for a few years, Cach began courting the muse again in 1996, and she says she sold her first book, *The Changeling Bride*, "over the transom" to Dorchester in 1999. *The Changeling Bride* features Elle, a modern-day heroine who is transported back into the past to assume the life of Eleanor Moore, an heiress about to wed the Earl of Allsbrook. Fairies and magic play a role in bringing these two together, but Cach also has Elle struggle with more practical concerns such as birth control in the 1790s and a distinct lack of modern plumbing conveniences. Cach's debut romance demonstrated her talent for witty dialogue and original plotting.

Cach followed *The Changeling Bride* with two historical paranormals: *Bewitching the Baron* (2000) and *Of Midnight Born* (2000). *Bewitching the Baron* is a historical in which an English baron finds himself bewitched by a woman with unusual healing gifts. In *Of Midnight Born,* Cach demonstrates a willingness to blend different elements by giving her story a heroine who has been a ghost for 500 years. When the hero with an interest in astronomy shows up to take residence, the heroine does everything she can to scare him off.

Cach's next two books, *The Mermaid of Penperro* (2001) and *The Wildest Shore* (2001), were both more traditional historical romances, but they also demonstrate her inventive plotting and gift for humor.

Cach tried her hand at chick lit with her first contemporary romance, *Dating without Novocaine* (2002), one of Harlequin's then-new series of books released under their Red Dress Ink line. At that time, most of the other books in the Red Dress Ink series were set in New York and featured big-city heroines, but Cach put a unique stamp on her book by giving it a West Coast setting in Portland, Oregon, and a heroine with a career as a seamstress.

With *George and the Virgin* (2002), Cach returned to mixing elements from several romance subgenres by sending the hero, a twenty-first-century professional wrestler, back to the Middle Ages to fight a dragon that has been holding a small village for ransom for years. Each year, the village of Markesaw must provide the dragon with one virgin to eat. Alizon, the heroine, "won" the lottery 12 years earlier, but proved to be too tough for the dragon. Unbeknownst to the village, she has worked out an arrangement whereby she saves each young girl sent to feed the dragon. From the opening chapter in which Cach narrates Alizon's attempts to get a young shepherd to rid her of her virginity to her plotting to keep the hero, George, unaware of what is really going on, the wit and originality of this story delights readers.

Given the paranormal elements in much of Cach's writing, it might seem highly improbable that her books would be a reflection of her own life, but readers can see touches of Cach in each of her romances. The author's love of desserts and sweets surely provided a source of inspiration for the heroines in two of her short stories, "Eliza's Gateau" (2000) and "Puddings, Pastries, and Thou" (2001). In particular, the luscious descriptions of chocolate in "Eliza's Gateau" could only have come from someone who shares a fondness for this sweet treat. Cach must also have drawn on her own experience when she gave the heroine in *Dating without Novocaine* a friend who works as a crisis counselor, and her use of Portland as a setting in the book reflects Cach's own love of that city.

Cach's love of travel often provides a source of inspiration for her books as well. A trip to Southeast Asia and the island of Borneo gave the author the opportunity to experience the area that would serve as the setting for her book *The Wildest Shore*. When Cach went to Nepal, she intended to use her trip to gather background information for a historical romance, but instead, her own adventures would eventually be incorporated as bits and pieces of her contemporary spy spoof, *Dr. Yes* (2003). Even though Cach wrote *Dr. Yes* as one of the titles in Dorchester's B.L.I.S.S. series, she still manages to evoke the splendid beauty of Nepal. Many of the settings of Cach's other books also have a real-world counterpart inspired by the author's travels.

Whether writing about time-traveling professional wrestlers, opera singers masquerading as mermaids, or contemporary girls searching for love and friendship, Cach brings her own unique touch to each of her protagonists. And although she writes romances that do not always fit neatly into one subgenre, they are always impossible to put down.

BIBLIOGRAPHY

Books: *The Changeling Bride.* New York: Dorchester, 1999; *Bewitching the Baron.* New York: Dorchester, 2000; *Of Midnight Born.* New York: Dorchester, 2000; *The Mermaid of Penperro.* New York: Dorchester, 2001; *The Wildest Shore.* New York: Dorchester, 2001; *Dating without Novocaine.* Toronto: Harlequin, 2002; *George and the Virgin.* New York: Dorchester, 2002; *Dr. Yes.* New York:

Dorchester, 2003; *Come to Me.* New York: Dorchester, 2004; *Dream of Me.* New York: Dorchester, 2004; *Have Glass Slippers, Will Travel.* New York: Pocket, 2005; *A Babe in Ghostland.* New York: Pocket, 2006; *The Erotic Secrets of a French Maid.* New York: Pocket, 2006.

Novellas: "A Midnight Clear" in *Mistletoe and Magic.* New York: Dorchester, 2000; "Eliza's Gateau" in *Seduction by Chocolate.* New York: Dorchester, 2000; "Puddings, Pastries, and Thou" in *Wish List.* New York: Dorchester, 2001; "The Breeding Season" in *A Mother's Way.* New York: Dorchester, 2002; "Return to Sender" in *Christmas Cards from the Edge.* New York: Dorchester, 2005.

JOHN CHARLES

LAURIE SCHNEBLY
CAMPBELL

Laurie Campbell. Courtesy of Laurie Campbell.

Laurie Schnebly Campbell's talent for writing contemporary romances was apparent from the release of her first published novel, *And Father Makes Three,* which was named the Silhouette Special Edition Premiere title of 1995 and was nominated by *Romantic Times* as Best First Series Romance. Her second novel, *Unexpected Family,* was also a hit and was named *Romantic Times'* Best Special Edition Romance of 1999. Campbell joined others at the top of the field by being named to *Romantic Times'* "200 Best Books of 1980–2000." Her subsequent novels continue to capture the hearts and loyalty of her readers, leaving them waiting anxiously for her next release.

The fourth generation of her family to call Arizona home, Campbell, daughter of Larry Schnebly, a noted local broadcaster, and Lee Schnebly, a singer, writer, and marriage and family counselor, grew up in Tucson. Campbell's great-grandfather was T. Carl Schnebly, who settled in Arizona wilderness territory with his wife in 1902. They started one of the area's first fruit orchards and operated a small store. Carl established the region's first post office and named the town, which is still known today for its breathtaking beauty, after his wife, Sedona.

Campbell holds a bachelor's degree in journalism from the University of Arizona and a master's degree in counseling from Arizona State University. By profession, Campbell works for an advertising agency in Phoenix, writing and producing brochures and television commercials and occasionally providing voice tracks. In addition, she records books for the blind, counsels newly diagnosed diabetics, and enjoys conducting writer's workshops. Her counseling expertise provides a unique insight into human behavior and the art of character development.

Although always a writer at heart, Campbell did not consider becoming a romance novelist until her early thirties. Her interest was piqued by an article in the newspaper about a novel-writing workshop sponsored by Romance Writers of America , and although she wasn't a reader of romance novels, she decided to give romance writing a try. Her apparent lack of experience in the genre prompted her RWA mentor to very diplomatically advise, "You might want to *read* some." In doing so, Campbell found that the genre she had never noticed actually had merit. The stories she read had an optimistic worldview and the reassuring certainty of a happy ending, which were qualities that appealed to Campbell.

A writing style that flows as naturally as spoken narration is one of Campbell's hallmarks. Her plots occur in the present-day and are derived from her observations of real-life events or from creative adaptations of classic stories. In *Home at Last* (2001), for example, a woman's ex-husband disappears with her three children. *Unexpected Family* (1999) follows the *Madame Butterfly* story of a man who leaves his pregnant love and marries an American, but in this book, the heroine is the American wife. Campbell prefers to develop the story idea first and then create characters to fill the roles. Her hometown of Phoenix has become her favorite setting. She enjoys casting her characters in places that she can easily visit to personally experience the ambience.

Campbell's novels usually involve characters who doubt themselves and don't believe they're good enough, but ultimately discover that they are. True to the genre, her novels reinforce the notion that people who love each other and work together to build a mutually rewarding relationship will always gain more than they give. This can be seen in *His Brother's Baby* (2003), where Conner Tarkington assumes responsibility for his brother's ex-wife and infant daughter.

The greatest part of being a writer, according to Campbell, is the sense of being in control of the outcome. She enjoys crafting the plot and characters and making them come to life as the story unfolds. She says her greatest motivations are the excitement and "absolute primal joy" she derives from the writing process. Campbell is inspired by writers whose work touches her so deeply that she wants to give the same experience to her own readers. She cites Patricia Coughlin, Susan Howatch, and Eloise Jarvis McGraw as longtime favorites. Campbell also admits that she gains a measure of encouragement from books written so poorly that they restore her faith in her own writing ability.

Campbell believes that the hardest of her books to write is always the one she's currently working on. She says the easiest book to write by far was her first one, because it was written with no awareness of "The Rules," such as "have a reasonable number of chapters" and "don't expect readers to remember things you haven't yet told them." For the same reason, this book is also her sentimental favorite. It's the one-of-a-kind, unpublished manuscript that she would rescue first from a burning building.

Campbell says her free time is reserved for her husband, Pete, who is "the inspiration for every romantic hero I've ever written," and their son, Christopher. Her hobbies are reading and writing, and she teaches fourth-grade religious education at her church. Her popularity with other authors is based on her cheery disposition, her readiness to help, and her sometimes quirky sense of humor. After all, when choosing a holiday to feature in her story for the anthology *Romancing the Holidays, Volume II,* who else would select National Pickle Week?

BIBLIOGRAPHY

Books: *And Father Makes Three.* New York: Silhouette, 1995; *Unexpected Family.* New York: Silhouette, 1999; *Good Morning, Stranger.* New York: Silhouette. 2000; *Home at Last.* New York: Silhouette, 2001; *His Brother's Baby.* New York: Silhouette, 2003; *Wrong Twin, Right Man.* New York: Silhouette, 2004.
Novella: "Criscross" in *Romancing the Holidays, Volume II.* Phoenix, AZ: Elan Press, 2002.

SANDRA VAN WINKLE AND SHELLEY MOSLEY

ANN CARBERRY. *See* Maureen Child

SUSANNAH CARLETON

When she was 33 years old, Susannah Carleton discovered Regency romances. It was love at first sight. Carleton loved the vivid sense of history, the fascinating characters, and most of all, the sparkling dialogue and witty conversations that serve as the foundation for almost every traditional Regency romance. This newfound love for Regency-era novels would eventually inspire Carleton to write her own books.

Carleton was born Susan A. Lantz in Hamilton, Ohio, in 1953. Her father was an engineer, and Carleton's mother, after raising her children, went back to college when she was in her forties to get a degree and become a nutritionist. Because her father worked in several different divisions of General Electric over the course of his career, Carleton and her family lived in different parts of the Midwest, including Cincinnati, Ohio; Glen Ellyn, Illinois; and Carmel, Indiana. Since her family spent the most time in Louisville, Kentucky, Carleton considers this town her home.

Carleton attended the University of Kentucky, where she received a bachelor of science degree in both mechanical engineering and science in 1976. While at the University of Kentucky, she went on to complete her master's degree in science in 1979 and another master's degree in mechanical engineering. Carleton later attended the University of Illinois in Chicago, where, in 1984, she received her PhD in engineering mechanics, with a specialization in orthopedic biomechanics.

While in college, Carleton worked as a pianist, a typist, and an assistant in an anatomy research lab. She worked as an intern for both General Electric and IBM, and after receiving her bachelor's degree in science, Carleton was hired by IBM as a test engineer. While pursuing her master's degree in science, Carleton not only worked as a graduate research assistant at the University of Kentucky but also as a part-time cocktail waitress and bartender. After graduating with her master's degree in science, Carleton accepted a job as a biomedical engineer for the Rehabilitation Institute of Chicago. When Carleton decided to concentrate on her PhD, she again worked as a graduate research assistant and also took a job as a secretary to two Methodist ministers. It was while working for the one of the ministers that

Carleton met her husband, Timothy Lloyd Jones. After completing her PhD, Carleton went on to the world of academia, working as an assistant professor and an associate professor for several different universities, including Wayne State University and the University of Utah.

In December 1987, after grading what Carleton calls "a truly horrible set of final exams," she decided to stop by one of the branches of the Detroit Public Library for something enjoyable to read. Carleton recalls, "I browsed through the shelves and found four or five books, two of which—Georgette Heyer's *Regency Buck* and Martha L. Thomas's *Waltz with a Stranger*—looked particularly appealing. I read *Waltz with a Stranger* first, and then *Regency Buck,* and was immediately hooked. The following week, I was back at the library again, looking for more of those Walker Regency romances. Fortunately for me, the Detroit Public Library system has (or had at the time) a lot of them. I read them all—every single one and any book that appeared to be similar." Thus began Carleton's lifelong love affair with Regency romances.

Eventually, just reading Regency-era novels wasn't enough, and Carleton decided to try writing one herself. From 1996 to 1998, Carleton worked on *A Scandalous Journey,* which was originally titled *The Perfect Bride,* and entered the completed manuscript in both the Beau Monde's Royal Ascot contest and the Romance Writers of America's Golden Heart contest. Carleton then wrote a novella, "The Viscount's Angel," and submitted it to the Regency Press's Regency Sampler contest, where it took second place and was published in the summer of 1999. Carleton also began working on the prologue for what would become her book *The Marriage Campaign* (2003), which was originally titled *The Chosen Bride.*

Carleton again submitted *A Scandalous Journey* to the Royal Ascot contest, where it placed third. She wrote her second novella, "The Unexpected Guest," which was published by Regency Press in their *Winter Holiday Sampler* in late 2000, and she continued working on *The Marriage Campaign.* Despite repeated urging from several published Regency authors, it took Carleton some time before she worked up the courage to submit *The Marriage Campaign* to an editor.

I might not have done it then had Hilary Ross not mentioned at the 2000 RWA conference that she was looking for new Regency authors. (And I wouldn't have had that conversation with her had she not gotten lost in the conference hotel!) The first time I sent the manuscript, it was lost between the mailroom and her office. I inquired about it several months later, learned that she hadn't received it, and resent it. Hilary asked that I revise *A Scandalous Journey* to include a male coconspirator for the villainess, which I did, although not as quickly as Hilary wanted it. I was going to wait until I finished *The Marriage Campaign,* but at the RWA conference in 2001, she practically begged me to send it to her as soon as I could. So I started working on it when I got home and sent it to her about two weeks later. She bought it and two other books in October 2001.

The year 2001 proved to be a very good year for Carleton. Not only did editor Hilary Ross buy three books from her for Signet's traditional Regency line, but *A Scandalous Journey* was a finalist in RWA's Golden Heart contest, and *The Marriage Campaign* won the Royal Ascot contest. Carleton says *The Marriage Campaign* won "even though my mother thought the first chapter was slow and kind of boring compared to my first book … needless to say, that chapter and the following one were rewritten long before Hilary Ross ever saw the book!" Published in 2002 by Signet, *A Scandalous Journey* is the first in a series of loosely connected books Carleton refers to as The Six. The story focuses on George Winterbrook, the Earl of Weymouth, who is kidnapped by an eccentric divorcee intent on blackmailing him into marriage, only to escape her clutches with a little help from American Beth Castleton.

With *A Scandalous Journey*, Carleton introduces Beth Castleton, the founder of The Six, a group of six musically inclined young ladies who are making their debuts into society in 1813. It isn't until Carleton's second book, *The Marriage Campaign*, that the friendship, based partly on their shared love of music, becomes an important part of the story. The six members of the group include Beth Castleton *(A Scandalous Journey)*, Karolina "Karla" Lane *(The Marriage Campaign)*, Deborah Woodhurst *(Twin Peril)*, Sarah Mallory *(A Rake's Redemption)*, Christina "Tina" Fairchild, and Harriet Broughton. Since books in The Six series are set roughly at the same time, a scene that appears in one book can also show up in another book, though from a different character's point of view. For example, the attempted kidnapping of Sarah Mallory by Sir Edward Smithson turns up not only in *A Rake's Redemption* (2004) but also in *Twin Peril* (2005). Writing a concurrent set of books can be a difficult task, but Carleton does a particularly skillful job at integrating each of these shared scenes.

Many authors use their own character traits or interests when creating their heroes and heroines, and Carleton is no exception. The heroines' love of music in The Six series is one trait that definitely comes from their creator. Carleton says her interest in science is also evident in some of her characters: "Several [characters] have been mathematical, and most of the heroes are scholars, but each in a different area. A number of characters are also shy. The heroine of *A Scandalous Journey* is very like me—the Regency equivalent of a woman engineer—and was, to a certain extent, based on me. (An example of writing what you know.) There is also, in a very different way, a lot of me in the heroine of *A Twist of Fate*. But my characters are more daring than I."

Carleton's third book, *A Twist of Fate*, published in 2003, is not really a part of The Six series, but it is connected to Carleton's first book through its hero, Lord David Winterbrook, who is related to the hero of *A Scandalous Journey*. In *A Twist of Fate*, the book's heroine, Madeline Graves, still bears the scars of an abusive first marriage, and all she wants to do is live peacefully by herself in her little cottage. When Madeline is rescued during a snowstorm by David Winterbrook, politeness demands that she let him stay with her until the storm abates. Legend has it that the Winterbrook men will recognize their loves at first sight, and one glimpse of Madeline is enough to convince David that she is the only woman for him. Now all he has to do is convince Madeline that he is the one man she can trust. Carleton subtly invests a tremendous depth of emotion into the beautifully written, richly poignant *A Twist of Fate*.

Carleton is passionate about Regency romances.

I can't pinpoint one thing about Regency romances that most appeals to me—the era, with its rules that everyone had to follow or suffer the consequences; the fact that most Regencies are lighthearted comedy-of-manners stories that capture the elegance of that glittering but fleeting romantic era; [or] the happy endings. I love the way the words flow in Regencies and the witty banter. I like the richness of detail about etiquette, customs, clothing, and scenery. I love the plethora of characters. And all of these people talk. Some are witty; some are arrogant; some speak eloquently, some irreverently, some eruditely, some foolishly. Some speak without listening or speak before thinking, but they all talk. I love the dialogue in Regencies, which, in my admittedly prejudiced opinion, is far superior to that in most romance novels. I like the variety of plots—mistaken identities, long-lost heirs, long-lost spouses, unexpected inheritances, expected inheritances that don't materialize, love at first sight, or marriages of convenience. Maybe their appeal is as simple as the fact that Regencies provide such a lovely framework for the standard romance formula or such a delightful diversion from my everyday world. Maybe it's a combination of all the things I mentioned above. I don't really know why they so appeal to me, but they do.

Love is like that. Sometimes, it isn't one grand gesture but rather a combination of many little things that makes us fall in love. This is perfectly exemplified by Carleton's passion for Regency romances, an affair that continues to flourish nearly twenty years after she first fell in love.

BIBLIOGRAPHY

Books: *A Scandalous Journey.* New York: Signet, 2002; *The Marriage Campaign.* New York: Signet, 2003; *A Twist of Fate.* New York: Signet, 2003; *A Rake's Redemption.* New York: Signet, 2004; *Twin Peril.* New York: Signet, 2005.

Novellas: "The Viscount's Angel" in *A Regency Sampler.* Cleveland Heights, OH: Regency Press, 1999; "The Unexpected Guest" in *Winter Holiday Sampler.* Cleveland Heights, OH: Regency Press, 2000.

John Charles and Joanne Hamilton-Selway

LIZ CARLYLE

Liz Carlyle. Photo by Christopher J. Happel/Studio 16. Courtesy of Liz Carlyle.

Liz Carlyle's books are a literary treasure trove of riches. From the richly nuanced characters she creates to the richly detailed settings she evokes to the rich sensuality that imbues all of her books, Carlyle's love stories are historical romance at its best. Add to that her elegant writing style, which is always rich in sharp wit.

Carlyle was born in Nansemond County, near the eastern shore of Virginia, "way back" in 1958. Her mother was a native Virginian, who worked as a bookkeeper for the Virginia State Department of Transportation until she retired from her job to start a family. Carlyle spent her earliest years growing up on the eastern shore and in northern Virginia, around Alexandria. Carlyle's father traveled a great deal with his business. Eventually, the frequent relocations became a bit much, so the family moved south to the Blue Ridge Mountains to be near Carlyle's mother's family.

Carlyle was in the seventh grade when she was first introduced to the joys of writing by a distinctly original teacher, Mr. Jim Epperly. Carlyle says, "He was one of those instructors who struck fear into the hearts of children everywhere. You would spend your last two or three years prior to the seventh grade praying he would retire. His class was a bit like academic boot camp, and at the tender age of 12, I found myself writing at least one essay and giving at least one extemporaneous speech before my class every week—those were terrifying. But I read twice as much and worked twice as hard in that class than in my freshman year of college. And I learned more—much more." Carlyle says Epperly was skilled at recognizing a child's budding talent: "He had a knack for finding each student's gift and bringing it out by sheer force of will. He told me early on that I had a talent for writing, and that he was going to help me cultivate it—*whether I liked it or not.*"

Carlyle learned about the discipline needed for writing from Epperly.

[He] didn't care about your handwriting or your margins or the globs of ink on the pages. He would scrawl a topic on the chalkboard and give us one hour to write a four-page critical essay. He wanted to make you think on your feet. He wanted to see if you could take a clear position and defend it. And he wanted to build utter confidence inside each one of us. And it worked. Writing and self-discipline became second nature for me, and from that day to this, I have never suffered a moment of writer's block or worried that I might fail. Of course I might fail. I *have* failed, and I will again. But I know that failure is only temporary if you have the guts to rethink, retool, and keep slogging.

With a scholarship from the Scripps-Howard Foundation, Carlyle later went on to enroll in the journalism school at Radford University, where she earned some extra money freelancing for a local newspaper. Because Carlyle began to have a few doubts about her ability to find a job as a journalist, she minored in business management, receiving her bachelor of science degree in journalism.

After finishing college, Carlyle entered the workforce and found employment in the automotive and chemical industries, primarily in human resources and labor relations. Carlyle soon became an expert in shutting down unproductive plants. For more than fifteen years, Carlyle helped close down factories for corporations until she finally could not take it anymore. Carlyle says, "It was boredom, really, that drove me. I was between jobs, a workaholic who'd just finished relocating a manufacturing facility from New Jersey to Virginia. It had been very stressful. Many good people were being let go, and we'd spend months hiring new workers and transferring as many of our old employees as possible. At the end, I just could not see relocating myself, and I was very tired of the travel; so I took my little parachute—it wasn't a golden one, more like tinfoil—left my job, and found a new one. But the position did not start until April. This, unfortunately, was December."

Carlyle says she found it difficult to be at home: "In about eight days, I'd driven my husband to the brink cooking and cleaning. I did not understand why he couldn't come home every night at seven for beef stroganoff or meatloaf or whatever culinary delight I'd cranked out, until he politely reminded me that *he* still had a job which required him to work 12 hours a day. The 'time off' I'd craved was turning into a nightmare, and the workaholic needed a new plan." It took the playful kidding of her coworkers to get Carlyle thinking about writing. "Before resigning my old job, I'd been joking with some of the union stewards about leaving heavy industry for good and becoming a romance novelist," says Carlyle.

Carlyle decided to use the "awful boredom" to start reading books in the romance genre again. She recalls, "I hadn't read a romance since polishing off Georgette Heyer in sixth grade. But out of desperation, I started reading, and oh, what a treat it was. Many were exceptional novels. I trotted off to Barnes and Noble and bought another bagful. On and on it went." Her so-called research into the genre started to become expensive for someone who was unemployed, so she stopped buying books. Carlyle says, "Finally, I sat down and started writing. Twelve weeks later, I had this … *book*. It felt foreign, and I'd no clue what to do with it, but thank heaven my husband did. Soon query packages were winging their way to New York. I'd never heard of RWA, never learned how to format a manuscript, and had completely forgotten what point of view was. But I stumbled forward, and while, in the end, no one bought it, I did get a lot of nice letters and phone calls. One of the nicest was from [someone at] Pocket, who asked to see my next book."

With the start date of her new job looming, Carlyle doubted there would even be a next book: "I tossed the letter in a file." When her husband accepted a job offer and transfer to North Carolina, Carlyle thought it would be unfair to start her new job knowing she would be leaving. She says, "I called my new boss and gave him the news. But June was three months away, so of course, I got bored. What else was there to do save write another book?"

Carlyle's first book, *My False Heart,* was published in 1999. A captivating tale of murder and mistaken identity, it is the story of Elliot Armstrong, the rakish marquis of Rannoch, whose latest mistress, Antoinette Fontaine, has just publicly humiliated him. Seeking revenge, Elliot follows Antoinette to the countryside, but he becomes lost in the pouring rain and is forced to seek shelter at nearby Chatham Lodge, the home of beautiful artist Evangeline van Artevalde. When Evangeline mistakes Elliot for a new client who has recently commissioned a portrait from her, Elliot does nothing to set her straight. Just as Elliot is beginning to fall in love with Evangeline, Antoinette is found murdered, and Elliot is suspected of being the killer. One of the significant themes of *My False Heart* is redemption, in this case, the redemption of Elliot. Even though Elliot seems to be a wicked, dissolute rake, readers quickly discover that he does have his own inner core of honor. For, as Carlyle notes, "even a hero in need of redemption must, at base, be an honorable man, or the book won't be worth writing." Dark, lushly sensual, and delightfully written, *My False Heart* introduced readers to a new star on the historical romance horizon.

A Woman Scorned (2000), Carlyle's next book, proved that her mastery of characterization and plotting was no fluke. In the book, virtuous, noble Captain Cole Amherst at first resists his uncle's request that he look into the mysterious death of Cole's brother, Lord Mercer. When Cole realizes his brother's two young children might be in danger, he agrees to tutor the children. Cole soon becomes involved with their mother, the lovely and notorious Jonet Rowland, the Marchioness of Mercer, who is rumored to not only be an unrepentant adulteress but also to have played a role in her late husband's death. In *A Woman Scorned,* Carlyle brilliantly twisted the conventional sweet heroine/roguish hero combination found in so many historical romances and, in the process, created a beguilingly dark tale of danger, deception, and desire. Carlyle says, "Though it was by no means my most popular [book], I really liked the characters. The heroine was very dark, very driven. Some readers prefer a softer, more innocent sort of heroine, so she is not everyone's cup of tea. But she was definitely mine. The hero was worlds apart from the typical wicked rake, so he, too, was very unusual."

More irresistible Regency-era romances followed, including *No True Gentleman,* published in 2002. Like many of Carlyle's books, there is a strong element of mystery and intrigue in *No True Gentleman.* The book's heroine, Lady Catherine Wodeway, is riding in Hyde Park one morning, when a stranger unexpectedly kisses her. The stranger turns out to be Maximilan de Rohan, whose initial purpose in kissing Catherine is to keep from being noticed by a couple of dangerous men he has been following. The two meet again when Maximilan, a former policeman working in the Home Office, becomes involved in the investigation of the murder of Lady Julia Markham-Sands and Catherine's younger brother becomes his chief suspect. Because both Catherine and Max had appeared as secondary characters in a previous book, Carlyle found *No True Gentleman* to be easier to write than some of her other novels. She says, "I knew them. Their personalities and motivations were quite clear to me from the outset, so all I had to do was tell their story. It was also a lot of fun to write and garnered some of my best reviews."

Carlyle is especially gifted at creating connected novels, where a character is carried over from one book to the next. An excellent example of this is her loosely linked trilogy, *One Little Sin* (2005), *Two Little Lies* (2005), and *Three Little Secrets* (2006). The trilogy begins in *One Little Sin* with Sir Alasdair MacLachlan, his brother Merrick MacLachlan, and their friend Quin Hewitt as they try to escape an irate blacksmith after Alasdair is found enjoying the company of the man's wife. The three hide in a gypsy's tent, where she insists on telling them their fortunes. The futures the gypsy predicts will be the catalyst for each of their subsequent stories.

In *One Little Sin,* rakish Alasdair MacLachlan's past comes back to haunt him in the form of Miss Esmee Hamilton, who turns up on his doorstep with her baby sister, Sorcha, whom Esmee insists is Alasdair's child. In *Two Little Secrets,* Quin Hewitt is all set to assume his responsibilities as the new Earl of Wynwood by marrying the proper Miss Esmee Hamilton, when his former mistress, the celebrated opera singer Contessa Viviana Bergonzi di Vicenza, turns up at the engagement party. In *Three Little Lies,* a disastrous elopement 13 years earlier sours Merrick MacLachlan on the idea of love until Merrick discovers that the woman buying one of his homes is none other than the recently widowed Lady Madeleine Bessett, his former "wife." On its own, each book is a wonderfully wrought story featuring Carlyle's superior characterization and skillful plotting, but even more delightful is the way all three books neatly connect together to create a tapestry of stories.

For readers, the rewards of Carlyle's novels are especially satisfying, in the form of books whose wickedly witty characters with their sinfully sensual relationships are romance at its most treasured. For Carlyle, leaving a career in corporate downsizing for one of writing romances has proven to be equally rewarding, as it gives her the opportunity to create gracefully written novels that celebrate the theme of "Love Conquers All."

BIBLIOGRAPHY

Books: *My False Heart.* New York: Pocket, 1999; *A Woman Scorned.* New York: Pocket, 2000; *Beauty Like the Night.* New York: Pocket, 2000; *A Woman of Virtue.* New York: Pocket, 2001; *No True Gentleman.* New York: Pocket, 2002; *The Devil You Know.* New York: Pocket, 2003; *A Deal with the Devil.* New York: Pocket, 2004; *The Devil to Pay.* New York: Pocket, 2005; *One Little Sin.* New York: Pocket, 2005; *Two Little Lies.* New York: Pocket, 2005; *Three Little Secrets.* New York: Pocket, 2006.

Novellas: "Hunting Season" in *Tea for Two.* New York: Pocket, 2002; "Let's Talk about Sex" in *Big Guns Out of Uniform.* New York: Pocket, 2003; "Much Ado about Twelfth Night" in *The One That Got Away.* New York: Avon, 2004.

JOHN CHARLES

EMILY CARMICHAEL

For Emily Carmichael, as far as writing is concerned, it's a dog's life. Especially if the dog is a corgi named Piggy, one of Carmichael's most famous and beloved characters. Piggy, a reincarnated femme fatale turned matchmaking canine, appears in several of Carmichael's fabulously funny novels (*Finding Mr. Right,* 1999; *Diamond in the Ruff,* 2001; *Gone to the Dogs,* 2003).

Carmichael was born Emily Christine Bradshaw in 1947, and grew up in Mesa, Arizona. Her father was a teacher and the head of the English department at Mesa High School, and later Westwood High in Phoenix. Her mother worked as a school librarian in Scottsdale, Arizona. Carmichael graduated from Westwood and earned her bachelor's and master's degrees in geology from Northern Arizona University in Flagstaff, Arizona. In 1975, she married Michael Krokosz, whom she met in graduate school at Northern Arizona University. Both of them are licensed pilots. Carmichael's work with canines over the years, training and showing a multitude of family dogs (including a Welsh corgi) inspired her to create Piggy.

Carmichael served as a geologist in the United States Army for three years, stationed first in the Women's Army Corps for one year at Walter Reed Army Medical Center, and finally, 18 months in a Seattle recruiting office. Back in civilian life, Carmichael continued to work as a geologist but realized in the mid-1980s that her profession was beginning to "fossilize." She was laid off from five different companies that went out of business as the domestic oil and mining industries disappeared. It was during this time that she decided to give romance writing a try, presuming that it would be easy to do.

According to Carmichael, she "stands corrected" on her initial assumption that writing romance novels was easy. She says her first three books were "hammered out" on an electric typewriter, and it took two years and five submissions to sell her first manuscript. She

---

also writing as Emily Bradshaw

chose Carmichael, her great-grandmother's name, for her nom de plume and began writing full-time after her first novel, *Devil's Darling* (1987), was published.

Between 1992 and 1996, Carmichael wrote several books as Emily Bradshaw, her maiden name, including *Heart's Journey* (1992), *Halfway to Paradise* (1993), *Midnight Dancer* (1994), *Sweet Sorcery* (1995), and *Bounty Bride* (1996). These titles were published by Dell; Carmichael was writing for Warner at the same time. Whereas most of her other books were set in the Old West, *Sweet Sorcery* is set in medieval times, when the Saxons are battling the Franks. Despite her best efforts, Giesela, a landed healer with a second sight, can't stop her properties from falling into the hands of the Saxon rebels. Charlemagne sends Rutgar of Beltane to get the lands for the Franks. Giesela doesn't like this arrangement either. All she wants is to live in peace on her manor, and she finds Rutgar, at best, unsettling.

Carmichael writes for eight hours a day, usually beginning very early in the morning, producing 2,000 to 2,400 words daily. She prefers to write from a plot outline and finds new story ideas everywhere. Carmichael enjoys the uplifting, positive outcome of romance novels. Her favorite setting is the American West, both modern and frontier historical, but she has been known to use settings from other centuries, such as the Klondike, Saxony, and Normandy.

Her heroines are self-reliant women who bear a strong resemblance to Carmichael herself, but they also possess other qualities that she admires and would like to have. Rachel Dorsett, the title character of *Bounty Bride* (1996), would rather live in the middle of Apache Territory than stay with her abusive, alcoholic spouse. However, she has her nine-year-old son with her, and her husband is willing to pay handsomely for their return. J. C. Tyler can't pass up the $4,000 reward offered for Rachel and her boy, but when he finally finds them, he changes his mind about taking them back. Even after Rachel's husband divorces her, other bounty hunters come, and the Apaches decide to attack. Although J. C. protects Rachel, she gets involved in the shoot-outs and is even shot herself. Her other weapon of choice, a skillet, comes in handy for hitting the bad guys over the head. Rachel, like Carmichael's other heroines, is brave, resourceful, and spunky.

Two of Carmichael's books feature madams as major characters. *A Ghost for Maggie* (1999), a paranormal romance set in modern-day Jerome, Arizona, a former mining town, is the story of Maggie Potter. A sex scandal with Ohio governor and presidential hopeful Jack Kilbourne leaves Maggie as the scapegoat. Tired of the political arena and the media circus, Maggie flees to Jerome to open a bed-and-breakfast with her stepsister, Catherine, in one of the ghost town's out-of-the-way mansions. Robin Rowe, also known as "Red Robin," was Jerome's most famous madam until her murder. As though under a curse, Robin's female descendants have one horrible relationship after another. Coincidentally, Maggie is Robin's last living relative, and now that she's in Robin's house, the matchmaking ghost takes the opportunity to shower her with otherworldly advice. Reporter Colby Drake wants the dirt on Jack Kilbourne, so he checks into Maggie's inn to look for a scoop, knowing that if she finds out his true occupation, he will be out on the street. Red Robin doesn't care what Colby does for a living. All she knows is that one of the women in her family finally has a chance to be with a decent man.

Carmichael's other story that features a madam, *Jezebel's Sister* (2001), is set in 1866 and shows what happens when sinners and saints live in close proximity for any length of time. At the insistence of her younger sister, Cass, Lila McAllister, the madam of a brothel, and her ladies of the night join a wagon train full of religious people for a new life in the West. The leader of the wagon train, Preacher Homer Pernell, seems interested in Cass, and she's attracted to him, too. However, the preacher isn't a man of the cloth at all, but rather Nathan Stone, who found the minister dead and assumed his identity. Carmichael tells the story through Cass's journal entries, which adds to the believability of this laugh-out-loud tale.

Windfall (1997), the third installment of the O'Connell family saga, is the book Carmichael names as the most difficult for her to write. Set in England and Montana at the turn of the century, this is the story of Dr. Ellen O'Connell, another one of Carmichael's courageous heroines. Lord Chesterfield's younger brother is dying, and Ellen is the only doctor in the vicinity. Ellen has only recently finished her studies in medicine, but if she doesn't tend to George Chesterfield's near-fatal head wound, he will die. During George's recuperation, Ellen falls in love with George's brother, Lord Chesterfield. Lord Chesterfield is about to enter an unwanted marriage, so he asks Ellen to marry him instead. The two of them go back to Ellen's home in Montana, where the pampered nobleman learns ranching from her father. Carmichael throws a twist into the story when a man from Ellen's past catches up with her.

Carmichael's first contemporary novel, *Finding Mr. Right* (1999) was her easiest to write, and it's also her favorite for its blend of romance and humor. This is the book that introduced the corgi Piggy to the world. Animals play an important part in Carmichael's other books, too. There's Drover, Piggy's corgi friend (*Diamond in the Ruff,* 2001); tomboy Katie O'Donnell's pet wolf, Hunter (*Gold Dust,* 1996); Chesty, the world's smartest dog (*The Good, the Bad, and the Sexy,* 2002); and Titi, amnesiac Mckenna Wright's communicative cat (*The Cat's Meow,* 2004).

A RITA finalist in 1996, Carmichael has garnered three *Romantic Times* Reviewer's Choice Awards and has received a number of other nominations and awards for her romance writing excellence. However, for Carmichael's many fans, the accolades are of little or no importance. What matters to them is that Carmichael is an author who entertains them, stirs their imaginations, makes them laugh, and leaves them with a smile. And she never fails to deliver.

BIBLIOGRAPHY

Writing as Emily Carmichael

Books: *Devil's Darling.* New York: Warner, 1987; *Autumnfire.* New York: Warner, 1987; *Surrender.* New York: Warner, 1988; *A Touch of Fire.* New York: Warner, 1989; *Vision of the Heart.* New York: Warner, 1990; *Lawless.* New York: Warner, 1993; *Outcast.* New York: Warner, 1995; *Gold Dust.* New York: Warner, 1996; *Windfall.* New York: Warner, 1997; *A Ghost for Maggie.* New York: Bantam, 1999; *Finding Mr. Right.* New York: Bantam, 1999; *Diamond in the Ruff..* New York: Bantam, 2001; *Jezebel's Sister.* New York: Jove, 2001; *The Good, the Bad, and the Sexy.* New York: Bantam, 2002; *Becoming Georgia.* New York: Berkley, 2003; *Gone to the Dogs.* New York: Bantam, 2003; *The Cat's Meow.* New York: Bantam, 2004; *The Courageous Corgi.* New York: Cherokee, 2004; *A New Leash on Life.* New York: Bantam, 2005.

Novellas: "Wheels of Love" in *A Message from Cupid.* New York: St. Martin's Press, 1998; "Pride" in *Opposites Attract.* New York: Jove, 2000; "Touched for the Very First Time" in *More Lipstick Chronicles.* New York: Berkley, 2004; "Tombstone Tess" in *How to Lasso a Cowboy.* New York: Berkley, 2004.

Writing as Emily Bradshaw

Books: *Heart's Journey.* New York: Dell, 1992; *Halfway to Paradise.* New York: Dell, 1993; *Midnight Dancer.* New York: Dell, 1994; *Sweet Sorcery.* New York: Dell, 1995; *Bounty Bride.* New York: Dell, 1996.

Novella: "The Gift" in *A Country Christmas.* New York: Signet, 1993.

SANDRA VAN WINKLE AND SHELLEY MOSLEY

JAYNE CASTLE. *See* Jayne Ann Krentz

CATHRYN HUNTINGTON CHADWICK. *See* Kate Huntington

SAMANTHA CHASE. *See* Rebecca York

MAUREEN CHILD

Maureen Child has a natural talent for creative expression. During her prewriting days she held a variety of banking positions, but she also dabbled in window painting, professional clowning, and delivering singing telegrams. She recalls that "even as a kid, I played with words and wrote stories for my own amusement." Ultimately, Child determined writing to be her creative outlet of choice, and has made it her full-time career since her first book sold in 1990.

A native Californian, Child was born and raised in Downey. Her parents met at Seal Beach Naval Base when her father was discharged at the end of World War II. They married three months later. Child's father worked as a police detective, and Child says her mother "took care of everything else" for the family. Child and her husband, Mark, have been married for over thirty years and have two grown children.

Romance has always been Child's favorite reading genre. She is fascinated by the mechanics of relationships: "I enjoy exploring relationships, tearing them apart to see what makes them tick, and then slapping them back together again." She finds the genre's greatest appeal to be the happy endings. Child says, "I love that in a romance you know that the story will end well—the main players will find love; justice will be served; the good guys will win; and … when you close the book, you'll smile."

For Child, the characters always precede the plot. She says, "My books are really character driven in that the people I write about decide where the story will go rather than intricate plots that push the people around." In addition, Child commonly uses the theme of family in her plots. "I think my books are all about family, finding one, making one, or losing one," she says, "because family really is at the center of all the individual worlds that surround us."

---

also writing as Kathleen Kane
also writing as Ann Carberry
also writing as Sarah Hart

Though Child has written some magazine articles, her primary work has been romance novels. "For many years, I wrote both historicals (writing primarily as Ann Carberry and Kathleen Kane) and contemporaries, not to mention paranormals, so there was plenty of variety to keep me on my toes," she says.

The preferred locale for Child's historicals is the Old West. She finds that contemporary romances offer a far greater variety of settings, "and the fun side of that is the travel to do the research." She adds, "I actually prefer writing contemporary romance, though I admit to a stirring every once in awhile to go back in time and experience the way things once were."

In Child's 1995 historical romp *The Bandit's Lady,* set in Yellow Dog, Texas, in 1870, schoolmarm Winnifred Matthews is taken hostage by Quinn Hawkins during a bank robbery—or at least that is how it appears. The ensuing adventure of living on the lam, eluding the law, and escaping peril at every turn is even more exhilarating than Winnifred's dime novels. Quinn, however, is hardly the dangerous criminal that Winnifred initially believes him to be. He's simply a rancher trying to save his spread from a greedy banker. Of course, Quinn falls for his accidental hostage, and she for him.

In the 1990s, Child began writing unique romances under the pseudonym Kathleen Kane. These tales of the American West—delectable blends of humor, pathos, and paranormal elements—make for an enchanting look at a brief but colorful chapter of history. Each story has its own touch of magic: an exiled angel (*A Pocketful of Paradise,* 1997); a Dreamweaver (*Dreamweaver,* 1998); a woman who dies before her time and comes back as someone else (*This Time for Keeps,* 1998); a wish-granting tinker (*Simply Magic,* 1999); a cowboy who doesn't know he's a warlock (*Wish Upon a Cowboy,* 2000); a bargain with the devil (*Catch a Fallen Angel,* 2000); and an angel made mortal when her halo is knocked off (*When the Halo Falls,* 2002).

Just West of Heaven (2001), another of these Western paranormal novels, is set in Tanglewood, Nevada, in 1880. Sophie Dolan and her young sister, Jenna, are new in town, having escaped to the West to hide from those seeking to exploit Jenna's unusual gift of the Sight. Sophie accepts the position of town schoolmarm and immediately goes to work whipping into shape both the rough-and-tumble students and the dilapidated schoolhouse. The town's stoic sheriff, Ridge Hawkins, suspicious of the persuasive, beautiful stranger and her so-called daughter, senses they're hiding something. When a "Wanted" poster arrives that features a woman fitting Sophie's description, he's more intent than ever to get at the truth. These stories and characters sum up all of the things Child likes about the romance genre: love, justice, and a happy ending.

Child considers a good sense of humor to be the defining quality in all of her heroes and heroines: "Humor makes everything easier—even bad times don't look so bad if you can still laugh." When asked how many of her own qualities can be found in her characters, Child replies, "A lot. I don't know if you can actually prevent your own personality from shining through in your characters. And my heroines always tend to have a smart-aleck sense of humor, which is definitely me."

Many of Childs' novels involve military men and women. In *The Man Beneath the Uniform* (2004), Kimberly Danforth, a marine biologist and daughter of a U. S. senate candidate, is placed reluctantly under the protection of a bodyguard. The Navy SEAL appointed to guard her is Zach Sheridan, who received the 30-day "babysitting" assignment as punishment for disobeying an order. Zach fumes, anticipating that the scientist entrusted to him will probably be some sort of nerdy egghead. Kimberly isn't exactly thrilled either since she presumes she'll be cooped up with a lecherous sailor. They couldn't be more wrong about each other, and things couldn't turn out more right.

In 2001's *Did You Say Twins?!* Gunnery Sergeant Sam Pearce suddenly becomes a father to his twin, nine-month-old goddaughters when their parents die tragically. While he's adjusting to fatherhood and creating a home for the girls, he encounters a former love, Michelle Guillaire, and breaks the exciting news to her. Sam had always wondered why Michelle ended their relationship so abruptly and dropped out of his life 10 years earlier. Now that she's resurfaced, he's determined to find out her secret, and more importantly, to not let her slip away again. Child skillfully blends the elements of relationship and family into a humorous and heartwarming tale.

Child's sense of humor and her sense of irony shine through in Three-Way Wager, her 2005 series about the Reilly brothers *(The Tempting Mrs. Reilly, Whatever Reilly Wants,* and *The Last Reilly Standing).* The Reilly triplets, all sexy, alpha-male Marines, stand to inherit several thousand dollars each. However, Father Liam Reilly, their older brother, a priest blessed with a diabolical mind, needs a roof for his church. He bets his younger siblings that they can't stay celibate for three months. Each brother who loses the bet forfeits his share of the inheritance. If all three fail, the church gets its much-needed renovation. The men pride themselves on their self-discipline, but the women of Baywater, South Carolina, are a determined lot. Sibling rivalry is at its finest as these macho brothers fight a valiant but futile battle against nature.

Inspiration has never been a problem for Child. She recalls, "In school, I was the kid who got in trouble for staring out the window. My imagination has always been excellent. Ideas come from songs, movies, overheard conversations, or sitting at the mall people watching."

Child says the most difficult novel for her to write is "always the one I'm working on now. Because as a writer, I'm always trying to be a little bit better than my last book." She doesn't believe that any of her novels was easier to write than the others: "There are some books that flow. They come like a gift—but easier? Not so much." Asking Child to choose her most favorite novel is like asking her to choose between her children. She says, "I love several of them—all for different reasons. So I think that's like asking a mother which of her kids is her favorite. They all are, for different reasons."

Child's philosophy about writer's block is frank and direct: "I don't believe there is writer's block. I do think there's a stalling disease that we all experience from time to time. It's when you know you have to start that next book, but you've thought about it so much, from so many different angles, that now you've paralyzed yourself. It happens to me a lot. But there is a cure—work anyway. If you're a full-time writer, then writing is your job. You can't just quit working because it got tough. You have to work through and trust yourself. Trust your instincts."

For aspiring writers, Child offers these words of encouragement: "I hope this book and others like it help people to reach for their dreams. When I was a kid, my parents convinced me that I could be anything and do anything. But I still thought writers were 'magical' people who were born somewhere far more fabulous than my hometown. Well the truth is, writing itself is the magic. And being able to make your living by making magic is the greatest gift in the world."

BIBLIOGRAPHY

Writing as Maureen Child

Books: *The Bandit's Lady.* New York: William Morrow & Company, 1995; *The Surprise Christmas Bride.* New York: Silhouette, 1997; *Have Bride Need Groom.* Toronto: Harlequin, 1997; *A Husband* *in Her Stocking.* New York: Silhouette, 1997; *Oldest Living Married Virgin.* New York: Silhouette, 1998; *The Non-Commissioned Baby.* New York: Silhouette, 1998; *The Littlest Marine.* New York: Silhouette, 1998; *Maternity Bride.* New York: Silhouette, 1998; *Mom in Waiting.* New York: Silhouette, 1999; *Colonel Daddy.* New York: Silhouette, 1999; *Marine Under the Mistletoe.* New York: Silhouette, 1999; *The Last Santini Virgin.* New York: Silhouette, 2000; *The Daddy Salute.* New York: Silhouette, 2000; *Marooned with a Marine.* New York: Silhouette, 2000; *The Next Santini Bri*de. New York: Silhouette, 2000; *Did You Say Twins?!* New York: Silhouette, 2001; *His Baby!* New York: Silhouette, 2001; *Prince Charming in Dress Blues.* New York: Silhouette, 2001; *Last Virgin in California.* New York: Silhouette, 2001; *The Royal Treatment.* New York: Silhouette, 2002; *The Marine and the Debutante.* New York: Silhouette, 2002; *The Seal's Surrender.* New York: Silhouette, 2002; *Sleeping with the Boss.* New York: Silhouette, 2003; *Beauty and the Blue Angel.* New York: Silhouette, 2003; *Loving You.* New York: St. Martin's Press, 2003; *Finding You/Knowing You.* New York: St. Martin's Press, 2003; *Kiss Me, Cowboy!* New York: Silhouette, 2003; *Lost in Sensation.* New York: Silhouette, 2004; *And Then Came You.* New York: St. Martin's Press, 2004; *Forever…Again.* New York: Silhouette, 2004; *The Man Beneath the Uniform.* New York: Silhouette, 2004; *Some Kind of Wonderful.* New York: St. Martin's Press, 2004; *The Tempting Mrs. Reilly.* New York: Silhouette, 2005; *Whatever Reilly Wants.* New York: Silhouette, 2005; *The Last Reilly Standing.* New York: Silhouette, 2005; *Turn My World Upside Down.* New York: St. Martin's Press, 2005; *Society-Page Seduction.* New York: Silhouette, 2005; *A Crazy Kind of Love.* New York: St. Martin's Press, 2005; *Satisfying Lonergan's Honor.* New York: Silhouette, 2006; *Strictly Lonergan's Business.* New York: Silhouette, 2006; *Expecting Lonergan's Baby.* New York: Silhouette, 2006; *Fortune's Legacy.* New York: Silhouette, 2006.

Novellas: "In Too Deep" in *Love Is Murder.* Toronto: Harlequin, 2003; "With a Twist" in *Summer in Savannah.* New York: Silhouette, 2004.

Writing as Kathleen Kane

Books: *Mountain Dawn.* New York: Diamond, 1992; *Small Treasures.* New York: Diamond, 1993; *Coming Home.* New York: Diamond, 1994; *Keeping Faith.* New York: Diamond, 1994; *Charms.* New York: Diamond, 1995; *Wishes.* New York: Jove, 1995; *Still Close to Heaven.* New York: St. Martin's Press, 1997; *A Pocketful of Paradise.* New York: St. Martin's Press, 1997; *Dreamweaver.* New York: St. Martin's Press, 1998; *This Time for Keeps.* New York: St. Martin's Press, 1998; *The Soul Collector.* New York: St. Martin's Press, 1999; *Simply Magic.* New York: St. Martin's Press, 1999; *Catch a Fallen Angel.* New York: St. Martin's Press, 2000; *Wish Upon a Cowboy.* New York: St. Martin's Press, 2000; *Just West of Heaven.* New York: St. Martin's Press, 2001; *When the Halo Falls.* New York: St. Martin's Press, 2002.

Novellas: "Paper Hearts" in *Sweet Hearts.* New York: Penguin, 1993; "Betrayed Hearts" in *Hearts of Gold.* New York: Penguin, 1994; "Across a Crowded Room" in *Perfect Secrets.* New York: St. Martin's Press, 1999.

Writing as Ann Carberry

Books: *Frontier Bride.* New York: Penguin, 1992; *Shotgun Bride.* New York: Diamond, 1993; *Nevada Heat.* New York: Diamond, 1993; *Runaway Bride.* New York: Diamond, 1994; *The Scoundrel.* New York: Jove, 1995; *Maggie and the Gambler.* New York: Avon, 1995; *Alice and the Gunfighter.* New York: Avon, 1996; *Frannie and the Charmer.* New York: Avon, 1996.

Writing as Sarah Hart

Book: *Whispers from Heaven.* New York: Penguin, 1996.

SHELLEY MOSLEY AND SANDRA VAN WINKLE

KATHY CHWEDYK. *See* Kate Huntington

NICOLE CODY. *See* May McGoldrick

JAN COFFEY. *See* May McGoldrick

JUSTINE COLE. *See* Susan Elizabeth Phillips

PATRICIA COX. *See* Pat Warren

EMMA CRAIG. *See* Alice Duncan

JENNIFER CRUSIE

Jennifer Crusie. Courtesy of Jennifer Crusie.

J ennifer Crusie's best-selling contemporary romances are known for their sharp sense of wit and delightfully acerbic writing, but there is more to this award-winning author's novels than just a fabulous sense of humor. While Crusie's books are deftly imbued with a generous measure of her tart humor, they are really a celebration of life's most important things: family, friends, hope, and, above all else, love.

Crusie was born Jennifer Smith in the small Ohio town of Wapakoneta in 1949 to Jack and JoAnn Smith. She grew up in Ohio, where she attended grade school and high school. While a teenager, Crusie had a number of different jobs, including waitressing and car-hopping at the Happy Humpty Drive-In and running a switchboard. Crusie enrolled in Bowling Green State University, where she graduated in 1973 with a bachelor's degree in art education. After getting married in 1971, Crusie and her husband lived briefly in Texas, before they settled down in Dayton, Ohio.

Crusie taught preschool for several years until her daughter was born. After taking some time off to be with her child, Crusie went back to teaching, and spent 10 years teaching art to elementary and high school students. While holding down a full-time teaching job,

also writing as Jennifer Smith
also writing as Jennifer Crusie Smith

Crusie also attended Wright State University, where she earned a master's degree in professional writing and women's literature.

In 1986, Crusie took a sabbatical from teaching to work on completing her PhD in feminist criticism and nineteenth-century British and American literature at Ohio State University. After her sabbatical ended, Crusie returned to the Dayton area to teach high school. In 1991, Crusie began working on her dissertation, which centered on the theme of the impact of gender on narrative strategies. As part of her research, Crusie planned to read 100 romance novels and 100 men's adventure novels.

While Crusie had read some romances as a teen, including books by Georgette Heyer and Mary Stewart, her reading tastes shifted more toward literary fiction after she began college. When Crusie began reading romances again for her dissertation project, she was amazed to discover just how truly empowering the books were for women. Crusie had so much fun reading romances that she figured writing one would be equally enjoyable, and so she set aside her dissertation to begin her own romance novel.

While working on her book, Crusie used *Writer's Market* to identify potential publishers. When she sent for a tip sheet from Silhouette, she discovered the publisher was running a novella contest in which the top winners would be published. Crusie's novella *Sizzle,* which later became a book, was chosen as one of the contest winners by Silhouette, who published it as part of their Stolen Moments series in 1994. At that time, authors writing for Silhouette and Harlequin were required to adopt pseudonyms, so Crusie chose her maternal grandmother's maiden name as her literary pseudonym.

In between teaching high school and working nights at a bookstore, Crusie continued working on her writing. She submitted another manuscript to Silhouette, who rejected it, but the book found a home at Silhouette's sister publisher, Harlequin, who published *Manhunting* in 1993. While *Manhunting* was not the first book Crusie wrote or sold, she says it was the "first thing I wrote that I liked." And it became her first published novel. In *Manhunting,* Kate Svenson realizes that she is not as successful in love as she is at climbing the corporate ladder. With three failed engagements to her credit, Kate is determined to find Mr. Right. Of course, Kate approaches the task the same way she does everything: with an organized schedule involving a visit to The Cabins resort, the premier vacation destination for plenty of wealthy, successful men. Kate's best-laid plans don't go quite according to her schedule, though, since all the men she seems interested in become "injured" in different ways. The only man who seems to be paying her any attention is commitment-phobic Jake Templeton, brother of the resort's owner. The potent sexual chemistry Crusie creates between Kate and Jake is one of the highlights of the book, and Crusie brilliantly blends her trademark sense of humor with a cast of realistically quirky characters, making *Manhunting* a truly stellar first book.

With *Manhunting,* Crusie found a home at Harlequin's Temptation line, and more books followed, including 1994's *Getting Rid of Bradley,* for which she won her first Romance Writers of America's RITA award for Best Short Contemporary Romance. When Lucy Savage discovers her husband, Bradley Porter, is cheating on her, she divorces him, despite his protests of innocence. What Lucy doesn't know about Bradley is that he might be an embezzler, and when the police turn up to investigate him, she finds herself attracted to sexy cop Zack Warren. When it seems as if someone might be trying to kill her, Zack offers Lucy 24/7 protection, but no one is going to keep Lucy safe from falling for Zack. Featuring a heroine who manages to overcome both a bad divorce and a series of bad hair days, *Getting Rid of Bradley* is an excellent example of Crusie's early brand of sharp, snappy writing.

In 1996, Crusie helped launch Harlequin's Love and Laughter line, with *Anyone but You.* Crusie's characteristically humorous writing style was a natural fit with Harlequin's new line, which focused on comic contemporary romances. The book's heroine, Nina Askew, starts over after divorcing an overambitious husband, whose control of her extended to even forbidding Nina from getting a dog since it might have messed up their perfect showplace of a home. Her first act of defiance as a single woman is to adopt a perky puppy, but what Nina ends up with is Fred—part basset hound, part beagle, and part manic-depressive. Much to her surprise, Nina finds herself "falling in love" with the personality-plus pooch, until Fred decides to play matchmaker and introduces Nina to her way-cute, way-younger downstairs neighbor, Alex Moore. While Crusie had incorporated pets into the plots of many of her previous books, such as the three dogs in *Getting Rid of Bradley* and the cat in *Strange Bedpersons* (1994), Fred, the lovable basset-hound mix in *Anyone but You* is such a strong character that he steals the show. In fact, when Crusie first turned in the manuscript for the book, she wanted to call it *The Importance of Owning Fred* since it was really Fred's book. As with all of Crusie's books, it is more than just a humorous contemporary love story. It is also about friendship, family, new beginnings, and even the debate about the value of literary fiction versus commercial fiction.

Crusie probably would have continued merrily on writing contemporary series romances for Harlequin and Bantam but for two small things. Shortly after she began writing for Bantam, the publisher's Loveswept line folded (Crusie swears she had nothing to do with this), and authors writing for Harlequin were presented with a new contract by the publisher, which contained several clauses with which Crusie did not agree. Crusie had always promised herself that some day, when she was ready and could handle something more complicated, she would write the "book of her heart." It seemed that day had arrived. Crusie began work on that book, which she found to be one of the most difficult things she had ever written, *Tell Me Lies* (1998).

Set in the small town of Frog Point, Ohio, *Tell Me Lies* is the story of Maddie Faraday, who has spent her whole life always doing the right thing. Maddie has been juggling many things in her life, including her eight-year-old daughter Emily, who wants a dog; a mother who insists on interfering in her life; busybody neighbors; and a best friend with a secret. Then one day, while cleaning out her husband's car, Maddie discovers a pair of women's underwear, and they aren't hers. This turns out to be the straw that breaks Maddie's marriage. When C. L. Sturgis, Maddie's dreamy former high school boyfriend, turns up on the same day her husband disappears, Maddie finally realizes just what a high price she has paid for living her life the way others expected her to. The strong feminist theme that is at the core of all of Crusie's books comes into full bloom in *Tell Me Lies,* the story of a woman who is finally learning how to claim her own identity, separate from being a wife, mother, and daughter. With her usual sharp, clever writing and an insightful look at the intricacies of modern-day relationships, Crusie's first single-title romance not only proved to be a hit with readers, but was also a 1998 RWA Top Ten Favorite Romance of the Year.

In Crusie's next book, *Crazy for You* (1999), the author continues with the theme of a woman changing her life. The heroine, high school art teacher Quinn McKenzie, has a perfectly nice, perfectly bland existence. Quinn decides to add just a little color to her beige world by adopting a stray dog, which she names Katie. Quinn never expects the adoption to become the catalyst that would change her boring life forever, but she is even more surprised when the lives of her nearest and dearest friends and relatives are also affected. Of course, there are those around Quinn, like her fiancé, Bill Hilliard, and her parents, who don't want her to change. When she dumps Bill and takes up with Nick Ziegler, the bad-boy mechanic formerly married to Quinn's sister Zoë, Quinn discovers that change is never easy or pretty but always worth the pain. Crusie's own experiences teaching high school art and drama provide a nice touch of realism to the laughter-laced and often quite poignant story. *Crazy for You* was a RITA finalist for Best Contemporary Romance and a 1999 RWA Top Ten Favorite Romance of the Year.

A book a year followed until 2002. Then, Crusie's writing muse took a vacation, and she fell behind on her deadline. She searched among her older, unpublished works for any material she could update and adapt. Crusie had written the original version of what would become *Bet Me* in 1992, but it was the one book she was never able to sell. Her agent was happy to sell the unpublished novel, but when Crusie went back and read her old draft of *Bet Me,* she realized that there was a good reason the manuscript had never sold in the first place—it was bad, or as Crusie puts it, "The book stunk on ice." She began cutting and revising, writing and rewriting until she finally had an almost completely new book, one with which she fell in love.

Submitted 11 months past her deadline, *Bet Me* was Crusie's return to pure romance, the kind of book she had written earlier in her career. The book focuses on Minerva "Min" Dobbs, a sturdy statistician, who overhears her then boyfriend betting another man, Cal Morrisey, that Cal can't bed Min in a month. At first, Min is furious, and then she decides to turn the tables on Cal by dating him for a month and dumping him before he can bed her. But the best-laid plans of Cal and Min go romantically astray once the two, much to their dismay, realize they are falling in love with each other. The joy is watching cynicism and optimism battle and knowing that love will win. *Bet Me* is not just the story of the romance that develops between Cal and Min, it is also about Min finally coming to terms with being a curvy woman in a world that doesn't accept anything but thin and finding a man who accepts her and loves her just the way she is.

After finishing *Bet Me,* Crusie began writing a book tentatively titled *You Again,* but once more, she hit a wall in her writing. While attending a writers' conference in Maui, Crusie met Bob Mayer, a writer of thrillers, science fiction, and nonfiction. When Mayer first suggested that the two of them collaborate on a novel, Crusie thought he was kidding. Once she realized that Mayer, the author of over thirty books, was serious, she realized that this was her chance at being saved from a dark and crippling writer's block. Crusie seized the opportunity. Inspired by her original master's dissertation on the impact of gender on narrative strategies, Crusie suggested writing a romantic thriller told from both the female and male perspectives. Mayer agreed. The partnership produced the suspense thriller *Don't Look Down* (2006).

In *Don't Look Down,* commercial film director Lucy Armstrong agrees to finish directing an action thriller movie in Savannah, because she thinks it will offer her both easy money and a chance to spend time with her sister and young niece. When Lucy shows up on the set, she discovers that her ex-husband is the film's stunt coordinator; half the cast has walked off the set: and the script is incoherent, even by Hollywood standards. And, to top it all off, the star of the film, Bryce McKay, has hired his own private stunt double/military consultant, Special Forces captain J. T. Wilder. The only reason Lucy agrees to keep J. T. on the payroll is because it really annoys her ex-husband. But, when things start getting dangerous on the set, Lucy discovers that there is no one she would rather have on her side than J. T.

When they first began writing *Don't Look Down,* Crusie and Mayer divided the writing responsibilities. Crusie was in charge of the heroine, and Mayer created the hero. Each author wrote his or her own character's story. As they finished a section, Crusie and Mayer shared with each other what they had written, and they had the chance to comment on each other's scenes. Between the writing and rewriting, editing and revising, they completed the first draft of the book, which was then further polished by both Crusie and Mayer. The resulting book proved to be a perfect blend of Crusie's comic talent for creating memorable characters, romantic situations, and inspired dialogue and Mayer's skill with plotting, riveting suspense, and guns—a lot of guns.

Readers cherish Crusie's novels for their quirky, yet realistically flawed characters; the sharp, clever writing and snappy dialogue; and the wicked wit that flavors everything she writes. But what they treasure most about Crusie's books is that they embrace the truly essential things in life—the power of friendship, the joy of pets, the love of family—and demonstrate that there is no situation that can't be improved by food.

BIBLIOGRAPHY

Writing as Jennifer Crusie

Books: *Manhunting*. Toronto: Harlequin, 1993; *Sizzle*. New York: Silhouette, 1994; *Getting Rid of Bradley*. Toronto: Harlequin, 1994; *Strange Bedpersons*. Toronto: Harlequin, 1994; *What the Lady Wants*. Toronto: Harlequin, 1995; *Charlie All Night*. Toronto: Harlequin, 1996; *Anyone but You*. Toronto: Harlequin, 1996; *The Cinderella Deal*. New York: Bantam, 1997; *Trust Me on This*. New York: Bantam, 1997; *Tell Me Lies*. New York: St. Martin's Press, 1998; *Crazy for You*. St. Martin's Press, 1999; *Welcome to Temptation*. New York: St. Martin's Press, 2000; *Fast Women*. New York: St. Martin's Press, 2001; *Faking It*. New York: St. Martin's Press, 2002; *Bet Me*. New York: St. Martin's Press, 2004.

Essays: "Happily Ever After: Writing Romantic Comedy for Women" in *Romance Writer's Marketplace*. Cincinnati, OH: Writer's Digest Press, 1996; "Why I Occasionally Think about Not Writing Romance Any More/ Why I Know I'll Continue Writing Romance until They Pry My Cold Dead Fingers from around My Keyboard" in *North American Romance Writers*. Lanham, MD: Scarecrow Press, 1999; "Dating Death" in *Seven Seasons of Buffy: Science Fiction and Fantasy Writers Discuss Their Favorite Television Show*. Dallas, TX: Benbella Books, 2003; "The Assassination of Cordelia Chase" in *Five Seasons of Angel: Science Fiction and Fantasy Writers Discuss Their Favorite Vampire*. Dallas, TX: Benbella Books, 2004; editor, *Flirting with Pride and Prejudice: Fresh Perspectives on the Original Chick Lit Masterpiece*. Dallas, TX: Benbella Books, 2005; editor, *Totally Charmed: Demons, Whitelighters, and the Power of Three*. Dallas, TX: Benbella Books, 2005.

Writing as Jennifer Smith

Book: *Anne Rice: A Critical Companion*. Westport, CT: Greenwood Press, 1996.
Essay: "Ngaio Marsh" in *Dictionary of Women Mystery Writers*. Westport, CT: Greenwood Press, 1994.

Writing as Jennifer Crusie Smith

Essays: "The Romantic Suspense Mystery" in *Mystery and Suspense Writers: The Literature of Crime, Detection, and Espionage*. New York: Scribners, 1998; "This Is Not Your Mother's Cinderella: The Romance Novel as Feminist Fairy Tale" in *Romantic Conventions*. Madison, WI: University of Wisconsin Press, 1998.

Writing with Bob Mayer

Book: *Don't Look Down*. New York: St. Martin's Press, 2006.

JOHN CHARLES AND JOANNE HAMILTON-SELWAY

CLAUDIA DAIN

RITA finalist Claudia Dain first considered being a writer as a 12-year-old, when she found the assignments in her seventh grade writing class to be like "an open door, inviting me to explore the world of words." She was hooked. When she mentioned to her mother that she'd love to be a writer, her mother was sympathetic but encouraged her to pursue a career with a bit more stability. Fortunately for her readers, this is one piece of maternal advice that Dain ignored.

Dain was born in Los Angeles, California, in 1956. Her father, Richard, a Marine in World War II, became a paraplegic at the age of 21. He met Dain's mother, Norma, in the Veteran's Administration Hospital in New York City; she was one of the nurses on his floor. Richard, who had dropped out of college on December 8, 1941—the day after the attack on Pearl Harbor—to enlist, went back to college on the GI Bill, attending UCLA, where he got his degree in social work. Norma worked as a nurse until Dain was adopted in 1956, making her the first child in the California state adoption system to be placed in a home where one of the parents was disabled.

The first 10 years of Dain's life were spent in Los Angeles, before her parents moved to a small town in Connecticut. Dain says she has vivid memories of both places, and while she feels like a "California girl to the bone," she thinks of that Connecticut town as home. Dain attended public schools until she went to the University of Southern California. She graduated with a degree in English and a lifetime credential to teach secondary-education English. She and her husband, Tom, were both teachers at the time of their wedding. Dain taught 10th grade English before quitting to become a home-schooling, stay-at-home mom to the couple's three children: Paul, Morgan, and Daniel.

Dain says she began to consider writing when she kept reading things that left her "slightly dissatisfied." She didn't think she could do it better, but she did feel that she could write "differently." At the time, her three children were still small, but her husband urged her to give writing a try. Six months later, Dain had completed her first novel, finding it "a lot harder" than she thought it would be. Dain wrote three full novels before she tried to find a publisher. Realizing that most publishers only look at unsolicited manuscripts that come to them by way of an agent, Dain found someone to represent her. In the meantime, Dain wrote a fourth and fifth novel. Disheartened because book number three still hadn't sold, Dain and the agent parted ways. Not ready to give up, Dain retained a second agent, and this one sold Dain's fourth manuscript, *Tell Me Lies*. Eventually, manuscripts three and five sold too, but manuscripts one and two remain unpublished. It took five years from the time Dain started writing until she sold her first novel, *Tell Me Lies,* for publication.

Dain says she writes "by the seat of her pants." She adds that the development of her works is "organic," with no outlines and "no clear idea of what's coming or where it's going or even if it will work. Ideas just seem to come, and they're so thin and indistinct at first that they can't be identified or classified." Dain comes up with the conflict first, with the characters quickly following. Dain's plots then flow from the characters and the conflict.

The recurrent themes in Dain's works fall under one general category: you are worthy and deserving of love. On the surface, Juliane of Stanora and Ulrich of Caen, the protagonists of *The Fall* (2004), the fifth and final book of Dain's medieval series (*The Holding,* 2001; *The Marriage Bed,* 2001; *The Willing Wife,* 2002; *The Temptation,* 2003), don't seem either worthy or deserving of love. Juliane, also known as Juliane le Gel, the "Lady of Frost," is a renowned beauty who can make a man impotent with a single, icy glance. Ulrich, "Lord of Nothing," is a poor but charming knight, not to mention famed lover, who sets his sights on the fair but aloof maiden. As Juliane and Ulrich play their flirtatious game, the rest of the court place wagers on whether he can win her hand. On the surface, this is a simple tale of a harmless round of courtly love; but then Dain ingeniously twists the story with political intrigue, secret scandals, and Machiavellian moves. Suddenly, people aren't what they seem, even the priest. Humor, pathos, and adventure fill this tale of a woman who is fighting for her independence and her lands, and a man who comes to value her more than her property.

There is just enough of Dain in her heroines that she can relate to them. Strength is the one trait found in all of her female protagonists. There are few heroines stronger and more courageous than Melania in *To Burn* (2002). With her father dead in battle, Melania is left alone in their isolated Roman villa in what used to be Saxon land but is now Britannia. Wulfred, a ferocious Saxon warrior, has come to reclaim the lands that were stolen from them by the Roman invaders. He burns Melania's home, and when faced with the choice of being conquered or dying in the inferno, she chooses a certain death. Wulfred refuses to let her commit what amounts to suicide. Their relationship is one of captive/captor, yet in her hatred, Melania doesn't hesitate to tell Wulfred what she really thinks, which results in sharp, piercing dialogue. Wulfred feels that his victory won't be complete until he conquers his unbending slave, but she refuses to acknowledge him as her lord and master. Since Melania is one of the early Christians, there's a slight religious overtone to this sensual book, but Dain never allows it to become didactic.

As for setting, Dain likes to write about places she's been—places for which she has a strong visual reference. She enjoys writing books set in a variety of time periods. Dain says she loves the medieval period "because it is so very different from the modern period, and that makes for a fun journey." She also enjoys contemporary stories, because it takes "no effort at all to get there." Two of Dain's novellas, "Every Square Inch" in *Unwrapped* (2000) and "Tracked" in *Silent Night* (2004), both tales of romantic suspense, are set in the present day.

According to Dain, the romance genre appeals to her as a writer because of the "focus on the male/female relationship; the inherent differences men and women bring to the table; and the excitement of emotionally weighted interaction." Dain likes the focus on the relationship in a romance, but she can imagine herself also writing many other types of fiction.

Many things about the writing process appeal to Dain: "the discovery, the play, the endless path of imagination and revelation." When asked where she gets her inspiration, Dain replies, "*Everything* is inspiration." She believes writer's block is a nice way of saying, "Scared to death." She has never actually experienced writer's block, but comments that "it has sniffed at my heels a few times."

Dain says she found *A Kiss to Die For* (2003) the hardest book for her to write, because there were "too many cooks" on that project. Both her agent and editor had ideas about what should happen in the story, and as Dain tried to please them both, she lost her own vision for the book. She says the "shadowy" journey back to her initial concept was worth it; Dain was able to make the book what she wanted it to be and says that "made all the difference." In *A Kiss to Die For,* Dain created a serial killer on the loose, and then she very cleverly set his bloody route in the Old West. The murderer is following a definite path—he's working his way up the Chisholm trail, leaving a series of lovely, youthful female corpses in his wake. Jack Scullard, also known as "Jack Skull," a legendary but despised bounty hunter, is always a step behind the killer, until Jack gets to Abilene. There, Jack befriends a young woman, one who perfectly fits the profile of the killer's victims, so the search becomes both more urgent and more personal. Anne Ross enjoys being courted by two men—dapper, sweet-talking Bill Tucker and rugged, rough-edged Jack. Bill, unknown to the oblivious Anne, is Jack's prime suspect. Lots of tension, suspense, and an unexpected twist make this another one of Dain's inimitable, highly entertaining stories.

If *A Kiss to Die For* was the most difficult book for Dain to write, *The Temptation* (2003) was the easiest. Dain says the words just "spilled out" of her, almost faster than she could get them down on paper. After she sees her mother die during childbirth, Elsbeth of Sunnandune plans to enter the convent, heeding her mother's final words about the "snare" of men and the need to avoid it. But her father wants to use his daughter to expand his wealth and power, and against her will, Elsbeth is to wed Knight of the Levant, Hugh of Jerusalem, a golden Adonis, not to mention a favorite of the king. Although Hugh acts as though he were a romantic suitor, Elsbeth knows that she's merely a pawn, and that her marriage has robbed her of her precious freedom. She cleverly uses her well-timed monthly courses as an excuse not to consummate their union. While Hugh waits for her cycle to end, he has a chance to get to know how intelligent his bride is as they discuss religious dogma and various philosophies, concepts he didn't know women were capable of grasping. During their conversations, Elsbeth comes to respect the man she was forced to wed. Dain began this novel with the standard plotline of an arranged marriage during medieval times, but, as is the case with her other books, made it uniquely hers. This book is a celebration of a woman's body: her blood—menstrual, maiden, and childbirth; and what it all symbolizes. More than that, it celebrates a woman's intellect and her ability to be an equal partner to any man. Deep with philosophical thought, this is one of Dain's most introspective novels.

RITA finalist *The Willing Wife* (2002), set in twelfth-century England, is Dain's favorite book from her oeuvre. She knew it as she was writing it, and she knew it when it was finished. Dain says she loves "everything" about this book. Nicolaa of Cheneteberie knows all about men and how little they can be trusted. She and her properties have been given to Rowland, "The Dark of Aquitaine," by a grateful king, making this fierce knight her fifth husband. Her other marriages were terminated when she didn't bear a child, and she hopes this, too, will be a short union. Rowland doesn't want the king's generous gift of a new wife and lands; he will always love the perfect, idealized Lubias. As with Dain's other heroes,

Rowland shares the trait of self-sacrifice. Dain takes this story of two people who literally want to run from each other and deftly turns their characters around so completely that all they want is each other. In this book, as is the case with her other novels, Dain's talent for characterization and character development shines.

The Holding (2001) runs a very close second as Dain's favorite book that she has written. Emotionally tied to this work, Dain comments that she cries every time she reads it. Brave and bold, Lady Cathryn of Greneford, the heroine of *The Holding,* like so many women of the medieval period, is in danger of losing her lands. Cathryn has already been raped, and her people abused by the greedy, amoral nobleman who wants everything she has. To defend what is hers, Cathryn devises the ingenious plan of making her holdings and her servants seem so run-down and meager that no man will covet them. William le Brouillard, a knight known as "The Fog," is given Cathryn and her holdings as a reward for service to the king. William, as well as Cathryn, hides behind a facade, and only trust can give them a clear vision of each other's true self. With a theme of the replenishing nature of two-way trust, reading this novel is analogous to watching a rose open from a tight bud to a beautiful, velvety flower.

As far as other authors who inspire Dain, she says she admires "Charles Dickens for his ability to change the world by using fiction as the vehicle; Mark Twain for his way with words; Jane Austen for her light touch; and William Shakespeare for his portrayal of character-driving plot." To the list of these authors and their strengths, Dain can add her own forte, that of taking a commonplace theme or a well-used plotline and making it sparkle with her own special kind of magic.

BIBLIOGRAPHY

Books: *Tell Me Lies.* New York: Dorchester, 2000; *The Holding.* New York: Dorchester, 2001; *The Marriage Bed.* New York: Dorchester, 2001; *To Burn.* New York: Dorchester, 2002; *The Willing Wife.* New York: Dorchester, 2002; *A Kiss to Die For.* New York: Dorchester, 2003; *The Temptation.* New York: Dorchester, 2003; *The Fall.* New York: Dorchester, 2004.
Novellas: "Every Square Inch" in *Unwrapped.* New York: Dorchester, 2000; "Union" in *Wish List.* New York: Dorchester, 2001; "Tracked" in *Silent Night.* New York: Dorchester, 2004.

SHELLEY MOSLEY

MAX DANIELS. *See* Roberta Gellis

GERALYN DAWSON

Geralyn Dawson. Courtesy of Geralyn Dawson.

Best-selling author Geralyn Dawson is as much a part of Texas as the Alamo, the longhorn steer, and the bluebonnet. Dawson's family moved to Texas when she was five days old, and she has never left. Her parents, John Dawson, a U.S. Air Force civilian employee, and Pauline, a homemaker, lived in Wichita Falls during her childhood. Dawson later attended Texas A&M University, where she earned a bachelor's degree in business administration. She married Steve Williams, and the two of them have three children: Steve, John, and Caitlin.

Before embarking on a writing career, Dawson aspired to be a corporate marketing executive and worked for a time as an advertising and marketing representative. She was drawn to writing romances because of their emphasis on relationships, family, and happy endings. Dawson confesses, "I'm a sap for happy endings." Family, love, and laughter are all recurrent themes in her novels. She says the writers who inspire her include "Nora Roberts for her talent and work ethic and Christina Dodd because she tells me I'm good." Dawson is good—she has won several prestigious awards, including the National Reader's Choice Award; Romance Writers of America's Top Ten Favorite Books of the Year (for *The Wedding Ransom,* 1998); and the *Romantic Times* Career Achievement Award.

Not surprisingly, Dawson says her favorite plot setting is her home state of Texas "because that's what I know." An avid Texas Aggie football fan, loyal to her alma mater, Dawson created a couple of male characters in her contemporary series who epitomize the rivalry between Texas A&M and the University of Texas. In the first of these novels *My Big Old Texas Heartache* (2003), the Aggie is the hero; but in the sequel, *My Long Tall Texas Heartthrob* (2004), the hero is a "sorry T-sip," as Dawson calls University of Texas fans. "I don't know that I'll ever live that down," she commented.

Dawson's stories originate with the characters rather than plot ideas. She believes her characters reflect her own love of family. Her heroines are always bright, intelligent women. Christina Delaney from *Simmer All Night* (1999) is one such woman. Christina scandalizes her prim, prissy Victorian society mother by becoming the Chili Queen of San Antonio. To teach her headstrong daughter good manners, proper behavior, and social graces, Christina's mother sends her to England to live with her grandfather, who happens to be an earl. Cole Morgan, Christina's adopted sibling, accompanies her to England; but he's there to find the lost copy of the Republic of Texas's Declaration of Independence. One thing he does discover is that his love for Christina is definitely not brotherly. Funny, fast-paced, and full of excitement, *Simmer All Night* became the first of two books (*Sizzle All Day,* 2000) about the search for the hidden document.

The heroes in Dawson's books are known for their sense of humor. Jake Delaney, the hero of *Sizzle All Day,* the sequel to *Simmer All Night,* is in Scotland, continuing the search for the lost copy of the Republic of Texas's Declaration of Independence. Flora Dunbar, the owner of the castle where he's staying, is pregnant, and his off-and-on attraction to her puzzles him. Little does he know that she has an identical, albeit nonpregnant twin, Gillian Ross, who haunts the castle as the "Headless White Lady of Rowanclere." After Gillian drugs Jake and discovers his true mission, she forces him to leave, only allowing him to return for the document once he promises to pretend to be a specter, too, so she can sell her holdings. Humor and charm abound as Gillian tries to teach Jake the ins and outs of being a ghost.

Dawson's novels alternate between contemporary settings and Victorian-era historicals set in 1880s Texas. She finds that the variety keeps the writing process fresh and interesting. In addition to her romances, Dawson has written a women's fiction novel, *The Pink Magnolia Club* (2002), which she considers her personal favorite. "It was truly the book of my heart," she says. While Dawson was doing volunteer work for the Making Memories Breast Cancer Foundation, an elderly man donated his only daughter's wedding gown. He said she had died from breast cancer at age 36, and he wanted another woman to be able to wear the beautiful gown. His story inspired Dawson to write a book featuring a Making Memories wedding gown and three women who become friends while one of them is battling breast cancer. This poignant, yet hopeful tale touched many readers and showed that the talented Dawson could write more serious prose as well as her trademark humor.

Dawson's most difficult novel to write was 1995's *Tempting Morality,* because her vision of the story was quite different than her editor's and resulted in major revisions. She adds, "I hadn't yet learned how to take a creative stand." Morality Brown, the title character of this book, is attracted physically to Zachary Burkett, also known as the "Burkett bastard," but is put off by this smooth-talking flimflam artist's personality. Morality needs to stay away from Zach because her miracle-man uncle has endowed her with the Sight, and she testifies at his revivals. Zach has returned to town for revenge, not to find love. Dawson takes the theme of opposites attract and plays it to perfection with these totally different people. Her subtext of the redemptive power of true love is a subtle message and doesn't overpower the plot or keep Dawson from sprinkling the story with a bit of humor now and then. Despite the book's rocky beginnings, the finished product is a fine one.

Perhaps Dawson is best known for her Bad Luck series. *The Bad Luck Wedding Dress* (1996) was followed by *The Bad Luck Wedding Cake* (1998). Although books one and two are about the McBride family, book three in the series, *The Bad Luck Wedding Night* (2001), brings in the Ross family, who are characters in *Simmer All Night* and *Sizzle All Day*. When Harlequin wanted Dawson to write books for each of the three young girls in *The Bad Luck Wedding Dress,* Dawson came up with a new trilogy, The Bad Luck Brides, which she refers to as "The McBride Menaces." This trilogy includes *Her Bodyguard* (2005), *Her Scoundrel* (2005), and *Her Outlaw* (in press).

Dawson says the least difficult novel for her to write was *Her Bodyguard*, although she observes, "None are easy." Dawson feels this book flowed so smoothly because the heroine, who had been in other titles in the series, was so familiar to her: "I knew her very well going into it." The heroine of *Her Bodyguard,* Mari McBride, owns a candy shop and considers herself well past her hellion days. Texas Ranger Luke Garrett likes Mari but stays away from her. However, when his half brother and Mari's sister disappear, Mari goes after them, leaving Luke no choice but to go along as her bodyguard. Dawson uses her trademark humor describing the couple's wild adventures as they search for their siblings, and Luke discovers that Mari is still a menace.

Dawson writes full-time and describes her techniques as "a seat-of-my-pants" writing style. For Dawson, the most appealing part of a writing career is the independence and "going to work in my pajamas." She is never troubled by writer's block but does occasionally experience what she refers to as "writer's laziness." Dawson's cure? "I look at the calendar and my deadlines to get over it," she says. Her inspiration can come from anywhere—even a casual remark made by her brother-in-law one Fourth of July, which became an idea for the plot of a book in her new contemporary romance series for NAL. As Dawson says, "It's never safe to speak freely around a writer." It's also not safe for people who don't like to laugh to read Dawson's delightfully humorous books, because her novels are guaranteed to tickle the funny bone.

BIBLIOGRAPHY

Books: *Capture the Night.* New York: Bantam, 1993; *The Texan's Bride.* New York: Bantam, 1993; *Tempting Mortality.* New York: Bantam, 1995; *The Bad Luck Wedding Dress.* New York: Bantam, 1996; *The Wedding Raffle.* New York: Pocket, 1996; *The Wedding Ransom.* New York: Pocket, 1998; *The Bad Luck Wedding Cake.* New York: Pocket, 1998; *The Kissing Stars.* New York: Pocket, 1999; *Simmer All Night.* New York: Pocket, 1999; *Sizzle All Day.* New York: Pocket, 2000; *The Bad Luck Wedding Night.* New York: Pocket, 2001; *The Pink Magnolia Club.* New York: Pocket, 2002; *My Big Old Texas Heartache.* New York: Pocket, 2003; *My Long Tall Texas Heartthrob.* New York: Pocket, 2004; *Her Bodyguard.* Toronto: Harlequin, 2005; *Her Scoundrel.* Toronto: Harlequin, 2005; *Her Outlaw.* Toronto: Harlequin, in press.

Novellas: "Castaway" in *Under the Boardwalk.* New York: Pocket, 1999; "Cold Feet" in *A Season in the Highlands.* New York: Pocket, 2000.

SANDRA VAN WINKLE AND SHELLEY MOSLEY

ROZ DENNY. *See* Roz Denny Fox

EILEEN DREYER

Eileen Dreyer. Courtesy of Eileen Dreyer.

As an author, Eileen Dreyer finds herself torn between two genres. Not only does she enjoy writing emotionally hopeful love stories, but she also finds herself perfectly suited to fashioning darker novels of suspense. Writing as Kathleen Korbel, Dreyer has written more than twenty-two contemporary romances for Silhouette. Under her own name, Dreyer has written seven medical thrillers for HarperCollins and St. Martin's Press. Along the way, she has garnered numerous awards, including five RITAs from the Romance Writers of America, which earned her the fourth spot in their prestigious Hall of Fame.

Dreyer was born Mary Eileen in 1952 in Brentwood, Missouri. The eldest daughter, Dreyer grew up with five brothers, a younger sister, a father who gave up his career as a big band singer to become an accountant, and a mother who was a talented writer herself. As a young child, reading was always an important part of Dreyer's life. Nancy Drew was a particular favorite of hers, and when she ran out of Nancy Drew mysteries to read, Dreyer wrote her own stories, featuring twin sisters who lived in a boarding school and solved crimes.

Dreyer attended Catholic schools as a child; a fact to which she attributes how she later turned out in life. While attending grade school, Dreyer rediscovered how much fun writing

---

also writing as Kathleen Korbel

could be, and that writing stories featuring her friends was one sure way to popularity. Dreyer credits one of her grade school English teachers, Sister Mary Alice, as being her first real writing instructor. After finding one of Dreyer's notebooks of stories, the Dominican nun announced that if little Eileen thought she was going to be an author, she should know what she was doing, and Sister Mary Alice proceeded to drill the basics of grammar and language into her.

Theater was another one of Dreyer's early passions, and she participated in the dramatic arts all through high school. Dreyer eventually abandoned any dreams of becoming a professional actress after her ever-practical mother convinced her that she would need a real education that would lead to a steady job. Dreyer enrolled in the Maryville University School of Nursing, where she eventually received her RN and AA degrees, but she also had another, more personal reason for becoming a nurse. Like many people, Dreyer was deeply affected by the Vietnam War, and her eldest brother had been serving in the United States Marine Corps in Vietnam. Dreyer was convinced that becoming a nurse was a way of helping her brother; however, by the time Dreyer had completed her training and was ready to go overseas, the war had ended.

It was while Dreyer worked as a nurse that she met her husband, through a blind date that was set up by one of her friends. That friend had recently married, but she never seemed to have any time alone with her new husband since one of her husband's friends kept coming over to work on cars with him. In desperation, Dreyer's friend insisted that Dreyer must date her husband's friend just to get him out of her house. Apparently the blind date was fun, because Dreyer married Rick Dreyer, an engineer, in 1974. Getting married also convinced Dreyer that it was time she put away her youthful dreams of a career in theater and writing to devote herself to her job as a nurse, her new husband, and eventually, their two children.

Despite her best efforts to quit, the fickle muse of writing kept calling to Dreyer. Over the years, the everyday wear and tear of nursing got to her, so when a friend and fellow nurse suggested in 1982 that they write a romance together, Dreyer thought the idea worth exploring. Because she had grown up reading mysteries, Dreyer was not familiar with the romance genre, but she began reading some of the newly published authors of the time, including Jayne Ann Krentz and Lisa Gregory. One of the first things Dreyer noticed about the romance genre was that it delivered happy endings to its readers, something Dreyer did not always get enough of in her nursing career. When her husband gave her a typewriter, it provided the last push Dreyer needed to begin writing again.

While Dreyer was serious about writing romance, it seems publishers were equally serious about rejecting her first efforts. Because Dreyer's own distinctive style of romance fiction was so different from much of what was being published at the time, it was difficult for publishers to conceive of her work finding a ready audience with romance readers. Eventually, one perceptive editor at Silhouette saw the literary worth in Dreyer's writing and plucked Dreyer's manuscript out of the slush pile in which it had been patiently waiting.

Like many romance writers publishing with Harlequin and Silhouette at that time, Dreyer was encouraged to adopt a pseudonym, under which her books would be released. Thus, while visiting with some of the cast and crew of the old television show *Combat* in California, Dreyer was inspired by the brand of champagne they happened to be drinking one night and came up with her new pen name of Kathleen Korbel.

Playing the Game, which was actually the second book Dreyer wrote, was published by Silhouette as part of their Desire line in 1986. Dreyer's unique voice, tart sense of wit, and talent for evoking a wide range of emotions from readers are all readily apparent in *Playing the Game.* In the book, nurse Kelly Bryne finds her quietly routine life changing in more ways than one when a handsome stranger jumps into her car and asks her to rescue him. The stranger turns out to be movie star Matt Hennessy, who somehow convinces Kelly—one of the few women in America who doesn't recognize him—to pretend to be his new girlfriend to fool the press. It is all fun until Kelly, who is still mourning the relatively recent loss of her husband, realizes she is falling in love with Matt and doesn't know what to do about it. Dreyer gives her first published heroine a few of her own talents and interests, including a nursing job and love of the theater. In addition, her familiarity with the St. Louis area gives the book's setting a vivid sense of place. Most importantly of all, Dreyer uses her deep understanding of human emotions to create a sweetly poignant and richly emotional tale of grief and love.

While Dreyer believes that "your first book is written on guts, the rest is on fear," she shouldn't have been afraid that she would never be published again. *A Stranger's Smile,* also published in 1986, followed *Playing the Game,* and soon, Dreyer was publishing two or more titles a year. In 1987, Dreyer won her first award from *Romantic Times,* which named her best new Contemporary Romance Author of the year. In 1990, Dreyer not only won her first RITA award from the Romance Writers of America for her contemporary romantic suspense novel, *Perchance to Dream* (1989), but she also garnered a second coveted RITA award that same year for *The Ice Cream Man* (1989) for Best Long Contemporary Romance. Soon, Dreyer's emotionally intense romances not only became regulars on the genre award lists but also much loved and treasured "keeper" books by readers.

Dreyer considers herself an organic writer, and like any oyster, she needs some kernel of sand around which she can begin building a story. For Dreyer, however, the inspiration for each book can come from completely different sources. Sometimes a particular scene will unfold in her imagination, prompting Dreyer to write a story that fits that scene. Such was the case with *Worth Any Risk* (1987), in which the heroine sees her life flash before her eyes when she is taken hostage during a drug holdup and vows that should it happen again, she will have something better to remember. Occasionally, a character will invade Dreyer's thoughts, demanding that she write his or her story, such as Jake Kendall in *Jake's Way* (1992). Other times, a particular setting can serve as a source of inspiration, such as the beautiful and exotic locale of Molokai in *Sail Away* (1998). Dreyer firmly believes inspiration for an author can come from anywhere and everywhere, but it is the implementation of the idea that tells you exactly who has written that particular book.

For Dreyer, plotting is a necessary evil, but one that she has learned to master. Dreyer remains convinced that her best plots have a mix of both internal and external motivations, such as those in her book, *Princess and the Pea.* Published in 1988, and loosely connected to *A Prince of a Guy* (1987), the book pairs up Crown Princess Cassandra Catherine Anna Marie Von Lieberhaven and newly retired spy Paul Phillips. The book's internal motivation centers on Cassandra's attempts to learn how to become a real, ordinary woman, while the external motivation comes from the fact that both Cassandra and Paul are being chased by some very bad guys for a valuable roll of microfilm.

Published in 1991, *A Man to Die For,* the first book Dreyer wrote under her own name, won the RITA award for best romantic suspense novel in 1992. In the book, Dr. Dale Hunsacker joins the staff of the hospital in which savvy trauma nurse Casey McDonough works, and he soon has everyone charmed, except for Casey, who senses there is something not quite right about the good doctor. When nurses who oppose Hunsacker suddenly begin dying, Casey takes her concerns to sexy police detective Jack Scanlon, who joins forces professionally, and personally, with Casey to stop the clever killer. Dreyer had been waiting a long time to incorporate her own views about medicine into one of her books, and *A Man to Die For* allowed her to finally give voice to both her love for and concerns about the profession. Dreyer's own experiences as a trauma-room nurse give the story a vivid sense of realism, and Casey is an excellent example of Dreyer's brand of tough and clever heroines.

While Dreyer is known for her ability to infuse a riveting sense of suspense into her books, such as *Walk on the Wild Side* (1992), she is also loved by readers for her contemporary romances that tackle difficult subjects, including adult illiteracy, suicide, and eating disorders, in a truthful and emotionally honest way. Dreyer consistently gets away with using topics such as these in her romance novels both because of the outstanding quality of her writing and because no matter what her characters might have to endure, readers are assured that it is going to be all right in the end. A beautiful illustration of this is Dreyer's best-known book, *A Rose for Maggie*. It is the story of a mother who is struggling to raise her Down syndrome baby and doesn't believe there is room in her life for romance, until she meets a reclusive author who proves her wrong. Published in 1991, *A Rose for Maggie* won Dreyer her much-deserved third RITA award.

After *Sail Away* was published in 1998, the next few books Dreyer wrote were medical suspense novels, such as *With a Vengeance* (2003) and *Head Games* (2004), which were published under her own name. But readers need not have feared that Kathleen Korbel had disappeared completely. In 2003, *Some Men's Dreams* was published under her Korbel pseudonym, and it became the third book in her Kendall Family series, preceded by *Jake's Way* and *Simple Gifts* (1994). Like each of the previous Kendall books, *Some Men's Dreams* deals with some serious issues—guilt, grief, and eating disorders—but Dreyer flawlessly integrates these topics into a superbly written, richly emotional love story.

One of the things that first drew Dreyer to the romance genre was the message of hope it gives its readers. Or as Dreyer herself puts it, "What, after all, is needed more in this world that seems to be spinning out of control than the reinforcement in the belief of hope? And that's just what romance reinforces. The belief that together, we can overcome anything. That as women we have power over our lives and the lives of our loved ones, and ultimately, our destiny. Pretty impressive stuff. It's the repetition of the message, not the plot, that keeps drawing people back and keeps writers writing." Dreyer truly believes in this message of hope, which is reflected in each of her splendidly rewarding love stories.

BIBLIOGRAPHY

Writing as Eileen Dreyer

Books: *A Man to Die For.* New York: Harper, 1991; *If Looks Could Kill.* New York: Harper, 1992; *Nothing Personal.* New York: Harper, 1994; *Bad Medicine.* New York: Harper, 1995; *Brain Dead.* New York: HarperCollins, 1997; *With a Vengeance.* New York: St. Martin's Press, 2003; *Head Games.* New York: St. Martin's Press, 2004; *The Sunken Sailor.* New York: Berkley, 2004; *Saints and Sinners.* New York: St. Martin's Press, 2005.

Novellas: "Double Jeopardy" in *Malice Domestic Anthology 5: An Anthology of Original Traditional Mystery Stories.* New York: Simon and Schuster, 1996; "Fantasy" in *Marilyn: Shades of Blonde.* New York: Tom Doherty Associates, 1997; "Crayons and Pink Giraffes" in *Mothers and Daughters: Celebrating the Gift of Love with Twelve New Stories.* New York: Penguin, 1998; "The Most Beautiful Place on Earth" in *Jessica Fletcher Presents: … Murder They Wrote II.* New York: Penguin, 1998; "Fun with Forensics" in *Irreconcilable Differences.* New York: HarperCollins, 1999; "Safe at Home" in *Fathers and Daughters.* New York: Penguin, 1999; "Variations on a Theme" in *Mothers and Sons: A Celebration in Memories, Stories, and Photographs.* New York: Penguin, 2000.

Genre-Related Essay: "And I Still Write Romance" in *North American Romance Writers*. Lanham, MD: Scarecrow Press, 1999.

Writing as Kathleen Korbel

Books: *Playing the Game*. New York: Silhouette, 1986; *A Stranger's Smile*. New York: Silhouette, 1986; *Worth Any Risk*. New York: Silhouette, 1987; *A Prince of a Guy*. New York: Silhouette, 1987; *Edge of the World*. New York: Silhouette, 1988; *Princess and the Pea*. New York: Silhouette, 1988; *Perchance to Dream*. New York: Silhouette, 1989; *The Ice Cream Man*. New York: Silhouette, 1989; *Hotshot*. New York: Silhouette, 1990; *Lightning Strikes*. New York: Silhouette, 1990; *A Rose for Maggie*. New York: Silhouette, 1991; *A Fine Madness*. New York: Silhouette, 1991; *Jake's Way*. New York: Silhouette, 1992; *Isn't It Romantic*. New York: Silhouette, 1992; *Walk on the Wild Side*. New York: Silhouette, 1992; *Simple Gifts*. New York: Silhouette, 1994; *A Soldier's Heart*. New York: Silhouette, 1995; *Don't Fence Me In*. New York: Silhouette, 1996; *Sail Away*. New York: Silhouette, 1998; *Some Men's Dreams*. New York: Silhouette, 2003.

Novellas: "The Road to Mandalay" in *Summer Sizzlers*. New York: Silhouette, 1989; "Timeless" in *Silhouette Shadows*. New York: Silhouette, 1993.

JOHN CHARLES

KAREN DROGIN. *See* Carly Phillips

REBECCA DRURY. *See* Jane Toombs

ALICE DUNCAN

Versatile, industrious, and persistent are three good words to describe author Alice Duncan. Along with her literary alter egos, Anne Robins, Emma Craig, Rachel Wilson, and John Sharpe, Duncan has written more than forty novels, ranging from historical romances to Westerns. The publishing business can be brutal to authors, but since 1992, Duncan has been industriously writing books for a variety of publishers, demonstrating versatility in her willingness to weather the changing tides of the business and showing remarkable persistence in pursuing her dream of becoming a published author.

Duncan was born in Pasadena, California, in 1945. Her parents had met in San Francisco, where her father served in the U.S. Navy and her mother worked as a cook for a wealthy family who lived in the city. Duncan grew up in Altadena, California, and graduated from John Muir High School. Her insatiable thirst for knowledge led her to attend Pasadena City College, the University of California at Los Angeles, and even the University of Phoenix, though she never received formal degrees from these institutions.

Ever since she was a young girl, being a writer was the one thing Duncan had truly wanted to do. Duncan got married and had two daughters, but when a divorce left Duncan a single parent, she put away her dreams of a writing career and instead focused on supporting herself and her children. She worked in a variety of secretarial and administrative assistant positions, sang in a Balkan women's choir called Zena, and eventually became a member of two different international folk dance groups, Avaz and Gypsy. With her children grown and her dancing career on hiatus due to arthritis, Duncan revisited the idea of

---

also writing as Emma Craig
also writing as Rachel Wilson
also writing as John Sharpe
also writing as Anne Robins

becoming an author. A friend convinced Duncan, whose only experience with romance novels up to that time had been the books of Georgette Heyer, to read a few romance titles. Duncan fell in love with the genre. Duncan says that romance novels "had everything she looked for in a good read: history, entertaining yarns, fulfilling relationships, and happy endings."

With her very first historical romance, Duncan demonstrated a flair for humor and an interest in the American West as a setting. Her first book, *One Bright Morning* (1995), was set in 1876 in the New Mexico Territory. The story of a young widow, Maggie Bright, who discovers a wounded stranger on her porch one day, *One Bright Morning* is imbued with Duncan's wonderfully tart sense of wit and her love for the landscape of New Mexico. *Texas Lonesome* (1996), Duncan's second published romance, takes readers to San Francisco circa 1895 for the humorous tale of a female newspaper columnist who responds to a letter from a Texas rancher requesting her advice on how he might find a wife. For her third romance, *Wild Dream* (1997), Duncan returned to 1868 New Mexico Territory, where a rancher heroine desperately tries to use her Southern charms to entice the leader of a gang of robber-musicians into sticking around.

As an author, Duncan frequently finds inspiration for her stories in the lesser-known and lesser-used (in the romance genre) periods of American history. For example, her Meet Me at the Fair trilogy—consisting of *Coming Up Roses* (2002), *Just North of Bliss* (2002), and *A Bicycle Built for Two* (2002)—is set in Chicago during the Columbian Exposition of 1893. With these three books, Duncan not only gives readers her usual humor-tinged love stories, but also provides readers with a vivid taste of what this colorful World's Fair must have been like by neatly integrating real historical figures, such as Buffalo Bill Cody and Annie Oakley, into her plots. Duncan's The Dream Maker quartet of books—*Cowboy for Hire* (2001), *Beauty and the Brain* (2001), *The Miner's Daughter* (2001), and *Her Leading Man* (2001)—are not only four entertaining historical romances, they are also a fascinating introduction to the early days of the silent-film industry in Southern California.

Occasionally, a dash of magic or a bit of fairy tale charm turns up in Duncan's books. For example, in *Christmas Pie* (1997), set in San Francisco in 1899, when the book's heroine, typist Polly MacNamara, stops off in Chinatown to buy her mother a Christmas present, the old shopkeeper gives Polly an ancient coin as a gift. Not only does the coin help bring Polly and lawyer James Drayton together, its "special" property adds a generous measure of humor to the story. Readers familiar with juvenile literature will especially appreciate Duncan's loving tribute to the classic children's fantasy book, *Half Magic*. With *Cooking Up Trouble* (2000), Duncan offers her own special twist on the fairy tale "Rumplestiltskin." The book's heroine, culinary-challenged Heather Mahaffey, finds she must accept the help of a mysterious stranger, Mr. D. A. Bologh, if she is to have any hope of keeping her new job as cook for wealthy, handsome Philippe St. Pierre. From the clever name Duncan gives the book's Rumplestiltskin stand-in to her neat incorporation of New Mexico's culinary heritage into the story, *Cooking Up Trouble* proved to be another of Duncan's bewitching literary confections.

In addition to romances, Duncan had long wanted to try writing a mystery. With *Strong Spirits* (2003), Duncan thought she just might have the chance to cross genres. Set in Pasadena, California, in the 1920s, the book introduced readers to Desdemona Majesty, also known as "Daisy Gumm," a spiritualist to the rich and famous of Southern California. When one of Daisy's clients is accused of bank fraud, Daisy becomes mixed up in the case and involved with detective Sam Rotondo. Duncan initially tried to sell *Strong Sprits* as a mystery, but she was persuaded by her publishers to "take out a few of the dead bodies," and the resulting book became something of a hybrid between a historical mystery and a historical romance. Duncan followed up *Strong Spirits* with *Fine Spirits* (2003), in which Daisy becomes tangled with a teenage runaway while investigating a so-called haunted mansion. While the two books might have been difficult to classify and market, they remain two of Duncan's personal favorites.

Interestingly enough, one of the hardest books for Duncan to write and one of the easiest are part of the same trilogy of books. Duncan found *A Perfect Stranger* (2004), the first in her Perfect trilogy, featuring three female survivors of the sinking of the *Titanic*, the most difficult book she has ever had to write. "I hated that book," Duncan remembers. "I wanted to be writing more Spirits books, but due to marketing errors, the books flopped big-time. I was in deep mourning for the characters and the setting and the time period. Also, the Perfect series was not my idea. It was suggested to me, but I couldn't think of a plot, didn't care about the characters, and wished they'd all go down with the ship."

Eventually with a little help from her editor and a lot of her own grit and determination, Duncan finished *A Perfect Stranger.* While Duncan hated the whole process involved with *A Perfect Stranger,* the next book in the trilogy, *A Perfect Romance* (2004), turned out to be the easiest book she has ever written. She recalls, " For one thing, I had the plot and characters floating around in my brain for about ten years, and for another thing, I *loved* them both. *A Perfect Romance* was a fun book to write, and I like it ever so much better than *A Perfect Stranger.*"

Writing for a living can be tough, demanding, and, all too frequently, exhausting for both the mind and the spirit. Those hardy souls willing to undertake these challenges for the opportunity to share their stories are a rare breed. Fortunately for readers who value expertly crafted tales of love and laughter, Alice Duncan is one of those unique individuals.

BIBLIOGRAPHY

Writing as Alice Duncan

Books: *One Bright Morning.* New York: Harper Monogram, 1995; *Texas Lonesome.* New York: Harper Monogram, 1996; *Wild Dream.* New York: Dell, 1997; *Secret Hearts.* New York: Dell, 1998; *Cowboy for Hire.* New York: Kensington, 2001; *Beauty and the Brain.* New York: Kensington, 2001; *The Miner's Daughter.* New York: Kensington, 2001; *Her Leading Man.* New York: Kensington, 2001; *Coming Up Roses.* New York: Kensington, 2002; *Just North of Bliss.* New York: Kensington, 2002; *A Bicycle Built for Two.* New York: Kensington, 2002; *Strong Spirits.* New York: Kensington, 2003; *Fine Spirits.* New York: Kensington, 2003; *Phoebe's Valentine.* Ostego, MI: PageFree Publishing, 2003; *Sierra Ransom.* Ostego, MI: PageFree Publishing, 2003; *A Perfect Stranger.* New York: Kensington, 2004; *A Perfect Romance.* New York: Kensington, 2004; *A Perfect Wedding.* New York: Kensington, 2005; *Pecos Valley Diamond.* Coral Springs, FL: New Age Dimensions Inc., 2005; *Lost Among the Angels.* Farmington Hills, MI: Five Star, 2006.

Writing as Emma Craig

Books: *Rosamunda's Revenge.* New York: Dorchester, 1997; *Christmas Pie.* New York: Dorchester, 1997; *Enchanted Christmas.* New York: Dorchester, 1998; *A Gentle Magic.* New York: Dorchester, 1999; *A Gambler's Magic.* New York: Dorchester, 2000; *Cooking Up Trouble.* New York: Dorchester, 2000; *Gabriel's Fate.* New York: Dorchester, 2001.

Novellas: "MacBroom Sweeps Clean" in *Midsummer Night's Magic.* New York: Dorchester, 1997; "Jack of Hearts" in *The Magic of Christmas.* New York: Dorchester, 1998; "Merry Gentlemen" in *Winter Wonderland.* New York: Dorchester, 1999.

Writing as Rachel Wilson

Books: *Sweet Charity.* New York: Jove, 1997; *Restless Spirits.* New York: Jove, 1998; *Heaven's Promise.* New York: Jove, 1998; *Bittersweet Summer.* New York: Jove, 1999; *Spirit of Love.* New York: Jove, 1999; *My Wild Irish Rose.* New York: Jove, 2000; *Heaven Sent.* New York: Jove, 2001.

Writing as John Sharpe

Books: *Pecos Belle Brigade.* New York: Signet, 1999; *California Crusader.* New York: Signet, 2000.

JOHN CHARLES

ELISABETH FAIRCHILD

The enchanted world of the Regency era has provided rich inspiration to the imagination of author Elisabeth Fairchild. The grace and poetry of that time period comes to life in her deft hands, and her expertly crafted romances have proved to be a magical reading experience for Regency lovers of all ages.

Fairchild was born in Albuquerque, New Mexico. Her father was a builder, and her mother was a British war bride. Her father raised Fairchild to believe that she had the ability to do anything that she set her mind to. As a child in suburban Dallas, Texas, Fairchild says she "wrote and illustrated stories as soon as I could spell." She realized that, from the very beginning, romance would play a part in her books. In fact, she says, "my first children's book [was] about snails under a trash can—a girl snail and a boy snail got married and had baby snails." In high school,

Elisabeth Fairchild. Photo by James Bland, photographer. Courtesy of Elisabeth Fairchild.

Fairchild's creative writing teacher submitted some of the poems Fairchild had written to a contest, and they were published. "I was euphoric!" Fairchild recalls. She attended North Texas State University, where she majored in commercial art and minored in English, graduating with a bachelor's degree in fine arts. She eventually married her high school sweetheart.

Fairchild says that before becoming a writer, she held a variety of interesting jobs.

> I've worked as a babysitter [and] a grocery checker. I waited tables for one day (not the job for me). I worked one summer as a maid in a castle in Denmark. I interned as a

photo stripper (checking photo negatives of insurance forms) for an in-house advertising agency (yawn). I interned at a small advertising agency where I drew the bubbly hands that used to be on almost every public bathroom soap dispenser in the U.S. I interned at a catalog company, doing photo shoot set-up and design work. I was a designer at a national gift wrap company. I was creative director at an in-house art department for a party goods company. And all that time, I was writing on weekends and on coffee breaks.

At this time, Fairchild's writing took the form of scripts for her favorite television shows. She recalls, "I boldly sent the scripts to several Hollywood agents. One offered to represent the work as soon as I moved to LA! But my husband's job was in Dallas, and our marriage was, and still is, of highest priority, so I focused on writing novels." With that priority in mind, Fairchild quit her job as an art director to concentrate on finishing her novel. About the romance genre, she says, "I never really decided to write romances; that's just what the stories in my head are about—relationships, how they form, why they work. Each book/short story I have written has a theme. Many have more to do with the human condition rather than romance, but love factors in somehow."

Manuscripts in hand, Fairchild entered the 1991 Greater Dallas Writer's Association/University of Texas at Dallas Craft of Writing Competition.

I had been writing two books at the time, a Western and the Regency that became *The Silent Suitor* (then called *Blind Love*). I had pushed the writing as far as I knew how to on my own, so I entered both pieces in a writing contest that would be judged by published authors, agents, and editors. I was looking forward to getting the promised professional critique that was part of the contest. It never occurred to me that both entries might win awards or that the agent who read the Regency would approach me afterwards to tell me she could sell my work. Or that within the year I would have a publishing contract. I was incredibly fortunate. Right place. Right time. Right agent.

The agent sold *The Silent Suitor*, which was released by Signet in April 1994. Featuring an unusual heroine, Sarah Lyndle, a beautiful but blind debutante in her first season in London, *The Silent Suitor* is the story of a young woman who must learn to see with her heart when she is forced to choose romantically between two cousins.

More traditional Regency romances followed, including *Miss Dornton's Hero* (1995), which Fairchild found inspiration for in an unusual historical footnote: "I read a passage about Waterloo teeth. There were men who went onto the battlefields, in France and America, and yanked the teeth of the dead for sets of false teeth. They [the teeth] were sent back to England by the barrelful. That one little horrific tidbit of history started me wondering, 'What if they tried to pull the teeth of a man who was still alive?' In my imagination, he sat up and said, 'I've still need of them!' And thus began *Miss Dornton's Hero*." Two wounded souls are perfectly matched this a poignant tale of Evelyn, Lord Dade, haunted by his memories of Waterloo and known by the sobriquet "Lord Dead." When he rescues Miss Margaret Dornton, he has no interest in becoming anyone's hero, but Margaret's gentle love and devotion inspires him to take a second chance on life and love. Richly emotional, thoroughly moving, and with subtly nuanced characters and historical depth, *Miss Dornton's Hero* became a favorite among readers.

As an author, Christmas holds a special appeal for Fairchild, as evidenced by the themes in several of her works, including her novels *The Holly and the Ivy* (1999) and *Sugarplum*

Surprises (2001) as well as the three novellas she wrote for the Signet Regency Christmas Anthologies. "I do love Christmas," says Fairchild. "It is such a delicious jumble of Christian significance deliberately overlapping pagan winter chasing. For most people it is a time of warmth and celebration in the bleakest time of year, a time for feasting and family gatherings. For others it is a time of crushing loneliness. Great thematic potential. Also, the history of Christmas is fascinating."

In *The Holly and the Ivy,* Fairchild pairs a Scrooge-like hero with a Pollyanna-ish heroine to charming results. When Charles Thornton Baxter, fifth Viscount Balfour, is forced to take on the responsibility of giving his family's annual Christmas ball, a holiday he despises, the last thing he wants is any help from his cheery and optimistic neighbor, Mary Rivers. The more time he spends with the lovely Mary, the more his perpetual cynicism about the holidays fades away. Sweetness is matched with cynicism, and love triumphs, in this charming and heartwarming holiday romance.

Another holiday, this time Valentine's Day, provides the background for *Captain Cupid Calls the Shots* (2000), when Alexander Shelbourne, a war-weary soldier whose nickname is "Captain Cupid," visits a friend's home in Cumbria. He never expects to find a kindred spirit in the form of Miss Penny Foster, but the two find their romantic fate sealed when they are matched together in a local Valentine's Day custom. Fairchild once again demonstrates her gift of subtly complex characterization and her lyrical writing style.

Captain Cupid Calls the Shots is loosely connected to *Valentine's Change of Heart* (2003), in that the hero, Mr. Valentine Wharton, is the friend that Captain Cupid visited in Cumbria. Observing Alexander Shelbourne and Penny Foster and their interaction with their family, Valentine's change of heart occurs when he is inspired to be a better parent and decides to take a more active role in raising his illegitimate daughter, Felicity. He hires Elaine Deering, a teacher at his daughter's school, to become Felicity's new governess. Aware of Valentine's wild reputation, Elaine is reluctant to accept the offer, but her devotion to Felicity and her concern for the girl's welfare prompts Elaine to take the position. As Elaine travels with Valentine and Felicity to his estate in Wales, she discovers that Valentine is no longer the rakehell of his past. Instead, she realizes that he is a man with whom she could fall in love. In *Valentine's Change of Heart,* Fairchild writes beautifully and poetically about a man who is struggling to change and be a better father and person.

When given the opportunity to pay homage to her hero Jane Austen, Fairchild jumped at the chance. In *Flirting with Pride and Prejudice* (2005), Fairchild's essay "Any Way You Slice It" tells of the joy of Austen and her gift for plotting and characterization. Using vegetable analogies, Fairchild explains that the key to Austen's work is much like an onion, with layers and nuances built around a central theme or core truth. In this sparkling and insightful essay, Fairchild's love of Austen is evident in each sentence. Says Fairchild, "So much of her work appeals. Her use of theme, densely layered and yet subtle, her sense of humor, wit, great comic characters, the voices that beg to be read aloud. The intelligence that shines through her work. Her barbed digs at the follies of her time." Fairchild acknowledges the influence of Jane Austen on so many other readers as well as in her own books. She says, "She leaves the reader who truly comprehends her work chuckling, thoughtful, and feeling clever all at the same time. I love that."

For millions of readers, Jane Austen has created magical love stories chronicling the Regency era. Fairchild follows in her footsteps with her poetically written and captivating romances. Fairchild says, "There is a magic to the process of imagination. Sometimes I get so swept up in what I am writing, that it is as if I am transported back in time. I can see and hear and smell the place I am writing about with such clarity. Characters' voices flow in conversations so fast that my fingers fly upon the keys to catch it all. Time has no meaning in such moments. Much of the writing process is more mundane than that; it's work, word after word. But when the words flow—and my imagination rules—it's breathtaking."

BIBLIOGRAPHY

Books: *The Silent Suitor.* New York: Signet, 1994; *Counterfeit Coachman.* New York: Signet, 1994; *Miss Dornton's Hero.* New York: Signet, 1995; *Lord Endicott's Appetite.* New York: Signet, 1995; *The Love Knot.* New York: Signet, 1995; *Lord Ramsay's Return.* New York: Signet, 1996; *A Fresh Perspective.* New York: Signet, 1996; *The Rakehell's Reform.* New York: Signet, 1997; *Marriage a la Mode.* New York: Signet, 1997; *The Holly and the Ivy.* New York: Signet, 1999; *Breech of Promise.* New York: Signet, 2000; *Captain Cupid Calls the Shots.* New York: Signet, 2000; *Sugarplum Surprises.* New York: Signet, 2001; *A Game of Patience.* New York: Signet, 2002; *Valentine's Change of Heart.* New York: Signet, 2003.

Novellas: "The Mistletoe Kiss" in *A Regency Christmas Carol.* New York: Signet, 1997; "Felicity's Forfeit" in *A Regency Christmas.* New York: Signet, 1998; "A Christmas Canvas" in *A Regency Christmas Present.* New York: Signet, 1999; "Love Will Find the Way" in *The Grand Hotel.* New York: Signet, 2000.

Genre-Related Essay: "Any Way You Slice It" in *Flirting with Pride and Prejudice: Fresh Perspectives on the Original Chick-lit Masterpiece.* Dallas, TX: Benbella Press, 2005.

JOANNE HAMILTON-SELWAY

DIANE FARR

Diane Farr. Courtesy of Diane Farr.

Traditional Regency romances and Regency historicals written with stylish wit and superb characterization are Diane Farr's gift to the romance genre. Born in San Jose, California, Farr is the youngest of five sisters. Being the daughter of a Methodist minister meant Farr grew up living all over California, primarily in the Bay Area. Both her father and mother gave all their children a love of music and books and impressed on their daughters that individuals should not only make a difference in the world, but should also follow their inner light without regard to what is popular or currently in fashion.

Even if Farr didn't realize it at first, her family knew she was destined to become a writer. As a young girl, Farr would spend hours telling anyone who would listen (and occasionally this meant only her beloved stuffed animals) fanciful stories. She read voraciously, loved to write long letters, and, of course, kept diaries.

Farr received a bachelor of art degree in drama (with an emphasis on acting/directing as opposed to technical theater) from California State University at Hayward and had minors in English, psychology, and foreign language. Farr attended the American Conservatory Theater in San Francisco, where she worked on but did not complete a master's degree in fine arts.

Farr's first passion was the theater, and she pursued it while working a number of secretarial jobs to keep financially afloat. Even while trying to establish a career as an actress, Farr still found time for her writing muse. She wrote a humor column for a tiny newspaper in Idyllwild, California, and published plays.

For Farr, her first novel, *The Nobody* (1999), turned out to be a hard book to write. Not having written a book before, Farr was not quite sure how the process worked and says she found herself "fishing around a lot with it, endlessly rewriting the beginning because I couldn't figure out where the book should actually begin." With *The Nobody*, Farr ended up opening her story with her heroine, Caitlin, a nobody suffering through her first season in London, experiencing an unexpected kiss from Lord Kilverton, a most eligible bachelor. The kiss awakens an attraction between the two that is then played out within the familiar boundaries of the traditional Regency romance. *The Nobody* would go on to earn Farr two RITA nominations—one for Best Regency and one for Best First Novel—from the Romance Writers of America. In an almost unprecedented recognition of a new author, Farr's second novel, *Fair Game* (1999) was also nominated for a RITA for Best Regency that same year.

Farr believes that her early romances "sounded a lot like Georgette Heyer," but as she continues to write she is "finding her own voice". Her novels are often described as light-hearted but poignant, with a generous dash of drama and humor. For a while, Farr did try to conform to writing in a more masculine style—terse and muscular and adverb-free—but she gave up. Whether it is her theatrical background, where adverbs and punctuation are appreciated as hints to the actors of what the playwright intends, or her own fruitful imagination, Farr's writing is rich in descriptive notes, such as exclamation points, redundant adjectives, and the occasional dreaded adverbial dialogue tag. Even if some editors might criticize such a style of writing, Farr sighs, "I just can't help it. That's the way I write."

As a writer, Farr finds characters come more easily than plot. Perhaps it is again because of her acting background, but Farr says she begins her books by "dreaming up a compelling character—male or female—in great detail, and then [thinking] about the kind of person who would be that character's ideal match. Once I have the couple fully formed, so to speak, with character traits that complement each other perfectly, I have to put them in a situation where they will encounter each other. That's the easy part. What is a bit tougher is finding reasons to keep them from just living happily ever after starting on page 12. In other words: plot!"

In the plot of the engrossing *Fortune Hunter* (2002), Farr's first foray into the longer Regency historical format, Farr pairs her heroine, Lady Olivia Fairfax, a wealthy young woman whose life is centered around rewarding charity projects, with Lord Rival, a noble-man in search of a wealthy wife. Farr raises the interesting question of a woman's independence in Regency times and her lack of it once she marries.

Farr's heroes seem to share three distinctive traits. She says that they "all have an innate moral compass, a wicked sense of humor, and a kind heart. Sometimes the kind heart is well hidden, but the heroine always finds it. Sometimes the moral compass is so idiosyncratic that even the hero doesn't know he has it, but all my heroes live by a strict code of honor—even if they don't recognize it, and even if no one else recognizes the code by which they live." Farr's heroines also share three common traits: honesty; a cheerful temperament; and insight, specifically into the hero's character, but in other ways as well. "Even if my heroines don't always perceive themselves accurately, they are always in tune with other people," she says. "As for a cheerful temperament, I have created several heroines whose unshakeable optimism turns out to be a real thorn in the hero's side. Mind you, they are not 'perky'; they are just serenely confident in their rosy worldview."

As difficult as the writing process might be, Farr still finds it impossible to resist the siren call of her muse: "When you write a book, you get to make everything perfect. Wonderful people who deserve each other find each other. Meanies are punished. The wonderful, witty ripostes that always seem to occur to you the following morning in real life occur to your heroes and heroines on the spot, and they say them. Jewels glitter, gowns swish, and music plays exactly the way you want them to. The kisses are earth shattering, and the gardens are always in full bloom. Believe me, it's irresistible."

The charm of her characters, her captivating plots, the sparkling wit of her dialogue, and the accurate use of Regency manners all combine beautifully in Farr's delightful books, which can usually be found on the top of many readers' lists of favorite romances.

BIBLIOGRAPHY

Books: *The Nobody.* New York: Signet, 1999; *Fair Game.* New York: Signet, 1999; *Falling for Chloe.* New York: Signet, 2000; *Once Upon a Christmas.* New York: Signet, 2000; *The Fortune Hunter.* New York: Signet, 2002; *Duel of Hearts.* New York: Signet, 2002; *Under the Wishing Star.* New York: Signet, 2003; *Under a Lucky Star.* New York: Signet, 2004.
Novella: "Reckless Miss Ripley" in *A Regency Christmas Eve*. New York: Signet, 2000.

JOHN CHARLES

COLLEEN FAULKNER

The circumstances of Colleen Faulkner's birth and her early childhood read like something out of a book. Faulkner was born in New Jersey, only because her mother, Judith E. French, another best-selling romance author, didn't make it over the Delaware state line before giving birth. It took years for her family to forgive her mother for marrying Gary French, a computer analyst. They never trusted any man who wasn't a farmer. Over the years, Faulkner's father became accepted, mostly because he learned to drive a tractor, smoke fish, and herd goats whenever necessary.

Faulkner was raised on a small farm in Delaware, mere miles from the area where her mother's family settled more than three hundred years earlier. She grew up among numerous relatives, including her great-great-grandparents. Her father made her take a job in a Jell-O factory one summer when she was in high school to prove to her that she needed a college education. This work experience convinced her of the benefits of a good education, and she attended both the University of Delaware and the University of Alaska. When she was living in Kodiak, Alaska, bored with her college classes, her mother sent her a box of historical romances, and Faulkner fell in love with them. Faulkner married her high school sweetheart, and the two of them had three boys and one girl.

The theater called to Faulkner, who wanted to be a stage actress, not a writer; but she had children, and she knew the acting life wasn't conducive to motherhood. She decided if her mother could write a book, so could she. French sold her first book one year before Faulkner sold hers, titled *Forbidden Caress* (1987), and through the years, Faulkner says her mother has been her "best supporter and best critic" when she needed it. Faulkner feels writing takes the same type of energy and creativity as acting. She figures she must have made the right career choice, because she loves what she's doing.

Faulkner has written full-time since 1986. Like her mother, Faulkner considers herself to be more of a storyteller more than a writer. As she put it, she simply tells her readers a story

---

also writing as Hunter Morgan

in the same way she would if she were "sitting next to them on her back porch." What the reader sees in her books is quite close to what Faulkner puts on the paper the very first time.

The first books Faulkner wrote were historical romances. In 2000, with the book *Maggie's Baby*, she tried her hand at contemporary romances. She always loved tales of suspense, so writing romantic suspense was a natural progression. In 2003, using the name Hunter Morgan, Faulkner published her first romantic suspense, *The Other Twin*. At the time, her 12-year-old daughter was playing competitive softball. Inspired by her daughter's activities, Faulkner included a softball player in this story as a secondary character who has a vital role in the plot resolution.

Faulkner says she always starts writing her stories with a situation: "What if … a woman followed her husband to war and became a soldier? What if … a woman thought a serial killer who murdered her sister was now after her daughter and no one would believe her?" Once the initial concept is established, Faulkner builds her plot and characters. She asks herself, "What kind of woman would do this? How would she react? What would she do?"

In Faulkner's books, good always triumphs over evil. Faulkner says her female protagonist "gets what she wants in the end because she is inherently good and just and feels a certain responsibility to mankind. And of course, she always realizes that love is the greatest gift of all." Elen Burnard of Dunblane, the title character of *Highland Lady* (2001), is one such person. On his deathbed, Elen's father goes against tradition and names her Laird of Dunblane. Elen's sister is kidnapped by the clan's deadly enemies, the Forrests, so in retribution, Elen captures Monroe Forrest, the Earl of Rancoff, hoping to trade him for her sister. However, life is harsh in medieval Scotland, and although Elen finds herself falling in love with her prisoner, she knows she must never marry, or the Dunblane Clan will lose its land.

Her heroes are just, righteous men who come to realize that the women they love make them better human beings. Carpenter Zack Taylor, the hero of *Tempting Zack* (2000), the third and final book of the Bachelors Inc. series (*Taming Ben,* 2000; *Marrying Owen,* 2000), doesn't like career women. After all, his workaholic wife left both him and their young daughter, Savannah. Dr. Kayla Burns, Savannah's physician, needs new kitchen cupboards. Kayla is attracted to the handsome woodworker Zack, but he tries his hardest not to get interested in her. Zack has to overcome his prejudices against women, and Kayla is just the woman to help him do this.

Although Faulkner prefers changing her settings and favors whatever she's working on at the moment, she does have a preference for time periods. Restoration England is one of her favorites. Faulkner's novel *Once More* (1998) is set in the court of King Charles II. The heroine of the book, Lady Julia Thomas, has been ordered to marry the cold, distant Earl of St. Martin to save her mother and disabled sister from a life of poverty. Julia's heart, however, belongs to Griffin, Baron Archer. Like the Scarlet Pimpernel, Griffin plays the fop to hide his true mission and personality. Court intrigue, murder, passion, and seduction blend to create this captivating story.

Faulkner doesn't suffer from writer's block, but admits that some days, the words come easier than others. She does, however, believe writers can get burned out by working too hard and not taking time to recharge their creative energy. Being very careful to protect her own creativity, Faulkner won't overcommit, even though she usually has more than one book contract running at a time. She says loves "sitting alone in her office, spinning tales to share with others." Faulkner says she hopes that in her writing, she "somehow can give back something of what has been given to her."

Bibliography

Writing as Colleen Faulkner

Books: *Forbidden Caress.* New York: Kensington, 1987; *Raging Desire.* New York: Kensington, 1987; *Snowfire.* New York: Kensington, 1988; *Traitor's Caress.* New York: Kensington, 1989; *Passion's Savage Moon.* New York: Kensington, 1989; *Temptation's Tender Kiss.* New York: Kensington, 1990; *Love's Sweet Bounty.* New York: Kensington, 1991; *Patriot's Passion.* New York: Kensington, 1991; *Savage Surrender.* New York: Kensington, 1992; *Sweet Deception.* New York: Kensington, 1992; *Flames of Love.* New York: Kensington, 1993; *Forever His.* New York: Kensington, 1993; *Captive.* New York: Kensington, 1994; *O'Brian's Bride.* New York: Kensington, 1995; *Destined to Be Mine.* New York: Kensington, 1996; *To Love a Dark Stranger.* New York: Kensington, 1997; *Fire Dancer.* New York: Kensington, 1997; *Angel in My Arms.* New York: Kensington, 1998; *Once More.* New York: Kensington, 1998; *If You Were Mine.* New York: Kensington, 1999; *Highland Bride.* New York: Kensington, 2000; *Maggie's Baby.* New York: Kensington, 2000; *Marrying Owen.* New York: Kensington, 2000; *Tempting Zack.* New York: Kensington, 2000; *Taming Ben.* New York: Kensington, 2000; *Highland Lady.* New York: Kensington, 2001; *Highland Lord.* New York: Kensington, 2002; *A Shocking Request.* New York: Silhouette, 2002; *Barefoot and Pregnant.* New York: Silhouette, 2004.

Novellas: "Lovespell" in *Spellbound Kisses.* New York: Kensington, 1993; "The Other Christmas Story" in *A Christmas Embrace.* New York: Kensington, 1994; "Man of My Dreams" in *To Love and to Honor.* New York: Kensington, 1995; "A New Beginning" in *Deck the Halls.* New York: Kensington, 1996; "Highland Blood" in *After Midnight.* New York: Kensington, 1998; "If Wishes Came True" in *Castle Magic.* New York: Kensington, 1999; "The Pleasures of a Wager" in *Only with a Rogue.* New York: Kensington, 2002.

Writing as Hunter Morgan

Books: *The Other Twin.* New York: Kensington, 2003; *She'll Never Tell.* New York: Kensington, 2004; *She'll Never Know.* New York: Kensington, 2004; *She'll Never Live.* New York: Kensington, 2004; *What She Can't See.* New York: Kensington, 2005; *Unspoken Fear.* New York: Kensington, 2006; *Unspoken Danger.* New York: Kensington, 2007.

SANDRA VAN WINKLE, SHELLEY MOSLEY, AND MARION EKHOLM

J. A. FERGUSON. *See* Jo Ann Ferguson

JO ANN FERGUSON

The versatile, award-winning Jo Ann Ferguson has written for different publishers and in a variety of subgenres, but one thing that is common to all of books is her dedication to the craft of storytelling.

Ferguson was born in Granville, New York, in 1953, to Nelson "Nick" Brown, a farmer, and Verna Loveland Brown, a seamstress. Ferguson grew up in Salem, New York, and earned a bachelor of arts degree in American and English history from State University College at Potsdam, New York. After receiving her bachelor's degree, she accepted a direct commission into the U.S. Army as quartermaster officer. Ferguson attended Marywood College in Scranton, Pennsylvania, and then the University of Cincinnati in Ohio, where she did graduate work in library science. In 1976, she married Bill Ferguson, an industrial engineer at Procter and Gamble at the time.

Ferguson always wanted to write. In middle school, she wrote short stories, starring her friends. In high school and college, she worked on the school newspapers. While she was in high school, she wrote her first book—a time travel/*Dungeons and Dragons*/medieval young adult novel—about which she humorously comments, "Gee, I wonder why that never found a market!"

Many authors inspired Ferguson's eventual decision to write romance novels, but perhaps the most powerful influence was legendary romance writer Laurie McBain, whose ability to successfully combine suspense, adventure, and romance would echo in Ferguson's own novels. Ferguson began writing for publication in 1984. She signed with an

---

also writing as J. A. Ferguson
also writing as Jo Ann Brown
also writing as Joanna Hampton
also writing as Rebecca North
also writing as Jocelyn Kelley

agent in 1985, and by April 1987, she had sold her first book, *Nothing Wagered,* which was published in 1988.

As far as settings, Ferguson prefers to write about England and Wales, with Regency and medieval time periods running neck and neck for a favored spot. While Ferguson has written romances set in a variety of historical time periods, she is best known for her traditional Regency romances, including *A Model Marriage,* written in 1998. The Duke of Exton, artist Patrick Fairchild, is searching for the perfect model for his next painting, a version of Boticelli's *Venus,* when he catches a glimpse of musician Antonia Locke. Antonia's lush curves are far from fashionable but just what Patrick desires. Convincing the practical but naive schoolmaster's daughter Antonia to bare her body for art requires all of Patrick's skills in seduction. In *A Model Marriage,* Ferguson deftly plays the traditional Regency ideal of physical perfection against the Renaissance's appreciation for a voluptuous woman and, in the process, cleverly demonstrates that beauty comes in all shapes and sizes.

As a writer, Ferguson has skillfully created a number of connected books, including her six-part series of traditional Regency romances featuring Lady Priscilla Flanders and Sir Neville Hathaway. In the first book of the series, *A Rather Necessary End* (2002), readers are introduced to Lady Priscilla Flanders, a beautiful widow who is finally ready to give up her widow's weeds and leave the small town of Stonehall-on-Sea, when the body of the Duke of Meresden is found her in garden. A prime suspect in the murder, Priscilla decides to pursue her own investigation. Fortunately for Priscilla, one of her late husband's good friends, Neville Hathaway, has arrived for a visit and offers his own skills as a former Bow Street Runner to help catch the killer. In *A Rather Necessary End,* Ferguson deftly sets the scene for the romantic relationship between Priscilla and Neville, which plays out in the next four books—*Grave Intentions* (2003), *Faire Game* (2003), *The Greatest Possible Mischief* (2003), and *Digging Up Trouble* (2004)—until their eventual marriage in the sixth book, *The Wedding Caper* (2004). Ferguson's gift for creating memorable characters includes a lively cast of secondary players, especially Priscilla's interfering Aunt Cordelia. Engaging and amusing, this series is a most entertaining blend of mystery and romance.

In 2005, Ferguson adopted yet another pseudonym, Jocelyn Kelley, with the publication of *A Knight Like No Other,* the first in the series The Ladies of St. Jude's Abbey. Founded and protected by Eleanor of Aquitaine, St. Jude's is more than just a cloister; it is a training ground for female warriors, such as Avisa de Ware. Avisa has been given the task of keeping the Queen's godson, Christian Lovell, from becoming entangled in the power struggle between the king and the Archbishop of Canterbury. Avisa's assignment is even more difficult than just protecting Christian—she must keep her warrior skills hidden and adopt the guise of a weak female. Filled with action, adventure, and heroines who are more than capable of taking care of themselves, Ferguson describes her series as "Lara Croft in the twelfth century." *A Knight Like No Other* was followed by *One Knight Stands* in 2005 and *A Moonlit Knight* in 2006. A fourth book in this series, *My Lady Knight,* is scheduled for publication in 2007.

According to Ferguson, her emotional historicals are the hardest for her to write. But although they drain her, she loves that aspect of writing. One such book is the compelling novel, *Her Only Hero* (2000), which tells the story of Arielle Gardiner, who tricks Captain Stephen Lightenfield into taking her to find her missing fiancé. Unfortunately, the fiancé is somewhere in Nicaragua, and Arielle and Stephen find themselves in the middle of a revolution and running for their lives. Along the way, Arielle discovers what a real hero is—and it's certainly not her errant fiancé. Ferguson mixes a concoction of romance, danger, and adventure, and the result is unforgettable.

Woven Dreams, written in 2000 under the name Joanna Hampton, was another emotionally difficult book for Ferguson. Set in New York City in 1863, Sarah Granger, manager of the Second Avenue Mission for Needy Children in the poor Irish neighborhood of Five Points, tries to keep her charges safe when the Southern-agitated race riots put the whole area at risk. Police officer Benjamin McCauley finds a murdered woman and takes her now motherless children to Sarah. Ferguson builds the tension in this story in a romantic way, as Benjamin and Sarah develop feelings for each other, and also in a suspenseful way, as the danger comes nearer and nearer to the orphanage. This powerful book chronicles the New York City Draft Riots, a much-neglected and horrible event in Civil War history.

The easiest book for Ferguson to write was *Rebecca: The Foxbridge Legacy #2* (1988), which was written in only 10 days. Ferguson says it just "exploded out of my fingers." *Ride the Night Wind* (1995) is Ferguson's favorite book from her many works because it has characters who deal with the themes she loves to write about—trust between two people who don't have any reason to trust each other, and duty and honor at the cost of personal happiness.

Ferguson has also written nonfiction works, which include both articles and contributions to reference books. In addition to her writing, Ferguson has donated thousands of hours to Romance Writers of America, both on a local and national level. She served as a chapter president, national director, and national president (1998 to 2000). She was also the recipient of the Emma Merritt Award (the highest honor for volunteer work from RWA). Whether volunteering on behalf of the genre or adding to its literature, Ferguson is an integral part of the contemporary romance scene.

BIBLIOGRAPHY

Writing as Jo Ann Ferguson

Books: *Nothing Wagered.* New York: Tudor, 1988; *Sybill: The Foxbridge Legacy #1.* New York: Tudor, 1988; *Rebecca: The Foxbridge Legacy #2.* New York: Tudor, 1988; *Mariel: The Foxbridge Legacy #3.* New York: Tudor, 1989; *At the Rainbow's End.* New York: Tudor, 1989; *Under the Outlaw Moon.* New York: Tudor, 1989; *The Fortune Hunter.* New York: Kensington, 1993; *The Smithfield Bargain.* New York: Kensington, 1994; *An Undomesticated Wife.* New York: Kensington, 1994; *Ride the Night Wind.* New York: Harper, 1995; *The Wolfe Wager.* New York: Kensington, 1995; *Miss Charity's Case.* New York: Kensington, 1996; *Wake Not the Dragon.* New York: Harper, 1996; *The Counterfeit Count.* New York: Kensington, 1997; *Rhyme and Reason.* New York: Kensington, 1998; *A Model Marriage.* New York: Kensington, 1998; *Raven Quest.* New York: Kensington, 1999; *Destiny's Kiss.* New York: Kensington, 1999; *Just Her Type.* New York: Kensington, 1999; *The Convenient Arrangement.* New York: Kensington, 1999; *O'Neal's Daughter.* New York: Kensington, 1999; *The Jewel Palace.* New York: Kensington, 1999; *No Price Too High.* New York: Kensington, 1999; *Lord Radcliffe's Season.* New York: Kensington, 1999; *An Offer of Marriage.* New York: Kensington, 1999; *Her Only Hero.* New York: Kensington, 2000; *An Unexpected Husband.* New York: Kensington, 2000; *Anything for You.* New York: Kensington, 2000; *The Captain's Pearl.* New York: Kensington, 2000; *A Daughter's Destiny.* New York: Kensington, 2000; *Lady Captain.* New York: Kensington, 2000; *A Brother's Honor.* New York: Kensington, 2000; *A Christmas Bride.* New York: Kensington, 2000; *A Sister's Quest.* New York: Kensington, 2000; *Faithfully Yours.* New York: Kensington, 2001; *A Highland Folly.* New York: Kensington, 2001; *The Perfect Match.* New York: iPublish, 2001; *His Lady Midnight.* New York: Kensington, 2001; *A Guardian's Angel.* New York: Kensington, 2002; *Twice Blessed.* New York: Kensington, 2002; *His Unexpected Bride.* New York: Kensington, 2002; *Moonlight on Water.* New York: Kensington, 2002; *After the Storm.* New York: Kensington, 2002; *A Rather Necessary End.* New York: Kensington, 2002; *Grave*

Intentions. New York: Kensington, 2003; *Faire Game*. New York: Kensington, 2003; *The Greatest Possible Mischief*. New York: Kensington, 2003; *Digging Up Trouble*. New York: Kensington, 2004; *The Wedding Caper*. New York: Kensington, 2004; *The Perfect Bride*. New York: Kensington, 2004; *A Primrose Wedding*. New York: Kensington, 2005.

Novellas: "Lord Chartley's Lesson" in *A Mother's Joy*. New York: Kensington, 1994; "Game of Harts" in *Valentine Love*. New York: Kensington, 1996; "The Winter Heart" in *A Winter Kiss*. New York: Kensington, 1997; "Spellbound" in *Spellbound Hearts*. New York: Kensington, 1997; "Beneath the Kitten Bough" in *Mistletoe Kittens*. New York: Kensington, 1999; "Not His Bread-and-Butter" in *Sweet Temptations*. New York: Kensington, 2000; "The Dowager's Dilemma" in *A Kiss for Mama*. New York: Kensington, 2001; "The Best Father in England" in *A Kiss for Papa*. New York: Kensington, 2002; "Invitation to Trouble" in *Murder at Almack's*. New York: Kensington, 2003; "My Dearest Daisy" in *A Valentine Waltz*. New York: Kensington, 2004; "Belling the Kitten" in *Valentine Kittens*. New York: Kensington, 2005; "Something Old, Something Mew" in *Wedding Day Kittens*. New York: Kensington, 2005.

Writing as J. A. Ferguson

Books: *Dreamsinger*. Canon City, CO: ImaJinn Books, 1999; *Timeless Shadows*. Canon City, CO: ImaJinn Books, 2000; *Dreamshaper*. Canon City, CO: ImaJinn Books, 2000; *My Lord Viking*. Canon City, CO: ImaJinn Books, 2001; *Daughter of the Fox*. Canon City, CO: ImaJinn Books, 2001; *DreamMaster*. Canon City, CO: ImaJinn Books, 2001; *Callback Yesterday*. Canon City, CO: ImaJinn Books, 2002; *DreamTraveler*. Canon City, CO: ImaJinn Books, 2004; *Luck of the Irish*. Canon City, CO: ImaJinn Books, 2006; *Sworn Upon Fire*. Canon City, CO: ImaJinn Books, 2006; *The Wrong Christmas Carol*. Canon City, CO: ImaJinn Books, 2006.

Writing as Jo Ann Brown

Book: *Seasons of the Heart*. Whidbey Island, WA: Mountain View, 1999.

Writing as Joanna Hampton

Books: *The Coming Home Quilt*. New York: Berkley/Jove, 1999; *Woven Dreams*. New York: Berkley/Jove, 2000.

Writing as Rebecca North

Novella: "Chloë's Elopement" in *A June Betrothal*. New York: Kensington, 1993.

Writing as Jocelyn Kelley

Books: *A Knight Like No Other*. New York: Signet, 2005; *One Knight Stands*. New York: Signet, 2005; *A Moonlight Knight*. New York: Signet, 2006; *My Lady Knight*. New York: Signet, 2007; *The Mistress School*. New York: Signet, 2007; *Gentleman's Master*. New York: Signet, 2008.

Marion Ekholm, Sandra Van Winkle, and Shelley Mosley

CHRISTINE FLYNN

When Christine Flynn was 12 years old, the answer to "What will I be when I grow up?" included a colorful variety of career choices: "I've wanted to be a ballerina, a cardiologist, a translator for the United Nations, a wedding-gown designer, a race-car driver, and the proprietor of a bed-and-breakfast—among other things." Even though romance writing wasn't on the agenda, with over forty novels to Flynn's credit and repeated appearances on national best seller lists, writing appears to be her true calling.

Flynn, who was born in Los Angeles in 1949 and grew up in Oregon, dabbled in a number of her early career aspirations, many of which would later appear in her books. While attending college, after one semester of hotel and service industry management, Flynn's interest in owning a bed-and-breakfast was effectively quashed, although she uses one as a setting in her novel *The Sugar House* (2005). Flynn raced in a couple of autocrosses; designed wedding gowns for three family members; and spent 12 years working as a paralegal, the occupation she chose for the heroine in her novel, *The Home That Love Built* (1999). Although Flynn never became a cardiologist, her daughter is a cardiac nurse, and several of her plots involve medical professionals. Flynn credits her success as a writer to her varied interests. "Writers get to research and explore it all," she says.

Her first exposure to the romance genre was a Silhouette novel that came free with the gift wrap of a Mother's Day present Flynn received from her husband. Neither of them can remember what the gift was, but Flynn clearly recalls that she fell in love with the book. It marked the beginning of her writing career. Besides romances, she has written a number of articles about the writing profession, but romance remains her forte. Flynn likes the assurance that everything will work out happily in the end.

Flynn's story inspiration comes from everywhere, but she makes it a point not to over-analyze what sparks her imagination. "I just look at each idea as a gift and feel grateful and excited for it," she says. Flynn begins the writing process with character ideas that determine the course of the plot. Many of her novels use family as a recurrent theme and take place in contemporary settings. Flynn doesn't have a favorite locale, because she enjoys researching new places, or better yet, visiting them. "Researching new places, their history, local culture, architecture, [and so forth], is half the fun of being a writer," says Flynn.

When Flynn encounters writer's block, she either spends a couple of hours away from writing or switches into a revising or editing mode instead until her creativity is revived. She also rereads chapters to find a logical progression that might help move the plot forward. Flynn says her favorite novel is always the one on which she will be working next. Her easiest novel to write was her first, *When Snow Meets Fire* (1985), because at the time, she didn't realize how difficult writing could be.

The heroes in Flynn's novels are noble men. They possess the moral character to protect those they care about, even at the risk of great personal cost. They can also be quite stubborn. In *The Sugar House* (2005), the second book of the Going Home trilogy (*Trading Secrets*, 2005; *Confessions of a Small Town Girl*, 2005), the young and handsome commercial developer Jack Travers attempts to atone for a wrong committed by his father years before by returning some land to Emmy Larkin, the proprietor of a local bed-and-breakfast, and a maple sugar operation in Maple Mountain, Vermont. Emmy's father had been ruined by the elder Travers, when a portion of the Larkin family's sugar bush property was sold to settle a debt. Emmy's resentment toward the Travers family and her mistrust of Jack run deep, and she wants nothing to do with them. However, when the weather causes Jack and Emmy to become stranded together, they're forced to confront what happened between their families in the past, and more importantly, what's beginning to happen between the two of them now. This beautiful story of healing reflects Flynn's firm belief in the ability of the human heart to forgive, and eventually, to love.

Gallantry takes a humorous turn in *Prodigal Prince Charming* (2004), the third installment of the Kendricks of Camelot trilogy (*The Housekeeper's Daughter*, 2004; *Hot August Nights*, 2004). Cord Kendrick, a wealthy international playboy, takes full responsibility for a construction-site accident in which caterer Madison O'Malley's lunch truck is crushed by a crane. Cord goes to great lengths to help her recover from her loss and prevent her from reporting the incident to the tabloids. Madison agrees to the arrangement, but soon the two are mixing business with pleasure, and exchanging more than trade secrets, as the attraction between them intensifies. Despite her inability to resist him, Madison expects that the adventurous and footloose Cord will only leave her and break her heart. Meanwhile, Cord is experiencing emotions and feelings for Madison that he's never felt before, and he suspects his playboy days may be over. In this twist on a classic fairy tale, Flynn shows that every princess can expect a prince, but sometimes he comes riding in on a piece of heavy equipment.

The heroines in Flynn's novels are described as nurturers. Dr. Margaret Matthews of *Jake's Mountain* (1995) delivers her nurturing on a large scale when she becomes "Dr. Maggie" to the poor people in an isolated area of the hills of Kentucky. One of the people to whom she reaches out, Jake Harris, isn't sure if he wants to risk opening his heart again. With Dr. Maggie, Flynn has created a strong, independent woman who isn't afraid to share her emotions. Flynn's sympathetic descriptions of the hardworking, spirited people in this economically depressed area make them three-dimensional rather than just a group of stereotypical characters, which would have been an easy thing to do.

In *The Baby Quilt* (2000), Flynn's personal favorite of the books she's written, powerful Chicago attorney Justin Sloan is at the top of his game, until his car breaks down on a country road in rural Illinois. At a nearby farm, he meets Emily Miller, a young, gentle Amish widow. While Justin is stranded in the country with Emily and her newborn child, he finds for the first time the contentment of a simpler, unhurried lifestyle. Justin is attracted to Emily's natural beauty and her goodness, and as he falls in love with her, he begins to reevaluate his priorities and rethink his high-pressure career. However, Justin is accustomed to the fast pace and competition of city life, and he questions if he could ever adjust to the countrified life of a farming community. Flynn recalls this story idea had been brewing for some time, "about a young Amish widow who had been shunned by her community, to live in a secular and, by her standards, more modern society." Flynn adds, "I mentioned the idea to my editor at the time, who said, 'Add a baby,' and the entire story was suddenly there."

Family and nurturing are the prominent plot and character elements in *Another Man's Children* (2001). After the tragic death of her sister-in-law, Lauren Edwards takes time out from her busy career to care for her young niece and nephew, while her brother, Sam, recovers from his shattering loss. Sam's friend and business partner, Zach McKendrick, has also promised to help with the children and joins Lauren at the wilderness cabin where the two surrogates soon develop feelings for each other. Mothering agrees with Lauren and brings out new and surprising instincts that the workaholic career woman has never before experienced. Zack, too, discovers his nurturing side and would like to think that perhaps he and Lauren have a future together. However, his disfiguring scars leave him doubting that a woman like Lauren could ever love a man like him. In this marvelously heartwarming book, the talented Flynn deftly brings home the point that love is indeed blind.

Flynn takes the traditional secret baby story and makes it her own in *Daughter of the Bride* (1994). Abby Sinclair was wildly in love with high school bad-boy Marc Maddox. Unbeknownst to Marc, their youthful passion resulted in twins, a boy and a girl. Twelve years later, Abby returns to Stowebridge, Vermont, for a wedding. Much to her shock, she discovers that Marc, no longer the small town's cautionary tale, is now a man of the cloth. Flynn takes the reader on Abby's journey from not knowing whether to share the information with Marc to finally coming to the decision to do the right thing. Once again, Flynn expertly avoids stereotypes by giving Pastor Marc all-too-human reactions to both Abby's arrival and the news of his fatherhood.

For Flynn, the best parts of the writing process are researching, editing, and typing the words *The End*. Although Flynn finds that the creative part of the process can be a struggle, her readers would never know it. She plots her books with the skill of a master choreographer and artfully crafts her characters with the grace of a ballerina.

BIBLIOGRAPHY

Books: *When Snow Meets Fire*. New York: Silhouette, 1985; *The Myth and the Magic*. New York: Silhouette, 1986; *Stolen Promises*. New York: Silhouette, 1986; *Meet Me at Midnight*. New York: Silhouette, 1987; *A Place to Belong*. New York: Silhouette, 1987; *Silence the Shadows*. New York: Silhouette, 1988; *Renegade*. New York: Silhouette, 1989; *Courtney's Conspiracy*. New York: Silhouette, 1989; *Walk Upon the Wind*. New York: Silhouette, 1990; *The Healing Touch*. New York: Silhouette, 1991; *Out of the Mist*. New York: Silhouette, 1991; *Beyond the Night*. New York: Silhouette, 1992; *Daughter of the Dawn*. New York: Silhouette, 1993; *Lonely Knight*. New York: Silhouette, 1993; *Luke's Child*. New York: Silhouette, 1993; *When Morning Comes*. New York: Silhouette, 1994; *Daughter of the Bride*. New York: Silhouette, 1994; *Remember the Dreams*. New York: Silhouette, 1995; *Logan's Bride*. New York: Silhouette, 1995; *A Father's Wish*. New York: Silhouette, 1995; *Jake's Mountain*. New York: Silhouette, 1995; *The Black Sheep's Bride*. New York: Silhouette, 1996; *The Rebel's Bride*. New York: Silhouette, 1996; *From Housecalls to Husbands*. New York: Silhouette, 1998; *Hannah and the Hellion*. New

York: Silhouette, 1998; *Her Child's Father*. New York: Silhouette, 1998; *Father and Child Reunion*. New York: Silhouette, 1998; *The Home That Love Built*. New York: Silhouette, 1999; *Finally His Bride*. New York: Silhouette, 1999; *Christmas Anthology*. New York, Silhouette, 2000; *The Baby Quilt*. New York: Silhouette, 2000; *Dr. Mom and the Millionaire*. New York: Silhouette, 2000; *Forbidden Love*. New York: Silhouette, 2001; *Another Man's Children*. New York: Silhouette, 2001; *Suddenly Family*. New York: Silhouette, 2002; *Royal Protocol*. New York: Silhouette, 2002; *Four Days, Five Nights*. New York: Silhouette, 2003; *The Housekeeper's Daughter*. New York: Silhouette, 2004; *Hot August Nights*. New York: Silhouette, 2004; *Prodigal Prince Charming*. New York: Silhouette, 2004; *Trading Secrets*. New York: Silhouette, 2005; *The Sugar House*. Toronto: Harlequin, 2005; *Confessions of a Small Town Girl*. New York: Silhouette, 2005.

Novella: "Christmas Bonus" in *36 Hours*. Toronto: Harlequin, 2000.

SANDRA VAN WINKLE AND SHELLEY MOSLEY

GAELEN FOLEY

Gaelen Foley. Courtesy of Gaelen Foley.

In a relatively short time, Gaelen Foley has created a prized collection for romance readers partial to Napoleonic England from 1790 to 1820. Having personally traveled Europe and absorbed the local scenery and culture of Regency London, she is well qualified to capture its essence in her writing.

Foley, the oldest of four daughters born to James Foley and Patricia Kennedy Foley Wilson, grew up in a working-class neighborhood in Pittsburgh, Pennsylvania. Her parents were both college educated and understood the value of introducing their daughters to culture and the arts early in life. Foley recalls that instead of a game room in their Pittsburgh home, they had a library.

Foley's earliest works were childhood stories, plays, and poems that she says she would share with "anyone who would listen." She began to seriously consider herself a writer at the age of 17, while a junior at Shaler Area High School in Pittsburgh. She recalls being inspired by a scene in James Joyce's *Portrait of the Artist as a Young Man,* in which the protagonist, Stephen, is watching a girl wading on the beach where a ray of sunshine has broken through the clouds to shine on her. His considerable personal problems seem insignificant in this moment of beauty. Foley has adopted this scene as her personal outlook on life.

Foley admits, however, to a turbulent, rebellious time as a tortured "adolescent-artist." She enrolled as an English major at the University of Pittsburgh and fiercely resisted the urging of literature and creative writing professors to channel her talents into literature. It was during this self-described period of "girls gone wild," that she met Eric, the man who would become her husband. He managed to "tame" her and refocus her energy into study-ing and writing. She and Eric transferred to State University of New York at Fredonia, a small liberal arts school in upstate New York where the social scene was far less chaotic and more conducive to studying. There, she earned her bachelor's degree in English literature and discovered an avid interest in romantic poetry, philosophy, and history that combined to create a powerful background of elements essential to the historic romance genre.

As college graduation approached, Foley was torn between entering graduate school for a teaching career and becoming a professional writer. The fates intervened when she over-heard a professor lamenting that it would take 10 years before a graduate student could make a decent living as a professor. Foley decided that if she would have to be poor for 10 years, she would rather do it as a writer. She and Eric moved to Atlanta, where he attended graduate school and she worked nights as a waitress, keeping her mornings open for writ-ing. It was during this time that Foley joined Romance Writers of America and found a lifelong kinship with other "scribbling women" who shared her passion for writing. Foley experimented for a while to find a writing genre best suited to her talent and temperament. She was intrigued by the history in the gothic novels she read in college, and attracted to the uplifting and positive messages found in romances. Historic romance was the obvious answer.

In 1998, Ballantine Books published Foley's first novel, *The Pirate Prince,* which earned her the *Romantic Times* Reviewer's Choice award as the Best First History Novel of the year. Foley followed *The Pirate Prince* with two more historical romance novels filled with in-trigue, danger, and passion: *Princess* (1999) and *Prince Charming* (2000). These three books form the author's Ascension trilogy, set on a fictional island nation in the Mediterranean Sea near Italy, continue the romantic adventures of the island's royal family.

With her fourth novel, *The Duke* (2000), Foley began a new series focused on the differ-ent members of the Knight family. Each book features a different Knight sibling, all of whom are related through their scandalous mother, Georgiana, whose affairs with a variety of men where notorious during her time. The Knight Miscellany series begins with *The Duke,* in which the eldest Knight brother, the Duke of Hawkscliffe, tries to trap a murderer by engag-ing in an affair with a celebrated courtesan. Each book in the Knight's Miscellany series deftly blends danger and desire, as each Knight—Lucian in *Lord of Fire* (2002), Damien in *Lord of Ice* (2002), Jacinda in *Lady of Desire* (2003), and near-sibling Lizzie in *Devil Takes a Bride* (2004)—will find their newfound love tested by deception and deadly intrigue.

Foley's books have earned her a variety of awards including the National Readers Choice, Beacon, and Golden Leaf awards. She has also been nominated for a *Romantic Times* Career Achievement award for her Knight Miscellany and Ascension Trilogy series.

Flynn gains her inspiration from such notable romance authors as Laura Kinsale, Mary Jo Putney, Judith McNaught, and Anne Stuart, whose writing she says she admires for its "from the heart" quality. Foley applies this same creative ethic to her own books, believing that her readers deserve nothing less than a carefully crafted, well-told tale. While Foley explores a variety of themes in her writing, some of her favorites include love's power to heal and transform, a prodigal's return and forgiveness, and redemption gained through acts of heroism or self-sacrifice.

Foley infuses her characters with some of her own personality traits—their reaction to struggles, their anxieties, and their penchant for dark curiosity. The heroes are often edgy, intense and engaging, with irresistible bad-boy qualities. Despite gnawing emotional pain, they maintain their macho image with dry, disarming, and self-deprecating humor. One such hero is Devil Strathmore in *Devil Takes a Bride* (2004). Her heroines provide an effective counterbalance of sensitivity and risk taking, such as Devil's perfect match, the clever, capable Elizabeth Carlisle. They see through the macho pretenses and uncover the deeper needs, longings, and vulnerabilities of their men.

Foley's favorite parts of the writing process are the so-called aha moments, those flashes of inspiration that occur when conscious thought catches up with creative intuition. She describes it as the "mysterious magic" that weaves the plot and enriches the characters. She also enjoys the process of planning and researching a new story. Foley finds that her favorite book is always the one she's working on, being "blissfully immersed" in writing.

Foley's view on writer's block is realistic and simple. She believes that writer's block and fear are synonymous. To overcome writer's block, she applies a Zen-style detachment that reduces the block to its most basic element. She finds in doing so a writer is able to see that there is really nothing to fear at all. She also feels that anxiety is the opposite of creativity, stifling the flow of creative thought. She recommends finding the source of the anxiety and facing it; often it's merely a phantom.

In choosing a career in writing, Foley believes that Divine Providence will intervene for those who wholeheartedly pursue their destiny. "You do your part; he'll do his," she says.

BIBLIOGRAPHY

Books: *The Pirate Prince*. New York: Ballantine, 1998; *Princess*. New York: Ballantine, 1999; *Prince Charming*. New York: Ballantine, 2000; *The Duke*. New York: Ballantine, 2000; *Lord of Fire*. New York: Ballantine, 2002; *Lord of Ice*. New York: Ballantine, 2002; *Lady of Desire*. New York: Ballantine, 2003; *Devil Takes a Bride*. New York: Ballantine, 2004; *One Night of Sin*. New York: Ballantine, 2005; *His Wicked Kiss*. New York: Random House, 2006.

SANDRA VAN WINKLE

GWYNNE FORSTER

Gwynne Forster. Photo by David M. Brown, photographer. Courtesy of Gwynne Forster.

W hen Gwynne Forster began writing fiction and romance in the mid-1990s, she had the enviable distinction of already being an accomplished author. Having worked nearly twenty years as a demographer with the United Nations in New York City, Forster had 27 published articles and books to her credit on the topic of demographics. Forster would later add 3 books of general mainstream fiction, over 20 romance novels, and several novellas to her body of literary work. "Since early childhood, I've been motivated to succeed at whatever I do. It's the same with writing," she comments.

Forster was born in North Carolina to parents King D. and Vivian Williams Johnson, who made their careers in education; her mother was a secondary school principal, and her father was a high school math teacher. When Forster was still quite young, her family moved to Washington, D.C., where she grew up. She went on to earn both a bachelor's and a master's degree in sociology from Howard University, and a second master's degree in economics/demography from American University in Washington, D.C. Forster has traveled extensively during her career with the United Nations and has served as the senior UN Population Officer in charge of nonmedical research in fertility and family planning, and the chairperson of the International Programme Committee of the International Planned Parenthood Federation in London. Forster's husband, Dr. George T. F. Acsádi, is a retired professor of demography. Her stepson, Peter Acsádi, is a managing electronic engineer.

Unlike nonfiction, Forster says she enjoys the surprises that occur with fiction writing, relishing those times "when I look on the screen and say, 'Where did that idea come from?'" She finds that the romance genre is more tastefully written than much of general fiction, which she says often contains "obscene language and immorality for shock purposes." Forster also believes the quality of the writing in the romance genre is generally superior to that found in "erotica and urban scene books."

Writer's block has never bothered Forster to the extent that she has been completely unable to write. She finds that leaving the computer for a while and turning instead to a pad and pen helps her to get the ideas flowing again. She enjoys the writings of the incomparable Langston Hughes and finds him inspirational.

Forster has won many awards for her fine writing. Her book, *Beyond Desire* (1999), was chosen as a Doubleday Book Club and Literary Guild selection in 2001. She was named Author of the Year by the Romance in Color Internet Reviewers in 1999 and was also awarded the Black Writers Alliance Gold Pen Award in 2001.

In her early novels, Forster's writing technique began with character development. She now says that she begins her stories with a theme and then adds characters and a story premise. "I go from there," she comments. Her books are contemporaries, usually set in slower-paced and genteel small towns in Maryland or North Carolina, or in Washington, D.C. In her book *Ecstasy* (1997), Forster took her readers around the world as she revisited many of the places to which she had traveled.

Forster says her novels most often focus on families, "what glues them, and what can rend them." Her heroines are independent women who often reflect Forster's personal values, and her heroes are men of honor. These types of characters are evident in her 2003 novel, *Flying High*. U.S. Marine Colonel Nelson Wainwright must balance honor and family when he suddenly becomes the guardian of his four-year-old nephew, Ricky, causing Nelson to postpone his goal of becoming a four-star general. To complicate matters, a potentially career-ending neck injury that he receives when the helicopter he pilots in Afghanistan crashes brings sports-medicine specialist, Audrey Powers, into his life, and they fall deeply in love. When Nelson receives military orders to return to active duty in Afghanistan, health, love, honor, and duty collide, forcing him to reevaluate his priorities and his future.

The novels *Whatever It Takes* (2005) and *Love Me or Leave Me* (2005) were Forster's most difficult to write. She says that's because she was "trying very hard to write the best book I'd ever written." Considering that many of her previous novels have won national awards, this was an ambitious goal. In *Whatever It Takes,* thirty-something twins Lacette and Kellie Graham, compete for everything from money to men, with the selfish and scheming Kellie usually emerging the winner. When their grandmother dies and their parents suddenly separate, Kellie ramps up her manipulative ways, and Lacette must fend for herself. Using her education, Lacette opens a successful marketing firm and, in the process, meets Douglas Rawlins, the man of her dreams. Lacette is confounded by his unexplained, standoffish behavior toward her, unaware that her jealous, conniving twin has stooped to new lows in deception. It takes a tragic event to finally force Kellie to stop thinking about herself and instead do the right thing.

Love Me or Leave Me is about Drake Harrington, the youngest of three brothers, who wants to cement his career before settling down with a wife. Local television newscaster Pamela Langford knows her biological clock is ticking and wants a baby as soon as possible. With Drake taking things slowly and Pamela wanting marriage and a family immediately, it's clear that there's going to have to be a lot of compromise before the two of them can have a meaningful relationship. *Love Me or Leave Me* is the third book in Forster's Harrington Brothers trilogy, following *Once in a Lifetime* (2002) and *After the Loving* (2005), which feature the other two brothers.

In *Once in a Lifetime,* Forster's easiest novel to write and her favorite, Alexis Stevenson, a recently divorced single mom, is hired sight unseen to move in and manage the home of wealthy and single Telford Harrington, who is a successful builder, and his two brothers, an architect and an engineer. From their very first meeting, the tension and chemistry between Alexis and Telford is undeniable, despite their best efforts to resist it. Their relationship is complicated by the secrets that Alexis harbors; Telford's suspicions about her past; and the antics of his two brothers, Drake and Russ, who do their worst to undermine Alexis's work. It is four-year-old Tara, Alexis's daughter, who holds the key to their stubborn hearts in this touching story.

After the Loving is the story of Russ Harrington and Velma Brighton, an ample-figured caterer who constantly compares her body to her thin, beautiful sister's. Never is her insecurity more acute than when she becomes the maid of honor in her sister's wedding and must wear a form-fitting gown that showcases her glorious curves. What's worse, she learns that Russ Harrington is her escort, and she fears that he will be turned off when he sees her full figure. Little does Velma realize, Russ has strong feelings for her as well, and he happens to like her contours just the way they are. However, he is turned off by Velma's apparent insecurity and lack of self-confidence. Velma blames his reaction on her weight, not realizing that losing pounds isn't the answer to keeping her from losing the man she loves.

Of these novels in the Harrington Brothers trilogy, Forster says, "I fell in love with the characters and didn't want to leave them for a minute, not even to sleep and eat." She's not the only one. With a host of loyal fans who devour her every page, it's obvious that Forster's readers feel the same way.

BIBLIOGRAPHY

Books: *Sealed with a Kiss.* New York: Kensington, 1995; *Against All Odds.* New York: Kensington, 1996; *Ecstasy.* New York: Kensington, 1997; *Obsession.* New York: Kensington, 1998; *Naked Soul.* Columbus, MS: Genesis Press, 1998; *Beyond Desire,* New York: BET Books, 1999; *Fools Rush In.* New York: BET Books, 1999; *Against the Wind.* Columbus, MS: Genesis Press, 1999; *Swept Away.* New York: BET Books, 2000; *Midnight Magic.* Columbus, MS: Genesis Press, 2000; *Secret Desire.* New York: BET Books, 2000; *Scarlet Woman.* New York: BET Books, 2001; *Once in a Lifetime.* New York: BET Books, 2002; *When Twilight Comes.* New York: Kensington/Dafina Books, 2002; *Blues from Down Deep.* New York: Kensington/Dafina Books, 2003; *Flying High.* New York: BET Books, 2003; *Last Chance at Love.* New York: BET Books, 2004; *If You Walked in My Shoes.* New York: Kensington/Dafina Books, 2004; *After the Loving.* New York: BET Books, 2005; *Love Me or Leave Me.* New York: BET Books, 2005; *Whatever It Takes.* New York: Kensington/Dafina Books, 2005; *Her Secret Life.* Toronto: Harlequin/Kimani Press, 2006.
Novellas: "Christopher's Gifts" in *Silver Bells.* New York: Kensington, 1996; "A Perfect Match" in *I Do.* New York: Kensington, 1997; "Love for a Lifetime" in *Wedding Bells.* New York: Kensington, 1999; "Miracle at Midnight" in *Midnight Clear.* Columbus, MS: Genesis Press, 2000; "Learning to Love" in *Going to the Chapel.* New York: St. Martin's Press, 2001; "The Journey" in *Destiny's Daughters.* New York: Kensington/Dafina Books, 2006.

SANDRA VAN WINKLE

PATRICIA FORSYTHE. *See* Patricia Knoll

PATTI FORSYTHE. *See* Patricia Knoll

LORI FOSTER

Lori Foster. Photo by Don Schenk Studios. Courtesy of Lori Foster.

When readers and reviewers describe Lori Foster's works, there's a cacophony of Ss—sexy, sassy, sizzling, steamy, spicy. While Foster is best known for writing for the more sensual lines (Silhouette Desire, Harlequin Blaze, Kensington Brava), she also understands how to mix humor and a more innocent kind of sensuality, as typified in her novels written for the Harlequin Duets line, such as her two-in-one *Annie Get Your Guy / Messing Around with Max* (2001).

Foster was born in Ohio, and grew up in a rural area. She married her high school sweetheart, Allen Foster, shortly after graduation, and they have three children, Aaron, Jake and Mason.

Never much of a reader, Foster held a number of small jobs in her prewriting days, working as a material handler, a clerk, and a salesperson. She realized at thirty-something that she wanted to be a romance writer when she was bedridden with pneumonia, and her sister, Monica, brought a bag of romance novels to help her pass the time. Foster says she was "cheesy enough to skip through the first historical until I found a sex scene. But the problem with that is that I got so engrossed in the story, I finished the book, then had to go back and read it from the beginning to see what I had missed." Foster devoured the entire bag of novels during her recuperation. Later, when she couldn't find enough of the type of romance novel she preferred to satisfy her reading tastes, she began writing her own books, considering it a natural transition.

With her head full of stories, Foster, a self-confessed daydreamer, wrote more than ten complete manuscripts, which she recalls sending to "every available publisher," suffering "too many rejections to count." Detesting how-to books, she taught herself writing by simply doing it. In 1996, Foster's tenacity and hard work paid off when Harlequin published her first book, *Impetuous,* the story of a shy schoolteacher who dares to spend one night with the man of her dreams. Foster's second novel, *Outrageous* (1997), the tale of an undercover cop trying to find out who is selling defective guns on the street, launched Harlequin's Temptation Blaze line. Foster's 25th book, *Sex Appeal* (2001), launched another line, Temptation Heat. An incredibly prolific writer, Foster routinely produces 6 to 10 releases a year. In Foster's case, high quantity doesn't mean low quality. Her book *Too Much Temptation* (2002) was named Amazon.com's number-one best seller, and *The Secret Life of Bryan* (2004) became Border's Bestselling Single Title Romance that year.

The greatest appeal of the romance genre for Foster is the certainty of a happy ending. As a writer, she gets pleasure from having the power to ensure the couple she created will be together in the end. Although she doesn't use a recurring theme in her novels, she does like to show that making mistakes and learning from them is part of the human experience. Foster writes full-time, and often works overtime when a book project becomes particularly captivating. She enjoys the full creative experience of writing, from developing the characters and constructing the scenes to presenting the crises and providing the resolutions. Foster has written in other genres for her own amusement but hasn't attempted to have them published.

For Foster, story ideas are anywhere and everywhere. Scenes from movies or other books, television commercials, and people on the street all provide potential story ideas that trigger Foster's imagination. As an avid reader, she gains insight into how other writers develop their plots, and contemplates how she might have taken the story in a different direction. She believes that writer's block is actually boredom that stems from a flawed plot, and, she says, if the writer is bored, "the readers will be bored, too." Her cure is to review the story to fix the flaw. "If I'm jazzed about writing the story, readers will be jazzed about reading," says Foster.

Foster develops each new plot idea in her head but creates her characters and settings on paper. Her character list contains the physical traits and occupations of the characters as well as the town's name, the season, and other specific plot elements. Many of Foster's novels contain familiar faces from previous stories (such as the characters from her series set in Visitation, North Carolina: *Say No to Joe?* 2003; *The Secret Life of Bryan,* 2004; *When Bruce met Cyn … ,* 2004; *Just a Hint—Clint,* 2004; and *Jamie,* 2005), which enables her to thoroughly know and understand how they will think and react in each new scenario. Once the basic plot is in place, she says the chapters "just come to me as I write."

Foster develops her novels by first having her characters appear in one particular scene, which then serves as inspiration for the rest of the plot. Her preferred setting is a contemporary small town, preferably located on or near water. Foster has always been a watersports enthusiast, so it's no surprise that she included her love of water in her *Buckhorn Brothers* series, featuring a fictitious lake identical to the one where she spent her childhood summers.

The heroes in Foster's books are protective and strong, and they value children and family. She prefers to portray men in a positive light, respecting their unappreciated sensitivity and gallantry, contrary to the way she feels that popular culture often bashes and ridicules them. Foster's heroines possess these same qualities, but they still allow the hero's gallantry to shine through. Foster's personal values and morals are reflected in her characters: the sanctity of marriage, the importance of family, and the top priority of parenting. The importance of family and the need for family members to protect each other is an element that runs throughout many of Foster's books. In *The Secret Life of Bryan,* for example, a bounty hunter, to find the perpetrators, takes the place of his identical twin brother, a street preacher who's been attacked and seriously injured by gangs.

Foster's most difficult novel to write was her 2004 book, *When Bruce Met Cyn ... ,* because of the intense emotion surrounding Cynthia Potter, or "Cyn." A former prostitute, Cyn has been sexually abused as a child, and Foster shared her pain when writing many of the scenes. "There were a lot of places where I cried, but there were places where I smiled a lot, too," she says. The ironic humor that the man of Cyn's dreams turns out to be a preacher isn't lost on the reader. Foster's knack for irony is showcased in other books as well. For example, in *Unexpected* (2003), when the hero advertises for a mercenary to rescue his younger brother, he gets Ray Veeker, a tough, fearless, muscular, and hard-bodied ... woman.

On the other hand, the easiest book for Foster to write was her 1998 novel, *Taken!* It is the story of a security expert who goes undercover to clear his brother of embezzlement charges. The idea came to Foster during an emergency milk run to the grocery store. Like many of her novels, she says this book "practically wrote itself" and was completed in a couple of weeks. Once again, Foster used the theme of family and the importance of taking care of each other. When the hero of *Taken!* discovers that the heroine is in danger, too, he adds her to his list of people to protect.

Of her numerous novels, Foster has several favorites. She specifically names *Beguiled* (1999), which holds a special place in her heart because it was originally published as a two-in-one with a Jayne Ann Krentz reissue, and the heroine, Angel Morris, was particularly inspiring for her. In *Beguiled,* prodigal son Dane Carter returns to his family to find out who murdered his twin brother. When he meets the woman who was involved with his twin, Angel Morris, who incidentally has a child, Dane pretends to be his brother to protect her from the killer. Foster also chooses her novella, "Tangled Dreams," from the anthology, *Charmed* (1999), as a favorite because it was her first venture into the paranormal (matchmaking ghosts), and the lead character, Chase Winston, was a joy for her to write. As seen from Foster's long list of novellas, this is one format in which she excels.

Foster's three-dimensional characters linger in the mind like old friends, long after the story ends. With her trademark fast-paced stories; witty dialogue; and unexpected, often humorous plot twists, Foster's style makes her an author who truly engrosses the reader from page one.

BIBLIOGRAPHY

Books: *Impetuous.* Toronto: Harlequin, 1996; *Outrageous.* Toronto: Harlequin, 1997; *Scandalized.* Toronto: Harlequin, 1997; *Fantasy.* Toronto: Harlequin, 1998; *Taken.* Toronto: Harlequin, 1998; *Tantalizing.* Toronto: Harlequin, 1999; *Little Miss Innocent.* New York: Silhouette, 1999; *Beguiled.* Toronto: Harlequin, 1999; *Wanton.* Toronto: Harlequin, 1999; *Charmed.* New York: Berkley Publishing, 1999; *In Too Deep.* Toronto: Harlequin, 2000; *Say Yes.* Toronto: Harlequin, 2000; *Sawyer.* Toronto: Harlequin, 2000; *Morgan.* Toronto: Harlequin, 2000; *Gabe.* Toronto: Harlequin, 2000; *Jordan.* Toronto: Harlequin, 2000; *Married to the Boss.* Toronto: Harlequin, 2000; *Annie Get Your Guy/Messing Around with Max.* Toronto: Harlequin, 2001; *Sex Appeal.* Toronto: Harlequin, 2001; *Caught in the Act.* Toronto: Harlequin, 2001; *All Through the Night.* New York: Kensington, 2001; *Treat Her Right.* Toronto: Harlequin, 2001; *Mr. November.* Toronto: Harlequin, 2001; *The Winston Brothers.* New York: Jove, 2001; *Wild.* New York: Jove, 2001; *Too Much Temptation.* New York: Kensington, 2002; *Once & Again.* Toronto: Harlequin, 2002; *Forever &*

Always. Toronto: Harlequin, 2002; *Never Too Much.* New York: Kensington, 2002; *Casey.* Toronto: Harlequin, 2002; *Men of Courage.* Toronto: Harlequin, 2003; *Riley.* Toronto: Harlequin, 2003; *Say No to Joe?* New York: Kensington, 2003; *Unexpected.* New York: Kensington, 2003; *The Secret Life of Bryan.* New York: Kensington, 2004; *When Bruce Met Cyn ...* New York: Kensington, 2004; *Just A Hint—Clint.* New York: Kensington, 2004; *Jamie.* New York: Kensington, 2005; *Wildly Winston.* New York: Kensington, 2006; *Jude's Law.* New York: Kensington, 2006; *Truth or Dare.* New York: Kensington, 2006.

Novellas: "Tangled Sheets" in *Hot Chocolate.* New York: Berkley, 1999; "Body Heat" in *Sizzle.* Toronto: Harlequin, 1999; "Tangled Dreams" in *Charmed.* New York: Penguin, 1999; "Tangled Images" in *Sinful.* New York: Berkley, 2000; "Christmas Bonus" in *All I Want for Christmas.* New York: St. Martin's Press, 2000; "Luring Lucy" in *Hot and Bothered.* New York: St. Martin's Press, 2001; "Indulge Me" in *I Love Bad Boys.* New York: Kensington, 2002; "Drive Me Wild" in *I Brake for Bad Boys.* New York: Kensington, 2002; "My House My Rules" in *Bad Boys on Board.* New York: Kensington, 2003; "He Sees You When You're Sleeping" in *Jingle Bell Rock.* New York: Kensington, 2003; "Bringing Up Baby" in *Bad Boys to Go.* New York: Kensington, 2003; "Good with His Hands" in *Bad Boys in Black Tie.* New York: Kensington, 2004; "Some Like It Hot" in *Perfect for the Beach.* New York: Kensington, 2004; "Tail Spin" in *The Truth About Cats and Dogs.* Toronto: Harlequin, 2004; "Once in a Blue Moon" in *Star Quality.* New York: Kensington, 2005; "He Sees You When You're Sleeping" in *Jingle Bell Rock.* New York: Kensington, 2005; "White Knight Christmas" in *The Night Before Christmas.* New York: Kensington, 2005; "Luscious" in *Bad Boys of Summer.* New York: Kensington, 2006; "Playing Doctor" in *When Good Things Happen to Bad Boys.* New York: Kensington, 2006.

SHELLEY MOSLEY AND SANDRA VAN WINKLE

ROZ DENNY FOX

Roz Denny Fox. Courtesy of Roz Denny Fox.

To anyone thinking of making writing a career, best-selling author Roz Denny Fox gives this advice: "Remember, it's hard work. But like most hard work, there are many rewards." Fox knows a lot about both.

Born in 1939 to homesteaders Wilber and Anna Loban in McMinnville, Oregon, Rosaline Fox spent her childhood in Yamhill County, Oregon, a small rural community where the major industries were millwork, logging, and farming. Her father logged and operated a machine shop that has since become a winery. Fox graduated from Yamhill/Carlton Consolidated High School and later completed a two-year degree in travel and tourism from Edmonds Community College in Washington State. She has been married for more than forty years to Denzell "Denny" Fox, who was a Marine at the time of their wedding. Later, he became a telephone engineer. A true love match, Fox uses her husband's nickname, Denny, as part of her nom de plume. They have two daughters, Kelly and Korynna, both of whom are married with families of their own.

Fox didn't always want to be a writer. Instead, she thought about being a lawyer or a reporter. She worked at other jobs before she began to write—medical records clerk, office secretary for three pediatricians, elementary-school secretary, and secretary to a

---

also writing as Roz Denny

college dean. Fox started writing when she worked full-time. After penning six books, she switched to part-time work, and when her husband retired, she decided to write full-time.

A disciplined writer, Fox works four to six hours a day, usually seven days a week. Influenced by Zane Grey and other writers of early Westerns, Fox thought she would like to write Western novels. Fortunately for her readers, she ultimately chose the romance genre instead. Although Fox enjoyed reading historical fiction, she gravitated toward writing contemporary romances, something for which she proved to have great talent.

A recurrent theme in Fox's books is home and family. She likes to add pets and children to her stories, many of which are based on the trials and tribulations endured by women or men raising children. One such book is *A Mom for Matthew* (2005), the story of the single father trying to raise a deaf son by himself. Zeke Rossetti's wife, Trixie Lee, deserted him, leaving Zeke to raise Matthew, a deaf, sickly baby. Zeke struggles as a mechanic to provide for the two of them and pay Matthew's medical bills until Zeke lands a position as manager for off-site oil locations in the Texas gulf. Schoolteacher Grace Safford wants to be in the same waters where Zeke is drilling, but Zeke has other ideas. Grace wants to find the downed plane that would clear her grandfather's military record, so she ignores Zeke's requests for her to leave. Resigned to her presence in the area, Zeke decides if he helps Grace, her search will be over sooner and she'll be out of his hair. However, during their time together, Grace falls in love with Zeke and his little boy. Fox adds emotional depth to the story with Zeke's reluctance to trust again and Matthew's need for a mother. The novel packs an emotional wallop, never once stooping to the maudlin.

For Fox, characters always come first. Once she gets to know them, she finds an appropriate setting and plot for them. Her characters are multidimensional and so well developed that they could almost step out of the pages of her books. People of all ages fill the pages of Fox's novels. Senior citizens play important roles in her plots. In *Sweet Tibby Mack* (1997), an entire retirement community plays matchmaker to their very sweet but single postal clerk. *Mad About the Major* (1998) features older characters who literally save the day when a Special Forces officer and a U.S. Air Force pilot become involved in an undercover operation that holds more danger than they originally thought.

Fox's characters are ethnically diverse. Her book *The Cinderella Coach* (1991) was one of the few at the time to feature Asian Americans. Unfortunately, with few exceptions, this continues to be true. Not one for conformity, Fox also created an Asian American heroine for her riveting suspense *She Walks the Line* (2005), in which Houston Police lieutenant Mei Lu Ling investigates a Chinese smuggling ring with Interpol agent Cullen Archer.

The Basque-American community, another group overlooked in the romance genre, is featured in Fox's powerful novel *Someone to Watch Over Me* (2003), the most difficult book for her to write. "A similar tragedy happened to a co-worker of mine, and the situation haunted me until I decided to write it out of my mind by providing a satisfying ending." Isabella Navarro has suffered the worst loss possible. Her husband, intent on killing himself and their children, puts them into the family car, closes the garage door, and turns on the engine. He survives, but the children don't. This tragedy becomes the defining event in Isabella's life, which is filled with bitterness and depression. Gabe Poston is attracted to the morose Isabella, and makes it his mission to cheer her up and give her hope. But when Gabe tries to move their relationship into something more permanent, something that includes children, Isabella balks, full of the fear that she's now incapable of love. This poignant tale of the healing power of love shows Fox's keen insights and observations, as well as her ability to transfer them skillfully and lyrically onto the written page.

Real-life events inspire Fox and give her ideas for her stories. "I'm a big clipper of news articles (human interest pieces)," says Fox. "Many times, I never see how the real story turned out, so I fictionalize the story and write my own ending." As far as writer's block, Fox says she's never experienced it, "although I'm always sure when I finish a last book under contract that I'll never think of a new idea. Somehow, they show up out of nowhere."

Hiking, skiing, and handcrafts are Fox's hobbies. They appear in some of her books, because, as she says, her characters "live full lives." Fox's heroes are honest and sensitive to others. Her heroines are usually gutsy, strong-minded women. One such heroine is nurse Faith Hyatt of *Baby, Baby* (2000). It's been a long time since Faith has seen her sister, Lacey. When Lacey decides to make an appearance in the hospital where Faith works, Lacey is pregnant and very close to her due date. But Lacey, a heart-transplant patient, hasn't taken her antirejection drugs for fear of losing her child and now she's dying. Lacey begs Faith to take care of the baby after she's gone and has Faith sign guardianship papers. Lacey gives birth to a boy and a girl and then dies. When, much to Faith's amazement, two men claim to be the father of the twins—one of whom is Lacey's ex-husband, Dr. Michael Cameron—an already tense situation grows even more stressful. Grief, custody, and paternity, each a serious issue in its own right, are treated by Fox with compassion and sensitivity. The myriad, intricate emotions are starkly realistic, making for a powerful and compelling story.

Fox's first book, *Red Hot Pepper* (1990), was the easiest for her to write. She says, "The book had fun characters, and I was filled with enthusiasm for writing a publishable book." *Red Hot Pepper* showcases Fox's keen comedic timing and her well-honed sense of humor. When asked to name her favorite book of all those she has written, Fox comments diplomatically, "Like my children, they all own a piece of my heart. But I could never love one more than another."

There is no one setting Fox prefers above others. She uses many different locales: "It's one of the things I most like about doing research—finding new places and delving into the lives of the people who have lived there for a long time." She enjoys "digging into backgrounds, careers, and situations that may make a good story and finding a new place to set a book." The depth of Fox's research can be seen in everything from the diverse cultures she writes about to the varied career choices her characters have made. For her book *Anything You Can Do …* (1998), for example, Fox researched the Santa Fe Trail, both in books and on location, so she could use it as a setting for a romance featuring a historic reenactment.

The romance genre has many things that appeal to Fox. She comments, "I like the happy endings. I like that our characters encounter and overcome real problems, and that love is part of that equation. Basically, I believe all humans are looking for someone to love and who will love them in return."

BIBLIOGRAPHY

Writing as Roz Denny

Books: *Red Hot Pepper.* Toronto: Harlequin, 1990; *Romantic Notions.* Toronto: Harlequin, 1991; *The Cinderella Coach.* Toronto: Harlequin, 1991; *Stubborn as a Mule.* Toronto: Harlequin, 1993; *Island Child.* Toronto: Harlequin, 1994; *Some Like It Hotter.* Toronto: Harlequin, 1994.

Writing as Roz Denny Fox

Books: *Major Attraction.* Toronto: Harlequin, 1995; *Christmas Star.* Toronto: Harlequin, 1995; *The Water Baby.* Toronto: Harlequin, 1996; *Trouble at Lone Spur.* Toronto: Harlequin, 1996; *Sweet*

Tibby Mack. Toronto: Harlequin, 1997; *Anything You Can Do ....* Toronto: Harlequin, 1998; *Having It All.* Toronto: Harlequin, 1998; *Mad About the Major.* Toronto: Harlequin, 1998; *Family Fortune: The Lyon Legacy.* Toronto: Harlequin, 1999; *Welcome to My Family.* Toronto: Harlequin, 2000; *Baby, Baby.* Toronto: Harlequin, 2000; *Mom's the Word.* Toronto: Harlequin, 2000; *Who Is Emerald Monday?* Toronto: Harlequin, 2001; *The Baby Cop.* Toronto: Harlequin, 2001; *Lost but Not Forgotten.* Toronto: Harlequin, 2001; *Wide Open Spaces.* Toronto: Harlequin, 2002; *The Seven Year Secret.* Toronto: Harlequin, 2002; *Someone to Watch Over Me.* Toronto: Harlequin, 2003; *The Secret Daughter.* Toronto: Harlequin, 2003; *Married in Haste.* Toronto: Harlequin, 2003; *A Cowboy at Heart.* Toronto: Harlequin, 2004; *Daddy's Little Matchmaker.* Toronto: Harlequin, 2004; *Too Many Brothers.* Toronto: Harlequin, 2004; *She Walks the Line.* Toronto: Harlequin, 2005; *A Mom for Matthew.* Toronto: Harlequin, 2005; *The Secret Wedding Dress.* Toronto: Harlequin, 2005; *More to Texas Than Cowboys.* Toronto: Harlequin, 2006; *Hot Chocolate on a Cold Day.* Toronto: Harlequin, 2006; *Angels of the Big Sky.* Toronto: Harlequin, 2006; *On Angel Wings.* Toronto: Harlequin, 2006.

SHELLEY MOSLEY AND SANDRA VAN WINKLE

THEA FREDERICK. *See* Judith Arnold

BARBARA FREETHY

As the only girl (aka "Dick's little sister") growing up in an all-boy neighborhood in the 1960s, Barbara Freethy remembers spending most of her play time reading and writing. Her mother, an avid romance reader and aspiring writer, introduced Freethy to the works of some of the genre's pioneering novelists. From those early influences, Freethy went on to become a *USA Today* best-selling author, a RITA award winner, and a four-time RITA award finalist.

Freethy grew up in Southern California, where she later attended the University of California at Santa Barbara, earning a bachelor's degree in communications. She has always been a voracious reader and story crafter, but she didn't seriously pursue a writing career until she was in her twenties, using the pseudonym Kristina Logan, a combination of her children's names. Romance, her favorite genre, seemed the logical choice. "I knew I would be putting a strong love story into my novels," she says. Freethy adds that she enjoys making the reader believe in romance, hope, love, and "all the good things in life." In addition to romance novels and women's fiction, Freethy has also written a number of press materials and magazine articles.

Inspiration for stories and characters can be found "everywhere and anywhere," says Freethy. She encourages writers to "stay out in the world," and find inspiration in the experiences of life. "You never know what is going to spark a good idea," says the author. Freethy now writes full-time, but before beginning her writing career, she spent several years working in public relations for a number of agencies, including the Women's Pro Tennis Tour and the March of Dimes.

For Freethy, the writing process begins by creating a basic story idea and several key points and expanding from there. She finds most often that the character ideas occur first, followed by plot. Freethy avoids overplanning and outlining the plot, which she believes

also writing as Kristina Logan

stifles creativity. "I'm the kind of writer who likes to discover the story as I go along," she says. Freethy prefers to write contemporary romances and has penned several popular novels set in San Francisco, just north of Freethy's home where she lives with her husband, Terry, and their two children, Logan and Kristen.

Freethy's novels frequently include secrets harbored between the characters and woven together with a good family story "into a suspenseful, page-turning plot." She adds, "My stories tend to be big and complicated in range and emotion." They are a blend of several plot elements that cross over a variety of categories, from romance to comedy to suspense.

The heroes in Freethy's books are known for being the rugged, handsome, athletic types. They're adventurous risk-takers. In *Some Kind of Wonderful* (2001), reporter Matt Winters discovers an abandoned baby in the hall outside his door, with a note attached that specifically asks for Matt to take care of her. The note is signed by "Sarah," whom Matt believes is his younger sister. They had become separated in the foster-care system 13 years before, and Matt has been searching for her ever since. Convinced that his sister must be in some kind of trouble, Matt enlists the aid of Caitlyn Devereaux, the bridal-shop proprietor who lives across the hall. She reluctantly agrees to help, knowing that mothering Emily will only bring back painful memories for her. In their quest for Sarah, Matt and Caitlyn find themselves falling for each other. Matt would like nothing more than a future with Caitlyn, but she struggles to resist the attraction, unwilling to risk repeating the sorrows of her past. As in her other books, Freethy writes a poignant, emotionally charged story without becoming maudlin or unrealistically optimistic.

Freethy describes her heroines as creative and nurturing but also capable, courageous, and determined in the face of conflict. She observes, "I've tried to create lots of interesting characters that come from my imagination and bits of myself and others." In *Summer Secrets* (2003), teenage sisters Kate, Ashley, and Caroline McKenna and their father, Duncan, are the past winners of the Winston Around the World Sailing Challenge. Now eight years later, reporter Tyler Jamison has come to Castleton Island asking probing questions about the voyage that the sisters had sworn never to discuss. Tyler suspects that his eight-year-old niece, Amelia, was born at sea during the expedition and later given away in an illegal adoption to his brother, Mark, and Mark's wife. However, when Mark's wife is killed in a car accident, Mark risks losing Amelia in a custody battle unless he is able to find the girl's birth mother. In Tyler's crusade to determine which of the McKenna women is the girl's mother, he gains the trust of Kate and promptly loses his heart to her, not realizing that the truth is right in front of him.

Of her many novels, Freethy chooses *All She Ever Wanted* (2004) as the most difficult to write, though she adds, "every book is difficult and challenging in places." This one combines the subplots of three strong female characters into one main story. "I like books that are rich in details and have lots of twists and turns, so this one ended up being a satisfying venture for me," says Freethy. Three sorority sisters, Natalie, Laura and Madison, share a dark secret about the tragic death of their friend, Emily Parish, which took place a decade before. Now, incredibly, an aspiring author, Garrett Malone, has written a best-selling novel that strikes eerily close to home. The level of detail in his story leaves little doubt that he knows something about that night; his story suggests that there was foul play in Emily's death and that Natalie is guilty of the murder. Natalie sets out to learn more about this mysterious writer and his sources. In the process, she encounters Emily's brother, Cole, her former lover. In their quest to determine Garrett Malone's real identity, the two rekindle their intimate relationship. Meanwhile, Laura and Madison join the hunt, and the group endeavors to get to the truth about Emily, as they each discover a long-lost love.

According to Freethy, her easiest novel to write was RITA winner *Daniel's Gift* (1996), which she describes as "a very touching and emotional love story." The idea came from personal experience, when her young teenage niece died tragically after a short illness. "I wrote the book completely 'on spec,' and it was truly a story of my heart," says Freethy. In this novel, summer love brings Jenny St. Claire together with Luke Sheridan, and the resulting pregnancy is not welcome news to Luke or his family, who have ambitions for Luke's future in medicine. Despite feeling betrayed and brokenhearted, Jenny decides against an abortion and keeps her infant son, Danny. However, the boy eventually begins to ask questions about his father, and at the age of 12, decides to find Luke on his own. When a drunk driver puts Danny into a coma, Danny discovers that while his body is motionless, his spirit is lucid and free. While his life hangs in the balance, Danny traverses the spiritual plain, enlisting the help of his unorthodox guardian angel, Jacob, to reunite Jenny and Luke and mend their broken family. In this book, Freethy effectively blends this world with otherworldly elements, and the result is a powerful tale of true love's ability to transcend all boundaries and obstacles.

Freethy chooses her RITA finalist *Golden Lies* (2004) as her favorite of the novels she's written. The story was inspired by an article Freethy read about Chinatown and other San Francisco neighborhoods. She crafted it into the plot of three families from those diverse neighborhoods, who are unaware they have a connection that dates back 50 years. Priceless art and intrigue unite three strangers, Riley McAllister, Paige Hathaway and Alyssa Chen, in a quest to recover a stolen objet d'art. An old bronze Chinese dragon belonging to Riley's grandmother disappears from The House of Hathaway, a prestigious San Francisco antiquities appraisal firm. Riley discovers the apparent value of the dragon when the firm's owner and Chinese-art expert, David Hathaway, is found beaten in a Chinatown alley, and the statue missing. Paige Hathaway, David's daughter, joins Riley in attempting to recover the rare antiquity. As Paige and Riley forge ahead on their dragon safari, they learn that David was attacked while delivering the statue to a woman named Jasmine Chen. Probing further, they uncover family ties and a loyalty pact dating back 50 years to World War II. They also discover that Jasmine's daughter, Alyssa, is Paige's half sister. The three must do some appraising of their own as they are forced to choose between the loves they've found and the decades-old family pact that brought them together. Freethy comments, "I loved the characters Riley and Paige and their love story, which was filled with fun, romance, and a little suspense."

To Freethy, the appeal of the writing process is the ability to create realistic scenarios within the structure of romantic fiction. Freethy offers, "I love making up stories and people and their backgrounds. I have a big imagination, and I love to entertain with my books." The popularity of her novels is proof positive of that.

BIBLIOGRAPHY

Books: *Daniel's Gift.* New York: Avon, 1996; *Ryan's Return.* New York: Avon, 1996; *Ask Mariah.* New York: Avon, 1997; *One True Love.* New York: Avon, 1998; *The Sweetest Thing.* New York: Avon, 1999; *Almost Home.* New York: Avon, 2000; *Just the Way You Are.* New York: Avon, 2000; *Some Kind of Wonderful.* New York: Avon, 2001; *Love Will Find a Way.* New York: Avon, 2002; *Summer Secrets.* New York: Onyx, 2003; *Golden Lies.* New York: Signet, 2004; *All She Ever Wanted.* New York: Signet, 2004; *The Cuzzian Horse.* Frederick, MD: PublishAmerica, 2004; *Don't Say a Word.* New York: Penguin, 2005; *Taken.* New York: Penguin, 2006.

Writing As Kristina Logan

Books: *Promise of Marriage.* Toronto: Harlequin, 1990; *Hometown Hero.* Toronto: Harlequin, 1991; *Two to Tango.* Toronto: Harlequin, 1992; *Right Man for Loving.* Toronto: Harlequin, 1992; *To the Rescue.* Toronto: Harlequin, 1993; *Man Behind the Music.* Toronto: Harlequin, 1993; *Man Like Jake.* Toronto: Harlequin, 1994.

SANDRA VAN WINKLE AND SHELLEY MOSLEY

JUDITH E. FRENCH

Judith E. French. Photo by Theis Photography, Ltd. Courtesy of Judith E. French.

J udith E. French isn't the typical farmer's daughter. She grew up on a dairy farm in rural Kent County Delaware, a descendent of the first generation of American Faulkners who settled on the eastern shore of Maryland in the 1660s. She comes from a long line of oral storytellers, and as early as age five, French dreamed of becoming a writer and seeing her books on library shelves. Now, French is practically a literary household name, with more than thirty titles to her credit and legions of devoted readers. Mission accomplished!

Born in Dover, Delaware, in 1941, French is the daughter of Lester Forest Bennett, a farmer, electric lineman, hunter, and fisherman, with a strong Native American (Lenni Lenape/Eastern Delaware) heritage; and Mildred Faulkner, a homemaker with a passion for reading. French attributes her gift for writing to her grandfather, William H. Faulkner, who claimed to be "woodpile kin to that other writer fellow" of the same name. French grew up surrounded by grandparents, aunts, uncles, cousins, and great-grandparents. Her sense of family, the importance of tradition, and Christian faith have remained very strong. For French, family and personal life come first, and out of these values and traditions come her stories.

French writes about ordinary people thrown into extraordinary situations, who rise to meet whatever challenges life offers. She says her grandfather taught her "to be responsible for her own mischief, to think before she acted, and not to back down from bullies."

French applies this wisdom in her Civil War novel *Rachel's Choice* (1998), in which pregnant Yankee widow Rachel Irons devises a way to save her farm by enlisting the help of the enemy. She discovers William "Chance" Chancellor, a badly wounded Confederate soldier who had escaped from a Union prison, hiding on her property. Rachel takes him into her home and nurses him back to health, with the understanding that if Chance will stay and plant Rachel's crops, she will continue to hide the Rebel fugitive on her land. The symbiotic arrangement is complicated when Chance's hidden agenda to escape is thwarted by Rachel going into labor, compounded by the irresistible attraction they've come to share. Chance is faced with a difficult decision—whether to honor an old blood vow to help a fellow Rebel prisoner escape, or to remain with Rachel and protect the woman and child he's come to love. "Love your enemy" takes on a whole new meaning in this powerful, emotionally introspective novel.

In *The Taming of Shaw MacCade* (2001), love conquers generations of bad blood between the MacCades and the Raeburns when fate brings Shaw MacCade and Rebecca Raeburn together. Returning to Missouri after four years of prospecting in the California gold rush, the rebellious Shaw plans to take care of some unfinished business, which includes avenging the murder of his brother. But Shaw's vendetta takes an unexpected turn when he meets the sweet, spirited Rebecca, and the long, bitter feud between the two families morphs instead into a stormy and passionate romance.

Although her formal education ended after graduating with honors from Media High School in Media, Pennsylvania, French's personal education didn't stop there. She learns constantly through her intense love of reading and her fascination with subjects ranging from Native American language and culture to genealogy and history to medicine to Delmarva and Scottish folklore. French's nonstop research ensures that her personal bank of knowledge is always increasing.

Over the years, French has had many jobs. She spent 12 years as a teacher, beginning in a one-room Amish schoolhouse and later serving as a substitute public school teacher. She has also been a census worker, a professional storyteller, a farmer, a newspaper columnist, and a freelance writer. A collection of her folk tales and ghost stories assembled from interviews with senior citizens appeared in a local magazine as "Ghosts Along the Delaware." French has also written action thrillers and, for the nonfiction market, practical tips on raising children. Currently, she is a full-time writer of best-selling romances.

French and her high school sweetheart, Gary, celebrated their 45th wedding anniversary in 2004. They have four children, including daughter Colleen Faulkner, who is a popular romance novelist (also writing as Hunter Morgan)carrying on the family tradition of award-winning storytelling. French has 10 grandchildren, some of whom also show promise as writers.

In French's writing, she says the plot, or rather "the situation," comes first. She thinks, "What would a person do if …". From this question, she formulates the characters, the conflict, and the conclusion. A recurrent theme in French's novels is the irresistible power of love. She philosophizes, "It's the greatest force in the universe, and it can make heroes of us all." French's heroes have moral courage, and her heroines are known for their emotional strength, but they share the common trait of loving hearts.

This is evident in French's Alexander Trilogy (*The Conqueror*, 2003; *The Barbarian*, 2004; and *The Warrior*, 2005), set in the fourth century B.C. Princess Roxanne, heir to the tiny mountain kingdoms of Bactria and Sogdiana, is conquered and captured by Alexander the Great. He takes Roxanne for his bride, far away from her homeland and her longtime love, Kayan. The stormy political alliance sweeps across the continent, conquering everything in its path.

The saga continues in the second book, *The Barbarian,* where Roxanne finds herself in the pharaoh's harem, stricken with amnesia and unable to remember her identity, her life with Alexander, or the son she bore. Deceived by the pharaoh's lies, Roxanne becomes comfortable with her life in the harem, until a barbaric ally rescues her and challenges her to remember her past and embrace her future.

In *The Warrior,* the third book of the trilogy, Alexander, son of Roxanne and Alexander the Great, returns to Persia and the Twin Kingdoms of Bactria and Sogdiana to regain the throne of his ancestors. Searching for a suitable bride to share his throne, Alexander abandons his quest for a princess when he encounters beautiful, beguiling Kiara, an Egyptian slave girl who captures his heart. With danger and deception at every turn, the two forge ahead into history.

French considers herself a storyteller and a sensuous writer. In her writing, all of the senses are involved so that the reader is immersed in the worlds and characters she creates. If her readers aren't part of the story, French feels she's failed them.

As a romance writer, French deals fairly with the righteous and with the wicked. However, unlike real life, where the villain sometimes lives to enjoy the spoils, in French's stories, justice is served—along with generous helpings of heart-stopping romance and colorful history.

BIBLIOGRAPHY

Books: *Tender Fortune.* New York: William Morrow & Co., 1986; *By Love Alone.* New York: William Morrow & Co., 1987; *Starfire.* New York: William Morrow & Co., 1987; *Bold Surrender.* New York: William Morrow & Co., 1988; *Windsong.* New York: William Morrow & Co., 1988; *Scarlet Ribbons.* New York: William Morrow & Co., 1989; *Moonfeather.* New York: William Morrow & Co., 1990; *Lovestorm.* New York: William Morrow & Co., 1991; *Highland Moon.* New York: William Morrow & Co., 1991; *Moon Dancer.* New York: William Morrow & Co., 1992; *Fortune's Flame.* New York: William Morrow & Co., 1993; *Fortune's Mistress.* New York: William Morrow & Co., 1993; *This Fierce Loving.* New York: William Morrow & Co., 1994; *Fortune's Bride.* New York: William Morrow & Co., 1994; *Shawnee Moon.* New York: William Morrow & Co., 1995; *McKenna's Bride.* New York: Random House, 1995; *Fire Hawk's Bride.* New York: William Morrow & Co., 1996; *Sundancer's Woman.* New York: William Morrow & Co., 1996; *Rachel's Choice.* New York: Random House, 1998; *Morgan's Woman.* New York: Random House, 1999; *Irish Rogue.* New York: Random House, 2000; *The Taming of Shaw MacCade.* New York: Random House, 2001; *Falcon's Angel.* New York: Random House, 2002; *The Conqueror.* New York: Dorchester, 2003; *The Barbarian.* New York: Dorchester, 2004; *At Risk.* New York: Dorchester, 2005; *The Warrior.* New York: Dorchester, 2005; *Blood Kin.* New York: Dorchester, 2006.

Novellas: "Bride of Wildcat Purchase" in *Avon Books Presents: To Love and to Honor.* New York: William Morrow & Co., 1993; "Gifts of the Heart" in *Avon Books Presents: Under the Mistletoe.* New York: William Morrow & Co., 1993; "Bride of the Red Wolf" in *Castle Magic.* New York: Kensington, 1999; "MacKenzie's Bride" in *Wedded Bliss.* New York: Kensington, 2003.

SANDRA VAN WINKLE, SHELLEY MOSLEY, AND MARION EKHOLM

PATRICIA GAFFNEY

Patricia Gaffney. Courtesy of Patricia Gaffney.

Despite moving from romances to women's fiction, Patricia Gaffney says, "Long live romance!" As the best-selling author of 12 romances and 4 mainstream titles, Gaffney recognizes her romance roots when she writes, "Everything I know about writing, I learned from writing romance novels. I don't write them anymore, but I still love them."

Gaffney was born in Tampa, Florida, to father who was an administrative law judge for the Interstate Commerce Commission and a mother who was a homemaker. She and her older brother grew up in Bethesda, Maryland, and she eventually earned a bachelor's degree in English and philosophy from Marymount College in New York. After college, Gaffney taught 12th grade English for one year. She also worked as a freelance photographer for a small newspaper and was a court reporter for 17 years.

The love of writing came early in Gaffney's life. From the time she was about eight years old, she had dreamed of becoming a writer; but as with many authors, life happened, and her childhood dreams were put up on the shelf. Then in 1984, cancer changed Gaffney's life. After discovering a malignant lump in her breast, she re-evaluated her life up to that point. Gaffney decided it was time to leave her job as a court reporter, and she moved to the country to become the writer she had always dreamed of being. At first, writing mysteries interested her. Then she wanted to write novels, then romances. Now, she says, "I'm back to novels."

Her first book, a romance, was published in 1989. *Sweet Treason,* set in Jacobean England, features Lady Katherine MacGregor, a gentlewoman turned Scottish spy who poses as a prostitute, and her love-hate relationship with James Burke, the English officer assigned to bring her to justice. *Sweet Treason* won the Golden Heart award from the Romance Writers of America. Her second novel, *Fortune's Lady* (1989) soon followed, and fans appreciated the fully developed characters, crisp dialogue, and simmering sexual tension that would become Gaffney's trademark. More historical romances followed, from the gothic-like *Lily* (1991) to the more humorous *Crooked Hearts* (1994), in which she asks the question, What if two con artists tried to con each other? And more readers became fans.

With *To Love and to Cherish,* published in 1995, Gaffney began the first of what would become a trilogy set in the small Victorian village of Wyckerley. While many authors tie the books of their trilogies together by means of the characters, Gaffney also used the setting of Wyckerley and its environs as a common connection among the three books. *To Love and to Cherish* focuses on the romance between Anne Verlaine and the vicar of the village, Reverend Christian Morrell, a man tormented by his growing desire for Anne, who just happens to be his friend's wife. Intensely emotional and lyrically written, many readers name this title, which was a finalist for a RITA award, as the one that started them reading Gaffney's work.

The second book in the Wyckerley trilogy, *To Have and to Hold* (1995), was inspired by Gaffney's research into the appalling prison conditions that existed in Victorian England. Gaffney employs an unexpected plot twist when the heroine, Rachel Wade, is the one who has spent time in prison for the murder of her husband. Rachel is brought before magistrate Sebastian Verlaine, a bored, debauched, and beautiful specimen of a man—the complete opposite of Gaffney's previous hero, the virtuous Christian Morrell. Sebastian's appeal lies in his redemption through his love for the vulnerable and psychologically wounded Rachel.

With *Forever and Ever* (1996), the last book in the Wyckerley trilogy, Gaffney introduces two more denizens of the quiet English village, Sophie Deene and Conner Pendarvis. Sophie has inherited her father's copper mine, and is determined to run it alone. Connor wants to expose the dangers involved in mining and goes undercover to investigate hazardous working conditions in Sophie's mine. Both characters are strong-willed and determined, and their eventual romance is both emotionally complex and brilliantly written. Gaffney's Wyckerley books beautifully illustrate her interest in writing stories that have a strong moral center and something to say about the human condition.

When Gaffney reexamined her career in romance writing and decided that the genre no longer offered the inspiration it once did, she turned to writing the kinds of books that are now in the genre called women's fiction. Gaffney wanted to write a different kind of story, one that did not focus solely on the relationship between the hero and heroine, but rather that explored the many relationships that define a woman's life. The resulting book, *The Saving Graces,* published in 1999, is the story of the close relationship among four women who are lifelong friends and their reactions to one of them being diagnosed with cancer. *The Saving Graces* quickly became a word-of-mouth favorite with readers and appeared on a variety of best seller lists, including *The New York Times, Publishers Weekly* and *USA Today.* It also introduced a new audience of readers to Patricia Gaffney.

With *Circle of Three* (2000), Gaffney once again explored themes that resonate with female readers. In this book, three generations of women must cope with their complicated relationships with each other. Carrie is newly widowed and has returned to the small town in which she grew up and where her mother, Dana, still resides. Carrie brings her difficult daughter, Ruth, with her. Gaffney's writing technique of allowing each woman to contribute to the story in her own voice brings the book to life. *Circle of Three* is not just about the relationships between daughters and mothers. Gaffney dipped into her romance background and added another layer, in this case, a love story, by reuniting Carrie with her high school sweetheart. One perceptive critic called it a "poignant story of growing up and growing old."

Flight Lessons (2002), also a coming-home story, is set against the background of a small, family-owned Italian restaurant. After discovering that her boyfriend is having an affair with her boss, Anna Catalano returns home to Maryland's eastern shore. This is especially ironic because an infidelity is what drove Anna away in the first place; her aunt Rose slept with her father. It is only after she arrives home that Anna can begin the difficult emotional journey from blame to forgiveness. Gaffney explores family relations from every angle. In *Flight Lessons* things come in twos—two tortured heroes, two affairs, two prodigal sons, and most importantly, two happy endings.

In *The Goodbye Summer* (2004), Gaffney once again explores the complexities of family life as she asks and answers the question, How much change can one summer bring? For Caddie Winger, who his 32 years old and still living with her grandmother, one season brings a world of difference as Caddie learns to love, trust, let go, and live a little. Once again, Gaffney's lovely, lyrical style of writing enhances the story as she takes a standard plotline and transforms it into something uniquely expressive.

For Gaffney, the appeal of the romance genre is "emotional intensity, sharply defined characters on a unambiguous quest for love and commitment, and a guaranteed and unapologetic happy ending." Fortunately for readers, Gaffney's books are rich with these very same elements.

BIBLIOGRAPHY

Books: *Sweet Treason.* New York: Dorchester, 1989; *Fortune's Lady.* New York: Dorchester, 1989; *Thief of Hearts.* New York: Dorchester, 1990; *Lily.* New York: Dorchester, 1991; *Another Eden.* New York: Dorchester, 1992; *Sweet Everlasting.* New York: Penguin, 1993; *Crooked Hearts.* New York: Penguin, 1994; *To Love and to Cherish.* New York: Penguin, 1995; *To Have and to Hold.* New York: Penguin, 1995; *Forever and Ever.* New York: Penguin, 1996; *Wild at Heart.* New York: Penguin, 1997; *Outlaw in Paradise.* New York: Penguin, 1997; *The Saving Graces.* New York: Harper-Collins, 1999; *Circle of Three.* New York: HarperCollins, 2000; *Flight Lessons.* New York: Harper-Collins, 2002; *The Goodbye Summer.* New York: HarperCollins, 2004.
Novella: "Second Chance" in *A Victorian Christmas: Five Stories.* New York: Penguin, 1992.
Genre-Related Essay: "Coming Out of the Closet and Locking It Behind Us" in *North American Romance Writers.* Lanham, MD: Scarecrow Press, 1999.

JOANNE HAMILTON-SELWAY

LISA GARDNER

Lisa Gardner knows how to plumb the depths of fear. In *The Perfect Husband* (1998), Tess Beckett can't escape from her psychotic husband. In *The Survivors Club* (2002), Jillian, Carol, and Meg are stalked by a serial rapist. And in *Alone* (2005), Catherine Gagnon, was kidnapped, raped, and almost murdered as a child. But Gardner also knows how to write about courage and resiliency when she creates her female protagonists, who might experience fear but are never victims. Each of her heroines is smart, brave, and, in the end, a true survivor.

Although she was born in Hawaii in 1971 to two accountants who, she says, "had no idea how they ever produced a writer," Gardner grew up in Oregon. Gardner says her love of reading came naturally, as her mother was "a big fan" of romances. It was while Gardner was attending college and waitressing that she first explored the idea of writing a novel. As an unsuccessful waitress, who actually caught her hair on fire, Gardner thought that she needed to explore other less-hazardous career options. She says she started writing a book "simply to see if I could write a novel. I knew nothing about publishing [and] had never even met another author, so I confess it didn't immediately occur to me to try to publish. Instead, a year later, a good friend of mine who knew I had written a manuscript gave me a guide to publishing romance. As a big reader of Silhouette Intimate Moments romance novels, I thought my manuscript would be a good fit for that line." Gardner says the process of submission seemed easy enough to her. She recalls, "I blithely followed the steps outlined" in the guide. "I'd like to say I sold the next day, but it was more like three years and three massive revisions later that I finally sold that first manuscript to Silhouette."

Gardner was only 20 when *Walking After Midnight,* written under the pseudonym of Alicia Scott, was published by Silhouette for their Intimate Moments line in 1992. While Gardner was excited to be a published author, she discovered that "it was hardly enough

---

also writing as Alicia Scott

money to make a living." She continued on with her college work, and, after graduating magna cum laude with a bachelor or arts degree in international relations from the University of Pennsylvania, she worked as a management consultant with a firm in Boston. While working 12-hour days and developing a vehement dislike for pantyhose, Gardner continued to write romance novels after work, from 11:00 P.M. to 1:00 A.M. "Oh, to be young again," she opines.

As Alicia Scott, Gardner wrote 13 books for the Silhouette line. A favorite of readers was the trilogy Maximillian's Children. Maximillian Ferringer fathered three children by three different women and then disappeared in a mysterious plane crash. In *Maggie's Man* (1997), the heroine is a held hostage by an escaped convict trying to clear his name. In *MacNamara's Woman* (1997), the second book in the series, Tamara Allistair has lost her family in a horrific hit-and-run accident. With the help of ex-Marine C. J. MacNamara, the "child" of the Maximillian's Children's series, she fights to bring the man responsible to justice. This book was a finalist for the Romance Writers of America's RITA award. The last book, *Brandon's Bride* (1998), features the eldest half sibling, Brandon, who while investigating a clue to his father's disappearance becomes involved with a divorced lady rancher.

A strong thread of suspense runs through all of her books written for Silhouette. For example, in *The One Who Almost Got Away* (1996), a sexy millionaire becomes entangled with a female FBI agent who is investigating a series of art thefts. Reminiscent of Daphne du Maurier's classic *Rebecca,* Gardner's *At the Midnight Hour* (1995) features a nanny who is suspicious of the death of her employer's first wife, while fighting her attraction to him.

In *Marrying Mike ... Again* (1998), an heiress becomes the new police chief, and her ex-husband's boss and must investigate a cop killing. Using a gritty urban backdrop, Gardner deftly handles the reality of police work with the rekindling of a failed relationship. With *The Quiet One* (1996), part of her Guiness Clan series, Gardner takes readers to a small Southern town where a violent murder brings together a beautiful artist and a local sheriff.

In 1998, Gardner decided she needed a change from writing short romances for Silhouette, so she turned her sights to mainstream romantic suspense and wrote *The Perfect Husband.* The inspiration for this book was Anne Rule's classic true-crime book about Ted Bundy, *The Stranger Beside Me.* Gardner realized that sometimes at first glance, the villain could look just like the hero, as is the case with the husband in *The Perfect Husband.* When Tess Williams married Jim Beckett, she was young; naive; and unaware of the dark, psychotic side of her husband, who is eventually convicted of being a serial murderer. When Tess learns that her now ex-husband has escaped from maximum security, she knows that he will be coming for her to seek revenge for Tess's help in convicting him. Refusing to be a victim and tired of living in fear, she hires J. T. Dillon, a burned-out ex-mercenary to train her to protect herself and her daughter. In a dark, thrilling tale of a horrifying villain pitted against a resourceful woman, Gardner created a gripping and spine-tingling page-turner of a novel. *Publishers Weekly* gave *The Perfect Husband* a rave review, calling it a "streamlined bang-up addition to the oeuvre of Tami Hoag, Karen Robards, Elizabeth Lowell and, these days, even Nora Roberts."

The Perfect Husband was followed by another suspense tale, *The Other Daughter,* published in 1999. Even though Gardner had moved to mainstream suspense, many of her novels still contained a strong element of romance within them. An excellent example is *The Third Victim* (2001), in which Rainie Conner, a police officer in a small town based on Tillamook, Oregon, must overcome her tragic past and investigate the shootings of two children and a teacher by the son of the town sheriff. Rainie finds herself attracted to FBI agent Pierce Quincy, sent to help with the investigation. Gardner creates a strong and haunted heroine in Rainie, and the blossoming relationship between Rainie and Pierce is a welcome relief from the dark, suspenseful story of a Columbine-like situation. Both Rainie and Quincy are featured in *The Next Accident* (2001), when Quincy's daughter Amanda is killed in a car accident that turns out to be a murder staged by a fiend. Rainie is now a private investigator and must help Quincy discover who is targeting his loved ones. Readers were delighted to have both characters return in *The Killing Hour* (2003), though Quincy's daughter Kimberley takes center stage. A rookie FBI agent, Kimberley discovers a body during her training at Quantico and takes a leave of absence to team up with Georgia Bureau of Investigations special agent Michael McCormack to investigate. *Publishers Weekly* wrote, " with tight plotting, an ear for forensic detail and a dash of romance, this is a truly satisfying sizzler."

Gardner's early romances and her more recent best-selling suspense books provoke a frisson of fear when read late at night or at any time in the day, but each of her heroines is smart and resilient enough to survive, and the reader knows that. "All of my heroines are very strong, some, though, in different ways than others," she says. Gardner succeeds in matching up these capable women with men who are their equals in every way. She is drawn to intelligent heroes because, as she says, "stupidity is boring to me."

"I have always loved romance novels," says this best-selling novelist. This is readily apparent in the strong characters and nuanced relationships she has created in both her early romantic suspense novels, written as Alicia Scott, as well as in her wildly popular suspense books, written as Lisa Gardner. Readers and fans who appreciate Gardner's skillful mix of danger and romance wait eagerly for each new novel by this master of suspense.

BIBLIOGRAPHY

Writing as Lisa Gardner

Books: *The Perfect Husband.* New York: Bantam, 1998; *The Other Daughter.* New York: Bantam, 1999; *The Third Victim.* New York: Bantam, 2001; *The Next Accident.* New York: Bantam, 2001; *The Survivors Club.* New York: Bantam, 2002; *The Killing Hour.* New York: Bantam, 2003; *I'd Kill for That.* New York: St. Martin's Press, 2004; *Alone.* New York: Bantam, 2005; *Gone.* New York: Bantam, 2006.

Writing as Alicia Scott

Books: *Walking After Midnight.* New York: Silhouette, 1992; *Shadow's Flame.* New York: Silhouette, 1994; *Waking Nightmare.* New York: Silhouette, 1994; *At the Midnight Hour.* New York: Silhouette, 1995; *Hiding Jessica.* New York: Silhouette, 1995; *The Quiet One.* New York: Silhouette, 1996; *The One Worth Waiting For.* New York: Silhouette, 1996; *The One Who Almost Got Away.* New York: Silhouette, 1996; *Maggie's Man.* New York: Silhouette, 1997; *MacNamara's Woman.* New York: Silhouette, 1997; *Brandon's Bride.* New York: Silhouette, 1998; *Partners in Crime.* New York: Silhouette, 1998; *Marrying Mike ... Again.* New York: Silhouette, 1998.

JOANNE HAMILTON-SELWAY

ROBERTA GELLIS

Roberta Gellis. Courtesy of Roberta Gellis.

When legendary writer Roberta Gellis states that she "loves to tell stories," millions of her fans realize what an understatement that is. Gellis, author of over forty novels, is the recipient of a Lifetime Achievement Award from Romance Writers of America. She has successfully crossed over to other genres, delicately blending fantasy, historical fiction, and mythological elements, among others, with romance. From her first published book, *Knight's Honor* (1964), she has created characters of honor and integrity. Using the richly recreated backdrops of such diverse locales and time periods as Medieval England, Ancient Greece, and Renaissance Italy, she has become a major influence on a generation of writers.

Gellis was born in 1927 in Brooklyn, New York, to a chemist father and a mother who taught elementary school. Her father, the chief chemist for the City of New York, gave Gellis her interest in science. Gellis's love of literature can be traced to her mother, who was a classics major in college. Gellis attended Hunter College, Brooklyn Polytechnic Institute, and New York University, where she received a bachelor of arts degree in chemistry, a master of science degree in biochemistry, and a master of arts degree in medieval literature, respectively. Gellis worked as a research chemist

also writing as Max Daniels
also writing as Priscilla Hamilton

and microbiologist, and though she was interested in writing, it was not a driving force until after the birth of her son in 1959. At home with her young son, she started writing and says she "rapidly became addicted."

Published in 1964, *Knight's Honor* was actually the second novel Gellis wrote. *Bond of Blood,* her first novel, was published a year after *Knight's Honor,* and both novels gave readers their first taste of Gellis's expertise in bringing the medieval era to life. With these books and the others that followed, Gellis not only developed a reputation for crafting romances with vivid and richly detailed historical settings, but also became recognized for her use of ordinary people as protagonists, along with the more popular lords and ladies. For example, *The Rope Dancer,* published in 1986, features a minstrel, a dwarf, and the title character of a rope dancer who had once been part of a group of traveling players in twelfth-century century England. Another example is her *Masques of Gold,* published in 1988. In this thirteenth-century medieval romance, Gellis draws her two lead characters from London's growing middle class, with an apothecary heroine and a hero who is not only a merchant but also the leader of the London Watch.

Many fans name her Roselynde Chronicles as their favorite Gellis books. Written in the 1970s, these books trace the history of a family through generations and are named for their extraordinary heroines: *Alinor* (1978), *Joanna* (1978), *Gillaine* (1980), *Rhiannon* (1982), and *Sybelle* (1983). Set in Gellis's beloved thirteenth-century England, each book in the series mixes historical figures, such as Eleanor of Aquitaine and Richard the Lionhearted, with fictional characters. While readers love the lush historical details in the Roselynde books, they know that Gellis never wavers from the emotional center of the story, the relationship between the hero and heroine. Wildly popular when they were published (*Roselynde* alone sold over 300,000 copies), Gellis choose to retire the series after the last book, *Sybelle,* because, realistically, Alinor would be in her sixties, which usually meant dead by medieval standards. Fans were delighted to discover that, in 2005, the series was revived with *Desiree,* and all the books in the Roselynde Chronicles were reissued, reuniting readers, new and old, with the family that captured hearts and imaginations 30 years ago.

Considering her love of myths and legends, it was not surprising that Gellis would turn to Greek mythology for inspiration. In the early 1990s, Gellis wrote five books based on characters from Greek mythology: Hecate in *Thrice Bound* (2001), Eros and Psyche in *Shimmering Splendor* (1995), Eurydice and Orpheus in *Enchanted Fire* (1996), Ariadne and the Minotaur in *Bull God* (2000), and Hades and Persephone in *Dazzling Brightness* (1994). Gellis's deft handling of Persephone's relationship with Hades in *Dazzling Brightness* gives the reader new insight into the myth of Persephone leaving her mother for six months of each year to join Hades in the Underworld. Once again, it is Gellis's skill in creating a deeply romantic relationship between the hero and heroine, whether god or mortal, that is key to the book's believability.

While best known for her historical romances, Gellis has brought her deft writing to other genres. She wrote several science fiction novels as Max Daniels in the late 1970s. In 1999, she began a historical mystery series, featuring Magdalene de la Batard, the owner of a brothel in twelfth-century England. In the first book, *A Mortal Bane* (1999), Magdalene becomes involved in the investigation of the murder of a papal messenger found stabbed in the church next to her elegant house of ill repute. A fanatical monk from the priory of St. Mary Overy accuses the women of Magdalene's brothel of being accomplices in the murder, in an attempt to close down Magdalene's business. Magdalene is forced to work with the Bishop of Winchester's knight, handsome Sir Bellany of Itchen, in order to clear her name. The relationship between Magdalene and Bellamy evolves in the next two books,

A Personal Devil (2001) and *Bone of Contention* (2002), giving a romantic flavor to the intricately plotted mysteries. In addition to science fiction and historical mysteries, Gellis demonstrated a flair for fantasy in a series of books published in the 2000s, which she coauthored with legendary fantasy writer Mercedes Lackey.

"I have always believed that human relationships direct and sometimes distort lives, that all the activities in a person's life are to some degree affected by relationships," says Gellis. "Romance is one of these relationships, and whether I write history or mystery or fantasy, love plays a part in the lives of my characters." From ancient mythology to medieval adventures, from science fiction to family sagas, Roberta Gellis has enchanted and influenced a generation of readers and romance authors. Her skillful use of historical details and her ability to create believable characters and emotionally satisfying relationships make her preeminent in each of the genres in which she writes.

BIBLIOGRAPHY

Writing as Roberta Gellis

Books: *Knight's Honor*. New York: Doubleday, 1964; *Bond of Blood*. New York: Doubleday, 1965; *Sing Witch, Sing Death*. New York: Bantam, 1975; *Dragon and the Rose*. New York: Playboy, 1977; *Sword and the Swan*. New York: Playboy, 1977; *Roselynde*. New York: Playboy, 1978; *Alinor*. New York: Playboy, 1978; *Joanna*. New York: Playboy, 1978; *Gilliane*. New York: Playboy, 1980; *The English Heiress*. New York: Dell, 1980; *The Cornish Heiress*. New York: Dell, 1981; *Siren Song*. New York: Playboy, 1981; *The Kent Heiress*. New York: Dell, 1982; *The Winter Song*. New York: PBJ Books, 1982; *Rhiannon*. New York: Playboy, 1982; *Sybelle*. New York: Jove, 1983; *Fortune's Bride*. New York: Dell, 1983; *Fire Song*. New York: Jove, 1984; *A Woman's Estate*. New York: Dell, 1984; *Tapestry of Dreams*. New York: Berkley, 1985; *The Rope Dancer*. New York: Berkley, 1986; *Fires of Winter*. New York: Jove, 1987; *Masques of Gold*. New York: Jove, 1988; *A Silver Mirror*. New York: Berkley/Jove, 1989; *A Delicate Balance*. New York: Dorchester, 1993; *Dazzling Brightness*. New York: Pinnacle, 1994; *Shimmering Splendor*. New York: Pinnacle, 1995; *Enchanted Fire*. New York: Pinnacle, 1996; *A Mortal Bane*. New York: Tor/Forge, 1999; *Bull God*. Riverdale, New York: Baen Books, 2000; *Thrice Bound*. Riverdale, New York: Baen Books, 2001; *A Personal Devil*. New York: Tor/Forge, 2001; *Bone of Contention*. New York: Tor/Forge, 2002; *Lucrezia Borgia and the Mother of Poisons*. New York: Tor/Forge, 2003; *Overstars Mail*. Waterville, Maine: Five-Star Press, 2004; *Desiree*. Toronto: Harlequin, 2005; *Chains of Folly*. New York: Thomson Gale, 2006.
Novellas: "Rarer Than a White Crow" in *Irish Magic*. New York: Pinnacle, 1995; "Bride Price" in *Irish Magic II*. New York: Pinnacle, 1997.

Writing as Roberta Gellis with Mercedes Lackey

Books: *This Scepter'd Isle*. Riverdale, New York: Baen Books, 2004; *Ill Met by Moonlight*. Riverdale, New York: Baen Books, 2005.

Writing as Max Daniels

Books: *Space Guardian*. New York: Pocket, 1977; *Offworld*. New York: Pocket, 1978.

Writing as Priscilla Hamilton

Book: *The Love Token*. New York: Playboy, 1979.

JOANNE HAMILTON-SELWAY

TESS GERRITSEN

Tess Gerritsen. Courtesy of Tess Gerritsen.

The most common bit of advice given to aspiring authors is to write what they know, but author Tess Gerritsen began her career differently, by writing the kind of romances she herself liked to read.

Gerritsen was born in 1953 in San Diego, California, to a social worker mother who immigrated from Kunming, China, and an American restaurateur father of Chinese descent. She always wanted to be a writer, even as a young child: but she instead followed the path to medical school and a career as a physician. She attended Stanford University, graduating Phi Beta Kappa with a bachelor of arts degree in anthropology, and received her medical degree from the University of California, San Francisco.

After working for five years as a physician in Honolulu, Gerritsen was on maternity leave when she began writing short stories, which were received with a flurry of rejection letters since, she says, "there are so few markets." She then turned to writing novels, but her first three collected a drawer full of rejection slips. SOS Publications, a small press, did buy two romances from Gerritsen. *Adventure's Mistress* was published in 1986, but only a few copies were ever distributed. The second book she sold, *Love's Masquerade,* was never published as the publisher went bankrupt soon afterward. Undaunted by this and the repeated rejections she had received from other publishers, Gerritsen decided to try writing a romantic suspense novel for Harlequin's Intrigue line, which she loved, and thus she began writing what she liked reading.

Gerritsen's *Call After Midnight,* published in 1987, became the first of eight novels she would write for the Harlequin Intrigue line. She quickly developed a reputation for her ability to write chillingly suspenseful romances featuring keenly intelligent heroines and heroes with integrity, and plots that frequently begin with some kind of unexpected twist. A perfect example of this is *Keeper of the Bride,* published in 1996, which opens with the heroine, Nina Cormier, being left at the altar when her fiancé, Dr. Robert Bledsoe, cancels their wedding at the last minute. Nina thinks her life is over, but when she narrowly escapes an explosion in the church mere moments after she leaves the building, Nina realizes she has a lot to live for, especially after meeting detective Sam Navarro.

While Gerritsen found creating romantic suspense for Harlequin extremely satisfying, the rapid writing pace demanded of series romance authors didn't fit her personal writing style. What Gerritsen wanted to write was a bigger, more in-depth novel. A dinner conversation that she overheard, about orphans being kidnapped in Russia and sold as organ donors in the United States, provided Gerritsen with the inspiration for her first suspense novel, *Harvest.* Published in 1996, *Harvest* combined Gerritsen's knowledge of medicine and her training as a physician with the taut writing style she had developed while writing for Harlequin. *Harvest* became a *New York Times* best seller, and Gerritsen's career changed forever.

Gerritsen's next three books, *Life Support* (1997), *Bloodstream* (1998), and *Gravity* (1999), were stand-alone novels, and all were best sellers. Each book incorporated a seamless blending of suspense and medicine, with neither element overshadowing the other. Though these books focused more on suspense than passion, Gerritsen frequently found a way to include a measure of romance in the story. For example, in *Bloodstream,* even though the book centers around Dr. Claire Elliot's attempts to connect with her own troubled son and find out what is causing the teenagers in Tranquility, Maine, to become lethally violent, a romance gradually blossoms between Claire and the town's police chief, Lincoln Kelly. Gerritsen says it took years for her to realize that readers would be interested in her experiences as a physician. Readers were more than just interested. Her legions of fans grew with each new book.

With 2001's *The Surgeon,* Gerritsen began a series combining medicine and serial killers. "The Surgeon" is a serial killer who preys on women, raping them, mutilating them by surgically removing their wombs, and then slitting their throats. Dr. Catherine Cordell believes that the murderer she thought she killed two years earlier has resurfaced as the Surgeon in Boston, where she relocated after her trauma. Gerritsen's descriptions of the fears rape victims face and Cordell's terror of having her safety zone violated again are some of the most riveting and emotionally draining scenes of the book. Gerritsen added an equal portion of romance into this suspenseful story by bringing Cordell and detective Thomas Moore into a close and protective relationship, even though Cordell, emotionally damaged by her assault and her self-defense murder of the serial killer, is reluctant to fall in love with Moore. Gerritsen's deft mix of medical suspense and romance in *The Surgeon* won her the RITA award for best romantic suspense novel in 2001. Reviewers called it "top grade," and Stephen King, a self-proclaimed fan, deemed her "better than Palmer and Cook and, yes, even better than Crichton."

With *The Apprentice* (2002), Gerritsen continued the story of some of the characters from *The Surgeon,* and she soon had another huge hit on her hands. In *The Apprentice,* Jane Rizzoli, a police detective who played a secondary role in *The Surgeon,* takes center stage to investigate a series of copycat murders, which look like the work of the Surgeon, who is in prison. Rizzoli is a complex and fully developed heroine whose intensity and tragic past make her a fascinating character. The subplot, a romance with an FBI special agent, does not soften the character of Rizzoli but instead emphasizes her unyielding nature and forces her to confront her feelings. Gerritsen believes that an element of romance can add an extra measure of excitement to any suspense novel and says that "the relationship between men and women is the greatest mystery of all, and I never get tired of exploring it."

Her next book, *The Sinner* (2003), features medical examiner Maura Isles, who appeared in a small role in *The Apprentice* and is known by her colleagues as "the Queen of the Dead." Jane Rizzoli and Isles are called on to investigate a grisly murder of two nuns in a convent. Clues and suspects are everywhere, from the multinational chemical company to Isles's ex-husband, as Gerritsen deftly weaves suspense and romance and medical details into what *Publishers Weekly* called "an assured, richly shaded seventh novel."

When asked about the writing process and what appeals to her, Gerritsen responds that she loves the beginning of a book, "when the ideas are fresh and new … when the possibilities are shining out there like a distant goal post." And as long as there are intriguing medical stories in the news or disturbing or fascinating situations that need to be explained, readers can depend on Gerritsen to continue to write captivating novels of suspense and romance.

BIBLIOGRAPHY

Books: *Adventure's Mistress.* Santa Monica, CA: SOS Publications, 1986; *Call After Midnight.* Toronto: Harlequin, 1987; *Under the Knife.* Toronto: Harlequin, 1990; *Never Say Die.* Toronto: Harlequin, 1990; *Whistleblower.* Toronto: Harlequin, 1992; *Presumed Guilty.* Toronto: Harlequin. 1993; *In Their Footsteps.* Toronto: Harlequin, 1994; *Peggy Sue Got Murdered:* New York: HarperCollins, 1994; *Thief of Hearts.* Toronto: Harlequin, 1995; *Keeper of the Bride.* Toronto: Harlequin, 1996; *Harvest.* New York: Simon and Schuster, 1996; *Never Say Die.* Toronto: Harlequin, 1996; *Life Support.* New York: Simon and Schuster, 1997; *Bloodstream.* New York: Simon and Schuster, 1998; *Gravity.* New York: Simon and Schuster, 1999; *The Surgeon.* New York: Ballantine, 2001; *The Apprentice.* New York: Ballantine, 2002; *The Sinner.* New York: Ballantine, 2003; *Body Double.* New York: Ballantine, 2004; *Vanish.* New York: Ballantine, 2005; *Mephisto Club.* New York: Random House, 2006.

JOANNE HAMILTON-SELWAY AND JOHN CHARLES

RACHEL GIBSON

When Rachel Gibson was a child, if someone had told her that she would grow up to be a writer, she says she would have "fallen off my little reading chair laughing." Always in the last reading group in her class, Gibson struggled with dyslexia, developing a strong dislike for the written word. Gibson recalls, "To me, books were scary things. Traps. Bound pages to mess up and make me cry and confuse me with words like *was* and *saw; were* and *where* and *there;* and *how* and *who..*"

Gibson was born and raised in the Northend in Boise, Idaho, in 1962. Her father worked for the telephone company but was also an adventurer who enjoyed hunting big game and driving race cars. Her mother, a full-time homemaker, still lives in the same house where Gibson was born and raised. As a child, Gibson preferred to be outside than in the class-room, and she wanted people to call her Donna. Riding motorcycles and horses were more of a draw than anything that school could offer. At first, Gibson dreamed of becoming a professional tetherball player. After that, she set her sights on becoming a nurse but decided, "Giving shots sucked." Having discarded her first two dream careers, she became undecided about her future.

Reading might have given Gibson trouble, but she certainly had no problem telling stories. Her first major outing as a storyteller occurred when she and her best friend took the family's blue Chevy Vega, skipped school, went off the beaten path, and drove into the side of a mountain. The car was hurt, but the girls weren't. Gibson took the pieces of the automobile to the car wash, and left the parts with the wrecked car in the school parking lot. When she told her parents the car was damaged while she was in class, they believed her. Thus, a storyteller was born.

Despite her learning disability, Gibson managed to graduate from high school. She had several jobs, mostly secretarial. She says she also worked for a hazardous materials company "for about three hours, once ... that job was hell." She married her husband, James, and had three children in fairly rapid succession by the time she was 24 years old. A broken television set provided a paving stone on the path to publication. As Gibson waited for it to be repaired, she discovered the joy of reading, in the form of *David Copperfield*, part of a set of classics her husband's grandmother had given her, and the only adult reading material in the house. Surprised that books could be entertaining, she began to devour the rest of the set. However, she says, the "male chauvinist" writers had begun to get on her nerves.

Fate intervened, and Gibson took the next step toward publication when a friend gave her a copy of Shirley Busbee's *The Spanish Rose*. At that point, Gibson fell in love with romance novels. Eventually, her passion for the genre lead her to try her hand at writing a romance. In fact, at age 31, Gibson says she "just sat down with an old typewriter and started to write." Initially, she wanted to rewrite *Gone with the Wind* with a different ending, where Rhett returned to Scarlett because she had morphed into a nice person. Gibson wrote four romances, all of which were rejected, but that provided a good learning experience.

Six years later, Gibson sold her first book, *Simply Irresistible* (1998), which won the *Romantic Times*' Best Love and Laughter Award and became the first of her four Romance Writers of America's Top Ten Favorite Books of the Year. Like Scarlett O'Hara, Georgeanne Howard, the heroine of *Simply Irresistible* is a Southern belle on her way to the altar. She decides to leave her rich, albeit elderly fiancé minutes before the wedding. Hockey star John Kowalsky, forced to attend the ceremony, prefers nursing his hangover to sticking around for the wedding. When he leaves, a beautiful woman asks if he'll take her with him. Georgeanne spends what would have been her wedding night with John instead. Unfortunately, it's too late when John figures out that his mystery woman is the would-be bride. Since the groom is the team owner and John's boss, John's career is on the line. Seven years later, John meets Georgeanne again. Much to his surprise, she now has a daughter, the result of their one night of passion. Georgeanne fell in love with John the first time she saw him, but John, a celebrity playboy, is just now ready to settle down. However, if John follows his heart, he once again risks his career, because Georgeanne's former fiancé is still his boss. In this book, Gibson incorporates both of her favorite themes: a secret child and unrequited love. Gibson also made Georgeanne dyslexic, a condition with which Gibson was all too familiar.

Truly Madly Yours (1999), another one of Gibson's books honored by RWA as a Top Ten Favorite Book of the Year, showcases her keen sense of humor and expert comic pacing. When hairdresser Delaney Shaw returns home for the reading of her stepfather's will, she is shocked to learn that he included the stipulation that she must remain in Truly, Idaho, for one year and stay away from Nick Allegrezza the entire time. Ten years earlier, Nick and Delaney were an item, but whereas Delaney considered Nick her true love, Nick only thought of her as a fling. Now, Nick's interested in Delaney again, but Delaney is bound by the terms of the will. *Truly Madly Yours* also reflects Gibson's favorite theme of unrequited love.

Gibson's stories are character driven. Her heroes are larger-than-life alpha males. Undercover cop Joseph Shanahan is one such man. In *It Must Be Love* (2000), Joe's cover is blown by art dealer Gabrielle Breedlove when she suspects him of being a stalker. Gabrielle is actually a crime suspect, and Joe really is shadowing her; but once she knows his identity, Joe poses as her boyfriend to continue his investigation into the art theft. The fact that Joe is such an alpha male doesn't impress Gabrielle one bit, and soon, their pretend romance starts feeling awfully real. Sheriff Dylan Taber (*True Confessions,* 2001) is another one of Gibson's alpha-male heroes. California tabloid journalist Hope Spencer, burned out on men, relocates to the small town of Gospel, Idaho, where she intends to do nothing but write. Dylan, always on the run from Gospel's available women, gets on Hope's bad side immediately with his theory that she'll want to return to big-city life in less than a week. Ironically, although both of them are intentionally avoiding people of the opposite sex, they're somehow drawn together in their battle of the sexes. Once again, Gibson fills her book with sparkling dialogue and unforgettable characters. *True Confessions* won both a RITA and a Top Ten Favorite Books of the Year award from Romance Writers of America.

The heroines in Gibson's books are strong, determined women who are equal to any task. They would "never consider letting anyone walk over them," says Gibson. She adds, "If you write alpha heroes, you have to write strong heroines." Although Gibson says that not much of her personality is reflected in her heroines, like the female protagonists in her books, she would "never consider letting anyone walk all over" her, either. Gibson's heroines are smart, clever, and more than capable of holding their own during verbal sparring matches. One of these women is writer Jane Alcott from *See Jane Score* (2003), a book that was on both the *New York Times* and *USA Today* best seller lists. It also won Gibson RWA's Top Ten Favorite Books of the Year award. Instead of a small town, Gibson sets this story of Jane and hockey goalie Luc "Lucky" Martineau in a series of large cities, including Seattle, Washington, and Phoenix, Arizona. Jane, a journalist who writes a love-advice column, is also penning serialized pornography for a men's magazine to make some extra money. A colleague's illness causes Jane to be moved from her position as columnist to that of reporter covering the sports beat, specifically the Chinooks, Seattle's hockey team. No one on the team is happy that the press contact is a woman, but Luc Martineau is the unhappiest of all. When Jane, pushed to her limit by the team's rude behavior, calls Luc "a big dodo," and the Chinooks win their first game of the season, her status is elevated from pariah to the team's lucky charm. A superstitious bunch, the team requires Jane to repeat her epithet before every game. Once in the team's good graces, Jane gets to know them, a lot better, especially Luc; but she's still not afraid to stand down one man, or the whole team for that matter, even if they're in the locker room.

In *The Trouble with Valentine's Day* (2005) Gibson returns to Gospel, Idaho, the setting of *True Confessions*. The 5-foot 11-inch private detective, Kate Hamilton, decides to visit her grandfather in Gospel to escape the chaos of a big city and the stress of her job. However, on the way there, she stops at Sun Valley ski lodge, and on a whim, for the first time in her life, tries to pick up a man in the bar. After he rejects her, he gives her a long lecture on her risky behavior. When Kate arrives at her grandfather's house she meets his good friend, Rob Sutter, the same man who had rebuffed her proposition. Humiliated by what she has done, Kate prays that Rob won't repeat the story of their encounter. More than that, she wants him to see her as more than the promiscuous woman that she's sure he believes she is. Rob, a former professional hockey player, was first introduced as a secondary character in *See Jane Score* (2003). His career has been ended by a woman he met in a bar, a psychologically unbalanced stalker who shot him in the chest and knee, almost killing him.

Readers expect light comedy, witty repartee, sexy banter, and quirky characters from Gibson, but she can also show a darker side in her works, as can be seen in her novel *Lola Carlyle Reveals All* (2002). Gibson claims this was the most difficult book for her to write, because, whereas her books tend to be purely character driven, this book was more plot driven, with a story line more involved than what she normally writes. Lola Carlyle, a former supermodel, decides to go into hiding when her ex-boyfriend publishes nude pictures of her on the Internet. Unfortunately, the yacht she's chosen as her safe haven becomes an object of hot pursuit, when Max Zamora, a government agent/spy, hijacks it. A major storm tosses the two of them on an island, where their relationship takes off. Gibson compares the experience of writing the hero, Max, to juggling 10 balls and keeping them all in the air at once. Lola's struggle with bulimia provides a serious subtext, resulting in a more intensely written story. In this book, Gibson makes a departure from her small-town settings and places the action in Nassau Harbor; the Bermuda Triangle; and Baltimore, Maryland.

According to Gibson, the easiest novel for her to write was RITA finalist *Daisy's Back in Town* (2004), which Gibson calls "her most personal work." In this novel, Gibson used people in her real life as the basis for the characters, something she hadn't done in any of her previous works. She patterned some of the characters after her own family, so she felt as though she already knew them, right down to Daisy's mother's pink flamingos, an homage to Gibson's mother. Nathan, Daisy's 15-year-old, is based on Gibson's son. In this book, Daisy Lee Brooks, former Lovett, Texas, cheerleader, leaves town and vows never to return. Fifteen years pass, and Daisy Lee (now Daisy Lee Monroe) returns home to give vintage car restorer Jackson Lamott Parrish a letter her deceased husband, once Jackson's best friend, asked her to deliver. Daisy has something else for Jackson—Nathan, the son he didn't know he had. Although Jackson wants Daisy to stay away from him, he's forced to get along with her because of Nathan. In this book, Gibson once again uses the underlying themes of unrequited love and a secret child.

For Gibson, plot ideas can come from movies, books, and even world events. She prefers to write about small-town settings (*Truly Madly Yours,* set in Truly, Idaho; *True Confessions* and *The Trouble with Valentine's Day,* set in Gospel, Idaho; *Daisy's Back in Town,* set in Lovett, Texas) to provide a more personal feel to her stories. All of Gibson's books to date have contemporary settings. Gibson admits to getting writer's block: "I have days where writing is like pulling my own teeth. After 10 hours of work, I get one paragraph. One *bad* paragraph. I write anyway."

Tragedy is easy, but comedy is hard. If anyone knows that writing contemporary romance is more difficult than it looks, it is Gibson. She overcame her fear and disdain of the written word to become one of the romance genre's most inventive and popular authors. Triumphing over her dyslexia against great odds has made her an excellent role model for others with the same condition. Beloved by readers, recognized by peers, Gibson is a study in determination and perseverance.

BIBLIOGRAPHY

Books: *Simply Irresistible.* New York: Avon, 1998; *Truly Madly Yours.* New York: Avon, 1999; *It Must Be Love.* New York: Avon, 2000; *True Confessions.* New York: Avon, 2001; *Lola Carlyle Reveals All.* New York: Avon, 2002; *See Jane Score.* New York: Avon, 2003; *Daisy's Back in Town.* New York: Avon, 2004; *The Trouble with Valentine's Day.* New York: Avon, 2005; *Sex, Lies, and Online Dating.* New York: Avon, 2006.
Novella: "Now and Forever" in *Secrets of a Perfect Night.* New York: Avon, 2000.

SHELLEY MOSLEY AND SANDRA VAN WINKLE

AMANDA GLASS. *See* Jayne Ann Krentz

JEANNE GRANT. *See* Jennifer Greene

ELIZABETH GRAYSON

Elizabeth Grayson. Courtesy of Elizabeth Grayson.

Relationships are at the core of every Elizabeth Grayson book. Whether it is her richly nuanced historical romances or her recent transition to powerfully written women's fiction, Grayson is a master at exploring relationships. "I am fascinated by what draws a man and a woman together and what makes those individuals tick," she says.

Grayson was born Karen Witmer in 1947, in Jamestown, New York. When she was 10 days old, Grayson was adopted by a family from Niagara Falls. Even though her adopted father studied mathematics in college, he ended up working in the family lumber company. Her mother was a stay-at-home mom, and Grayson has many fond memories of her childhood growing up in Niagara Falls. They lived in a big Dutch colonial house, built by carpenters from the family lumber company. It was close to parks, and Grayson reminisces that she could walk across a bridge and be in Canada, marveling that a foreign country was so nearby.

Grayson attended public schools in Niagara Falls, and after winning an academic scholarship, she went on to study at the State University of New York at Geneseo. While she had many academic interests, she eventually graduated with a bachelor of science degree in

also writing as Elizabeth N. Kary
also writing as Karyn Witmer

education, with a certification to teach art. Grayson later pursued postgraduate work at several colleges while she was teaching at a rural school outside of Rochester. She received her master of science degree in education from Nazareth College in Rochester. In 1977, Grayson married Tom Gow, an advertising art director.

Grayson taught elementary school art for 12 years in the Wayne Central School District, outside of Rochester. She and her husband then moved to St. Louis, Missouri, where she was hired by the St. Louis Art Museum to teach in their nationally recognized program, "Arts in the Basic Curriculum." Grayson loved the intellectual stimulation the job provided, as well as the opportunities it offered her to work with children and meet visiting artists.

Grayson says she was always interested in writing: "I am addicted to stories. Always have been, always will be. Before I went to school, I'd write stories with scribbles, then 'read' them back to my mother and father." And romance was in her blood. She says, "I started writing boy-girl stories in grade school—and by the time I was 15, I had finished my first full-length historical novel, *Forever and Always.* It was a love story set during the Civil War and was an outgrowth of my fascination with the period, spurred by reading [the book] and seeing the movie *Gone with the Wind.*"

Years passed before Grayson returned to her love of writing. She recalls, "I was working as an art teacher when I started my first adult novel, *Love, Honor and Betray,* written as Elizabeth Kary. I came home after a less-than-great day with the kids, sat down, and started a novel with nothing more than a first line and a setting I was familiar with—the Niagara frontier on the eve of the War of 1812."

Grayson says she found that "the writing bug bit me immediately. I was working full-time when it did, so I wrote between school and dinnertime. I wrote at school during breaks and lunch. I wrote when I should have been doing report cards and between appointments during parents' conferences. Writing a first book with the hope of publication is a learning experience, and I wrote and researched and rewrote in every minute of my spare time for four years."

While Grayson found that the story flowed and filled her waking hours, how to get her novel published initially was a mystery to her. "I had no idea how long books were supposed to be and let *Love, Honor and Betray* just take its course," she says. "Finally, I gathered my courage and took all 26 handwritten, spiral-bound notebooks to a typing service. What resulted was a 1,203 page manuscript."

Grayson bundled up her epic work, *Love, Honor and Betray,* and sent it to her agent, who, after several rejections, gave the manuscript back to her, explaining that it was too long and would never sell. "Then, through a friend of a friend, the manuscript ended up on Nancy Coffey's desk at Berkley Books," says Grayson. "Luckily, Nancy loved long books and bought it immediately. The novel was published [in 1986] and went on to win the Waldenbooks Award for the Bestselling Romance by a New Author."

While the first book Grayson wrote and submitted to a publisher was *Love, Honor and Betray,* her first published book was *Portrait of a Lady,* written under the pseudonym Elizabeth N. Kary. Published in 1985 as part of Dell's Second Chance at Love series, the book features museum conservator Paige Fenton, who has discovered that one of the Tri-City art museum's recent donations, *The Lady of Dordrect* by Frans Hal, is a fake. Of course, the painting's owner, wealthy local CEO Grant Hamilton, is not pleased to hear that his donation may be worthless and doesn't want the news of the potential fraud leaked to the press. At first, Grant refuses to believe Paige's professional assessment, but the more time he spends with her, the more impressed he is by her dedication and expertise and the more attracted he is to the woman herself. In *Portrait of a Lady,* Grayson does a superb job of incorporating her own extensive knowledge of art history and her experiences working in an art museum. Details of how museums acquire art and how they authenticate it give the book its stunning sense of realism. Grayson excels at developing the simmering sexual tension between Paige and Grant, making *Portrait of a Lady* a stellar debut.

Love, Honor, and Betray, also published by Berkley, followed in 1986. Grayson's first historical novel, set during the tempestuous years of the War of 1812, was the kind of big, lush, and richly detailed historical romances that were popular during the 1980s but have all but disappeared from the current publishing scene. *Love, Honor, and Betray* is the story of beautiful American Charlotte "Charl" Beckworth and Seth Porterfield, the illegitimate son of an English duke, and the passionate romance that blossoms between them. Grayson says of her inspiration for the book, "My adopted father's family was one of the first to settle in Niagara County. These family stories were very much a part of my growing up and, I think, they are a part of why history seems so real to me. One family story that took place during the War of 1812 spurred me to set my first historical novel, *Love, Honor, and Betray,* in that period."

For her next historical, *Let No Man Divide* (1987), Grayson chose the turbulent time period of the American Civil War as a backdrop to the romance between independent, spirited Leigh Pennington, who volunteers with the nursing corps and whose fiancé is a confederate soldier, and Hayes Banister, a Yankee engineer who is secretly working on the Ironclads for the Union. Grayson recalls, "When we moved to St. Louis from upstate New York, I knew very little about the history of the Mississippi Valley. Having finished *Love, Honor and Betray,* I was ready to start another historical novel, and it made sense to explore some of the history of the St. Louis area. After reading several general histories, I decided one of the most interesting eras was the Civil War. You see, Missouri was every bit as divided a state as Virginia during the war, and while only a couple of battles were fought there, St. Louis was involved in everything from building the Ironclads that eventually opened up the Mississippi and divided the Confederacy to being a major depot for medical supplies and personnel in the western theater of the war." With *Let No Man Divide,* Grayson once again uses her splendid storytelling skills to bring this period of American history vividly to life.

After two more historical romances, Grayson turned to the western frontier for inspiration for her first book written as Elizabeth Grayson, *Bride of the Wilderness* (1995). This sweeping novel uses the backdrop of the French colonial period in the Mississippi Valley to tell the story of young, beautiful widow Celene Bernard, whose fate becomes entwined with English trapper Burke Cardwell. The two meet at the Prairie du Chien fur trade rendezvous, when Celene confronts Burke as he argues with a Native American woman. Celene comes to the woman's rescue by pushing Burke into a mud hole, thus setting the stage for their fractious, yet deeply romantic relationship. "I think one of my strengths as a writer is creating both realistic and complex characters, as well as the historical period they inhabit," says Grayson. "I work hard on this and do in-depth research to each period I write about." In *Bride of the Wilderness,* Grayson combines her gift for creating compelling characters with a fully realized, refreshingly original historical setting to fashion a love story that is truly memorable.

Several more Westerns followed, as Grayson explored the expansiveness of the frontier and the complex relationships of the men and women who settled the land: "In the early books (most of the Karys), I wrote with a close focus on the love story and sexual attraction between hero and heroine. As I developed as a writer (and as a person), I began to take a broader view, widening my scope beyond the growing love relationship to include children, family, and friends. The latter stories (mostly the Graysons) are more complex—and more fascinating for me to write."

An excellent example of this is Grayson's beautifully poignant *Moon in the Water*, published in 2004. Set in St. Louis, just after the Civil War, the book opens with Chase Hardesty, a riverboat pilot who has been offered his own steamboat, the *Andromeda*, in exchange for marrying the owner's stepdaughter, Ann Rossiter. Ann, who has embarrassed the family by becoming pregnant, refuses his offer. Though Chase initially promises Ann that he will decline her father's offer, he breaks that promise when the temptation of owning his own steamboat is too great. Much to Chase's surprise, his new wife insists on accompanying him on the *Andromeda*'s maiden voyage to Montana Territory. Somewhere during the long and dangerous journey, their marriage of convenience becomes a love match. Grayson's subtle, spare writing style perfectly complements her quietly intense story of two emotionally wounded and deeply conflicted individuals who find new hope and love when they learn to trust each other.

In *Moon in the Water*, as with her other historical Westerns, Grayson captures the restless spirit of America's pioneers and the grandeur of the land they come to call home.

> I believe that all of us are shaped by the places we live. We discover things about ourselves—strengths and weaknesses, skills, and the capacity for creativity—as we learn to live in new environments. I think that happens today just as it did in the past. Certainly the records that have come down to us from those involved in the Westward Movement repeatedly underscore the need to change and adapt to their new lives if they mean to survive. That said, I look at the books I wrote as Elizabeth Grayson [and see they] are not so much books about the West, but books about the expanding American frontier. Each subsequent move West demanded that characters rise to the challenge of this new place, and the novels reflect that.

After *Moon in the Water*, Grayson changed genres (to contemporary women's fiction) and pseudonyms (to Karyn Witmer) with her next book, *A Simple Gift*, published in 2006. Ever since her daughter, Fiona, ran away from home, Avery Montgomery has spent each day hoping for a phone call or letter or some contact that would let her know that her daughter is safe. So when Avery discovers that Fiona is working in the local grocery store and that Avery's husband, Mike, knew about it and didn't tell her, she is devastated. Now all Avery wants to do is put the broken pieces of her family back together, hopefully before Christmas. In this emotionally powerful story, Grayson writes skillfully of family and forgiveness, and the complex nature of the relationship between mothers and daughters.

Grayson says, "I find relationships between men and women are integral to almost any story I want to tell, so I can't ever imagine myself writing anything else." Historical novels, contemporary women's fiction, contemporary romances—no matter what genre she chooses to write, Grayson's great versatility is apparent, and her talent shines through.

BIBLIOGRAPHY

Writing as Elizabeth Grayson

Books: *Bride of the Wilderness*. New York: Berkley, 1995; *A Place Called Home*. New York: Avon, 1995; *So Wide the Sky*. New York: Avon, 1997; *Color of the Wind*. New York: Bantam, 1999; *Painted by the Sun*. New York: Bantam, 2000; *Moon in the Water*. New York: Bantam, 2004.

Writing as Elizabeth N. Kary

Books: *Portrait of a Lady.* New York: Berkley, 1985; *Love, Honor and Betray.* New York: Berkley, 1986; *Let No Man Divide.* New York: Berkley, 1987; *From This Day Onward.* New York: Jove, 1989; *Midnight Lace.* New York: Jove, 1990.

Writing as Karyn Witmer

Book: *A Simple Gift.* New York: Dell, 2006.

JOHN CHARLES

JENNIFER GREENE

Jennifer Greene. Courtesy of Jennifer Greene.

Jennifer Greene is an author who truly appreciates the power of love to transform lives. As an award-winning author of over sixty books, Greene brings emotional depth, fresh situations, and tart humor to her contemporary love stories. She crafts subtly nuanced characters whose struggle to survive and find love in a complex world resonate with readers both young and old.

Greene, the pseudonym for Alison Hart, was born in Grosse Pointe, Michigan, in 1948. Greene's parents were divorced, and she grew up mainly in Grosse Pointe but also spent part of the year with her father either in Florida or Michigan. Her mother's side of the family goes all the way back to the *Mayflower*, and it was her mother who gave Greene her love of reading and, as she puts it, "my belief in the wonder and joy of family, and the whole concept that a woman could do anything with enough commitment and willingness to work." Greene says her father's side of the family gave her "a rich background in faith, a huge range of interests, and a love and fascination for people."

Greene attended school in Grosse Pointe, and after graduating from high school went on to Michigan State University (MSU), where she received a multidisciplinary degree in

---

also writing as Jeanne Grant
also writing as Jessica Massey

English and psychology. While at MSU, Greene received the college's Lantern Night Award, an honor given for service rather than academics, for being one of their 50 outstanding women graduates.

Greene recalls, "I always wrote, from the time I could string two words together. I look back now and easily realize that every class in school, every job, every outside activity I can think of involved writing—that I always was steered in that direction." While Greene was interested in writing, she says her mother "wasn't about to raise a daughter who couldn't support herself, so my goals and education were geared toward a 'serious' career."

Before succumbing to the muse, Greene held a variety of different jobs. She worked as a counselor and resident assistant in college, as a teacher, and for several years as a labor relations manager. In between working, Greene married her very own hero, in 1970, and raised two children. When she was home with her firstborn, though, Greene says she "couldn't keep the writing hound tethered any longer," and she decided to give her dream a chance.

While she didn't always want to write romance fiction, Greene says what drew her to the genre was its focus on "women's issues and interests—that these books were by women and for women, covered problems women were and are struggling with." Greene worked diligently, and by 1980, she had sold her first romance, written under the pseudonym Jeanne Grant, for Berkley.

The first Grant book published by Berkley was *Man from Tennessee,* which came out in 1983, but it was actually the second book Greene wrote. The first book Greene wrote, *A Daring Proposition,* was published by Berkley next, in 1983 as well. Because the subject of *A Daring Proposition* (artificial insemination) was somewhat controversial at that time, Greene's publisher suggested she might want to start her writing career with a more normal romance.

While *A Daring Proposition* might have been daring for the times, this first book just poured out of her heart. At first, Greene says she didn't realize how unusual this was for a novice writer and that she should have been "scared witless." Fortunately as Greene remembers, "by the time I did realize this and became scared witless, thankfully I also had a better understanding of point of view, transitions, and conflicts, and all the other craft issues that writers need to master." One thing writing her first book did teach Greene was "how much loving writing—and loving a story—affects the outcome. It was a book that I didn't know how to write, that supposedly 'couldn't sell' … but it taught me that those kinds of rules aren't always true. What matters most for an author—and for a reader—I believe is to have a book that comes from the writer's heart. An author can always edit or fix point of view. There is no fixing a book that doesn't have emotion."

Greene would go on to write a total of 15 books as Jeanne Grant for Berkley's Second Chance at Love and To Have and to Hold lines. As Jessica Massey, she wrote one romance for Dell before she moved to Harlequin, where she adopted the pseudonym Jennifer Greene.

From the beginning of her writing career, Greene's books were recognized as being something special and wonderful. Greene received the Romance Writers of America's Silver Medallion for her book *Silver and Spice* in 1984. *Ain't Misbehaving* was a RWA Gold Medallion finalist in 1986, as was *Secrets* in 1989. *Night of the Hunter* became Greene's first RITA award winner in 1989, and she would continue on to win RITAs for *Single Dad* in 1996 and *Nobody's Princess* in 1998. Greene's three RITAs earned her a place in RWA's prestigious Hall of Fame in 1998.

Greene also became known as an author willing to tackle different, or even tough, topics that did not often appear in romances. With her book *Ain't Misbehaving* (1985), Greene consciously chose to reverse the frequently used romance genre convention of the sexually inexperienced heroine who is tutored in the art of romance by the more experienced hero by making her book's hero the one who is sexually innocent. In *Conquer the Memories* (1984), the book's hero struggles with the guilt he feels after his wife is assaulted and he was not able to protect her. *Broken Blossom* (1990) deals with child custody, but in the case of this particular book, it is the heroine who has lost custody of her child.

After 20 years of writing category romances, Greene wanted to try something different. Her first single-title romance, *The Woman Most Likely To ...*, was hotly sought after by several publishers before Avon successfully won the bid to publish the book in 2002. *The Woman Most Likely To* has several of the signature elements—including passion, humor, and richly defined characters—readers had come to expect from Greene in her category romances. The longer length allowed in single-title romances gave Greene the room to explore several secondary themes in her story of a woman who returns home to deal with the changes going on in both her mother's and her daughter's lives.

Many writers return to a particular theme that resonates with them in their work. For a long time, Greene really didn't think she was one of these writers, until she had written somewhere over twenty books. At that point, she says, "readers starting identifying some of these themes to me (and for me). I tend to write about vulnerable women who are seeking to find their individual source of strength—women in trouble because they haven't resolved something in their past. My heroes tend to function as catalysts who throw them off the cliff, rather than leap in and rescue them. I like to write about people who've made serious mistakes—because I think good people do just that—and a definite reoccurring theme for me is how people can grow, change, and forgive themselves for mistakes they may have made."

An excellent example of this is Greene's recent The Scent of Lavender trilogy, which she wrote for Silhouette's Desire line. The first book in the trilogy, *Wild in the Field* (2003), features the youngest Campbell sister, Camille, who has returned to her family's farm in White Hills, Vermont. Camille has just suffered through the outcome of the trial of the young robbers who killed her husband, and she is burdened with a sense of grief so deep that it has left her emotionally numb and turned her into a recluse. It takes her neighbor, Pete MacDougal, and his two teenage sons to give Camille the push she needs to get back into life and love. *Wild in the Moonlight* (2004), the second book of the trilogy, focuses on middle sister Violet, whose seemingly ditzy ways don't fool Cameron Lachlan, a chemist from a French perfume company who is interested in Violet's special strain of lavender. *Wild in the Moment* (2004), the third book, brings the oldest Campbell girl, glamorous Daisy, into the forefront when she returns home to White Hills after a bitter breakup in France. Each of the Campbell women must come to terms with choices they have made in the past and the women they have become. With a little help from each of the book's heroes though, Camille, Violet, and Daisy all discover that change is possible, no matter where you might be in life.

Another illustration of Greene's recurring themes of growth, change, and forgiveness is her book *Where Is He Now?* (2003). The book's heroine, Jeanne Claire Cassidy, had always wondered why her high school sweetheart, Nate Donneli, dumped her right after graduation instead of loving her forever as he promised. The arrival of their 15-year high-school reunion gives Claire the impetus to contact Nate and ask him just why he did abandon her. The answers surprise Claire, but what is even more surprising is that once Nate connects with Claire again, he realizes he doesn't want to let her go this time around. The reactions of Nate's young daughter to his dating Claire, as well as the interactions of other members of Nate's family, add a nice dash of realism to Greene's beautifully written story of dreams discarded and rediscovered, and love lost and found.

"Honestly, I don't think anyone wants to be a writer ... at least, if the person is sane," says Greene. "Sometimes I think sanity is vastly overrated, but still, the nature of writing is a complicated mix of joy and trial. Most jobs don't leech so much emotional energy, nor do they require the person to dig so hard for the kind of honesty that most people are thrilled to bury deep in the closet. Nevertheless, for me the Peace Corps' famous phrase really applies to writing—it's the hardest work I've ever loved." While for Jennifer Greene, writing is emotionally draining and endlessly demanding, fortunately for her many readers, it is the one job she wouldn't trade for anything in the world.

BIBLIOGRAPHY

Writing as Jennifer Greene

Books: *Body and Soul.* New York: Silhouette, 1986; *Foolish Pleasure.* New York: Silhouette, 1986; *Madam's Room.* New York: Silhouette, 1986; *Dear Reader.* New York: Silhouette, 1987; *Minx.* New York: Silhouette, 1987; *Lady Be Good.* New York: Silhouette, 1987; *Secrets.* New York: Silhouette, 1987; *Love Potion.* New York: Silhouette, 1988; *The Castle Keep.* New York: Silhouette, 1988; *Lady of the Island.* New York: Silhouette, 1988; *Night of the Hunter.* New York: Silhouette, 1989; *Devil's Night.* New York: Silhouette, 1989; *Dancing in the Dark.* New York: Silhouette, 1989; *Heat Wave.* New York: Silhouette, 1990; *Slow Dance.* New York: Silhouette, 1990; *Broken Blossom.* New York: Silhouette, 1990; *Night Light.* New York: Silhouette, 1991; *Falconer.* New York: Silhouette, 1991; *Just Like Old Times.* New York: Silhouette, 1992; *It Had to Be You.* New York: Silhouette, 1992; *Pink Topaz.* New York: Silhouette, 1992; *Quicksand.* New York: Silhouette, 1993; *Bewitched.* New York: Silhouette, 1994; *Bothered.* New York: Silhouette, 1994; *Bewildered.* New York: Silhouette, 1994; *Groom for Red Ridinghood.* New York: Silhouette, 1994; *Single Dad.* New York: Silhouette, 1995; *Arizona Heat.* New York: Silhouette, 1995; *The Unwilling Bride.* New York: Silhouette, 1996; *Bachelor Mom.* New York: Silhouette, 1996; *Nobody's Princess.* New York: Silhouette, 1997; *The 200% Wife.* New York: Silhouette, 1997; *Baby Chase.* Toronto: Harlequin, 1997; *A Baby in His In-box.* New York: Silhouette, 1998; *Her Holiday Secret.* New York: Silhouette, 1998; *The Honor Bound Groom.* New York: Silhouette, 1998; *Prince Charming's Child.* New York: Silhouette, 1999; *Kiss Your Prince Charming.* New York: Silhouette, 1999; *Rock Solid.* New York: Silhouette, 2000; *You Belong to Me.* Toronto: Harlequin, 2000; *Millionaire M.D.* New York: Silhouette, 2001; *The Woman Most Likely To ....* New York: Avon, 2002; *Wild in the Field.* New York: Silhouette, 2003; *Where Is He Now?* New York: Avon, 2003; *Wild in the Moonlight.* New York: Silhouette, 2004; *Wild in the Moment.* New York: Silhouette, 2004; *Lucky.* New York: Silhouette, 2005; *Hot to Touch.* New York: Silhouette, 2005; *Blame It on Chocolate.* Toronto: Harlequin, 2005; *Soon-to-be-Disinherited Wife.* New York: Silhouette, 2006; *Sparkle.* Toronto: Harlequin, 2006.

Novellas: "Riley's Baby" in *Birds, Bees, and Babies.* New York: Silhouette, 1993; "The Twelfth Night" in *Santa's Little Helpers.* New York: Silhouette, 1995; "Diana" in *Big Sky Brides.* New York: Silhouette, 2000; "The Christmas House" in *Gifts of Fortune.* New York: Silhouette, 2001.

Genre-Related Essay: "The Key Formula in Romance: A Woman's Quest" in *North American Romance Writers.* Lanham, MD: Scarecrow Press, 1999.

Writing as Jeanne Grant

Books: *Man from Tennessee.* New York: Jove, 1983; *A Daring Proposition.* New York: Jove, 1983; *Kisses from Heaven.* New York: Jove, 1984; *Sunburst.* New York: Jove, 1984; *Wintergreen.* New York: Jove, 1984; *Trouble in Paradise.* New York: Jove, 1984; *Silver and Spice.* New York: Jove, 1984; *Cupid's Confederates.* New York: Jove, 1984; *Conquer the Memories.* New York: Jove, 1984; *Ain't*

Misbehaving. New York: Berkley, 1985; *Can't Say No.* New York: Berkley, 1985; *Pink Satin.* New York: Berkley, 1985; *Sweets to the Sweet.* New York: Berkley, 1986; *No More Mr. Nice Guy.* New York: Berkley, 1986; *Tender Loving Care.* New York: Berkley, 1987.

Writing as Jessica Massey

Book: *Stormy Surrender.* New York: Dell, 1984.

JOHN CHARLES

LEIGH GREENWOOD

Leigh Greenwood. Courtesy of Leigh Greenwood.

Award-winning author Leigh Greenwood is somewhat of an anomaly among romance writers. "Leigh" is a he. His readers don't appear to hold that against Greenwood, whose real name is Harold Lowry. Since 1987, Greenwood has written more than 40 historical romance novels, including three Western series, The Cowboys, The Night Riders and The Seven Brides. For his prolific, yet high-quality efforts, he has twice been awarded the Carolina Romance Writers Author of the Year Award, two Maggie's, three Bookrak Bestseller Awards; and has been nominated for a Holt Medallion and a Romance Writers of America's RITA. Six of his characters have been awarded the *Romantic Times*' K.I.S.S. award. His loyal fans keep him in constant demand, and his works appear regularly on national best seller lists.

In his prewriting life, Greenwood attended the University of North Carolina, where he earned a bachelor's degree in voice, with a minor in history, and later, a master's degree in musicology. He was employed for 32 years as a professional music teacher. His wife was an avid romance reader, and Greenwood recalls that her novels were all over the house. Greenwood had long been a fan of the classics and considered romance novels to be condescending, until his wife challenged him to stop judging the covers and actually read one. The book was Georgette Heyer's *These Old Shades*. For Greenwood, it was an epiphany.

Until reading his first romance novel, Greenwood had never considered writing one. He didn't know much about the profession or the genre, but he was intrigued to learn that successful romance writers actually made more money than he made as a music teacher. Armed with this motivation, his interest in history, and the guidance he received from his involvement in Romance Writers of America, he began writing historic romances set in the Old West. His first published novel, *Wyoming Wildfire,* was released in 1987. Greenwood's relationship with RWA is reciprocal—he's donated great quantities of time and effort to the organization that got him started down the right path, even serving a two-year term as national president.

Greenwood writes full-time, with a daily goal of 12 to 16 pages. His greatest satisfaction as a writer is knowing that he alone controls the quality and success of his own work. He finds the words *The End* most gratifying to write.

The reason most other men don't share his interest in the romance genre, Greenwood believes, is simply because they've never read one, threatened by the repercussions of being outed as a romance reader. Some of his female fans have confided that their husbands also read Greenwood's novels, and he has several men on his mailing list.

Greenwood's advice to new writers is to "write every day and research diligently." Greenwood notes, "It takes much more than a few cowboys and dirty saloons to capture the flavor of a western town." He has visited each state that he has used as a setting in his novels and discovered that each has a uniqueness not found elsewhere in the country. He creates settings that are colorful, rich in detail, and historically accurate. In his preferred setting of the Old West, some towns are built around mining, others around cattle. Immigrant populations help to shape the culture and identity of the place, as well. By learning historical details about a prospective setting and weaving them into his plots, Greenwood adds realism to his stories that brings them to life. His careful research is evident in such books as those in his series The Cowboys. Greenwood is also known for his strong heroines. This includes Rose, from the book of the same name in the Seven Brides series, the first Randolph bride, a Yankee who brings order to a chaotic, Confederate, all-male household. Greenwood's later heroines are just as competent and determined. For example, Abby Pierce, a city girl and the heroine of *The Independent Bride* (2004) leaves St. Louis for a new life in the rugged wilds of Colorado, where Col. Bryce McGregor thinks she's too "civilized" to last.

The heroes in Greenwood's books often have emotional obstacles to overcome. In his books set after the Civil War, many of them are still affected by vivid memories of the battles and the animosities caused by the conflict. One of his heroes, Jeff Randolph, in *Violet* (1996) from the Seven Brides series, has lost his arm during the war and is drowning in a mixture of self-pity and hostility. The Seven Brides and The Cowboys series highlight two other themes found throughout Greenwood's works—ranching and the intricacies of family relationships.

Although he's best known for them, Greenwood doesn't limit himself to historicals. He has also written contemporary novels, such as *Family Merger* (2003), *Married by High Noon* (2000), and *Undercover Honeymoon* (2001) No matter what the setting, Greenwood's wit, subtle sense of humor, and insightful observations make his stories shine with creativity and originality.

Greenwood's wife of more than thirty years is a nurse who works in health-care maintenance, and they have three grown children. When he isn't writing, and sometimes when he is, Greenwood is the doorman for the family cat. A self-described househusband, he performs most of the household chores. Like most seasoned writers, Greenwood enjoys reading. In the meantime, Greenwood's fans are reading, too, devouring his wonderful Westerns and captivating contemporary novels and wanting another one as soon as they finish the one they have.

BIBLIOGRAPHY

Books: *Wyoming Wildlife.* New York: Kensington, 1987; *The Captain's Caress.* New York: Kensington, 1988; *Wicked Wyoming Night.* New York: Kensington, 1989; *Seductive Wager.* New York: Kensington, 1990; *Colorado Bride.* New York: Kensington, 1990; *Sweet Temptation.* New York: Kensington, 1991; *Scarlet Sunset, Silver Nights.* New York: Kensington, 1992; *Rebel Enchantress.* New York: Kensington, 1992; *Arizona Embrace.* New York: Kensington, 1993; *Rose.* New York: Dorchester, 1993; *Fern.* New York: Dorchester, 1994; *Iris.* New York: Dorchester, 1994; *Laurel.* New York: Dorchester, 1995; *Daisy.* New York: Dorchester, 1995; *Violet.* New York: Dorchester, 1996; *Lily.* New York: Dorchester, 1996; *Jake.* New York: Dorchester, 1997; *Ward.* New York: Dorchester, 1997; *Only You.* Toronto: Harlequin, 1997; *Buck.* New York: Dorchester, 1998; *Chet.* New York: Dorchester, 1998; *Just What the Doctor Ordered.* New York: Silhouette, 1999; *Sean.* New York: Dorchester, 1999; *The Winner's Circle.* New York: Kensington, 1999; *Pete.* New York: Dorchester, 1999; *Married by High Noon.* New York: Silhouette, 2000; *Love on the Run.* New York: Kensington, 2000; *Drew.* New York: Dorchester, 2000; *Luke.* New York: Dorchester, 2000; *Undercover Honeymoon.* New York: Silhouette, 2001; *Matt.* New York: Dorchester, 2001; *Texas Homecoming.* New York: Dorchester, 2002; *Texas Bride.* New York: Dorchester, 2002; *Family Merger.* New York: Silhouette, 2003; *Born to Love.* New York: Dorchester, 2003; *The Independent Bride.* New York: Dorchester, 2004; *The Reluctant Bride.* New York: Dorchester, 2005; *The Mavericks.* New York: Dorchester, 2005; *Bret.* New York: Dorchester, 2006; *A Texan's Honor.* New York: Dorchester, 2006.

Novellas: "Fairy-Tale Christmas" in *An Old-Fashioned Southern Christmas.* New York: Dorchester, 1994; "Father Christmas" in *Their First Noel.* New York: Dorchester, 1995; "Bah, Humbug!" in *The Christmas Spirit.* New York: Dorchester, 1997; "Here Comes Santa Claus" in *Winter Wonderland.* New York: Love Spell, 1999.

SANDRA VAN WINKLE

SHIRLEY HAILSTOCK

Shirley Hailstock. Courtesy of Shirley
Hailstock.

As a child growing up in Buffalo, New York, Shirley Hailstock set her goals high, some would even say lofty, as she aspired to become the first female astronaut. Toward that end, Hailstock went on to study chemistry and math in college, and earned a bachelor's degree from Howard University. She rounded out her education with an associate of business administration degree from Benjamin Franklin University and a master's degree in business administration from Fairleigh Dickinson University. Even though Hailstock hasn't made it to the stars yet, she has sent her readers on wonderful trips around the globe.

Hailstock was born in Newberry, South Carolina, in 1948 to Hattie and Eugene Hailstock, and has two children, Ashleigh and Christopher. Although she has always enjoyed writing, she never dreamed she would become an accomplished novelist. When asked about what started her writing, Hailstock says, "I wrote my first book on a dare from a fellow romance reader." She focuses on writing romances and suspense novels, the types of books she most enjoys reading, although she has also written short stories, novellas, poetry, and various nonfiction articles.

Hailstock's novels are known for their multidimensional African American characters, who effectively destroy any racial stereotypes the reader might have. Rich in multiculturalism, Hailstock's books are among the very few novels published by Silhouette that feature African Americans on the cover.

Hailstock often includes the themes of "truth, justice and the American way" in her novels, and finds that using suspenseful plots enables justice to prevail and the bad guys to always get their due. Along with these themes go the qualities of honor and courage, two traits her heroes and heroines have in abundance. Her first published novel, *Whispers of Love* (1994) was a romantic suspense in which Robyn Richards, a former FBI agent must enter the federal Witness Protection Program. In order to protect her family from retaliation after she exposes an assassination ring, Robyn's death is faked, and she receives facial surgery and a new identity, plunging her into protective anonymity. However, years later, she learns her daughter has developed a life-threatening illness that requires a rare compatible donor. To save her daughter's life, she is compelled to resurface and reconnect with her husband, who thinks she is dead. Meanwhile, the assassins have not forgotten or forgiven Robyn, and they menacingly stalk the resurfaced agent and her daughter. With this debut novel, Hailstock demonstrated a true flair for mixing desire and danger.

The federal Witness Protection Program is also used in Hailstock's novel *You Made Me Love You* (2005), in which Rachel Wells returns to the town of Lake Como, where she and her family were declared dead in a boating accident nine years earlier. Tired of living a lie, Rachel wants to return to her old life and restore the family's abandoned cabin. Meanwhile, the town sheriff, Samuel Hairston, has more than a few questions for the resurrected Rachel, along with a strong attraction to her. Rachel finds herself with these same feelings of desire, except, oddly, she doesn't like the man. The fine blend of passion, tension, intrigue, and peril is quintessential Hailstock.

For Hailstock, the writing process is based in plotting. She says, "I usually get the plot first. I have to find the characters to go with the story." Even though the plot comes to Hailstock first, she says that creating the characters is the best part of the process. She loves discovering the people and finding out who they are and how they act in each situation. She says it is like discovering a new friend or a sister, and for the heroes, it's like finding the ideal man. Occasionally, when a character develops in her mind first without a story, she says it can take years to discover a plot that will fit.

She recalls, "The character Michael in my book *Legacy* (1997) was like that. It took me three years to find a book for him." In *Legacy,* Erika St. James, the poster girl of bad relationships, discovers that her late guardian has named her coheir to his fortune, but there's a catch. She must share his mansion for 12 months with his grandson, attorney Michael Lawrence, or lose the inheritance. Not a problem, except that Michael never knew his grandfather or that he had an inheritance he stood to gain, and his bitterness over his irreparably damaged career has left him withdrawn and jaded. He declines the lovely Erika's proposal, until he discovers that in doing so, she will be disinherited, and the family fortune will fall into the hands of his nemesis, Frank Mason, a murderous psychopath. Thrust together into this odd co-ed arrangement, the reluctant heroine and the wounded hero find romance and healing amid the suspense. The family unit, even one like Michael and Erika's, which has been fractured and put back together, is a recurring theme in Hailstock's novels.

Of her heroines, Hailstock says, "[They] tend to be strong, take-charge women. I would say they get that from me." This is evident in her novels *Clara's Promise* (1995); *Mirror Image* (1998); and *His 1–800-WIFE* (2001). In *Mirror Image,* Aurora Alexander, the spitting image of actress and talk-show host Marsha Chambers, receives a death threat from a menacing stalker intended for the haughty, mean-spirited actress. After being a guest on the Chambers show, Aurora is nearly kidnapped outside the studio by the stalker. Gallant, handsome television producer Duncan West comes to her rescue, and she falls hard for him. The attraction between them is immediate and intense. In order to catch the stalker, Aurora agrees to become the bait, and she fills in on Chamber's talk show to lure the stalker back into the open. Meanwhile, Duncan can only watch and wait, yearning to have sweet Aurora safe again in his arms.

The romance genre appeals to Hailstock because of the variety of subgenres. She notes that for every type of writing, there is a romance version: historical, paranormal, futuristic, science fiction, mystery, inspirational, and suspense. Hailstock says, "I don't have to leave the genre in order to find the kind of books I like to read." Hailstock's favorite time period varies between contemporary and historical. She notes, "I have a book (*Clara's Promise*) set in Montana in 1899." In *Clara's Promise,* a runaway girl becomes a teacher in Waymon Valley, Montana, where her matchmaking aunt tries to pair her up with sworn bachelor, architect/carpenter Luke Evans. Hailstock goes on to say, "I also have a mainstream [novel] I'm working on that's set during the Depression of the 1930s. There are so many interesting periods of time that I wouldn't want to limit myself to one, although going back in time past the sixteenth century is difficult for me."

In the beginning, Hailstock thought that writing would be easy, but she now knows it's the most difficult thing she's ever tried. Hailstock says the hardest of her novels to write was her unsold mainstream book. She says, "It took me years to work through formatting, characters, point-of-view preferences … Many frustrations happened with that book, but it's finished now, and I'm proud of the blood I spilled to get it in the shape it's in." Ironically, this is also Hailstock's favorite work.

Hailstock says the book that took the least amount of time to write was *White Diamonds* (1996) because she was up against a short deadline. Of that experience, she says, "I didn't angst over the right words. I just wrote. I made the deadline, and I believe it's one of my best books." *White Diamonds* is the story of Senator Wyatt Randolph, who has a hit on his life because his murdered friend left him a fortune in diamonds. When he finds out about the hit and tries to figure out who's been hired to kill him, he's stabbed and left for dead during a terrible snowstorm. College professor Sandra Rutledge has gone to her family's cabin in the mountains to study for her PhD. When she finds Wyatt, wounded and bleeding, she takes him inside and nurses him to health. Wyatt is attracted to Sandra, but his feelings are tempered by the fact that she's the daughter of the man whom he suspects wants him dead. Hailstock weaves a tight tale of suspense as she explores a variation of the theme, Is the friend of my enemy, my enemy? Hailstock says, "The government is so ripe for fiction. It can be the good guys or bad guys. The government has its hands in everything, so using it as a backdrop is always interesting."

The inspiration for each of Hailstock's books is different. Her muse comes from a love of what she does—writing and creating characters and stories. She is also inspired by her fans. She says, "[The fans] get very involved in the characters' lives and want more stories, not necessarily about the same people, but about people they can connect with. I find this a great reason to produce new stories." With that kind of inspiration, Hailstock has never had writer's block. She says, "I have so many plots that need writing that I could keep busy for years. I hope I never run out."

For example, the recent state of corporate layoffs was the inspiration for *Opposites Attract* (1999). In this book, Averal Ballantine is hired as a professional hatchet man to cut the workforce in the corporation where Nefertiti Kincaide is employed. Even though her job is at risk, she feels an odd attraction toward him. She discovers this cold-hearted hatchet man has a soft side, when she learns that he helps those who have lost their jobs find even better ones. However, Averal has his own problems and emotional demons from a troubled past that he must face before he can commit to a relationship with the beautiful Nefertiti. In a world where job displacement is an everyday occurrence, many of Hailstock's readers could identify with the characters in the novel.

Hailstock has won many awards: the *Romantic Times* Career Achievement Award; the Holt Medallion (for *Whispers of Love*); Waldenbooks Bestselling Multicultural Romance; and inclusion in the "100 Greatest Romances of the 20th Century" (for *Legacy*). Hailstock has won more than awards, though—she has won a legion of fans, and for her, that's more important than all of her accolades combined.

BIBLIOGRAPHY

Books: *Whispers of Love*. New York: Kensington, 1994; *Clara's Promise*. New York: Kensington, 1995; *White Diamonds*. New York: Kensington, 1996; *Legacy*. New York: Kensington, 1997; *Mirror Image*. New York: BET, 1998; *Opposites Attract*. New York: BET, 1999; *More Than Gold*. New York: BET, 2000; *His 1–800 WIFE*. New York: BET, 2001; *A Family Affair*. New York: BET, 2002; *A Father's Fortune*. New York: Silhouette, 2003; *Love on Call*. New York: Silhouette, 2004; *You Made Me Love You*. New York: Kensington, 2005; *Magnetic Hearts*. New York: BET, 2005; *The Secret*. New York: Kensington, 2006; *My Friend, My Lover*. New York: Kimani Press, 2006.

Novellas: "Invitation to Love" in *Holiday Cheer*. New York: Kensington, 1995; "The Engagement" in *I Do!* New York: Kensington, 1998; "Kwanzaa Angel" in *Winter Nights*. New York: Kensington, 1998; "An Estate of Marriage" in *Island Magic*. New York: St. Martin's Press, 2000; "The Bad Penny" in *Where There's a Will*. New York: Kensington, 2004.

SANDRA VAN WINKLE, SHELLEY MOSLEY, AND SHANNON PRESCOTT

PRISCILLA HAMILTON. *See* Roberta Gellis

JOANNA HAMPTON. *See* Jo Ann Ferguson

SARAH HART. *See* Maureen Child

ROBIN LEE HATCHER

Robin Lee Hatcher. Courtesy of Robin Lee Hatcher.

Robin Lee Hatcher is a veteran storyteller of contemporary, historical, and Christian fiction, with over forty published works and an estimated six million copies in print worldwide. Her impressive list of awards and achievements spans two decades, including two RITA awards for Best Inspirational Romance and two *Romantic Times* Career Achievement Awards for Inspirational Romance and Americana Historical Romance. She has also earned a Christy Award for Excellence is Christian Fiction, a Romance Writers of America Lifetime Achievement Award, and a host of other accolades.

Hatcher recalls from her childhood in Boise, Idaho, that she had developed a talent for storytelling early in life. In what was perhaps her first attempt at historical romance, she convinced her fifth grade schoolmates that her mother was born in a covered wagon traveling west on the Oregon Trail. Clearly, fiction was in her future. Her colorful imagination was fueled by an insatiable love of reading, and throughout high school, she wrote habitually, covering her notebooks with doodled stories and poems. Other creative interests included ballet dancing, which she studied for seven years, performing in school and local theater productions. She was also an avid horse enthusiast, raising them and riding them competitively.

---

also writing as Robin Leigh

Hatcher continued dabbling in her writing pursuits into adulthood, while also working in a local business office and raising two daughters. It was during this time that she began developing a story idea for her first book, *Stormy Surrender* (1984). She completed the book in only nine months, despite having handwritten it on legal pads and then having transcribed it during her lunch breaks. Two years after it was completed, the book was published, and her career as a writer was officially underway.

Hatcher finds that plot ideas are easy to come by, with possibilities popping up everywhere—in ordinary places, everyday events, and human struggles. Rather than planning the plot's outcome, Hatcher lets each story develop as she writes and watches the plot unfold on its own, often branching out in unexpected directions. She is just as curious as her readers to discover how the story will end. The history of the American West provides inspiration for many of her books, including the suffrage movement (*Kiss Me Katie,* 1996; *Catching Katie,* 2003) and Spanish and Mexican land grants (*Midnight Rose,* 1992, which features a masked hero much like Zorro). The struggle of immigrants to create a new life in a new land forms the basis for her Coming to America series: *Dear Lady* (1997)—about an English immigrant to Montana; *Patterns of Love* (1998)—about a Swedish immigrant to Iowa; and *In His Arms* (1998)—about an Irish immigrant to Idaho.

The heroines in Hatcher's books are strong and resourceful. *Liberty Blue* (1995), for example, features a woman who flees her domineering father, comes west, and runs her own ranch. *Ribbon of Years* (2001) chronicles a woman from ages 15 to 80, and once again, the heroine's strength is evident at all stages of her life.

Among her many notable accomplishments, Hatcher feels that her most inspired works are her Christian fiction books. She experienced a turning point in 1991, when she realized the power and opportunity she possessed as a writer to enlighten and change the lives of her readers, and she made the transition from secular to inspirational works, producing award-winning books in both areas. Her unshakable belief and her close relationship with God are immediately evident in her writing and lectures, and she is happy to share her story of faith and inspiration with others. She has rewritten and reissued several of her older, more sensual novels to reflect her change in philosophy. Examples of this are *Kiss Me Katie,* her 1996 novel about a suffragist, which was reworked into *Catching Katie* in 2004, and her Coming to America series, which she revised and published with Zondervan, a major religious press. She encourages readers to select the revised versions of her books. In short, faith has become the major emphasis of her writing.

Hatcher defines good fiction, as writing that "will provide a memorable reading experience that captures the imagination, inspires, challenges, and educates." In the Christian genre, the storyteller uses the temptations and conflicts found in everyday life to lead the reader toward spiritual growth and hope. Hatcher finds this calling most rewarding.

BIBLIOGRAPHY

Writing as Robin Lee Hatcher

Books: *Stormy Surrender.* New York: Dorchester, 1984; *Heart's Landing.* New York: Dorchester, 1984; *Thorn of Love.* New York: Dorchester, 1985; *Heart Storm.* New York: Dorchester, 1986; *Passion's Gamble.* New York: Dorchester, 1986; *Pirate's Lady.* New York: Dorchester, 1987; *Gem Fire.* New York: Dorchester, 1988; *The Wager.* New York: Dorchester, 1989; *Dream Tide.* New York: Dorchester, 1990; *Promised Sunrise.* New York: Dorchester, 1990; *Promise Me Spring.* New York: Dorchester, 1991; *Devlin's Promise.* New York: Dorchester, 1992; *Midnight Rose.* New York: Dorchester, 1992; *The Magic.* New York: Dorchester, 1993; *Where the Heart Is.* New York: Dorchester, 1993; *Forever,*

Rose. New York: Dorchester, 1994; *Remember When.* New York: Dorchester, 1994; *A PurrFect Romance.* Farmington Hills, Michigan: Wheeler, 1995; *Liberty Blue.* New York: Harper, 1995; *Chances Are.* New York: Harper, 1996; *Kiss Me Katie.* New York: Harper, 1996; *Dear Lady.* New York: Harper, 1997; *Patterns of Love.* New York: Harper, 1998; *In His Arms.* New York: Harper, 1998; *The Forgiving Hour.* Colorado Springs, CO: Waterbrook, 1999; *Hometown Girl.* New York: Silhouette, 1999; *Taking Care of the Twins.* New York: Silhouette, 1999; *Whispers from Yesterday.* Colorado Springs, CO: Waterbrook, 1999; *Daddy Claus.* New York: Silhouette, 1999; *The Shepherd's Voice.* Colorado Springs, CO: Waterbrook, 2000; *Ribbon of Years.* Wheaton, IL: Tyndale House, 2001; *Firstborn.* Wheaton, IL: Tyndale House, 2002; *Promised to Me.* New York: Zondervan, 2003; *Speak to Me of Love.* Wheaton, IL: Tyndale House, 2003; *Catching Katie.* Wheaton, IL: Tyndale House, 2003; *Legacy Lane.* New York: Revell, 2004; *Beyond the Shadows.* Wheaton, IL: Tyndale House, 2004; *Veteran's Way.* New York: Revell, 2005; *The Victory Club.* Wheaton, IL: Tyndale House, 2005; *Loving Libby.* New York: Zondervan, 2005; *Another Chance to Love You.* New York: Steeple Hill, 2006; *Diamond Place.* New York: Baker, 2006.

Novellas: "A Christmas Angel" in *A Frontier Christmas.* New York: Dorchester, 1992; "Heart Rings" in *The Story Jar.* New York: Multnomah, 2001.

Writing as Robin Leigh

Books: *Rugged Splendor.* New York: Avon, 1991; *The Hawk and the Heather.* New York: Avon, 1992.

SANDRA VAN WINKLE

RACHEL HAWTHORNE. *See* Lorraine Heath

LORRAINE HEATH

Lorraine Heath. Courtesy of Lorraine Heath.

Lorraine Heath was a budding novelist at the age of seven, when she began writing her first story about a man who fell in love with a mermaid. The story was never finished, but an important lesson was learned years later, after the hit movie *Splash!* was released, and Heath observed, "unfinished stories don't have any chance of finding success." A decade and more than twenty novels later, she hasn't missed another opportunity.

It is no small irony that Lorraine Heath, one of the premiere writers of romances set in the Old West, is from Great Britain. Heath was born in Watford, Hertfordshire, England, in January 1954, where her parents met following World War II. The family later moved to the United States, settling in Angleton, Texas, where Heath grew up. While in school, she worked summers at a recreational vehicle campground, and she was employed for a time in food service while attending the University of Texas at Austin. In 1976, she earned a bachelor's degree in psychology and married the love of her life. After graduation, Heath spent the next 24 working for the federal government, holding various positions with the Internal Revenue Service and the Veteran's Administration, "none of which," she says, "will ever appear in one of my stories."

---

also writing as Rachel Hawthorne

Heath's degree in psychology, on the other hand, would prove to be useful to her as a writer, helping her create believable people with real problems. She enjoys exploring her characters' emotions and pasts. Heath allows her characters to emerge on their own, usually beginning with a situation or simple dialogue that only the character can explain. "I try to give the characters the freedom to tell the story, in their own way—which probably makes me sound a bit unbalanced; but my characters are very real to me," says Heath.

As in real life, Heath's characters have issues. In *As an Earl Desires* (2005), for example, the problems of spousal abuse and illiteracy are both explored. Other titles deal with such issues as single parenthood, dying, and infidelity. Heath digs deep into each character's psyche, creating three-dimensional heroes and heroines that come to life on the pages of her books, and these strong characterizations engage all of the reader's emotions.

Heath had always enjoyed writing relationship stories but never considered them to be romances. She was an admitted cover-judger who had little interest in the genre. It wasn't until she accidentally discovered LaVyrle Spencer's *Morning Glory,* that she realized the stories in her head were romances. She was so impressed by the depth of the characters and the strength of the emotions that she began reading two and three romances every week. She recalls thinking, "If only I could write as well as these authors." After frequent appearances on a variety of national best seller lists, her legion of avid readers would say she has arrived.

Heath has two locales she prefers to use in her novels, returning to her roots in England and Texas. Most of her stories are set in the late nineteenth century, often focusing on the importance of family and always involving experiences relevant to the time period. However, in 2003, Heath made a surprising departure from her popular historical romances with *Hard Lovin' Man,* the first book in the Hard Lovin' series, her contemporary romance trilogy. Even with this change of venue, it was apparent that her strong characterizations and stories that engaged all the reader's emotions were just as successful in a different time period. Set in the aptly named Hopeful, Texas, this is the story of schoolteacher Kelley Spencer, who has come home to raise Madison, her orphaned 16-year-old sister. Police chief Jack Morgan sees Kelley for the first time in years when he arrests Madison for underage drinking. Jack, a former student of Kelley's and now divorced, had a relationship with her after his graduation. Kelley called it off when they found out that his former girlfriend was pregnant. This tale of second-time-around love shows that Heath's creativity and versatility shine, no matter what the setting.

As a reading hobbyist, Heath often references the classics in her novels or portrays one of her characters reading. One such heroine, 21-year-old Lydia, from *Love with a Scandalous Lord* (2003), has come to England with her stepfather, Grayson Rhodes (first introduced in *A Rogue in Texas,* 1999). Fourteen years have passed since Grayson, the illegitimate son of a duke and an actress, has been exiled to Fortune, Texas. Now Grayson's been called back to his father's ancestral home to be at his deathbed, and he's brought his family. With the duke's oldest legitimate son drowned, the second son, Rhys, the Marquess of Blackhurst, will inherit the title. Lydia is smitten by the rakish Rhys and is confident she can hook him, because she's brought *Blunders in Behavior Corrected,* her trusty guidebook, to help her deal with London society. Although Rhys is quite taken by his half brother's stepdaughter, the "Gentleman Seducer," as he's come to be called, believes his past is far too scandalous to begin a relationship with her. Wanting to find a better man for Lydia than himself, Rhys sponsors her for a season on London's marriage market. Unimpressed by Rhys' peers, Lydia refuses to give up her goal of marriage to him. As so many of Heath's heroines, this obstinate, persistent woman will settle for nothing less than the man she wants.

Heath's heroes and heroines both exhibit some of Heath's own personality traits, but mainly reflect those that she only wishes she had. Her heroes adore the women they love and would do anything for them. This is certainly true of Houston Leigh from *Texas Destiny* (1997). A broken leg prevents Houston's brother, Dallas, from meeting his mail-order fiancée, Miss Amelia Carson, at the train station, so he sends Houston to take his place. Dallas figures it's safe for Houston to make the long journey with Amelia because his face is so scarred and disfigured from a Civil War battle that no woman could possibly want him. What Dallas hasn't taken into account is Amelia's ability to see past a man's appearance to his inner character and beauty. Houston falls in love with the woman who has courageously survived war-torn Georgia, has come to a strange land, and is willing to marry Dallas, a man she only knows through his correspondence. As much as Houston loves Amelia, and she loves him, their honor stands in the way of a relationship. This powerfully written book is the first of the emotionally gripping Leigh Brothers series: *Texas Destiny* (1997), *Texas Glory* (1998), and *Texas Splendor* (1998).

The heroines in Heath's books long for love and acceptance. They're usually strong, determined, and fearless, as is the case with Serena Hamilton, the heroine of *Smooth Talkin' Stranger* (2004), the second book of her contemporary series. Serena is the widow of the hero's best friend in *Hard Lovin' Man*, book one of the series. Her mother has died, and Serena has come home to help her father. Serena's husband has been dead for six years, but she's still grieving for him. Feeling lonely one evening, she stops into a bar and goes home with a stranger, something she's never done before. Hunter Fletcher, an operative for the CIA, is secretive both by nature and training, so he can't bring himself to open up to Serena. Between guilt on both their parts and Hunter's reluctance to share his past, their relationship looks hopeless. The sensitively written descriptions of their innermost thoughts and the poignancy of Serena's grief and healing is quintessential Heath.

Although Heath doesn't have a favorite among her novels, she says she is "incredibly proud" of her 1996 work, *Always to Remember*. Based on an actual incident of a Civil War prisoner who avoided execution when he said a heartfelt prayer for the firing squad, this is the story of sculptor Clayton Holland, a conscientious objector who supported neither the North nor the South during the War between the States. Because of his beliefs, Clayton is branded a traitor and sentenced to be executed. Like the real-life prisoner, Clayton's prayers touch the hearts of his would-be executioners, and they let him live. When the war ends, Clayton returns to his home in Cedar Grove to much ridicule and tormenting. Everyone thinks he's a coward, including Meg Warner. To make him pay for his cowardice, Meg commissions a memorial for the town's fallen heroes in hopes that as Clayton carves the names of her father and brothers, among others, he'll be overwhelmed by guilt. Although set in the period directly after the Civil War, this book, with its theme that sometimes it takes more courage not to fight than to take up arms, has a timelessness and universality that make it ring true for any postwar period. Heath won both a RITA and a Holt Medallion for this deeply moving tale.

In 2002, Heath began to write historical romances for the young adult market under the name Lorraine Heath. (At the time, she was already writing contemporary romances for teens as Rachel Hawthorne.) Heath's 2002 book, *Samantha and the Cowboy*, an historical Western, launched Avon's True Romance line, specifically designed for that age group. Heath also wrote *Amelia and the Outlaw* (2003) for the same line. As Rachel Hawthorne, Heath continued to write contemporary romances for teens, including *Caribbean Cruising*, 2004; *Island Girls (and Boys)*, 2005; *Love on the Lifts*, 2005; and *Thrill Ride!* 2006.

Heath finds story ideas from her own experiences, from the people she knows or reads about, and she enjoys sharing these touching stories with her readers. Heath compares beginning a new novel to the experience of childbirth, saying there's "a lot of screaming, sweating, [and] pain; but when you hold the baby in your arms, it's all worth it." For Heath, a story starts slowly, an impossible task, and she wonders how it will ever be completed. In time, however, the novel begins to take shape, until eventually it's finished, and she thinks, "That wasn't so hard."

BIBLIOGRAPHY

Writing as Lorraine Heath

Books: *Parting Gifts.* New York: Diamond, 1994; *Sweet Lullaby.* New York: Diamond, 1994; *The Ladies' Man.* New York: Jove, 1995; *Always to Remember.* New York: Jove, 1996; *Texas Destiny.* New York: Topaz, 1997; *Texas Glory.* New York: Topaz, 1998; *Texas Splendor.* New York: Topaz, 1998; *A Rogue in Texas.* New York: Avon, 1999; *Never Love a Cowboy.* New York: Avon, 2000; *Never Marry a Cowboy.* New York: Avon, 2001; *The Outlaw and the Lady.* New York: Avon, 2001; *Samantha and the Cowboy.* New York: Avon, 2002; *To Marry an Heiress.* New York: Avon, 2002; *Love with a Scandalous Lord.* New York: Avon, 2003; *Amelia and the Outlaw.* New York: Avon, 2003; *Hard Lovin' Man.* New York: Pocket, 2003; *An Invitation to Seduction.* New York: Avon, 2004; *Smooth Talkin' Stranger.* New York: Pocket, 2004; *As an Earl Desires.* New York: Avon, 2005; *A Matter of Temptation.* New York: Avon, 2005; Promise *Me Forever.* New York: Avon, 2006.

Novellas: "Long Stretch of Lonesome" in *To Tame a Texan.* New York: St. Martin's Press, 1999; "The Reluctant Hero" in *My Heroes Have Always Been Cowboys.* New York: Kensington, 2006.

Genre-Related Essay: "Gentle Heroes" in *North American Romance Writers.* Lanham, MD: Scarecrow Press, 1999.

Writing as Rachel Hawthorne

Books: *London: Kit and Robin.* New York: Bantam, 2000; *Paris: Alex and Dana.* New York: Bantam, 2000; *Rome: Antonio and Carrie.* New York: Bantam, 2000; *The Older Guy.* New York: Bantam, 2000; *Nick and the Nerd.* New York: Bantam, 2001; *Caribbean Cruising.* New York: Avon, 2004; *Island Girls (and Boys).* New York: Avon, 2005; *Love on the Lifts.* New York: Avon, 2005; *Thrill Ride!* New York: Avon, 2006.

SHELLEY MOSLEY AND SANDRA VAN WINKLE

CANDICE HERN

Candice Hern. Courtesy of Candice Hern.

Candice Hern was born to write Regency romances, despite being 200 years too late to actually live the Regency lifestyle. Using her extensive knowledge of the Regency era, her research skills, and her own witty writing style, Hern brings the glittering and graceful era alive.

Hern was born in Houston, Texas, in 1950. Her parents were married during World War II, a week before her father was shipped to England as a member of the Army Air Corps. Three weeks later, his plane was shot down over the Netherlands. He bailed out and was rescued by the Dutch underground, who kept him hidden for several months until the Allies liberated the town. All that time, her mother did not know that he was safe. She still has the MIA telegram from the Army.

Hern grew up in Houston and moved to Southern California when she was eight. She attended the University of California at Santa Barbara, where she received her bachelor's degree in art history. She continued on to the University of California at Berkeley, where she completed her master's degree in art history.

Before becoming a writer, Hern worked in the high-tech industry in Silicon Valley. Her last job, before quitting to write full-time, was as the directory of marketing operations for a software company. "I was 40 before the notion [of wanting to be a writer] entered my mind," says Hern. "But once I began, I realized that I had found, at last, what I truly wanted to do in life."

Hern actually sold her first novel before it was completed. The book, *A Proper Companion,* began life as an entry in several local Romance Writers of America contests, where it drew the attention of an editor at Berkley/Jove. The editor liked the entry so much that she requested the whole manuscript. *A Proper Companion* was published by Jove in 1995 and became the first in a loosely connected trilogy of books featuring three best friends: Robert Cameron, Jack Raeburn, and Colin "Sedge" Herriot. In *A Proper Companion,* newly affianced Robert Cameron, the Earl of Bradleigh, agrees to assist his grandmother, the Dowager Countess, in finding a suitable husband for her paid companion, Emily Townsend. What Robert doesn't suspect is that the Countess has already chosen a husband for Emily, and that it is Robert. *A Proper Companion* demonstrated Hern's gift for sparkling dialogue, deft characterizations, and elegant writing style, wrapped around a sweetly satisfying love story.

After completing the two other books in the trilogy, *A Change of Heart* (1995) and *An Affair of Honor* (1996), Hern began work on *A Garden Folly* (1997), which she says was inspired by the classic 1953 movie *How to Marry a Millionaire.* Hern noted the similarities between the film characters' search for rich husbands and the necessity in the Regency era for women to marry well: "Because all my heroines are products of their time, several are actively seeking a husband, like Catherine in *A Garden Folly* or Isabel in *Her Scandalous Affair* (2004). It was difficult to be a woman alone during the Regency [era]. Women were financially dependent upon the men in their lives, but, in the case of Catherine and Isabel, the need is for security, not romantic love. In the end, they happily find both."

A Garden Folly features the two Forsythe sisters, smart and sensible Catherine and sweet but simple Susannah. Catherine believes that the key to their family's financial future is for the sisters to both marry well. When, by chance, the two receive invitations to the Duke of Carlisle's house party, the sisters seize the opportunity to go husband hunting. Their hopes for advantageous matches are first dashed when Susannah falls in love with the impoverished but respectable cousin of the Duke of Carlisle. Their hopes are destroyed yet again when Catherine finds herself torn between accepting a worthy offer from a wealthy earl or succumbing to the kisses of the Duke's handsome gardener. In *A Garden Folly,* Hern used her extensive research into the estates and gardens of the Regency era to create a fascinating backdrop for her witty, wonderful, and richly emotional romance.

In her last traditional Regency romance, *Miss Lacey's Last Fling* (2001), Hern decided that she was going to write about a young woman who believes she has six months to live. Hern says of the character, "Rather than fret, she decides to use every minute and live it to the fullest extent possible. For her hero, I decided her opposite would be a man who had seen it all and done it all, a man who had spent a lifetime living it up, but now was so bored, he was contemplating ending it all." In this book, Rosalind Lacey has devoted her life to caring for her father and her motherless siblings, forgoing a season in London and a marriage and family of her own. When she believes she has contracted the same disease that killed her mother, she decides to take what time she has left to live the life she has always wanted. Her first step is a trip to London to visit her scandalous Aunt Fanny, who introduces her to jaded rake Max Davenant, who, to his own surprise, proves to be a willing volunteer to help Rosalind with her plan to do everything on her list before she dies. While the initial idea of a heroine facing her own demise might seem depressing, Hern brilliantly uses the plot to make this romance a heartwarming and laughter-laced tale of a woman finally realizing her own worth and the need to explore all of life's opportunities.

In 2002, with the publication of *The Bride Sale,* Hern made the switch from traditional Regencies to Regency historicals and never looked back. Inspired by an article of a real-life incident in a London newspaper of 1814, Hern opens *The Bride Sale* with a memorable scene of a young wife, Verity Osborne, about to be auctioned off to settle her husband's debts. James Harkness, known as "Lord Heartless," is unexpectedly touched by the young woman's plight and appalled by the thought of her being purchased by the town's most repugnant bachelor, so he steps in with the winning bid. But now, James has no idea what he is going to do with Verity, his new bride. The setting of the book, beautiful and bleak Cornwall, perfectly complements Hern's compelling tale of old secrets and the healing power of love.

The Bride Sale was a radical departure from her previous sparkling Regency romances. Hern says, "[It was] the most difficult book for me to write. The themes of pain and redemption and healing are much darker than my usual light comedies. My natural voice is lighthearted, and I had to rein in that tendency in writing a darker book. It was a story I wanted to tell though, and I am glad I wrote it; but it did require a modification of my writer's voice, and I was not as comfortable with it. However, *The Bride Sale* is so far my best-selling book. Perhaps, I should dip my toe into dark waters once again someday."

Hern followed *The Bride Sale* with a loosely connected trilogy featuring a Regency-era ladies fashion magazine. In *Once a Scoundrel* (2003), the second book of the trilogy, rakish Anthony Morehouse initially thinks he has won a piece of furniture when he wins The Ladies Fashionable Cabinet in a card game. After discovering that he is actually the new owner of a popular women's fashion magazine, Anthony intends to turn over ownership to the magazine's current editor, whom he believes is a dried-up spinster. When Anthony meets the magazine editor, lovely Edwina Parrish, and realizes that she is his old childhood friend and nemesis (and far from dried-up), he decides to use this opportunity to pay her back for all the humiliations she inflicted on him in their youth. Spirited and strong-willed, Edwina Parrish is an excellent example of Hern's brand of an independent, self-sufficient heroine. The book's sparkling dialogue, luscious sensuality, lively writing, and fascinating use of historical details earned *Once a Scoundrel* a place on the Romance Writers of America's Top Ten Favorite Romances of 2003.

In 2006, Hern's first book in her Merry Widows trilogy, the elegantly written *In the Thrill of the Night,* was published. The trilogy features five friends and widows, all members of the Benevolent Widows Fund. Since the women are all financially secure, they need never marry again; but a few of the widows are reluctant to give up the physical aspects of marriage. At a board meeting, they debate the merits of taking a lover. After listening to one of the women discuss the pleasure derived from her latest lover, Marianne Nesbitt, who loved her late husband dearly, now wonders if something had been missing from her "perfect" marriage. Once Marianne decides to take a lover, she realizes that she doesn't know how to go about getting one, so she asks her best friend, renowned rake Adam Cazanove, to teach her the art of seduction. With her book *In The Thrill of Night,* Hern uses both Marianne's strong friendships with the other women of the club and her growing romantic relationship with Adam to subtly and skillfully explore the roles of friendship and love in a woman's life.

With Candice Hern, writing about the Regency era has proved to be a perfect fit. But, while she is known and loved for the sparkling wit, expertly crafted settings, and beautifully nuanced characters in both her traditional Regency romances and her Regency historicals, perhaps the most important ingredient in all of her books is hope. Hern says, "Romance novels provide a measure of hopefulness that appeals to me. Yes, there are times when we like to tug [at readers'] heartstrings and make them cry, but we never leave them heartbroken. Moments of sadness and poignancy will ultimately lead to a fulfilling, satisfying, uplifting, happy ending."

BIBLIOGRAPHY

Books: *A Proper Companion.* New York: Jove, 1995; *A Change of Heart.* New York: Signet, 1995; *An Affair of Honor.* New York: Signet, 1996; *A Garden Folly.* New York: Signet, 1997; *The Best Intentions.* New York: Signet, 1999; *Miss Lacey's Last Fling.* New York: Signet, 2001; *The Bride Sale.* New York: Avon, 2002; *Once a Dreamer.* New York: Avon, 2003; *Once a Scoundrel.* New York: Avon, 2003; *Once a Gentleman.* New York: Avon, 2004; *Her Scandalous Affair.* New York: Avon, 2004; *In the Thrill of the Night.* New York: Signet, 2006; *Just One of Those Flings.* New York: Signet, 2006.

JOHN CHARLES AND JOANNE HAMILTON-SELWAY

ALEXIS HILL. *See* Rebecca York

SANDRA HILL

I n Sandra Hill's best-selling books, Vikings travel through time, pigs have five legs, fairy
godmothers are really fairy godfathers who think they're Elvis reincarnated, and
St. Jude gives heavenly advice for every occasion. It doesn't matter what kind of character Hill has created, whether hot Cajuns or cool Vikings, the one thing Hill's readers are
guaranteed is plenty of laughs.

The daughter of John and Veronica Cluston, Hill was born and raised in Lock Haven,
Pennsylvania. She attributes her writing inspiration to her mother, who had always believed
in her daughter's ability to accomplish anything she endeavored. A shy child, Hill had a
strict Catholic upbringing, some of which shows up in her books from time to time in the
form of nuns, novenas, and St. Jude. It's hard to believe that the girl under the direction of
the nuns of St. Agnes School is now the writer of some of romance's steamiest novels.

Hill attended Lock Haven and Penn State Universities, and holds degrees from both.
She spent her postcollege career as a print journalist, writing news articles and features and
editing for publications in New Jersey and Pennsylvania. During this time, she met her
husband, Robert Hill, a former political aide who became a stockbroker and eventually vice
president of an international financial firm. The Hill's are antiquing hobbyists, with a
particular interest in jewelry, old paintings, and Roseville pottery, which have made appearances in her novels *Frankly, My Dear* (1996) and *Tall, Dark, and Cajun* (2003). They have
four grown sons—Beau, Rob, Matt and Daniel—and make their home in Pennsylvania.

With a genealogy that traces Hill's earliest ancestors to the Vikings, dating back to the first
Duke of Normandy, it is no wonder she's written two separate series of Viking books. The
Viking Series I includes Holt Medallion winner, *The Reluctant Viking* (1994); *The Outlaw
Viking* (1995); *The Tarnished Lady* (1995); *The Bewitched Viking* (1999); *The Blue Viking*
(2001); *My Fair Viking* (2002); and *A Tale of Two Vikings* (2004). These books sparkle with
wit and humor. In *The Reluctant Viking*, businesswoman Ruby Jordan has a floundering marriage. She finds herself transported to tenth-century Norseland, where she meets Thork Haralds-
son, a Viking warrior with an amazing resemblance to her husband. When Thork dies, Ruby

is sent back to the future. *The Outlaw Viking* features Ruby and Thork's daughter, six-foot-tall Dr. Rain Jordan. Rain never really believed her mother's tales of time travel, but when Rain receives a blow to the head that transports her to a tenth-century Norse battleground, she knows her mother told the truth. She finds Selick the Outlaw outnumbered by Saxons and saves him with a riderless horse she finds on the battleground. The ungrateful Viking takes her prisoner and, against his better judgment as well as that of the priest and the healer, allows Rain to use her medical training to save the life of her half brother who was injured during the fight. *The Tarnished Lady* features Lady Eadyth, a medieval merchant and bee-keeper who is also a single mother. Eirik of Ravenshire doesn't seem to be a suitable mate for Eadyth, but somehow, as in all of Hill's books, love finds its way to them.

The Viking Series II includes: *The Last Viking* (1998); *Truly, Madly Viking* (2000); *The Very Virile Viking* (2003); 2005 RITA finalist *Wet and Wild* (2004); *Hot and Heavy* (2005); and *Rough and Ready* (2006). The first book in Series II, ironically named *The Last Viking*, is the story of Dr. Meredith Foster, a modern scholar and expert on ancient Norse culture who gets the research opportunity of her life when "Rolf" Ericsson, a tenth-century Viking warrior, lands in the twentieth century. Rolf had no idea that the mission his father sent him on in the year 997, would end a thousand years later in a world full of curious things, such as indoor showers and Oreos. Jorund Ericsson, the hero of *Truly, Madly Viking,* has a time-traveling experience that ends in a modern mental hospital under the care of psychologist Maggie McBride, who calls him "Joe." Magnus Ericsson, the title character of *The Very Virile Viking,* is suffering from depression. He's raising 10 children on his own, and his 11th child, whom he didn't know existed, has just been delivered to him. Magnus decides to curb his potency by taking a vow of celibacy, so he gathers his children and leaves for Vinland. On the boat, Magnus has a vision of an old lady praying over some kind of religious beads, and before he knows it, he and his rowdy, undisciplined children are in twenty-first-century California. Rose Abruzzi is desperate for great-grandchildren, a bunch of them, so they can fill every nook and cranny of her large vineyard estate. Every night, she prays a novena that her granddaughter, Angela, a Hollywood real-estate agent, whom Rose raised from child-hood, will get married and have children. Angela, whose first marriage was a disaster, has lost her interest in men and doesn't believe in happily ever afters. One look at Angela, and Magnus promptly forgets his vow of celibacy. In his rough, first-millennium manner, he proceeds to woo her. This third book in the trilogy about the time-traveling Ericsson brothers neatly ties the story lines together as the three of them are reunited.

Hill brings her tenth-century Vikings to the world of the Navy SEALs in her next three books, *Wet and Wild, Hot and Heavy,* and *Rough and Ready.* In *Wet and Wild,* a finalist for the Romance Writers of America's RITA award, Ragnor Magnusson, the son Magnus Ericsson (*The Very Virile Viking*) left behind, is bored and decides to go "a'Viking," hoping this will include many bloody battles. During one especially gory conflict, a Saxon warrior drags Ragnor from his ship, and the two of them begin to drown. Instead of going to Valhalla, as he expected, Ragnor regains his consciousness in a SEAL training camp. Every-one there mistakes Ragnor for Torolf, his half brother, who bears an uncanny resemblance to Ragnor. Torolf has developed amnesia while performing a heroic feat and is now AWOL. Lieutenant Alison MacLean, a Navy doctor, is SEAL Instructor Master Chief Ian MacLean's sister; but that doesn't stop Ragnor from pursuing his superior officer. *Hot and Heavy* is a departure from Hill's other books in that the time traveler is a woman, Madrene Olgadottir. Madrene, the last of Magnus Ericson's many offspring left in Norseland, is taken captive during an invasion and sold into a harem. Ian MacLean, now a lieutenant with the Navy SEALs, is on a special operations mission in Iraq. He believes the woman who hit him over the head and tied him up is a terrorist. When Ian finally figures out that the tart-tongued Madrene is not the enemy, despite her belligerent actions, he knows he can't leave her in the war-torn country. Unfortunately, the most expedient, obvious method of getting her out of Iraq and into the United States is marriage. The humor of this married couple's bizarre courtship is offset by the presence of real terrorists. *Rough and Ready* (2006) is the sixth book in Hill's Viking Series II, with more Viking Navy SEALs to come.

The heroes in Hill's books are usually tortured individuals who maintain a sense of humor through adversity, and her heroines are strong women who are often insecure about their bodies. Helga the Homely, from *A Tale of Two Vikings*, has an axe to grind. She suffered years of ridicule because of the hurtful nickname Toste Ivarsson gave her. Toste's identical twin brother, Vagn, made liberal use of the moniker, too, so when Vagn is wounded in battle, and the no longer plain Helga nurses him back to health, he realizes the hard way that Helga has never forgiven him. Helga's father, on the other hand, feels that his daughter is too old to be picky about a husband, and he insists she marry Vagn. Toste, wounded in the same battle, finds himself in a convent under the care of Esme, a novice who still hasn't taken her final vows after 11 years. Separated for the first time in their lives, and each believing that the other is dead, these hardheaded Norse twins are forced to do individual battles in the war of the sexes with these two equally strong-willed women.

Two of Hill's early books, RITA finalist *Frankly, My Dear,* 1996; and *Sweeter Savage Love,* 1997, have many things in common. They are both set in the old South in Creole society. Each of the books parodies a classic romance novel. *Frankly, My Dear* finds its inspiration in *Gone with the Wind,* while *Sweeter Savage Love* pays homage to Rosemary Rogers' *Sweet Savage Love.* The heroine in *Frankly, My Dear,* Sandra Selente, also known as Selena, wants a man just like Rhett Butler. Similarly, Dr. Harriet Ginoza, the heroine of *Sweeter Savage Love,* dreams of a hero just like the one Rosemary Rogers wrote about. The heroines of both books are modern women longing for a larger-than-life hero from the past. Both books are time-travel stories that feature twentieth-century heroines thrust back into a different era. Both books, not coincidentally, display Hill's zesty, over-the-top sense of humor.

Two years later, Hill switched from the past world of the Creoles to the present world of the Cajuns. The wonderful characters of Hill's Cajun Contemporary series were introduced in 1999 with *The Love Potion.* Lucien LeDeux, "Bad Boy of the Bayou," also known as "The Swamp Solicitor," accidentally eats jelly beans that change his life after Dr. Sylvie Fontaine, a brilliant chemist, injects them with a love potion she's just developed. Although humorous in nature, this book begins a strand of a serious nature dealing with the abuse the LeDeuxs suffered at the hands of a brutish father. In *Tall, Dark, and Cajun,* feng shui expert Rachel Fortier, who lives in Washington, D.C., breaks up with her shallow fiancé, who judges people by their appearance and weight. When Rachel's gun-toting, tobacco-chewing grandmother, Gizelle Fortier, invites her to rural Louisiana, Rachel jumps at the chance. Once there, Rachel meets up with Remy LeDeux, the scarred but sexy owner of a helicopter charter business who wants to purchase part of Grandma Gizelle's expansive Bayou spread. Hill expertly blends humor and poignancy in this "true beauty has nothing to do with outward appearances" themed novel.

Raoul Lanier, the title character of *The Cajun Cowboy* (2004), was Charmaine LeDeux's first husband. Four divorces later, Charmaine decides to be a born-again virgin, although her skintight Spandex clothes shout otherwise. Raoul's devious father wills half of his cattle ranch to his son and the other half to Charmaine. Raoul delivers this message with proof that they are still married. Terms of this will specify that the two need to live together. Tante Lulu, another swamp granny, albeit a matchmaking one, and her interfering cowhands set themselves up as matchmakers. Even Tante Lulu's beloved St. Jude chimes in with an opinion when one is needed. Tante Lulu and St. Jude return in *The Red-Hot Cajun* (2005). Washington, D.C. environmental lobbyist, René LeDeux, is worn down after losing case after case to big business and interest groups, so he retreats to the sanctuary of Louisiana's Bayou Black. René's well-meaning activist friends kidnap Trial TV celebrity Valerie "Ice" Breaux and bring her to Bayou Black to get media attention for their environmental causes. To further complicate matters, Valerie, a Creole, and René, a Cajun, share an unpleasant history, including a badly bungled "first time" as teenagers. Once again, Hill mixes humor and serious themes (bayou ecology and the changing environment, and child abuse) with a deftness and sensitivity that make this series so unique.

Hill has always aspired to be a writer. She chose the romance genre because it has always appealed to her as an avid romance reader. She enjoys the romantic relationships in romance novels and the happy, hopeful endings. Hill chooses her first novel set in Scotland, *The Blue Viking,* as the most difficult to write because of the level of research it required. The easiest for her to write was *The Last Viking.* "[It] just wrote itself," she says. According to Hill, her sentimental favorite is her first novel, *The Reluctant Viking,* because of the joy of completing a first novel and the satisfaction of having it published. Her writing style has become less structured than the detailed outlines and synopses used in her early books. She says she now writes "by the seat of my pants," and finds the two approaches equally effective. The process of polishing and self-editing a completed manuscript is Hill's favorite part of writing. Her cure for writer's block, or in her case, "writer's malaise," is to just do it.

From the hot Cajuns of the humid bayous of Louisiana to the sexy Vikings of the icy reaches of Scandinavia to the sinewy SEALs of the sunny coast of California, Hill's heroes and spitfire heroines have garnered critical praise. According to reviewers, Hill, with her extensive comedic talent, is "wonderfully imaginative" and "entertaining." Quintessential Hill is outrageous, side-splittingly funny, naughty, hilarious, steamy, and outlandish. Her sexy, wacky, sassy style tickles funny bones, eliciting chuckles, guffaws, and giggles from those who love to read her books. If best seller lists (*New York Times,* Waldenbooks, and *USA Today*) are any indication, Hill's fan base is growing, and they can't wait for her next cast of crazy characters.

BIBLIOGRAPHY

Books: *The Reluctant Viking.* New York: Dorchester, 1994; *The Outlaw Viking.* New York: Dorchester, 1995; *The Tarnished Lady.* New York: Dorchester, 1995; *Frankly, My Dear.* New York: Dorchester, 1996; *Desperado.* New York: Dorchester, 1997; *Sweeter Savage Love.* New York: Dorchester, 1997; *Love Me Tender.* New York: Dorchester, 1998; *The Last Viking.* New York: Dorchester, 1998; *The Bewitched Viking.* New York: Dorchester, 1999; *The Love Potion.* New York: Dorchester, 1999; *Truly, Madly Viking.* New York: Dorchester, 2000; *The Blue Viking.* New York: Dorchester, 2001; *My Fair Viking.* New York: Dorchester, 2002; *The Very Virile Viking.* New York: Dorchester, 2003; *Tall, Dark, and Cajun.* New York: Warner, 2003; *A Tale of Two Vikings.* New York: Dorchester, 2004; *The Cajun Cowboy.* New York: Warner, 2004; *Wet and Wild.* New York: Dorchester, 2004; *The Red-Hot Cajun.* New York: Warner, 2005; *Hot and Heavy.* New York: Dorchester, 2005; *Rough and Ready.* New York: Berkley, 2006; *Pink Jinx.* New York: Warner, 2006.

Novellas: "Heart Craving" in *Lovescape.* New York: Dorchester, 1996; "Naughty or Nice" in *The Night Before Christmas.* New York: Dorchester, 1996; "Fever" in *Blue Christmas.* New York: Dorchester, 1998; "Sam's Story" in *Here Comes Santa Claus.* New York: Dorchester, 2001.

SHELLEY MOSLEY AND SANDRA VAN WINKLE

VICKI HINZE

Vicki Hinze. Courtesy of Vicki Hinze.

RITA finalist Vicki Hinze is a self-described "writing junkie." Everything about the process appeals to her, "the creating, the editing, the revising—all of it," which is evident in her prolific body of work.

She recalls always having an interest in writing, although not necessarily aspiring to becoming an author. As a child, she would play "library" while her friends would play "school," and she planned to one day become a doctor or a lawyer or an ambassador; but writer wasn't on her list of things to be. In fact, Hinze didn't seriously consider writing until the age of 30.

Hinze was born in Denver, Colorado, to Victor and Edna Martin Sampson, and she grew up in Gretna, Louisiana. Her education credentials include a master's degree in creative writing and a PhD in philosophy, theocentric business, and ethics. Before becoming a full-time writer, her occupations included director of operations for a corporate chain, certified escrow officer, legal assistant, and cosmetologist. Her husband, Lloyd Hinze, was an Air Force officer who did airborne hurricane research and was later assigned to Special Operations. The Hinze's have three children, Raymond, Michael and Kristen.

Hinze has written a variety of business documents and nonfiction articles and books about professional writing, along with novels in the suspense and mystery genres. She hadn't considered writing romances until her mother introduced her to the genre. Hinze says she

also writing as Victoria Barrett

was captivated by their "unity of mind, body, and spirit"; and how the hero and heroine somehow manage to end up together. "I like the family values; the importance placed on children; the acknowledgement of emotions, positive and negative; and the characters working through challenges constructively" she says.

The theme of healing and overcoming challenges from painful past experiences is a recurrent theme in Hinze's works. She isn't afraid to tackle difficult themes: child custody (*Shades of Gray,* 1998); post-traumatic stress syndrome (*Acts of Honor,* 1999); spousal abuse (*All Due Respect,* 2000); and terrorists in the United States ("Total Recall" in *Smokescreen,* 2005). Honor, courage, and loyalty are also themes interwoven throughout all of her books.

Inspiration for her stories is something Hinze finds "everywhere," especially when interacting with other people. Each of her books originates from a specific scenario cast with likely characters in various roles. She most often weaves romance into plots of suspense and mystery; however, writing as Victoria Barrett, she has also written purely romantic stories in a more cozy, comfortable, and conversational style.

Hinze's heroes are honorable men, respected and admired, who value the dignity of others. Such is the case of Special Operations Major Jake Logan in *Shades of Gray* (1998). In order to keep his son, Timmy, safely away from the custody of his alcoholic ex-wife, Jake accepts his friend Laura Taylor's offer of marriage, forsaking true love to protect his child. His loyalty to his son takes precedence over his own need for romantic love. Parental love is a strong theme in this story of a self-sacrificing father, who despite his noble actions, finds his soul mate.

"Strong, spirited women," is how Hinze describes her heroines. Dignified and graceful despite their flaws, they try to do the right thing. They've also been known to do the wrong thing, but always for the right reason. Hinze sees herself in her heroines, whom, she says, are her vision of "real women striving to be better women and better human beings." One of Hinze's "strong, spirited women" is military attorney Captain Tracy Keener, the heroine of *Duplicity* (1999). Tracy has been assigned to defend Captain Adam Burke at his court-martial. Burke, who works in Intelligence, has been accused of the worst crimes possible: treason and killing his own men. However, once Tracy meets Adam, she's truly convinced that he's innocent, especially later, when she hears that he's been murdered. The rumors of his death are premature, and Tracy, risking her own life, is determined to help Adam find the real perpetrators and clear his name.

Another one of Hinze's "strong, spirited women" is Captain Amanda West, the heroine of RITA finalist *Body Double* (2004), which is part of Hinze's War Games series. Captured by the enemy, much of Amanda's memory has been erased. Agent Mark Cross is a victim of the same nefarious treatment. Together, they try to re-create what has happened and discover what it is that neither of them can remember.

Hinze's favorite locales for her contemporary romances have varied over the years, from Maine to New Orleans (where she grew up) to her home state of Florida, with its gorgeous "sugar-white" beaches. Military bases are common in her books, and she recently began including settings in the Middle East.

Writer's block isn't something that Hinze has experienced, but her theory for those who do, is that it stems from fear and doubt or from pushing too hard to produce without stopping to "refill their creative well." Hinze refills her well with leisure activities that she enjoys, such as home decorating and shooting pool with her husband.

Hinze considers her 1996 book *Maybe This Time,* written as Victoria Barrett, to be her hardest to write because she wrote it to mourn the passing of her father. A paranormal story, it required a great deal of raw emotion from Hinze, although in the end, it brought her peace.

Shades of Gray is the novel Hinze names as her easiest to write. It was inspired by a young soldier and his wife debating whether to buy a jar of peanut butter or a can of tuna, because they couldn't afford both. The scene she witnessed moved Hinze to make a statement through her writing. The story also contains a number of other events that she experienced in real life, knowing firsthand the reactions and emotions they evoked.

Of all her books, Hinze's favorite is her 1997 novel (written as Victoria Barrett), *Festival*. She wrote this novel for her mother, a lifelong avid reader, rolling all of her favorite story elements into one book. Hinze completed the work and was able to read it to her mother shortly before she died. "It was her book, and she loved it," says Hinze. For that reason, it will always be Hinze's favorite, too.

Hinze is one of a handful of romance writers who use military settings, complete with tough, brave female protagonists; men willing to die for their honor; and realistic portrayals of violence in their books. None of this was anticipated or expected in the romance genre, but Hinze, with her quality military romantic suspense novels, has helped expand the romance genre itself and has attracted a whole new segment of readers in the process.

BIBLIOGRAPHY

Writing as Vicki Hinze

Books: *Shades of Gray.* New York: St. Martin's Press, 1998; *Duplicity.* New York: St. Martin's Press, 1999; *Acts of Honor.* New York: St. Martin's Press, 1999; *All Due Respect.* New York: St. Martin's Press, 2000; *Lady Liberty.* New York: Bantam, 2002; *Lady Justice.* New York: Bantam, 2004; *Body Double.* New York: Silhouette, 2004; *Double Vision.* New York: Silhouette, 2005; *Double Dare.* New York: Silhouette, 2005; *Invitation to a Murder.* New York: Silhouette, 2005; *Her Perfect Life.* Toronto: Harlequin, 2006; *Bulletproof Princess.* New York: Silhouette, 2006.

Novella: "Total Recall" in *Smokescreen.* New York: Silhouette, 2005.

Writing as Victoria Barrett

Books: *Mind Reader.* New York: St. Martin's Press, 1993; *Beyond the Misty Shore.* New York: St. Martin's Press, 1996; *Maybe This Time.* New York: Kensington, 1996; *Upon a Mystic Tide.* New York: St. Martin's Press, 1996; *Beside a Dreamswept Sea.* New York: St. Martin's Press, 1997; *Festival.* New York: Kensington, 1997.

Novellas: "Summer Fling" in *Seeing Fireworks.* New York: St. Martin's Press, 1997; "Cupid's Arrow" in *A Message from Cupid.* New York: St. Martin's Press, 1998.

SHELLEY MOSLEY AND SANDRA VAN WINKLE

ALYSSA HOWARD. *See* Rebecca York

KATE HUNTINGTON

Kate Huntington. Courtesy of Kate Huntington.

If Kate Huntington had not been forced to read Jane Austen's *Pride and Prejudice* as a high school sophomore, she might never have written her own Regency romances later on. Fortunately though, like so many high school students, Huntington was introduced to Austen's immortal prose, and she immediately fell in love with the witty and wonderful world of Regency England.

Huntington was born Kathy Hoch in Huntington, Indiana, and she spent her childhood years growing up in the small Midwestern town. Huntington later attended St. Francis College (now St. Francis University) in Fort Wayne, Indiana, where she received her bachelor of arts degree in English and secondary education.

Huntington always dreamed of becoming a writer but majored in education because she thought teaching would be a good career to fall back on just in case she didn't become a "successful, world-renowned novelist right away." Ironically, Huntington never did teach, but before turning to writing full-time she worked as a nurses' aid in college and, after graduating, become a reporter for her community newspaper, eventually going onto to

also writing as Cathryn Huntington Chadwick
also writing as Kate Ivers
also writing as Kathy Chwedyk

work as an editor for a variety of newspapers in Huntington, Fort Wayne, and the suburbs of Chicago. Even now, writing full-time, Huntington does occasionally take on the odd freelance or temp job to help with the somewhat erratic cash-flow situation with which most authors struggle.

Huntington has written short stories and novellas under her real name, Kathy Chwedyk, in science fiction, fantasy, and horror. She wrote one contemporary romance as Kate Ivers, but she is best known for her sparkling Regency comedies of manners under her pseudonyms Cathryn Huntington Chadwick and Kate Huntington.

While all of her books were challenging to write in their own individual way, Huntington believes *The Captain's Courtship* (1999), her first book written under her Kate Huntington pseudonym, was the hardest to write in many ways. *The Captain's Courtship* would become her third published book, but was actually the fifth book Huntington completed. After writing two Regency romances as Cathryn Huntington Chadwick, Huntington completed two more books, which didn't sell until years later. She says, "I was discouraged by the fact that these two books were not selling and was beginning to lose confidence as a writer. It took me one year to complete *The Captain's Courtship,* and I didn't show it to anyone for a long time because writing it was like crawling along a tunnel lined with jagged glass." Huntington says a "wonderful" new agent sold *The Captain's Courtship* almost immediately.

As a Regency writer, Huntington has done many stories based on popular themes in the subgenre. An example is *The Poor Relation* (1990), her first book published as Cathryn Huntington Chadwick, which uses the much-loved plot of a plain heroine who feels overshadowed by her more beautiful and popular sister. Kate, the heroine of *The Poor Relation,* initially spurns captain Mark Verelst's advances, thinking he prefers her sister. Kate is used to being overlooked in favor of her "diamond of the first water" sister, but Mark is only pretending to be interested in her sister to get to know Kate better. In her book, *Mistletoe Mayhem* (2000), Huntington deftly uses the much-loved theme of a second chance at love when Lady Madelyn Rathbone meets up again with Robert Langtry at a holiday country house party. After appearing as a secondary character in two of Huntington's previous books, Madelyn's hopes of finally finding true love at last with Robert also depends on her willingness to take on the role of mother to Robert's orphaned nephews and nieces.

With *Town Bronze* (2003), Huntington takes up the theme of two people who resist being romantically paired up by others only to discover that they really do belong together. Christopher Warrender, the hero of the book, realizes he does want to wed his grandfather's ward, Cassandra Davies. In addition to having a realistic military background for the time period, Christopher is a perfect example of Huntington's preferred brand of male: responsible, brave, and equipped with a good sense of humor. As Huntington herself says, "I can't imagine anything worse than being married for years to a man who isn't good for a laugh or two on a daily basis."

Huntington's heroines tend to be independent, sensible, and direct. "They don't do guile well, and if they have got something to say, they come right out and say it," she says. An excellent example of this is Catriona Grant from *To Tempt a Gentleman* (2005). When the will of his elderly cousin, Sophie Tilden, is read and Sir Michael Stewart discovers he has "inherited" Catriona, her dedicated and loving companion, as his new housekeeper, Catriona intends on honoring Sophie's wishes and refuses to listen to Michael's offer of pensioning her off somewhere else. Instead, strong, opinionated, plain-speaking Catriona moves into Michael's home and immediately begins giving his house, and his life, the much-needed cleaning they both deserve. Huntington's superb sense of characterization extends not only to Michael and Catriona, but also to many of the secondary characters in the book, including Michael's two grown daughters Marguerite, Lady Redgrave; and Mrs. Dorothea Walbridge. Huntington resists turning the women into mere villains out to break up the blossoming romance between their father and Catriona, but instead shows them as three-dimensional people, with their own hopes and dreams. Imbued with a sharp, yet subtle sense of wit and gifted with a wonderfully diverse cast of characters, *To Tempt a Gentleman* is Huntington at her best.

For Huntington, the appeal of the romance genre isn't just about the happy ending. It is also about justice. "In my romance novels, the good people are rewarded, and the bad people are not," she says. "No wonder people love romances." Thus, with her sensible, plain-speaking heroines; her heroes who know how to laugh at themselves and the world around them; and her ability to see to it that everyone receives the ending they deserve, it is no wonder that discerning readers love Huntington's books.

BIBLIOGRAPHY

Writing as Kate Huntington

Books: *The Captain's Courtship.* New York: Kensington, 1999; *The Lieutenant's Lady.* New York: Kensington, 1999; *Lady Diana's Darlings.* New York: Kensington, 2000; *Mistletoe Mayhem.* New York: Kensington, 2000; *A Rogue for Christmas.* New York: Kensington, 2001; *The Merchant Prince.* New York: Kensington, 2002; *Town Bronze.* New York: Kensington, 2003; *The General's Daughter.* New York: Kensington, 2004; *Hero's Homecoming.* New York: Kensington, 2004; *To Tempt a Gentleman.* New York: Kensington, 2005.

Novellas: "The Royal Kitten" in *Spring Kittens.* New York: Kensington, 2000; "A Breath of Scandal" in *Untameable.* New York: Kensington, 2002; "The Husband Hunt" in *On Bended Knee.* New York: Kensington, 2003; "The Awakening" in *His Immortal Embrace.* New York: Kensington, 2003.

Writing as Cathryn Huntington Chadwick

Books: *The Poor Relation.* New York: Kensington, 1990; *A Cruel Deception.* New York: Kensington, 1990.

Writing as Kate Ivers

Books: *Midsummer Lightning.* New York: Berkley, 2000.

Writing as Kathy Chwedyk

Novellas: "Qadishtu" coauthored with Laura Resnick in *Warrior Enchantresses.* New York: DAW, 1996; "Terrible Monkey" coauthored with Laura Resnick in *Return of the Dinosaurs.* New York: DAW, 1997; "The Dowry" in *Highwaymen: Robbers and Rogues.* New York: DAW, 1997; "She of the Night" coauthored with Laura Resnick in *Urban Nightmares.* New York: Baen, 1997; "Dead Woman's Things" in *365 Scary Stories: A Horror Story a Day.* New York: Barnes and Noble Books, 1998.

JOHN CHARLES

KATE IVERS. *See* Kate Huntington

ELOISA JAMES

Eloisa James. Courtesy of Eloisa James.

When Eloisa James burst onto the historical Regency scene with her first book, *Potent Pleasures* (1999), critics greeted her as the next Amanda Quick. James, who specializes in sexy, witty historical Regencies, has created memorable characters in her clever, intelligent, unconventional heroines who seem to fall for heroes poisoned by an "overabundance of testosterone," to quote James.

James, the pseudonym for Mary Bly, was born in a small town in the Midwest in 1962, where she grew up with parents who were both writers. Her father is world-renowned poet Robert Bly, author of the best-selling book, *Iron John;* and her mother is short-story writer Carol Bly. James remembers her parents encouraging her and her siblings to read and use their imaginations. As a child, James wrote plays starring her siblings, for which she would charge her parents admission. These childhood experiences would definitely play a part in James's decision to become a writer as an adult.

James's first experiences writing a romance came in the 1980s. After graduating from Harvard, James tried writing a romance that involved "storms at sea, pirates, several sheiks, and a heroine whose journey from Europe to the Middle East included at one point being blinded by camel spit." She even thought up a pseudonym for herself, "Penelope Blaze." With the help of her then-boyfriend's secretary, James sent her first romance out; but being unfamiliar with the submission process, James didn't get much interest from publishers. However, her rejection letter from the Sierra Club did say they thought it was "frisky," and they were "truly sorry it wasn't in their line" of publishing.

In her early twenties, James decided to go to England to study, prompted, she says, by her love of "rain, English men, Cornish pasties, and long baths." It was in England that she encountered someone who would change her reading life forever: Georgette Heyer. Introduced to Heyer's classic Regencies by her friend, Sarah, James found refuge from the difficulties of being an American studying at Oxford University in the timeless tales of this romance master.

Yet James put aside any dreams of being a writer to enter the workforce as a professor of English literature. She eventually married and had a baby, but thoughts of writing a romance would come sneaking back into her life. Along with graduate degrees from Oxford and Yale, James had acquired many student loans. Her husband insisted that before they could have another child, they first had to pay off what James owed. After discovering that her next-door neighbor was a romance writer, James revisited her dreams of writing a romance, thinking that it would provide some additional income.

It was while she was coming up with the plot for her romance *Potent Pleasures* that James first discovered that her academic research could come in handy. One of the topics she had explored for her PhD was the life of the Earl of Essex, whose marriage in 1613 was annulled due to impotency. Using this snippet of history as a source of inspiration, James came up with her heroine, Charlotte Daicheston, who stumbles across the hero, Alexander Foakes, in London one day, only to discover he doesn't remember her or their first romantic encounter three years earlier. Alexander's new passionate pursuit of Charlotte is somewhat complicated by the misperception of others in society that he is impotent, since his first marriage to an Italian woman was annulled on those grounds.

James says the year she spent writing her first book, *Potent Pleasures,* will remain in her memory as "one of the most charmed experiences" of her life. Despite juggling a teaching job, a three-year-old child, and all the other assorted details of running a household, James put aside all the madness, and at every day at four o'clock, sank into the story of Alexander and Charlotte.

When the book was finished, James adapted a more professional approach to submitting it to publishers. She sent queries out to five agents and quickly got rejections from four, primarily because of her unconventional use of impotency as a plot device. The fifth agent asked to see James's whole manuscript. Eventually, *Potent Pleasures* was the object of a bidding war between publishers, and James ended up with a contract for three books from Dell publishers—and an advance that nicely covered her student loans.

While James's experiences writing her first book, were ones of pure pleasure, once the book was published, she discovered the many challenges facing a published author. Regency readers are sticklers for accuracy, and after a few of those readers pointed out some historical inconsistencies in the story that had slipped by the author and her editor, James found time in between taking care of her new baby, her teaching career, and working on the next book in her contract to revise and correct these errors for the paperback edition of *Potent Pleasures.*

James frequently finds ideas for her books in Renaissance literature. Her second book, *Midnight Pleasures* (2000), was inspired by a relatively unknown play "The Hog Has Lost His Pearl"—especially the scene in which James's hero, Patrick, climbs up a ladder to fetch the heroine so she can elope with his best friend, but doesn't return from her room as quickly as he should. That opens the door to a romance between Patrick and his friend's fiancée.

As with *Potent Pleasures,* another snippet from the Earl of Essex's life would act as a catalyst for a scene in *Duchess in Love* (2002). In the 1590s, the Earl returned home from a long trip to the continent. Observing a beautiful lady dancing at a ball, he turned to a stranger and asked for the name of that lovely woman. Readers quickly saw echoes of this historical scene when James's hero falls in love with a woman he sees at a party, only to discover that the complete stranger is his wife, whom he hasn't seen in 12 years.

One of James's strengths as a writer is the way she emphasizes the importance of female friendships in her books. Or as her editor says, "Her stories are partly about the heroine's love for a man and partly about her love for her girlfriends." An excellent example of this is Gabby in *Enchanting Pleasures* (2001), who turns to Sophie, heroine of *Midnight Pleasures,* for advice on how to seduce her husband. In *Duchess in Love*, Gina's friendships with Helene, Carola, and Esme, each of whom have their own romantic problems, are an important part of the story; together these friends help Gina find a solution to her own difficult choice between a new fiancé and an absent husband who has returned to claim her affections. With *Much Ado About You* (2005), James began a new series centering on four sisters whose complex relationships with each other figure in the series almost as clearly as do their love stories.

With the publication of *Much Ado about You,* James decided that the secrecy surrounding her identity was no longer necessary. Rather than have the press "out" her, she did it herself in February 2005, with a full-page op-ed column in the *New York Times* titled "A Fine Romance" and signed by "Mary Bly." James, a Shakespearean scholar with degrees from Oxford, Harvard, and Yale, and who teaches at Fordham University, proudly acknowledged her own love of reading and writing romances and her respect for the readers of the genre.

As an author, James tries to remain true to human emotion rather than solely focusing on strict historical accuracy. While she strives to remain as true to the Regency time period as she can, James's interest as an author is more in her characters and their stories. As James continues to write her wonderfully humorous and potently sensual Regency historicals, she gathers more readers who readily agree with the critics, such as the one from *People* magazine, who states, "romance writing does not get much better than this."

BIBLIOGRAPHY

Books: *Potent Pleasures.* New York: Delacorte, 1999; *Midnight Pleasures.* New York: Delacorte, 2000; *Enchanting Pleasures.* New York: Delacorte, 2001; *Duchess in Love.* New York: Avon, 2002; *Fool for Love.* New York: Avon, 2003; *A Wild Pursuit.* New York: Avon, 2004; *Your Wicked Ways.* New York: Avon, 2004; *Much Ado about You.* New York: Avon, 2005; *Kiss Me Annabel.* New York: HarperCollins, 2005; *The Taming of the Duke.* New York: Avon, 2006; *Pleasure for Pleasure.* New York: Avon, 2006.

Novellas: "A Fool Again" in *The One That Got Away.* New York: Avon, 2004; "A Proper English-woman" in *The Talk of the Ton.* New York: Penguin, 2005.

JOANNE HAMILTON-SELWAY AND JOHN CHARLES

STEPHANIE JAMES. *See* Jayne Ann Krentz

ELLEN JAMISON. *See* Jane Toombs

SUSAN JOHNSON

Susan Johnson. Courtesy of Susan Johnson.

F or some, history may be thought of as a mere collection of dull and dry facts, but for author Susan Johnson, it is a rich source of inspiration. Johnson combines her passion for history with her love of romance, and together, these two elements translate into a steamy writing style that makes her premier amongst authors who embrace the sensual side of romance.

Johnson was born Susan Aho in Hibbing, Minnesota, in 1939. Her mother, Gertrude, was a nurse; her father John was an industrial engineer for U.S. Steel. She grew up in the small towns of Minnesota, including Ely and Virginia, and eventually attended the University of Minnesota, where she received a bachelor of arts degree in studio art in 1960. She married Pat MacKay in 1957 and had two children. Her second marriage, in 1966, to history teacher Craig Johnson produced another child. She went on to receive her master's degree in art history in 1969. Before beginning her writing career, she worked as a slide librarian at the University of Minnesota for 13 years. Her expertise in her chosen fields of art and history would later play a prominent role in her writing career.

Johnson didn't really start writing until she was 37, when, she says, "the romance market inspired me [because] you can make a living and not work outside the house." Johnson's

also writing as Jill Barkin

first book, *Seized by Love* (1979), was published by Playboy Press. While Playboy Press was not known for its romance novels, it permitted authors to explore the full range of sensuality in their writing without restraint, and Johnson proved to be a perfect fit for this publisher. *Seized by Love* became the first work in a trilogy featuring three generations of a wild and tempestuous Russian family, the Kuzans, and introduced readers to the sensual writing style of Johnson and the opulent world of czarist Russia. *Seized by Love* was followed by *Love Storm* (1981) and *Sweet Love Survive* (1985), which concluded with the story of Kitty Radachek and Captain Apollo Kuzan.

After the story of the Kuzan family, Johnson took readers to the American West with *Blaze* (1986), in which a Boston heiress finds first lust and then love with a Harvard-educated son of an American Indian chief. She continued the saga of the Braddock-Black clan with *Silver Flame* (1988), *Forbidden* (1991), and *Brazen* (1995). Eight years later, Johnson returned to the story of Blaze and Jon Hazard Black with *Force of Nature* (2003), featuring Jo, the illegitimate daughter of Hazard Black and Lucy Attenborough.

With her background in history and an interest in research, historical detail is important to Johnson and plays an integral part in her books. Recognizing that there is often more background to a story than can be used in a book, Johnson often adds detailed endnotes that explain rituals, battles, and real-life characters, which allows her readers to understand the historical context of a particular book without bogging down the fast-moving plot in an overabundance of detail.

Johnson is known for a lush writing style that brilliantly balances both history and sensuality. With her lavish descriptions and vivid images, Johnson explores all the senses in her books, incorporating them into sensually detailed love scenes, through the use of food, fragrances, music, and tactile pleasures. Against these richly developed backdrops, she adds fully fleshed out characters whose extraordinary personalities affect the reader both visually and emotionally. Her unconventional heroines are strong and independent, and her commanding heroes are, as she says, "willing to go that extra mile for the heroine."

An excellent example is *Pure Sin* (1994), in which a beautiful aristocrat, Lady Flora Bonham, meets Adam Serre, a half Native American count, when their passionate natures collide in nineteenth-century Montana. On the same night that Adam's pampered and money-loving wife has left him, he meets Lady Flora, who is visiting from England with her father. Lady Flora finds a sensual and adventurous kindred spirit in Adam, and, though battling her feelings while fearing a loss of independence, she eventually acknowledges the growing love and commitment to Adam and his young daughter Lucy. Filled with expressive descriptions of Montana and vivid love scenes between her strong-willed characters, *Pure Sin* is an erotic journey through the Wild West that beautifully exploits Johnson's signature searing sensuality.

Given Johnson's academic background in art history, it isn't surprising that she would use the art world as a setting for one of her next books. Such is the case with *Seduction in Mind* (2001), in which the painting of a beautiful nude woman intrigues the book's hero, Samuel Lennox, Viscount Ranelagh. After tracing the model to artist Frederic Leighton, Lennox discovers the lovely lady in the canvas is none other than Alexandra Ionides, a wealthy widow, model, and artist herself. When Alex refuses Samuel's invitation to indulge in a no-strings-attached erotic liaison, he finds he must call on all his powers of seduction to convince her otherwise. While rife with Johnson's trademark love scenes, *Seduction in Mind* is also filled with fascinating tidbits about the art world in the late nineteenth century, cameo appearances from famous people of the time, and intriguing details about such other subjects as golf.

While best known for creating richly depicted historic backdrops, Johnson has written several contemporary romances, still replete with the sensual and seductive details that readers know and expect from her. Johnson's first contemporary romance, *Hot Streak,* was originally published in 1990 by Berkley, under the pseudonym Jill Barkin. *Hot Streak* introduces a bride-to-be, Molly Darian, who falls in love with summer love Cary Fersten but chooses to marry her high school sweetheart. Years later, when they have a second chance at happiness, Molly, now a single mother, and Cary, successful and famous, find their love threatened. In 2004, Johnson revised *Hot Streak,* and it joined *Hot Pink* (2003), *Hot Legs* (2004), and *Hot Spot* (2005) as part of Johnson's growing list of sexy contemporary romances.

From the French Revolution to czarist, from the American West to modern-day settings, Susan Johnson takes readers to the heights of passion, from which they hope never to return. When it comes to blending passion and desire and celebrating the power of romance through playful, yet erotic sensuality, Johnson is in a class by herself.

BIBLIOGRAPHY

Writing as Susan Johnson

Books: *Seized by Love.* New York: Playboy Press, 1979; *Love Storm.* New York: Playboy Press, 1981; *Sweet Love Survive.* New York: Berkley, 1985; *Blaze.* New York: Berkley, 1986; *The Play.* New York: Fawcett, 1987; *Silver Flame.* New York: Berkley, 1988; *Golden Paradise.* Toronto: Harlequin, 1990; *Sinful.* New York: Bantam, 1991; *Forbidden.* New York: Bantam, 1991; *Outlaw.* New York: Bantam, 1993; *Pure Sin.* New York: Bantam, 1994; *Brazen.* New York: Bantam, 1995; *Wicked.* New York: Bantam, 1997; *Taboo.* New York: Bantam, 1997; *A Touch of Sin.* New York: Bantam, 1999; *To Please a Lady.* New York: Bantam, 1999; *Legendary Lover.* New York: Bantam, 2000; *Temporary Mistress.* New York: Bantam, 2000; *Tempting.* New York: Kensington, 2001; *Seduction in Mind.* New York: Bantam, 2001; *Again and Again.* New York: Kensington, 2002; *Blonde Heat.* New York: Bantam, 2002; *Force of Nature.* New York: Kensington, 2003; *Hot Pink.* New York: Berkley, 2003; *Pure Silk.* New York: Kensington, 2004; *Hot Legs.* New York: Berkley, 2004; *Hot Spot.* New York: Berkley, 2005; *When You Love Someone.* New York: Kensington, 2006; *French Kiss.* New York: Berkley, 2006.

Novellas: "Playing with Fire" in *Rough around the Edges.* New York: St Martin's Press, 1998; "Bound and Determined" in *Captivated.* New York: Kensington, 1999; "A Tempting Wager" in *Naughty, Naughty.* New York: St Martin's Press, 1999; "Risking It All" in *Fascinated.* New York: Kensington, 2000; "Out of the Storm" in *Delighted.* New York: Kensington, 2002; "From Russia, With Love" in *Taken by Surprise.* New York: Kensington, 2003; "Natural Attraction" in *Strangers in the Night.* New York: Kensington, 2004; "American Beauty" in *Not Just for Tonight.* New York: Kensington, 2005.

Genre-Related Essay: "The Joy of Writing" in *North American Romance Writers.* Lanham, MD: Scarecrow Press, 1999.

Writing as Jill Barkin

Book: *Hot Streak.* New York: Berkley, 1990.

Writing with Jasmine Haynes

Book: *Twin Peaks.* New York: Berkley, 1990.

JOANNE HAMILTON-SELWAY

ALEX HILL JORDAN. *See* Rebecca York

NICOLE JORDAN

Nicole Jordan. Courtesy of Nicole Jordan.

For Nicole Jordan, it's all about passion: the passion of writing, the passion between her characters, and the passion she evokes in her readers. With her signature use of sensuality and an eye for historical detail, Jordan makes every book a fresh mixture of passion and romance.

Nicole Jordan was born Nicole Bushyhead in Norman, Oklahoma, in 1954. Her father was a career Army officer, and her mother was from Louisiana. Bushyhead is a Cherokee name, coming from her great-great-great-grandfather, a principal chief in the Cherokee tribe who helped lead his people across the tragic Trail of Tears. Jordan credits her mother "with instilling in me my love of romance. I was 10 years old when she started reading *Pride and Prejudice* and *The Scarlet Pimpernel* aloud to me. I soon graduated to Mary Stewart and Victoria Holt."

As an Army brat, Jordan grew up around the world. She attended high school in Germany, but, because she lived most of her life in Georgia, she considers Georgia home.

Jordan earned a degree in civil engineering from Georgia Tech. She says she "honestly never expected to become a writer after earning a civil engineering degree. I spent eight years working as an engineering manager for Procter and Gamble, making Pampers diapers and Charmin toilet tissue. I started writing as an escape from my high-stress job and, over the years, taught myself to write, essentially from scratch." The romance that started her career was Laurie McBain's *Tears of Gold:* "I stayed up all night devouring that book and, afterward, began dreaming of writing my own stories. What kept me going was simply that I love romance, and I consider myself fortunate to have discovered work that is also a passion."

Jordan's first published book was a Regency historical titled *Velvet Embrace.* It took four years of writing and rewriting and receiving dozens of rejection letters before Zebra Books bought and published it in 1987. *Velvet Embrace,* the story of Brie Carringdon, an innocent beauty, and Dominic Serrault, an untamed rake, features many of the elements that would become her signature trademark: sizzling sensuality, lush descriptions, and strong sexual conflict between the hero and heroine.

Velvet Embrace was followed by more Regency historical novels, such as *Desire and Deception* (1988) and *Moonwitch* (1991), which was a finalist for the Romance Writers of America's RITA award. Despite her love of the Regency era, Jordan branched out into other time periods with books like *The Warrior* (1995), a medieval romance and one of the more difficult books she has written. Along with *The Warrior,* she cites 1992's *Lord of Desire* (about a desert sheik and a willful English noblewoman) and 1994's *The Savage* (the tale of a Comanche loner and a Texas belle) as being among the most challenging books to write. According to Jordan, "Those stories were larger in scope than some of my other romances, with more historical depth and with life and death issues at stake. Plus, they were brand-new periods for me, which required extensive research."

Jordan delved into the Old West with her Rocky Mountain books, *The Outlaw* (1996) and *The Heartbreaker* (1998), two connecting novels featuring the McCord brothers. Set in Colorado, with the backdrop of a range war, Jake McCord and Caitlin Kingsly fall in love, despite the opposition of their feuding families. When Jake accidentally kills Caitlin's brother, he is forced to run from the law. Caitlin tries to forget him, but when he returns to clear his name, she must confront her feelings for Jake. *The Outlaw's* sizzling sensuality pervades both this book and the second book in the Rocky Mountain trilogy, *The Heartbreaker.* In *The Heartbreaker,* Jordan introduces another McCord brother, Sloan McCord, a widower with an infant daughter. When her father's gambling debts force her to close her all girls' school, well-bred Heather Ashford must choose between marrying a man she hates and a complete stranger, Sloan McCord.

While the sensuality is strong, it's more than just sex for Jordan's characters. Jordan uses the sexual chemistry and sizzling love scenes to further character development and the relationship of the hero and heroine. It is an integral part of her stories. "My books are known for their scorching sensuality and to-die-for heroes," says Jordan. "I write what I love to read—spicy, emotional, historical romances with strong, appealing characters; powerful conflict; sharp-edged wit; and riveting sexual tension." The third book in the Rocky Mountain trilogy is planned but not yet published.

In 1990, Jordan began writing *The Seduction,* which would be the first of five novels in her Notorious series. Jordan says, "My Notorious series is set during the Regency era and features sexy heroes who are members of the Hellfire League, a gentlemen's club dedicated to pleasure and sensual adventure. And, of course, these guys are all notorious in some way." In *The Seduction* (2000), Baron Damien Sinclair finds his plans of revenge for his sister's injury complicated by his growing love for Vanessa, Lady Wyndham. Known to the *ton* as "Lord Sin," Damien epitomizes the seductive rakehell at his wicked best, and "as for romantic conflict, there's nothing like the clever, cutting wit of the Regency era to create sizzling sexual tension," says Jordan. Another favorite in the Notorious series is *The Prince of Pleasure* (2003), whose hero is first introduced to readers in *The Seduction* and appeared in *The Passion* (2000), *Desire* (2001), and *Ecstasy* (2002). *The Prince of Pleasure's* title character is Jeremy Adair North, the Earl of Clune, known as "Dare" to his friends, who is one of the leaders of the Hellfire League. He wagers that the beautiful actress and French émigré Julianne Laurent will be his mistress, but secretly he wants revenge for her betrayal seven years earlier. When Julianne takes his wager, they work together to uncover the identity of a spy and a traitor to the Crown. With her Notorious series, Jordan skillfully blends dangerous intrigue with sizzling sexual tension to create books filled with passion and adventure.

In 2004, Jordan began a new series featuring a secret society of dangerous rakes, bold adventurers, and a sun-drenched island called Cyrene. "My Paradise series also takes place during the Regency [era]," says Jordan. "But in addition to England, the Paradise romances are set partly on a wonderful Mediterranean island and feature a secret society of protectors sworn to fight evil and tyranny across Europe." The society of protectors is called the Members of the Guardians of the Sword, operating with the approval of the British Foreign Office, with roots in the legend of King Arthur and his knights. Mixing real Regency settings and her own fictional world allows Jordan to "offer something fresh and different to pique [readers'] interest." The series begins with *Master of Temptation* (2004), the story of Max Leighton, a veteran of the Peninsula Wars, and Caro Evans, the unconventional daughter of one of the ruling families of the island of Cyrene and one of the few female members of the society. Max comes to the island with a wounded soldier, and Caro nurses the man back to health but yearns for Max. When Max has the chance to help the Guardians by planning the rescue of a kidnapped noblewoman, he willingly returns to the island to see Caro again. Each book in the series features one of the Guardians of the Sword and Jordan's signature sensuality and breathtaking intrigue. "Writing a romance series allows me to use connecting characters, which readers love," she says. "And I can give fascinating secondary characters their own stories in future books with revisiting previous heroes and heroines."

In the end, it all comes back to passion for Jordan. The process of writing in the romance genre allows her to, as she says, "indulge my passion. It's hard to describe the mental and emotional exhilaration I get from writing. I guess what I find most satisfying is my total absorption in my work. Sometimes I can write for two hours and think 10 minutes have gone by. And meeting a difficult challenge is always satisfying. After hours of pulling out my hair, finding just the right words or making a scene finally work [gives] me a definite sense of triumph. There are few greater thrills than writing. For me, it truly is a passion."

BIBLIOGRAPHY

Books: *Velvet Embrace.* New York: Zebra, 1987; *Desire and Deception.* New York: Zebra, 1988; *Moonwitch.* Toronto: Harlequin, 1991; *Tender Feud.* Toronto: Harlequin, 1991; *Lord of Desire.* New York: Avon, 1992; *Wildstar.* New York: Avon, 1992; *Touch Me with Fire.* New York: Avon, 1993; *The Savage.* New York: Avon, 1994; *The Warrior.* New York: Avon, 1995; *The Outlaw.* New York: Avon, 1996; *The Lover.* New York: Avon, 1997; *The Heartbreaker.* New York: Avon, 1998; *The Seduction.* New York: Ballantine, 2000; *The Passion.* New York: Ballantine, 2000; *Desire.* New York: Ballantine, 2001; *Ecstasy.* New York: Ballantine, 2002; *The Prince of Pleasure.* New York: Ballantine, 2003; *Master of Temptation.* New York: Ballantine, 2004; *Lord of Seduction.* New York: Ballantine, 2004; *Wicked Fantasy.* New York: Ballantine, 2005; *Fever Dreams.* New York: Ballantine, 2006.

JOANNE HAMILTON-SELWAY

KATHLEEN KANE. *See* Maureen Child

ELIZABETH N. Kary. *See* Elizabeth Grayson

JOCELYN KELLEY. *See* Jo Ann Ferguson

JULIE KENNER

Julie Kenner. Courtesy of Julie Kenner.

Ademon-hunting soccer mom, the author of testosterone-laden spy novels, a school librarian who discovers she has X-ray vision, and a code-cracking twenty-something with a passion for fashion—while at first glance these characters could not be any more different from one another, they do have one thing in common. They are all creations of the wildly inventive and delightfully clever Julie Kenner.

Kenner was born Julia Beck in Mountainview, California, in 1965. Her father was an aeronautical engineer, and her mother worked as a secretary. Kenner grew up in Austin, Texas, where she attended Lyndon Baines Johnson High School, graduating as valedictorian of her class. She went on to the University of Texas, where she received a bachelor's degree in communications (radio-television-film). Afterward, Kenner worked as a media specialist for a community college, before enrolling in Baylor Law School. Coincidently, her father was attending Baylor and earning his law degree at the same time. She graduated second in her class.

After graduating from law school, Kenner clerked for two years for a federal appellate judge. After this, she spent several years practicing general litigation, including entertainment law, in California. She worked as a production executive for a Beverly Hills production company; met and married her future husband, Don; and discovered the joys of scuba diving. Kenner taught part-time as an adjunct professor of torts in Orange County, before moving back to Texas with her husband.

While Kenner always loved creating stories, which she fondly remembers "always had a happy ending," it was years before she embraced the idea of writing a romance book. After a good deal of hard work, Kenner sold her first two romances to publishers by submitting the manuscripts to contests in 1999. By June of that year, Kenner had received her first offer from Harlequin, which published *Nobody Does It Better* in 2000 as part of their Temptation line. By the following year, Kenner had sold six books, including several more titles to Harlequin's Temptation line.

In *Nobody Does It Better,* the heroine, author Paris Summers, is forced by her publishers to adopt the pseudonym Montgomery Alexander, since they believe it will be easier to market Paris's testosterone-rich espionage thrillers to male readers if the readers think a man wrote the books. The only problem is that Paris's publishers want her to go on tour for her new book. Obviously, readers are going to expect a man signing the books, so when Paris bumps into sexy bar owner Devlin O'Malley, who looks exactly like her idea of what Montgomery would look like if he was real, Paris convinces him to pretend to be Montgomery for the upcoming tour. From its inspired title, which not only cleverly spoofs the kind of books Paris writes but also hints at the relationship that develops between her and Devlin, to its brilliant blend of simmering sexual chemistry and sharp wit, *Nobody Does It Better* beautifully demonstrates Kenner's sexy, sassy writing style.

The Cat's Fancy, Kenner's second book, was published by Dorchester in 2000 and became the author's first paranormal romance. In the book, when Maggie the cat falls in love with her owner, attorney Nicholas Goodman, she is granted one week in human form to get Nicholas to say he loves her, without Maggie having to tell him the truth about her real identity. With the publication of the utterly charming, sexy, and laughter-laced *The Cat's Fancy,* Kenner proved she had a real gift for blending fantasy and romance, and her inspired take on fairy tales quickly won her a dedicated group of readers.

After writing *The Cat's Fancy,* Kenner wanted to try writing another light, paranormal romance, but coming up with just the right concept took some time and a bit of thought. Kenner's next published book was *Reckless* (2000), another contemporary romance for Harlequin's Temptation line, which featured Rachel Dean, Paris Summer's best friend in *Nobody Does It Better,* as the heroine. Inspired by the popular theme of returning home for a school reunion, Kenner constructed the humorous and sexy story of Rachel, a former high school wallflower who is determined to show the high school hunks who rejected her just what they missed out on. Rachel's plan backfires, though, when she mistakes Garrett MacLean for his brother Carl, and Garrett decides he isn't content with just one night with Rachel but wants her every night from now on.

Somehow, the idea of a heroine with superpowers presented itself to Kenner, and she began writing *Aphrodite's Kiss* (2001), the first in what would become her Protector series. In *Aphrodite's Kiss,* school librarian Zoe Smith discovers right before her 25th birthday that she is only half mortal. Since Zoe is also half immortal, she now has the chance to become a member of the Venerate Council of Protectors, a race of superheroes descended from the Greek gods and goddesses, who use their powers to protect mankind. If Zoe accepts the opportunity, she will be able to use her powers of X-ray vision, flight, and a heightened sensitivity to save the world. But doing so would mean giving up any dreams Zoe might have of a normal life and any chance at a romance with private investigator George Taylor. Kenner's fresh and funny take on contemporary romance meets the world of Greek mythology not only won over readers, but also earned her a RITA nomination from the Romance Writers of America for best paranormal romance.

Other Protector books would follow, as Kenner paired up Zoe's superhero brother Hale with mortal Tracy Tannin in *Aphrodite's Passion* (2002); reunited protector Jason Murphy with his long-lost love Lane Kent and their six-year-old son, Davy, in *Aphrodite's Secret* (2003); and gave bad-boy and sometime-villain protector Mordichai Black his own chance at redemption and love with half-ling Isole Frost in *Aphrodite's Flame* (2004). With her Protector books, Kenner demonstrates a distinct gift for combining sexy romance, quirky humor, and a generous measure of fantasy in a delightfully fun series of paranormal romances.

Kenner's wicked sense of humor plays an important role in two of her recent contemporary romances, *Nobody but You* (2003) and *The Spy Who Loves Me* (2004). In *Nobody but You*, Kenner takes the conventional noir detective novel and adds her own brand of smart, witty romantic chemistry and snappy writing as she tells the story of David Anderson, a struggling private investigator with a taste for 1940s pulp novels; and Jacey Wilder, the femme fatale who offers Anderson the case of his career. Quotes from Anderson's own detective novel open each of the chapters in *Nobody but You,* further enhancing the tongue-in-cheek tone of the book.

If *Nobody but You* was inspired by the detective films of the 1940s, then James Bond had to be the catalyst for *The Spy Who Loves Me,* the tale of Finn Teague, a lawyer whose dull life changes forever when he stumbles into the exotic and dangerous world of espionage. Kenner neatly twists the Bond formula by making the heroine—cool, efficient, and deadly Amber Anderson—the real spy in the story. The book's colorful cast of characters includes the usual Bond suspects, including a villain out to destroy the world and his gorgeously evil henchwoman. Both *Nobody but You* and *The Spy Who Loves Me* delightfully demonstrate Kenner flair's for combining acerbic humor, witty dialogue, and clever plot twists into one terrifically entertaining story.

With the publication of *The Givenchy Code* and *Carpe Demon: Adventures of a Demon-Hunting Soccer Mom* in 2005, Kenner expanded her literary horizons to include both chick lit and women's fiction. In *The Givenchy Code,* graduate student Melanie "Mel" Prescott becomes caught up in a deadly game when she is forced into solve a series of clues being left by a madman. The use of first-person narration; the witty, humor-tinged writing; and the hint of romance that blossoms between Mel and Stryker, the ex-Marine who helps protect Mel from her assassin, give *The Givenchy Code* its chick-lit flavor. In *Carpe Demon,* the book's heroine, Kate Connor, is a retired demon hunter turned suburban housewife and mother; but when Kate crosses paths with a powerful demon, she is forced out of retirement and back into the demon-hunting business. Much of the humor in *Carpe Demon* comes from watching Kate juggle the normal duties of any mom—carpools, kids, and housework—while trying to keep her old identity a secret from her family. The book gleams with Kenner's distinctive brand of wit.

Humor is one of the most important ingredients in any of Kenner's many different kinds of books. Whether readers are enjoying one of Kenner's wild and witty contemporary romances, one of her whimsical paranormal love stories, or even one of her stylish blends of chick lit and modern-day romance, they know they can count on at least a laugh or two from this gifted writer.

BIBLIOGRAPHY

Books: *Nobody Does It Better.* Toronto: Harlequin, 2000; *The Cat's Fancy.* New York: Bantam, 2000; *Reckless.* Toronto: Harlequin, 2000; *Aphrodite's Kiss.* New York: Bantam, 2001; *Intimate Fantasy.* Toronto: Harlequin, 2001; *L. A. Confidential.* Toronto: Harlequin, 2001; *Aphrodite's Passion.* New York: Bantam, 2002; *Undercover Lovers.* Toronto: Harlequin, 2002; *Nobody but You.* New York: Pocket, 2003; *Silent Confessions.* Toronto: Harlequin, 2003; *Aphrodite's Secret.* New York: Bantam, 2003; *Silent Desires.* Toronto: Harlequin, 2003; *Dangerous Desires.* Toronto: Harlequin, 2004; *Stolen Kisses.* Toronto: Harlequin, 2004; *The Spy Who Loves Me.* New York: Pocket, 2004;

Aphrodite's Flame. New York: Bantam, 2004; *Carpe Demon: The Adventures of a Demon-Hunting Soccer Mom.* New York: Berkley, 2005; *The Givenchy Code.* New York: Downtown Press, 2005; *Night Moves.* Toronto: Harlequin, 2005; *First Love.* New York: Signet, 2005; *The Manolo Matrix.* New York: Downtown Press, 2006; *California Demon: Further Adventures of a Demon-Hunting Soccer Mom.* New York: Berkley, 2006; *The Perfect Score.* Toronto: Harlequin, 2006; *The Prada Paradox.* New York: Downtown Press, 2007.

Novellas: "Seeking Single Superhero" in *A Mother's Way.* New York: Bantam, 2002; "Dangerous Desires" in *Beyond Suspicion.* Toronto: Harlequin, 2004; "Wild Thing" in *Essence of Midnight.* Toronto: Harlequin, 2004; "Today's Secret" in *The Hope Chest.* Toronto: Harlequin, 2005; "Those Were the Days" in *Perfect Timing.* Toronto: Harlequin, 2006.

JOHN CHARLES

CORY KENYON/KEATON. *See* Vicki Lewis Thompson

LYNN KERSTAN

Lynn Kerstan. Courtesy of Lynn Kerstan.

Readers can readily discern the influence of both William Shakespeare and Georgette Heyer in Lynn Kerstan's writing. Like Shakespeare, Kerstan believes an entertaining story will often contain a mix of comedy and tragedy. From Heyer comes an appreciation for witty writing and sparkling dialogue. Nowhere are these two elements more brilliantly combined than in Kerstan's frequently fast-paced, occasionally risky, sometimes elegant, and always superbly written romances.

Kerstan was born in Paris, Tennessee. Her father was a career Navy man, a so-called mustang officer who was promoted from the ranks during World War II. Kerstan's mother was a journalist, who in the latter part of her life saw the world by teaching bridge on cruise ships. Kerstan grew up wherever the Navy sent her father, including Eritrea, Panama; Albuquerque, New Mexico; and Pacific Grove, California—where, Kerstan says, "we had the good fortune to stay for five years. It was an idyllic place for kids."

Kerstan attended mostly Catholic schools from the second grade through graduate school. After high school, she entered the religious order of the Sisters of St. Joseph of Carondelet, where she became known as Sister Michael Damien. After leaving the convent three years later, Kerstan attended the University of San Diego and graduated with majors in English and theater. She then accepted a doctoral teaching fellowship at the Catholic University of America in Washington, D.C.

I'd always loved Shakespeare, and circumstances helped me find my specialty straightaway. My advisor, an Elizabethan scholar, recommended me for a part-time job at the Folger Shakespeare Library as an assistant to the editor of *Shakespeare Quarterly,* a position I held for five years. Also, my first year in grad school, I was awarded a scholarship for a summer Shakespeare study program at Stratford-upon-Avon. Every morning before classes, I joined the queue at the theatre to buy standing room for that evening's production by the Royal Shakespeare Company. It was in Stratford, by the way, that a fellow student handed me Georgette Heyer's *The Grand Sophy,* assuring me that I'd like it. Oh, I did! My love for Regency and for romance novels was born, and at a time when the high drama and splendid characterization of Shakespeare influenced the love stories I began making up in my head. Of course, many years passed before I actually wrote a story.

Before becoming a writer, Kerstan held a variety of jobs. To help pay her tuition for school, she waitressed, babysat, and mowed lawns. For several years, she was a folk singer. She worked at the *Washington Post* (in a totally "menial" capacity, she recalls) and taught English literature, drama, and writing at both the Catholic University of America and the University of San Diego. Kerstan hast been a travel manager, a technical writer, and a professional bridge player. "Guess I couldn't hold a job!" she laughingly observes.

While Kerstan had always loved dreaming up stories, the thought of transcribing and rewriting them on a typewriter, she says, "was more work than I wanted to do." She did write lots of articles, scholarly papers, and the like, as well as a couple of plays and TV scripts when she was studying theater. "Oh, and four or five pretentious short stories as an undergraduate. That's it, until the PC became affordable," says Kerstan.

Kerstan had been working in isolation for three years on what she calls "my rambling, convoluted, but highly dramatic masterpiece, also known as *The Book of My Apprenticeship,*" when she discovered Romance Writers of America and went to a conference.

There I pitched my story to a Zebra (Kensington) editor, who agreed to look at it; but I also learned enough at that conference to know my masterpiece was unmarketable … not to mention awful. It would have to be rewritten. [In the meantime], with the arrogance of inexperience, I decided to toss off a short Regency comedy of manners—a bit of fluff—just so I'd have something to offer for a quick sale. But very soon, I became invested in my Regency characters and their story. The book wound up being as long as a historical, and only Zebra was publishing the longer Regencies. So I sent the entire manuscript to that Zebra editor I'd met, with a cover letter that apologized for sending the book a whole year later, and not even the same book I'd pitched! She graciously passed the manuscript on to the Regency editor, and within a few weeks, I got "The Call."

Kerstan's first book, *A Spirited Affair,* was published by Kensington in 1993 as part of their traditional Regency line. In Kerstan's debut romance, after Miss Jillian Lamb's allowance stops coming, she goes to London to confront her guardian, Mark Delacourt, the Earl of Coltrane, who insists on giving her a season of her own. With her very first book, Kerstan demonstrated her flair for sparkling dialogue and her sharp sense of wit. *A Spirited Affair* was nominated for RITA awards for both best first book and best Regency romance by Romance Writers of America.

Kerstan contributed several novellas to Zebra's Regency anthologies before collaborating with fellow Zebra Regency authors Alicia Rasley and Julie Caille on *Lessons in Love* (1994). The three became acquainted in 1992 on the Genie Romance Exchange, a DOS-based server that drew a large community of romance writers and readers. Kerstan recalls, "The collaboration on an anthology of three 'braided' Regency novellas was Julie's idea. We shared an editor at Zebra, so I pitched the idea to her, and we had a sale before we started. Next we created a 'room' on the Genie RomEx for brainstorming and critiquing and welcomed other authors to watch us making sausage. What were we thinking! Anyway, Julie, an engineer with an organized mind and way of working, found herself collaborating with a pair of loosey-goosey writers in front of an audience; but we three pioneers muddled through and even made our deadline."

Kerstan's next book, *Lady in Blue* (1995), was her first historical romance. "As proven by the length of my early Regencies, my imagination tends to serve up stories that require space," says Kerstan. "But only one publisher was open to longer traditional Regencies at that time, and soon after, they stopped accepting them. In part, I was making a practical business decision." Set in the early Victorian era, *Lady in Blue* is the story of Clare Easton, who is so desperate for money to help support her brothers that she accepts the position of mistress to Brynmore Talgarth, the Earl of Caradoc. Brynmore finds himself captivated by the intelligent and graceful Clare, so much so that he decides he no longer wants Clare as his mistress—he wants her as his wife.

Kerstan partnered with Rasley again in 1995 to write *Gwen's Christmas Ghost,* another traditional Regency romance with a twist. In *Gwen's Christmas Ghost,* the hero, Valerian Caine, is a Georgian rake who has been killed in a duel with Richard Sevaric. Valerian's dalliance with Sevaric's wife precipitated the duel, which in turn caused a hundred year feud between the two families. Now Valerian's ghost is being given another chance at life if he can put to rights, by Christmas Day, the damage he has caused. Valerian finds himself back on earth with only his clothes and his wits, but when he rescues Gwendolyn "Gwen" Sevaric from a near accident with a runaway carriage, it gives him the opportunity to become involved with Gwen, Max Sevaric, and his own descendant, Dorothea Caine. Valerian's mission to avenge his past becomes complicated by his growing love for Gwen. *Gwen's Christmas Ghost* won Kerstan her first RITA award in 1996.

After *Raven's Bride* (1996), another long historical romance, was published in 1996, Kerstan focused on writing traditional Regencies for Fawcett, including the delightful *Francesca's Rake* (1997). Miss Francesca Childe, an unfashionably tall bluestocking, and at age 31, more than a bit long in the tooth, has been roped into chaperoning her two nieces during the London Season. Galen Pender, Viscount Clayburn, is being forced by his ruthless father to marry a spinster so her property holdings can be added to theirs. Galen decides to thwart his father's plans by finding the most unsuitable woman possible and marrying her. Francesca seems to fit the bill perfectly. Reforming a rake was never so much fun as when Francesca and Galen go toe-to-toe to match wits and gleefully engage in verbal sparring. An unapologetic rogue and a woman society considers unmarriageable turn out to be the perfect couple in Kerstan's charming, merry romp.

Celia's Grand Passion (1998), a traditional Regency that earned Kerstan another RITA nomination, is the story of Lady Celia Greer, a young widow. Now that her very odd husband is dead, a newly emancipated Celia is looking for an affair, not another marriage. Diplomat Lord Kendal is the best in the business. Although he is able to create and mend relationships with people in power, the protective wall of ice he's built around his heart prevents him from having a meaningful relationship of his own. Celia falls for the cool, calm nobleman; but once Kendal finds out that, despite her marital status, she is still a virgin, he refuses to "ruin" her. Devastated by Kendal's rejection, Celia returns to her home to settle her dead husband's estate. Fate steps in, and Celia and Kendal are once more drawn together, but this time, he's smart enough not to let her go. Kerstan's keen sense of irony shines as she takes an innocent woman and a glacially frosty man and gives them a Grand Passion.

Kerstan turned her talents to the historical Regency market in 2002, with the publication of *The Golden Leopard,* the first in her Big Cat trilogy. *The Golden Leopard* proved to be a special joy for Kerstan to write because it allowed her to draw on her own love of travel and her interest in the experiences of the British who traveled to and lived in India in the eighteenth and early nineteenth centuries. The book is based on the premise of "what it would be like to be under a death sentence and be forced to live in close proximity, while completing a task, with your executioner." *The Golden Leopard* is the spellbinding story of Lady Jessica Carville, who has channeled all of her former passion for Lord Hugo Duran into her work as an antiquities expert for Christie's auction house. When Hugo turns up in England needing Jessica's help to find a fabulous Indian icon, a jewel-encrusted golden leopard, Jessica finds herself not only working with the man who once abandoned her, but also falling in love with him all over again.

Kerstan followed *The Golden Leopard* with *Heart of the Tiger* (2003), which she found to be one of the most challenging books she has written. The book's wonderfully complex heroine, Mira Holcombe, is bent on revenge against the Duke of Tallant, who has done everything he can to ruin Mira's life, including driving Mira and her father out of their home. Michael Keynes, the duke's brother, wants to destroy Tallant as well, and he has just arrived in England from India with that very goal in mind. Mira's and Michael's paths keep crossing as the two formulate their individual plans of retribution; but when the duke is murdered and Mira becomes the prime suspect, Michael discovers there are better things worth pursuing than revenge. In *Heart of the Tiger,* Kerstan contemplates the idea of "good people compelled to do bad things in order to protect others and being willing to take the consequences." With this book, as with the other two of her Big Cat historical romances, Kerstan skillfully explores themes of sacrifice, retribution, and honor—all within the framework of a sublimely sensual love story.

What would happen if a truly good man with a perfect life made a serious mistake that brought him down? This became the core theme of *The Silver Lion* (2003), the third book in Kerstan's Big Cat trilogy. In order to obtain a job as secretary to the book's hero, Derek Leighton, the Earl of Varden, Helena Pryce promises to use her connections to get Derek a piece of property he desires. Helena has a zeal for reform legislation, and she is certain that working with Derek will provide the opportunity to get her ideas before Parliament. The only problem is that after sharing one intense, unplanned night of passion with Derek, Helena finds herself falling in love with the one man she can never hope to have. Kerstan says writing *The Silver Lion* presented her with several unique challenges: "As the third book of the trilogy, it had to tie up several other continuing story lines, such as the identity of the 'Secret Master Villain.' But the real problem was with Derek, the book's hero, a good man struggling with his own unexpected failures. He had a tendency to fade into the woodwork, mainly because my favorite hero ever (Michael Keynes of *Heart of the Tiger*) was also a major character in the book. But Lord Varden came into his own, and readers really liked him." It is difficult to imagine how readers could not like the subtly nuanced Derek, who meets his match in the sharp-witted and sharp-tongued Helena. *The Silver Lion* not only brought Kerstan's Big Cat trilogy to a splendidly triumphant conclusion, it also earned the talented author yet another RITA nomination.

"Mostly, I try to find ways to make the happy ending both inevitable and impossible," says Kerstan. "And then I have to find a way to bring it off convincingly." Nowhere is this more evident than in Kerstan's Black Phoenix books, beginning with *Dangerous Deceptions,* published in 2004. In *Dangerous Deceptions,* Jarrett, Lord Dering, is "invited" by the Black Phoenix Society, a secret organization dedicated to righting wrongs perpetrated by high-ranking members of the *ton,* to infiltrate Paradise, a decadent pleasure resort where men's darker desires are fulfilled. He is paired with Kate Falshaw, an actress with a tortured past, and together they must use the cover of a passionate affair as a disguise for their real mission: shutting the gates of Paradise. Kerstan continues the adventures of the Black Phoenix Society in *Dangerous Passions* (2005). Lady Eve Halliday finds her personal plans of vengeance against Lord Marcus Cordell compromised when she is forced to collaborate intimately with him while on a mission for the Black Phoenix. Kerstan deftly blends danger, deception, and desire into a heady mix in both of her Black Phoenix books, as she continues to explore the themes of honor, retribution, and redemption.

Even with Shakespeare, Heyer, and Dorothy Dunnett as inspiration, Kerstan still faces the challenge of crafting stories that realistically balance laughter and tears. But for her, writing has always been a labor of love: "Every once in a while, I get in the zone. A scene, sometimes an unexpected one, pours out as if I actually knew what I was doing. It's rare, and it's magic. I live for those times. Primarily I love that I am creating something out of nothing, telling a unique story with unique characters and inviting readers to share it. I love what I do and am blessed to be a writer."

BIBLIOGRAPHY

Books: *A Spirited Affair.* New York: Kensington, 1993; *Lessons in Love* (with Alicia Rasley and Julie Caille). New York: Kensington, 1994; *Lady in Blue.* New York: Harper, 1995; *Gwen's Christmas Ghost* (with Alicia Rasley). New York: Kensington, 1995; *Raven's Bride.* New York: Harper, 1996; *Francesca's Rake.* New York: Fawcett, 1997; *A Midnight Clear.* New York: Fawcett, 1997; *Celia's Grand Passion.* New York: Fawcett, 1998; *Lucy in Disguise.* New York: Fawcett, 1998; *Marry in Haste.* New York: Fawcett, 1998; *Lord Dragoner's Wife.* New York: Signet, 1999; *The Golden Leopard.* New York: Onyx, 2002; *Heart of the Tiger.* New York: Onyx, 2003; *The Silver Lion.* New York: Onyx, 2003; *Dangerous Deceptions.* New York: Onyx, 2004; *Dangerous Passions.* New York: Onyx, 2005.

Novellas: "The Runaway Bride" in *A June Betrothal.* New York: Kensington, 1993; "A Change of Heart" in *A Mother's Joy.* New York: Kensington, 1994; "The Marriage Scheme" in *Wedding Belles.* New York: Signet, 2004.

Genre-Related Essay: "In Praise of Love and Folly" in *North American Romance Writers.* Lanham, MD: Scarecrow Press, 1999.

JOHN CHARLES

APRIL KIHLSTROM

April Kihlstrom gave up the analytical world of operations research for the glittering social whirl of the Regency *ton,* and her readers couldn't be more grateful. They love Kihlstrom's strong heroines; the heroes who learn to value their worth; and her enchanting stories, which celebrate the power of love to shape people's lives.

Kihlstrom was born in Buffalo, New York. Her father was an engineer, while her mother, a statistician, was a stay at home mom when Kihlstrom was growing up. Kihlstrom attended Purdue University, receiving bachelor of science degree in honors math and later earning her master's degree in operations research from Cornell University in New York.

Ever since college, Kihlstrom dreamed of writing romance novels. After completing her degrees, Kihlstrom and her new husband went to Paris on his NATO postdoctoral fellowship. Kihlstrom was not allowed to work due to the conditions of her visa. This presented her with the ideal opportunity to begin writing her first book. Upon their return to the United States, Kihlstrom gave birth to a child with Down Syndrome. Because Kihlstrom needed and wanted to spend time with her son, she decided to seriously pursue writing as her career.

Kihlstrom's publishing career began with *Paris Summer,* written for Avalon and published in 1977, the first of three contemporary romances. Inspired by the year Kihlstrom and her husband spent in Paris after they finished graduate school, *Paris Summer* features two mathematicians as the lead characters. Kihlstrom followed *Paris Summer* with *Trondelaine Castle* (1979), which was set in England, and *My Love Betrayed* (1980), set in Mexico.

Citing Georgette Heyer as one of her favorite authors, Kihlstrom began writing the Regency romances for which she later became known and loved. "When the market opened up, I decided to write them," says Kihlstrom. "Of course, I tried pitching my manuscript just as the market was collapsing back then but … eventually I was lucky to have my manuscript read and bought by Signet." Her first Regency romance, *A Choice of Cousins* (1982), features Edward Fambrough, the Earl of Danvers, and Sara Farthingham, two cousins who, though enemies, must unite to save two younger relatives from scandal.

More Regency romances followed, including *The Wary Spinster* (1983), which showcases Kihlstrom's skill at characterization. She gives her heroine, thirtyish spinster-by-choice Anthea Marwood, excellent reasons for not getting married. After growing up with an abusive father, Anthea vows never again to be under the thumb of any man, until she meets Viscount Giles Radbourne. Despite his rakish reputation and his disappointing first marriage, Giles proves to be surprisingly sensitive, and he can't resist the challenge of winning the love of a woman like Anthea. Kihlstrom not only crafts an endearing hero and heroine, but she also extends her gift for characterization to creating a deliciously evil villain and a cast of engaging secondary characters in this fine early effort.

While Kihlstrom has written her share of lords and ladies, she especially shines when writing about unconventional characters, such as the heroes in *The Reckless Barrister* (1999), *The Wily Wastrel* (1999), and *The Sentimental Soldier* (2000), a trilogy featuring the Langford brothers. The three brothers are not typical noblemen and in fact earn their livelihoods in more unusual professions. Philip Langford is the reckless barrister of the title, who has been hired by Miss Emily Ashbourne to seek justice for industrial workers. James Langford, the hero of *The Wily Wastrel,* has a natural talent for inventions. He meets his match in Miss Juliet Galsworth, a lady whose curiosity and lively mind equals his own. For her third Langford brother, Kihlstrom turns to the military and introduces Col. Harry Langford, a career soldier who must collaborate with Miss Prudence Marland when the two are caught behind enemy lines in France. With her Langford Brothers trilogy, Kihlstrom introduces readers to a world beyond the glittering social swirl of the *ton.*

While Kihlstrom is known for crafting colorful characters, perhaps her most famous creation of all is the remarkable Miss Tibbles. As the governess in charge of the five Wescott sisters, Miss Marian Tibbles first appeared in *The Wicked Groom* (1996), in which the intrepid Jeremy, Duke of Berenford, is betrothed to the spirited Lady Diana Wescott, a young woman he has never met. He decides to disguise himself as a groom in her father's stables, to better know his bride-to-be. While the focus of the story is on Diana and Jeremy, Miss Tibbles is a secondary character, who steals the show in the first book in which she appears. "She was just going to be a prop, totally unimportant, and then … she appeared and took over," says Kihlstrom. "It was as if she wrote her own lines. She became a delight to include in my stories!" More books about the Wescott sisters followed, until the sixth book elevated Miss Tibbles to leading-character status.

In the sixth book in the Wescott series, *Miss Tibbles' Folly* (1998), the resourceful governess finds herself the object of a gentleman's attention, when she is courted by a retired soldier, Col. Andrew Merriweather, who served with her late fiancé. She has successfully married off all of her charges and is now enjoying a vacation in Bath, courtesy of her grateful employers. Miss Tibbles blossoms under the Colonel's attention, but she fears that her diminished social status as a governess dooms any chances of marriage between them. Despite opposition from society, the Wescott sisters, and his family, Andrew devises a campaign worthy of Wellington to win Miss Tibbles' heart. *Miss Tibbles' Folly,* a charming conclusion to the Wescott saga, opens the door for the further adventures of the newly married Miss Tibbles.

"The changing roles of men and women seemed the most important thing that I, as a feminist, could write about," says Kihlstrom. "How do two people come together with love and kindness and mutual respect in a way that empowers them both?" Kihlstrom brilliantly explores this theme in her many books. Her heroines not only survive, but thrive and prove to be more than a match for the men they meet. According to Kihlstrom, "Romances are powerful stories that help to shape the world we live in and reflect the challenges we all, men *and* women, face."

BIBLIOGRAPHY

Books: *Paris Summer.* New York: Avalon, 1977; *Trondelaine Castle.* New York: Avalon, 1979; *My Love Betrayed.* New York: Avalon, 1980; *A Choice of Cousins.* New York: Signet, 1982; *A Scandalous Bequest.* New York: Signet, 1982; *An Improper Companion.* New York: Signet, 1983; *The Wary Spinster.* New York: Signet, 1983; *The Mysterious Governess.* New York: Signet, 1984; *Twice Betrothed.* New York: Signet, 1984; *The Charming Imposter.* New York: Signet, 1985; *The Counterfeit Betrothal.* New York: Signet, 1986; *The Nabob's Widow.* New York: Signet, 1987; *Captain Rogue.* New York: Signet, 1988; *Miss Redmond's Folly.* New York: Signet, 1988; *The Scholar's Daughter.* New York: Signet, 1989; *The Reckless Wager.* New York: Signet, 1991; *Dangerous Masquerade.* New York: Signet, 1992; *The Wicked Groom.* New York: Signet, 1996; *The Widowed Bride.* New York: Signet, 1996; *An Honorable Rogue.* New York: Signet, 1997; *The Reluctant Thief.* New York: Signet, 1998; *An Outrageous Proposal.* New York: Signet, 1998; *Miss Tibbles' Folly.* New York: Signet, 1998; *The Reckless Barrister.* New York: Signet, 1999; *The Wily Wastrel.* New York: Signet, 1999; *The Sentimental Soldier.* New York: Signet, 2000; *Miss Tibbles Investigates.* New York: Signet, 2000; *The Ambitious Baronet.* New York: Signet, 2001; *The Widower's Folly.* New York: Signet, 2001; *The Soldier's Bride.* New York: Signet, 2002; *Miss Tibbles Interferes.* New York: Signet, 2002.

JOANNE HAMILTON-SELWAY

SANDRA KITT

Sandra Kitt. Photo by John Penderhughes, photographer. Courtesy of Sandra Kitt.

Sandra Kitt is a trailblazer who proved to the publishing world that true love doesn't come in one color. With her book *Adam and Eva* (1984), Kitt became the first African American writer published by Harlequin. Ten years later, her book *Serenade* (1994) helped launch Kensington's Arabesque line, the first effort by a major publisher to feature African American romance novels. Many other writers now walk down the path that Kitt paved for them.

Kitt comes by her creativity naturally. She was born and raised in Harlem, New York City, in 1947 to parents from Charleston, South Carolina. They met in high school and married after Kitt's father returned from serving four years in the Navy in Hawaii. Her father was very artistic, writing poetry and songs, drawing cartoons, and singing. He formed his own trio called The Associations, and they performed in small clubs around Harlem. Kitt says, "I got my talents and sensibilities from my father, and my sense of individual style and confidence from my mother."

Following in the footsteps of her father, Kitt wanted to be an artist from the age of 8 and was actively encouraged to study it by both her parents and teachers. She took classes at the Museum of Modern Art in New York when she was 11 and attended the High School of Music and Art. After attending Bronx Community College, Kitt graduated with an associate's degree in liberal arts. She then spent the next semester at the University of Guadalajara, Mexico, in order to study art and to perfect her Spanish. Upon returning to New York, she finished her bachelor's degree in fine arts at City College of New York. She went on to work in advertising for two years before deciding to return to school for a master's degree in fine arts, specializing in printmaking and illustration. After completing her graduate degree, Kitt worked as a graphic designer and freelance illustrator, exhibiting around the country. Her work is now on the cover of UNICEF cards as well as in several corporate collections, the Institute of American Illustrators, and the Los Angeles Museum of African American Art.

As a youngster, Kitt's goal was to become a children's book author and to illustrate her own stories. She wrote her first children's books at the age of 15 and has written seven stories for the children's and young adult market, but they remain unpublished. She hadn't considered writing and publishing for adults until about 1981, and she had completed three manuscripts before contacting a publisher.

When she began writing professionally, Kitt was still doing limited freelance artwork and participating in print exhibits. She was also working full-time as a librarian/information specialist in astronomy and astrophysics at the American Museum of Natural History in New York City. She retired from that position to become a full-time writer after writing and publishing 26 books. Her creative focus shifted from art—except for Christmas cards, which she has designed and made by hand for close friends and family since she was 18—to the written word. Of her artwork, Kitt says, "I have every intention of returning to art in the near future."

Kitt's writing style is fairly "loose and easy." She explains, "I've never felt the need to write every single day, as many writers claim is necessary. Because of my many other interests, I've been able to compartmentalize my time and attention to my different projects. When I'm working on a new story, I let it happen as slowly or as quickly as the plot develops in my head." However, if Kitt is under a tight deadline, she says she can "crank up the heat" and write very rapidly, working straight through from early morning until evening. In those cases, Kitt has written as much as one hundred pages in one day.

Kitt began her career writing in longhand, in the days before personal computers. She had to learn to create at the computer when she found herself faced with deadlines for two books in the same month. Now, she prefers to write on a computer because of the speed and ease of making changes. With the advent of the laptop, Kitt says, "Many nights, I enjoy sitting up in bed and working."

At first, Kitt didn't consider her books to be romance novels. She says, "I thought I was writing pretty mainstream stories that incorporated some romance. I began publishing first with Harlequin because there was no other publishing house producing the kind of stories I was writing." Although Kitt enjoyed writing for Harlequin, the editors felt that Kitt always had a much bigger story in mind than just a linear exploration of a relationship between a man and a woman. She wrote several books and novellas that were strictly romances, but they were still infused with a degree of realism that was uncommon at the time. When she stopped writing for Harlequin, it was only because she wrote a novel that was "out of scope for what they were publishing at the time." She comments, "There was no place for me to advance to."

Kitt keeps a notebook of ideas and themes for novels, a list of potential titles, and names for male and female protagonists. She also completes a character sketch of each important character in her novels. Years ago, she kept a folder of pictures of men, women, and children, torn from catalogs and magazines, that she used as an aid for finding the right image for her characters and the names she had chosen for them. Usually it's the characters that come to Kitt first, but in a few instances, she has had a great theme, premise, or "what if" that acted as the catalyst for a new novel.

Kitt enjoys writing books that show extensive emotional change and growth in her main characters. She likes to see them struggle with very human issues, including doubt, fear, anger, loss, forgiveness, and love—while having the character become a better person in the end. In her 1994 novel *Serenade,* singer Alexandra Morrow is finally making it big in the jazz business only to be unexpectedly reunited with music legend Parker Harrison, an old flame from her past. Alexandra must contend with the tender feelings that resurface for Parker, despite the turmoil and heartache he caused her 10 years earlier, when she was young and naive.

The exploration of racial and social issues is also common in Kitt's books because she is fascinated with social change and speculation as to how an "American" will be defined in 30 or 40 years. Kitt likes to give readers a story that is more than just entertaining; she asks questions through her characters' actions and motivations, with the intention of provoking her readers to think about and consider those issues. Kitt says, "The response I get from my reader base lets me know that I've not only succeeded, but that my ideas make the books thoughtful as well as romantic or entertaining."

In *The Color of Love* (1995), Kitt examines the concept of interracial relationships. Leah Downey, a gifted black artist, is trapped in a lonely, empty relationship. She meets Jason Horn, who is a white police officer struggling with painful experiences from his past. The chemistry between them is undeniable, but they each have obstacles to overcome in order to forge a relationship. In her 1996 novel, *Significant Others,* Kitt examines the racial issue of light-skinned versus dark-skinned African Americans. In this story, a Brooklyn high school counselor, Patricia Gilbert, who is light-skinned, must confront the color bias when one of her students, who is also light-skinned, is being pressured by peers to choose sides. Patricia's own racial identity is called into question when she meets the student's father, who is suspicious of her ethnicity and motives, until love renders the point moot.

The men in Kitt's stories are very centered, strong, and smart; but they are also capable of being vulnerable and unsure at times. To Kitt, the greatest strength a man can possess is his ability to be gentle. Her male characters are capable of being introspective, meaning they can think and consider other people before themselves. In Kitt's 1996 novel *Suddenly,* Maxwell Chandler is a doctor who operates a clinic for infants with AIDS. He meets professional New York model Christine Morrow (who is the younger sister of Alexandra Morrow from Kitt's novel *Serenade*). Maxwell is completely unimpressed with the beautiful Christine, whom he considers shallow and frivolous. Christine comes to realize how self-centered and superficial her life has been, and by becoming involved with Maxwell and his work, she finds meaning in her life, and he finds his soul mate.

Kitt's heroines are fair, thoughtful, and kind; but they also have a very healthy suspicion of other people's motives. The women are self-protective without being paranoid or defensive. They are also somewhat fearless, in that they are not afraid to take a risk. Kitt says some people claim that her heroines are a lot like her. In *Between Friends* (1998), two childhood friends, Dallas and Valerie, find themselves reunited at the funeral of a mutual friend from the old neighborhood. Even though they grew up in the same community, they each came from very different cultural backgrounds; Dallas is a biracial African American and Valerie is Irish. During this bittersweet reunion, the heroine, Dallas, and her best friend, Valerie, find themselves both falling for the same man, Alex, the brother of the deceased. Now, for the first time, the women question their friendship and racial differences as they compete over the handsome Italian, Alex.

Preferring to write about the northeastern United States, Kitt especially likes New York because that is the area with which she is most familiar. She notes, "New York being such a 'melting pot' lends itself perfectly to the kind of stories I like to tell, but I have written books that have taken place in other cities; sometimes that depends on the subject of the story." Kitt prefers writing about the present, so her writing is mostly contemporary fiction. Because there are so many changes taking place in American culture, Kitt feels that when one of her books explores them, she is also writing about the future.

Among her hobbies, Kitt includes a love of travel and adventure. A true Renaissance woman, besides making her own greeting cards, Kitt cooks; sews; and hones her skills in photography, pottery, and silversmithing. While she does not read other fiction while working on a book, Kitt takes time between projects to catch up on novels.

When asked what one particular book was harder to write than the others, Kitt said, "I can't think of any book I've written that I would consider as having been 'hard' to write. Some of my stories have been fairly complex, especially when I introduce multiple points of view or there are more than one or two subplots. I just take my time thinking about how it all fits together." Sometimes there is a need to rewrite a chapter or eliminate or add another scene or character to make it work, but Kitt does not consider that "hard." Some books have been very easy for Kitt to write. From the first page until the last, the story just flows smoothly, easily and quickly. According to Kitt, *The Color of Love,* her first mainstream novel, was the easiest book for her to write. She feels that she was meant to write that book, and it remains her best-selling. Published more than a decade ago, the novel is in its 10th printing. It is also her favorite book, although *Close Encounters* (2000) is a close second.

Kitt finds inspiration for her work by observing people around her, reading newspapers and books, watching movies, and sometimes, listening to songs. She doesn't start a book without knowing the characters. For Kitt, writer's block occurs when she becomes distracted or tired, or when there are other things happening in her life that interfere with her ability to concentrate on her work. When that happens, she tries to pull back, deal with the problem at hand, and then relax and do something fun. She says, "I know that it doesn't help me to try and push through the 'block' and write. For me, that's counterproductive. I simply leave it alone and go do something else. This action usually works perfectly to free up my mind and allow the creative juices to start flowing again."

For Kitt, the fact that she is creating people out of thin air and breathing life into them with her words so that readers will believe in them the way she does is the most appealing part of writing. She says, "I love exploring their emotions, and I love writing about a topic or issue that really interests me. I don't mind the isolation of being a writer because I'm very good at breaking away from that and engaging in other activities. Writing is like having another little room in my life where I go alone to interact with make-believe people, places, and things." With an imagination as fertile as Kitt's, that little room must be awfully crowded.

BIBLIOGRAPHY

Books: *All Good Things.* New York: Doubleday, 1984; *Adam and Eva.* Toronto: Harlequin, 1984; *Rites of Spring.* Toronto: Harlequin, 1984; *Only with the Heart.* Toronto: Harlequin, 1985; *Perfect Combination.* Toronto: Harlequin, 1985; *With Open Arms.* Toronto: Harlequin, 1987; *An Innocent Man.* Toronto: Harlequin, 1989; *The Way Home.* Toronto: Harlequin, 1990; *Someone's Baby.* Toronto: Harlequin, 1991; *Love Everlasting.* New York: Odyssey, 1993; *Serenade.* New York: Pinnacle, 1994; *Sincerely.* New York: Pinnacle, 1995; *The Color of Love.* New York: Signet, 1995; *Significant Others.* New York: Onyx, 1996; *Suddenly.* New York: Pinnacle, 1996; *Between Friends.* New York: Signet, 1998; *Family Affairs.* New York: Signet, 1999; *Close Encounters.* New York: Signet, 2000; *She's the One.* New York: Signet, 2001; *Just Passing Through.* New York: Washington Square Press, 2003; *Southern Comfort.* New York: BET, 2004; *The Next Best Thing.* New York: BET, 2005.

Novellas: "Love Is Thanks Enough" in *Friends, Family, Lovers.* Toronto: Harlequin, 1993; "Sweet Dreams" in *For the Love of Chocolate.* New York: St. Martin's Press, 1996; "Celebration" in *Merry Christmas, Baby.* New York: HarperCollins, 1996; "Homecoming" in *Sisters.* New York: Signet, 1996; "Heart of the Matter" in *Girlfriends.* New York: HarperCollins, 1999; "Love Changes Everything" in *Back in Your Arms.* New York: BET, 2006; "Survival Instinct" in *Have a Little Faith.* New York: Pocket, 2006.

Genre-Related Essay: "Telling Tales Out of School" in *North American Romance Writers.* Lanham, MD: Scarecrow Press, 1999.

SANDRA VAN WINKLE, SHELLEY MOSLEY, AND SHANNON PRESCOTT

PATRICIA KNOLL

RITA finalist Patricia Ann Knoll was born Patricia Forsythe in 1951 in Morenci, Arizona. Her parents were both from the Kiamichi Mountains in southeastern Oklahoma, where Knoll's father originally worked as a rancher. He was drafted into the Army, served in World War II, and was awarded a Silver Star for bravery. Following his military stint, he moved his wife and daughter, Alice, to the copper mining town of Morenci, Arizona, in search of better work prospects with the Phelps Dodge company. Knoll's mother was a schoolteacher and a homemaker for Knoll and her two sisters, Alice and Betty.

Knoll recalls her mother was a lifelong reader who fostered the love of books in her children. It helped develop Knoll's wild imagination, early storytelling skills, and the desire to write. As a child, Knoll would make up stories so vivid she would frighten herself and have to crawl into bed with her parents.

Her parents were insistent that their daughters would have college educations. Knoll earned her degree in elementary education and worked for a few years as a teacher, a librarian, and a secretary, while raising her own four children. She opened a care home for disabled children in 1981, dividing her time between family, writing, and working.

Knoll defines her writing style as romantic comedy, but some of her books are also serious. She began her writing career in 1981, when she took a writing class in San Diego that focused on romances. She didn't necessarily want to write romances—she just wanted to write. After a couple of years with no sales, Knoll partnered with Barbara Hicks, and together, they sold two novels to Silhouette. Their first book, *For Love of Mike,* won the Romance Writers of America Golden Medallion Award (the precursor of the RITA) in 1984.

---

also writing as Patricia Forsythe
also writing as Patti Forsythe
also writing as Charlotte Nichols

Knoll's writing process begins with an interesting conflict, such as the McCoy/Hatfield feud (RITA finalist *The Real McCoy*, 1993), which develops into a plot idea. In *Clanton's Woman* (1996), she depicts the present-day descendents of the Earp family and the Clantons.

Knoll doesn't have a recurrent theme in her books, other than the fundamental premise that "love conquers all, changes you, and brings understanding." Her heroes are smart alecky, tough guys who find themselves in adverse situations that they must overcome. They're baffled by the heroines, who are bright, successful women.

Her heroines don't always fit the mold. The librarian in *Wedding Bells* (1998), for example, is 5-feet 10-inches tall. Knoll sees many of her own traits in her heroines, who personify what Knoll aspires to be. Some of them are even-modern day royalty, as seen in *The Runaway Princess* (2001) and *Protecting the Princess* (2003).

Knoll prefers to set her novels in California, Arizona, or other regions in the western United States with big, open spaces and clear skies. She believes her characters in that setting are more real, with odd peccadilloes and crazy habits like the everyday people in Calamity Falls, Arizona. She writes in the contemporary time period, preferring the immediacy of modern challenges for her characters.

To Knoll, the appeal of the romance genre is its fantasy and the way the characters are able to overcome their differences and conflicts to form a stronger bonds. Fellow writers who inspire her are Tony Hillerman; Elmore Leonard, with his talent for dialogue; and Harper Lee, author of her all-time favorite, *To Kill a Mockingbird*.

Knoll names her novel *Bachelor Cowboy* (1999) as the easiest to write as well as the fastest. The novel took one month to write and did well in sales. Her favorite is *The Tenderfoot* (1993). She doesn't have one particular book that was harder to write than the others. They all had difficulties and challenges. When she experiences writer's block, she returns to the beginning and rereads what she's written. The block is often removed by developing a stronger conflict to propel the story forward. Knoll finds the rereading and revising phase of the writing process to be part of its appeal.

Most of her books are "sweet" romances, but Knoll says she gets the "greatest rush" from a well-written comedy scene. In fact, Knoll is known for her romantic comedies and has written for Harlequin's Love and Laughter line (*Delightful Jones,* 1998), and later, their Duets line (*Meant for You,* 1999; *Calamity Jo,* 2000; *Perk Avenue, 2002*). Whether she has written a work intended to be a romantic comedy, or a more serious book that she sprinkles with enticing snippets of humor, Knoll's novels are a mirror of her own quick wit and creativity.

BIBLIOGRAPHY

Writing as Patricia Knoll

Books: *Gypsy Enchantment.* Toronto: Harlequin, 1988; *Always a Bridesmaid.* Toronto: Harlequin, 1989; *Send in the Clown.* Toronto: Harlequin, 1989; *Cats in the Belfry.* Toronto: Harlequin, 1992; *The Real McCoy.* Toronto: Harlequin, 1993; *The Tenderfoot.* Toronto: Harlequin, 1993; *Clanton's Woman.* Toronto: Harlequin, 1996; *Desperately Seeking Annie.* Toronto: Harlequin, 1996; *Two Parent Family.* Toronto: Harlequin, 1996; *A Double Wedding.* Toronto: Harlequin, 1997; *Another Chance for Daddy.* Toronto: Harlequin, 1998; *Delightful Jones.* Toronto: Harlequin, 1998; *Wedding Bells.* Toronto: Harlequin, 1998; *Meant for You.* Toronto: Harlequin, 1999; *Bachelor Cowboy.* Toronto: Harlequin, 1999; *Resolution: Marriage.* Toronto: Harlequin, 1999; *Calamity Jo.* Toronto: Harlequin, 2000; *Project: Daddy.* Toronto: Harlequin, 2000; *Perk Avenue.* Toronto: Harlequin, 2002.

Writing as Patricia Forsythe

Books: *The Runaway Princess.* Toronto: Harlequin, 2001; *Protecting the Princess.* Toronto: Harlequin, 2003.

Writing as Patti Forsythe

Book: *Love in the Afternoon.* New York: Kensington, 2000.

Writing with Barbara Hicks as Charlotte Nichols

Books: *For the Love of Mike.* New York: Silhouette, 1984; *Eye of the Beholder.* New York: Silhouette, 1985.

SHELLEY MOSLEY AND SANDRA VAN WINKLE

KATHLEEN KORBEL. *See* Eileen Dreyer

BETINA KRAHN

Betina Krahn. Courtesy of Betina Krahn.

Award-winning author Betina Krahn always wanted to write. She began to write seriously in junior high school. But as for publishing novels and fiction—she says that was "a dream, one which always seemed unattainable." In 1980, Krahn read a romance novel and decided she wanted to write one. The rest is history.

Born in Huntington, West Virginia, in 1949, Krahn's parents were the first in their families to attend college. Her mother, Regina Triplett, a teacher, and her father, Dors Maynard, a World War II veteran of the Pacific theater, both went on to obtain their master's degrees. They were employed in the public schools and fostered in Krahn "a huge love of learning and a curiosity about the world."

Krahn lived in Charleston, West Virginia, until the age of 15, when she moved with her family to Newark, Ohio. She attended Ohio University, earning a bachelor of science degree in education in biological science comprehensive. She then moved on to Ohio State University, where she did graduate work in counseling. Krahn completed her college education at Southwestern Oklahoma State University, where she earned her master's degree in counseling.

Krahn's first husband, Donald Krahn, a physicist, was a graduate student in physics when they met. They were married 23 years when he succumbed to cancer. Several years after his death, she met and fell in love with Rex Rountree, the senior vice president of a construction firm. Krahn has two sons, Nathan and Zebulun, and at current count, she has two grandsons, Nicholas and Michael, with a third one on the way.

Like so many other authors, Krahn has had other careers. She taught science in both junior high and high school, wrote school curriculum in career development at Ohio State University, and performed personnel work and administration at New Horizons Comprehensive Mental Health Center in Oklahoma. Finally, she achieved her dream of becoming a full-time writer.

In her writing, Krahn says she strives for "a conversational, personal storytelling style that embodies the humor and paradoxes of life and portrays the playful side of loving as well as the soulful side." Krahn unerringly meets this goal in her books, and it shows marvelously in such works as *Sweet Talking Man* (2000). Suffragist Beatrice Von Furstenburg has more fights on her hands than just the battle for the vote. She is the guardian of Priscilla, her rebellious 16-year-old niece. Priscilla wants to marry Jeffrey, who is 18. Frantic to prove their competence and maturity to Beatrice, the young couple hires criminals to attack Beatrice so she can be rescued by Jeffrey. Nothing goes right, and the kidnappers stash Beatrice in a brothel. Realizing they're in over their heads, Jeffrey begs his cousin, attorney Connor Barrow, for help. Known for his gift of gab, the silver-tongued Irishman negotiates Beatrice's release. Of course, Connor and Beatrice experience a strong physical attraction to each other, but she finds his expeditious politics as distasteful as he does her modern ideas. The palpable sexual tension between Connor and Beatrice, their witty (and sometimes sneaky) battle of wills, and wonderful secondary characters keep the reader entertained from the first page to the last.

As an author, Krahn finds that sometimes characters come to her first, and sometimes plot ideas come first. However, she says, "I never proceed with an idea until I have characters that engage my imagination and give me a laugh or two." Barton "Bear" McQuaid and Diamond Wingate, the protagonists of *The Soft Touch* (1999), do both. Bear, who desperately needs funding for his Montana Railroad, meets with Diamond, an heiress to a fortune and an ardent philanthropist, to see if he can get some financial support from her. Unfortunately, lots of other people have the same idea, and Bear finds himself running interference between them and the oh-so-softhearted Diamond. Then there are the three fiancés Diamond has been too nice to turn down … Bear, a tough westerner who lives up to his name, and Diamond, who, unlike her namesake, has no hard edges, make perfect foils for each other as Bear learns that Diamond's true treasure has nothing to do with her money. Krahn softens the sometimes slapstick comedy of the book with well-placed touches of poignancy, and the result is a perfect balance of humor and pathos.

Krahn claims that "theme is probably in the eye of the beholder." She adds, "But over time, I think the idea of love triumphing over the prescribed roles and attitudes that keep men and women apart has been the most common in my books. Men and women need each other and have so much to offer each other—and society. Our socialization creates artificial barriers between us … teaches us to treat each other like objects, not persons. Love is the only thing I know that can break through such barriers." It is almost impossible to have two characters more different or socially separated than the hero and heroine of Krahn's *The Princess and the Barbarian* (1993); however, she somehow manages to bring them together in a humorous but believable way. This is made even more difficult because of the fact that Saxxe Rouen, the barbarian of the piece, heroically rescues Princess Thera and then unheroically demands three nights in her bed as his reward. The charming scoundrel in furs eventually wins the heart of Princess Thera's court as well as that of the fair damsel herself. The humor in the book is outrageously wonderful, and Saxxe's alpha-male antics add to the lively pace.

There are three major traits found in Krahn's heroes: strength, intelligence, and need. Likewise, there are three major traits found in Krahn's heroines: intelligence, strength, and need. The order and the pattern are not accidental. Krahn explains, "Dull/arrogant/ unevolved men don't interest me. I prefer men who have already had a few eye-opening experiences. Life should have given them a kick or two and gotten their attention, prepared the way for the important lessons of love. The women should be educated enough and self-possessed enough to command respect and make their own way in the world, yet should be capable of admitting that career, success, and station in life are only the start of a fulfilling life." Krahn also believes that there is "probably a great deal" of herself is in her heroines and heroes.

Krahn's hobbies often show up in her novels: "I used to cook fabulously. With every deadline, a few more of my skills seem to hit the dust. But I love to include food in my books … like the cook in *The Marriage Test* (2004)." Krahn deftly sprinkles numerous fascinating details about food and cooking in medieval England into this superbly entertaining novel. The third book in the Convent of the Brides of Virtue trilogy (*The Husband Test*, 2001; *The Wife Test*, 2003), *The Marriage Test* is a wonderfully witty and deliciously sexy story. Julia of Childress, a cook at the convent, is matched with Griffin de Grandaise, a nobleman whose heightened sense of smell means he is rarely able to eat anything. When Griffin tastes some of Julia's heavenly dishes, he realizes that he has found the solution to his culinary problems. Readers are treated to a splendidly amusing battle of wits between Julia, who is determined to become a nun, and Griffin, who'd do anything to secure her services as a cook.

Most of Krahn's books are set in England, but she also enjoys setting her stories in colonial America and "warm, exotic climes like the Caribbean." For *The Book of the Seven Delights* (2005), Krahn moves the action to the Sahara Desert. Librarian Abigail Merchant knows that she's as competent as any of the men running the British Museum, and she intends to prove it. Her golden opportunity to do just this occurs when she stumbles across the journals of an unorthodox scholar, which chronicle his quest for the remains of the Great Library of Alexander. Abigail travels to Casablanca, where she meets Apollo Smith, a sexy ex-legionnaire with a questionable past. Apollo meets his match in the feisty librarian, and together, they face the many challenges and obstacles that stand between them and their goal. With Abigail, Krahn neatly blows away the stereotype of "Marian the Librarian."

The librarian stereotype isn't the only one this author destroys. In her 2006 book, *The Book of True Desires,* the hero, Hartford Goodnight, is a butler, who is, according to Krahn, "a snarky, delicious British ex-pat—who needs liberation in the worst way." Set in turn-of-the-century Havana, Florida, and the jungles of Mexico, this exciting romantic adventure also features a courageous, daring, and resourceful explorer as the heroine, Cordelia O'Keefe Blackburn. Cordelia and Hartford are in search of the Gift of the Jaguar, a Mayan legend that may or may not be based on fact. In a neat twist, the Book of True Desires turns out to be Hartford's journal, which grows as the story progresses. In it, his changing feelings about Cordelia are revealed. The Book of True Desires takes the place of a sidekick, and when writing in it, Hartford allows his innermost feelings, desires, and even doubts to surface. At one point, Cordelia is abducted, and thinking that Hartford is dead, she is tempted to give up—until she reads his journal. Krahn's clever literary device, as well as this unforgettable couple, show yet another aspect of her impressive creativity.

Krahn writes in many time periods, but finds the Victorian era (which she says she "avoided for a long time because of my unfair prejudices about those times") in England and America "quite fascinating." Krahn made a captivating discovery about the time period she had tried so hard to avoid: "Every major social and societal movement that exists today—from women's rights to social reform to ecological responsibility to health consciousness—began in Victorian England. There was a tremendous amount going on there, and it's exciting to dig out some of the roots of our current thinking and practices and weave them into a story narrative."

For Krahn, the romance genre has many appeals: "I love the journey aspect of the genre—the change that overcomes the characters as they learn about each other, become vulnerable, and make decisions to put another's good and welfare above their own. What results is the slow, entrancing surrender of self to something bigger and finer ... over currents of delicious sexual tension ... and in full recognition of the divine foolishness we humans engage in as we stumble and squirm our way into love."

According to Krahn, every book presents obstacles to overcome: "Some are difficult because of craft issues ... starting the story in the wrong place or stubbornly hanging on to a scene or situation that just doesn't fit ... characters that outgrow a story line. Others are hard because of personal issues and events that occur during the writing. One quarter of the way through *The Unlikely Angel* (1996), my husband of 23 years died of cancer. I missed the deadline by a thousand miles; but my publisher patiently waited for me and kept the book in the schedule, and I had to write three-quarters of that book in the two months after my husband died. The words flowed like manna from heaven ... but when I wasn't writing, I was in agony." Six weeks before the loss of her husband, Krahn earned her first spot on the *New York Times* Best Seller List. "It was a difficult and emotional time for me, while I was hopelessly behind on a deadline and caring for my dying husband 24 hours a day at home," says Krahn. "It was a strange sort of gift that helped me see through some very tough days. It also made it possible for me to continue writing later, when it seemed there was no romance left in the world for me."

On the other hand, some of Krahn's books were relatively easy to write. An example of this is *The Husband Test*, which Krahn says, "just flowed from my brain to my fingertips. I was in Florida for the winter with family ... lots of joy and pleasure ... no responsibilities except putting out pages and making the occasional lasagna. It was damn near heaven." In this book, Peril, the Earl of Whitmore, travels to the Convent of the Brides of Virtue to find the perfect woman, a wife who can save his estate. Even though the purpose of the convent is to train young women to become ideal wives, it's not his first venue of choice for the right spouse. Although the abbess of the convent sees this as a chance to get rid of Eloise, an enthusiastic but disastrous novice, she does require that her trouble-prone trainee put Peril through a husband test. Eloise creates as much chaos in Peril's keep as she did in the convent, but her unflagging spirit appeals to him. Once again, Krahn's trademark humor, irony, and wit shine through as this mismatched pair find unexpected happiness and love in each other.

Of the books that she's written, Krahn has several favorites: *Passion's Treasure* (1989), which was rereleased in 2000 as *Just Say Yes; Midnight Magic* (1990), which was rereleased in 2002 as *Luck Be a Lady; and My Warrior's Heart* (1992), which was rewritten and rereleased in 2005 as *The Enchantment. The Last Bachelor* (1994) and *The Husband Test* also rank among her favorites.

Krahn gets her inspiration from "lots of things." Her own relationships with her family and friends teach and inspire her. She says, "Music is a vital part of my life. Water inspires me, comforts, and calms me. Natural colors and textures are very important in my environment, including plant scapes and genuine earth-source materials. Meditation. Reading. Travel. Sunshine. The birth of babies, particularly grandchildren. Flowers, especially from my beloved, Rex."

According to Krahn, "Writer's block is me indulging in procrastination and avoiding the hard work of meeting myself and my ideas on the blank page. It's also a fear of committing to one course of action, because to do so cuts off other lovely possibilities for a story. There are lots of cures, but nothing snaps me out of it like the sound of the Doppler Shift as a deadline goes flying by."

Krahn finds the process of writing to be an exciting one: "The freedom of imagination … the chance to roam and create people and landscapes that are interesting … experiencing the power of the written word as it's being written. I also love the exhilaration of reading a scene I've written and knowing that it's exactly what the story/book needed." Krahn has realized her youthful dream of becoming an author, and she's had the good fortune of finding that what she wished for was the very right thing.

BIBLIOGRAPHY

Books: *Rapture's Ransom*. New York: Kensington, 1983; *Passion's Storm*. New York: Kensington, 1985; *Rebel Passion*. New York: Kensington, 1987; *Hidden Fires*. New York: Kensington, 1988; *Love's Brazen Fire*. New York: Kensington, 1989; *Passion's Ransom*. New York: Kensington, 1989; *Passion's Treasure*. New York: Kensington, 1989; *Midnight Magic*. New York: Kensington, 1990; *Caught in the Act*. New York: William Morrow, 1990; *Behind Closed Doors*. New York: William Morrow, 1991; *My Warrior's Heart*. New York: William Morrow, 1992; *The Princess and the Barbarian*. New York: Avon, 1993; *The Last Bachelor*. New York: Bantam, 1994; *The Perfect Mistress*. New York: Bantam, 1995; *The Unlikely Angel*. New York: Bantam, 1996; *The Mermaid*. New York: Bantam, 1997; *The Soft Touch*. New York: Bantam, 1999; *Sweet Talking Man*. New York: Bantam, 2000; *The Husband Test*. New York: Bantam, 2001; *The Wife Test*. New York: Berkley, 2003; *The Paradise Bargain*. New York: Kensington, 2003; *The Marriage Test*. New York: Berkley, 2004; *Not Quite Married*. New York: Bantam, 2004; *The Book of the Seven Delights*. New York: Jove, 2005; *The Book of True Desires*. New York: Berkley, 2006.

Novellas: "Six Little Angels" in *Christmas Romance*. New York: Avon, 1990; "A Certain Magic" in *Haunting Love Stories*. New York: Avon, 1991; "Kidnapped for Christmas" in *A Victorian Christmas*. New York: Bantam, 1992; "A Touch of Warmth" in *Stardust*. New York: Bantam, 1994.

SHELLEY MOSLEY AND SANDRA VAN WINKLE

JAYNE ANN KRENTZ

N *ew York Times* best-selling author Jayne Ann Krentz is one of very few writers who are completely comfortable writing romances set in the past, the present, and the future. As Amanda Quick, Krentz fashions deliciously witty, intrigue-steeped tales of love in the past. As Jayne Ann Krentz, she delivers humor-tinged contemporary romances and sizzlingly sexy novels of romantic suspense. As Jayne Castle, Krentz offers readers bewitching stories of danger and passion set in the future. Whatever the time period, and whatever the name, readers know they can always count on Krentz for a captivating story.

Krentz was born Jayne Ann Castle in San Diego, California, in 1948. She grew up in Borrego Springs and Cobb, California, where she attended local schools. Krentz enrolled in the University of California at Santa Cruz, where she graduated with a bachelor of arts degree in history. Krentz went on to San Jose State University, where she received her master of library science degree. With her library degree in hand, Krentz spent one year working as a elementary school librarian, an experience she fondly recalls as "an unmitigated career disaster," before settling into the world of corporate and academic librarianship.

As a child, Krentz entertained thoughts of becoming an author. Realistically, she knew that she would have to have a "real" job to make a living. Krentz recalls, "When I was growing up, it was generally accepted that the odds of being able to pay the rent as a writer were not very good, so I made no plans for this kind of career. On the other hand, I'm not sure

---

also writing as Amanda Quick
also writing as Jayne Castle
also writing as Jayne Bentley
also writing as Stephanie James
also writing as Jayne Taylor
also writing as Amanda Glass

anyone could actually plan a career as a writer, anyway. This is a very odd business. Five year plans don't work very well."

Eventually, though, the siren call of the writing muse proved to be impossible to resist. Despite her unmistakable talent, publication did not come easily for Krentz: "Sadly, I was not an overnight success. Much as it pains me to report it, the embarrassing truth is that it took six (very long) years to get a book into print. I lost count of the proposals I sent out and of the rejections I received. To keep my spirits up, I managed to sell a couple of short stories to one of the 'true confession' magazines. I know you will be shocked, *shocked,* to hear that my stories were not actual true confessions. I confess that I made them up, which may explain why I didn't do particularly well in that market niche. But that is another part of my murky writing past that I prefer to forget."

While Krentz modestly insists she was no overnight success, when her literary career was finally born, it took off with a bang. Writing as both Jayne Bentley and Jayne Castle, Krentz had seven contemporary romances published by McFadden in 1979 and 1980. In addition, when Dell began a new line of category romances, Candlelight Ecstasy, Krentz became one of their first authors, writing as Jayne Castle.

Earlier in her career, Krentz had submitted several of her manuscripts to Silhouette, but the publisher was not interested in her at the time. "I had a hard time breaking into Silhouette. My first book with that publisher, *A Passionate Business,* was title # 89 in the series, which means there were 88 other books by other authors published before they finally bought one from me! Sad truth is that I had been submitting to them regularly from the start under the name Stephanie James, and they had been rejecting me just as routinely. Then, one of the Silhouette editors discovered that I was publishing merrily along over at Dell Ecstasy as Jayne Castle, and all of a sudden, my style became acceptable to the Silhouette editorial staff. That kind of thing has happened to me a lot over the course of my career." In 1981, Krentz published her first book with Silhouette, *A Passionate Business,* which began a decade-long publishing partnership, with 29 titles having been published over the years.

Among the books Krentz wrote for Silhouette as Stephanie James was *Night of the Magician,* published in 1984. Ariana Warfield is concerned about her aunt's obsession with a psychic claiming to be in contact with aliens. Ariana decides that she needs a magician to help expose the fraud. When she partners with Lucian Hawk, a handsome magician with a rough past, she is attracted to him despite her best intentions to keep it a business relationship. *Night of the Magician* is a wonderful introduction to Krentz's irresistible brand of sexy contemporary romance. Another of Krentz's works writing as Stephanie James, was *Nightwalker* (1984), in which Cassie Bond opposes her sister Alison's relationship with charismatic ex-casino owner Justin Drake. When she forces their breakup, Justin sets his sights on seducing Cassie. Krentz creates plenty of sparks with the smoldering relationship between financial expert Cassie and the man she thinks of as a "creature of the night."

Krentz continued to write more fast-paced, sensually-charged contemporary romances for Silhouette, including *The Devil to Pay,* published in 1985. While searching for evidence to extricate her brother from a blackmailer's clutches, Emelina Stratton's investigations are hampered by the presence of Julian Colter. Colter has been watching Emelina, and when he catches her breaking into the blackmailer's empty cottage, he forces her to accept his help. Her concern is that Julian's help comes with a price that she is not sure that she is willing to pay. Readers will find Krentz's trademark humor in the irony of the heroine's occupation, an aspiring author trying to break into publishing with genre-blending books (ones that mix romance and science fiction), something about which Krentz herself knows a thing or two. With its simmering sexual chemistry, mysterious alpha hero, and potent blend of danger and desire, *The Devil to Pay* is an excellent example of Krentz's early works, which would form the foundation for her later best-selling suspense novels.

Krentz had been selling books as Stephanie James to Silhouette for several years when British-based Harlequin made a big pitch to recruit U. S. authors. Krentz recalls, "They were opening up a new line, Temptation, aimed at the American market, and it sounded like an exciting project, so I switched houses. I had to use a new name as the Stephanie James name was tied up at Silhouette. A short time later, of course, Harlequin bought out Silhouette; but by then, I had established my Jayne Ann Krentz name, so I stayed with it. It was the first time in my career with either Silhouette or Dell Ecstasy that I finally had the clout to keep all the rights to a name!"

With her own interest in science fiction as a young reader (Krentz counts Andre Norton as one of her favorite authors), and given the fact that the first type of book that Krentz tried her hand at was a futuristic romance, it isn't surprising that she would eventually write this kind of story. However, it was 10 years and more than a dozen contemporary romances later, before Krentz's first futuristic romances, her Colony series, were published. The first book, *Sweet Starfire,* which came out in 1986, featured ethereal Cidra Rainforest, raised by one race but actually a member of the savage Wolf race. She teams up with Teague Severance, one of the Wolves, and together, their dangerous quest forces Cidra to battle both human and alien dangers as well as her own dark desires awakened by the handsome fortune hunter.

Krentz followed *Sweet Starfire* with *Crystal Flame* (1986), another passionate futuristic adventure tale in her Colony series. Set in the great Northern Continent of Zantalia, Kalena, the last daughter of the Great House of the Ice Harvest, is on a mission of vengeance to assassinate the man responsible for the deaths of the men of the House of the Ice Harvest. Standing in her way is Fire Whip, a soldier who has been commanded to tame the cold-hearted beauty. In her second futuristic romance, Krentz created a colorful and imaginative tale, and her inspired pairing of an icy heroine and a hot-blooded hero produced an exotic and sensual love story that delighted readers looking for something different in the romance genre. Three years later, writing as Amanda Glass, Krentz completed her Colony trilogy with *Shield's Lady,* the fascinating story of cool, confident businesswoman Sariana Dayne, who joins forces with psychic, soldier-for-hire Gryph Chassyn on a dangerous quest to save the world.

In 1987, Krentz made the transition from category romances to single title books, with the publication of *A Coral Kiss.* Science fiction writer Amy Slater is haunted by the scuba diving death of her last boyfriend, a death that she thinks might not have been accidental. In order to return to the South Pacific island where he died, Amy needs the help and support of Jed Glaze, a friend who has a dangerous secret of his own. When Amy and Jed arrive on Orleana Island, they discover that beneath the deceptively serene blue waters lurk both peril and passion. With *A Coral Kiss,* Krentz brilliantly uses the exotic locale of the fictional Orleana Island as a backdrop for her suspenseful story of a woman who must face her fears before she can begin to love again.

Midnight Jewels (1987) followed *A Coral Kiss,* both published by Popular Library. Krentz was obviously inspired by her own experience as a librarian when she created her next heroine, Mercy Pennington. Mercy is an ex-librarian turned bookseller whose quiet little world is both shaken and stirred by Croft Falconer, a martial arts expert who is not used to taking no for an answer. Mercy has in her possession a rare edition of the *Valley of the Secret Jewels,* a book of erotica. Croft is extremely unhappy to discover that Mercy has already promised the book to another customer, and he will do whatever it takes get it. With *Midnight Jewels,*

Krentz once again proves her mastery at creating compelling sexual tension between her strong hero and equally strong heroine, and she deftly infuses her writing with a rapier-sharp sense of wit. In addition, Krentz spices up her suspense-driven plot with some fascinating details about martial arts and rare books.

The next big development in Krentz's literary career came in 1990 with the publication of her first historical romance, *Seduction*, and the birth of her pseudonym Amanda Quick. Krentz recalls, "When I first started doing historicals I was not at all sure that I would be able to write successfully for that market. I wasn't even a fan of historical romances—I preferred contemporary settings—so what did I know about writing them? I chose a pen name [Amanda Quick] in case I failed. I didn't want the poor sales figures to hurt my Jayne Ann Krentz name."

The impetus for Krentz to try her hand at historicals came after she had written her first three futuristic romances: "I realized as I was finishing the last book in that series, *Shield's Lady*, that the story I was telling—the arranged-marriage-of-convenience story—was a classic historical plot. It dawned on me that maybe I should give the genre a whirl. What can I say? I tried it; I loved it."

In *Seduction*, Krentz uses the classic marriage-of-convenience plot, as she introduces readers to Sophy Dorring, innocent country girl and budding feminist, who agrees to wed brooding and dangerous Julian, the Earl of Ravenwood. Rumors surround Julian, one of which is that he murdered his first wife, but Sophy has her own reasons for marrying him. In Sophy, a woman who not only reads Mary Wollstonecraft but also actively embraces Wollstonecraft's "radical" theories, Krentz gives readers another of her strong heroines who is well suited to the task of civilizing and taming a dark and passionate hero.

Readers loved Krentz's first foray into the historical romance subgenre, and more books followed, including *Surrender*, published in 1990. Victoria Huntington, tired of being sought after for her money, is determined to resist the romantic overtures of all men, until fortune hunter Lucas Colebrook, the Earl of Stonevale, tempts her with the promise of feeding Victoria's appetite for risky adventures. Krentz's next book, *Scandal* (1991), focuses on 24-year-old spinster Emily Faringdon and Simon Traherne, who are romantically brought together through their shared love of poetry, but whose fledgling relationship is endangered by Simon's thirst for revenge against Emily's family. *Seduction, Surrender, Scandal*, and each historical romance that followed all displayed Krentz's flair for wonderfully witty writing and sexy romance.

As Quick, Krentz continued to write more historical romances, most of them set during the glittering period of Regency England. With *Desire*, however, published in 1994, Krentz tried her hand at medieval romance. Lady Clare, ruler of the exotic, perfume-producing island kingdom of Desire, is forced to find a husband. She meticulously compiles a list of requirements for the man of her dreams, including "a man of cheerful continence and well-mannered, pleasing disposition." Of course, the hero of the piece, Sir Gareth of Wyckmere, also known as the "Hellhound of Wyckmere," meets none of them, and the fun begins. Krentz's right-on comedic timing and keen sense of humor fill the pages of this book, making it a laugh-aloud treat for readers.

Slightly Shady, published in 2001, introduced two of Krentz's best-loved characters, sleuths Tobias March and Lavinia Lake. With their quick wit, clever repartee, and rapid-fire dialogue, the two soon become an unstoppable crime-solving team. Both their professional and personal relationships grow over the course of the three historical Regencies that feature Lavinia and Tobias (*Slightly Shady*, 2001; *Don't Look Back*, 2002; *Late for the Wedding*, 2003). By the third novel, there's a running joke about how hard it is for this couple to find a place for a tryst.

In 2005, Krentz, after writing 19 historical Regencies as Quick, changed time periods and wrote *Wait Until Midnight,* her first Victorian historical romance. She says, "The switch from the Regency era to the Victorian was done because I wanted to tell a somewhat darker mystery. I also wanted to be able to tap into the Victorian taste for the paranormal for my stories." Spiritualist Elizabeth Delmont is brutally murdered in the underbelly of Victorian London. Wealthy Adam Hardesty and novelist Caroline Fordyce team up to find the person who killed Elizabeth. Their own secrets are at stake as they become partners in investigation … and passion. Krentz's versatility once again shone as she deftly switched her setting from the England of the Prince Regent to that of Queen Victoria.

In 1996, writing as Jayne Castle, Krentz returned to the futuristic romance subgenre with *Amaryllis,* the first book in a trilogy. Set on the imaginary world of St. Helens, Krentz created a society where matched marriages are the norm and almost everyone is psychically gifted to some degree. *Amaryllis* centers on security expert Amaryllis Lark, who is hired by businessman Lucas Trent to uncover a security leak in his company, Lodestar Exploration. The two find themselves mixing business and pleasure when they are forced to use their psychic gifts to catch a murderer. Krentz followed *Amaryllis* with *Zinnia* (1997) and *Orchid* (1998), both of which were also set in St. Helens and featured a similar mix of romance, suspense, and a generous measure of the paranormal.

With *After Dark* (2000) also written as Jayne Castle, Krentz began another series, this time set on the planet of Harmony. She followed up this with a sequel, *After Glow* (2004). Both books feature the adventures of para-archaeologist Lydia Smith and ghost hunter Emmett London. With each of these clever and imaginative books, Krentz proved she could transfer her potent brand of sensuality, subtle characterization, and sharp humor from her traditional historical and contemporary settings to a future-world setting.

For Krentz, the significant challenges her heroines face are the heroes themselves, a theme at the center of each of her books, whether contemporary, historical, or paranormal. As an author, she is extremely fond of the "dangerous hero," who is tamed or "civilized" by the adventurous heroine. Krentz's "beauties" are sometimes the only characters in the books brave enough to approach, let alone speak to, their "beasts." In Krentz's literary world, the reason these heroines are able to civilize these bad boys is because they are every bit as strong as her heroes, especially where it counts most, in intelligence.

Even when she is not writing futuristic romances, Krentz's interest in the paranormal figures into several of her contemporary romances. One example is Krentz's two Whispering Springs books: *Light in Shadow* (2003) and *Truth or Dare* (2004). In *Light in Shadow,* Krentz introduces readers to psychic interior designer Zoe Luce. Zoe can intuit emotions or so-called psychic cobwebs in a room. When she enters the bedroom of her new client, Davis Mason, she senses that he has murdered his wife. Zoe seeks the help of private investigator Ethan Truax to help her uncover the evidence needed to prove Davis guilty of the crime. However, Zoe never expected Ethan would also uncover a dark secret in her own past. In *Truth or Dare,* Krentz picks up the relationship between Zoe and Ethan, who are now married, as past events from both of their lives threaten to destroy their new happiness. Zoe's ability to discern emotions and her own experiences in Candle Lake Manor, a private psychiatric hospital, lend an effectively eerie edge to Krentz's more traditional blend of romance and suspense.

In *Falling Awake* (2005), the paranormal topic is lucid dreaming, from which Krentz skillfully fashions another of her compelling tales of deception and desire. The book's heroine, dream analyst Isabel Wright, is about to lose her job at the Belvedere Center for Sleep Research, when she is given the chance to work for a shadowy government agency by Ellis

Cutler, one of her anonymous clients from the sleep research center. Ellis hopes that Isabel will help the agency be able to use "extreme dreaming" as an investigative technique, but their mutual attraction may make it difficult to keep things between them strictly professional. Krentz seamlessly blends fascinating information about lucid dreaming and sleep research into the plot of *Falling Awake,* and each of these books, *Light in Shadow, Truth or Dare,* and *Falling Awake,* are superb examples of Krentz's brilliance at blending danger, desire, and the paranormal into a riveting story.

Krentz is not only an award-winning and best-selling author of romance fiction, she is also a noted scholar and dedicated advocate of the genre. Krentz was the first recipient of *Romantic Times* Jane Austen Award, which is given out to "those in the romance community who have significantly impacted our genre." In addition, Krentz is the only author to date to have received the Romance Writers of America's Industry Award, given to an individual for his or her outstanding contributions to the romance industry.

One of Krentz's greatest contributions to the romance genre, though, is her work as the editor and a contributor to *Dangerous Men and Adventurous Women: Romance Writers on the Appeal of Romance.* The perpetually dismissive and scornful attitude of the academic community toward romantic fiction is what initially gave Krentz the idea for a book like *Dangerous Men and Adventurous Women.* Krentz explains, "I like to think it was my own academic background and training in librarianship, but maybe I was just in a bad mood that day. All I know is that I finally got fed up with the fact that books in the romance genre received no proper academic or critical attention, let alone respect. Sure, popular literature, in general, doesn't get much respect; but the romance genre was the only one in which critics not only condemned the books, but the readers [did] as well! Women who read romance novels were widely perceived by academics and the media to be uneducated and unsophisticated. That last bit really ticked me off."

Up until that time, other books had been written about the romance genre, but most of them perpetuated the myths about the lack of quality of the books themselves and the stereotype of the genre's readers. For Krentz, these books were less than helpful: "There was, of course, plenty of academic junk written about the romance novel. The authors of those silly papers and books did not even bother to distinguish the popular titles from the unpopular ones, let alone question why some books hit the best seller lists and other did not. Talk about a lack of intellectual integrity! I wanted to produce a volume that explained the appeal of the romance novel to those who just didn't get it. Academics, for instance."

Both angry and inspired, Krentz gathered together an eclectic and distinguished group of contributors for the project, including such fellow romance authors as Laura Kinsale, Susan Elizabeth Phillips, and Mary Jo Putney. Each one was given the task of writing an essay that would help explain the appeal of romances to those unfamiliar with the genre, "that this appeal is as complex as it is powerful." Krentz says she found a fairy godmother for her project in the form of a "brilliant, insightful editor named Patricia Reynolds Smith. She [Smith] was working at the University of Pennsylvania Press at the time. I knew that she not only loved reading romance novels but had also edited books in the genre for one of the major publishers. When I called her at the University of Pennsylvania Press and asked her where I could take such a project as *Dangerous Men and Adventurous Women,* her exact words were, 'Right here.'"

Dangerous Men and Adventurous Women was published by the University of Pennsylvania Press in 1992. It proved to be a groundbreaking book on the romance genre that helped pave the way for other enlightened and informed academic studies of romance fiction and was awarded the PCA/ACA (Popular Culture Association/American Culture Association)

Women's Caucus Susan Koppelman Award for Excellence in Feminist Studies of Popular Culture and American Culture.

The key to Krentz's success as a romance writer is that she knows exactly what her readers want, and she consistently delivers it. Readers know that, no matter what name she is writing under—Krentz, Quick, or Castle—or in which subgenre she is working—contemporary, historical, or futuristic—the story will be riveting, the characters will be well-defined and appealing, and the passion will be unforgettable.

Writing as Jayne Ann Krentz

Books: *Uneasy Alliance.* Toronto: Harlequin, 1984; *Call It Destiny.* Toronto: Harlequin, 1984; *Ghost of a Chance.* Toronto: Harlequin, 1985; *Legacy.* Toronto: Harlequin, 1985; *Man with a Past.* Toronto: Harlequin, 1985; *The Waiting Game.* Toronto: Harlequin, 1985; *True Colors.* Toronto: Harlequin, 1986; *The Ties That Bind.* Toronto: Harlequin, 1986; *Between the Lines.* Toronto: Harlequin, 1986; *Sweet Starfire.* New York: Popular Library, 1986; *Crystal Flame.* New York: Popular Library, 1986; *Twist of Fate.* Toronto: Harlequin, 1986; *The Family Way.* Toronto: Harlequin, 1987; *The Main Attraction.* Toronto: Harlequin, 1987; *A Coral Kiss.* New York: Popular Library, 1987; *Chance of a Lifetime.* Toronto: Harlequin, 1987; *Midnight Jewels.* New York: Popular Library, 1987; *Test of Time.* Toronto: Harlequin, 1987; *Full Bloom.* Toronto: Harlequin, 1988; *Joy.* Toronto: Harlequin, 1988; *Gift of Gold.* New York: Popular Library, 1988; *Dreams: Part One.* Toronto: Harlequin, 1988; *Dreams: Part Two.* Toronto: Harlequin, 1988; *Gift of Fire.* New York: Popular Library, 1989; *A Woman's Touch.* Toronto: Harlequin, 1989; *Lady's Choice.* Toronto: Harlequin, 1989; *The Golden Chance.* New York: Pocket Books, 1990; *The Pirate.* Toronto: Harlequin, 1990; *The Adventurer.* Toronto: Harlequin, 1990; *The Cowboy.* Toronto: Harlequin, 1991; *Silver Linings.* New York: Pocket Books, 1991; *Too Wild to Wed?* Toronto: Harlequin, 1991; *The Wedding Night.* Toronto: Harlequin, 1991; *Sweet Fortune.* New York: Pocket Books, 1991; *The Private Eye.* Toronto: Harlequin, 1992; *Perfect Partners.* New York: Pocket Books, 1992; *Family Man.* New York: Pocket Books, 1992; *Wildest Hearts.* New York: Pocket Books, 1993; *Hidden Talents.* New York: Pocket Books, 1993; *Grand Passion.* New York: Pocket Books, 1994; *Trust Me.* New York: Pocket Books, 1995; *Absolutely, Positively.* New York: Pocket Books, 1997; *Deep Waters.* New York: Pocket Books, 1997; *Sharp Edges.* New York: Pocket Books, 1998; *Flash.* New York: Pocket Books, 1999; *Eye of the Beholder.* New York: Pocket Books, 1999; *Soft Focus.* New York: Putnam, 2000; *Eclipse Bay.* New York: Jove, 2000; *Lost and Found.* New York: Putnam, 2001; *Dawn in Eclipse Bay.* New York: Jove, 2001; *Smoke and Mirrors.* New York: Putnam, 2002; *Summer in Eclipse Bay.* New York: Jove, 2002; *Light in Shadow.* New York: Putnam, 2003; *Truth or Dare.* New York: Putnam, 2004; *Falling Awake.* New York: Putnam, 2005; *All Night Long.* New York: Putnam, 2006.

Nonfiction: (Editor) *Dangerous Men and Adventurous Women: Romance Writers on the Appeal of Romance.* Philadelphia: University of Pennsylvania Press, 1992.

Writing as Amanda Quick

Books: *Seduction.* New York: Bantam, 1990; *Surrender.* New York: Bantam, 1990; *Scandal.* New York: Bantam, 1991; *Rendezvous.* New York: Bantam, 1991; *Ravished.* New York: Bantam, 1992; *Reckless.* New York: Bantam, 1992; *Dangerous.* New York: Bantam, 1993; *Deception.* New York: Bantam, 1993; *Desire.* New York: Bantam, 1994; *Mistress.* New York: Bantam, 1994; *Mystique.* New York: Bantam, 1995; *Mischief.* New York: Bantam, 1996; *Affair.* New York: Bantam, 1997; *With This Ring.* New York: Bantam, 1998; *I Thee Wed.* New York: Bantam, 1999; *Wicked Widow.* New York: Bantam, 2000; *Slightly Shady.* New York: Bantam, 2001; *Don't Look Back.* New York: Bantam, 2002; *Late for the Wedding.* New York: Bantam, 2003; *The Paid Companion.* New York: Putnam, 2004; *Wait Until Midnight.* New York: Jove, 2005; *Lie by Moonlight.* New York: Putnam, 2005; *Second Sight.* New York: Putnam, 2006.

Writing as Jayne Castle

Books: *Vintage of Surrender.* New York: McFadden, 1979; *Queen of Hearts.* New York: McFadden, 1979; *Gentle Pirate.* New York: Dell, 1980; *Bargain with the Devil.* New York: Dell, 1981; *Right of Possession.* New York: Dell, 1981; *Wagered Weekend.* New York: Dell, 1981; *A Man's Protection.* New York: Dell, 1982; *A Negotiated Surrender.* New York: Dell, 1982; *Affair of Risk.* New York: Dell, 1982; *Power Play.* New York: Dell, 1982; *Relentless Adversary.* New York: Dell, 1982; *Spellbound.* New York: Dell, 1982; *Conflict of Interest.* New York: Dell, 1983; *Double Dealing.* New York: Dell, 1984; *Trading Secrets.* New York: Dell, 1985; *The Desperate Game.* New York: Dell, 1986; *A Chilling Deception.* New York: Dell, 1986; *The Sinister Touch.* New York: Dell, 1986; *The Fatal Fortune.* New York: Dell, 1986; *Amaryllis.* New York: Pocket Books, 1996; *Zinnia.* New York: Pocket Books, 1997; *Orchid.* New York: Pocket Books, 1998; *After Dark.* New York: Jove, 2000; *After Glow.* New York: Jove, 2004; *Ghost Hunter.* New York: Jove, 2006.

Novellas: "Connecting Rooms" in *Everlasting Love.* New York: Pocket, 1995; "Bridal Jitters" in *Charmed.* New York: Jove, 1999.

Writing as Jayne Bentley

Books: *A Moment Past Midnight.* New York: McFadden, 1979; *Turning Towards Home.* New York: McFadden, 1979; *Maiden of the Morning.* New York: McFadden, 1979; *Hired Husband.* New York: McFadden, 1979; *Sabrina's Scheme.* New York: McFadden, 1979.

Writing as Stephanie James

Books: *A Passionate Business.* New York: Silhouette, 1981; *The Dangerous Magic.* New York: Silhouette, 1982; *Stormy Challenge.* New York: Silhouette, 1982; *Corporate Affair.* New York: Silhouette, 1982; *Velvet Touch.* New York: Silhouette, 1982; *Lover in Pursuit.* New York: Silhouette, 1982; *Renaissance Man.* New York: Silhouette, 1982; *A Reckless Passion.* New York: Silhouette, 1982; *The Price of Surrender.* New York: Silhouette, 1983; *To Tame the Hunter.* New York: Silhouette, 1983; *Affair of Honor.* New York: Silhouette, 1983; *Gamesmaster.* New York: Silhouette, 1983; *The Silver Snare.* New York: Silhouette, 1983; *Battle Prize.* New York: Silhouette, 1983; *Bodyguard.* New York: Silhouette, 1983; *Serpent in Paradise.* New York: Silhouette, 1983; *Gambler's Woman.* New York: Silhouette, 1984; *Fabulous Beast.* New York: Silhouette, 1984; *Night of the Magician.* New York: Silhouette, 1984; *Nightwalker.* New York: Silhouette, 1984; *Raven's Prey.* New York: Silhouette, 1984; *Devil to Pay.* New York: Silhouette, 1985; *Wizard.* New York: Silhouette, 1985; *Golden Goddess.* New York: Silhouette, 1985; *Cautious Lover.* New York: Silhouette, 1985; *Green Fire.* New York: Silhouette, 1986; *Second Wife.* New York: Silhouette, 1986; *The Challoner Bride.* New York: Silhouette, 1987; *Saxon's Lady.* New York: Silhouette, 1987.

Writing as Jayne Taylor

Book: *Whirlwind Courtship.* New York: Tiara, 1979.

Writing as Amanda Glass

Book: *Shield's Lady.* New York: Popular Library, 1989.

JOHN CHARLES, SHELLEY MOSLEY, JOANNE HAMILTON-SELWAY, AND SANDRA VAN WINKLE

SUSAN KRINARD

Susan Krinard. Courtesy of Susan Krinard.

S usan Krinard has always had natural artistic ability. In fact, her earliest career aspiration was to become a professional illustrator—of book covers. Now, with over twenty titles in print, it's apparent that she possesses quite a talent for filling the pages in between, too.

Born in Long Beach, California, Krinard grew up in the San Francisco Bay Area, in the community of Concord. Her father worked as a computer programmer and systems analyst, and her mother's career was in child care, as a teacher, administrator, and freelance advisor. Krinard attended both San Francisco State University and Diablo Valley College, later graduating from the California College of Arts and Crafts with a bachelor's degree in fine arts, specializing in illustration.

After marrying her husband, Serge, a native of Beauport, Quebec, the couple relocated to Toronto for a few years, before returning to California, and then finally settling in Albuquerque, New Mexico. Serge, now a U. S. citizen, is employed as a computer programmer for Wells Fargo. The couple has no children "unless you count our three dogs and two cats," says Krinard.

Recalling her childhood, Krinard says, "I thought I'd be an artist, since I drew and painted constantly." Although she sometimes wrote stories for her own amusement, she never considered the possibility of being published. Eventually, she says, "the circumstances just came together that way, quite unexpectedly."

Before becoming a writer, Krinard worked in a series of clerical and library jobs: "I hated the clerical jobs, but I enjoyed being around books." She now writes full-time in the genres of romance and fantasy, averaging about seven pages per day and generating two novels a year. Though she isn't often troubled by writer's block, she admits, "I had horrible writer's block when I was writing my fantasy and wasn't sure I could pull it off. I struggled to write one or two pages a day for a couple of months. It was all fear." Krinard advises prospective writers, "The pressure to produce, not only quickly but well, can be very great," and Krinard still experiences it, even as a professional.

As a lifelong avid reader, Krinard admits, "I'd read very little romance before I began writing it. Although I enjoyed romantic plots in movies and books, I didn't know much about the romance genre per se, and read mainly science fiction and fantasy. However, the relationships were always the important part of any story for me. Since I'd grown up reading the old-fashioned types of romantic adventure stories, that's the way I tackled romance." By the time Krinard began writing her first manuscript, *Prince of Wolves* (1994), romance came to her naturally. "I love stories about relationships and the psychology of human beings," says Krinard. "I'm happiest writing about these aspects in a romance—not just the physical relationship, but the way two unique individuals find a way to come together and create a lasting relationship."

For Krinard, the writing process begins with the setting, determining the ideal time and location for her novel. "I get lots of ideas just from researching setting and period," she says. Krinard has set stories in historical England, both Regency and Victorian, and the American West (*Once A Wolf*, 2000). The time periods that interest her most, however, are those that are out of the ordinary, the ones not often found in the romance genre, such as ancient Rome and Egypt. One of these unusual settings appears in her alternate historical fantasy *Shield of the Sky* (2004), set in 300 B.C. In this story, Rhenna of the Free People is becoming more and more uneasy about changes she sees in her world. Isolated as she patrols the tribal borders, she notices that the mountain-dwelling shape-shifters, longtime allies of her people, are vanishing, and an evil new god has begun to overtake the land. This Stone God's followers carry mysterious and dangerous red rocks that possess destructive powers, in a world that is becoming increasingly angry and violent. When Rhenna learns that one of the shape-shifters has been captured by this wicked horde, she sets out to rescue him and becomes tangled in a life-and-death struggle between nature and evil. The future of the Free People hangs in the balance as Rhenna and her unusual militia—Tahvo the shaman, Quintus the rebel, and Cian the panther shape-shifter—travel the world to prevent its annihilation. Casting paranormal shape-shifters with primitive cultures in a dark and little-documented era adds to the tension and uncertainty of the story. Some of the same elements that are found in Krinard's fantasies (shape-shifting; strong, resourceful heroines; life and death struggles; fantastical landscapes; etc.) also appear in her paranormal romances.

In casting her romances, the choice of characters is of utmost importance to Krinard—whether vampires (*Prince of Dreams,* 1995); werewolves (*Prince of Wolves,* 1994; *Prince of Shadows,* 1996; *Touch of the Wolf,* 1999; *To Catch a Wolf,* 2003; *To Tame a Wolf,* 2005); or aliens (*Star Crossed,* 1995; *Kinsman's Oath,* 2004)—because each of them inspires the next. "I often develop the second protagonist, male or female, based on the first one," says Krinard.

Perhaps Krinard is best known for her werewolf books. In *To Catch a Wolf,* book four of the Forster Werewolf series, the heroine, Athena Munroe, lives her life from her wheelchair. Despite her disability, Denver society accepts Athena—after all, her brother is wealthy, and she devotes her time to charity. Morgan Holt, a werewolf who has served time for the murder of his father, is part of a sideshow in French's Fantastic Family Circus. Morgan meets Athena when she hires the circus to perform for a group of orphans. Morgan embraces the fact that he's a werewolf, and Athena, in spite of her strong denial, is a werewolf, too. Ironically, in her Wolf persona, Athena is physically sound, her movements athletic and fluid; but her self-acceptance is a long emotional journey away. For their relationship to work, however, Morgan and Athena must decide which lifestyle they want to lead—that of "civilization," or the way of the Wolf. The circus freaks and social outcasts in this book are more human than the humans, and Krinard's werewolves, going against Hollywood stereotypes, are actually compassionate characters rather than terrifying monsters. Like her other werewolf novels, Krinard has penned an incredibly gripping story, filled with multi-layered, three-dimensional characters and many poignant moments.

Krinard's plot ideas evolve out of the settings and the characters she's chosen. Krinard begins by asking herself: "What sorts of things can happen in that place and time between those particular people? How does the paranormal issue drive the relationship?" The answers to these questions form the framework of the plot and story line.

Nature and the wilderness are among Krinard's favorite settings. She says, "Cities don't interest me so much, except when they represent a wilderness of danger and uncertainty—for instance, when the protagonist isn't familiar with the city and suddenly finds herself having to deal with a world she doesn't understand." Krinard often places her characters in situations that force them to confront their fears and inner demons, in remote locations such as deserts, jungles, forests, and mountains. She comments, "These places tend to strip away the outer shell and bare the soul." The harsh Arizona wilderness is the setting for Krinard's *To Tame a Wolf*. Chantal "Tally" Bernard's brother is missing in this dangerously rugged land, so she hires Simeon "Sim" Wartrace Kavanaugh to help locate her sibling. Tally has one condition of employment—Sim has to take her with him on the hunt. Although she's disguised as a boy, Sim knows Tally is actually a woman, and he can't figure out why no one else has discovered this secret. Sim has a secret, too—he's a shape-shifter who prefers to run with his wolf brethren rather than associate with humans. This intense, yet touching tale of redemption has a hero and a heroine who have fallen so far from grace that neither of them believes forgiveness and acceptance are in the realm of possibility. Krinard writes with such emotional realism that the reader forgets her werewolves aren't entirely human.

Themes of intolerance and the challenges of parenthood can be found in many of Krinard's novels, but the main recurring theme is "outsiders finding a place in the world through love." Her heroes aptly fit this profile. Krinard says they're "almost always outsiders, loners, intensely emotional but afraid to reveal their vulnerability. Some of the heroes cover their vulnerability with cynical humor, others with anger." However, not all of Krinard's heroes are emotionally troubled. "I do like to vary heroes, and sometimes I 'lighten them up' for the sake of contrast," she says.

In a personal observation of the genre, Krinard offers, "Heroes can often express emotions still not considered 'acceptable' [by] women in our society. Heroes are also permitted to be more 'flawed' in romance novels than are heroines," a bias Krinard finds exasperating. Krinard says the heroines in her stories are "all strong women who aren't afraid to buck the system, whether it be Victorian English society or modern expectations that women should be beautiful and ultimately compliant. I like to write flawed heroines, not perfect ones."

Krinard believes that some of her own personality traits can be found in her characters: "Both my heroes and heroines are made up of various bits of me—isolated elements of my own personality, scrambled and rearranged. I feel as close to my heroes as my heroines, sometimes closer." Krinard candidly reveals, "Rebelliousness—refusal to fall in with what everyone else is doing—is probably a trait of mine that appears in many of my heroines."

Of all of her novels, Krinard names her first fantasy, *Shield of the Sky*, as her most difficult to write. She explains, "It was on a much grander scale with many more important characters and a more complex plot and included a huge amount of research and world-building. I almost thought I wouldn't make it."

Krinard's first novel, *Prince of Wolves*, was her easiest to write. She recalls, "I didn't know what I was doing, I had no real expectation of selling, and I wrote exactly what I wanted with no commercial concerns whatsoever. That never happened again!" In this book, years after Joelle Randall's parents are killed in a plane crash in the Canadian Rockies, she is finally ready to face the awful reality of their death, so she can get on with her life. She travels to Lovell, British Columbia, and enlists the help of a local guide, Luke Gevaudan, to lead her to the remote site of the accident. Joelle feels an irresistibly strong attraction toward this dark, mysterious loner, not realizing his heritage—Luke is the last survivor of a race of werewolves. But the passion between Joelle and Luke doesn't recognize their difference, and the two find themselves in an unlikely romance. With Luke, Krinard skillfully introduces her magnificent but believable werewolf heroes and sets the stage for more to come.

Among her romances, Krinard chooses *Kinsman's Oath* as her favorite: "It combines all the elements I love—romance; adventure: science fiction with starships, distant worlds, and an alien race. I love being able to write about alien cultures, whether on Earth or other planets." When Cynara D'Accorso, a human and the captain of the Starship Pegasus, finds Ronan ValKalevi, a telepath and fellow human, adrift in space, she offers him sanctuary aboard her ship. Ronan, a badly scarred fugitive, had been kidnapped as a child 20 years earlier by the dreaded shaauri, ferocious catlike warriors. Now, he is running for his life … or so he says. Cynara's crew doesn't trust Ronan—they think he's one of the traitorous Kinsmen. Neither Cynara nor Ronan had anticipated the passion that would grow between them, a love that could ultimately lead to their mutual demise.

Kinsman's Oath also draws on Cynara's backstory, including her odyssey, thanks to an inheritance of a spaceship, from a place where women are forced to wear veils over their faces and are barely considered human. Ronan's backstory is one of an outsider forced to live in an alien culture where literally everyone hates him and where inflicting pain on him is almost a local sport. While Ronan and Cynara are different in many ways, they share in common that they were both considered inferior to the dominant culture in their earlier years. As in Krinard's other works, the characters are three-dimensional, and easy to relate to, despite the paranormal, futuristic setting.

For Krinard, story inspiration comes from both external and internal influences. External sources are everywhere. "The inner ones come from my emotions and my curiosity about people, how my characters will turn out," she says. "I never know exactly who they are at the beginning of a book." Krinard adds, "I'm also very inspired if I'm able to explore unusual themes or develop my own culture. Frankly, getting away from the real world is the ultimate inspiration!"

Krinard describes the writing process as "a fascinating journey." But it's her fertile imagination that provides the fuel and drives the story, cover to cover.

BIBLIOGRAPHY

Books: *Prince of Wolves.* New York: Bantam, 1994; *Prince of Dreams.* New York: Bantam, 1995; *Star Crossed.* New York: Bantam, 1995; *Prince of Shadows.* New York: Bantam, 1996; *Twice a Hero.* New York: Bantam, 1997; *Body and Soul.* New York: Bantam, 1998; *Touch of the Wolf.* New York: Bantam, 1999; *Once a Wolf.* New York: Bantam, 2000; *Secret of the Wolf.* New York: Berkley, 2001;

The Forest Lord. New York: Berkley, 2002; *To Catch a Wolf.* New York: Berkley, 2003; *Kinsman's Oath.* New York: Berkley, 2004; *Shield of the Sky.* New York: Luna, 2004; *To Tame a Wolf.* New York: HQN, 2005; *Hammer of the Earth.* New York: Luna, 2006; *Lord of the Beasts.* New York: HQN, 2006.

Novellas: "Angel on my Shoulder" in *My Guardian Angel.* New York: Bantam, 1995. "Saving Serena" in *Bewitched.* New York: Jove, 1997; "Kinsman" in *Out of This World.* New York: Jove, 2001; "Kiss of the Wolf" in *When Darkness Falls.* New York: Silhouette, 2003; "Murder Entailed" in *Murder by Magic.* New York: Warner Books, 2004; "…Or Forever Hold Your Peace" in *My Big, Fat Supernatural Wedding.* New York: 2006.

SANDRA VAN WINKLE AND SHELLEY MOSLEY

MARY ALICE KRUESI. *See* Mary Alice Monroe

LESLIE LAFOY

Award-winning author Leslie LaFoy didn't choose to become a writer—it was something that chose her. She recalls, "As a child, I would lie awake in bed at night and mentally rewrite the scripts of television shows." She finds the entire writing process to be fun and "magical," as her characters twist the plot in completely unplanned and unexpected directions. She observes, "I don't write a book, I discover one." She is delighted to be able to share the fun with her readers.

LaFoy credits her creativity to her parents, Donald and Joyce Voss, whom she describes as great oral storytellers. Her father, a former Ranger and Pathfinder with the 101st and the 82nd Airborne Infantries, and a garment industry executive, is now a retired cattle rancher. Her mother is a retired registered nurse who is a highly active community volunteer. LaFoy also credits her parents for teaching her to believe in herself, persevere, and follow her dreams.

LaFoy was born in Clarksville, Tennessee, in 1955. Growing up in a military family, LaFoy has lived in a variety of places, including Kentucky, Germany, Texas, North Carolina, Florida, and finally Kansas, where she has spent more than thirty years. She attended Johnson County Community College in Overland Park, where she earned an associate of arts degree in administration of justice, followed by a bachelor of arts degree from Wichita State University. She also holds a master of arts degree in sociology from Wichita State, with emphasis on criminology, as well as a social studies teaching certificate with emphasis on American history. LaFoy's husband, David, operates a business that engineers and installs industrial heating systems.

Before beginning her writing career, LaFoy was employed in a number of occupations. She briefly worked as a law enforcement VISTA volunteer, then took a job as a floor director for a local PBS station, which she describes as a "rather cool job." She later managed a furniture store before returning to school for her teaching certificate, while also managing a quilt shop and working for a friend in his custom picture-framing store. After receiving her certification, LaFoy taught high school for more than ten years.

LaFoy's earliest writing efforts predate the romance genre, but she had always included romantic relationships in her stories to make them more enjoyable. When the genre came into its own in the 1970s, LaFoy was a natural. She now writes full-time, beginning each novel with a rough idea of the characters, settings, and plot. "The story unfolds as it wills," she says. According to LaFoy, everything that occurs between the opening scene and the closing scene is serendipity, "a mystery I get to solve as I go along." LaFoy finds that planning every step of the story takes the fun out of writing it. "Every book I write begins with a leap of faith," she says.

LaFoy finds character and story ideas everywhere, with inspiration often coming "from out of the blue." A few of her sources include snippets of overheard conversations, strangers that trigger character ideas, scenes on television, or lyrics from a song. On occasions when she experiences writer's block, or "writer's confusion," she steps away from the project to let her subconscious work on it. "The subconscious is a marvelous percolator, and it almost always provides a, 'Duh! Of course!' moment," LaFoy explains. If the confusion stems from a flaw in the plot mechanics, she returns to the spot where the story first went off track, and rewrites from there. "Works every time," she says.

LaFoy's preferred setting is the American West, a region and culture this Kansan and history major knows very well. Her expertise shines through in such books as *Maddie's Justice* (2000), an intense historical novel set in Fort Larned, Kansas, in 1871. Maddie, a young teacher in a school for Cherokees, stops a high-ranking official from raping one of her students, killing him in the process. Wrongfully convicted of murder, Maddie is destined to be the recipient of frontier justice. U. S. Marshall Rivlin Kilpatrick, the lawman assigned to accompany Maddie to prison, has a less-than perfect past himself; but the longer the two of them are together, the more he doubts her guilt. Despite the trumped-up charges, Maddie is a true LaFoy heroine, courageous and willing to put herself on the line to protect someone else.

LaFoy's favorite time period for her American historicals is pre-Civil War, the antebellum period, an era of fundamental decency and nobility that was lost in the conflict. *Jackson's Way* (2001) takes place in 1838, and the action occurs in both Texas and New York City. When Lyndsay MacPhaull's father dies, he leaves their business, of which she's been part for years, to Jackson Stennet, a cowboy. They have only 60 days to prove their claim. However, there's an unknown but nefarious enemy who comes into play, so the two of them have to team up for protection.

For her European historicals, LaFoy prefers the later years of the Victorian era, when social attitudes were undergoing substantial change. Set in 1864 London, *The Perfect Temptation* (2004) is the story of Alexandra Radford, the governess for a rajah's son, who falls in love with Aiden Terrell, a private investigator who swore off women after the death of his fiancée. LaFoy's recurring theme in this book, as in her other works, is the hallmark of all romances, "the hero and the heroine overcome obstacles to love and commitment."

LaFoy invests considerable time in developing her characters, believing that they are the key to a truly good story. She notes, "A good plot is utterly wasted if you don't have solid, likable, fully dimensional characters to move through it." LaFoy's heroes and heroines both share common traits of intelligence and a good sense of humor. "It takes a long time to write a good book, and I refuse to spend months of my life in the company of dimwits and humorless trolls," says LaFoy. Much of LaFoy's own personality is in her characters, she says, noting, "My friends and family tell me that they can sometimes actually hear my voice saying some of the things in my books."

LaFoy finds the greatest appeal and challenge of writing romances to be the genre's depth and adaptability. She continues, "I think romance writers are some of the most diversely talented in the publishing world." Romance writers not only develop solid characters in meaningful relationships and engaging plots, but also adapt them to subgenera such as suspense, paranormal, fantasy ,and humor. "There's a niche for every style," says LaFoy.

LaFoy doesn't have a favorite among her own novels: "They're all my babies, and each has its own endearing qualities." The one she names as the hardest to write is her first Victorian historical, 2003's *The Perfect Seduction,* the first book in a trilogy (*The Perfect Temptation; The Perfect Desire,* 2005). The story of Seraphina Treadwell, a widowed artist, and Carden Reeves, a wealthy, aristocratic rake, took a great deal of time to research since historical accuracy is very important to LaFoy.

Her easiest novel to write was 1999's *Daring the Devil,* in which a private investigator sets himself up as a mark for pickpockets and blackmails the woman who tries to rob him into helping with his investigation. "It practically wrote itself," LaFoy says.

LaFoy maintains a home office and tries to keep regular hours, making it a point to live a healthy, well-rounded life apart from her writing. She finds doing that is "one of the best ways to keep your writing fresh." She describes herself as "a Real World version of Martha Stewart." Her crafting interests include quilting, sewing, cross-stitch, and needlepoint. She enjoys cooking and baking and is an avid gardener and interior designer. She also collects antique silver, the by-product of researching an occupation for a heroine. Other interests waiting in the wings include cake decorating, watercolor, and returning to school for a degree in interior design. On the eighth day, she rests!

BIBLIOGRAPHY

Books: *It Happened One Night.* New York: Bantam, 1997; *Lady Reckless.* New York: Bantam, 1998; *Daring the Devil.* New York: Bantam, 1999; *Maddie's Justice.* New York: Bantam, 2000; *Jackson's Way.* New York: Bantam, 2001; *Come What May.* New York: Bantam, 2002; *The Perfect Seduction.* New York: St. Martin's Press, 2003; *The Perfect Temptation.* New York: St. Martin's Press, 2004; *The Perfect Desire.* New York: St. Martin's Press, 2005; *Grin and Bear It.* Toronto: Harlequin, 2005; *Blindsided.* New York: Silhouette, 2005; *Her Scandalous Marriage.* New York: St. Martin's Press, 2006.

Novella: "The Proposition" in *My Scandalous Bride.* New York: St. Martin's Press, 2004.

SANDRA VAN WINKLE AND SHELLEY MOSLEY

JILL MARIE LANDIS

Jill Marie Landis. Photo by Sara Wall Photography. Courtesy of Jill Marie Landis.

To say that Jill Marie Landis loves to write is an understatement: "My dream would be to take off for Tonga, stay there for a few months and write, walk on the beach, eat fresh fish and coconut and fruit, sleep when I want to, and then come back with a finished book under my arm." She would also like to come back tan, thin and, maybe taller. Life keeps interrupting the dream.

Her earliest writing project was a handwritten newspaper she wrote under the dining room table at age 10, which reported the birth of her little brother. Now a best-selling novelist, Landis has 20 novels, half a dozen novellas, and numerous accolades to her credit. She enjoys the freedom that writers have, working at home and choosing their own hours. Landis says of her writing career, "This is not really a job. They pay me to make things up."

Landis was born in 1948 in Clinton, Indiana. Her paternal grandparents were midwesterners. Her maternal grandparents were Italian immigrants who moved to America in the early 1920s, settling in Clinton, where Landis's mother, Margaret Baima Davis, was born. In 1958, when Landis was 10, her family moved to Long Beach, California, where she grew up. She worked summers in various jobs, selling shave ice in Hawaii, cleaning vacation homes, and operating rides at Disneyland during college. Landis holds a bachelor's degree in history and a lifetime California teaching credential in elementary education. She taught kindergarten full-time for 9 years, and taught part-time English as a second language (ESL) classes. Her husband, Steve Landis, taught high school English and coached football for several years but now works as an actor and model. They have no children. "We taught school too long to want any kids of our own," she laughs.

Drawn to the romance genre both because of the happy endings and because the genre celebrates hope, love, family, and adventure, Landis was hooked on romances, as she puts it, "from the minute I read the last page of the first one I ever read." It was obvious from the beginning that Landis would be a star in the field of romance writing. Her very first book, *Sunflower,* published in 1988, is a historical about Analisa Van Meeteren, a Dutch immigrant who makes her living as a seamstress. Analisa has a child conceived from a rape during an Indian attack in which her beloved family was massacred. Caleb Storm, a half-Sioux frontiersman, is Analisa's romantic interest. More than just a love story, this book also explores the tenuous relationship between the Native American population and the white settlers. *Sunflower* won the Romance Writers of America's 1989 Golden Medallion (the precursor of the RITA) for Best Historical.

Landis's heroes tend to be victims of their past, wounded in different ways, with no intention of falling in love. "They're the worst possible choice for the heroine," she says. This is definitely the case for wealthy Jemma O'Hurley in *Just Once* (1997). Her parents have selected a proper husband for her, one of their own class and social strata, but Jemma wants to marry for love. When she goes to New Orleans to meet her husband-to-be, she finds that he's died in the interim. So with her new freedom, Jemma decides to go on a grand adventure … and immediately gets into trouble. Hunter Boone, an independent, spirited frontiersman, comes to the rescue, and grudgingly agrees to escort her to Canada. Unfortunately, on the way, Jemma gets kidnapped by the Choctaws, and Boone has to get her out of yet another situation. Landis uses the *Perils of Pauline*-ish trip to draw the young society girl and the previously unshackled adventurer together and prove that opposites do indeed attract.

Recurrent themes in Landis's novels involve prejudices that need to be faced and overcome, heroines who are down on their luck, or heroines who are at a turning point in their lives. Landis's heroines are women caught in desperate situations, running away from something and barely hanging on as they resolutely endure the slings and arrows of life. *Blue Moon* (1999), which has been called Landis's darkest novel, is a good example of both. This book has the unique setting of the Illinois backwoods in 1820. Olivia Bond, an 18-year-old runaway, meets up with Noah LeCroix, a tortured soul and lonely recluse with a disfigured face and only one eye. Noah, who originally appeared as a secondary character in *Just Once,* received his physical wounds performing a superhuman act of heroism. This unlikely pair are strangely drawn to each other, and with their two imperfect halves, make the perfect whole.

For Landis, the writing process begins with a character idea in an opening situation. The plot gets more refined and becomes more layered and polished with each successive draft. As a compulsive draft reviser, Landis admits, "Eventually I have to stop myself." She gets story ideas from the things she reads or sees on television, by observing life situations, and by just listening to people. "I'm always watching people's emotions and thinking … how can I write that down?" she says. Landis deals with writer's block by either confronting it and forcing herself to write or surrendering to it and spending time doing things she enjoys to refresh her muse.

According to Landis, her easiest novel to write was 1992's *Come Spring,* which virtually wrote itself. "It all fell together easily, and I laughed through it all," says Landis. Readers also enjoyed the hilarious tale of Buck Scott, the recluse who kidnaps the wrong woman from the train and is stuck with her in his mountain cabin until the spring thaw. In fact, the book won a RITA award and was chosen as one of RWA's Top Ten Favorite Books of the Year.

Landis is her own worst critic. She claims that the hardest novel for her to write is "always the one I'm working on." She believes that all writers are neurotic, and she experiences her biggest doubts "around page 350, when I'm sure it's the dumbest idea I ever came up with, I have no conflict, and the characters all need to have lobotomies." This is typical of Landis, who continues to exhibit genuine humility about her work, despite best sellers, two RITA winners, and four RITA finalists (*Rose*, 1990; *Summer Moon*, 2001: *Magnolia Creek*, 2002; and *Lover's Lane*, 2003). *Summer Moon* was also named one of *Library Journal*'s Top Five Romance Fiction Novels of 2001.

Landis doesn't have a favorite novel, but she is partial to her 1998 work *Glass Beach*, simply because it was set in Hawaii. An unwavering look at spousal abuse, this book is set on the Mauna Noe Ranch on the island of Kauai in the year 1888. Elizabeth Bennett is an abused wife. Fortunately, her monster of a husband dies fairly early in the book, but just as she celebrates her freedom, his illegitimate son, whom she didn't know existed, arrives on the scene. Spence Laamea, per his father's will, has been tapped to run their problem-ridden cattle ranch until Elizabeth's daughter, Hadley, turns 18. Elizabeth, who's never recovered emotionally from the abusive treatment by her husband, sees Spence as a threat, both physically and financially. Landis tackles this difficult subject with empathy and honesty. She shows the reader that the healing process is possible, reaching deep into her character's psyche to do so. In a world where Regency England, medieval England, and the American West are settings of choice for most historical romances, Landis, true to form, took a chance by selecting an uncommon setting—turn-of-the-century Hawaii.

A favorite with romance readers is the younger man/older woman story. For Landis, this didn't create quite enough conflict for her story. In *Last Chance* (1995), she makes the older woman, Rachel Albright McKenna, a newly widowed schoolmarm; and the younger man, Lane Cassidy, a gunslinger who used to be Rachel's student. Although the book is filled with humorous situations, Landis balances the tale by adding a custody battle over Rachel's son when she is deemed an unfit mother because of her choice of men—this, despite the fact her sheriff-husband died in another woman's bed. Rachel faces down the town and her in-laws, proving that she's a worthy addition to Landis's collection of feisty heroines.

Landis sees herself in the optimistic, determined, can-do attitudes of her characters. This is true of the title character in *Rose*. Despite her family's warnings, Rosa Audi leaves Italy for Busted Heel, Wyoming, where her husband waits for her. Alas, when she arrives in the untamed western town alone and penniless, she discovers that her husband has been shot and killed. Marshall Kase Storm tells her to return to her home in Europe. Rosa, a vivacious woman with a mind of her own, stays and opens a restaurant instead, showing that she has the grit to succeed. Kase has no choice but to admire the spirited Italian widow, and this admiration turns to love. However, he needs to resolve his own past and his relationship with his father before he can truly open his heart to her.

One of Landis's most independent heroines is Joya Penn from *The Orchid Hunter* (2000). Raised on a remote jungle island by a father who spends more time searching for his precious flowers than he does parenting her, Joya grows up a free spirit. Without any societal guidelines except those of the island's original, laid-back inhabitants, she lives her life wild and uninhibited. When Trevor Mandeville comes to offer Joya's father a contract with his import company, he sees Joya and realizes that she looks exactly like his adopted sister. Convinced that they're twins, he takes Joya from her jungle paradise to London, where she comes face-to-face with Janelle, the twin she never knew she had ... and the rigid confines of Victorian society. Joya's unrestrained ways and untamed behavior, as well as her passion for Trevor, turn the Mandeville household on its collective ear. Landis resolves the cultural conflict quite nicely, never losing respect for Joya's unique individuality. As usual, Landis creates a perfect blend of humor and poignancy.

In 2003, Landis tried her hand at contemporary romance. *Lover's Lane,* a romantic suspense, follows private investigator Jake Montgomery as he looks into the "accidental" death of his friend, Richard Saunders, and the disappearance of Richard's baby and the baby's mother. Six years later, he finds the Caroline Graham, now "Carly Nolan," living with her son in Twilight Cove, California. Landis followed this book with 2004's *Heat Wave,* which features Jake's partner, Kat Vargas, who's been wounded while apprehending a suspect. A third contemporary romance, *Heartbreak Hotel* (2005), completes the Twilight Cove trilogy and tells the story of widow Tracy Potter, who opens a supposedly haunted inn that becomes a sanctuary for famous writer Wade MacAllister.

Landis writes many of her hobbies and personal interests into her stories. She enjoys quilting, playing the ukulele, hula dancing, kayaking, and tropical gardening. This vivacious writer is also an avid swimmer and loves any form of water recreation.

Landis offers this observation of the writing profession: "Writers have no choice. They must write, or they would have to be locked away somewhere on a permanent basis." Although she emphasizes that this is just her opinion, many would nod in agreement. Landis's fans are happy that she's driven to write, since whether she's penning unforgettable historical novels or expertly crafted contemporaries, Landis continues to entertain her readers with stories that stay with them long after they finish the last page.

BIBLIOGRAPHY

Books: *Sunflower.* New York: Jove, 1988; *Wildflower.* New York: Jove, 1989; *Rose.* New York: Jove, 1990; *Jade.* New York: Jove, 1991; *Come Spring.* New York: Jove, 1992; *Past Promises.* New York: Jove, 1993; *Until Tomorrow.* New York: Jove, 1994; *Last Chance.* New York: Jove, 1995; *After All.* New York: Jove, 1995; *Day Dreamer.* New York: Jove, 1996; *Just Once.* New York: Jove, 1997; *Glass Beach.* New York: Jove, 1998; *Blue Moon.* New York: Jove, 1999; *The Orchid Hunter.* New York: Jove, 2000; *Summer Moon.* New York: Ballantine, 2001; *Magnolia Creek.* New York: Ballantine, 2002; *Lover's Lane.* New York: Ballantine, 2003; *Heat Wave.* New York: Ballantine, 2004; *Heartbreak Hotel.* New York: Ballantine, 2005.

Novellas: "Faithful and True" in *Loving Hearts.* New York: Berkley, 1992; "Picture Perfect" in *Sweet Hearts.* New York: Berkley, 1993; "Cradle Song" in *Three Mothers and a Cradle.* New York: Silhouette, 1995; "Josie's Story" in *Heartbreak Ranch.* Toronto: Harlequin, 1997; "Summer Fantasy" in *Summer Love.* New York: Kensington, 1997.

Genre-Related Essay: "Everything Looks New Again" in *North American Romance Writers.* Lanham, MD: Scarecrow Press, 1999.

SHELLEY MOSLEY AND SANDRA VAN WINKLE

CATHIE LINZ

Cathie Linze. Courtesy of Cathie Linz.

Best-selling, award-winning author Cathie Linz says she got her love of words "from the lyrics of Paul McCartney" and her sense of pacing from the "Uncle Wiggly" children's books, "because at the end of each book there was always a sneak peek at the next story, which made you want to read more." Building on these two trademark skills, she has developed a reputation for writing contemporary category romances that frequently feature sexy alpha-male heroes with a sense of humor, heroines who discover inner strengths they never knew they had, and plots that are always leavened with a generous measure of laughter.

Born in Chicago to an electrical engineer father who wrote great poetry and funny essays in his spare time, and a mother who was also an artist, Linz grew up in the Chicago area. From the time she won a writing award in the third grade, Linz knew writing was something special for her; but her path to romance writer would take a slight detour along the way. After graduating from college, she worked as the head of acquisitions at Northern Illinois University Law Library.

Linz began writing her first book, *Remembrance of Love* (1982), while working at the law library. She would write during her breaks and lunch hours, after work, and on weekends. Linz finally came to the realization that if she wanted to write, she just needed to do it, so she decided to take some time off from work and write full-time. She gave herself one year to get published, and one week before the end of her deadline, she received a call from Dell Publishing, asking to buy *Remembrance of Love*.

With Linz's own background in library work, it isn't unusual that several of her books would feature librarian heroines. In *Flirting with Trouble* (1992), a hunky cop goes undercover as a librarian, and much of the humor in the story comes from watching this macho man assume the stereotypical persona of a meek and mild librarian. In *Between the Covers* (2001), Linz again pairs a librarian with a cop. In this case, librarian Paige Turner finds herself giving romantic advice to policeman Shane Huntington.

As a prolific writer of category romances, Linz has explored a number of themes popular with readers in her books. With her Men of Honor series of books, each of which features a U. S. Marine Corps hero, she explores the concepts of courage, honor, and commitment. Beginning the series with *Daddy in Dress Blues* (2000), the hero, marine Curt Blackwell discovers he has a daughter he never knew about and needs the help of preschool teacher Jessie Moore to learn how to become a daddy. *Stranded with the Sergeant* (2001) Linz's 40th book, continues the military theme and introduces the first of her Wilder brother heroes, Joe Wilder, who is stranded with his commanding officer's daughter on a wilderness trip. Other Wilder brothers would get their own chance at romance, as Mark Wilder finds true love with a European princess in *The Marine and the Princess* (2001), and Justice Wilder, while recovering from an accident, falls in love with an old family friend in *Married to a Marine* (2002).

Royalty is another familiar theme in category romances, and Linz used this for several of her books. *A Prince at Last* (2002), features Luc Dumont, who turns out to be the missing heir to the throne of St. Michel. American Juliet Beaudreau is given the task of teaching him royal protocol, but Luc has trouble concentrating on his studies with a teacher as lovely as Juliet. With her fictionalized St. Michel, Linz creates her own lovely fairy-tale-like setting for this charming love story.

One of Linz's most-loved trilogies with readers, and an excellent example of her ability to write sexy, sassy, humorous contemporary romances, is her three Marriage Maker books. A trio of all-too-charming fairy godmothers—Betty, Muriel, and Hattie Goodie—is given the task of watching over triplets. Like all fairy godmothers, each one gives a sibling a special gift, but comical romantic difficulties ensue when each Knight triplet is given a bit too much of the qualities represented in each title: *Too Sexy for Marriage* (1998), *Too Stubborn to Marry* (1998), and *Too Smart for Marriage* (1998).

Though she prefers to write romances with contemporary settings, Linz created a love story in 1995 that included a historical setting. Her time-travel love story, *A Wife in Time,* features a book editor and a computer executive who, while attending a convention in Savannah, are sent back in time 111 years by a ghost who wants them to prove she didn't commit suicide.

As with many other authors, Linz's own personal interests can provide a bit of needed inspiration for the plot of one of her books. For example, Linz's love of travel shows up in *Continental Lover* (1986), as the book's heroine Mary Ellen Campbell finds her tour of Europe interrupted by Ty Stevenson, the playboy she thought she had left behind in Chicago.

By mixing humor and poignancy, crisp dialogue, and engaging characters, the prolific Linz continues to hone her writing skills and gather new fans along the way.

BIBLIOGRAPHY

Books: *Remembrance of Love.* New York: Dell, 1982; *Wildfire.* New York: Dell, 1983; *A Summer's Embrace.* New York: Dell, 1983; *A Charming Strategy.* New York: Dell, 1984; *A Private Account.*

New York: Dell, 1984; *Winner Takes All.* New York: Dell, 1984; *Pride and Joy.* New York: Dell, 1985; *A Glimpse of Paradise.* New York: Dell, 1985; *Tender Guardian.* New York: Dell, 1985; *Lover and Deceiver.* New York: Dell, 1986; *Continental Lover.* New York: Dell, 1986; *A Handful of Trouble.* New York: Dell, 1987; *Change of Heart.* New York: Silhouette, 1988; *A Friend in Need.* New York: Silhouette, 1988; *As Good as Gold.* New York: Silhouette, 1989; *Smiles.* New York: Silhouette, 1990; *Handyman.* New York: Silhouette, 1991; *Smooth Sailing.* New York: Silhouette, 1991; *Flirting with Trouble.* New York: Silhouette, 1992; *Male Ordered Bride.* New York: Silhouette, 1993; *Escapades.* New York: Silhouette, 1993; *Midnight Ice.* New York: Silhouette, 1994; *Bridal Blues.* New York: Silhouette, 1994; *One of a Kind Marriage.* New York: Silhouette, 1995; *Baby Wanted.* New York: Silhouette, 1995; *A Wife in Time.* New York: Silhouette, 1995; *Michael's Baby.* New York: Silhouette, 1996; *Seducing Hunter.* New York: Silhouette, 1996; *Abbie and the Cowboy.* New York: Silhouette, 1996; *Husband Needed.* New York: Silhouette, 1997; *Too Sexy for Marriage.* New York: Silhouette, 1998; *Too Stubborn to Marry.* New York: Silhouette, 1998; *Too Smart for Marriage.* New York: Silhouette, 1998; *The Rancher Gets Hitched.* Toronto: Harlequin, 1999; *The Cowboy Finds a Bride.* Toronto: Harlequin, 1999; *The Lawman Gets Lucky.* Toronto: Harlequin, 2000; *Daddy in Dress Blues.* New York: Silhouette, 2000; *Between the Covers.* Toronto: Harlequin, 2001; *Stranded with the Sergeant.* New York: Silhouette, 2001; *The Marine and the Princess.* New York: Silhouette, 2001; *A Prince at Last.* New York: Silhouette, 2002; *Married to a Marine.* New York: Silhouette, 2002; *Sleeping Beauty and the Marine.* New York: Silhouette, 2003; *Her Millionaire Marine.* New York: Silhouette, 2004; *Cinderella's Sweet-Talking Marine.* New York: Silhouette, 2004; *The Marine Meets His Match.* New York: Silhouette, 2004; *The Marine and Me.* New York: Silhouette, 2005; *Good Girls Do.* New York: Berkley, 2006.

Novella: "Brides Gone Wild" in *Catch of the Day.* New York: Berkley, 2006.

Genre-Related Essay: "Setting the Stage: Facts and Figures" in *Dangerous Men and Adventurous Women: Romance Writers on the Appeal of the Romance.* Philadelphia: University of Pennsylvania Press, 1992.

JOHN CHARLES

AMANDA LEE. *See* Rebecca York

ROBIN LEIGH. *See* Robin Lee Hatcher

KRISTINA LOGAN. *See* Barbara Freethy

MERLINE LOVELACE

M any popular romance authors grew up in military families, but Merline Lovelace took it a step further. She herself is a decorated veteran. Inspired by her father, a career Air Force aircrew member who served in the European theater in World War II, Lovelace has earned a number of awards during her 23 years of meritorious service. Among them are a Bronze Star, a Defense Superior Service Medal, and an Air Force Legion of Merit with one Oak Leaf Cluster. Lovelace continues to garner awards in her postmilitary career as a writer, having earned, among accolades, a coveted RITA award from the Romance Writers of America.

Growing up in an Air Force family, Lovelace recalls moving often as a child, living in Newfoundland and France, and at bases in New York, New Mexico, Kansas, Wisconsin, and Tennessee, to name just a few. Lovelace recalls, "I remember going to three different schools one year. Leaving friends behind was tough, but meeting new ones and moving to new locations was always exciting." She credits her mother with the daunting task of frequently relocating the family: "Mom was a real trooper. She packed up kids, dogs, cats, turtles, and parakeets and moved us all across country and across oceans dozens of times."

The well-traveled Lovelace acquired an interest in languages at an early age. She earned a bachelor's degree in German and Russian from Ripon College in Ripon, Wisconsin, and spent a year at Princeton University and two summers at Middlebury College in Vermont, studying Mandarin Chinese as part of the Critical Languages Program. She also earned a master's degree in personnel counseling and guidance from Troy State University in Alabama. Her Air Force credentials enabled her to attend Harvard University's Kennedy School of Government, under the Senior Officials in National Defense program. On her second day of active military duty, Lovelace met the man who would become her husband of more than thirty years. In true romantic form, they married in Taipei and honeymooned in Hong Kong. The couple has two sons and one grandson.

Lovelace says that she Lovelace held an assortment of jobs to work her way through college, including "car-hopping, slogging in the tobacco fields, shelving books in libraries, cocktail-waitressing, clerking at Sears, [and so forth]." After joining the Air Force, Lovelace moonlighted for a couple of semesters teaching German at a junior college but says that eventually "the responsibilities of rank and military duties caught up with me, and I spent the next twenty-plus years working on national defense issues."

It wasn't until after Lovelace retired from the Air Force that she considered becoming a writer, and within six months, she had sold her first novel, *Maggie and Her Colonel* (1994), to Harlequin. Lovelace hit the publishing ground running. Before *Maggie and Her Colonel* was actually published, Meteor came out with her book, *Bits and Pieces* (1993); and Silhouette published *Dreams and Schemes* (1994). Lovelace explains, "I had always loved books and reading. My earliest childhood memory is my mom rocking and reading to me. Everyone in my family always had their nose buried in a book, and I worked part-time in libraries during high school and college. At one point, I'd thought about becoming a librarian, then considered opening a bookstore after leaving the Air Force." However, it appears Lovelace has found her destiny as an author.

Her writing style focuses on action rather than introspection: "I work from a basic structure of two scenes per chapter, with something dramatic happening in each scene to move the plot or the romance along." Lovelace writes full-time, rising early in the morning and writing until midafternoon. This is followed by an exercise break, and then three to four hours are spent tending to business matters.

As one might expect of a world traveler, Lovelace's stories usually begin with a setting. She explains, "I guess it's the wanderlust in me, but I'm always traveling and exploring new places. When I stumble on some spot that grabs my interest, I immediately start populating it with characters and visualizing what happened there." Lovelace prefers not to use a recurring setting. Her favorite is "the next one that grabs my interest. I'm not good at series set in one locale, as I tend to get bored with it. I prefer to be off exploring new settings."

Lovelace's book *Alena* (1994) was inspired during a cold, misty morning stroll with her husband along Hadrian's Wall in north England. At that point, she was still in the military and had never thought about writing a book. It was here Lovelace had the epiphany that she would write when she retired, and that her first historical would be set at that spot. Her novel *The Horse Soldier* (2001) got its impetus from the windswept parade ground at historic Fort Laramie. It was another eerie experience—she knew she had to set a book there, too. Lovelace remembers, "I could almost hear the bugles calling." Other sites that Lovelace has visited and used as settings in her books include the Ritz Carleton at Cannes, the Russian Fort on California's coast, and the medieval walls of Valetta, Malta. "I love researching the history of such sites and incorporating them into my books," says Lovelace.

Lovelace uses a variety of time periods in her novels: "I've set books in ancient Egypt, classical Greece, Roman Britain, medieval France, the western United States, and at modern military bases around the world." To keep her writing fresh and interesting, Lovelace varies her time settings from one novel to the next. Lovelace says, "I enjoy alternating between a lush historical, full of detail about another time, and a fast-paced, modern-day thriller. That gives me a chance to exercise a different voice, and hopefully, keep from getting stale."

In a publishing world where the preferred setting for a historical romance novel was medieval England or France, Regency England, or the American West, Lovelace's decision to use ancient Egypt for *Lady of the Upper Kingdom* (1996) was a bold choice. Although the primary romance is between Philip, a Greek, and Farah, his Egyptian captive, the story also contains a wonderful secondary, star-crossed love affair between an older woman and a younger man. In another departure from the norm, Lovelace's time travel, *Somewhere in Time* (1994), has U.S. Air Force pilot Aurora Durant taking off from a base in Saudi

Arabia, being caught in a terrible storm, and ending up with a Roman centurion in the first century A.D.

Lovelace has had offers to write in other genres, but her heart is in romances: "I'm a sucker for a happy ending. I also believe in the power of love to get us through the worst of times—war, illness, death. I especially love romances because they appeal to the woman in me and represent the triumph of love over tragedy and/or evil." Lovelace enjoys the challenge of weaving the plot together with the emerging romance between the characters. She observes, "There's a real art to blending the two into a seamless whole. It's like writing a book inside a book."

Lovelace frequently writes about the role of women in national defense. "Women have participated in our country's military history from day one, yet receive little coverage in the history books. I've written a number of historical and contemporary novels featuring women, either on active duty or serving in vital support roles." In her novel *The Horse Soldier*, Lovelace explores the unique role played by Army laundresses whose service dates back to the Revolutionary War. In *The Captain's Woman* (2003), Lovelace pays tribute to the civilian contract nurses who served during the Spanish-American War. The book got its genesis from a single, grainy black-and-white photo of the nurses aboard the hospital ship *Relief*. "There they were, in their starched aprons and caps, with all those petticoats, going off to wallow in mud and blood. Having served with and witnessed the heroic actions of the nurses in Vietnam, I knew I had to write about these incredible women," she explains. Lovelace also has plans to write the story of the Hello Girls, who were French-speaking American women serving in France during World War I with Black Jack Pershing's Allied Expeditionary Force (AEF).

Lovelace names *The Captain's Woman,* the third in the Garrett Family saga (*The Horse Soldier,* 2001; *The Colonel's Daughter,* 2002), which is set during the Spanish-American War, as her favorite. "Teddy Roosevelt was such a fascinating figure, as was Clara Barton, both of whom appear as sub-characters in the book," says Lovelace. In *The Captain's Woman,* Captain Sam Garrett makes the mistake of forbidding his true love, Victoria Parker, from going to war-torn Cuba, although he's bound for the same destination. Victoria, an independent-minded newspaper reporter, dutifully sees him off at the docks, and then she defiantly sets sail for the forbidden island on another ship. The idealized romance and adventure of war die almost immediately for Victoria when she sees the grim reality of seriously wounded soldiers and finds herself in the middle of a deadly yellow fever epidemic. Lovelace skillfully manages to create an admirable heroine who is enthusiastic and naive, yet doesn't seem scatterbrained or ditzy. The young Victoria proves her mettle time and time again as she helps others survive the horrors of war and plague.

The heroes in all of Lovelace's novels are patterned after her husband. She observes, "You'll find they all share certain traits—a crooked grin, a slightly overdeveloped protective streak, a rock-solid dependability, and a maddening tendency to do the opposite of what's expected." Lovelace describes her heroines as independent women, written true to their time. For example, she says, "I would never have a medieval heroine nattering on about marrying for love. But I would have her determined to influence the marriage settlements to make sure they're in her best interests." She adds, "There's something of me in all of them. I've tried to do shy, retiring heroines; also meek, frightened ones. They always seem to reach inside for a spark of courage and/or stubbornness that can't be quelled."

One such heroine is *After Midnight's* (2003) Col. Jessica Blackwell. Jessica is reassigned to Elgin Air Force Base in Florida, a place that is, coincidentally, near her childhood home. She has no desire to return to the community where she and her promiscuous mother were pariahs. But she's a good soldier, and she obeys the relocation orders without voicing her deeply ingrained concerns. A series of killings coincide with her arrival. Small towns have long memories, and Jessica becomes a suspect in the murders. Local sheriff Steve Paxton knows Jessica has both the motive and the means, but despite the mounting evidence, he senses her innocence. Steve's faith in Jessica is substantiated when someone tries to kill her, and he appoints himself her bodyguard. This book, with its unflinchingly brave heroine and the man who believes in her, the white-knuckle suspense, and an intricate plot show why Lovelace is one of the leading names in romantic military thrillers.

According to Lovelace, the most difficult novel for her to write was *The 14th …and Forever* (1997), the story of the chief financial officer of a major hospital who gets called to Washington, D.C., to testify during a Senate committee's medical reform hearings. Unfortunately, the CFO's new love interest, the senator's aide, has been implicated in the violent events designed to interrupt the proceedings. Lovelace comments, "I have to admit, I struggled with [this] part of the Holiday Honeymoons series. I didn't feel there was enough plot to sustain the action and wasn't sure who the heck the villain was almost until the last chapter." Her hard work paid off, however, as this book turned out to be one of her best sellers.

According to Lovelace, several of her novels "almost wrote themselves." She recalls being so captivated by the medieval setting and characters in *His Lady's Ransom* (1994), a tale of a man who unsuccessfully tries to dominate a woman during the reign of Henry II, that she "could hardly type fast enough to keep up with them." In addition to her extensive travels, Lovelace finds story inspiration just about everywhere: "I've been known to weave a whole novel from a one-paragraph news item or blurb." Her novel *A Man of His Word* (1999) was born from a few lines in a *National Geographic Magazine* article about a town in Italy that was submerged in the 1950s when the government constructed a nearby dam. In a neat twist to this story, Lovelace writes about an ancient Anasazi cliff dwelling emerging from the water when a man-made lake in Arizona is drained to make repairs to a dam. The heroine, a documentary filmmaker, and the hero, the engineer in charge of the project, find themselves in a romantic relationship—and a lot of danger—as someone resorts to murder to interrupt the work on the dam. Adventure and suspense fill this page-turner as Lovelace once again shows that no matter what the setting, her books can entertain and enthrall.

For Lovelace, the best part of the writing process is the research. She observes, "I can get lost in other worlds and cultures. I also love the way characters take on unforeseen dimensions, and plots spin off in unexpected directions." Lovelace's cure for the occasional writer's block is to continue writing every day, regardless of the quality. "Even on the bad days, when I have to pry out every word. I'm constantly amazed at what comes out of my head once I get into a story and it starts to flow," she says.

Lovelace's military career has given her a unique perspective as a writer, and the passion and motivation to pay tribute to those women who risk their lives for freedom. Lovelace proclaims, "I was proud as heck to serve my country and am thrilled to write about the men and women I served with—ordinary people sometimes called upon to perform extraordinary deeds."

BIBLIOGRAPHY

Books: *Bits and Pieces.* New York: Meteor, 1993; *Dreams and Schemes.* New York: Silhouette, 1994; *Maggie and Her Colonel.* Toronto: Harlequin, 1994; *Somewhere in Time,* 1994; *His Lady's Ransom.* Toronto: Harlequin, 1994; *Siren's Call.* Toronto: Harlequin, 1994; *Sweet Song of Love.* Toronto:

Harlequin, 1994; *Alena.* Toronto: Harlequin, 1994; *Cowboy and the Cossack.* New York: Silhouette, 1995; *Night of the Jaguar.* New York: Silhouette, 1995; *Undercover Man.* New York: Silhouette, 1995; *Perfect Double.* New York: Silhouette, 1996; *Lady of the Upper Kingdom.* Toronto: Harlequin, 1996; *Line of Duty.* New York: Penguin Press, 1996; *Halloween Honeymoon.* New York: Silhouette, 1996; *Wrong Bride, Right Groom.* New York: Silhouette, 1996; *Beauty and the Bodyguard.* New York: Silhouette, 1996; *The 14th ... and Forever.* New York: Silhouette, 1997; *Duty and Dishonor.* New York: Penguin Press, 1997; *The Tiger's Bride.* Toronto: Harlequin, 1998; *Countess in Buckskin.* Toronto: Harlequin, 1998; *Call of Duty.* New York: Penguin Press, 1998; *If a Man Answers.* New York: Silhouette, 1998; *Return to Sender.* New York: Silhouette, 1998; *Undercover Groom.* New York: Silhouette, 1999; *Mercenary and the Mom.* New York: Silhouette, 1999; *River Rising.* New York: NAL, 1999; *Two Tickets to Paradise.* New York: Silhouette, 1999; *A Man of His Word.* New York: Silhouette, 1999; *The Harder They Fall.* New York: Silhouette, 2000; *Mistaken Identity.* New York: Silhouette, 2000; *The Horse Soldier.* Toronto: MIRA, 2001; *Dark Side of Dawn.* New York: NAL, 2001; *Twice in One Lifetime.* New York: Silhouette, 2001; *The Spy Who Loved Him.* New York: Silhouette, 2001; *Texas Hero.* New York: Silhouette, 2002; *Hot as Ice.* New York: Silhouette, 2002; *The Colonel's Daughter.* Toronto: MIRA, 2002; *A Savage Beauty.* Toronto: MIRA, 2003; *The Captain's Woman.* Toronto: MIRA, 2003; *A Question of Intent,* 2003; *After Midnight.* New York: NAL, 2003; *To Love a Thief.* New York: Silhouette, 2003; *Texas Now and Forever.* New York: Silhouette, 2003; *The Right Stuff.* New York: Silhouette, 2004; *Untamed.* Toronto: MIRA, 2004; *Full Throttle.* New York: Silhouette, 2004; *Eye of the Beholder.* Toronto: MIRA, 2005; *The Last Bullet.* Toronto: MIRA, 2005; *The Middle Sin.* Toronto: MIRA, 2005; *The First Mistake.* Toronto: MIRA, 2005; *Diamonds Can Be Deadly.* New York: Silhouette 2006; *Devlin and the Deep Blue Sea.* New York: Silhouette, 2006; *I'll Walk Alone.* New York: Silhouette, 2006.

Novellas: "Rogue Knight" in *Renegades Three.* Toronto: Harlequin, 1995; "A Drop of Frankincense" in *The Gifts of Christmas.* Toronto: Harlequin, 1998; "Final Approach ... to Forever" in *Special Report.* New York: Silhouette, 2000; "Mismatched Hearts" in *Bride by Arrangement.* Toronto: Harlequin, 2000; "The Major's Wife" in *The Officer's Bride.* Toronto: Harlequin, 2001; "Undercover Operations" in *The Heart's Command.* New York: Harlequin, 2002; "A Military Affair" in *In Love and War.* Toronto: Harlequin, 2003; "Sailor's Moon" in *April Moon.* Toronto: Harlequin, 2004; "A Bridge for Christmas" in *A Soldier's Christmas.* New York: Silhouette, 2004.

SHELLEY MOSLEY AND SANDRA VAN WINKLE

KATIE MACALISTER

Popular with readers, prolific in output, and possessing a wicked sense of humor, Katie MacAlister has quickly earned a reputation in the romance genre for her versatility. The award-winning, *USA Today* best-selling author has the ability to write a variety of types of romances, including historical romances, contemporary romances, paranormal romances, and, writing as Katie Maxwell, young adult romantic comedies.

MacAlister was born in the Seattle, Washington, area in 1962. She got her love of books from her mother, an artistic soul who instilled in all her children the joys of reading. MacAlister grew up in Seattle, where she attended grade school; but after a couple of weeks in high school, she left Seattle. MacAlister eventually wound up at the University of Washington, where she spent seven years pursuing a double degree in physics and astronomy.

MacAlister had no idea she wanted to be an author, and she worked at a variety of jobs, including genealogist, wave machine solderer, Fortran programmer, and sales associate for Harrods. MacAlister didn't start writing until she was in her early thirties, and at first, all of her writing projects were nonfiction, including three books on genealogy. Then in her midthirties, MacAlister discovered how much fun writing fiction could be. She says that with her "passion for mystery, fascination with alpha males, and deep love of history," she turned out to be a natural at writing romance fiction.

Even before she received any contracts for her work, what kept MacAlister writing was her love of storytelling and her love of romances. MacAlister's first novel, a historical romance published under the name Marthe Arends, was *The Lion's Shadow* (1999), the story of stubborn, intelligent suffragette Cassandra Whitney who meets her match in explorer Griffin St. John. Published by a small press, *The Lion's Shadow* has some wonderfully

---

also writing as Katie Maxwell
also writing as Marthe Arends

unique characters, plenty of passion, delightful humor, and a dash of suspense; all ingredients that would show up in MacAlister's later books.

While MacAlister was pleased with *The Lion's Shadow,* she did recognize the flaws in her first work of fiction. When she sold her second novel, *Noble Intentions* (2002), to Dorchester, she decided to go with the pen name of Katie MacAlister. With *Noble Intentions,* MacAlister refined all the ingredients present in her first book into a wonderfully witty, sexy historical romance. In search of a docile, tranquil woman to marry, the book's hero, Noble Britton, instead finds Gillian Leigh, who turns his hopes for a quiet life upside down.

Noble Intentions would become the first in a series of historical Regency romances by MacAlister, who found her second historical romance, *Noble Destiny* (2003), to be one of her more difficult books to write because the story features a heroine who first appeared as a secondary character in *Noble Intentions,* Lady Charlotte "Char" Collins. MacAlister found Char to be "fine as a wacky sidekick but difficult to write as a main protagonist."

Improper English (2003), MacAlister's first contemporary romance, is told from the viewpoint of the book's heroine, Alexandra Freemar, and proved that MacAlister is one of those rare authors who is perfectly comfortable writing in the first-person voice. An American living in London, Alexandra has three months to prove she isn't a complete failure by writing a romance novel; only her plans keep getting interrupted by her sexy upstairs neighbor, Scotland Yard detective Alexander Black. A great deal of the humor in the book comes from Alexandra's efforts to write a romance and find a publisher for her book, giving MacAlister the opportunity to gleefully skewer a number of misperceptions about the romance genre.

Using the pseudonym of Katie Maxwell, MacAlister began writing young adult romances with, *The Year My Life Went Down the Loo,* published in 2003. The book's heroine, 16-year-old American Emily Williams, must spend a year abroad with her family. Three more books chronicle Emily's humorous adventures as she not only tries to adapt to life in Europe, but also enjoys a bit of romance with assorted hunky European boys. One of MacAlisters other young adult romances written under the pen name Katie Maxwell, *Got Fangs? Confessions of a Vampire's Girlfriend* (2005), has a small connection to MacAlister's adult romances in that the author puts her teen protagonist, Francesca, in a traveling GothFaire that also appeared in *The Girl's Guide to Vampires* (2003). While written for a younger audience, MacAlister's young adult books share the same outrageous sense of humor that flavors her adult romances.

In 2003, MacAlister wrote her first paranormal romance novel by dabbling in the growing subgenre of romances featuring vampires. The Vamp series, as MacAlister calls it, began with *The Girl's Guide to Vampires* in which the heroine, Joy Randall, allows herself to be dragged along with her best friend, Roxy, on a trip to the Czech Republic. Roxy is determined to find the mysterious author of the Moravian Dark One romance novels, even though Joy is skeptical that such things as Dark Ones even exist. Then Joy meets a handsome stranger, Raphael Griffin St. John, who eerily resembles the sexy man who has been haunting her dreams, and Joy starts believing in vampires.

MacAlister firmly believes in placing her heroines in situations where they are on their own and must rely on themselves to get out of whatever sticky situation they've managed to get into. Each of the heroines of her Vamp series—Joy in *The Girl's Guide to Vampires;* Allie in *Sex and the Single Vampire* (2004); and Nell in *Sex, Lies, and Vampires* (2005)—are excellent examples of this. "I'm very big on self-reliance, and I think that this filters through to the plots of my books," she says.

MacAlister is also known for her imperfect heroines, and Tessa Riordan of *The Corset Diaries* (2004) is a perfect illustration of this author's realistically flawed, yet utterly lovable heroines. Tessa, unlike most romance heroines, is a plus-size, thirty-something woman hired to play the part of a duchess in a British reality television show. Told in diary form, Tessa narrates her hilarious experiences while filming the show; her deepening relationship both on and off camera with the man who plays her husband, Max Edgerton, the duke; and her attempts to befriend Max's truculent teenage daughter. Like all of MacAlister's heroines, and most of her heroes, Tessa has a strong sense of humor, which helps immensely as she deals with the many things that go wrong on the show and the things that go right, such as her discovery that Max, the man of her dreams, really loves her for who she is and not the character she is playing.

"I regret I can't amuse the entire world, but I am resigned to just pleasing those who share my rather warped sense of humor," says MacAlister. She may not be able to please everyone, but her outrageously humorous, deliciously sexy romances continue to offer love and laughter to a growing number of readers.

BIBLIOGRAPHY

Writing as Katie MacAlister

Books: *Noble Intentions.* New York: Dorchester, 2002; *Improper English.* New York: Dorchester, 2003; *Noble Destiny.* New York: Dorchester, 2003; *The Girl's Guide to Vampires.* New York: Dorchester, 2003; *Men in Kilts.* New York: Onyx, 2003; *Sex and the Single Vampire.* New York: Dorchester, 2004; *The Corset Diaries.* New York: Onyx, 2004; *The Trouble with Harry.* New York: Dorchester, 2004; *You Slay Me.* New York: Onyx, 2004; *Sex, Lies, and Vampires.* New York: Dorchester, 2005; *Hard Day's Knight.* New York: Eclipse, 2005; *Fire Me Up.* New York: Signet, 2005; *Blow Me Down.* New York: Signet, 2005; *Even Vampires Get the Blues.* New York: Signet, 2006; *Light My Fire.* New York: Signet, 2006.

Novellas: "Bird of Paradise" in *Heatwave.* New York: Dorchester, 2003; "Bring Out Your Dead" in *Just One Sip.* New York: Dorchester, 2006.

Writing as Marthe Arends

Book: *The Lion's Shadow.* New York: Avid Press, 1999.

Writing as Katie Maxwell

Books: *The Year My Life Went Down the Loo.* New York: Dorchester, 2003; *They Wear What Under Their Kilts?* New York: Dorchester, 2004; *What's French for "Ew"?!* New York: Dorchester, 2004; *Eyeliner of the Gods.* New York: Dorchester, 2004; *The Taming of the Dru.* New York: Dorchester, 2004; *Got Fangs? Confessions of a Vampire's Girlfriend.* New York: Dorchester, 2005; *Circus of the Darned.* New York: Dorchester, 2005.

JOHN CHARLES

DEBBIE MACOMBER

Debbie Macomber. Courtesy of Debbie Macomber.

Debbie Macomber recently found a journal entry that she had written on January 1, 1973. It said, "Since the greatest desire of my life is to somehow, some way be a writer, I'll start with the pages of this diary." In 2000, Macomber had 60 million books in print worldwide. She writes full-time and has an office outside of her home and a staff of three. As Macomber puts it, "This is the power of a dream."

Macomber is a strong believer in dreaming. She has always dreamed of being a writer, even as a child. But, Macomber says, she was dyslexic "before they had a word for it. I never told a soul about my fragile dream for fear someone would discourage me. I couldn't bear that. I kept this desire buried in my heart until I lost a cousin in 1978. After David died, it was as if God was telling me I couldn't stuff my dreams into the future."

A native of Yakima, Washington, Macomber was born in 1948 to Ted and Connie Adler. Her father had his own upholstery business, and her mother was a waitress at the Chinook Hotel. When Macomber was four or five years old, her mother would take her to the library for story hour. Macomber says she loved the library "because it was built like a castle, and I felt like a princess. That story hour librarian who first instilled in me a love of books later went on to write books of her own. Her name is Beverly Cleary."

In the eighth grade, Macomber's first book was sold, when her brother and two cousins stole her diary and offered it to their classmates for a price. Although humiliating at the time, it was a sort of foreshadowing that people were willing to pay for her writing.

Macomber went to St. Joseph Academy, a Catholic girls' high school. After graduation, she moved to Seattle and married Wayne Macomber in 1968, making a union that has lasted through the years. At the time of their wedding, Macomber worked for PEMCO Insurance at the fire desk, and Wayne was an electrician. He continued with electrical/construction work until he retired at the age of 50. Macomber didn't go to college until after the birth of her four children, when she attended a community college and took night courses.

Despite her desire to write, Macomber's first priority was motherhood. She waited until her youngest (and last) was born before deciding that she could do both. Macomber recalls, "In 1978, I rented a typewriter and set it up on the kitchen table to begin my dream, moving it for meal times. When the older kids left for school, supermom turned into the struggling young writer." Macomber, who considers herself a storyteller, says that she doesn't know how to describe her writing style. She feels her readers are the "best people to ask" for that information.

When queried as to why she chose the romance genre, Macomber, with her typical humor, explained, "I enjoyed reading romances. After potty training four kids, I needed a story with a happy ending and found escape from the trials and tribulations of motherhood in a good romance. They were what I wanted to write because they were what I enjoyed reading the most."

Early in Macomber's career, she had the opportunity to novelize ten of the scripts for *Knot's Landing,* a popular nighttime soap opera that ran from 1979 to 1993. Besides providing financial support for her family, those assignments began to build her name as a romance writer. Later, the optimistic writer also became a much-sought-after motivational speaker.

Macomber says she loves to write: "I love everything about it. I am so blessed to be able to work at what I love. It doesn't matter if I am just starting a book or if I am doing revisions for the second time on the same manuscript. I love every aspect when it comes to writing. My readers are a constant blessing to me, and I treasure their feedback." Writer's block has never been an issue for the prolific Macomber: "I have far too many plot ideas spinning around in my head. This is not a problem for me. Over the years, I've discovered that if I have what many attribute to writer's block, there's actually something wrong with the story, and all I need to do is go back and figure that out. As soon as I do, the story progresses."

There is a running joke in Macomber's family that when she is lying on the living room sofa for an afternoon nap, no one is to disturb her because she is "plotting." For Macomber, the plot comes first. She says, "This is the easiest part of writing for me. I get plot ideas from the simplest of things. I could be reading the newspaper or watching TV, and something will click in my head, and the ideas will start to roll. The characters will come later. My plots guide me to the characters."

Macomber says about her heroes: "My heroes all share one common trait. They might possess flaws, but they are honorable." All of the heroines she creates have a touch of her in them. "Quite a bit of me is in each character," says Macomber. "How can they not—I've created them!"

Macomber writes a romantic comedy every year with a Christmas theme. Perhaps her most famous—and favorite—Christmas stories are those starring three angels: Shirley, Goodness, and Mercy. *A Season of Angels* (1993); *The Trouble with Angels* (1994); *Touched by Angels* (1995); *Shirley, Goodness, and Mercy* (1999); and *Those Christmas Angels* (2003) all feature this winsome trio of eccentric celestial beings who find unconventional ways of answering prayers. They each have their foibles. Goodness, for example, likes to see herself on movie screens. Mercy has a penchant for anything mechanical, especially motor scooters and escalators. Even though they prefer to help humans in need, Shirley, Goodness, and Mercy aren't the most skilled angels, and at one point, the three of them mess up so badly on Earth that they are banished to the Heavenly Host Choir by the Archangel Gabriel himself.

According to Macomber, her favorite books to write are the Christmas romantic comedies. She says, "*When Christmas Comes* (2004) came to me after watching an episode of *Trading Spaces;* only I decided to have everyone trade *places*." In this story, two people trade homes for the Christmas holidays, and the results are hilarious.

On a more serious note, for the past few years at Christmas, Macomber has penned a new book for the Cedar Cove series—heartwarming tales of family life in a small town. Macomber says, "I like to write about small towns. They're what I'm familiar with, having been born and raised in one. Wayne and I chose to raise our family in a small town, which is why we moved to Port Orchard, Washington. My ongoing Cedar Cove series, which is actually Port Orchard in disguise, takes place in [such] a community." The Cedar Cove books include the following titles: *16 Lighthouse Road* (2001), in which a female judge refuses to grant a divorce to a young couple whose baby has died; *204 Rosewood Lane* (2002), about a librarian who helps her two daughters cope with the disappearance of their father; *311 Pelican Court* (2003), in which a judge awards the kids the house in a divorce settlement and requires the newly divorced parents to make alternating visits; *44 Cranberry Point* (2004), in which a Vietnam vet is murdered in the local bed-and-breakfast; and *50 Harbor Street* (2005), in which a couple solves a mystery from their past and their daughter opens a new clinic in town. The strong sense of community that flavors all of Macomber's books is an especially important part of her Cedar Cove series, and it is one of the things her readers love best about these books.

Macomber counts the state of Alaska among her favorite places. Midnight Sons, a series set in Hard Luck, Alaska, tells the story of the members of this small community, population 150 and growing. Funny and poignant, this series includes the following titles: *Brides for Brothers* (1995), about a librarian and her two children who move to town; *The Marriage Risk* (1995), in which a grandmother comes between a man and woman; *Daddy's Little Helper* (1995), in which the daughter of a single father matches him up with her teacher; *Because of the Baby* (1996), in which a divorced couple has one night of passion for old times' sake that results in a pregnancy; *Falling for Him* (1996), about a bush pilot who hates the woman who loves him, or so he thinks; and *Ending in Marriage* (1996), in which a plane crash brings a man and woman together. The anthology *Born in a Small Town* (2000) contains a final Midnight Sons novella, "Midnight Sons and Daughters."

Macomber's current favorite book is *The Shop on Blossom Street* (2004), the story of a cancer survivor who is also the owner of a yarn shop and who begins to conduct knitting classes for her patrons. Macomber says, "I love to knit and could easily relate to the women in the book. If I wasn't writing, I would probably own a yarn store, which I could easily do considering the stash of yarn in my home!" She adds diplomatically, "I love all the books I've written. Each book is special to me for some reason or another, so it's impossible to pick a favorite."

The hardest book for Macomber to write was *Between Friends* (2002). The entire story is told as though reading the scrapbook of two women's lives, and there is no description or dialogue. It begins with a birth announcement dated 1948 and ends with September 11, 2001, when the terrorists attack New York City. Macomber comments, "There is a lot of history in the book, and I tried to touch on most of the major historical events during the years covered."

All books require research, something at which Macomber has become very adept. For her book *Changing Habits* (2003) she says, "I read everything I could get my hands on about being a nun and the Catholic Church. I spent many hours reading and interviewing former nuns, all before I started writing the book." In this story, three nuns of St. Bridget's Sisters of the Assumption leave their order to find their destinies.

Years later, Macomber switched from writing category romances to the longer format of mass-market paperback novels. Eventually, she entered the world of women's fiction, where a variety of a women's relationships (sister, daughter, friend, etc.) are explored as well as the women's love lives. However, Macomber says whatever she writes "will always have an element of romance in the story line." The setting will also stay in the present. "I write contemporary novels," she says. "I don't write historicals, although I enjoy reading them."

The following is Macomber's take on what being a romance writer means to her: "I am passionate about the written word and the power of story. My readers inspire me with their letters and their comments on how my books touch their lives. The happy ending in a romance is important to me. Life can be full of doom and gloom. I enjoy the escape romance offers, the same way I did when my children were little. We never outgrow our need for love, and that's what romance offers—that promise of a happy-ever-after [that] we all seek on one level or another."

BIBLIOGRAPHY

Writing as Debbie Macomber

Books: *Starlight.* New York: Silhouette, 1983; *Thanksgiving Prayer.* New York: Silhouette, 1984; *Undercover Dreamer.* New York: Silhouette, 1984; *Heartsong.* New York: Silhouette, 1984; *The Gift of Christmas.* New York: Silhouette, 1984; *That Wintry Feeling.* New York: Silhouette, 1984; *A Girl Like Janet.* New York: Silhouette, 1984; *Promise Me Forever.* New York: Silhouette, 1985; *Borrowed Dreams.* New York: Silhouette, 1985; *Adam's Image.* New York: Silhouette, 1985; *Trouble with Cassi.* New York: Silhouette, 1985; *A Friend or Two.* New York: Silhouette, 1985; *Love Thy Neighbor.* New York: Silhouette, 1985; *Christmas Masquerade.* New York: Silhouette, 1985; *Reflections of Yesterday.* New York: Silhouette, 1986; *Shadow Chasing.* New York: Silhouette, 1986; *Yesterday Once More.* New York: Silhouette, 1986; *Yesterday's Hero.* New York: Silhouette, 1986; *White Lace and Promises.* New York: Silhouette, 1986; *Friends and Then Some.* New York: Silhouette, 1986; *Jury of His Peers.* New York: Silhouette, 1986; *Laughter in the Rain.* New York: Silhouette, 1986; *The Matchmakers.* Toronto: Harlequin, 1986; *Sugar and Spice.* New York: Silhouette, 1987; *No Competition.* New York: Silhouette, 1987; *All Things Considered.* New York: Silhouette, 1987; *Love 'n' Marriage.* New York: Silhouette, 1987; *Love by Degree.* Toronto: Harlequin, 1987; *Mail Order Bride.* New York: Silhouette, 1987; *Almost Paradise.* New York: Silhouette, 1988; *Cindy and the Prince.* New York: Silhouette, 1988; *Playboy and the Widow.* New York: Silhouette, 1988; *Some Kind of Wonderful.* New York: Silhouette, 1988; *Navy Wife.* New York: Silhouette, 1988; *Yours and Mine.* Toronto: Harlequin, 1989; *Navy Blues.* New York: Silhouette, 1989; *Any Sunday.* New York: Silhouette, 1989; *Almost an Angel.* New York: Silhouette, 1989; *Way to a Man's Heart.* New York: Silhouette, 1989; *Denim and Diamonds.* New York: Silhouette, 1989; *For All My Tomorrows.* New York: Silhouette, 1989; *The Sheriff Takes a Wife.* New York: Silhouette, 1990; *Rainy Day Kisses.* Toronto: Harlequin, 1990; *Country Bride.* Toronto: Harlequin, 1990; *Cowboy's Lady.* New York: Silhouette, 1990; *Fallen Angel.* New York: Silhouette, 1990; *Courtship of Carol Sommars.* New York: Silhouette, 1990; *A Little Bit Country.* Toronto: Harlequin, 1990; *First Comes Marriage.* Toronto: Harlequin, 1991; *Girl Like Janet.* Toronto: Harlequin, 1991; *The Forgetful Bride.* Toronto: Harlequin, 1991; *Father's Day.* Toronto: Harlequin, 1991; *Here Comes Trouble.* Toronto: Harlequin,

1991; *Navy Woman.* New York: Silhouette, 1991; *Navy Brat.* New York: Silhouette, 1991; *Navy Baby.* New York: Silhouette, 1991; *My Valentine.* Toronto: Harlequin, 1991; *Valerie.* Toronto: Harlequin, 1992; *Stand-in Wife.* New York: Silhouette, 1992; *Norah.* Toronto: Harlequin, 1992; *Stephanie.* Toronto: Harlequin, 1992; *Bride on the Loose.* New York: Silhouette, 1992; *My Hero.* Toronto: Harlequin, 1992; *To Have and to Hold.* Toronto: Harlequin, 1992; *The Man You'll Marry.* Toronto: Harlequin, 1992; *Marriage of Inconvenience.* New York: Silhouette, 1992; *Marriage Wanted.* New York: Silhouette, 1993; *Morning Comes Softly.* New York: Harper, 1993; *To Mother with Love.* New York: Silhouette, 1993; *Bride Wanted.* New York: Silhouette, 1993; *A Season of Angels.* New York: Harper, 1993; *Groom Wanted.* New York: Silhouette, 1993; *Lone Star Lovin'.* Toronto: Harlequin, 1993; *Ready for Romance.* Toronto: Harlequin, 1993; *Hasty Wedding.* New York: Silhouette, 1993; *Ready for Marriage.* Toronto: Harlequin, 1994; *The Bachelor Prince.* New York: Silhouette, 1994; *The Trouble with Angels.* New York: Harper, 1994; *One Night.* New York: Harper, 1994; *Baby Blessed.* New York: Silhouette, 1994; *Someday Soon.* New York: Harper, 1995; *Same Time Next Year.* New York: Silhouette, 1995; *Touched by Angels.* New York: Harper, 1995; *Wanted: Perfect Partner.* New York: Silhouette, 1995; *Brides for Brothers.* Toronto: Harlequin, 1995; *The Marriage Risk.* Toronto: Harlequin, 1995; *Daddy's Little Helper.* Toronto: Harlequin, 1995; *Just Married.* New York: Silhouette, 1996; *Because of the Baby.* Toronto: Harlequin, 1996; *Falling for Him.* Toronto: Harlequin, 1996; *Ending in Marriage.* Toronto: Harlequin, 1996; *Mrs. Miracle.* New York: Harper, 1996; *Sooner or Later.* New York: Harper, 1996; *Three Brides, No Groom.* New York: Silhouette, 1997; *This Matter of Marriage.* Toronto: MIRA, 1997; *Montana.* Toronto: MIRA, 1998; *Lone Star Baby.* Toronto: Harlequin, 1998; *Nell's Cowboy.* Toronto: Harlequin, 1998; *Dr. Texas.* Toronto: Harlequin, 1998; *Caroline's Child.* Toronto: Harlequin, 1998; *Texas Two-Step.* Toronto: Harlequin, 1998; *Lonesome Cowboy.* Toronto: Harlequin, 1998; *Can This Be Christmas?* Toronto: MIRA, 1998; *Shirley, Goodness, and Mercy.* Toronto: MIRA, 1999; *Promise, Texas.* Toronto: MIRA, 1999; *Moon Over Water.* Toronto: MIRA, 1999; *Orchard Valley.* Toronto: Harlequin, 1999; *Ready for Love.* Toronto: Harlequin, 1999; *Ready for Marriage.* Toronto: Harlequin, 1999; *Family Men.* Toronto: Harlequin, 2000; *Return to Promise.* Toronto: MIRA, 2000; *Dakota Born.* Toronto: MIRA, 2000; *Dakota Home.* Toronto: MIRA, 2000; *Mail-Order Marriages.* Toronto: Harlequin, 2000; *16 Lighthouse Road.* Toronto: MIRA, 2001; *Always Dakota.* Toronto: MIRA, 2001; *Buffalo Valley.* Toronto: MIRA, 2001; *Thursdays at Eight.* Toronto: MIRA, 2001; *An Ideal Marriage?* Toronto: Harlequin, 2001; *204 Rosewood Lane.* Toronto: MIRA, 2002; *The Christmas Basket.* Toronto: MIRA, 2002; *Between Friends.* Toronto: MIRA, 2002; *Angels Everywhere.* New York: HarperCollins, 2002; *The Snow Bride.* Toronto: MIRA, 2003; *Changing Habits.* Toronto: MIRA, 2003; *Those Christmas Angels.* Toronto: Harlequin, 2003; *311 Pelican Court.* Toronto: MIRA, 2003; *When Christmas Comes.* Toronto: MIRA, 2004; *The Shop on Blossom Street.* Toronto: MIRA, 2004; *44 Cranberry Point.* Toronto: MIRA, 2004; *Navy Husband.* New York: Silhouette, 2005; *50 Harbor Street.* Toronto: MIRA, 2005; *Mrs. Miracle.* New York: Avon, 2005; *There's Something about Christmas.* Toronto: MIRA, 2005; *A Good Yarn.* Toronto: MIRA, 2005; *Buffalo Valley.* New York: Thomas Gale, 2005; *This Matter of Marriage.* New York: Thomas Gale, 2005; *6 Rainier Drive.* Toronto: MIRA, 2006; *Christmas Letters.* Toronto: MIRA, 2006; *Susannah's Garden.* Toronto: MIRA, 2006; *The Wyoming Kid.* Toronto: Harlequin, 2006.

Novellas: "Let It Snow" in *Christmas Stories.* New York: Silhouette, 1986; "Christmas Masquerade" in *Christmas Treasures.* Toronto: Harlequin, 1990; "My Funny Valentine." Toronto: Harlequin, 1990; "First Man You Meet" in *To Have and to Hold.* Toronto: Harlequin, 1992; "Mail-Order Bride" in *Solution: Marriage.* New York: Silhouette, 1993; "The Apartment" in *To Mother with Love.* New York: Silhouette, 1993; "Family Affair" in *Purrfect Love.* New York: Harper, 1994; "Rock-a-Bye Baby" in *Three Mothers and a Cradle.* New York: Silhouette, 1995; "The Marrying Kind" in *A Spring Bouquet.* New York: Kensington, 1996; "Silver Bells" in *Christmas Kisses.* New York: Silhouette, 1996; "Private Paradise" in *That Summer Place.* Toronto: MIRA, 1998; "Midnight Sons and Daughters" in *Born in a Small Town.* Toronto: Harlequin, 2000; "Let It Snow" in *Midnight Clear.* New York: Silhouette, 2001; "My Funny

Valentine" in *Sealed with a Kiss*. Toronto: Harlequin, 2002; "The First Man You Meet" in *Harlequin Special #2*. Toronto: Harlequin, 2002; "What Amanda Wants" in *More Than Words*. Toronto: Harlequin, 2005; "5-B Poppy Lane" in *Hearts Divided*. Toronto: MIRA, 2006.

Shelley Mosley and Sandra Van Winkle

ANNETTE MAHON

Annette Mahon. Courtesy of Annette Mahon.

Author and master quilter Annette Mahon is best known for her Hawaiian romances—exotic books with small-town settings. According to Mahon, the *real* theme of her romances is *ohana*. *Ohana* is the Hawaiian term for family, but it refers to more than just the immediate family; it also includes good friends and *calabash,* or shirttail relatives.

Mahon knows *ohana*. She was born in Hilo, Hawaii, in 1947 to Agnes and Arthur Edwards, both second-generation islanders of Portuguese descent. Her mother, a native of Hilo, was a stay-at-home parent who later worked as a child-care provider. Mahon and her sisters not only wore the clothes this excellent seamstress made, but also learned their own sewing skills from her. Mahon's father, a talented musician, was well known locally for his ukulele and guitar playing. He worked for the state government in various capacities, mostly as a clerical worker in the Department of Corrections.

Although Mahon grew up in Hilo, the second-largest city in Hawaii, she considered herself a country girl, mainly because of Hilo's small-town atmosphere. The settings in her books, such as Malino, Hawaii, where her Secret series takes place and where the townsfolk are no strangers to matchmaking, reflect this love of small communities.

Mahon attended parochial schools in Hilo and then went on to the mainland for college. After earning a bachelor of arts degree in English from LeMoyne College in Syracuse, New York, she attended graduate school at Syracuse University, earning a master of science degree in library science. In 1973, she married George Richardson Mahon, a marketing manager for General Electric, and together, they have three daughters—Margo, Lindsey, and Cari.

Mahon's interest in books is long and abiding. Always a voracious reader, she worked for many years as a librarian after earning her library degree. Her career took her to different types of libraries: the Veteran's Administration Hospital Library, Syracuse University Library, and the Onondaga Public Library System, all of which were located in Syracuse; and the Allen County Public Library in Fort Wayne, Indiana, where she taped a series of 50 "story-times" for cable television.

But Mahon also wanted to be a writer. Eventually, she left the library field and began to write full-time. At first, she considered writing children's books, but her love of genre fiction led her to the romance novel. Her first novel, a romantic suspense, was never published; but her Hawaiian romances, beginning with *Above the Rainbow* in 1995, were published by Avalon literally one right after the other. Several of these have been featured in *Booklist*'s annual "Spotlight on Multicultural Romance." Later, Mahon also began to write cozy mysteries. Not limiting herself to book-length works, she drew on her expertise about Hawaiian quilting to write articles on that topic as well.

Writing her romances begins with the creation of the novel's characters, usually starting with the idea of how the hero and the heroine meet. As Mahon comes to know these two people, the plot develops. Her heroes have strong personalities but aren't necessarily alpha males. The one trait common to all of her heroines is their ability to take care of themselves, something Dr. Lani Kalima of *Maui Rose* (1996) does as she leaves her residency and begins to deal with her astronomically high medical-school loans.

Like Mahon, the heroine in *Above the Rainbow* is a Hawaiian quilter. Mahon says that this book was the hardest to write. She rewrote it many times and kept changing the original concept. About the only thing that didn't change was the heroine.

On the other hand, *Just Friends* (1998) seemed to flow. According to Mahon, "I was writing another book at the time, one that never quite gelled and did not sell. But for a plot device in that particular book, the heroine's relative and neighbor had to be called away unexpectedly. I wrote the scene where he left, then figured I'd decide later exactly what happened that would make him leave so quickly. Later—and I recall it was around midnight one night—I had this burst of creativity that told me what had happened. I could actually see him striding into the Hilo Medical Center, worrying about his friend. And I sat right down and wrote the first scenes."

Like all good writers, Mahon writes about what she knows. In each of her books, she tries to have one character who is also a stitcher, quilter, needleworker, or embroiderer. In *Lei of Love* (1996), for example, the heroine, Dana Long, is a seamstress who specializes in hula costumes, wedding outfits, and formal attire. Mahon says her other hobbies—collecting stamps, postcards, thimbles, and matchbooks—"may someday" show up in her novels.

Mahon's cozy mysteries are set in Arizona. All of her romances, on the other hand, take place in Hawaii. She feels that in addition to being her home state, it's a "supremely romantic place to fall in love." Her ulterior motive is to show the real Hawaii in her books—multiracial heroines, multiculturally named characters, island food, music, and hobbies. This is because, as much as she read as a child, she rarely found a book that matched her own experiences on Hilo. In addition to educating and entertaining mainlanders, Mahon likes to think that she's "providing some young island girl with a story she can relate to."

Mahon's books are contemporary, something known as a novel's "eternal present." In other words, the reader feels as though the story is taking place in the here and now. Her romances, considered "sweet" because there are no sex scenes, are appropriate for younger readers, too.

Mahon likes to read romance novels for the good feeling she gets as she follows the path of the main characters. She's drawn to the light stories with feel-good endings, and this is what she tries to write herself. Mahon cites Nora Roberts and Janet Evanovich as authors who inspire her as a writer—Roberts for her characters, and Evanovich for her humor.

Although Mahon lives in Arizona with her husband, she brings the beauty, magic, and wonder of her beloved Hawaii to her readers with her heartwarming stories. For those who will never have the privilege of visiting the magnificent Hawaiian Islands, Mahon's books are the next best thing to being there.

BIBLIOGRAPHY

Books: *Above the Rainbow.* New York: Avalon, 1995; *Lei of Love.* New York: Avalon, 1996; *Maui Rose.* New York: Avalon, 1996; *Chase Your Dream.* New York: Avalon, 1997; *Just Friends.* New York: Avalon, 1998; *A Phantom Death.* New York: Avalon, 2000; *The Secret Admirer.* New York: Avalon, 2001; *The Secret Wedding.* New York: Avalon, 2002; *The Secret Santa.* New York: Avalon, 2003; *The Secret Beau.* New York: Avalon, 2004; *The Secret Wish.* New York: Avalon, 2006; *An Ominous Death.* New York: Avalon, 2006.

SHELLEY MOSLEY

TESS MARLOWE. *See* Rebecca York

SANDRA MARTON

Sandra Marton. Photo by Marton Myles, photographer. Courtesy of Sandra Marton.

Four-time RITA finalist and Holt Medallion winner Sandra Marton says she has yet to experience writer's block, "knocking on wood, crossing fingers, tossing salt over my shoulder." After twenty years of romance writing, and with over sixty novels to her credit, it's not likely that she will be experiencing it any time soon.

Marton has always been a writer at heart, starting practically as soon as she learned the alphabet. Her earliest attempts were, as she describes them, "murky, depressing poetry," followed by "murky, depressing short stories." Eventually, she moved on to writing popular fiction and romance with marketable appeal. "I realized I wanted to write stuff people wanted to read," she says. Her first sales were made to confession magazines.

A true New Yorker, Marton was born and raised in the Big Apple. Both of her parents worked in the movie industry, her mother as an executive secretary to a producer, and her father as an industry sales representative for United Artists Films in the state of New York. Marton recalls spending time with her father as he traveled the state and taking family vacations each summer in a rental cabin near her uncle's farm in Troy, New York. "I had that dichotomy, the urban/country background, in me from the beginning, and it's definitely influenced my writing," says Marton.

Marton earned a bachelor's degree in creative writing with a minor in education from Hunter College (the City University of New York). She worked for a couple of years as an elementary-school teacher, and served as president of her town's board of education. Still, writing was her passion.

"Intense and layered" is how Marton describes her writing style. She says she writes about "the redemptive power of love," which is usually the theme of her novels. In *Raising the Stakes* (2002), attorney Gray Baron has been hired to find single mother Dawn Lincoln. Gray has some preconceived ideas about this runaway wife, but when he finds her, what he discovers is a woman who has been badly abused by her husband and who is afraid to return to him. Gray becomes attracted to Dawn, admiring the courage he knows it took for her to flee her sadistic spouse. Marton writes about this emotion-packed issue with great sensitivity and understanding.

Marton says another of her recurring themes is "what the French call *coup de foudre,* that incredible moment of passionate attraction that grows and deepens and becomes love that lasts forever." Marton cleverly finds the potential for *coup de foudre* in many situations. Like most writers, Marton discovers character and story inspiration everywhere, and confesses to being "an inveterate listener-to-conversations in restaurants, on planes, etc."

Marton's novels are contemporary romances that are often set in New York and Connecticut, but she also uses many of her favorite foreign locales, including London, Paris, Rome, South America, and the Caribbean. "I also love the hush of the deep woods and the breathtaking open expanse of the desert, and use those settings when I can," she says. Marton concludes, "I think I'd enjoy writing about almost any time period, and I'm open to all locales. It's the characters that matter." An ardent animal activist, Marton also takes every opportunity to put in a positive plug for animals and the wilderness in her novels.

Her heroes are men of honor who possess strength, courage, and kindness. Marton usually develops the heroes first, and they tend to drive the plot. One of Marton's most unique heroes is Matthew McDowell from *'Til Tomorrow* (1996). A nineteenth-century sea captain, Matthew's spirit is doomed to wander the halls of Charon Crossing. Manhattan businesswoman Kathryn Russell, who inherits the rundown Caribbean estate, is awakened from her sleep by someone trying to strangle her. The strangler is none other than Matthew, who mistakes her for Catherine, a woman from his past. It takes a lot to convince Matthew that he's trying to kill the wrong woman, and Kathryn is much more sympathetic toward the tortured spirit when she finds out that the other Catherine was responsible for not only Matthew's death but also the death of his crew. When Kathryn and Matthew find themselves falling in love, their new relationship faces unique challenges. For instance, an evil specter who also inhabits the decaying mansion is out to get them. The couple also has the unusual problem of being involved in a relationship that is neither earthly nor otherworldly. In Marton's ghost story, she cleverly shows that love is strong enough to provide a "happily ever after" ending to the lovers' tribulations, but not without a lot of effort on their part.

Once Marton becomes acquainted with a hero, she is able to match him with a suitable, unfailingly compassionate heroine. "I know my [characters] so well that I could tell you what they like to eat, what they read, what they're like intellectually and spiritually, who they vote for, [and so forth]," says Marton. Some of their traits and interests are also Marton's, but she says that "those things aren't necessarily visible." Lara Stevens, the heroine of *Slade Baron's Bride* (1999), wants a baby. What she doesn't want is a husband. She meets architect Slade Baron at the Denver airport and has a one-night stand with him. Eighteen months later, they meet again, this time on a business project. When he finds out that her nine-month-old son is his, he insists on marriage. Although they do things in the reverse order, Lara comes to realize that if she has to have a husband, she could do much worse than Slade.

Marton was inspired at an early age by the writing of Guy de Maupassant and Honoré de Balzac, which she found in her mother's collection. In particular, Marton says that de Balzac's short story *A Passion in the Desert* "touched me so deeply I never quite forgot it. I even paraphrased the title and gave it to my very first romance (*Rapture in the Sands,* 1985)." Today, she says she is inspired by "the dialogue of Elmore Leonard, the rich characterization of John Sandford, the intricate plotting of Michael Connelly, and the quirky stories of Anne Tyler."

According to Marton, there isn't one particular novel that was harder to write than the others, but she names 1994's *The Corsican Gambit* and *Roman Spring* as her easiest. "Every now and then, a book flies from my fingertips to the computer," she says. *The Corsican Gambit* is the story of Francesca Drury, who is lost in a card game by her shiftless, irresponsible stepbrother, Charles. Maximillian "Max" Donelly, Charles's business rival, wins Francesca, believing she's a cold, unscrupulous socialite. What Max doesn't know is that Francesca is actually a warmhearted, innocent virgin. Max becomes Francesca's tutor in the romantic arts, but she's looking for a deeper commitment. In *Roman Spring,* part of the Postcards from Europe series, supermodel Caroline hates her job and all the men looking at her, until Nicolo Sabatini becomes one of those admirers. Caroline thinks Nicolo just wants to use her, when all he wants is to be with her. In each of these two books, men and women have jaded stereotypes about the other sex, which they have to overcome, and Marton skillfully brings them to their senses.

To Marton, the greatest appeal of being a romance writer is the feedback she receives from her readers. She says, "I am truly amazed and humbled when I realize how many lives we romance writers touch." She also loves the intimate experience of bringing her characters to life. In general, her favorite part of a writing career is the freedom that writers enjoy: "Jeans, sweats, sandals, and sneakers. Oh, and no makeup. Nothing that even resembles a hairstyle. Where else could I go to work like this?" Marton and her family live in Connecticut. She and her childhood sweetheart, Marty, have been married for many years, and she says they have two grown sons, "a daughter-in-law, and the most brilliant, most beautiful grand-daughter and grandson in the world."

The tropical paradise of Hawaii, the crystal clear waters of the Caribbean, the romantic streets of Paris, or the rugged mountains of Peru—Sandra Marton's readers never know where she will take them next. One thing they can count on, though, is that every trip will be an adventure worth taking.

BIBLIOGRAPHY

Books: *Rapture in the Sands.* Toronto: Harlequin, 1985; *Out of the Shadows.* Toronto: Harlequin, 1987; *A Game of Deceit.* Toronto: Harlequin, 1987; *Lovescenes.* Toronto: Harlequin, 1988; *Intimate Strangers.* Toronto: Harlequin, 1988; *Cherish the Flame.* Toronto: Harlequin, 1989; *Deal with the Devil.* Toronto: Harlequin, 1989; *A Flood of Sweet Fire.* Toronto: Harlequin, 1989; *Heart of the Hawk.* Toronto: Harlequin, 1989; *Fly Like an Eagle.* Toronto: Harlequin, 1990; *Eye of the Storm.* Toronto: Harlequin, 1990; *From this Day Forward.* Toronto: Harlequin, 1990; *Garden of Eden.* Toronto: Harlequin, 1991; *Consenting Adults.* Toronto: Harlequin, 1991; *Night Fires.* Toronto: Harlequin, 1991; *Lost in a Dream.* Toronto: Harlequin, 1992; *By Dreams Betrayed.* Toronto: Harlequin, 1992; *Roarke's Kingdom.* Toronto: Harlequin, 1993; *That Long-Ago Summer.* Toronto: Harlequin, 1993; *Roman Spring.* Toronto: Harlequin, 1994; *The Corsican Gambit.* Toronto: Harlequin, 1994; *A Bride for the Taking.* Toronto: Harlequin, 1995; *A Woman Accused.* Toronto: Harlequin, 1995; *Hostage of the Hawk.* Toronto: Harlequin, 1995; *Spring Bride.* Toronto: Harlequin, 1996; *Hollywood Wedding.* Toronto: Harlequin, 1996; *Guardian*

Groom. Toronto: Harlequin, 1996; *An Indecent Proposal.* Toronto: Harlequin, 1996; *'Til Tomorrow.* New York: Kensington, 1996; *Master of El Corazon.* Toronto: Harlequin, 1997; *The Second Mrs. Adams.* Toronto: Harlequin, 1997; *No Need for Love.* Toronto: Harlequin, 1997; *Until You.* New York: Kensington, 1997; *A Proper Wife.* Toronto: Harlequin, 1997; *The Bridal Suite.* Toronto: Harlequin, 1998; *The Bride Said Never!* Toronto: Harlequin, 1998; *The Divorcee Said Yes!* Toronto: Harlequin, 1998; *The Groom Said Maybe!* Toronto: Harlequin, 1998; *Slade Baron's Bride.* Toronto: Harlequin, 1999; *More Than a Mistress.* Toronto: Harlequin, 1999; *Marriage on the Edge.* Toronto: Harlequin, 1999; *The Sexiest Man Alive.* Toronto: Harlequin, 1999; *Mistress of the Sheikh.* Toronto: Harlequin, 2000; *Romano's Revenge.* Toronto: Harlequin, 2000; *Emerald Fire.* Toronto: Harlequin, 2000; *The Taming of Tyler Kincaid.* Toronto: Harlequin, 2000; *The Alvares Bride.* Toronto: Harlequin, 2001; *Yesterday and Forever.* Toronto: Harlequin, 2001; *The Bedroom Business.* Toronto: Harlequin, 2001; *Dancing in the Dark.* Toronto: Harlequin, 2002; *Wedding of the Year.* Toronto: Harlequin, 2002; *Raising the Stakes.* Toronto: Harlequin, 2002; *The Pregnant Mistress.* Toronto: Harlequin, 2002; *Cole Cameron's Revenge.* Toronto: Harlequin, 2002; *Keir O'Connell's Mistress.* Toronto: Harlequin, 2003; *The Sheikh's Convenient Bride.* Toronto: Harlequin, 2004; *Claiming His Love Child.* Toronto: Harlequin, 2004; *The Sicilian Surrender.* Toronto: Harlequin, 2004; *Ring of Deception.* Toronto:Harlequin, 2004; *One Night Wife.* Toronto: Harlequin, 2004; *The Sicilian Marriage.* Toronto: Harlequin, 2005; *The Disobedient Virgin.* Toronto: Harlequin, 2005; *The Desert Virgin.* Toronto: Harlequin, 2006; *Captive in His Bed.* Toronto: Harlequin, 2006; *Naked in His Arms.* Toronto: Harlequin, 2006; *The Sicilian's Christmas Bride.* Toronto: Harlequin, 2006.

Novellas: "Miracle on Christmas Eve" in *Christmas Affairs.* Toronto: Harlequin, 1999; "Malone's Vow" in *Married in Spring.* Toronto: Harlequin, 2001; "The Borghese Bride" in *For Love or Money.* Toronto: Harlequin, 2003.

SANDRA VAN WINKLE AND SHELLEY MOSLEY

JESSICA MASSEY. *See* Jennifer Greene

KATIE MAXWELL. *See* Katie MacAlister

AMANDA MCCABE

Amanda McCabe specializes in writing Regencies and Regency historicals with a
twist. Featuring adventurous, unconventional heroines and strong, courageous
heroes, McCabe's romances offer Regency readers everything from unusual settings
to a measure of the supernatural; but the story is always brightened with a generous dash of
humor.

McCabe was born in Oklahoma in 1974. Raised by parents who were high school sweet-
hearts, McCabe lived in Oklahoma City and Albuquerque, New Mexico. She attended the
University of Oklahoma, where she graduated with a degree in English literature.

Ever since the third grade, when a short story she wrote won an award, McCabe dreamed
of becoming a writer. There were a few short detours, as a young McCabe entertained
thoughts of wanting to be an opera singer or an actress; but her desire to write would
overcome the lure of these other career possibilities. While writing full-time was her dream,
the reality was that McCabe had to work at a variety of different jobs, including bookstore
clerk in the materials selection office of the Oklahoma City Metropolitan Library System
while she attended college. Currently working part-time at a classical music radio station in
Oklahoma, McCabe writes part-time but has still managed to create an impressive list of
works.

McCabe's first book, *Her Kind of Man*, was published in 2000 by Kensington. Set in
New Mexico in 1872, *Her Kind of Man* was McCabe's first completed book, and she was a
bit surprised that anyone would want to buy it. McCabe had always read Regencies and had
planned on writing those kinds of stories, but the beautiful, mysterious, and romantic
landscape of New Mexico, where McCabe had lived at one time, inspired her to write *Her
Kind of Man*.

Her first Regency romance, *Scandal in Venice*, was published in 2001 and is a good
example of this author's willingness to mix new elements into the traditional Regency
romance. One of the most interesting things about McCabe's first Regency romance is
the setting—Italy. In addition, McCabe gives her heroine a talent for painting and a

rather outrageous female friend. The story begins in England as the book's heroine, Lady Elizabeth Everdean, flees the country after mistakenly thinking she has killed a man. The plot shifts to Venice as Elizabeth seeks refuge with her old school friend, artist Georgiana Beaumont. McCabe deftly evokes the color and beauty of Italy as the hero, Sir Nicholas Hollingsworth, tries to find some way to return Elizabeth to her brother in England.

McCabe continued to create new and different variations on the traditional Regency romance. Her next book, *The Spanish Bride* (2001), quickly followed *Scandal in Venice*. It features a Spanish heroine who arrives in England with her young daughter, seeking the Englishman she married during the Peninsular War. *Lady Rogue* (2002), McCabe's third Regency romance, uses the colorful artist Georgina Beaumont from McCabe's first Regency as the heroine of the story. McCabe says this was perhaps the most difficult book for her to write since she "had lived with Georgina as a secondary character for two books, and she wanted to be absolutely sure she found Georgina the right man."

McCabe's fourth book, *The Errant Earl*, published in 2002, is another wonderful example of her ability to humorously blend colorful, quirky characters and a creative plot. Marcus Hadley, the book's hero, is returning home after a four-year absence to take care of his new responsibility: Julia Barclay, a stepsister he has only met once before. Julia's first impression of Marcus is not a favorable one, and she is certain he won't appreciate the fact that she has been letting her actor friends stay at the Hadley estate. To keep Marcus from finding out, Julia has her friends impersonate servants, and the fun begins. *The Errant Earl* was nominated for a RITA award in 2003.

In her Regency novels that followed, McCabe continued to augment the classic Regency pattern by introducing unusual elements. For instance, the heroine in another 2002 title, *The Golden Feather*, is the owner of a gambling establishment. In addition, two of McCabe's books published in 2003, *A Loving Spirit* and *One Touch of Magic*, have an element of the supernatural. In *A Loving Spirit*, three matchmaking ghosts try to bring the heroine and hero together, while the archaeologist heroine of *One Touch of Magic* matches wits with the new owner of a reportedly haunted piece of land she is interested in excavating.

McCabe was one of the first Regency authors chosen to launch Signet's new Super Regency line in 2003 with her title *Lady in Disguise*, the story of an Englishwoman, Emma Weston, who is raised by her aunt and uncle in Russia. Emma returns to England and meets up with English nobleman and spy Jack Howard, who is delivering secret papers to her uncle. Howard is an excellent example of McCabe's signature type of hero—one who has some type of military experience and bravely faces danger, but who is frequently emotionally unsure of himself or emotionally scarred by some past event in his life.

McCabe finds that characters tend to come to her first when she begins plotting a new book. As she says, "Frequently, people just pop into my head and demand I find plots for them. I think this is why I write books for so many of my secondary characters—I want to know what happens to them!"

BIBLIOGRAPHY

Books: *Her Kind of Man.* New York: Kensington, 2000; *Scandal in Venice.* New York: Signet, 2001; *The Spanish Bride.* New York: Signet, 2001; *Lady Rogue.* New York: Signet, 2002; *The Errant Earl.* New York: Signet, 2002; *The Golden Feather.* New York: Signet, 2002; *A Loving Spirit.* New York: Signet, 2003; *One Touch of Magic.* New York: Signet, 2003; *Lady in Disguise.* New York: Signet,

2003; *The Rules of Love.* New York: Signet, 2004; *The Star of India.* New York: Signet, 2004; *Lady Midnight.* New York: Signet, 2005; *A Tangled Web.* New York: Signet, 2006.

Novellas: "A Partridge in a Pear Tree" in *A Regency Christmas.* New York: Signet, 2002; "Upon a Midnight Clear" in *Regency Christmas Magic.* New York: Signet, 2004.

John Charles

JUDI MCCOY

Judi McCoy. Courtesy of Judi McCoy.

Judi McCoy believes that "anything the mind can dream of can be told in a story." This means, that in the universe of McCoy's incredibly creative mind, the possibilities are endless. Whether her tales are "paranormals," as some people call them, or "whimsy," as the author herself refers to them, they are sure to contain the unpredictable, fantastic characters and inventive plots that have become McCoy's trademarks.

McCoy was born in Joliet, Illinois, in 1949. Her mother died when McCoy was only 13 years old, so her father raised McCoy and her sister. McCoy attended a Catholic grade school and an all-girl Catholic high school, St. Francis Academy. She married her high school sweetheart shortly after she graduated, beginning a partnership that has lasted more than thirty years. The couple has two daughters, Sara and Casey.

Always an avid reader, McCoy also did a great deal of writing throughout her high school years, but it wasn't until the mid-1990s that she set a goal for herself of creating a novel and getting it published. Before that, what she characterizes as her "wonderful" career as a woman's gymnastic judge and raising a family took up most of her time. Then, McCoy heard writing's clarion call. She was drawn to the ability to be in complete control of the story, at least, she says, "until her characters take it in a completely different direction." She adored sorting out the elements of a tale much like the pieces of a gigantic puzzle. McCoy says she decided that she would write in the romance genre because she "loves a happy ending."

Her debut novel, *I Dream of You* (2001), certainly had a happy ending—it won Waldenbooks' Bestselling Debut Romance of 2001 award. A twist on the story of Aladdin, *I Dream of You* is about Maddie Winston, who, after her fiancé dumps her, finds a bottle on the beach. The bottle, of course, is enchanted, and the inhabitant of the bottle, Prince Abban ben-Abdullah, otherwise known as "Ben," is more than happy to be freed from his prison. However, Ben has never had a female master before, so needless to say, he has to make as many adjustments to his new life as Maddie does. McCoy deftly mixed humor, magic, and a bit of mystery to create this superb combination of the everyday and the exotic.

"What if …" are the words that begin the creative process for McCoy. She says that once an idea has taken hold, the characters "pop into her head." An example of this is her conjecture, "What if angels lived among us?" which became the premise of her Heavenly series. *Match Made in Heaven* (2004), the third book in this series, is the story of Honoria Hewitt, the prissy, prudish, and uptight headmistress of her family's school, who reluctantly agrees to let herself be part of a fund-raising singles auction. Much to her surprise, devilishly handsome playboy Alexander Vandencort donates $20,000 and whisks her away to a tropical destination for a week. With a little heavenly help from angels Milton and Junior, Alex and Honoria find their own personal paradise, not to mention an eternity of love. Fun and fantasy fill the pages as McCoy cleverly shows that opposites not only attract—they can stay together.

McCoy doesn't write about alpha males. She says that all of her heroes are "nice guys who aren't afraid to admit when they're wrong." One of these nice guys is Paul Anderson of *Wanted: One Special Kiss* (2004), the second book in McCoy's Starlight trilogy. Paul, a small-town doctor, is the single father of two-year-old twin boys. When he hires Lila to be his new nanny and housekeeper, he has no idea that she's an alien from outer space. With *Wanted: One Special Kiss,* McCoy continues to deliver a beguiling blend of love and laughter.

Besides the "happily ever after" endings, what appeals to McCoy about the romance genre, she says, is that the heroine "always wins. She gets her man and a happy ending." McCoy says her heroines are like her in that they have a sense of humor, and none of them are "weak willed." These women have the ability to laugh at themselves. McCoy also comments that they're "strong women who don't need a man to get them out of trouble (or in it)."

McCoy enjoys writing in the present day. She likes to set her stories in isolated places because the characters have to interact more with each other than with their surroundings. The main theme of McCoy's books is that true love is the driving force in the world. "It overcomes pain, sorrow, greed, and a list of ills to triumph in the end," she says.

You're the One (2001), McCoy's second novel, was the easiest for her to write. She says that story came to her mind "fully formed." Cassandra Kinross, the heroine of *You're the One,* used to be a normal woman—that was before her nefarious fiancé put her into a closet and erected a brick wall in front of it. Now her fiancé's great-nephew, construction company owner Rand MacPherson, has inherited the decaying mansion and Cassandra's feisty spirit along with it. Cassandra wants to be left alone, but nothing she does scares Rand—he even laughs at her antics. As the two of them live together, they fall in love. Body and soul take on a whole new meaning as beings from two different planes try to find love and happiness. McCoy's delightfully written ghost story, although a comedy, does include quite a bit of pathos.

The most difficult book for her to write was the second book of her Heavenly series, *Heaven Sent* (2003). McCoy says she had a hard time "getting into the head" of her heroine,

Miss Starr. Eloise Starr is an angel of a teacher—literally. However, she has bungled so many of her earthly assignments that this stint as an educator is a definite demotion. Eloise has been put on probation, and if she fails, heaven help her. Phoebe Baxter, one of her kindergarten students, has no mother. Phoebe's father, Nathan, a homicide detective, isn't interested in dating. He's tired of his mother's incessant matchmaking efforts, which have been going on since his wife died, but he feels some sort of strange connection to his daughter's teacher. Nathan gets his second chance at love, but this is Eloise's last chance at being an angel. McCoy's "angel with a crooked halo" story, despite its rocky beginnings, turns into a charmingly poignant tale that is liberally sprinkled with humorous moments.

Of all her books, McCoy names *Say You're Mine* (2002) as her favorite. She adds, "Your books are like children—you love them all." In *Say You're Mine*, a handsome Irishman named Declan O'Shea woos Libby Grayson, an accountant and single mother whose life partner has left her. Declan tells Libby that he's an eighteenth-century sea captain who's come for his buried treasure. Libby knows Declan is a rogue with a brogue, but she can't bring herself to believe that he's actually 300 years old.

McCoy claims she's been lucky and has never been bothered by writer's block. She finds her muse from reading a story in the newspaper, hearing a snippet of gossip, or having a dream about her story. She says her active imagination just "takes off," and a new book is born.

Love is at the center of McCoy's philosophy: "Romance is the heart of life. Without it, the world would be a very small, sad place to live." Fortunately for readers, McCoy has brightened the literary horizon with her happy, hopeful, and heartwarming stories and has brought a bit of serendipitous sunshine into each of their lives.

BIBLIOGRAPHY

Books: *I Dream of You.* New York: Kensington, 2001; *You're the One.* New York: Kensington, 2001; *Say You're Mine.* New York: Kensington, 2002; *Heaven in Your Eyes.* New York: Kensington, 2003; *Heaven Sent.* New York: Kensington, 2003; *Match Made in Heaven.* New York: Kensington, 2004; *Wanted: One Special Kiss.* New York: Avon, 2004; *Wanted: One Perfect Man.* New York: Avon, 2004; *Wanted: One Sexy Night.* New York: Avon, 2005; *Almost a Goddess.* New York: Avon, 2006.
Novella: "The Twelve Frogs of Christmas" in *Mistletoe and Mayhem.* New York: Avon, 2004.

SHELLEY MOSLEY

JAMES AND NIKOO MCGOLDRICK. *See* May McGoldrick

MAY MCGOLDRICK

Nikoo and Jim McGoldrick. Courtesy of Nikoo and Jim McGoldrick.

It's been said that two heads are better than one. Jim McGoldrick and Nikoo Coffey, one of the romance genre's few writing teams, have done such a good job putting their heads together that they've been finalists for the RITA not once, but twice; won the Holt Medallion twice; been given the Golden Leaf Award twice; and received the *Romantic Times* Reviewers' Choice Award, just to name a few of their honors.

Nikoo was born in Tehran, Iran, the daughter of Iraj and Nassrin Kafi. Her father was a resort owner, and her mother a telephone company administrator. Jim was born to George McGoldrick, a lawyer, and his wife, Rosemary, a homemaker, in Meriden, Connecticut. While Jim grew up in Connecticut, Nikoo's childhood was spent in both Iran and the United States.

Jim attended Connecticut College, earning a bachelor's degree in English, and then went on to the University of Rhode Island, where he earned his master's degree and a PhD (his dissertation was titled *Sixteenth Century Scottish and English Literature*). Nikoo also attended the University of Rhode Island, earning a

---

also writing as Jan Coffey
also writing as Nicole Cody
also writing as James and Nikoo McGoldrick

bachelor's degree in mechanical engineering and applied mechanics. They met in 1979, while Nikoo was an engineering student and Jim was a submarine builder. A year later, they were married, and now they have two sons, Cyrus and Sam.

Jim finally got to use what he had studied in college when he was able to change his profession from submarine builder to college professor. Nikoo, on the other hand, found work in her field right after she graduated, as an engineering manager for various high-tech industries.

Although Nikoo's college studies were in the technical fields, she always had an interest in writing. Jim also had a lifetime passion for the written word. After one of their sons was born with a heart problem, the couple evaluated where they were in their lives, and decided it was time to make a change. They became full-time writers, adopting the name May McGoldrick, after Jim's grandmother, a woman they admired for her strength and integrity.

There aren't a lot of writing teams in the romance industry, and even fewer husband-and-wife combinations. While Nikoo provides the "bricks" for their writing projects, Jim adds the "mortar." Nikoo, the duo's self-described screenwriter, focuses on plot, dialogue, and characters. Jim, on the other hand, is more of the finishing writer, and polishes the passages. His strengths are narrative and descriptive passages.

Both Jim and Nikoo agree that the plot flows from their characters. Their books are about strong, intelligent people dealing with overwhelming challenges and circumstances. For example, in *Dreams of Destiny* (2004), the third book in the couple's Scottish Dream trilogy (which also includes *Borrowed Dreams,* 2003, and *Captured Dreams,* 2003), Gwyneth Douglas's scandalous secret—that she's a novelist who writes very descriptive adventure books—has been discovered by a blackmailer. Gwyneth decides that the only way to protect her honor and fortune is to elope with an old family friend. Although she sees this as her only escape, David Pennington, no stranger to scandal himself, finds out what Gwyneth is up to and refuses to leave her side, effectively squashing all plans for elopement.

The McGoldricks aren't afraid of dealing with difficult themes. In *Borrowed Dreams*, widowed Millicent Wentworth has to undo all the evil her slave-owning husband had perpetrated. Slavery, also a theme in *The Promise* (2001), made that book the most difficult for Jim and Nikoo to write, because in their desire to make everything and everyone as realistic as possible, the many hours spent in research evoked strong images of the horrors of that institution. Even more difficult, they had to incorporate this into their story.

All authors have certain places and time periods they like to use as settings for their books. For Nikoo and Jim, ideal locations are Scotland, England, New England, and Pennsylvania. They both cite contemporary America as their preferred era. Jim also adds medieval Scotland to his list of favorites.

Jim and Nikoo, who say they "never get writer's block," are passionate about their writing because of the connection to their readers and the "few moments of joy" readers add to their lives. They also find it exciting to bring characters to life on a page.

The uplifting theme and tone that is so typical of the romance novel drew the couple to that genre. Being multifaceted writers, they also coauthor suspense thrillers and mysteries under the pseudonym Jan Coffey. *Jan* is a combination of the first letters of the words in the phrase *Jim and Nikoo.* Writing under the pen name Nicole Cody, they wrote *Love and Mayhem* (2006), a sixteenth-century romp. The team also penned a young adult romance novel, *Tess and the Highlander* (2002) as well as a how-to book, *Marriage of Minds: Collaborative Fiction Writing* (2000). Regardless of the nom de plume or the genre, there is no question that this particular husband-and-wife team make a very talented combination.

Bibliography

Writing as May McGoldrick

Books: *The Thistle and the Rose.* New York: Penguin Press, 1995; *Angel of Skye.* New York: Penguin Press, 1996; *Heart of Gold.* New York: Penguin Press, 1996; *The Beauty of the Mist.* New York: Penguin Press, 1997; *The Intended.* New York: Penguin Press, 1998; *Flame.* New York: Penguin Press, 1998; *The Dreamer.* New York: Onyx, 2000; *The Enchantress.* New York: Onyx, 2000; *The Firebrand.* New York: Onyx, 2000; *The Promise.* New York: Signet, 2001; *The Rebel.* New York: Signet, 2002; *Tess and the Highlander.* New York: HarperCollins, 2002; *Borrowed Dreams.* New York: Signet, 2003; *Captured Dreams.* New York: Signet, 2003; *Dreams of Destiny.* New York: Signet, 2004.

Writing as Jan Coffey

Books: *Trust Me Once.* Toronto: MIRA, 2001; *Twice Burned.* Toronto: MIRA, 2002; *Triple Threat.* Toronto: MIRA, 2003; *Fourth Victim.* Toronto: MIRA, 2004; *Five in a Row.* Toronto: MIRA, 2005; *Tropical Kiss.* New York: HarperCollins, 2005; *Silent Waters.* Toronto: MIRA, 2006.

Writing as Nicole Cody

Book: *Love and Mayhem.* New York: Signet, 2006.

Writing as James and Nikoo McGoldrick

Book: *Marriage of Minds: Collaborative Fiction Writing.* Portsmouth, NH: Heinemann, 2000.

SANDRA VAN WINKLE AND SHELLEY MOSLEY

TERESA MEDEIROS

Teresa Medeiros. Courtesy of Teresa Medeiros.

There is a sprinkling of magic in everything Teresa Medeiros writes. From the real presence of magic in *Breath of Magic* (1996) and *Touch of Enchantment* (1997) to the fairy-tale-like magic of *Charming the Prince* (1999), *The Bride and the Beast* (2001), and *A Kiss to Remember* (2002) to her skilled writing that magically brings the past to life in such books as *Lady of Conquest* (1989), *A Whisper of Roses* (1993), and *Once an Angel* (1993), Medeiros has perfected her ability to cast a literary spell. Her readers just can't seem to get enough of her special brand of magic.

Born in Heidelberg, Germany, Medeiros was a so-called Army brat. Her father spent more than twenty-two years in the military, and she grew up in Germany, Tennessee, North Carolina, and finally, Kentucky. After retiring from the military, her father worked for the United States Postal Service for 20 years. She says her mother was "the quintessential Kool-aid mom, who made Popsicles for all the other kids in the neighborhood."

As an only child, Medeiros was very close to her parents. Like many other writers, she grew up loving to read and names Victoria Holt as being her favorite author. At age 12, Medeiros took her first step into the world of writing romances, when she penned one chapter of *The Pirates of Rocklyn Hill,* featuring her then-heartthrob Donny Osmond as Sir Donald Osmond. While Medeiros always dreamed of being a writer, she says she had other career aspirations too, including becoming "a movie star, a princess, and a secret agent."

Childhood dreams gave way to reality, and Medeiros went to Madisonville Community College, where she earned a degree in nursing in 1983. A year later, while working as a registered nurse, she decided to give writing another try: "I basically sat down at my mom's kitchen counter with an old Smith-Corona typewriter and a gallon of ice tea and started writing the book I wanted to read but couldn't find. I set a goal of three pages a day. I was working the afternoon shift at the time, so if I didn't finish my pages before I went to work at 2:30 P.M., I would come home at midnight and finish them. I was so swept up in that book! It was as if I actually *lived* the story."

That story was *Lady of Conquest*. Medeiros spent a year and three months working on the manuscript. In between, she got married, changed jobs, and moved; but she continued writing the story she wanted to read. When it was finally done, says Medeiros, "I popped it into an envelope and mailed the entire book to Avon, where it languished for a year. After it was rejected, I sent off 22 query letters to 22 different publishers and sold the book within three months."

Lady of Conquest was published by Bantam in 1989, and at the age of 21, Medeiros saw her first novel gain a place on the *New York Times* Best Seller List. It was marketed with "historical novel" on the spine, instead of "historical romance," and Medeiros says that "there was definite talk afterwards about which direction my career should go [in]." With its expert mix of history and romance, it is easy to see how *Lady of Conquest* could be targeted to either group of readers. Inspired by a real historical figure who once ruled ancient Ireland, Medeiros blended fact, myth, and her own vivid sense of imagination to create her version of Conn of the Hundred Battles, whose own romantic battles with Gelina O'Monaghan form the foundation of the book. Medeiros's vibrant descriptions of the mist-filled countryside, her sure sense of characterization, and her ability to evoke the past in all its beauty, brutality, and splendor imbue *Lady of Conquest* with a richness and depth readers find difficult to resist.

Medeiros's brand of literary magic quickly found favor with readers, and more historical romances followed, using a variety of settings and time periods. These included another medieval historical, *Shadows and Lace* (1990); a delectably entertaining Victorian-era romance, *Once an Angel*; and an eighteenth-century Scottish tale, *Whisper of Roses*, which earned Medeiros her first Romance Writers of America RITA nomination. "I have a very short attention span, so I tend to love whatever time period I'm *not* writing about at the moment," says Medeiros. "I do seem to keep coming back to the medieval and Regency time periods, though."

Magic plays a very real part in the plot of two of Medeiros's books, *Breath of Magic* and *Touch of Enchantment*. In *Breath of Magic*, Arian Whitewood is struggling to master the art of magic in a Massachusetts colony in 1689, when she is accused of practicing witchcraft and nearly killed by her fellow Puritans. With the help of a special amulet left to her by her mother, Arian escapes on her trusty broomstick, only to find that she has somehow managed to travel 300 years forward in time to contemporary New York City. Arian winds up in the offices of reclusive billionaire Tristan Lennox, who is willing to pay one million dollars to anyone who can prove to him that magic really exists. Medeiros's own love of such classic television sitcoms as *Bewitched* and *I Dream of Jeannie* inspired her to write this clever and witty genre-blending romance between a bumbling witch who travels through time and a no-nonsense boy billionaire. *Breath of Magic* garnered Medeiros her second RITA nomination.

Medeiros followed *Breath of Magic* with *Touch of Enchantment,* another sparkling time-travel romance, featuring Arian and Tristan's daughter, Tabitha Lennox. Tabitha has eschewed the magical inheritance she received from her mother in favor of concentrating on the practical world of science, represented by her father's computer business. However, the same amulet that once brought her mother forward in time sends Tabitha back 700 years to the medieval era and Sir Colin of Ravenshaw. Modern miss meets medieval knight in this delightful time-travel romance.

The world of fairy tales and folklore inspired Medeiros's next three books: *Charming the Prince, The Bride and the Beast,* and *A Kiss to Remember.* Medeiros based the heroine of *Charming the Prince,* Lady Willow of Bedlington, on Cinderella, and the Old Woman Who Lived in a Shoe became the source of inspiration for the book's hero, Lord Bannor the Bold. After spending years catering to the whims of her spoiled stepsiblings, Willow looks forward to living her own romantic dream. She arrives at Bannor Castle, only to find that the master of the manor is looking for a wife willing to clean his castle and take care of his 12 unruly children.

The Bride and the Beast is Medeiros's clever take on the classic "Beauty and the Beast" fable. Medeiros opens the book with the heroine, a young Gwendolyn "Gwen" Wilder, who is feeling like a beast herself, since everyone in the small village of Ballybliss, including her two beautiful, petite sisters, constantly mocks her appearance. Years later, when Ballybliss is being held hostage by the Dragon of Weyrcraig, the residents try offering up the sharp-tongued, sharp-witted Gwen as a virgin sacrifice to appease the monster's appetite. When Gwen finally encounters the "beast" she discovers a man on a mission of vengeance, whose plans are disrupted by the new "beauty" in his castle. One of the themes of *The Bride and the Beast* is that of redemption, a popular one with Medeiros. She says, "There is always someone who needs saving in my books, usually the hero. It gives my stories a sense of urgency. I want to give the reader the sense that if it weren't for the love the hero finds with the heroine, he would be lost forever."

The fairy tale inspiration for *A Kiss To Remember* is the much-loved story of "Sleeping Beauty," but as with her previous fairy tale romances, Medeiros gives this classic love story her own special twist. In this case, the hero, an unconscious Sterling Harlow, the "sleeping beauty" of the book, is awakened by a kiss from the heroine, Linda Fairleigh. When Linda realizes Sterling has no memory of who he is, she claims he is her fiancé, since she desperately needs to find a man to wed before her fast approaching 21st birthday. Deception, secrets, and the need to repair one's past all play important roles in Medeiros's humor-tinged, richly sensual love story. *A Kiss to Remember* earned Medeiros another RITA nomination.

The heroine of Medeiros's next book, *One Night of Scandal,* is Carlotta "Lottie" Anne Fairleigh, who was first introduced to readers as Linda's precocious and inquisitive younger sister from *A Kiss to Remember.* An aspiring novelist, Lottie finds her own life mirroring that of her beloved gothic novels when she becomes involved with the "Murderous Marquess," Hayden St. Clair. While writing *One Night of Scandal,* which was nominated for a RITA, gave Medeiros the chance to pay affectionate tribute to her beloved Gothic genre and her favorite author, Victoria Holt, it also proved to be one of the most difficult books she ever wrote. "It was a challenge because it was my most personal book," says Medeiros. "The hero's first wife suffered from manic-depression, and so does my mom. When I was writing a scene where I tried to absolve him from the guilt he felt for not being able to help her, I discovered tears were streaming down my own cheeks."

Medeiros says the following about being a romance writer: "Romance allows me to express my own heartfelt beliefs in optimism, faith, honor, and the timeless power of love to bring about a happy ending. In a society gutted by cynicism, romance writers have found the courage to stand up and proclaim that hope isn't corny, love isn't an antiquated fantasy, and dreams can come true for those still willing to strive for them." And if this isn't magic, what is?

BIBLIOGRAPHY

Books: *Lady of Conquest.* New York: Bantam, 1989; *Shadows and Lace.* New York: Bantam, 1990; *Heather and Velvet.* New York: Bantam, 1992; *Once an Angel.* New York: Bantam, 1993; *A Whisper of Roses.* New York: Bantam, 1993; *Thief of Hearts.* New York: Bantam, 1994; *Fairest of Them All.* New York: Bantam, 1995; *Breath of Magic.* New York: Bantam, 1996; *Touch of Enchantment.* New York: Bantam, 1997; *Nobody's Darling.* New York: Bantam, 1998; *Charming the Prince.* New York: Bantam, 1999; *The Bride and the Beast.* New York: Bantam, 2001; *A Kiss to Remember.* New York: Bantam, 2002; *One Night of Scandal.* New York: Avon, 2003; *Yours Until Dawn.* New York: Avon, 2004; *After Midnight.* New York: Avon, 2005; *The Vampire Who Loved Me.* New York: Avon, 2006.

JOHN CHARLES

LINDA LAEL MILLER

Linda Lael Miller. Courtesy of Linda Lael Miller.

S he's been called the Queen of the Western, but there's much more than that to the outstanding oeuvre of award-winning author Linda Lael Miller. This talented and multifaceted best-selling author crosses genre lines with both ease and skill, writing not only beautifully crafted contemporary love stories, but also romances featuring time travel, pirates, knights, vampires, and ghosts, just to name a few.

Born Linda Lael in 1949 in Spokane, Washington, Miller grew up in Northport, Washington, a wilderness town near the Canadian border. She graduated from high school, but mostly, as she puts it, "I've educated myself, and I have a PhD from the school of hard knocks." In 2005, however, she enrolled in the University of Phoenix's Criminal Justice Program. Before becoming a full-time writer, Miller was employed as a chart clerk in a medical clinic and a personnel clerk for Pan American Airlines. She also worked for various insurance agencies.

Miller's earliest writing ambition was simply to write books, any kind of books, but it wasn't long before she discovered and quickly fell in love with the romance genre. Her readers now have over sixty novels from which to choose. Miller, a frequent RITA award nominee whose novels have appeared on virtually every national best seller list, considers

also writing as Lael St. James

herself fortunate to be a full-time writer. She says she also feels fortunate to have the opportunity to "show young women what a healthy relationship looks like."

Only 10 years old when she set her sights on a writing career, Miller credits a very perceptive sixth-grade teacher, Bob Hyatt, for recognizing her potential and providing her with encouragement. She believes she inherited her talent with words and her love of reading from her mother, Hazel Bleecker Lael, and she credits her father, Grady "Skip" Lael, a former town marshal, for her tireless work ethic and persistence in the face of challenges. The writing tradition continues with Miller's grown daughter, Wendy, who is an aspiring screenwriter.

Miller's writing career took off with a bang with her 1983 novel, *Fletcher's Woman*. Set in a logging camp in Washington Territory in 1889, this is the story of a young doctor, Griffin Fletcher, who makes a deathbed promise to Rachel McKinnon's mother that he'll keep Rachel safe from Jonas Wilkes, the powerful owner of the lumber empire. *Fletcher's Woman* was quickly followed by the popular Corbin series.

According to Miller, the easiest novels for her to write were those in her Corbin series, set in Washington Territory and Oregon in the 1880s and 1890s. "They virtually wrote themselves," she says. *Banner O'Brien* (1984) features Banner O'Brien, a determined woman who earns her medical degree against all odds, and Dr. Adam Corbin, a man with a mysterious past. *Corbin's Fancy* (1985) tells the story of Fancy Jordan, who is stranded when the traveling carnival leaves without her, and Jeff Corbin, who is suffering from depression after being severely wounded when his ship was attacked. *Memory's Embrace* (1986) features Keith Corbin, who hides his identity and flees his life as one of Washington's wealthy elite, meeting Tess Bishop in a small lumber town in Oregon. The feisty little sister, Melissa Corbin, gets her own book in *My Darling Melissa* (1990), in which she leaves her groom at the altar after discovering he's brought everything with him from Europe—including his mistress. With her three persistent brothers on her trail, she cons Quinn Rafferty into helping her escape.

Miller's Western historicals are set in the late nineteenth century, often using Arizona as a backdrop. However, she doesn't limit herself to locales, as seen in her Australian books, *Just Kate* (1989) and *Wild About Harry* (1991). In *Wild About Harry*, Miller adds a touch of paranormal when Amy Ryan's deceased husband, Tyler, makes an appearance to tell her she'll meet a man named Harry.

Common in Miller's characters are the traits she values most: personal integrity and courage. Her heroines are strong and independent, much like herself. "I like to write about women finding their power," Miller says. Her highly popular Springwater series (*Springwater*, 1998; *A Springwater Christmas*, 1999; and *A Springwater Wedding*, 2001), which takes place in the fictional town of Springwater, Montana, inspired a spin-off series, Springwater Seasons (*Rachel*, 1999; *Savannah*, 1999; *Miranda*, 1999; and *Jessica*, 1999). The stories of these brave women led to the Women of Primrose Creek series (*Bridget*, 2000; *Christy*, 2000; *Skye*, 2000; and *Megan*, 2000). Throughout these books, Miller is true to her vision of the resilient, resourceful, and self-sufficient woman. Her heroes are men of honor who have to be worthy of her heroines. Miller says she never tires of "the surprises that unfold as I write and the unexpected things the characters do."

Miller describes her writing style as "free-wheeling, like a comet plunging through space." She writes her initial story quickly, without a lot of outlining, and then conducts thorough and repeated revisions until the finished product is to her liking. She says she finds story inspiration everywhere, from books and movies to "noodling" in her journal. Miller also creates collages as a visual inspiration for her tales and says she enjoys "the messy frenzy" of that art form. Another truly inspiring source of ideas for her is prayer: "When I need an idea, I ask for one. I've never been refused."

According to Miller, her 2003 novel *Don't Look Now* was her most difficult to write because it was a thriller written in the first person—a style different from all of her others. "I had to learn the form from the ground up," she says. Miller's favorite novel is always the one on which she's currently working. When asked if she ever experiences writer's block, Miller says, "I can't afford writer's block. I have a beagle to feed!"

The emotional intensity of Miller's books can be seen in such works as *Daniel's Bride* (1992). In this book, set in 1877 in Washington Territory, farmer Daniel Beckham saves Jolie McKibben, a stranger about to be hanged for robbery and murder, by marrying her. Although Jolie has been wrongfully accused, he treats her poorly and expects her to do more than her share of the work. Gradually, as Daniel comes to see what kind of a person Jolie really is, his feelings change toward her, making him feel disloyal to his dead wife.

On the other hand, Miller has been known to lace her books with humorous dialogue and situations. In *McKettrick's Choice* (2005), part of the McKettrick Brother series, Holt McKettrick leaves his mail-order bride at the altar in Arizona Territory when he hears that his friend is about to be hanged in Texas. Holt arrives in Texas, where he meets spunky Lorelei Fellows, who is busy burning her wedding gown in the town square to protest her unfaithful groom.

The first time-travel romances that Miller wrote were a duet for Silhouette's Beyond the Threshold series. In *There and Now* (1992), it's 1992, and newly divorced Elisabeth McCartney finds solace at Pine River. Little does she know that the house is a portal to the past, and her Aunt Verity's pendant necklace is the key. When uptight Victorian Dr. Jonathan Fortner, also divorced, finds Elisabeth in his kitchen in 1892 wearing a football jersey, he believes, in his best medical opinion, that she's a lunatic. The next morning, she escapes back to the present. However, stories of Jonathan Fortner and his small daughter dying in a fire a hundred years earlier cause Elisabeth to return and try to change the past. The follow-up novel, *Here and Then* (1992), has Elisabeth's cousin, Rue Claridge, anxiously searching for her missing relative and discovering the doorway to the past, too, where she becomes involved with Marshal Farley Haynes. This time, two-way time travel is explored, and Farley is introduced to the wonders of the modern world. Some of Miller's other ventures into the fantastic realm of time travel include *Pirates* (1996), *Knights* (1996), and *My Outlaw* (1997).

Miller's vampire quartet maintains a strong cult following. Her most famous vampire character, Valerian, shares celebrity status with such literary heroes as J. D. Robb's (Nora Roberts) Roarke and Jo Beverley's Rothgar and appears throughout the series. Set in a small town in Connecticut, *Forever and the Night* (1993) is the story of reclusive Aidan Tremayne, who meets Neely Wallace when she comes trick-or-treating with her nephew. An unwilling vampire, Aidan has been told by a gypsy that a woman will be either his damnation or his salvation. However, he doesn't know if Neely, a senator's aide, is the key to regaining his human existence. To complicate things, Neely knows too much about the senator, and she's become a target of the mob. Through all of this action, Miller's theme of redemption is telegraphed neatly to the reader.

The heroine of *For All Eternity* (1994) is Maeve Tremayne, who, unlike her twin, Aidan, enjoys her vampire status. A vampire with a conscience, she only feeds on humans who deserve it. Maeve finds love with nineteenth-century physician Calder Holbrook, who uses the powers he's received from their union, including time travel, to care for wounded soldiers on Civil War battlefields. This book also brings back Lisette, the nefarious (even for the undead) queen of the vampires introduced in book one. Furious at Aidan's rejection, Lisette summons the forces of darkness to earth, which threatens to begin an end-of-times battle between good and evil. Only Maeve can stop Lisette, although the effort threatens Maeve's very existence.

In *Time Without End* (1995), Valerian finally gets his own book. Now Las Vegas's biggest magician, Valerian is victimized when an unknown enemy starts killing his assistants. Homicide detective Daisy Chandler isn't just the cop on the case—she's the woman Valerian has loved in her many incarnations during his 600-year existence. Miller tells the reader the story of Valerian's doomed relationships with Daisy's former selves, starting with their medieval romance, and shows his sorrow each time she's wrenched from him. This technique makes *Time Without End* a tantalizing blend of a modern whodunit and exquisite period romance.

Kristina Tremayne Holbrook, Maeve and Calder Holbrook's daughter, is a hundred years old when *Tonight and Always* (1996) opens. Kristina is an immortal, but despite her roots, she is not a vampire. She also possesses the ability to move objects and time travel. The prospect of the family she's longed for comes with the appearance of widower high school coach Max Kilcarragh and his two young daughters. Kristina faces a dilemma—once she gets her wish, can she stand watching her loved ones age and die, as she has in the past? Miller explores this mortal/immortal issue from many angles, including the dangers mortals face from the capricious world of the immortals. Once again, characters from the other three novels, including Valerian, make appearances.

Since the beginning of her career, Miller has been known for her ability to write passionate, sensual love scenes. A perfect example of this is her Orphan Train trilogy, *Lily and the Major* (1990), *Emma and the Outlaw* (1991), and *Caroline and the Raider* (1992). These books take place in 1878 and deal with three sisters who were separated as children when they were adopted from the infamous "Orphan Train" by different people. In the first book of the trilogy, 18-year-old Lily Chalmers, a Tylerville, Washington, waitress, is saving money to find her sisters and buy her own land. Major Caleb Halliday wants Lily for his mistress, but she has her own agenda. *Emma and the Outlaw* introduces Emma Chalmers, an Idaho librarian raised by a madam. Although Emma is properly engaged, she forsakes her hard-won propriety for true love when she and her adopted mother are asked by the town doctor to care for Steven Fairfax, a roguish, wounded outlaw. *Caroline and the Raider* has more humor than the previous two books. When teacher Caroline Chalmers decides to get her fiancé sprung from a Wyoming jail cell, she hires Civil War raider Guthrie Hayes. Even though she falls in love with Guthrie, she's resolute about helping her fiancé—now former fiancé—escape. The three sisters' journey to find each other culminates in a most satisfying reunion in the third book. Each of the three books is filled with sizzling sexual tension between the, and their love scenes are sensual and vividly detailed.

Miller usually writes under her own name. However, she adopted the pseudonym Lael St. James for her two medieval romances, both of which came out in 2001. The name change was mandated by the publisher so readers could differentiate Miller's medieval romances from her Westerns. In *My Lady Wayward,* a wounded knight found within the walls of St. Swithin's Abbey changes Meg Redclift's life forever. *My Lady Beloved* tells about Meg's twin, Gabriella Redclift, a convent-raised bride who becomes a pawn in her betrothed's attempt to avenge an old wrong. Miller plans to finish the trilogy, possibly as an e-book on her Web site, with the proceeds going to her scholarship fund.

A self-proclaimed "Barn Goddess," Miller is an ardent animal lover, particularly favoring horses and dogs, and she manages to write one or the other into all of her stories. Miller lives on her five-acre Springwater Ranch outside of Scottsdale, Arizona, with her horses, a menagerie of pets, and a variety of desert creatures just passing through.

Animals aren't Miller's only passion. Her Linda Lael Miller Scholarships for Women, is a program she established in 2004 that provides educational assistance to women who are struggling to succeed. Now in her third decade as a best-selling author, it's safe to say that Miller has found her own success, and the romance genre is better for it.

BIBLIOGRAPHY

Writing as Linda Lael Miller

Books: *Fletcher's Woman.* New York: Pocket, 1983; *Desire and Destiny.* New York: Pocket, 1983; *Willow.* New York: Pocket, 1984; *Snowflakes on the Sea.* New York: Silhouette, 1984; *Banner O'Brien.* New York: Pocket, 1984; *Corbin's Fancy.* New York: Pocket, 1985; *Part of the Bargain.* New York: Silhouette, 1985; *State Secrets.* New York: Silhouette, 1985; *Memory's Embrace.* New York: Pocket, 1986; *Ragged Rainbows.* New York: Silhouette, 1986; *Lauralee.* New York: Pocket, 1986; *Wanton Angel.* New York: Pocket, 1987; *Used to Be Lovers.* New York: Silhouette, 1988; *Moonfire.* New York: Pocket, 1988; *Only Forever.* New York: Silhouette, 1989; *Angelfire.* New York: Pocket, 1989; *Just Kate.* New York: Silhouette, 1989; *Daring Moves.* New York: Silhouette, 1990; *My Darling Melissa.* New York: Pocket, 1990; *Mixed Message.* New York: Silhouette, 1990; *Escape from Cabriz.* New York: Silhouette, 1990; *Glory, Glory.* New York: Silhouette, 1990; *Lily and the Major.* New York: Pocket, 1990; *Emma and the Outlaw.* New York: Pocket, 1991; *Wild About Harry.* New York: Silhouette, 1991; *Caroline and the Raider.* New York: Pocket, 1992; *Here and Then.* New York: Silhouette, 1992; *There and Now.* New York: Silhouette, 1992; *Daniel's Bride.* New York: Pocket, 1992; *Yankee's Wife.* New York: Pocket, 1993; *Taming Charlotte.* New York: Pocket, 1993; *Forever and the Night.* New York: Berkley, 1993; *The Legacy.* New York: Pocket, 1994; *Princess Annie.* New York: Pocket, 1994; *For All Eternity.* New York: Berkley, 1994; *Time Without End.* New York: Berkley, 1995; *Pirates.* New York: Pocket, 1996; *Knights.* New York: Pocket, 1996; *Together.* New York: Avon, 1996; *Tonight and Always.* New York: Berkley, 1996; *My Outlaw.* New York: Pocket, 1997; *The Vow.* New York: Pocket, 1998; *Two Brothers.* New York: Pocket, 1998; *Springwater.* New York: Pocket, 1998; *Rachel.* New York: Pocket, 1999; *Savannah.* New York: Pocket, 1999; *Jessica.* New York: Pocket, 1999; *Miranda.* New York: Pocket, 1999; *A Springwater Christmas.* New York: Pocket, 1999; *One Wish.* New York: Pocket, 2000; *Bridget.* New York: Pocket, 2000; *Christy.* New York: Pocket, 2000; *Skye.* New York: Pocket, 2000; *Megan.* New York: Pocket, 2000; *Courting Susannah.* New York: Pocket, 2000; *Springwater Wedding.* New York: Atria, 2001; *My Lady Beloved.* New York: Pocket, 2001; *My Lady Wayward.* New York: Pocket, 2001; *The Last Chance Cafe.* New York: Atria, 2002; *High Country Bride.* New York: Pocket, 2002; *The Leopard's Woman.* New York: Silhouette, 2002; *The Women of Primrose Creek.* New York: Pocket, 2002; *Springwater Wedding.* New York: Pocket, 2002; *Don't Look Now.* New York: Atria, 2003; *Shotgun Bride.* New York: Pocket, 2003; *Second Hand Bride.* New York: Pocket, 2004; *Never Look Back.* New York: Atria, 2004; *McKettrick's Choice.* Toronto: Harlequin, 2005; *The Man from Stone Creek.* Toronto: Harlequin, 2006; *One Last Look.* New York: Simon & Schuster, 2006.

Novellas: "The Other Katherine" in *Haunting Love Stories.* New York: Avon, 1991; "Scent of Snow" in *A Christmas Collection.* New York: Avon, 1992; "Store-Bought Woman" in *To Love and to Honor.* New York: Avon, 1993; "A Midsummer Day's Dream" in *Timeless.* New York: Berkley, 1994; "Switch" in *Purrfect Love.* New York: HarperCollins, 1994; "Resurrection" in *Everlasting Love.* New York: Pocket, 1995; "Never Been to Anphar" in *In Our Dreams.* New York: Kensington, 1998.

Writing as Lael St. James

Books: *My Lady Wayward.* New York: Simon & Schuster, 2001; *My Lady Beloved.* New York: Simon & Schuster, 2001.

SHELLEY MOSLEY AND SANDRA VAN WINKLE

MARY ALICE MONROE

Mary Alice Monroe. Courtesy of Mary Alice Monroe.

Mary Alice Monroe's passion for the environment and her love of wildlife permeate the majority of her remarkable stories. Without stooping to didacticism, Monroe makes the reader care, too, about the world we all live in, with her haunting, expressive, and lyrical tales that linger long after the last page is read.

Monroe was born in Evanston, Illinois. Her father, Werner Cryns, grew up in Germany and came to America with his family as a young teen. He was raised in Chicago, went to medical school, and became a pediatrician. An accomplished pianist, he played for church and schools. Monroe's mother, Elayne, was born and raised in Chicago. She danced ballet and later decided to study nursing. She became a registered nurse before marrying Monroe's father and having 10 children. Monroe's parents passed on their love of music, art, and dance to their children.

Monroe says she spent her youth in the suburbs of Chicago, living in a "hectic" but "fabulous" environment with her nine brothers and sisters. She went to boarding school for high school. After 12 years in parochial school, Monroe entered Northwestern University. During that time, she married Markus John Potter Kruesi, a filmmaker, and moved to New Jersey, where her husband had been accepted to medical school. There, she finished her

---

also writing as Mary Alice Kruesi

bachelor's degree in Asian studies, with a Japanese-language minor, as well as a master of arts degree in education at Seton Hall University on a fellowship. Monroe credits her marriage of more than thirty years to the fact that both she and Kruesi went to school and worked toward their goals together, forming a bond with proven longevity. The couple has three children, Claire deLancey (Kruesi) Dwyer, Margaretta Elizabeth Kruesi, and Zachary Oscar Kruesi. Monroe and her husband, now a psychiatrist, live on the Isle of Palms, South Carolina.

Monroe wrote her first story when she was eight years old. While growing up, she and her many brothers and sisters wrote and performed in plays and musicals to wile away the long summer hours. Like many other novelists, Monroe has had what she calls "the usual eclectic selection" of jobs, several of which involved using her skills as a writer: working for the Japan Trade Center, freelance writing and ghost writing, starting an English program for Southeast Asian refugees (Vietnamese, Laotian, Hmong, and Cambodian) during the Carter administration; writing a series of survival-English texts, and teaching. Monroe says she began her "greatest career"—being a full-time mother—after moving to Washington, D.C. Monroe's children were older and in school when her first book sold. She has been writing full-time ever since.

Monroe spends a great deal of time doing research. Since each of her stories evolves from a theme, she says the story and characters "come alive" as she researches. For Monroe, the early stages of novel writing are "very distressing." She explains, "I feel unsettled and frustrated until my story takes shapes. Then, once I get the scent, I'm like a hound dog, nose to the ground, and I work furiously until the first draft is finished. Ideas flood my head. It seems everything I see or do is somehow connected to my story. My family has learned not to ask me anything of import during this phase, because though I'm physically there, mentally I'm in my story." According to Monroe, revisions are a pleasure "because the pain of creation is done, and it is fun to use craft and polish."

Monroe has been a member of Romance Writers of America since 1989 and a strong supporter of the romance genre and its followers, citing the fact that romance readers are among the most eclectic. Love stories play an important role in Monroe's works. Three of her novels—*The Beach House* (2002), *The Four Seasons* (2004), and *Girl in the Mirror* (2004)—have been nominated for RITAs, and her books have appeared on both the *New York Times* and *USA Today* best seller lists. Monroe has expanded her love stories to create books that are more like women's fiction—novels that explore the myriad relationships in women's lives. And although Monroe's novels are contemporary, she has plans to write a Japanese historical that she says has been "playing in my mind forever."

As mentioned, theme is always where Monroe begins her stories, and from this starting point comes the plot, followed by the characters. In the book *Girl in the Mirror,* for example, the classic ugly duckling theme led Monroe to create a female character with a hideous face who, after surgery, becomes a head-turning beauty. Her emotional adjustment to the change expands on the theme by asking, What price beauty?

Monroe's heroines have heart. They reflect the strengths and weaknesses of everyday women. Though her heroines may appear weak or troubled at the novel's start, during the course of the story their true character and strength is revealed in their ability to change or rise up to the challenge. Monroe believes there is a bit of her in many of her heroines, but only in the sense that she uses her experiences and insights to help her characters be real. Other people see this differently: "When I wrote *The Four Seasons,* my brother called me up and informed me which of the characters corresponded to which of my four sisters! It was amusing because the four sisters were all me and what I gleaned from being one of five sisters. After all, I had a lot to say on the subject of sisters! But I loved that he could read bits of us (and our experiences) in these fictional characters."

Passion for nature and conservation are more than just words in her books for Monroe. She actively volunteers to help loggerhead sea turtles and birds of prey. These experiences inspired her novels *The Beach House* and *Skyward* (2003) and have provided much of the rich texture found in them.

Monroe's concern for dwindling natural habitats is reflected in her prodigal son story, *Sweetgrass* (2005). The protagonist of the book, environmentalist Morgan Blakely, is typical of Monroe's heroes—compassionate, honest, and noble, even in the face of failure. Because of his strong sense of duty, Morgan grudgingly returns to the South Carolina low country to help run the aging family plantation, Sweetgrass, after his dictatorial father, Preston, suffers a debilitating stroke. Morgan, now an advocate for the endangered bison, had fled to Montana years earlier, consumed by guilt over his older brother's death. Morgan's mother, Mary June, has drifted away from her husband emotionally, believing that he loves his precious Sweetgrass infinitely more than he loves her. However, Preston's stroke has made Mary June reevaluate their past. Monroe deftly uses flashbacks to accomplish this introspection and, eventually, love rediscovered. While Morgan and his parents try to deal with their supercharged emotions and the extreme change in their circumstances, Morgan's Aunt Adele tries to take advantage of the situation and force them to sell Sweetgrass to developers. Monroe uses the metaphor of the region's Sweetgrass baskets throughout the book, delicately imparting her point about the urgency of conserving the environment—and the Gullah culture. Monroe's multi-layered characters are starkly real, their conflicts striking a chord with readers and packing an emotional punch.

Publisher's Weekly named *Skyward* as one of the six best mass-market novels of 2003. The hero of this novel, Harris Henderson, is a man who has created a sanctuary for injured birds of prey in the wilds of the South Carolina coast. Harris is so occupied with his beloved birds that he's lost much of his ability to connect with humans, including his daughter, Marion, who suffers from juvenile diabetes. He hires former emergency room nurse Ella Majors to care for Marion. In this story, both man and nature are at risk. Ella is burned out and guilt ridden. Both she and Harris are as emotionally wounded as Marion and the birds are physically damaged. These two battered souls come together and eventually find healing with each other. Interesting tidbits about owls, eagles, ospreys, and other birds of prey are woven throughout the fabric of the story. Secondary characters, such as Elijah, a man from the Gullah tradition of the African American culture, and Brady Simmons, a teen who shoots one of Harris's eagles and makes restitution by working at the center, add another layer to this gripping tale.

Monroe's home, the low country of South Carolina, is her setting of choice. She writes enchantingly detailed descriptions of the incredibly lush landscape that is so extraordinarily varied and home to many endangered species. It is also a stopover for many migrating species, so Monroe has a unique opportunity to observe those, too.

The one particular book that is harder for Monroe to write than others is always the book she's currently writing: "Until I'm well into the denouement, I'm convinced I'll never finish it. I'm sure I'm not easy to live with ... Once I'm on the final slide, however, it's thrilling, like sliding down a hill." The low-country novels (*The Beach House, Skyward,* and *Sweetgrass*) took more time than her other novels. Monroe says that is because of the "enormous amount of interviewing and research I did to present the information/background as accurately as possible as well as to confirm that my 'ear' for local dialect, such as Gullah, was true. This was where my background in linguistics proved useful."

Although *Second Star to the Right* (1999) came easiest to Monroe, she characterizes its evolution as the "strangest." According to Monroe, "'Crazy Wendy' in that book came to me in a dream. Inspired, I wrote the story in a rush of enthusiasm. It was also the only book I had difficulty revising. My editor wanted me to develop the romance more, and I balked. However, in the end, I believe my revision did make the novel a more enjoyable read. In this novel, I expressed a personal philosophy in the frame of a favorite fairy tale. *Second Star to the Right* remains very close to my heart." A charming twist on Sir James Barrie's *Peter Pan,* this story features Faye O'Neill, an American advertising executive who, following an acrimonious divorce, moves to London with her children, eight-year-old Maddie and six-year-old Tom. Faye moves into a flat in a delightful old house that she shares with Jack Graham, a physicist and fellow American, and Wendy Forrester, the elderly owner of the building, who is known around town as "Crazy Wendy." Wendy does have a few eccentricities, such as speaking to the stars at night and believing that she is Peter Pan's Wendy, but Faye and her children soon fall under the spell of her charms. In the meantime, Jack is falling for Faye. But the serpent enters their little paradise in the form of Wendy's prim, prissy daughter, who wants to sell the house. Fortunately, Wendy has a secret weapon, the magical power of goodness and love, which, mixed with a sprinkling of fairy dust, comes to the rescue.

Although Monroe is always most passionate about the book she's writing, she names *The Beach House* as her favorite. She says, "When I began writing it, I was told focusing on the environment and, in this case, sea turtles was risky in the publishing business. But I forged ahead, believing in the book. When finished, I knew I had written something special. When the readership responded, it was especially rewarding and opened up the door for writing more books set against an environmental theme."

Nature—both animal and human—provides much of the inspiration for Monroe's novels. She is fascinated by the parallels and explores the nuances. Monroe didn't believe in writer's block until recently: "I learned that it is not really a block at all, but rather, an emptiness. There are times when we writers must refill our creative well. Whatever it takes—whether walks on the beach, time playing with children or dogs or friends, reading voraciously, listening to music, working in our gardens, skydiving—whatever! We need to dare to be idle, to back off from deadlines and expectations and the crazed world of promotion, and to take time to figure out what we want or need to say … We have to believe that the stories still lie within us. We have to face that blank page. Ultimately, the story will reveal itself if you remain present to the story and keep writing."

The writing process itself is appealing to Monroe. She says, "My imagination is my playground. Only in stories can I be anything or do anything. Writers have the best job in the world!" Whether it is her contemporary fiction written as Mary Alice Monroe, which she creates with preserving the environment in mind, or her modern fairy tales penned as Mary Alice Kruesi, which are aimed at preserving that bit of magic in the human experience, Monroe's books are both unique and unforgettable.

BIBLIOGRAPHY

Writing as Mary Alice Monroe

Books: *The Beach House.* Toronto: MIRA, 2002; *Skyward.* Toronto: MIRA, 2003; *The Book Club.* Toronto: MIRA, 2004; *The Four Seasons.* Toronto: MIRA, 2004; *Girl in the Mirror.* Toronto: MIRA, 2004; *Sweetgrass.* Toronto: MIRA, 2005.

Writing as Mary Alice Kruesi

Books: *Second Star to the Right.* New York: Avon, 1999; *One Summer's Night.* New York: HarperCollins, 2000.

SHELLEY MOSLEY

HUNTER MORGAN. *See* Colleen Faulkner

CHARLOTTE NICHOLS. *See* Patricia Knoll

REBECCA NORTH. *See* Jo Ann Ferguson

BRENDA NOVAK

Brenda Novak. Courtesy of Brenda Novak.

Growing up, Brenda Novak never dreamed of being a writer. In fact, she went to school, graduated, started a career and a family, and still the thought of becoming a writer hadn't occurred to her. Then one day, as a young mother, she discovered that the caregiver of her children was drugging them with cough syrup and Tylenol to get them to sleep while Novak worked as a loan officer. She knew then that she could no longer trust someone else with the care of her children. Novak says, "I quit my job to stay at home with them, but I needed to help out financially. That was when I first got the idea to try my hand at writing, because it was something I could do from home while I raised my children." Fortunately, she had the talent for writing and discovered the passion later.

Novak was born in 1964 in Vernal, Utah. "My parents were responsible, hardworking people—solid citizens," she recalls. Novak grew up in Murray, Utah, and eventually, her family moved to Chandler, Arizona, where she attended Chandler High School and graduated second in her class. Novak return to Utah to attend Brigham Young University on a full academic scholarship. Before turning to writing, she held a variety of jobs, including commercial-real-estate agent, loan officer, and a field agent for a state senator. She always loved romances, and when the experience with the caregiver occurred, she decided to try her hand at writing what she loved to read.

Writing a historical romance was a natural fit for Novak, as one of her favorite books is Jude Devereaux's *Knight in Shining Armor*. Other than a few poems that according to Novak "aren't fit for others to see," she had never written fiction before. In 1994, Novak, who had just given birth to her third child, somehow managed to find the time to begin writing *Of Noble Birth,* which grew into an 800-page manuscript. She credits Romance Writers of America and one of their conferences in helping her realize that she needed to edit her book to a more sellable size. After editing the book to 400 pages, she started submitting it to a variety of publishers. When she received a call from one of them, she was ecstatic, but they backed out of the deal when Novak didn't have another book in the works. So she got an agent and realized that entering writing contests might be a way to get a foot in the door and set her apart from other fledgling authors. *Of Noble Birth* won the Great Confrontations Contest, sponsored by the Lake Country Romance Writers; the Aspen Gold; and the Beacon Award. It also reached the finals of RWA's Golden Heart contest for unpublished authors.

Despite her success with *Of Noble Birth,* Novak's next book, *Expectations* (2000), was a contemporary romance written for Harlequin's Superromance line, part of the Nine Months Later series. Novak recalls, "When I first started writing contemporaries, I planned to do it in addition to the historicals. I thought it would be a good career choice not to have all my eggs in one basket (to borrow a tired cliché). Turns out that was a better choice than I ever dreamed because I was orphaned at HarperCollins (they fired all their romance editors when they acquired Avon) before my first book ever came out. Without my editor, I had no advocate at that house, and I wasn't picked up at Avon. Fortunately, I'd already sold my first book to Harlequin, so it was natural for me to segue into writing for them full-time." In *Expectations,* Novak pairs the popular theme of reuniting with a lost love with a nicely detailed Mendocino setting. *Expectations* became the first of many Superromances Novak would write for Harlequin, since she found that the line's emphasis on character-driven narratives and stories that explore a range of different contemporary themes fit her own needs as an author.

One of her most popular books in the Superromance line was a series set in the small town of Dundee, Idaho. The first in the series, *A Baby of Her Own* (2002) is the story of Delaney Lawson, raised by her aunt and uncle in Dundee, who grew up always trying to be the "good girl." Now Delaney is 30 and realizes she wants more out of life, including a baby of her own. Enter Conner Armstrong, the grandson of a millionaire rancher, who seems to be the answer to Delaney's problem of creating a baby. But when he arrives in Dundee after their brief tryst, the scandal that ensues rocks the small town and threatens any chance of happiness that Delaney and Conner might have. With *A Baby of Her Own,* Novak does a particularly good job of evoking the small-town atmosphere, where everyone knows everyone else's business.

More Dundee books would follow, including *A Stranger in Town* (2005), a poignant and emotionally intense story of forgiveness and second chances. Gabe Holbrook's NFL career ended the day Hannah Price's car skidded into his on a snowy mountain road. Now wheelchair-bound, Gabe is rebuilding his shattered life the best he can, and when he is asked to coach his old high school football team, he can't refuse. Tortured by the memories of the accident, Hannah Price never expected to see Gabe again, but she is forced to deal with him and her guilt when her son joins the team. Novak's powerful story of two lonely, emotionally fragile people who are given a second chance at love is a richly satisfying and deeply moving romance.

Beginning with her first single-title romantic suspense novel, *Taking the Heat* (2003), Novak proved to not only have a talent for blending danger and passion but also for imbuing this book and her following suspense novels with a strong sense of place. She says, "To me, setting is like another character. I try to anchor the reader in the place where I set the book by pointing out a few things that are unique to the characters' surroundings without slowing the pace with an overload of detail. I like that settings can also work as metaphors and incorporate that when I can." In *Taking the Heat,* she uses her knowledge of Arizona and her research of the prison system to create the riveting story of escaped prisoner Randall Tucker and prison guard Gabrielle Hadley. Tucker is a convicted murderer serving a life sentence in a prison in Florence, Arizona, for killing his wife. When new guard Gabrielle watches Tucker being beaten by another prisoner with none of the guards interceding, she steps in to save him. Tucker escapes during his transfer to another prison, and Gabrielle follows him into the harsh Sonoran Desert to recapture him. The characters of Gabrielle, a single mother searching for her own birth mother, and Tucker, a man innocent of murder and desperate to reunite with his young son, are beautifully delineated. Their growing relationship, combined with the unforgiving heat of the desert, make *Taking the Heat* an unforgettable book.

Cold Feet (2004) was more difficult to write because of the intricate plot, says Novak, but it is one of her favorites. Madison Lieberman grew up under the shadow of everyone thinking her father was the notorious serial killer known as the Sandpoint Strangler. His suicide seems to confirm their accusations, but Madison always believed in her father's innocence, until she discovers a box of items belonging to the victims with her father's effects. After another victim is found murdered in the same manner, the question becomes is it a copycat killer at work or was her father innocent in the first place. When Caleb Trovato, an ex-cop turned crime writer, returns to Seattle, he seizes the chance to reopen his own investigation into the Sandpoint Strangler murders. Caleb believes Madison is the key to unlocking the case, but he isn't sure he can trust her. Against a brilliantly detailed Seattle setting, Novak has created a page-turning roller-coaster ride with an escalating sense of suspense that readers love.

If Novak's first two romantic suspense novels proved to be potent mixes of thrills and danger, her third foray into the subgenre established her as a master of the craft. *Every Waking Moment* (2005) is the powerful and intense story of a mother and the lengths to which she will go to protect her child. Emma Wright has finally escaped an abusive marriage and is on the run with her five-year-old son Max, who is a diabetic. Not only must Emma worry about eluding her powerful, vindictive husband, but she must also face having limited financial resources and the reality of dealing with a child on insulin. When her car breaks down in Nevada, Emma is forced to accept a ride from Preston Holman, a man tortured by his own demons. *Every Waking Moment* is a tour de force of survival, resourcefulness, and emotional connections that are forged by adversity.

While Novak is best known and loved for her contemporary romances and romantic suspense, she has also shown herself to be skilled in the art of short fiction. Her first novella, "What a Girl Wants," appeared in the anthology *Mother Please* (2004) and displayed a light, humorous side of Novak, who paired a flighty mother and her serious daughter. Her next novella was "Small Packages," which appeared in the *More Than Words* anthology, published in 2004. "Small Packages" features the story of Noelle Kane, who becomes involved in the Memory Box Artist Program, a real-life nonprofit charity that donates memory boxes to hospitals for their infant bereavement programs. Noelle has lost a child, and being part of the Memory Box Artist Program has helped her work through her grief. When she meets Harrison Ferrello, who has lost his wife and one of his twins in childbirth, Noelle hopes to help him with his sorrow and with raising the surviving twin. The *More Than Words* anthology includes five stories by five different authors who were inspired by ordinary women who made a difference, and the proceeds from the sale of the book were reinvested into Harlequin's More Than Words program to support causes of concern to women.

Despite the fact that she didn't initially plan on being a writer, now Novak cannot imagine doing anything else: "I like that each new book is another adventure—no two are the same. I like getting to know these imaginary characters and bringing them to life. I like being inspired by their larger-than-life approach to everyday problems." Novak's sense of adventure and rich characterizations shine through in every book that she writes.

Bibliography

Books: *Of Noble Birth.* New York: HarperCollins, 1999; *Expectations.* Toronto: Harlequin, 2000; *Snow Baby.* Toronto: Harlequin, 2000; *Baby Business.* Toronto: Harlequin, 2000; *Dear Maggie.* Toronto: Harlequin, 2001; *We Saw Mommy Kissing Santa Claus.* Toronto: Harlequin, 2001; *Shooting the Moon.* Toronto: Harlequin, 2002; *A Baby of Her Own.* Toronto: Harlequin, 2002; *Taking the Heat.* Toronto: Harlequin, 2003; *A Husband of Her Own.* Toronto: Harlequin, 2003; *Sanctuary.* Toronto: Harlequin, 2003; *Cold Feet.* Toronto: Harlequin, 2004; *A Family of Her Own.* Toronto: Harlequin, 2004; *A Home of Her Own.* Toronto: Harlequin, 2004; *A Stranger in Town.* Toronto, Harlequin, 2005; *Every Waking Moment.* Toronto: Harlequin, 2005; *Dead Silence.* Toronto: MIRA, 2005; *The Other Woman.* Toronto: Harlequin, 2006.

Novellas: "What a Girl Wants" in *Mother Please.* Toronto: Harlequin, 2004; "Small Packages" in *More Than Words.* Toronto: Harlequin, 2004.

Joanne Hamilton-Selway

JANEEN O'KERRY

The Gaelic "*Sonas!*" which means happiness and prosperity, is Janeen O'Kerry's trademark greeting. This is just one indication of her love for all things Celtic. This rich influence along with mysticism and stories of legendary feats are hallmarks of her writing.

O'Kerry was born Janeen Louise Sloan in 1953 in Washington, D.C. Her father was an Air Force senior master sergeant, and her mother divided her time between raising her family and working as a medical technician and a telephone operator. O'Kerry spent much of her Air Force childhood relocating, living in Washington D.C., California, Germany, and Texas. After graduating from high school, she attended two years of college at Southwest Texas State and was one of the first female students ever to attend Texas A&M University. In her prewriting career, O'Kerry worked as a riding instructor, having always had a love of horses. She also worked as a computer programmer and an office worker.

O'Kerry's writing career began in 1984 when she sold the first of her more than one hundred nonfiction magazine articles written for horse enthusiasts. It wasn't long before the notion of writing a novel began to intrigue her, and with the help of a friend, Hazel Williams, she decided to give it a try. On their third attempt, *April's Christmas* sold in 1994. Encouraged by this success, O'Kerry continued writing on her own, producing eight more novels in 10 years.

O'Kerry finds that blending romance and fantasy appeals to an entirely different audience, and it provides an endless supply of story ideas. "They're everywhere, it's just a matter of recognizing them," she says. O'Kerry enjoys the freedom and control that a writing career offers—choosing when to work, on what, and for how long.

Preferring to write from an outline, O'Kerry starts with a theme and develops a situation around it. She describes the recurrent theme in her stories as "finding your place in the world and where you belong." She often manages to work a horse or two into the plot, if not onto the cover. Her favorite setting is Ireland, perhaps 2,000 years ago in the Iron Age, but she has also explored time travel in three of her novels (*Lady of Fire*, 1996; *Queen of the*

Sun, 1998; and *Mistress of the Waters,* 1999). The heroes in her novels are steady and dependable, always there when they're needed. The heroines, while independent and self-sufficient, still need and welcome the comfort of a loving relationship in their lives.

According to O'Kerry, the most difficult of her books to write was the first one, when every step of the process was a learning experience. No particular books stands out as her easiest. She chooses her novel *Sister of the Moon* (2001) as her favorite. O'Kerry is inspired by the writing of fellow authors Marion Zimmer Bradley and Margaret Mitchell, whose writing, she says, contains such colorful detail that "it's like watching a movie."

O'Kerry and husband Scott Michael DeBoard live in Glendale, Arizona, and have two grown children. In addition to writing, O'Kerry offers a writer's critiquing service. She finds that while providing professional advice to her clients she also gains useful insights into her own writing.

Bibliography

Books: *April's Christmas.* New York: Avalon, 1994; *Lady of Fire.* New York: Dorchester, 1996; *Queen of the Sun.* New York: Dorchester, 1998; *Mistress of the Waters.* New York: Dorchester, 1999; *Sister of the Moon.* New York: Dorchester, 2001; *Spirit of the Mist.* New York: Dorchester, 2002; *Maiden of the Winds.* New York: Dorchester, 2003; *Keeper of the Light.* New York: Dorchester, 2003; *Daughter of Gold.* New York: Dorchester, 2004; *Goddess of Eire.* New York: Dorchester, 2006.

Sandra Van Winkle

KAYLA PERRIN

Kayla Perrin. Courtesy of Kayla Perrin.

Jamaican-born Kayla Perrin describes the romance genre as a celebration of love, hope, and family. She believes that with love, a person can do anything. Her passion for writing and her rapidly expanding list of award-winning novels are certainly a testament to that belief.

Reminiscing about her origins as a writer, Perrin recalls, "I've wanted to be a writer since I could hold a pencil. I always knew this is what I wanted to do." In fact, while growing up in Ontario, Canada, Perrin began writing and submitting illustrated children's books to publishers when she was just 13. She got rejection letters, but they were encouraging. When she was 18, Perrin's short story about a girl whose friend dies of cancer, "The Million Dollar Smile," won first place in the Silver Quill Literary Association's short-story contest. At the age of 20, Perrin wrote a mystery novel for middle school readers titled *The Disappearance of Allison Jones,* which was published several years later, in 2000.

Perrin worked in a variety of jobs, including waitress, actress, film editor, and substitute teacher. She has earned three bachelor's degrees: a bachelor of arts degree in English from the University of Toronto; a bachelor's degree in sociology from the University of Toronto; and a bachelor's degree in primary/junior education from York University. Perrin had originally planned for a career in teaching, but she completed her education degree at a time when budget cutbacks were forcing schools to lay off teachers. The soft job market forced Perrin to reassess her goals, and she decided to seriously pursue her lifelong dream of professional writing. It proved to be the right choice. In less than 10 years, Perrin has published over twenty books and novellas, with many of them winning national awards. Two of her novels, *Sweet Honesty* (1999) and *Say You Need Me* (2002), were voted part of the Romance Writers of America's Top Ten Favorite Books of the year.

Perrin finds inspiration anywhere and everywhere, from overhearing a conversation to seeing something on the news that sparks her creativity. The writing process for Perrin always begins with the plot, originating with an inciting incident and building from there. Her characters are developed through a series of questions—who, what, when, where, and why—that help to define their personalities and motives and bring them to life. When Perrin experiences writer's block, she overcomes it by simply jumping ahead to a different scene in the story and working her way backward.

For Perrin, the best part about writing is the ability to create a world out of thin air that touches other people's lives. She mentions one particular reader, who after reading *If You Want Me* (2001) found the strength to return home and face her mother after 15 years. In the novel, Alice Watson is a shy, overweight girl who is growing up in a dysfunctional home and is ridiculed in school. She finds comfort with high school classmate and confidant Marcus Quinn and grows very close to him, only to have him break her heart. In time, Alice matures into a stunningly beautiful woman who has parlayed her high school drama skills into a successful acting career. It isn't until her mother suffers a heart attack that Alice returns to Chicago for the first time in 13 years to finally mend their fractured relationship. When Alice is reunited with Marcus, who is now bitterly divorced, she finds that she still has feelings for him; but they each must learn to trust again before they can ever hope for love.

Perrin writes contemporary stories laced with mystery and suspense. She says, "There is definitely a fair bit of me in my heroines—some books more than others." Though Perrin's heroes don't necessarily share one common trait, her heroines do: in some way, each has been wronged by a man in her life. The main recurrent theme in Perrin's novels is the dangerous nature of secrets and their annoying tendency to resurface. All of these elements are present in *The Sisters of Theta Phi Kappa* (2001) and *The Delta Sisters* (2004). *The Sisters of Theta Phi Kappa* was Perrin's easiest novel to write, as well as one of her favorites. Perrin recalls that this novel "flowed out of me in five weeks, and I was writing about four different women! It was simply incredible." The novel tells the story of four Howard University sorority sisters—Shereen, Ellie, Yolanda, and Jessica—who pledge among themselves to protect a secret that involves one of the sisters and her connection to a professor's suicide. Ten years later, with their lives and careers well underway, the past returns to haunt them when an unknown adversary attempts to expose the truth. The once tight-knit Fabulous Four find their loyalty, friendship, and even their safety jeopardized over their nasty little secret.

Perrin chooses *The Delta Sisters* (2004) as her most difficult book to write because the story involves the mother-daughter relationships of three generations of women. The different sensibilities among the age groups required careful consideration to ensure that the characters were correctly developed. The story begins in 1953 in Lafayette, Louisiana, when Sylvia Grayson suffers through an experience so terrible that it haunts her for the rest of her life. Years later, she has a daughter, Olivia, whom she maintains careful control over to keep her from making the same mistakes. However, after 17 years of her mother's relentless manipulation, Olivia rebels one last time, and their relationship is destroyed. Eventually, Olivia has a daughter of her own, Rachelle. Now it's Olivia's turn to somehow protect her daughter from two generations of bad parenting. To complicate matters, a mysterious figure from their past is lurking in the shadows, willing to kill any one of them, but particularly Rachelle, to protect certain secrets.

In a departure from her often serious plots, Perrin has a humorous recurring character, inhibited sex specialist Lecia Calhoun, who appears in two novels (*Tell Me You Love Me,* 2003; and *Gimme an O!,* 2005). Lecia makes her cameo debut in *Tell Me You Love Me* as an ultraconservative, buttoned-down gynecologist who secretly aspires to become a writer. In her first full-length feature role in *Gimme An O!,* Lecia has become a celebrated sex therapist and a noted authority on female sexuality, with a best-selling women's book titled *The Big O.* The fact that Lecia's own love life could use more than a little "physical therapy" adds to the humor and irony of this wickedly funny, wonderfully sexy book.

Perrin's novels abound in deep, dark secrets. Characters hide things from each other and even themselves. Still, one thing isn't a secret—Perrin's popularity among romance readers. With the universality of her themes, her multicultural works have a broad appeal. The promise that Perrin showed as a very young writer has come to fruition.

BIBLIOGRAPHY

Books: *Everlasting Love.* New York: Kensington, 1998; *Again, My Love.* Mississippi: Genesis Press, 1998; *Midnight Dreams.* New York: Kensington, 1999; *Sweet Honesty.* New York: Kensington, 1999; *Holiday of Love.* New York: BET Books, 2000; *The Disappearance of Allison Jones.* Columbus, MS: Genesis Press, 2000; *Flirting with Danger.* New York: BET Books, 2001; *If You Want Me.* New York: HarperCollins, 2001; *The Sisters of Theta Phi Kappa.* New York: St. Martin's Press, 2001; *Say You Need Me.* New York: HarperCollins, 2002; *In an Instant.* New York: BET Books, 2002; *Fool for Love.* New York: BET Books, 2003; *Tell Me You Love Me.* New York: HarperCollins, 2003; *In a Heartbeat.* New York: BET Books, 2003; *The Delta Sisters.* New York: St. Martin's Press, 2004; *Gimme an O!* New York: HarperCollins, 2005; *Getting Even.* Toronto: Harlequin, 2006; *The Sweet Spot.* New York: Avon, 2006.

Novellas: "Perfect Fantasy" in *Wine and Roses.* New York: Kensington, 1999; "Maternal Instincts" in *Very Special Love.* New York: BET Books, 2000; "Kidnapped!" in *The Best Man.* New York: Penguin, 2003; "Hot and Bothered" in *Perfect for the Beach.* New York: Kensington, 2004; "Blind Faith" in *A Season of Miracles.* New York: BET Books, 2005; "Never Satisfied" in *An All Night Man.* New York: St. Martin's Press, 2005.

SANDRA VAN WINKLE AND SHANNON PRESCOTT

CARLY PHILLIPS

When is a couch potato not a couch potato? When her name is Carly Phillips. Despite television's questionable reputation among the literati, Phillips observes of this popular Drogin family pastime, "It's not just procrastination, it helps with my writing." In fact, she credits television as the source for many of her story ideas. The medium even became a boon to Phillips's career when her novel, *The Bachelor* (2002), was featured on the popular daytime show, *Live with Regis and Kelly,* as a pick for the Reading with Ripa Book Club. The novel spent six weeks on the *New York Times* Best Seller List.

Phillips didn't begin writing until after she had completed law school, having graduated cum laude with a bachelor's degree from Brandeis University in Waltham, Massachusetts, and a juris doctorate from Boston University School of Law. After graduation, when it became apparent to Phillips that she enjoyed studying law far more than practicing it, she began to consider a career in writing. As an avid romance reader, she noticed that many of the well-known romance authors got their start with Harlequin and Silhouette, and Phillips considered the possibilities for herself.

Harlequin published Phillips's novel, *Brazen,* seven years later, in 1999. In this story, when a wealthy older man asks Samantha Reed to marry him, she decides to accept the proposal, seeing it as an opportunity to help her father settle his considerable debts. Samantha decides, before committing to the marriage, to experience a weekend of cheap, meaningless sex by "picking up" the first man she meets. While on her manhunt, Samantha develops car trouble near a country tavern, and when she goes inside to seek help, she meets hunky bartender Mac MacKenzie and has an unexpected change in plans. Phillips's wicked wit draws the reader into the action as Samantha decides between the man of her dreams and the man with the money.

---

also writing as Karen Drogin

The writing process for Phillips begins with character development, using ideas she finds in magazines, newspapers, real life, and television. She adds, "I just pray the inspiration never stops coming!" Of her writing style, Phillips says, "I fly by the seat of my pants most of the time." For Phillips, the most rewarding and fascinating part of the process occurs "when a scene and the characters come together and all of a sudden I get a burst of inspiration and find that I've tied something together and astounded even myself."

Most of Phillips's novels are connected in series. In *Simply Sinful* (2000), the first installment of the Simply series (which also includes *Simply Scandalous,* 2000; and *Simply Sensual,* 2001), Kayla Luck's finishing school for inept businessmen is being investigated by detective Kane McDermott to determine if it's really a front for an escort service. Kayla's trusting nature makes the investigation easy, but what should be an open-and-shut case becomes complicated when Kane is beguiled by the lovely proprietor. Kane, a seasoned veteran in the police force can easily pull off the sting. However, Kayla is more than just a pretty face, and Kane fears what will happen to their relationship once she figures out what he's up to. With Phillips's fast-paced, clever style, the reader knows that Kayla's epiphany is bound to happen sooner or later.

The "Luck" continues for Assistant District Attorney Logan Montgomery in *Simply Scandalous* (2000), the second installment of the Simply series. Logan abhors politics and will go to any lengths to avoid carrying on this family tradition—including destroying his own reputation to prevent being elected. To do so, he carries on a tawdry, high-profile relationship with sexy siren Catherine Luck, whose family's reputation is dubious at best. However, Logan's clever charade becomes serious business when he falls in love with Catherine. Once again, Phillips's sensual love scenes and flawless comedic timing add much to the book.

Phillips believes that since all writers base their stories on things they know, they can't help but imbue their characters with some of their own traits . Phillips's heroines in her fun, contemporary novels are known for their strength, and her heroes, for their inherent goodness. She places them in the midst of past problems or family issues, which are recurrent themes in Phillips's books.

In *The Bachelor* (2002), the first book in the Chandler series (which also includes *The Playboy,* 2003; and *The Heartbreaker,* 2003), Roman Chandler has lost the coin toss to see which brother marries first. Ordered by their ailing mother to settle down and give her grandchildren before it's too late, Chandler brothers Chase, Rick, and Roman, the three most eligible bachelors in Yorkshire Falls, must now find suitable wives. Roman, the youngest of the brothers, already has a bride in mind—gorgeous Charlotte Bronson, a lingerie entrepreneur who has returned to town with plans to open a business and put down roots. Roman's job as a foreign news correspondent had gotten in the way of their romance in the past, but now that Charlotte is back, Roman gets a second chance at happiness, and they fall in love all over again. The secondary characters in this book, from the scheming mother to the eccentric townspeople, add to the entertainment and the fun.

The locales used in Phillips's stories are chosen from among the places she is familiar with or has at least visited. New England is a common locale for her books, she says, because "I lived there through college and law school." A native New Yorker since 1965, Phillips also uses fictional settings from New York. She currently lives there with her husband, Philip Drogin, a supermarket owner/businessman; the couples' two daughters, Jaclyn and Jennifer; and Phillips's constant companion, a soft-coated wheaten terrier named Buddy.

Phillips doesn't feel that any one of her novels was more difficult to write than another. "Every book as I am writing it is the hardest," she says. However, she does have a favorite,

The Bachelor. Phillips says that is "because I tried to just enjoy the first single-title experience." Her cure for writer's block, if it isn't a style problem that she can identify on her own, is to call her critique partners, "to bounce ideas in order to get past the block."

Phillips always writes from the heart with her readers in mind. She says, "When you read a Carly Phillips book, you're always getting a part of me as my gift to you."

BIBLIOGRAPHY

Writing as Carly Phillips

Books: *Brazen*. Toronto: Harlequin, 1999; *Simply Sinful*. Toronto: Harlequin, 2000; *Simply Scandalous*. Toronto: Harlequin, 2000; *Simply Sensual*. Toronto: Harlequin, 2001; *Secret Fantasy*. Toronto: Harlequin, 2001; *Body Heat*. Toronto: Harlequin, 2001; *Erotic Invitation*. Toronto: Harlequin, 2001; *The Bachelor*. New York: Warner, 2002; *Simply Sexy*. Toronto: Harlequin, 2002; *The Playboy*. New York: Warner, 2003; *The Heartbreaker*. New York: Warner, 2003; *Under the Boardwalk*. New York: Warner, 2004; *Hot Stuff*. Toronto: HQN, 2004; *Summer Lovin'*. Toronto: HQN, 2005; *Hot Number*. Toronto: HQN, 2005; *Hot Item*. Toronto: HQN, 2006; *Cross My Heart*. Toronto: HQN, 2006.

Novellas: "Naughty or Nice?" in *Naughty Under the Mistletoe*. Toronto: Harlequin, 2001; "Going All the Way" in *Invitations to Seduction*. Toronto: Harlequin, 2003; "Midnight Angel" in *Stroke of Midnight*. New York: Onyx, 2004.

Writing as Karen Drogin

Books: *Perfect Partners*. New York: Kensington, 1999; *The Right Choice*. New York: Kensington, 2000; *Solitary Man*. New York: Kensington, 2000.

SANDRA VAN WINKLE

SUSAN ELIZABETH PHILLIPS

Susan Elizabeth Phillips. Courtesy of Susan Elizabeth Phillips.

For Susan Elizabeth Phillips, romance novels are more than entertainment—she says they are "an expression of female empowerment" in which the heroines triumph because "guts and brains beat brawn every time." Phillips says she loves reading and writing romances because they are all about "strong, feisty heroines who overcome all obstacles life throws at them and become women who win." With her engaging combination of independent, sassy heroines and sharp, sexy writing, it isn't any wonder Phillips's books are among romance readers' favorites.

Born in Cincinnati, Ohio, Phillips grew up in Central Ohio, in the areas of Lancaster and Columbus. Her father, John Titus, was a management recruiter, a veteran, and, she says, a "man with a true feminist sensibility, although he would have shuddered at the label." Phillips's mother, Louesa, was an elementary school teacher, a musician, and an artist. Phillips attended Ohio University, where she received a bachelor's degree in fine arts. She met her husband, Bill, an engineering major, on a blind date while they were both in college. After graduating and getting married, Phillips taught high school English, speech, and drama for several years.

When her first child was born, Phillips quit teaching to become a stay-at-home mom. In 1976, the Phillips family moved from Ohio to New Jersey, where Phillips discovered a new

---

also writing with Claire Kiehl as Justine Cole

friend and fellow reader in her neighbor, Claire Kiehl. Both women loved discussing what they were reading, which ranged from literary novels to romances. One day, the two of them decided that they would try to write a book together, "just for fun." For three weeks, they talked and plotted. When they finally sat down to write though, they discovered they really had no idea how to begin. Ultimately, the two women came up with their own writing system. They would get together to plot a scene and would act out the dialogue. Kiehl would take notes and type them up. Phillips would either revise these notes or throw them out and start from scratch.

Eventually, the two had completed about half of a book when they decided to call an editor at Dell Publishing. The editor not only proved to be quite nice, but amazingly enough was also interested in seeing their work, despite the fact that their book was not yet finished. The editor asked Phillips and Kiehl to send her a synopsis. The two coauthors spent the next few weeks feverishly coming up with a conclusion to their story. They typed a copy of their manuscript and sent it to Dell. Three weeks later, the editor called to buy their manuscript, *The Copeland Bride,* which was published under the pseudonym Justine Cole in 1983. With the publication of *The Copeland Bride,* Phillips discovered that she had developed a taste for writing. Her writing partner, Kiehl, was not as addicted to crafting novels. When Kiehl and her family moved to the Southwest, where Kiehl would realize her own dreams of attending law school and becoming a successful lawyer, Phillips was left to figure how to write a book on her own. In time, all of her hard work and perseverance paid off when Phillip's second book, *Risen Glory,* was published under her own name a year later, in 1984, by Dell. Set during the Reconstruction era, *Risen Glory* is the story of Southern hellion Katherine Louise "Kit" Weston, who is determined to reclaim her family's plantation, Risen Glory, from the Northern war hero, Baron Cain. Cain not only owns the estate but, unbeknownst to Kit, is also her new guardian. Disguised as a boy, Kit travels to New York City, where she plans on killing Baron, but the Northerner proves surprisingly difficult to get rid of, especially when she falls in love with him.

The Copeland Bride and *Risen Glory* were both very much literary products of their time. Both books reflected Phillips's own love of the swashbuckling, larger-than-life, sexy romances of the late 1970s and early 1980s, in which men called all the shots and the lovemaking was often violent. By the 1990s, this style of historical romance was not considered politically correct and had fallen out of favor with readers. While Phillips realized that *Risen Glory* showed its age, the core of the story, the feisty heroine, and the brooding hero were still appealing, and according to Phillips, the book just needed some "freshening up." Phillips spent the summer of 2000 revising and rewriting *Risen Glory,* which was published the following year as *Just Imagine.*

Phillips followed up her two historical romances with *Glitter Baby* (1987), her first contemporary novel. This is the story of Fleur Savager, the daughter of a Hollywood starlet and an aging actor. *Glitter Baby* is more women's fiction in the vein of Judith Krantz and Rona Jaffe than it is romance; the focus of the book is on the heroine's journey to self-discovery rather than her romance with one man. *Fancy Pants* (1989), Phillips's next novel, is much along the same lines—a rags-to-riches, glitz-and-glamour tale of the romance between the once poor Francesca Day, a British beauty, and Dallas Beaudine, a down-on-his-luck golfer.

Hot Shot, another of Phillips's "big" novels, as she calls them, followed in 1991. This book focuses on four characters—Susannah Faulconer, a San Francisco socialite who gives up her social status to follow a dream; Sam Gamble, a visionary inventor; Yank Yankowski, a genius with electronics; and Mitch Blaine, a marketing guru. Phillips brings to life the exciting early years of the computer industry with these characters, who combine their talents to invent and market a prototype for a new kind of computer.

In *Honey Moon,* published in 1993, Phillips once again turned to the glamorous world of the entertainment industry for her story of orphan Honey Jane Moon, an aspiring actress from a poor background. Honey Jane comes to Hollywood and winds up the costar of a television show, but her dreams of a real family continue to elude her. While the focus of *Glitter Baby, Fancy Pants, Hot Shot,* and *Honey Moon* is definitely on the heroine, with each of these books Phillips moved closer to the kind of classic contemporary romance novels and the style of writing for which she is known and loved today.

For some time, Phillips had dreamed about writing a romance featuring a woman who knows nothing about football, but who inherits a professional sports team. In 1994, that dream came true when her book *It Had to Be You* was published. The book's heroine, beautiful, sexy Phoebe Sommerville, has just arrived from New York to take charge of her newly inherited Chicago Stars football team. The Star's head coach, Dan Celebow, would like nothing better than to have the football-clueless Phoebe pack her designer bags and return from whence she came. Despite the conventional wisdom of the publishing world that any romance featuring a sports figure as a hero would not be commercially successful, Phillips went with her instincts and wrote *It Had to Be You,* which became a bestseller. Readers loved the book's sharp, sassy heroine; its testosterone-rich hero; and Phillips's wonderful sense of humor. The success of *It Had to Be You* encouraged Phillips to embark on the Chicago Stars series, highlighting other members of Phoebe's football team, much to the delight of her fans.

Heaven, Texas (1995), the second book in the Chicago Stars series features lovable bad boy Bobby Tom Denton. A wide receiver for the team, Bobby Tom has led them to many victories, but a knee injury has ended his stellar career in football, forcing him to retire at age 33. When Bobby Tom is offered a part in an action movie, his agent is concerned he'll be sidetracked by women along the way and won't meet his obligation. To allay his fears, the agent hires a sort of bodyguard for the sexy playboy, a woman considered reliable and mature—in other words, one who is immune to Bobby Tom's legendary charms. Mousy, virginal Gracie Snow, an assistant in a nursing home who dresses more conservatively than a nun, is hired to escort Bobby Tom to his destination. However, somewhere along the way, Bobby Tom realizes Gracie's potential as a lover and teases and woos her incessantly. The changes in their personalities, as she becomes more playful and he becomes more serious, are a joy to behold.

Phillips has a delicious sense of irony, which comes across beautifully in her books, including *Nobody's Baby But Mine* (1997), the third of her Chicago Stars romances. In *Nobody's Baby But Mine,* the heroine, Dr. Jane Darlington, is a geeky genius who spent her childhood years being ostracized by the other kids because she was so much smarter than they were. Now an adult, Jane is ready to have children of her own, but she is determined that her offspring will be average so they do not have to suffer the same fate she did when she was young. Jane hits on the idea of having a so-called dumb jock father her baby, but little does she know that Cal Bonner, the Chicago Stars football player she has targeted as her "sperm donor," is also gifted with a superior intellect. Once the pregnant Jane discovers the truth about his IQ, she is furious with Cal, who is equally mad at her for stereotyping him. Nonetheless, Cal insists that Jane marry him so the baby will have a father. This book runs the gamut from sexy to funny to heartbreaking, just the sort of roller-coaster ride that Phillips's fans have come to expect.

While Phillips is known for her feisty, resilient heroines, she is equally loved by her readers for her testosterone-rich, bad-boy heroes, like pro-golfer Kenny Traveler, the hero of

Lady Be Good (1999). Suspended from the golf circuit, Traveler finds himself coerced by the wife of the acting PGA commissioner into escorting headmistress Lady Emma Wells-Finch around Texas. In order to avoid the romantic overtures of a persistent duke, who unfortunately has the power to ruin her beloved girls' school, Emma must find some way to lose her spotless reputation, and she sees Kenny as the perfect solution to all of her problems. In *Lady Be Good,* Phillips cunningly twists the expected conventions of the genre with her wickedly entertaining tale of a "good girl" heroine, who seeks to ruin her reputation with a "bad boy" hero, who is doing everything he can to avoid scandal. Phillips knows that women love bad boys, but she also wisely knows that what women really want is a good guy. Phillips's heroes are always an irresistible combination of both these qualities. On the outside, they are sexy rogues; but at their core, they are, like Kenny, truly honorable men.

Phillips says one of the themes that interests her most as an author is that "love triumphs and makes us better people. I'm never interested in writing characters who can't be redeemed." A perfect example of this is her book *Ain't She Sweet?* (2004), the story of Sugar Beth Carey. Fifteen years ago as a teenager in the small town of Parrish, Mississippi, Sugar Beth was the most popular girl in town, and she used this, along with her family's money, to get whatever she wanted. This included mercilessly tormenting fellow high school student Winnie Davis and having popular high school teacher Colin Bryne's career destroyed. Now Sugar Beth is returning to Parrish, thrice divorced, down on her luck, and out of money, to claim an inheritance left to her by a disapproving aunt. Much to her chagrin, everyone in Parrish, including Winnie, now the town's wealthiest citizen, and Colin, now a best-selling author, have long memories when it comes to Sugar Beth and the havoc she created. In *Ain't She Sweet?* Phillips daringly gives readers a heroine who is far from perfect. As a teenager, Sugar Beth is self-centered, manipulative, and vindictive. Over the years, Sugar Beth has learned a little bit about life and a lot about herself. When she comes back to her hometown, sharp-tongued Sugar Beth is still proud and definitely not perfect, but she tries to atone for her past and set things right with those she has wronged, including the infuriatingly sexy Colin. The path to redemption was never more deliciously funny than in this richly poignant, deeply romantic, and wonderfully witty romance.

One of the things readers love most about Phillips is her ability to create heroines who possess a realistic combination of strength and vulnerability. It is the flaws that make Phillips's characters so endearing and real. A perfect example of this is the main character of *Match Me if You Can* (2005), Annabelle Granger. When readers first meet Annabelle, she has inherited her beloved nana's matchmaking business, Matches by Myrna, and is doing her best to bring it into this century. Annabelle has pinned all of the company's economic hopes on landing Heath Champion, megarich sports agent for many of the Chicago Stars players, as a client. Before her first meeting with him, Annabelle manages to have car trouble, ruin her beautiful suit, break a nail, and destroy her shoes, making her late for her appointment. Despite all these setbacks, Annabelle perseveres and attends the meeting, where she convinces Heath to give her a chance to find him the perfect wife. Like all of Phillips's books, *Match Me if You Can* sparkles with her trademark saucy wit and winning characters.

Readers are not the only ones who have recognized Phillips's literary genius in the genre. Phillips is the only five-time winner of the Romance Writers of America's Favorite Book of the Year Award. In 2001, Phillips was inducted into the Romance Writers of America's Hall of Fame for her three RITA award-winning books—*Nobody's Baby but Mine, Dream a Little Dream* (1998), and *First Lady* (2000).

Not many writers can successfully mix rib-tickling humor and heartbreaking emotion in one story, sometimes within pages of each other, but Phillips can and does. Phillips, who started writing with a friend just for kicks and ended up at the top of her field, who defied conventional wisdom and used sports figures for romantic leads, and whose character development is as strong as her plotting, is definitely one of the romance genre's shining stars.

BIBLIOGRAPHY

Writing as Susan Elizabeth Phillips

Books: *Risen Glory.* New York: Dell, 1984; *Glitter Baby.* New York: Dell, 1987; *Fancy Pants.* New York: Pocket, 1989; *Hot Shot.* New York: Pocket, 1991; *Honey Moon.* New York: Pocket, 1993; *It Had to Be You.* New York: Avon, 1994; *Heaven, Texas.* New York: Avon, 1995; *Kiss an Angel.* New York: Avon, 1996; *Nobody's Baby but Mine.* New York: Avon, 1997; *Dream a Little Dream.* New York: Avon, 1998; *Lady Be Good.* New York: Avon, 1999; *First Lady.* New York: Avon, 2000; *Just Imagine.* New York: Avon, 2001; *This Heart of Mine.* New York: William Morrow, 2001; *Breathing Room.* New York: William Morrow, 2002; *Ain't She Sweet?* New York: William Morrow, 2004; *Match Me if You Can.* New York: William Morrow, 2005.

Genre-Specific Essay: "The Romance and the Empowerment of Women" in *Dangerous Men and Adventurous Women: Romance Writers on the Appeal of the Romance.* Philadelphia: University of Pennsylvania Press, 1992.

Writing with Claire Kiehl as Justine Cole

Books: *The Copeland Bride.* New York: Dell, 1983.

JOHN CHARLES, SHELLEY MOSLEY, JOANNE HAMILTON-SELWAY, AND
SANDRA VAN WINKLE

LISA PLUMLEY

Lisa Plumley. Photo by Jennifer Berry/ Studio 16. Courtesy of Lisa Plumley.

USA Today best-selling author Lisa Plumley likes to leave her readers smiling. Judging by the public's reaction to her sassy contemporary romances and humorous historicals, it's evident that this is one goal she has more than met.

Lisa Plumley was born in 1965 in a small town in Michigan. Her parents owned a music distribution business for a number of years. Her father also worked in a variety of other occupations, including salesman, heavy-equipment operator, and mine worker, in the various places they lived. Her mother was employed as a bookkeeper. Much of Plumley's childhood was spent in northwestern Michigan, but her family also lived in Wyoming and Arizona.

Plumley has always been an avid reader, finding entertainment and good company in books. Fortunately, most of the places her family moved had public libraries she could visit. Her interest in reading led to her desire to write at a very early age. Plumley recalls she wrote her first novel in grade school, "a Scooby-Doo style mystery with a pair of Nancy-Drew-ish junior sleuths," simply because she enjoyed making up stories to share with other people.

After graduating from high school in 1984, Plumley spent a few years working in such occupations as pharmacy technician, bookkeeper, and construction coordinator, before enrolling in college. It was during the course of her degree program she discovered she had a flair for writing and decided to make a serious attempt at becoming a novelist. She started writing when her children were preschoolers. They had been spending a lot of time at the library, visiting children's story time and checking out armloads of books. As Plumley says, "I found myself reading more than ever—both with my sons and in my downtime. I remembered exactly how much I loved books, and how fascinated I always was with the idea of creating stories on paper. One day, I just decided to give it a go …"

Plumley's first attempts at being a novelist were two full-length historical romances, which were rejected with words of encouragement. Ironically, her professional writing career began with a short romantic comedy, *Surrender* (1997), written for Kensington's Precious Gem line. She wrote three more Precious Gems (*The Honeymoon Hoax,* 1998; *My Best Friend's Baby,* 1999; and *Man of the Year,* 2000) for Hilary Sares, a Kensington editor who helped many new authors establish their careers, before the line folded. Although her career as a "Gemster" was short lived, she found her voice with the Precious Gem novels, and the exposure helped establish her as a strong voice in the field of romantic comedy. Plumley's first three Precious Gems were rereleased in the anthology *Once Upon a Christmas* (2005).

Plumley enjoys the entire writing experience, from character and plot development to scripting humorous dialogue and situations. Her writing is character driven, typically originating with a single character in a predicament that shapes the rest of the story. In *The Matchmaker* (2003), Sheriff Marcus Copeland finds himself in such a position when the men in his town insist he find out who the anonymous—and highly successful—matchmaker is. Furthermore, if he doesn't stop her, they will.

The writing process begins for Plumley by compiling a complete synopsis and character sketches meant to keep her story on track. Each scene is developed in order until the story is complete. Plumley revises as she writes, allowing her to address problems right away. She believes that writer's block is merely a signal that something needs reworking, "either in a writer's current project, or in her life." Plumley says the authors who have inspired her writing are "too many to count." She considers storytelling to be a gift, and treasures "all the experiences authors have given me over the years," from those who inspired and entertained her as a child to those she's met and whose books she adores.

Plumley's novels are humorous and lighthearted romantic comedies that focus more on the personalities of the characters than on the complexity of the plot. In *Perfect Together* (2003), a radio station's public relations department turns sportscaster Jake Jarvis, a single parent, into an unwilling sex symbol. When he ends up as a contestant on a reality dating game show, he's paired with the incognito Marley Madison, who, after eight years in a popular television show, wants to be recognized as a serious actress.

Marley's identical twin, Meredith, gets her own book in *Perfect Switch* (2004). Since Marley is on her honeymoon with Jake, Meredith agrees to take her place so the paparazzi doesn't tail the two lovebirds. However, Marley forgets to tell Meredith that she has agreed to be the featured star at an actor's fantasy camp. Meredith doesn't wear makeup and is cavalier when it comes to shaving her legs, so it takes everything she's got to pull off the deception. Tony Valentine, e-commerce genius, is trying to save his studio, so this camp is important to him. He didn't remember Marley swearing like a sailor or forgetting her lines, so he has no alternative but to turn her into the polished professional she's supposed to be. Plumley's contemporary version of the Pygmalion tale has hysterically funny results.

A recurring theme in Plumley's books is that love brings out the best in people, inspiring hope and motivating them to accomplish remarkable things. In *Making Over Mike* (2001) another modern take on the Pygmalion story, life coach Amanda Connor, faces the overwhelming task of turning unemployed slob Mike Cavaco into a civilized kind of guy as part of a televised publicity stunt.

The heroes in Plumley's romantic comedies approach life with a sense of humor and self-confidence that help them handle the challenges to come. They tend to be regular guys who can sometimes be baffled by women but are always fascinated by them. Riley Davis, the hero of *Reconsidering Riley* (2002), has no idea that he's the reason Jayne Murphy wrote the best-selling *Heartbreak 101: Getting Over the Good-bye Guys*. When the two of them end up at the same Arizona wilderness retreat, he eventually reaches enlightenment, albeit the hard way. With this book, Plumley has written a hilarious but insightful novel on the battle of the sexes.

Plumley says her characters exhibit only a little of her own personality; she finds part of the fun of writing is to explore other personas through her characters. Her heroines are headstrong and determined, often striving for something just beyond their reach. Plumley's heroines have a desire to connect with the people around them, and like her heroes, they also have a sense of humor. Traveling book saleswoman Amelia O'Malley, the heroine of *Outlaw* (1999) a tale of the Old West, is rescued by Mason Kincaid after the stagecoach he has just robbed leaves her behind in the sweltering Arizona desert. However, Amelia overcomes her fear of Mason almost immediately, and soon the two of them are verbally sparring their way to romance.

Writing has become Plumley's full-time occupation. She tries to stick to an eight-to-five schedule but says she is often tempted to "fiddle with a story" after hours in her home office. She finds the most difficult novel to write is whatever she's currently working on. She says the easiest to write is whatever she's currently plotting, while the possibilities are still endless: "The story in my mind is perfect!" Plumley has two favorite novels: the one she's just completed and the one she's just beginning. The former is fresh from what she calls the "writer's amnesia" stage, when all of the angst of writing it is forgotten. The latter feels filled with shining possibilities, and she can't wait to begin it.

Plumley credits her husband, John, as her romantic muse and dedicates every one of her books to him. She says, "My books are all about finding the truth in yourself while falling in love." The couple and their two sons live in Arizona. They enjoy hiking, watching classic movies, exploring historical sites, traveling, and of course, reading. Having accomplished her dream of becoming a novelist, Plumley recalls, "I never did finish college … but I just might find the time to do that eventually!"

Plumley chose to write in the romance genre for its endless variety and always satisfying endings. She still appreciates the character emphasis of romance novels and is amazed by the way men and women struggle to relate to each other through their radically different viewpoints. "It's fascinating and a little miraculous every time they manage to bridge the gender gap and find a piece of happiness together," she observes. Plumley's books have brought laughter into the homes of many. That's a miracle in itself.

BIBLIOGRAPHY

Books: *Surrender.* New York: Kensington, 1997; *The Honeymoon Hoax.* New York: Kensington, 1998; *Lawman.* New York: Kensington, 1999; *My Best Friend's Baby.* New York: Kensington, 1999; *Outlaw.* New York: Kensington, 1999; *Her Best Man.* New York: Kensington, 2000; *Man of the Year.* New York: Kensington, 2000; *Making Over Mike.* New York: Kensington, 2001; *Reconsidering Riley.* New York: Kensington, 2002; *The Drifter.* Toronto: Harlequin, 2002; *Falling for April.* New York: Kensington, 2002; *Perfect Together.* New York: Kensington, 2003; *The Matchmaker.* Toronto: Harlequin, 2003; *Perfect Switch.* New York: Kensington, 2004; *Josie Day Is Coming Home.* New York: Kensington, 2005; *The Scoundrel.* Toronto: Harlequin, 2006; *Lucy Logan Is Getting Lucky.* New York: Kensington, 2006; *Mad About Max.* New York: Kensington, 2006.

Novellas: "Winter Song" in *Timeless Winter.* New York: Kensington, 1999; "Chances Are" in *Timeless Spring.* New York: Kensington, 1999; "Merry, Merry Mischief" in *Santa Baby.* New York: Kensington, 2002; "Just Jennifer" in *I Shaved My Legs for This?!* New York: Kensington, 2006.

SANDRA VAN WINKLE AND SHELLEY MOSLEY

MARY JO PUTNEY

Mary Jo Putney. Photo by Franco, photographer. Courtesy of Mary Jo Putney.

Award-winning, best-selling author Mary Jo Putney takes special delight in torturing her characters. Putney doesn't do this simply because she enjoys watching them suffer; she has perfectly valid reasons for putting her heroes and heroines through their own personal hells. Putney firmly believes that any "good romance is about transformation," and that there is perhaps no more intriguing and compelling form of transformation than a wounded person who must overcome their own damaged past, their own pain, or their own sorrow in order to get their personal happy ending.

Putney was born in Batavia, New York, in 1946 and grew up in the farm country of western New York, between Buffalo and Rochester. Putney's father was the only prison guard in the state at the time with a college degree, and her mother was a schoolteacher. A voracious bookworm, Putney inherited her love of reading from both her parents. After attending local public schools, Putney skipped a year of high school to enter college early. She enrolled at Syracuse University and graduated with two bachelor's degrees, one in eighteenth-century British literature and the other in industrial design.

While Putney had always dreamed of writing, it seemed to her more like a vague fantasy rather than an achievable goal. Instead, Putney worked as a graphic and industrial designer

also writing as M. J. Putney

and also took a job as an art editor for a British magazine. Putney would later remember that working in the graphic arts field as a full-time freelancer "was excellent preparation for a writing career, since I was used to an erratic cash flow and no benefits."

After purchasing a computer for her business, Putney was suddenly reminded of her former writing dreams when she discovered her computer offered word processing. Once she realized what this meant, Putney happily began writing her first book, a traditional Regency romance called *The Diabolical Baron,* which was bought by Signet in a three-book contract and published in 1987. This first effort also became a finalist for the Romance Writers of America's Gold Medallion Award for Best Regency Romance.

Considering her academic background and interest in both Great Britain and the early nineteenth century, it isn't surprising that Putney would go on to write six more Regency romances for Signet. By the time she had written her third book, *The Would-Be Widow* (1988), Putney had "discovered her voice, and that voice was angst" as she states in the "The Writer's Journey: Like a Lemming Over a Cliff," an essay she contributed to *North American Romance Writers.*

Putney's fifth book, *The Rake and the Reformer* (1989), was inspired by her irritation with the way that many Regency romances of the time portrayed hard-drinking heroes as dashing instead of the dissolute, difficult-to-live-with drunks they more likely were in reality. Putney created an alcoholic hero, Reginald Davenport, for *The Rake and the Reformer,* but she wanted to give this self-indulgent rogue one last chance for redemption. That chance comes in the form of the novel's heroine, the sharp-witted and sharp-tongued Alys Weston, the reformer. Writing about the themes of alcoholic addiction, recovery, and the healing power of love turned out to be a very visceral experience for Putney, and this comes across powerfully in the book. *The Rake and the Reformer* was chosen as one of RWA's Top Ten Favorite books of 1989 and won Putney her first RITA award in 1990.

Like many romance writers, Putney has written her share of loosely connected books. Putney's first romance trilogy was her Silk books, comprised of *Silk and Shadows* (1991), *Silk and Secrets* (1992), and *Veils of Silk* (1992). Set in the early Victorian era, these books sweep readers around the globe from England to Central Asia and even India. With their marvelously exotic locales, Putney's Silk romances offered readers a refreshing alternative to the more familiar historical settings found in most other historical romances of the time.

After finishing up her Silk trilogy, Putney began a new series featuring the Fallen Angels, four men who meet as schoolboys and become lifelong friends. Putney says using the Fallen Angels as her heroes gave her the opportunity to explore the "kind of supportive, emotional relationship that is rare among men." *Thunder and Roses* (1993) introduces readers to the first of the Fallen Angels, Nicholas Davies, the "Demon Earl" who will only help Welsh schoolteacher Clare Morgan save her small village if she agrees to live with him for three months. While *Thunder and Roses* was initially intended to be the first in a trilogy, it was soon followed by six more titles, including *Dancing on the Wind* (1994), which earned Putney her second RITA award.

In the late 1990s, Putney, like such authors as Catherine Coulter, was given the opportunity to revise, adapt, and expand several of her earlier traditional Regency romances into the longer, more sensual Regency historical romances, for which she is now known and loved by readers. *The Rake,* published in 1998, is a reworking of Putney's early classic, *The Rake and the Reformer,* and *The Would-Be Widow* became the basis for *The Bargain,* published in 1999. In addition, two of Putney's Fallen Angel books had their origins in earlier books: *Petals in the Storm* (1994) was a reworking of *The Controversial Countess* (1989), and *Angel Rogue* (1995) was a revision of *The Rogue and the Runaway* (1990).

The Burning Point, set in Baltimore, and published in 2000, was Putney's first contemporary romance and proved to be an especially difficult book for her to write. Not only did Putney have to find her "modern voice," but she also had to explore the issue of domestic violence within one couple's relationship, which proved to be quite controversial with some readers. In *The Burning Point,* the book's heroine, Kate Corsi, returns home after her father's death to discover that his will stipulates she must live with her ex-husband, Patrick Donovan, for one year if she wants to inherit the family's demolition business. Patrick knows that because of his inability to contain his anger, he is to blame for the breakup of their marriage; but he wants another chance to prove to Kate that he has changed. Readers either loved or hated *The Burning Point,* but the mere fact that Putney could inspire such extreme emotions in readers proved to be one more sign of her own power as a writer.

The Burning Point became the first in Putney's Circle of Friends trilogy, which features a group of childhood friends who manage to remain connected with each other despite the different directions their lives have taken. *The Spiral Path* (2002) and *Twist of Fate* (2004) followed *The Burning Point,* and both of these books also explore some tough topics within the context of a contemporary romance. In *The Spiral Path,* dark, childhood secrets haunt the movie-star hero, who is working with the heroine, his estranged wife, on a new film. The attempt by a tabloid journalist to expose those secrets threatens the hero's hard-won sanity, and it is only with the help and love of the heroine, and the powers of the spiral path, that the hero is able to come to terms with his past. The death penalty and the current state of the American justice system play important roles in *Twist of Fate* (2004), in which corporate attorney Val Covington gives up her well-paying job to open her own practice. She then finds her life tangled up romantically and professionally with her new landlord, Rob Smith, as the two try to save an innocent man from being executed for a crime he did not commit.

Ever since she was a child, Putney has been a reader of science fiction and fantasy, so it isn't surprising that she would eventually explore the possibilities of the fantasy genre as a writer. In 1998, Putney published two novellas, "Avalon" in the *In Our Dreams* anthology and "Dangerous Gifts" in the anthology *Faery Magic,* both of which added a generous measure of fantasy to her signature brand of romance. Putney first introduced her readers to her Guardians—humans with magical powers who have pledged to use these gifts in the service of humanity—with her novella "The Alchemical Marriage" in *Irresistible Forces* (2004), in which the hero and heroine try to keep the Spanish Armada from invading England through the use of their special talents in manipulating the weather. In *A Kiss of Fate* (2004), Putney continued to draw from her Guardian world for inspiration. The book's hero is a Scottish nobleman, Duncan Macrae, who joins forces and powers with the heroine, English widow Gwyneth Owens, to try to stop a danger that threatens both of their countries.

By the time Putney wrote *Stolen Magic* (2005), the integration of fantasy and magic into her stories had been so important that she adopted a new pseudonym, M. J. Putney. She used this pen name for *Stolen Magic* and future titles in her Guardian series to help distinguish these fantasy romance books from her more traditional historical romances with only occasional elements of fantasy. In addition, *Stolen Magic* became the first of her Guardian titles to be published by legendary science fiction and fantasy publisher Del Rey.

Putney's dedication to her art and her willingness to try things in her romances that other writers would never consider doing have garnered her a reputation among readers as a remarkably creative and superbly entertaining storyteller. "Stories give shape to experience and help us cope with pain and the unknown as well as entertaining, educating, and inspiring,." she says. "To be a storyteller is an ancient and noble calling." Putney's belief in the power of stories is a beautiful reflection of her own master-storytelling skills.

BIBLIOGRAPHY

Writing as Mary Jo Putney

Books: *The Diabolical Baron.* New York: Signet, 1987; *The Would-Be Widow.* New York: Signet, 1988; *Lady of Fortune.* New York: Signet, 1988; *The Controversial Countess.* New York: Signet, 1989; *The Rake and the Reformer.* New York: Signet, 1989; *Carousel of Hearts.* New York: Signet, 1989; *The Rogue and the Runaway.* New York: Signet, 1990; *Dearly Beloved.* New York: Signet, 1990; *Uncommon Vows.* New York: Onyx, 1991; *Silk and Shadows.* New York: Onyx, 1991; *Silk and Secrets.* New York: Onyx, 1992; *Veils of Silk.* New York: Onyx, 1992; *Thunder and Roses.* New York: Signet, 1993; *Petals in the Storm.* New York: Signet, 1994; *Dancing on the Wind.* New York: Signet, 1994; *Angel Rogue.* New York: Signet, 1995; *Shattered Rainbows.* New York: Signet, 1996; *River of Fire.* New York: Signet, 1996; *One Perfect Rose.* New York: Ballantine, 1997; *The Rake.* New York: Signet, 1998; *The Bargain.* New York: Signet, 1999; *The Wild Child.* New York: Ballantine, 1999; *The China Bride.* New York: Ballantine, 2000; *The Burning Point.* New York: Berkley, 2000; *The Bartered Bride.* New York: Ballantine, 2002; *The Spiral Path.* New York: Berkley, 2002; *Twist of Fate.* New York: Ballantine, 2004; *A Kiss of Fate.* New York: Ballantine, 2004; *The Marriage Spell.* New York: Ballantine, 2006.

Novellas: "Sunshine for Christmas" in *A Regency Christmas II.* New York: Signet, 1990; "The Christmas Cuckoo" in *A Regency Christmas III.* New York: Signet, 1991; "The Christmas Tart" in *A Regency Christmas IV.* New York: Signet, 1992; "The Black Beast of Belleterre" in *A Victorian Christmas.* New York: Penguin, 1992; "Mad, Bad, and Dangerous to Know" in *Rakes and Rogues.* New York: Signet, 1993; "The Wedding of the Century" in *Promised Brides.* Toronto: Harlequin, 1994; "The Devil's Spawn" in *Dashing and Dangerous.* New York: Signet, 1995; "The Best Husband Money Can Buy" in *A Stockingful of Joy.* New York: Onyx, 1997; "Dangerous Gifts" in *Faery Magic.* New York: Zebra, 1998; "Avalon" in *In Our Dreams.* New York: Zebra, 1998; "The Stargazer's Familiar" in *A Constellation of Cats.* New York: DAW, 2001; "A Holiday Fling" in *Christmas Revels.* New York: Jove, 2003; "The Alchemical Marriage" in *Irresistible Forces.* New York: NAL, 2004; "The Stargazer's Familiar" in *The Journey Home.* Canon City, CO: ImaJinn Books, 2005.

Genre-Related Essays: "Welcome to the Dark Side" in *Dangerous Men and Adventurous Women: Romance Writers on the Appeal of the Romance.* Philadelphia: University of Pennsylvania Press, 1992; "The Writer's Journey: Like a Lemming Over a Cliff" in *North American Romance Writers.* Lanham, Maryland: Scarecrow Press, 1999.

Writing as M. J. Putney

Book: *Stolen Magic.* New York: Del Rey, 2005.

JOHN CHARLES

M. J. PUTNEY. *See* Mary Jo Putney

AMANDA QUICK. *See* Jayne Ann Krentz

TARA TAYLOR QUINN

Tara Taylor Quinn. Courtesy of Tara Taylor Quinn.

Emotionally intense contemporary romances that focus on the psychological journey of a character and the many variations a family can take are the specialty of author Tara Taylor Quinn. A disciplined and dedicated writer, in less than ten years, Quinn has written more than thirty-five books and earned a reputation for intriguing stories that deliver all the optimism and hope the romance genre promises its readers.

Tara Lee Gumser was born in Toledo, Ohio, in 1959 to a real-estate broker/school-board president father and a housewife mother. Quinn's family moved around Ohio when she was a young girl, but eventually, the Gumser family settled in Dayton. When it came time for Quinn to attend college, she chose Harding University in Arkansas, where she graduated with a bachelor of arts degree in English. Realizing her degree really did not offer much in the way of career options, Quinn continued her studies at Harding, where she also received her certification to teach.

Before she turned to writing, Quinn taught high school English, worked various clerical/office jobs, waitressed for a bit, and was a stringer for the *Dayton Daily News*. In 1984, she married Kevin Reames, and in 1985, her daughter, Rachel, was born.

Quinn had always wanted to be a writer. She wrote her first story at the age of seven. Published in her grade school's magazine, her story "It Happened One Night" featured a brave young heroine who woke her mother up after hearing the bogeyman one night. The two of them then sent the monster on his way. Quinn's own love of romance fiction began when she was 14 years old. While waiting in a supermarket checkout line, a bored Quinn picked up one of the free Harlequin romances that were being handed out that day and was immediately hooked. Quinn enjoyed her first romance so much that eventually she was reading at least one romance a day. Quinn's habit of reading romances in high school ultimately got her suspended from her typing class, when the instructor discovered that rather than doing the assignments from the text (with which Quinn was already familiar), she had hidden a romance book and was reading that.

Quinn's love of the romance genre did not immediately translate into success for her as a writer. While staying at home in 1985 with her new daughter, Quinn began writing her first romance. Two years later, she had a complete manuscript, but it was rejected. Quinn called Harlequin and asked to speak to the editor who had rejected her book. The editor turned out to be very encouraging and helpful. Quinn later met another Harlequin editor at a writers' conference , who sat down with Quinn and spent several hours telling her what she needed to do to get published with Harlequin's Superromance line.

Quinn's first book, *Yesterday's Secrets,* the story of a mother who would do anything to keep her powerful ex-husband from taking custody of her twins away from her, was published in 1993. This book held many of the appealing ingredients that readers would come to expect from her and went on to become a RITA finalist.

Early in her writing career, Quinn established herself as an author willing to try something different. In *Dare to Love* (1994), her third book published for Harlequin's Superromance line, drug abuse and prevention play an important part in the plot of the romance, as policewoman Andrea Parker trains Doug Avery, a former gang member himself, in the DARE program. At first, Doug doesn't think he is good enough for a woman like Andrea, but her love holds the promise of redemption.

Jacob's Girls (1995), the story of a single father raising triplet daughters, is a particular favorite with many of Quinn's readers. This beautifully written contemporary romance demonstrates Quinn's talent for incorporating gentle humor into a love story, as the hero, a handsome radio-show host whose wife has left him for her high-powered political career, searches for a mother for his daughters and finds a wife along the way. The sweetness and humor of this story of a friendship that gradually changes into something more romantic proved to be an irresistible combination that brought new readers to Quinn.

Another example of Quinn's use of modern issues that are not frequently found in series romances is in *Her Secret, His Child* (1999), Jamie Archer, the heroine and a former prostitute, has created a new life for herself and her daughter, Ashley; but when Kyle Radcliffe reappears in her life, her past may be exposed. With this book, Quinn gave herself the challenge of creating a love story in which the heroine is not the innocent woman readers are used to. Instead, Jamie must learn to separate sex from love. For this particular book, Quinn decided to forgo the traditional sex scenes altogether, which for a romance novel, can be risky.

The small town of Shelter Valley, Arizona, provides a geographic connection for several of Quinn's recent romances. Inspired by her husband's birthplace, South Haven, Michigan, Shelter Valley is a place where residents know and care about one another and where love lasts. Characters from one book in the Shelter Valley series often appear in small roles in other books, giving readers a strong connection to this warm and friendly place. A small town like Shelter Valley can seem too confining, as it does to Sam Montford, in *Sheltered in His Arms* (2001), who leaves because living up to his family's reputation as the town's founders proves to be difficult. However, the appeal of the place proves too strong to ignore as Sam returns home to the place and the ex-wife he loves.

Where the Road Ends, published in 2003, represented a change for the talented Quinn. The story of a mother's search for her missing child, *Where the Road Ends* was the first book by Quinn to be published by MIRA. This novel differs slightly from the author's previous, more traditional contemporary romances in that the plot centers more around the heroine, Amelia Wainscoat, and all of her relationships—mother, friend, member of the family. Quinn offers readers an element of romance in the story as Amelia finds help and emotional comfort from Brad Dorchester, the private detective she hires to help find her child.

With each new book, Quinn proves herself to be an accomplished and mesmerizing writer, creating strong characters, whose eventual redemption brings psychological depth to her works. From her books that feature an array of moral and ethical issues to those in which she smoothly blends women's fiction with suspense, Quinn always constructs emotionally involving and deeply compelling stories. Her books never fail to satisfy her readers and fans.

BIBLIOGRAPHY

Books: *Yesterday's Secrets.* Toronto: Harlequin, 1993; *McGillus V. Wright.* Toronto: Harlequin, 1994; *Dare to Love.* Toronto: Harlequin, 1994; *No Cure for Love.* Toronto: Harlequin, 1994; *Jacob's Girls.* Toronto: Harlequin, 1995; *The Birth Mother.* Toronto: Harlequin, 1996; *Another Man's Child.* Toronto: Harlequin, 1997; *Shotgun Baby.* Toronto: Harlequin, 1997; *Father Unknown.* Toronto: Harlequin, 1998; *The Heart of Christmas.* Toronto: Harlequin, 1998; *Her Secret, His Child.* Toronto: Harlequin, 1999; *My Babies and Me.* Toronto: Harlequin, 1999; *Maitland Maternity: Cassidy's Kids.* Toronto: Harlequin, 2000; *Tomorrow's Baby.* Toronto: Harlequin, 2000; *Becca's Baby.* Toronto: Harlequin, 2000; *My Sister, Myself.* Toronto: Harlequin, 2000; *White Picket Fences.* Toronto: Harlequin, 2000; *Sheltered in His Arms.* Toronto: Harlequin, 2001; *Just Around the Corner.* Toronto: Harlequin, 2001; *The Secret Son.* Toronto: Harlequin, 2002; *Trueblood Texas: The Rancher's Bride.* Toronto: Harlequin, 2002; *His Brother's Bride.* Toronto: Harlequin, 2002; *The Sheriff of Shelter Valley.* Toronto: Harlequin, 2002; *Born in the Valley.* Toronto: Harlequin, 2003; *Where the Road Ends.* Toronto: MIRA, 2003; *For the Children.* Toronto: Harlequin, 2003; *Nothing Sacred.* Toronto: Harlequin, 2004; *Street Smart.* Toronto: MIRA, 2004; *What Daddy Doesn't Know.* Toronto: Harlequin, 2004; *Somebody's Baby.* Toronto: Harlequin, 2005; *Hidden.* Toronto: MIRA, 2005; *A Child's Wish.* Toronto: Harlequin, 2006; *In Plain Sight.* Toronto: MIRA, 2006; *Merry Christmas Babies.* Toronto: Harlequin, 2006.
Novellas: "Gabe's Special Delivery" in *Valentine Babies.* Toronto: Harlequin, 2000; "Beth" in *Trueblood Christmas.* Toronto: Harlequin, 2002; "A Second Chance" in *From Here to Maternity.* Toronto: Harlequin, 2006.

JOANNE HAMILTON-SELWAY

FRANCIS RAY

Francis Ray. Photo by William Ray Photography. Courtesy of Francis Ray.

While growing up on her father's farm near the tiny town of Richland, Texas, with its population of almost five hundred at the time, it never occurred to young Francis Ray to become a novelist. In fact, the desire to write didn't surface until adulthood, when, in 1988, she finished reading her third Kathleen Woodiwiss romance. Ray became inspired, and within three years, she had sold her first novel.

After her first book was published, Ray lost her father, McClinton Radford, to cancer. She recalls, "He was so happy to see me published." Her mother, Verona, became a licensed vocational nurse after Ray suffered a serious injury at the age of eight. It was the beginning of a career her mother would continue for nearly forty years. To honor her parents, Ray dedicated her novel, *Fallen Angel* to them. *Fallen Angel* (1993) was reissued in 2003 as *Someone to Love Me.* In this novel, Michelle Grant is a highly successful Dallas real estate agent, and the brunt of a jealous rumor that the young, attractive realtor slept her way to the top. She suddenly finds herself bidding on a hot property against a new, equally skilled opponent, Brad Jamison, who happens to be an old flame from her past. Michelle must struggle to overcome the sordid rumor as well as her own ambivalence about renewing the romance. Brad, whose feelings for Michelle are stronger than ever, doesn't know what to believe, which adds tension to their slow-simmering relationship. Ray's combination of strong, believable characters and effective conflict enhance an already entertaining plot.

Ray says the appeal of the romance genre lies in "the idea of couples remaining faithful once committed; the monogamous relationships and high morals; the ability of the hero/heroine to work through problems; and of course, the happy endings." She considers it crucial to get to know her characters thoroughly before she begins to write about them and loves to see them come alive on the page. Ray describes her writing as "mainstream," but all of her stories have a strong measure of romance.

Ray finds that her stories originate with the characters as often as the plots. She comments, "It's a toss-up. I'm just pleased when it all comes together and solidifies in my mind." She prefers to work from a synopsis proportionate to the size of the piece, ranging in length from a few pages for a novella to several pages for a novel.

When Ray experiences writer's block, she attributes the cause to not knowing the story and characters well enough: "My characters can be very stubborn when I'm trying to get them down on paper. If I'm actually in the process of writing the story, I try to write through it [the block] or discuss the problem with another writer. Usually the reason is that I've taken a wrong turn in the story or written out of character." Regarding the source of her inspiration Ray confesses, "I wish I knew; then perhaps I could nurture it."

Core values are the foundation of Ray's books. She says, "Hopefully in every book you'll see the recurrence of core values, fighting for what you want no matter the odds, the healing power of love, and the importance of families." This is evident in her heroes and heroines, who are driven and determined individuals, always willing to defy the odds to get what they want. Ray confides, "They are who I want to be one day."

Ray's preferred time setting for her novels is contemporary, although she has written a historical romance set in the Regency period (*The Bargain,* 1995). She muses, "If I had time, I'd love to do a sequel, then a medieval." In *The Bargain,* Alexandria Carstairs is determined to maintain her independence in a man's world, during an era when women were nothing more than ornaments or chattel. The rebellious Alexandria sheds petticoats for breeches, and manages the business side of her father's farm. She's perfectly happy with her single life and unconventional ways, such as having a pet wolf, until she discovers that she had been promised to marry Thorne Blakemore, the dashing Earl of Grayson, in a contract her father had signed a decade before. Neither Alexandria nor Thorne wish to honor the contract, and they agree to strike a bargain to get out of it. Ultimately, however, love complicates the deal when they find themselves falling for each other. This delightful story demonstrates the talented Ray's versatility.

BET (Black Entertainment Television) based a made-for-TV movie on Ray's story *Incognito* (1997). Erin Corland, a corporate executive, gives testimony that puts a murderer in prison, but the murderer escapes and vows to kill both the judge in the case and Erin. She obviously needs a bodyguard, but the person her father picks for the position is none other than Jake Hunter, the man with whom she had a fleeting but memorable affair. Jake, a security expert, takes the job guarding Erin, the woman he can't get out of his mind. Their time together was short, but she made a lasting impression on his heart. The perfect blend of sensuality and suspense makes this thriller one that's not to be missed.

Ray says that most of her stories are set in the South and Southwest "because of the wonderful people and culture, the different terrain, and lifestyles." Her Graysons of New Mexico series (*Until There Was You,* 1999; *You and No Other,* 2005; *Dreaming of You,* 2006; *Irresistible You,* 2007) is set in Santa Fe. It chronicles the loves of the Grayson men, who were first introduced in Ray's novella "Until Christmas" in the 1998 anthology, *Winter Nights.* Luke Grayson, a former FBI agent, is the first of Ruth Grayson's four sons and destined, by his mother, to become the first to be married. After being repeatedly subjected to his scheming mother's awkward dating setups, he escapes her wedding crusade by heading for the family's retreat in New Mexico's Sangre de Cristo Mountains. His plans for peace and quiet are disrupted at the cabin doorstep when he comes face-to-gun-barrel with Dr. Catherine Stewart, who is already occupying the cozy lodge. Catherine, an accomplished child psychologist and UCLA professor, was invited by Luke's cousin to use the retreat as a quiet place to escape a stalker and to prepare for an upcoming lecture. Luke, however, wonders if this is yet another matchmaking attempt cooked up by the meddling matriarch. Gradually, the two warm to each other's presence as they share the romantic comforts of the secluded cabin. Lowering her defenses, Catherine confides in Luke about her stalker, and he suddenly realizes he would do anything to protect this woman. The strong family relationships, resourceful heroines, and engaging plots and wonderful love stories in this series are all quintessential Ray.

Her 2004 novel, *Like the First Time,* the first in her Invincible Women series (*Any Rich Man Will Do,* 2005; *In Another Man's Bed,* 2006), is set in Charleston, South Carolina. According to Ray, it was her most difficult to write: "There was a great deal of research on Charleston, including the history and culture; the making of bath and beauty products; and trying to balance the growing relationship of two couples and the deterioration of a third." The three heroines are friends on different paths who become business partners after two of them lose their jobs in a corporate downsizing. When shy, reserved Claire Bennett and vivacious Brooke Dunlap find themselves out of work, their friend, homemaker and empty nester Lorraine Averhart, suggests they launch Bliss, a business based on a line of scented candles and lotions using Claire's original creations. Lorraine, who helped her husband build a nationally known business, provides the capital; Claire provides the product line; and Brooke uses her feminine wiles and natural sales ability to develop Bliss into a resounding success. Along the way, Claire comes out of her shell and finds the courage to pursue her first love. The too-often superficial Brooke stops merely flirting and starts caring. And Lorraine learns independence and self-worth when her longtime marriage begins to unravel. Ray draws a parallel between the corporate growth of Bliss and the personal growth of the heroines as their lives change in ways they never expected. This ode to friendship and female empowerment is an excellent study in character development. Ray sends a message to women that anything is possible once they put their minds to it.

Unlike most romance authors, Ray also creates big, beautiful heroines in some of her stories. "The Wright Woman" from *A Whole Lotta Love* (2004) turns out to be size-20 Stephanie Wright, an assistant manager in a boutique. Her ample curves inspire wealthy Michael Dunbar, who has to get past his belief that women are always after his money before he can make their relationship work. In the 2005 anthology *Big Girls Don't Cry,* Ray's novella "His Everything Woman" is the story of a workaholic designer who hires a voluptuous woman to be his "wife." With both of these stories, Ray beautifully illustrates that love comes in all shapes and sizes.

Although most of Ray's characters are African American, there is universality to her writing that crosses cultural boundaries. Her heroines face the problems women across the country deal with—unemployment, separation, divorce, and financial problems—but Ray's books are also imbued with the themes of hope and optimism.

For Ray, none of her novels have come easily: "Writing is a difficult process for me, so each one seems more challenging ..." The proverbial book that practically wrote itself hasn't occurred yet. Rays says, "I haven't had that pleasure, but I haven't given up hope." She adds that "the anthologies are usually fun and less stressful."

Ray finds that naming her favorite book from those she has written is difficult, but she lists two: *Forever Yours* (1994), the first novel of her romantic Taggert series (*Only Hers,* 1996; *Heart of the Falcon,* 1998; *Break Every Rule,* 1998), and her first novel, *The Turning Point* (1991). *The Turning Point* was reissued in 2004 as *Trouble Don't Last Always* in her Against the Odds series, which also includes *Somebody's Knocking at My Door* (2003).

In *Forever Yours,* heroine Victoria Chandler is caught in a dilemma. Her grandmother, who provided the venture capital for Victoria's successful lingerie boutiques, demands that Victoria either marry or face losing the business. Having been betrayed by love in the past, Victoria is unwilling to complicate her life with a husband. Her solution is to approach an old acquaintance, Kane Taggert, with a business proposal: she will pay him to marry her for one year. She doesn't realize that Kane has secretly loved her for many years, and he accepts her proposition on his own terms—not as a marriage of convenience, but as a chance to be with her forever. Kane is determined to get past Victoria's demons and defenses and show her what love is supposed to be. Ray deftly gets the point across that marriage can indeed be an equal partnership.

In the Holt Medallion–nominated *The Turning Point,* Lilly Crawford escapes her abusive marriage and heads for Texas, where she is hired to be the caregiver to Adam Wakefield, a once-successful neurosurgeon who was blinded in a carjacking. Their initial relationship is one of hurt, mistrust, anger, and bitterness. However, in time, the two begin to care for each other, and a mutual healing occurs. Lilly finally experiences true love and tenderness, and Adam discovers that his blindness only ended his career, not his purpose. Ray's sensitive portrayal of the two victims is frank and realistic. The reader can feel the emotions of loss and betrayal experienced by characters, contrasted with the cathartic effect of love.

Ray also uses *The Turning Point* as an opportunity to help women who have been victims of domestic violence rebuild their lives, through her *Turning Point* Legal Fund, which debuted at the release event for the novel. The fund receives regular contributions from, among others, the proceeds of Ray's books.

Following her mother's example as a caregiver, Ray pursued a bachelor's degree in nursing from Texas Woman's University. She divides her time between writing and working as a school nurse practitioner with the Dallas Independent School District in Dallas, Texas, where she lives with her husband, William, and their daughter, Carolyn.

BIBLIOGRAPHY

Books: *The Turning Point.* New York: Kensington, 1991; *Fallen Angel.* New York: Kensington, 1993; *Forever Yours.* New York: Kensington, 1994; *Undeniable.* New York: Kensington, 1995; *The Bargain.* New York: Kensington, 1995; *Only Hers.* New York: Kensington, 1996; *Incognito.* New York: Kensington, 1997; *Silken Betrayal.* New York: Kensington, 1997; *Heart of the Falcon.* New York: Kensington, 1998; *Break Every Rule.* New York: Kensington, 1998; *Until There Was You.* New York: BET, 1999; *Rosie's Curl and Weave.* New York: St. Martin's Press, 1999; *I Know Who Holds Tomorrow.* New York: St. Martin's Press, 2002; *Somebody's Knocking at My Door.* New York: St. Martin's Press, 2003; *Rockin' Around That Christmas Tree.* New York: St. Martin's Press, 2003 (written with Donna Hill); *Like the First Time.* New York: St. Martin's Press, 2004; *You and No Other.* New York: St. Martin's Press, 2005; *Any Rich Man Will Do.* New York: St. Martin's Press, 2005; *Dreaming of You.* New York: St. Martin's Press, 2006; *In Another Man's Bed.* New York: St. Martin's Press, 2006; *Irresistible You.* New York: St. Martin's Press, 2007.

Novellas: "Sarah's Miracle" in *Spirit of the Season.* New York: Kensington, 1994; "Until Christmas" in *Winter Nights.* New York: Kensington, 1998; "A Matter of Trust" in *Della's House of Style.* New York: St. Martin's Press, 2000; "Sweet Temptation" in *Welcome to Leo's.* New York:

St. Martin's Press, 2000; "Southern Comfort" in *Going to the Chapel.* New York: St. Martin's Press, 2001; "The Wish" in *Gettin' Merry.* New York: St. Martins' Press, 2002; "Strictly Business" in *Living Large.* New York: Penguin, 2003; "The Wright Woman" in *Whole Lotta Love.* New York: Penguin, 2004; "Blind Date" in *Let's Get It On.* New York: St. Martin's Press, 2004; "His Everything Woman" in *Big Girls Don't Cry.* New York: Signet, 2005; "Then Sings My Soul" In *How Sweet the Sound.* New York: Steeple Hill, 2005; "A Chocolate Affair" in *Chocolate Kisses.* New York: Penguin, 2006.

SANDRA VAN WINKLE, SHELLEY MOSLEY, AND SHANNON PRESCOTT

JACLYN REDING

Jaclyn Reding wanted to be a writer for nearly as long as she can remember. As a child, she was obsessed with the children's fiction character Harriet the Spy. She created a spy tool belt for herself and would hide in her brothers' closets, spying on them and writing everything they did in her journal. Although her siblings might not have appreciated their sister's "espionage" efforts at the time, Reding's early efforts at writing certainly paid off in the long run.

Reding was born Jaclyn Adamowicz in 1966 and raised in northeastern Ohio. Her parents were first- and second-generation Americans whose families emigrated from Poland to the United States in the early 1900s. She holds a bachelor's degree in English history and literature from Arizona State University. Reding says, "I have always been fascinated by how people lived in history—what they did, what their everyday life was like. I took that fascination and turned it to researching and then writing my own stories about characters of my own creation in history."

Different things can inspire different people to become writers. Sometimes all it takes is a friendly nudge to push someone in the right direction. At least for Reding that's all it took. She recalls, "I started writing seriously after I attended the local Romance Writers of America conference in Phoenix, Arizona. I'd read about the conference in the newspaper … my husband, who had listened to me talk about writing 'someday' for too long, dared me to go. I haven't looked back since." Both her accountant husband, Steve, whom she married in 1984, and her sons, Joshua and Calum, enthusiastically support her choice of career.

Reding began her writing career in earnest during her lunch breaks at the insurance agency where she worked as an adjuster. By the age of 23, she was writing for publication, and she sold her first novel by the time she was 26. Soon, she became a full-time writer, realizing her goal "to write stories that readers will enjoy and remember long after they've closed the book."

Reding writes historical romances in a variety of styles—sometimes humorous, sometimes poignant, and sometimes dark. This keeps the process fresh and interesting to both her as an author and her audience. Her preferred setting is Scotland, and the time period she most enjoys is the Georgian era. She frequently uses the themes of perseverance and self-discovery, though she adds, "I like to think that each story has something new to offer the reader." She also weaves an element of mystery into many of her stories and would like to one day try her hand at mystery writing.

Reding's first book, *Deception's Bride* (1993), begins in her beloved Scotland. Chelsea Estwyck leaves her feckless fiancé and journeys to London, where she looks for her father, who lives there in exile. During her search, she meets a handsome stranger who captures both her fancy and her favor. *Deception's Bride* caught the attention of the public, and Reding's career as a romance writer began.

Tempting Fate (1995) became the first book of the Restoration Rogues trilogy. Set in 1658 Ireland, Mara Despenser has lost her castle and is determined to get it back at any cost. Unfortunately, this involves clever scheming and marriage to the new owner of the castle, Hadrian Ross (a nod to Reding's editor, Hilary Ross). In *Chasing Dreams* (1995), Cassia Montfort faces charges for the alleged murder of her abusive father. She hates him enough to kill him but claims that she's innocent. To make matters worse, Cassia is the sole heir to his fortune, which suggests that she has a motive for murder. Rolfe Brodrigan is assigned by the king to protect her and uncover the truth. The third book of the trilogy, *Stealing Heaven* (1996), is set in 1666 and showcases Reding's humor and wit. Gillian Forrester will do anything to flee the men who have abducted her. They are intent on taking her to Gretna Green, where she will be forced to marry a nefarious man. Unfortunately, she hits her head during her attempt to escape. Dante Tremaine, the "Rakehell Earl," finds Gillian on a country road. He rescues her, only to discover that she has amnesia. The Restoration Rogues series established Reding as a writer who creates smart, feisty, courageous women who are a match for any man.

In 1997, Reding began her Regency Rogues quartet with *White Heather,* the story of Robert, or Lord Devonbrook, a rake, rogue, art dealer, and British missions officer who loses almost everything he has, including his sight, in a fire and moves to Scotland. Robert takes up residence in an isolated castle where his self-induced exile is interrupted by Catriona, a crofter's daughter, who sneaks into the castle library to read his books. He discovers Catriona's visits because of her unique scent and his newly augmented sense of smell. Robert, now Laird of Rosmorigh, is frustrated by his blindness and has to teach himself even the most basic tasks in order to survive. Catriona, really an heiress in hiding, loves the new laird despite his disability.

Book two in the Regency Rogues quartet, *White Magic* (1998), has Noah Edenhall discovering his best friend's body. The only clue is a "Dear John" letter signed "A" in an envelope with Lady Augusta Brierley's seal on it, which the dead man clutches in his hand. Noah confronts the bluestocking Augusta, who has lived her life defying society, preferring her books and astronomical observations to the company of people. *White Magic* is as much about this brilliant woman's attempt to be recognized by the all-male scientific community as it is the hunt for the woman who actually sent the ill-fated note.

White Knight (1999), the third "Regency Rogue" novel, was written by Reding during the time of Princess Diana Spencer's untimely death. Reding's heroine, Lady Grace Ledysthorpe, has attributes of the late princess, but Reding granted her the "happily ever after" ending she felt Diana deserved. Lady Grace, who grew up on fairy tales and fantasies, finds herself in an arranged marriage with the stern knight, Christian Wycliffe, the Marquess Knighton, who refuses to allow her to have any children. Like the real Diana, Lady Grace suffers a cold, loveless relationship with her husband. Psychologically wounded, Lady Grace flees to Castle

Skynegal, her ancestral home, an ancient keep in ruins on the northwest coast of Scotland. There, she is guarded by a flock of fabled white-winged birds. A good-hearted woman, Lady Grace takes up the cause of the villagers, who have been victimized by an unscrupulous landlord. In the meantime, Christian searches for his missing wife, anxious to bring her back to England. With her independence, courage, and concern for others, Reding's Lady Grace is a heroine in the truest sense of the word.

The last book in the quartet, *White Mist* (2000), takes place in the Scottish Hebrides. Lady Eleanor Wycliffe, posing as Nell Harte, accepts a position as governess of viscount Gabriel MacFeagh's mute, estranged daughter, Juliana. Rumor has it that the viscount, also known as the "Devil of Dunevin," is the victim of an ancient curse. Typical of Reding's strong, brave heroines, Nell is not frightened away by the colorful stories and gossip about Gabriel and does her best to make Juliana's life better. In the Regency Rogues series, as in the earlier Restoration Rogues, Reding makes a strong case for female empowerment and its positive effect on a relationship.

Trying her hand at a novella-length work, Reding penned "Written in the Stars," set in Regency-era Scotland, for the *In Praise of Younger Men* (2001) anthology. As part of a family curse, Harriet Drynam has to find a man to marry. According to her psychic aunt, if Harriet doesn't manage to do so by her next birthday, she'll have a "miserably ever after" life. Tristan Carmichael, war hero and Harriet's true love, offers to marry her, but she refuses. Harriet doesn't want to ruin his life with her family curse. This welcome addition to the romance genre's younger-man theme (even though Tristan is only a "few seconds" younger than Harriet) features a clever paranormal twist.

Reding used a light touch for *The Pretender* (2002), the first book in the Highland Heroes series, a humorous novel about Lady Elizabeth Drayton, whose father, the Duke of Sudeleigh, discovers that she's the author of popular writings on female equality and sends her and her sister to live with her aunt. Unbeknownst to Elizabeth, the siblings are actually headed for Lord Purfoyle's Scottish estate, where she is to marry this aging nobleman. On the way to the arranged wedding, Elizabeth's sister, Isabella, confesses to being part of this terrible plot. When their carriage breaks down, a strong, handsome man helps them, and Elizabeth decides she would rather marry this commoner than wed the ancient nobleman her father has chosen for her. After she tricks the stranger into sleeping with her, he marries her. Elizabeth has no idea that her new husband is actually Douglas MacKinnon, a Scottish lord. To turn the tables on her for her blatant manipulation, Douglas allows Elizabeth to continue thinking that he's a poor commoner.

Reding considers her 2002 novel *The Adventurer,* the second book of the Highland Heroes series, her hardest to write. She started the novel just after the 9/11 World Trade Center attack, which she witnessed while in New York City delivering a manuscript to her publisher. She recalls, "I had a hard time sitting down to write a happy story after that." Near the completion of the novel, Reding fell on an icy driveway and broke her wrist. She says, "All in all, writing that book could be called an adventure in itself." Ironically, *The Adventurer* is one of Reding's funniest books. During her Paris holiday, Lady Isabella Drayton, the book's heroine, dines in Versailles with the king. While there, a mysterious man gives her a necklace with a fabled crystal and tells her to guard it with her life and let it lead her to "the real MacAoidh" (Reding's version of the Real McCoy). As she sails back to England, Jacobite privateers commandeer the ship. When they see the ancient clan charm stone in her necklace, they kidnap Isabella and take her to the isolated fortress of Cape Wrath, Scotland. The fortress is headquarters for Calum MacKay, "The Adventurer," who is the rescuer of Highlanders taken prisoner by the British. Isabella's feisty attitude wins the hearts of Calum and his band of "hairy Scottish pirates." However, at the same time, the man her parents have chosen to be her husband is searching Scotland for his missing fiancée. In this book, Reding created a wonderful mix of humor, history, and, of course, romance.

The Secret Gift (2003), although not part of the Highland Heroes series, forwards the story of Lady Isabella's magical necklace to the present and is Reding's first contemporary romance. Filled with scrumptious details of Scottish life, this superb, finely textured story of an inheritance lost—and found—features Graeme Arthur Frederick MacKenzie, who becomes both Viscount Kintail and the Marquess of Waltham when his mother and uncle die on the same day. Attracted to his titles—and the money that goes with them—women stoop to all sorts of trickery to make his acquaintance. Isabella Elizabeth "Libby" MacKay Hutchinson works in an antiquarian bookstore in Manhattan. When she inherits her mother's Victorian house in Massachusetts, Libby finds an unusual crystal necklace hidden in an aged chest. Also in the chest is a photograph of a man Libby doesn't recognize. Written on the back is simply "Wrath Village, Scotland." Intrigued by her mother's secret, Libby goes to Wrath Village and ends up at Graeme's remote castle, where he drives her away with his shotgun. However, when Libby discovers that the key to her past is in this very castle, not even Graeme can keep her at bay. Although the characters in this book live in the modern world, Reding gives them the same traits as their predecessors—grit, determination, and ingenuity. The fine writing in *The Secret Gift* was recognized by the Romance Writers of America when it became a finalist for the RITA.

The Second Chance (2006), sequel to *The Secret Gift,* also has a contemporary setting. Flora MacCallum, a widow with three children, feels as though she can never be truly happy again. However, when her friend asks her to take over a bed-and-breakfast on the Massachusetts shore, Flora accepts the offer. Her new home, new life, and new friends help the healing process, but it's not until she meets composer Gavin Matheson—who has lost his wife, son, and muse—that she finds love again. Hope is the dominant theme of this book, and Reding sends the message in a powerful way.

The romance genre attracted Reding because of the positive, uplifting messages the novels contain and the way they portray healthy relationships between men and women. The characters are allowed to grow through their experiences, and the stories guarantee a happy ending. "What's not to like in that?" Reding comments.

It usually takes from six to nine months for Reding to write a book. The inspiration for her stories usually begins with the characters. She observes, "I love writing characters [that] have to face sometimes seemingly insurmountable obstacles to get to their happy ending. Triumph through the strength of love just does it for me more than anything else." Both her heroes and heroines possess honor and strength, despite their human flaws. She finds story inspiration everywhere, from news articles to interesting facts about fascinating places that she discovers during research. Even songs can summon her muse, as was the case with *White Heather.*

To Reding, the greatest appeal of the writing process is the way she feels "when it's really working" and she can't get the words down fast enough. Reding says, "When the words are flying onto the page, I don't stop to look up a different word for 'slowly' in the thesaurus, because I'm just so anxious to get the story onto the page." Reding considers writer's block to be an occasional lapse in creativity, when she can't decide where the plot should go next. Her solution is to work through it by reading or finding some quiet time to really concentrate and focus on the story until her creativity returns.

Jaclyn Reding has brought Scotland to life for a generation of readers. Unlike many of the other writers who create tales set in that country, she doesn't rely on Scottish accents and men in kilts to set the stage for her Highland romances. Her pristine research skills make her historical romances vivid with details of the time and place. Like her heroines, Reding stubbornly adheres to the highest standards in everything she does, so when she writes a book, the results never fail to enchant.

BIBLIOGRAPHY

Books: *Deception's Bride.* New York: Berkley, 1993; *Tempting Fate.* New York: Topaz, 1995; *Chasing Dreams.* New York: Topaz, 1995; *Stealing Heaven.* New York: Topaz, 1996; *White Heather.* New York: Signet, 1997; *White Magic.* New York: Signet, 1998; *White Knight.* New York: Signet, 1999; *White Mist.* New York: Signet, 2000; *The Pretender.* New York: Signet, 2002; *The Adventurer.* New York: Signet, 2002; *The Secret Gift.* New York: Signet, 2003; *The Second Chance.* New York: Signet, 2006.

Novella: "Written in the Stars" in *In Praise of Younger Men.* New York: Signet, 2001.

SHELLEY MOSLEY AND SANDRA VAN WINKLE

EMILIE RICHARDS

Emilie Richards. Courtesy of Emilie Richards.

For Emilie Richards, no subject is taboo for her novels. From a disillusioned preacher (*Dragonslayer,* 1993) to an infertile man (*The Trouble with Joe,* 1994) to a boy with autism (*The Parting Glass,* 2003), Richards courageously explores all sides of the issue. She tackles these problems in such a sensitive way that they become an integral part of the story without overpowering it.

Richards, a RITA winner and a *USA Today* best-selling author, was born in Bethesda, Maryland, in 1948. Her parents. John and Emilie Richards, owned and operated a roofing company. She spent her childhood in St. Petersburg, Florida, and later attended Florida State University, where she earned a bachelor's degree in American studies, with a minor in music. She also holds a master's degree in family development from Virginia Tech. Richards is married to a minister, Michael McGee, and they have four children: Shane Michael, Jessamyn Emilie, Galen Timothy, and Brendan Carlyle.

Before becoming a writer in 1983, Richards worked in a number of humanitarian fields. She was a volunteer for VISTA, a therapist in a mental-health center, a part-time counselor, and a parent services coordinator for a Head Start program. Although she always enjoyed writing, she never seriously considered doing it professionally. Richards recalls, "Being a writer seemed like a lofty, unattainable goal until I was old enough to realize that trying, even with the possibility of failure, was better than the alternative." To spend hours every day living in her imagination is Richards's greatest reward as a writer.

Richards had always been interested in human interaction, the nuances of relationships, social issues, and moral dilemmas—in her words, "the things that separate us all and bring us together." She says that "romances were a wonderful place to begin" to write about these interests.

Over the years, Richards has seen her writing style evolve from romances into women's fiction, which has more characters and more story lines. An example of this is *The Parting Glass* (2003), the sequel to *Whiskey Island* (2000). The Donahue sisters, fifth-generation Irish Americans, are each at turning points in their lives. Megan, who runs the family's Whiskey Island Saloon, is about to be married. Casey is adjusting to being a newlywed … and a mother-to-be. The third sister, Peggy, quits pursuing her dream to be a doctor when she discovers that Kieran, her son, is autistic. The sisters' lives change dramatically when a distant relative in Ireland, Irene, asks the siblings to solve the riddle of her father's death, which had occurred 75 years earlier in Cleveland. Megan takes on the role of researcher, and, in exchange for room and board, Peggy flies to Ireland with Kiernan to care for Irene, whose health is failing. Irene's physician, widower Finn O'Malley, isn't sure of Peggy's intentions, but despite his distrust, he's attracted to her. Of course, their homes are an ocean apart, and this adds to the conflict. Richards has deftly crafted a lovely tale of an old mystery, a new love, and a hopeful future.

Richards's heroes and heroines share one common trait: intelligence. She hopes that this is a reflection of herself and adds, "My characters always grow and change, and I hope that's true of me as well." Richards frequently uses the theme of attaining personal growth by overcoming obstacles.

With a minister for a husband, it's no surprise that Richards has used men of the cloth as heroes in her books. Thomas Stonehill, a street preacher who has lost his faith, is the hero of *Dragonslayer* (1993). He no longer believes in himself, romantic love, or even God. Although cynical, jaded, and agnostic, Thomas continues to preach in "the Corners" to the gangs, the homeless, and the people the rest of the world has forgotten. Idealistic free-clinic nurse practitioner, Garnet Anthony, has somehow alienated herself from the gangs who live at the Corners. Thomas's initial instincts toward the feisty Garnet are protective ones, and through her persistence, tenacity, and can-do attitude, he eventually rediscovers his heart … and his soul. Richards's gritty, yet touching tale was awarded a RITA in 1994.

Unlike Thomas Stonehill of *Dragonslayer*, Sam Kinkaid, the hero of *Endless Chain* (2005), is happy to be a minister. There is no questioning his faith. He has a devoted congregation in rural Toms Brook, Virginia. His flock stays loyal until Sam makes the decision to integrate members of the rapidly growing Hispanic community into the church. When the new church sexton, an enigmatic woman named Elisa Martinez, enters the picture, Sam realizes how estranged from his standoffish, long-time fiancé he has become. However, as Sam gets closer to Elisa, she tries to keep her distance, hiding a secret she doesn't want to share—that she's a Guatemalan refugee. Richards, once again, deals with tough issues: prejudice in the Christian community; religious and political persecution; and the bravery of people who are willing to endanger their own lives for their beliefs. In this story, Richards parallels the contemporary tale of Elisa and Sam with that of lovers Sarah and Jeremiah, who risk everything to shelter a runaway slave in 1853. Without being didactic, Richards puts forth the message that social issues today need to be dealt with as courageously as they were back in the nineteenth century. Although this continuation of Richards's Shenandoah Album series packs an emotional wallop, it is sprinkled with humorous moments, such as when the delightful ladies of the church's quilting circle take the stage.

Her characters share other interests of Richards's that turn up frequently in her novels, including quilting, gardening, and traveling. The secondary characters of *Endless Chain* belong to a quilting circle, and Richards uses the symbol of a wedding ring quilt in *Wedding Ring* (2004), which is the story of three generations of women, their unhappy loves, and their relationships to each other.

Richard's novels are often set in Virginia "because it has so many different settings within one beautiful state: mountains, shore, rolling hills of horse country, the fertile Shenandoah Valley." Other locales used as settings for her novels include Australia (*Beautiful Lies,* 1999) and Louisiana (*Iron Lace,* 1996; *Rising Tides,* 1997). Her women's fiction, although contemporary, often contains connections to the past, from antebellum America to 1960s America.

For Richards, stories can originate from settings, but characters are often her inspiration, too. She believes that story inspiration is everywhere, and that writers just "have to pay attention." Richards says, "Sometimes it's something as mundane as a title." Her philosophy on writer's block is brutally simple: "If I was a teacher or a bank teller, I'd still be expected to work." On days when her motivation to write is flagging, she either writes anyway or spends time doing research or tending to the other business matters of a full-time writer.

Whichever book Richards is currently working on is the one she considers the hardest to write: "Giving birth to a book is like giving birth to a baby. Once it's over, you forget how difficult it was to bring into the world." For Richards, her easiest book to write was 2004's *Wedding Ring.* She says, "I just fell in love with the characters, and they felt so real to me they guided my hand." She is reluctant to choose a favorite novel because it would be "like choosing between her children." Richards says that in general, her favorite book is "the one I just finished." She concedes that she is particularly pleased with her foray into women's fiction, 1996's *Iron Lace,* because "I had wanted to tell that story for a long time." *Iron Lace* is the tale of a dying New Orleans matriarch with many dark secrets, which she chooses to divulge for her own reasons to an African American journalist.

In 2005, with *Blessed Is the Busybody,* Richards turned her talents to the field of cozy mysteries. As in her romances and women's fiction, she drew on her own experiences, this time making the heroine, Aggie Sloan-Wilcox, a minister's wife. Even as Richards expands her writing to other categories, she remains loyal to the romance genre, saying, "I believe in the power of love, in the importance of commitment, in people struggling to overcome their difficulties so they can build a life together."

BIBLIOGRAPHY

Books: *Sweet Georgia Gal.* New York: Silhouette, 1985; *Gilding the Lily.* New York: Silhouette, 1985; *The Unmasking.* Toronto: Harlequin, 1985; *Brendan's Song.* New York: Silhouette, 1985; *Sweet Sea Spirit.* Toronto: Harlequin, 1986; *Sweet Mockingbird's Call.* New York: Silhouette, 1986; *Sweet Mountain Magic.* Toronto: Harlequin, 1986; *Lady of the Night.* Toronto: Harlequin, 1986; *Angel and the Saint.* Toronto: Harlequin, 1986; *Season of Miracles.* Toronto: Harlequin, 1986; *Something So Right.* Toronto: Harlequin, 1986; *Bayou Midnight.* New York: Silhouette, 1987; *Sweet Homecoming.* Toronto: Harlequin, 1987; *Outback Nights.* New York: Silhouette, 1987; *Aloha Always.* Toronto: Harlequin, 1987; *From Glowing Embers.* New York: Silhouette, 1988; *All the Right Reasons.* Toronto: Harlequin, 1988; *Smoke Screen.* New York: Silhouette, 1988; *Rainbow Fire.* New York: Silhouette, 1989; *Island Glory.* New York: Silhouette, 1989; *Out of the Ashes.* New York: Silhouette, 1989; *The Way Back Home.* New York: Silhouette, 1990; *Fugitive.* New York: Silhouette, 1990; *Runaway.* New York: Silhouette, 1990; *All Those Years Ago.* Toronto: Harlequin, 1991; *Desert Shadows.* New York: Silhouette, 1991; *Twilight Shadows.* New York: Silhouette, 1991; *From* *a Distance.* New York: Silhouette, 1992; *One Perfect Rose.* Toronto: Harlequin, 1992; *Dragonslayer.* New York: Silhouette, 1993; *Somewhere Out There.* New York: Silhouette, 1993; *The Trouble with Joe.* New York: Silhouette, 1994; *Macdougall's Darling.* New York: Silhouette, 1995; *Iain Ross's Woman.* New York: Silhouette, 1995; *Duncan's Lady.* New York: Silhouette, 1995; *Woman without a Name.* New York: Silhouette, 1996; *Iron Lace.* Toronto: MIRA, 1996; *Once More with Feeling.* New York: Avon, 1996; *Twice Upon a Time.* New York: Avon, 1997; *Mail-Order Matty.* New York: Silhouette, 1997; *Rising Tides.* Toronto: MIRA, 1997; *A Classic Encounter.* Toronto: Harlequin, 1998; *Beautiful Lies.* Toronto: MIRA, 1999; *Good Time Man.* Toronto: Harlequin, 1999; *One Moment Past Midnight.* New York: Silhouette, 1999; *A Passionate Proposal.* Toronto: MIRA, 2000; *Whiskey Island.* Toronto: MIRA, 2000; *Fox River.* Toronto: MIRA, 2001; *Prospect Street.* Toronto: MIRA, 2002; *Wedding Ring.* Toronto: MIRA, 2004; *The Parting Glass.* Toronto: MIRA, 2003; *Endless Chain.* Toronto: MIRA, 2005; *Blessed Is the Busybody.* New York: Penguin, 2005; *Lover's Knot.* Toronto: MIRA, 2006.

Novellas: "Labor Dispute" in *Birds, Bees and Babies.* New York: Silhouette, 1990; "That Old Familiar Feeling" in *To the One I Love.* New York: Silhouette, 1993; "Naughty or Nice" in *Silhouette Christmas Stores.* Toronto: Harlequin, 1993; "A Stranger's Son" in *A Funny Thing Happened on the Way to the Delivery Room.* New York; Silhouette, 1997; "Billie Ray Wainwright" in *Southern Gentlemen.* Toronto: MIRA, 1998; "Nobody's Child" in *A Mother's Gift.* Toronto: Harlequin, 1998; "One Perfect Rose" in *Maybe This Time.* New York: Silhouette, 2003; "Hanging by a Thread" in *More Than Words.* Toronto: Harlequin, 2004.

SHELLEY MOSLEY AND SANDRA VAN WINKLE

EVELYN RICHARDSON

Evelyn Richardson. Courtesy of Evelyn Richardson.

B lame it on Jane Austen. At least that is the person whom author Evelyn Richardson credits for inspiring her own writing career. Like others before her, once Richardson discovered Austen's sterling prose and acerbic wit, she was hooked. Austen soon led to other writers, or as Richardson says, "one can only reread Austen so many times before one turns to Georgette Heyer, then to Clare Darcy; and by then, one is halfway down the slippery slope." Thus is a Regency author created.

Richardson, pseudonym for author Cynthia Johnson, was born in 1950 in Rochester, Minnesota. Her father, a plastic and reconstructive surgeon, was doing his residency at the Mayo Clinic at the time. Richardson's mother was a full-time homemaker, who instilled a love of reading and of libraries in all of her children. Her family soon moved to Illinois, and Richardson grew up in Rockford. While attending high school there, Richardson was introduced to and quickly became a devotee of Austen's books, not realizing at the time how much this interest in the author and her era would later influence Richardson's own life.

Richardson went on to Wellesley College, where she majored in French and English, concentrating mostly on late eighteenth- and early nineteenth-century literature in both languages. Richardson wrote her honors thesis on English novelist Fanny Burney while at Wellesley, and then later attended Simmons College, where she received her master of library science degree. After working a few years in different libraries, Richardson returned to academia to pursue studies in early nineteenth-century literature at Northwestern, where she received another master's degree, this time in English literature.

The younger Richardson had always enjoyed writing and even flirted with the idea of becoming an author. The older she got, the more Richardson realized she wasn't "quite as good" as she first thought. Deciding it was far more practical for her to get a so-called real job, Richardson became a reference librarian, since working in a library surrounded by books seemed like a good compromise in terms of her career goals. Ironically, it was the insecurity of being between library positions that Richardson says finally convinced her to take the plunge and begin writing her first Regency romance—"just to keep myself from going mad with worry about finding a job."

Once she had finished her first manuscript, Richardson began compiling a list of potential publishers. At first, Richardson thought she would target Walker and St. Martin's Press, since they published their Regency titles in hardcover, and she thought they had more cachet. So she sent off a synopsis and the first three chapters from her book to St. Martin's Press, and six weeks later, she received a form rejection letter. Richardson tried the same approach with Walker, with the same results.

Fortunately, just as Richardson was going through her submission trials and tribulations, a patron donated a "gazillion" paperback Regency novels to the library where she worked. After discovering a whole new potential market (the Regency publishers and readers) for her manuscript, Richardson sent it off to Fawcett and six weeks later received a familiar-looking rejection letter. Gathering up her resolve, Richardson sent another packet with her synopsis and the first three chapters of her book to Signet, and waited … and waited … and waited. When Richardson finally got up the nerve to call the publisher, she discovered they had lost the package. So they asked her to send it again, but this time, they asked for the full manuscript. "Guilt will make publishers do all kinds of things," Richardson recalls with amusement.

As Richardson was printing out a copy of her manuscript to send to Signet, she discovered "about a hundred corrections" she needed to make. Richardson recalls that since "this was before the days of spell-check," she nearly went crazy trying to fix the manuscript before she had to rush off to Europe for her sister's wedding. On the way back, Richardson stopped in New York City to visit the Signet offices: "They were terribly nice, and naturally, they hadn't made any sort of decision in that short of a time. But I tried to convey the impression that I was a businesslike sort of person."

A few months later, while she was working at the library reference desk, Richardson received a call from Signet asking if she would like a contract and if she could do two books for them: "I was so glad to have gotten one book done, I didn't even think beyond that, so I sort of sat dumbfounded as the editor explained [that] they wanted to be sure I was going to continue with Regencies and not veer off into science fiction or some other 'weird' genre. So there I was on the phone in the reference room agreeing to a contract—so much for anonymity and the carefully chosen pseudonym!" Richardson's first novel, *The Education of Lady Frances,* was published by Signet in 1989, and it became the first of her many sparkling, wonderfully witty Regency romances.

Richardson says that if there is one recurrent theme in her Regency-era novels, it is that she generally "returns to the plight of the independent, original, intelligent, and intellectually curious person caught in a society where fashion and social standing are the abiding preoccupations of his or her peers." She adds, "I examine how such a person comes to terms with being who they are and how they eventually find someone else who shares their values."

Several of Richardson's recent books provide excellent illustrations of this. For example, in *The Scandalous Widow* (2004), the book's heroine, Lady Catherine Granville, refuses to let her late husband's family tell her how to live her life. Catherine's dreams of opening a school for young ladies scandalizes her in-laws, since members of the *ton* were not suppose to engage in trade. Catherine could care less about her place in society; she wants to help girls develop their intellect and their sense of self-worth. Catherine's determination and plucky individuality are what first draws the book's hero, Lucian, the Marquess of Charlmont, to her. At first, he comes to admire her determination, and then to support her in achieving her goals.

Another good example of Richardson's brand of bright, principled heroines is Lady Harriet Fareham, in *My Wayward Lady* (1997), who demonstrates her own belief in the value of a good education by choosing to tutor so-called fallen women in reading and writing. The book's hero, Lord Adrian Chalfont, after indulging in a night of pleasure at Mrs. Lovington's Temple of Venus, stumbles across Harriet with the establishment's employees. His life is forever changed once he realizes that Harriet, and not the eminently refined Alicia De Villiers, is the only woman for him. Cecelia Manners, from *A Lady of Talent* (2005), is yet another of Richardson's original, intelligent heroines who refuses to be limited to the occupations society at that time considered proper for ladies. She takes up a brush to earn her living as an artist, thus attracting the attention of the book's hero, Sebastian, the Earl of Charrington.

One of the things about the writing process that appeals most to Richardson is the research involved in creating her stories: "I just love the words, and I love the research. I could spend hours on both, and I frequently do in order to soothe myself enough to write." Richardson enjoys the research involved in her work, but *A Foreign Affair* (2003) proved to be one of the more difficult books she has written, simply because the book's unusual setting was quite challenging. Richardson recalls, "It was about the Congress of Vienna, and the politics were so incredibly byzantine that it was difficult to keep them straight in my own mind, let alone keep them simple enough not to lose the reader's interest." While the task of neatly integrating a romance into politically tangled and scandal-ridden Vienna was a bold move for Richardson, she succeeded admirably with *A Foreign Affair*. Not only did Richardson beautifully capture the mood of Vienna at the time, but she also creatively used the political intrigues being played out in the city as an important source of tension in the book's plot.

In her expertly crafted Regency romances, Richardson has taken readers from London to Paris to Vienna and even to the Pyrenees. She has not only used the much favored glittering *ton* as a setting, but has also introduced the art world, the world of politics, and even the military world of the Regency era into her stories. Richardson has combined her subtle, yet sharp sense of wit, gift for nuanced characterization, and passion for history into stories that celebrate the reforming power of love and the innate strength of women. Jane Austen would be proud.

BIBLIOGRAPHY

Books: *The Education of Lady Frances.* New York: Signet, 1989; *Miss Cresswell's London Triumph.* New York: Signet, 1990; *The Nabob's Ward.* New York: Signet, 1991; *The Bluestocking's Dilemma.* New York: Signet, 1992; *The Willful Widow.* New York: Signet, 1994; *Lady Alex's Gamble.* New York: Signet, 1995; *The Reluctant Heiress.* New York: Signet, 1996; *My Wayward Lady.* New York: Signet, 1997; *The Gallant Guardian.* New York: Signet, 1998; *My Lady Nightingale.* New York: Signet, 1999; *Lord Harry's Daughter.* New York: Signet, 2001; *Fortune's Lady.* New York: Signet, 2002; *A Foreign Affair.* New York: Signet, 2003; *The Scandalous Widow.* New York: Signet, 2004; *A Lady of Talent.* New York: Signet, 2005

JOHN CHARLES

J. D. ROBB. *See* Nora Roberts

NORA ROBERTS

Nora Roberts. Courtesy of Nora Roberts.

F or millions of readers, Nora Roberts *is* romance. Her books, written both as Nora Roberts and J. D. Robb, have appeared on every major best-seller list in America, including the top spot on the *New York Times* Best Seller List. A powerful and prolific literary pacesetter, Roberts is more than a best-selling author—she's a megaselling author. Roberts' first book to make the *New York Times* Best Seller List was *Genuine Lies* in 1991. Since then, she's had 115 *New York Times* best sellers. In fact, according to *Publisher's Weekly,* Nora Roberts has written more best-sellers than anyone else in the world. There are more than 280 million of her more than 160 titles in print all over the globe. During the last 22 years, an average of 21 books written by Roberts were sold every minute. Roberts has won an amazing 16 RITA awards from the Romance Writers of America, and she is the only author who has twice been inducted into RWA's Hall of Fame. Honors and awards aside, what matters most to her readers is the simple fact that Roberts is an exceptional storyteller.

Roberts was born Eleanor Marie Robertson in 1950, in Silver Spring, Maryland, to Eleanor (Harris) and Bernard Edward Robertson. Roberts's father, a stagehand and a movie projectionist, started a lighting company in 1964. He was the firm's president, and Roberts's mother was vice president. The youngest of five children, Roberts was the only girl in the

---

also writing as J. D. Robb

family. She married Ronald Aufdem-Brinke in 1968, right after high school. Aufdem-Brinke worked at his father's sheet metal business, and she worked as a secretary in Keedysville, Maryland. After their marriage ended, Roberts married her second husband, Bruce Wilder, a carpenter who now owns a bookstore in Boonsboro, Kentucky, which features Civil War books as well as novels autographed by his wife. Roberts has two sons, Jason and Dan; one granddaughter, and one grandson.

It was because of bad weather in 1979 that Roberts became a writer. Actually, it was a combination of a blizzard, two young sons, and a week's worth of cabin fever. Although this doesn't sound like an ideal situation for a writer to pen her first novel, it worked for Roberts, who used writing as a means to calm her frayed nerves. She wrote this first effort, as well as five more manuscripts, in longhand. Robert's blizzard-based excursion into writing paid off—her first book, *Irish Thoroughbred,* came out in 1981, and she took the publishing world by storm. *Irish Thoroughbred* became the first of 100 novels Roberts would write for Silhouette and Harlequin.

Perhaps being around so many men her whole life is one of the things that enables Roberts do such an exceptionally fine job of writing a realistic masculine point of view. In the Chesapeake Bay Saga (*Sea Swept,* 1998; *Rising Tides,* 1998; *Inner Harbor,* 1999; *Chesapeake Blue,* 2002), four boys adopted by Ray and Stella Quinn grow up to be strong alpha males, committed to their family. Although The Chesapeake Bay Saga (also known as The Quinn Brothers series) was initially intended as a trilogy, public demand for "Seth's story" led Roberts to write the fourth book, *Chesapeake Blue.* In this novel, Seth Quinn has returned home from Europe after a five-year absence as a world-renowned artist. Tired of being away from home, he's ready to settle down in the same town as the three older step-brothers who helped raise him. Seth meets pulchritudinous, self-reliant Druscilla "Dru" Whitcomb Banks and falls for her almost immediately. Life couldn't be better, but then, a person from Seth's past begins blackmailing him again. Seth feels powerless, until, in a moving show of solidarity, his brothers come to the rescue. This insightful, poignant story has lots of Roberts's trademark humor and just a touch of the paranormal, when Ray speaks to his adopted clan from beyond the grave.

Roberts's heroines are resilient, resourceful, competent women who are always able to solve their own problems—finding a man worthy of them is just the icing on the cake. All three sisters in Roberts's aptly named Three Sister Island trilogy (*Dance Upon the Air,* 2001; *Heaven and Earth,* 2001; *Face the Fire,* 2002) have an inner strength, something they must draw on to break an age-old curse. In *Dance Upon the Air,* Nell Channing is on the run from her abusive husband, but her reluctance to share information intrigues Zack Todd, the sheriff of Three Sisters Island. During the course of the book, Nell is transformed from a helpless victim to a courageous survivor, and this volume becomes a paean to female empowerment. Deputy Sheriff Ripley Todd of *Heaven and Earth* is another example of Roberts's strong female leads. Ripley has the same incredible powers as her sisters, but she chooses to ignore them. MacAllister "Mac" Brooke, a paranormal researcher who's come to the island to research witchcraft, is sure that Mia Devlin qualifies as a real witch and that she should be studied. However, when Mac is around Ripley, his equipment registers off the chart, and he soon realizes that his real research material is the woman he's come to love. The trilogy concludes with *Face the Fire,* in which Mia Devlin and Sam Logan are reunited, and in which the three women—Mia, Ripley, and Nell—find the strength to unite, face down the evil, and break the spell that threatens to destroy the island.

In 1996, Roberts wrote her 100th book, *Montana Sky,* a hardcover published by G. P. Putnam's Sons. When Montana cattle baron Jack Mercy, dies, he leaves his ranch, which is worth almost twenty million dollars to his three daughters. However, the will stipulates that in order to receive their share of the ranch, the siblings must all live there together for one year. In this book, Roberts examines the connection between sisters as much as their romantic involvement with men. She deftly captures every nuance of the complex and complicated relationship that exists between sisters, making this book as realistic as those of hers that feature brothers.

Some of Roberts's villains are dead but continue to torment the living. *Blue Dahlia* (2004), the first in Roberts's eerie In the Garden trilogy, features Amelia, also known as the "Harper Bride," a criminally insane ghost who haunts Harbor House. She is the specter of a woman seeking vengeance. Stella Rothchild's relationship with Logan Kitridge, a landscape designer, is threatened by Amelia. In the second book of the series, *Black Rose* (2005), Roz Harper, who is trying to discover a way to help her distant relative Amelia find eternal rest, enlists the help of genealogist Dr. Mitchell Carnagie to do research. Instead of gratitude, the Harper Bride once again chooses revenge. The trilogy concludes with *Red Lily* (2005). This time, Amelia's attitude toward single parent Hayley Phillips changes for the worst, and Amelia adds possession to her bag of tricks when Haley becomes romantically involved with Roz' son, Harper Ashby. Lily, Hayley's child, is also at risk. With this trilogy, Roberts shows a talent for mixing romance with some extremely terrifying moments.

Paranormal elements, such as the troubled ghost Amelia, are present in many of Roberts's books. Her enchanting Irish trilogy (*Jewels of the Sun,* 1999; *Tears of the Moon,* 2000; and *Heart of the Sea,* 2000), also known as The Gallaghers of Ardmore, is set in the picturesque Irish village of Ardmore. The trilogy features a mourning ghost and the King of the Faeries, an estranged couple. The members of the Gallagher family are so real that they could almost step out of the pages of the books. In *Jewels of the Sun,* college professor Jude Murray comes to her grandmother's home in Ardmore, where she meets Aidan Gallagher, who owns the local pub. Aidan's siblings are introduced in this novel, and in true Roberts fashion, each one has a fully developed story. The second book of the series, *Tears of the Moon,* features Shawn Gallagher, Aidan's brother and the cook at the pub. Shawn has grown up with tomboy Brenna O'Toole, who is now the town's jack-of-all-trades. There isn't a thing Brenna can't fix, except her unrequited love for the irritatingly oblivious Shawn. Book three, *Heart of the Sea,* introduces entertainment mogul Trevor McGee, who comes to Ardmore and falls for Darcy Gallagher, Shawn and Aidan's sister. *Heart of the Sea* also resolves the broken relationship between the Faerie King and his beloved ghost. Full of Irish charm, this engaging series is quintessential Roberts.

Roberts is known for her family sagas, each exhibiting different, richly detailed cultural traits. These include the Ukrainian Stanislaskis, the Irish Donovans, and the Scottish MacGregors. The Stanislaskis, also known as "The Wild Ukrainians," are featured in *Taming Natasha* (1990), *Luring a Lady* (1991), *Falling for Rachel* (1993), *Convincing Alex* (1994), *Waiting for Nick* (1997), and *Considering Kate* (2001). The Irish Donovans, all of whom have paranormal powers known as "The Donovan Gift," are featured in *Captivated* (1992), *Entranced* (1992), *Charmed* (1992), and *Enchanted* (1999). However, Roberts's series The MacGregors is by far her longest. Her first MacGregor book, *Playing the Odds,* came out in 1985 and features Daniel MacGregor, a matchmaking patriarch. Other MacGregor stories followed: *Tempting Fate* (1985); *All the Possibilities* (1985); *One Man's Art* (1985); *For Now, Forever* (1987); *Rebellion* (a historical romance published in 1988); "In from the Cold" from *Harlequin Historical Christmas Stories 1990; The MacGregor Brides* (1997); *The Winning Hand* (1998); *The MacGregor Grooms* (1998); and *The Perfect Neighbor* (1999).

In 1995, the ever-creative Roberts began to write a series that fused romantic suspense and science fiction. For this series, she adopted the pseudonym, J. D. Robb. Robb is short for Roberts, and the letters *J* and *D* are the first letters of her sons' names—Jason and Dan. Set in the future, the heroine of the series, Eve Dallas, is a fearless NYPD lieutenant who, in between solving crimes, finds her life becoming entangled romantically with that of a mysterious Irish billionaire/businessman, Roarke. Eve meets Roarke in the first book of the series, *Naked in Death* (1995), when he becomes the prime suspect in the murder of a prostitute.

In 2003, Roberts wrote a book as both Nora Roberts and J. D. Robb, called *Remember When*. The first part of the story (written as Nora Roberts) is set in the present and features a diamond heist that brings together insurance investigator Max Gannon and Laine Tavish, the owner of an antiques and collectibles store. Laine is also the daughter of con man Jack O'Hara, whom Gannon suspects knows where the missing jewels can be found. The second part of the book (written as J. D. Robb) takes place nearly sixty years later, in 2059, when Laine's granddaughter, Samantha Gannon, writes a best-selling book about the missing diamonds. When Samantha's housekeeper is murdered, Lieutenant Eve Dallas begins searching for a killer who will do anything to get the stones. Not only did these two linked tales mark the hardcover debut of a J. D. Robb book, but both stories were also nominated for RITA awards in 2004, with *Remember When* (part one, by Nora Roberts) winning the award for Best Romantic Suspense.

Scandal found its way into Roberts's world when popular author Janet Dailey admitted to plagiarizing much of Roberts's work over a fairly long period of time. Dailey claimed that stress and psychological disorder caused her to do it, and she ended up paying a settlement and making a public apology. Roberts handled the difficult situation with her usual grace and professionalism by donating the settlement she received from Dailey to literacy-based charity groups.

Roberts has said, "Whatever we aim for has to be for ourselves, or the victory isn't nearly so sweet." A consummate storyteller, she is an author who has proven that quality and quantity aren't mutually exclusive. When all is said and done, Roberts has set the standard to which all other authors aspire.

BIBLIOGRAPHY

Writing as Nora Roberts

Books: *Irish Thoroughbred*. New York: Silhouette, 1981: *Blithe Images*. New York: Silhouette, 1982; *Song of the West*. New York: Silhouette, 1982; *Search for Love*. New York: Silhouette, 1982; *Island of Flowers*. New York: Silhouette, 1982; *The Heart's Victory*. New York: Silhouette, 1982; *From This Day*. New York: Silhouette, 1983; *Her Mother's Keeper*. New York: Silhouette, 1983; *Reflections*. New York: Silhouette, 1983; *Once More with Feeling*. New York: Silhouette, 1983; *Untamed*. New York: Silhouette, 1983; *Dance of Dreams*. New York: Silhouette, 1983; *Tonight and Always*. New York: Silhouette, 1983; *This Magic Moment*. New York: Silhouette, 1983; *Endings and Beginnings*. New York: Silhouette, 1984; *Storm Warning*. New York: Silhouette, 1984; *Sullivan's Woman*. New York: Silhouette, 1984; *Rules of the Game*. New York: Silhouette, 1984; *Less of a Stranger*. New York: Silhouette, 1984; *A Matter of Choice*. New York: Silhouette, 1984; *The Law Is a Lady*. New York: Silhouette, 1984; *First Impressions*. New York: Silhouette, 1984; *Opposites Attract*. New York: Silhouette, 1984; *Promise Me Tomorrow*. New York: Pocket, 1984; *Playing the Odds*. New York: Silhouette, 1985; *Partners*. New York: Silhouette, 1985; *The Right Path*. New York: Silhouette, 1985; *Tempting Fate*. New York: Silhouette, 1985; *Boundary Lines*. New York: Silhouette, 1985; *All the Possibilities*. New York: Silhouette, 1985; *One Man's Art*. New York:

Silhouette, 1985; *Summer Desserts*. New York: Silhouette, 1985; *Night Moves*. Toronto: Harlequin, 1985; *Dual Image*. New York: Silhouette, 1985; *The Art of Deception*. New York: Silhouette, 1986; *Affaire Royale*. New York: Silhouette, 1986; *One Summer*. New York: Silhouette, 1986; *Treasures Lost, Treasures Found*. New York: Silhouette, 1986; *Risky Business*. New York: Silhouette, 1986; *Lessons Learned*. New York: Silhouette, 1986; *Second Nature*. New York: Silhouette, 1986; *A Will and a Way*. New York: Silhouette, 1986; *For Now, Forever*. New York: Silhouette, 1987; *Mind over Matter*. New York: Silhouette, 1987; *Command Performance*. New York: Silhouette, 1987; *Hot Ice*. New York: Bantam, 1987; *Temptation*. New York: Silhouette, 1987; *The Playboy Prince*. New York: Silhouette, 1987; *Sacred Sins*. New York: Bantam, 1987; *Local Hero*. New York: Silhouette, 1988; *Irish Rose*. New York: Silhouette, 1988; *Brazen Virtue*. New York: Bantam, 1988; *The Last Honest Woman*. New York: Silhouette, 1988; *Dance to the Piper*. New York: Silhouette, 1988; *Rebellion*. Toronto: Harlequin, 1988; *Skin Deep*. New York: Silhouette, 1988; *Name of the Game*. New York: Silhouette, 1988; *Sweet Revenge*. New York: Bantam, 1989; *Loving Jack*. New York: Silhouette, 1989; *Gabriel's Angel*. New York: Silhouette, 1989; *Best Laid Plans*. New York: Silhouette, 1989; *Lawless*. Toronto: Harlequin, 1989; *The Welcoming*. New York: Silhouette, 1989; *Time Was*. New York: Silhouette, 1989; *Times Change*. New York: Silhouette, 1990; *Taming Natasha*. New York: Silhouette, 1990; *Public Secrets*. New York: Bantam, 1990; *Without a Trace*. New York: Silhouette, 1990; *Night Shift*. New York: Silhouette, 1991; *Night Shadow*. New York: Silhouette, 1991; *Courting Catherine*. New York: Silhouette, 1991; *A Man for Amanda*. New York: Silhouette, 1991; *For the Love of Lilah*. New York: Silhouette, 1991; *Suzanna's Surrender*. New York: Silhouette, 1991; *Genuine Lies*. New York: Bantam, 1991; *Luring a Lady*. New York: Silhouette, 1991; *Carnal Innocence*. New York: Bantam, 1992; *Captivated*. New York: Silhouette, 1992; *Entranced*. New York: Silhouette, 1992; *Charmed*. New York: Silhouette, 1992; *Divine Evil*. New York: Bantam, 1992; *Unfinished Business*. New York: Silhouette, 1992; *Honest Illusions*. New York: G. P. Putnam's Sons, 1992; *Falling for Rachel*. New York: Silhouette, 1993; *Nightshade*. New York: Silhouette, 1993; *Private Scandals*. New York: G. P. Putnam's Sons, 1993; *Night Smoke*. New York: Silhouette, 1994; *Convincing Alex*. New York: Silhouette, 1994; *Hidden Riches*. New York: G. P. Putnam's Sons, 1994; *Born in Fire*. New York: Jove, 1994; *Born in Ice*. New York: Jove, 1995; *The Return of Rafe MacKade*. New York: Silhouette, 1995; *The Pride of Jared MacKade*. New York: Silhouette, 1995; *True Portrayals*. New York: G. P. Putnam's Sons, 1995; *Megan's Mate*. New York: Silhouette, 1996; *The Heart of Devon MacKade*. New York: Silhouette, 1996; *The Fall of Shane MacKade*. New York: Silhouette, 1996; *Born in Shame*. New York: Jove, 1996; *True Betrayals*. New York: Jove, 1996; *Daring to Dream*. New York: Jove, 1996; *Montana Sky*. New York: G. P. Putnam's Sons, 1996; *The MacGregor Brides*. New York: Silhouette, 1997; *Captive Star*. New York: Silhouette, 1997; *Hidden Star*. New York: Silhouette, 1997; *Waiting for Nick*. New York: Silhouette, 1997; *Holding the Dream*. New York: Jove, 1997; *Finding the Dream*. New York: Jove, 1997; *Sanctuary*. New York: G. P. Putnam's Sons, 1997; *The MacGregor Grooms*. New York: Silhouette, 1998; *The Winning Hand*. New York: Silhouette, 1998; *Rising Tides*. New York: Jove, 1998; *Homeport*. New York: G. P. Putnam's Sons, 1998; *Secret Star*. New York: Silhouette, 1998; *Sea Swept*. New York: Jove, 1998; *The Reef*. New York: G. P. Putnam's Sons, 1998; *Inner Harbor*. New York: Jove, 1999; *The Perfect Neighbor*. New York: Silhouette, 1999; *Jewels of the Sun*. New York: Jove, 1999; *Enchanted*. New York: Silhouette, 1999; *Rivers End*. New York: G. P. Putnam's Sons, 1999; *Night Shield*. New York: Silhouette, 2000; *Heart of the Sea*. New York: Jove, 2000; *Tears of the Moon*. New York: Jove, 2000; *Irish Rebel*. New York: Silhouette, 2000; *Carolina Moon*. New York: G. P. Putnam's Sons, 2000; *Considering Kate*. New York: Silhouette, 2001; *Heaven and Earth*. New York: Jove, 2001; *Dance Upon the Air*. New York: Jove, 2001; *The Villa*. New York: G. P. Putnam's Sons, 2001; *Midnight Bayou*. New York: G. P. Putnam's Sons, 2001; *Face the Fire*. New York: Jove, 2002; *Cordina's Crown Jewel*. New York: Silhouette, 2002; *Three Fates*. New York: G. P. Putnam's Sons, 2002; *Chesapeake Blue*. New York: G. P. Putnam's Sons, 2002; *Key of Knowledge*. New York: Jove, 2003; *Key of Light*. New York: Jove, 2003; *Once Upon a Midnight*. New York: Berkley, 2003; *Birthright*. New York: G. P. Putnam's Sons, 2003; *Blue Dahlia*. New York: Jove, 2004; *Northern Lights*. New York: G. P. Putnam's Sons,

2004; *Key of Valor.* New York: Jove, 2004; *Red Lily.* New York: Jove, 2005; *Blue Smoke.* New York: G. P. Putnam's Sons, 2005; *Black Rose.* New York: Jove, 2005; *Angel's Fall.* New York: G. P. Putnam's Sons, 2006; *Morrigan's Cross Circle.* New York: Jove, 2006; *Dance of the Gods.* New York: Jove, 2006; *Valley of Silence.* New York: Jove, 2006.

Novellas: "Home for Christmas" in *Silhouette Christmas Stories.* New York: Silhouette, 1986; "Impulse" in *Silhouette Summer Sizzlers.* New York: Silhouette, 1989; "In from the Cold" in *Harlequin Historical Christmas Stories, 1990.* Toronto: Harlequin, 1990; "The Best Mistake" in *Birds, Bees and Babies.* New York: Silhouette, 1994; "All I Want for Christmas" in *Jingle Bells, Wedding Bells.* New York: Silhouette, 1994; "Spellbound" in *Once Upon a Castle.* New York: Jove, 1998; "Ever After" in *Once Upon a Star.* New York: Jove, 1999; "Christmas in Ardmore." New York: Jove, 2000 (promotional giveaway); "Christmas with the Quinns." New York: Jove, 2000 (promotional giveaway); "In Dreams" in *Once Upon a Dream.* New York: Jove, 2000; "Winter Rose" in *Once Upon a Rose.* New York: Jove, 2001; "World Apart" in *Once Upon a Kiss.* New York: Jove, 2002; "The Witching Hour" in *Once Upon a Midnight.* New York: Jove, 2003.

Genre-Related Essay: "The Romance of Writing" in *North American Romance Writers.* Lanham, MD: Scarecrow Press, 1999.

Writing as J. D. Robb

Books: *Naked in Death.* New York: Berkley, 1995; *Glory in Death.* New York: Berkley, 1995; *Immortal in Death.* New York: Berkley, 1996; *Rapture in Death.* New York: Berkley, 1996; *Ceremony in Death.* New York: Berkley, 1997; *Vengeance in Death.* New York: Berkley, 1997; *Holiday in Death.* New York: Berkley, 1998; *Conspiracy in Death.* New York: Berkley, 1999; *Loyalty in Death.* New York: Berkley, 1999; *Witness in Death.* New York: Berkley, 2000; *Judgment in Death.* New York: Berkley, 2000; *Betrayal in Death.* New York: Berkley, 2001; *Seduction in Death.* New York: Berkley, 2001; *Reunion in Death.* New York: Berkley, 2002; *Purity in Death.* New York: Berkley, 2002; *Portrait in Death.* New York: Berkley, 2003; *Imitation in Death.* New York: Berkley, 2003; *Divided in Death.* New York: G. P. Putnam's Sons, 2004; *Visions in Death.* New York: G. P. Putnam's Sons, 2004; *Survivor in Death.* New York: G. P. Putnam's Sons, 2005; *Memory in Death.* New York: G. P. Putnam's Sons, 2006; *Born in Death.* New York: G. P. Putnam's Sons, 2006.

Novellas: "Midnight in Death" in *Silent Night.* New York: Jove, 1998; "Interlude in Death" in *Out of this World.* New York: Jove, 2001; "Haunted in Death" in *Bump in the Night.* New York: Penguin, 2006.

Written as Nora Roberts and J. D. Robb

Book: *Remember When.* New York: G. P. Putnam's Sons, 2003.

SHELLEY MOSLEY, SANDRA VAN WINKLE, AND JOHN CHARLES

LAUREN ROYAL

Lauren Royal. Photo by Teri Royal. Courtesy of Lauren Royal.

The two great influences in Lauren Royal's young life were television's Marcia Brady and *Forever Amber*. Readers who have fallen in love with Royal's rich and wonderful historical romances are eternally grateful that Royal decided to follow the path of Kathleen Windsor and not the oldest Brady Bunch daughter.

Royal was born in Hollywood, California. She grew up in Los Angeles and later moved to Orange County, where her father owned a business that involved performing insurance inspections. Her mother was a homemaker, whom Royal fondly remembers as always "doing crafts with us and having snacks waiting every day when we got home from school." As a young girl in the third grade, Royal dreamed of one day becoming a writer: "That year, I won a 'Why My Mother is the Greatest' essay contest, and my essay was published in our big regional newspaper. Seeing my words in print did it … I was hooked!" Later, in the fifth grade, Royal honed her literary skills by writing and illustrating a hundred-page book about the adventures of a girl and her doll (told from the doll's viewpoint).

While in high school, Royal began reading historical romances, and she says she quickly became a fan of the genre and its "happily ever after" endings. After discovering the rich period details in Kathleen Windsor's classic romance, Royal began accumulating a research library in anticipation of the time she would begin writing her own novel.

Royal attended the University of California at Irvine and then transferred to UCLA, where she majored in motion picture and television production. Royal met her husband while they were both in college, when he happened to take one of the film classes that Royal had also enrolled in. At the time, Royal had a bet going with her girlfriend that they would each have to pick out a different boy in their class and see if they could get him to ask them out by the end of the semester. The man Royal selected not only asked her out but also became the love of her life.

While she was in college, Royal had planned her future around a career writing screenplays, directing television shows, or both. Royal was actually offered her dream job of directing a cable television show, but because she came from a family of entrepreneurs, Royal ultimately decided against going into the television industry in favor of opening her own jewelry store in a local shopping mall. Royal's store soon grew into six, and she eventually dragged her parents, brother, and husband into the business. Fourteen years later, Royal sold her flourishing group of jewelry stores to a national chain, thinking that would give her the opportunity to stay home with her three children. One short week later, Royal realized that simply staying at home would drive her insane, and it was then that she recalled her childhood dream of writing a book.

Because she loved to read romances, Royal decided to write a romance herself. Royal also recalled the famous words of advice, "Write what you know." She knew two things exceedingly well: jewelry and Restoration England. Thus, her first manuscript was set in Stuart England and featured a heroine who was a jeweler. Several years and twenty-some drafts later, the book was finished. Royal then began the search for an agent. She received 34 rejection letters before she found an agent willing to take her on as a client. Within one week of sending Royal's manuscript out to publishers, her agent had received an offer for a three-book contract.

Her first book, *Amethyst,* was published by Signet in 2000. In the story, jeweler Amethyst Goldsmith is fated to marry one of the apprentices in her father's jewelry shop. When the Great Fire of London destroys part of the city, Colin Chase, the Earl of Greystone, rescues Amethyst, and she finds her romantic future unaccountably tied to the handsome nobleman. Not only did Royal's first historical romance offer readers a refreshingly different time period—that of Restoration England—but her heroine, Amethyst, a strong, stubborn merchant-class artisan, was also a tantalizing change from the more popular noblewomen heroines found in other romance novels of the time.

Emerald (2000) and *Amber* (2001), two more fast-paced historical romances, soon followed. Brimming with adventure and passion, each of these novels features a different member of the Chase family. In *Emerald,* Royal matched Jason Chase, a nobleman, with Caithren Leslie, a young woman disguised as a lad. The two meet while Jason is pursuing Geoffrey Gothard, the villain who murdered several of Jason's villagers. Kendra Chase, the Chase brothers' younger sister, gets her own chance at romance in *Amber* when she finds herself falling in love with notorious highwayman Patrick "Trick" Caldwell after he stops her carriage one dark night.

With her Jewel trilogy, Royal quickly became known not only for her richly imagined historical settings, but also for her deft incorporation of historical details in her stories. For example, in *Amber,* the real-life sinking of King Charles I's baggage ferry, with its rumored horde of gold and silver, plays a small but important role in the story, when 35 years later, Kendra and Trick, of *Amber,* find the missing treasure. Royal also loves to provide historical figures—such as Charles II; Catharine of Braganza; and Barbara, Countess of Castlemaine— their own small secondary roles in her stories, giving her romances a splendidly real sense of the past. Readers loved the way Royal would mention or include real dishes or foodstuffs from the era, so much so that Royal began including recipes for the items on her Web site for the benefit of readers who wanted to recreate the dishes on their own.

Royal followed her Jewel trilogy of books with another trio of historical romances set in Restoration England: her Flower trilogy (*Violet,* 2002; *Lily,* 2003; *Rose,* 2003). *Violet,* the first book in the series, introduces readers to the Ashcroft sisters—Violet, Rose, and Lily— and the men with whom they will fall in love. The strong emotional bond between the sisters plays an important role in all three novels, as Royal explores the many different ways a family interacts. Royal provided a clever bridge between her Jewel and Flower books when she paired up Violet Ashcroft with her next-door neighbor, eccentric inventor Ford Chase. One memorable scene in *Violet* includes a party sequence where Isaac Newton, Robert Hooke, Robert Boyle, and other scientific luminaries of the time put in brief appearances, which lends a delightful air of vivid realism to the scene.

After writing six historical romances and one novella set in Restoration England, Royal turned her attention to the Regency period, with the publication of *Lost in Temptation* in 2005. *Lost in Temptation,* the first book in a trilogy, introduces readers to Griffin Chase, who is the Marquess of Cainewood and a descendant of the Chases featured in her Restoration books. With three marriageable sisters, Griffin Chase finds that all of his time is spent in a desperate search for eligible husbands for the headstrong girls. Griffin has the perfect man picked out for his sister Alexandra, but the always-correct Alexandra surprises everyone when she rejects Chase's choice in favor of pursuing a romance with Tristan Nesbitt, Lord Hawkbridge, the man she has loved since she was a child. While the time period might be different in *Lost in Temptation,* everything else that readers loved about Royal's Restoration romances is present: the lavishly imagined scenes; the incorporation of real-life historical figures; the fascinating details of everyday life of the time; and the sinfully sensual love story.

Royal says, "I love reading romances because they allow me to fall in love vicariously, along with the characters. As a writer, my goal is to make my own readers experience all those wonderful emotions." With her expertly crafted, splendidly imagined, and emotionally involving historical romances, Royal succeeds admirably in building on the grand and glorious tradition of her beloved *Forever Amber.*

Bibliography

Books: *Amethyst.* New York: Signet, 2000; *Emerald.* New York: Signet, 2000; *Amber.* New York: Signet, 2001; *Violet.* New York: Signet, 2002; *Lily.* New York: Signet, 2003; *Rose.* New York: Signet, 2003; *Lost in Temptation.* New York: Signet, 2005; *Tempting Juliana.* New York: Signet, 2006.
Novella: "Forevermore" in *In Praise of Younger Men.* New York: Signet, 2001.

John Charles

BARBARA SAMUEL

As a writer, Barbara Samuel is fascinated by the physical, emotional, and spiritual journeys women take. Her books written as Ruth Wind and as Barbara Samuel reflect this, both in the plot lines and in her strong female characters, whose lives are enriched by many different kinds of relationships.

Samuel was born in 1959 in Colorado Springs, Colorado. Her parents met in high school, when her mother was a painfully shy new student and her father had returned to school after being suspended for riding his motorcycle through the hallways. Samuel's father took her mother to lunch that day, and they have been married for 50 years.

Samuel grew up in Colorado Springs "under the burly shoulders of Pike's Peak," with three siblings. She says of her childhood, "I admire and respect my parents very much. For various reasons, neither of them had very stable childhoods, and it's funny how they gave the four of us a childhood out of books—it was so incredibly normal and stable and suburban, I used to want to scream. Now I see how valuable it was for me."

For Samuel, the desire to write started young: "I wanted to be a fiction writer starting in the fifth grade and spent my teen years writing a lot of bad novels and short stories. After high school, I took a year and tried to focus and sell my stories but was very frustrated by the whole idea of a 'market.' My father wanted me to be sensible and study something that could support me; thus the journalism focus."

Samuel attended the University of Southern Colorado (now Colorado State University), where she majored in mass communications and minored in psychology and sociology. She says, "I studied journalism in college, along with psychology, sociology, anthropology, and English literature. In the end, the journalism track was absolutely the right track for me—the discipline grounded me and helped me see how to tell a story in a clean, honest way." Samuel also worked on the student newspaper, called *The Today*, for four years and served as editor her final year.

---

also writing as Ruth Wind

When Samuel was in her last year at college, an incident occurred that changed her life forever: "I was tending bar to support myself, and I happened to overhear a reporter I absolutely adored telling another writer that one of these days, she was going to quit the newspaper and write her novels. It absolutely terrified me—I could see that I'd be that writer in a decade or two if I didn't act." Later, Samuel broached the topic with her husband. She recalls, "I went home and asked my husband if he'd give me five years to see if I could write and sell. He gulped bravely and agreed (we suffered a lot financially for that decision)."

Samuel focused only on her writing, honing her skills in writing fiction, and she eventually decided that the romance genre fit her writing style the best. Samuel recounts the following about her early efforts: "I'd been writing all kinds of things—literary short stories, a 'mainstream' novel (that eventually was published as a romance), even inspirational pieces. But I was reading a lot of romances and finally had the big 'duh!' moment: why not try my hand at that? It was like Cinderella's slipper—the form fit my voice and I wrote one, which went through the whole company at Harlequin/Silhouette, I think, and had letters from three editors. So I examined all the things they said, wrote a second romance, and sold it to Silhouette in 1988." Samuel came in under her five-year goal, selling her first book (her second romance) in the fourth year of her plan.

Written under the name of Ruth Wind, her first book, *Strangers on a Train* (1989), gave readers a taste of the vivid, multilayered characters and the emotionally intense storytelling for which she would become known. In *Strangers on a Train,* widow Heather Scarborough thought she had buried her love when she buried her husband, a Vietnam veteran whose suicide left Heather emotionally lost. Then, an unexpected meeting on a train with a handsome stranger, author Ben Shaw, reawakens her long-suppressed passion and her hope for a brighter future.

More books for Silhouette followed, including the poignant *Jezebel's Blues,* published in 1992. When Eric Putman is caught in a flash flood while trying to reach his sister's house, he seeks shelter, in the home of Celia Moon, from the overflowing Jezebel River. Ethereal Celia has lived in the shadow of her late father, legendary author Jacob Moon, but sees in Eric a kindred spirit and a troubled soul. Together, they wait out the storm in Celia's old Victorian house, and they discover a shared attraction and hunger that goes beyond the physical. Samuel creates a vulnerable, tormented hero in Eric, who is a handsome drifter looking for the connection of family. Celia is a winsome heroine with a will to survive. "I'm always exploring the notion of survivors," Samuel explains, "and the need to discover and claim the authentic person you are inside, where you are true and real." The lyrically beautiful *Jezebel's Blues* was a finalist for the RITA award. Writing as Ruth Wind, Samuel would go on to be a RITA award finalist six more times and would win twice for *Reckless* (1997) and *Meant to Be Married* (1998).

Marissa Pierce, the heroine of *Beautiful Stranger,* published in 2000, is an excellent example of Samuel's ability to create an authentic person with whom readers can readily relate. Marissa had always been the chubby twin until a dramatic weight loss changes her life. Robert Martinez always thought Marissa was beautiful, even before she lost weight, and as he gets to know her better, he finds himself irresistibly attracted to her. Samuel doesn't flinch from adding realistic subjects into her books, such as the issues of body image and teenage pregnancy in *Beautiful Stranger.* And by making the hero of *Beautiful Stranger* a Native American, she also brings an appealing multicultural element to her romance.

Beautiful Stranger is also a good example of Samuel's ability to create a strong sense of place in her books. Set in the Southwest, as many of Samuel's books are, *Beautiful Stranger* has an air of authenticity that readers begin to look forward to from Samuel. She says,

"I'm nearly always writing about the stretch of land that starts at Colorado Springs and ends at Santa Fe. It's the land and the people I know best, and not many other people write about it; so there is a lot of freedom for me to shape a vision of it and offer some insights and talk about the people and cultures I love here."

In 1993, she branched out into the historical romance genre, writing as Barbara Samuel. She was inspired to start writing historical romances by her own love of the past. "I was a Shakespeare fanatic as a teenager and fell in love with history over *Green Darkness,* Anya Seton's classic novel. When I'd written five books for Silhouette, I started to see that I could quickly start to repeat myself in a format if I didn't find ways to keep it fresh. And I loved reading historicals, so they seemed the logical choice. I found a great historical tidbit about St. Valentine in medieval Germany, and the idea for *Bed of Spices* bloomed."

In the compelling *Bed of Spices* (1993), Samuel uses the unusual setting of fourteenth-century Strasbourg, Germany, just as the Black Death is sweeping across Europe. The hero is Solomon, a physician in training and the son of a well-to-do Jewish businessman, who meets the heroine Frederika "Rica" der Esslingen. Rica is destined to marry a man of her father's choosing, her twin sister's lover. While religion, class, and family threaten to keep Solomon and Rica apart, their love for each other overcomes all these obstacles. In addition to her well-developed skill in creating fully realized characters, Samuel demonstrated a gift for intricate plotlines, brilliantly evoked settings, and vivid historical details as she crafted this powerful story about a love that overcomes prejudice and persecution.

No Place Like Home, published in 2002, marked Samuel's first foray into hardcover books. Heroine Jewel Sabatino has not made the best choices in her life. She left her home-town of Pueblo, Colorado, as a teenager and never looked back; but she is forced to return with her best friend Michael, who is dying of AIDS. Jewel, her teenage son, and Michael barely settle in to the old house she inherited from her aunt, when Michael's brother Malachi visits and stirs up feelings that Jewel did not expect to have. In *No Place Like Home,* Samuel fashions an exquisitely moving tale of redemption and reconciliation, deftly blended with love and loss.

Many things serve as inspiration for Samuel: "Stories come from all sorts of places, I'm never quite sure what lights the fire exactly. Often it's quite a few things coming together suddenly in a new way—my grandfather's restaurant and a little family-run Italian restaurant in Pueblo, the love and family connections in the town, a longing to write about a woman who hasn't necessarily made good choices; and a friend talking about her brother coming home to die of AIDS. The elements coalesced into *No Place Like Home,* but I can't say it was plot or character."

The Goddesses of Kitchen Avenue (2004) was by far the most difficult book for Samuel to write.

I was exploring my thoughts about marriage when my own marriage was obviously not going to make it, and that was hard. It was also hard to keep myself focused on the characters and let them tell their stories, which were very different than my own. I was also worried that there was too much raw emotion on the page, that some read-ers would find it hard to read. And knowing where the line was sometimes challenged me. In a previous book, I had written about a really bad divorce and had so many readers at signings come up and tell me what they had done during their own divorces that I really wanted to get that intensity of crazed brokenheartedness on the page in some way. Divorce is rough stuff, and all too often in fiction, the conflicting emotions of it aren't as raw as I saw in others and in my own situation.

In *Goddesses of Kitchen Avenue,* Samuel tells the stories of four different friends and neighbors living in Pueblo, Colorado, all of whom are at different stages in their lives. Trudy Marino has been married for 20 years when her husband Rick falls in love with a blowsy bartender and moves out of their family home, which devastates Trudy and forces her to reexamine the choices she has made in her life. Trudy's next-door neighbor Roberta has just lost her husband of 62 years, and Roberta's granddaughter Jade has returned to Pueblo to lend her support to her grandmother. Jade is recovering from a failed marriage to a charming cad who is serving a prison term for burglary. Shannelle is a young mother who dreams of becoming a writer, but whose husband does his best to subtly sabotage her dream. Samuel writes lyrically and tenderly about the challenges women of every age face and how their friendships can support and sustain them—in good times and bad.

While Samuel is known for her award-winning women's fiction and contemporary and historical romances, she has also written more than a few adrenaline-filled, action-driven stories, including her two Bombshell books (*Countdown,* 2005, and *The Diamond Secret,* 2006), written as Ruth Wind. Samuel has always written about strong female characters, but the Bombshell books gave her the opportunity to create some "action-adventure babes." In *Countdown,* Kim Valenti, a graduate of the Athena Academy who works for the National Security Agency, must team up with FBI agent Alexander Tanner to stop a terrorist attack. In *The Diamond Secret,* the heroine is gemologist Sylvie Montague, who has obtained a cursed diamond that her ex, Paul Maigny, will do anything to possess. Samuel was prompted to start writing for Silhouette's Bombshell line after meeting with her former editor at Silhouette, who was instrumental in birth of the Bombshell line. Samuel says, "We brainstormed ideas for the line at lunch one conference weekend, and it just sounded like so much fun, I wanted to give it a shot. Again, it's great to try something new, exercise new writing muscles, [and] let the work teach me something."

Samuel has written contemporary romance, historical love stories, women's fiction, and even a few "kick-ass" adventure tales, but she says that each of these books has one common element: "I've always liked writing all kinds of things, but most of my work does have a strong romantic thread, even if it isn't straight romance." In the end, for Samuel, the appeal of romance is the hopeful quality. "It's unfailing optimism." she says. "It says firmly [that] if we believe in this world, we're taking steps to create it—a good world where no one is unredeemable, where no teenagers can't be saved, where good triumphs over evil."

BIBLIOGRAPHY

Writing as Barbara Samuel

Books: *Bed of Spices.* New York: Avon, 1993; *Winter Ballad.* New York: Avon, 1994; *Lucien's Fall.* New York: Harper, 1995; *Dancing Moon.* New York: Harper, 1996; *Heart of a Knight.* New York: Harper, 1997; *Black Angel.* New York: Harper, 1999; *Night of Fire.* New York: Avon, 2000; *No Place Like Home.* New York: Ballantine, 2002; *A Piece of Heaven.* New York: Ballantine, 2003; *The Goddesses of Kitchen Avenue.* New York: Ballantine, 2004; *Lady Luck's Map of Vegas.* New York: Ballantine, 2005; *Madame Mirabou's School of Love .* New York: Ballantine, 2006.
Novellas: "The Harper's Daughter" in *Irish Magic.* New York: Kensington, 1996; "The Love Talker" in *Faery Magic.* New York: Kensington, 1998; "Earthly Magic" in *Irish Magic II.* New York: Kensington, 1999.
Genre-Related Essay: "The Art of Romance Novels" in *North American Romance Writers.* Lanham, MD: Scarecrow Press, 1999.

Writing as Ruth Wind

Books: *Strangers on a Train.* New York, Silhouette, 1989; *Summer's Freedom.* New York: Silhouette, 1990; *Light of Day.* New York: Silhouette, 1990; *A Minute to Smile.* New York: Silhouette, 1992; *Jezebel's Blues.* New York: Silhouette, 1992; *Walk in Beauty.* New York: Silhouette, 1994; *Breaking the Rules.* New York: Silhouette, 1994; *The Last Chance Ranch.* New York: Silhouette, 1995; *Rainsinger.* New York: Silhouette, 1996; *Marriage Material.* New York: Silhouette, 1997; *Reckless.* New York: Silhouette, 1997; *Her Ideal Man.* New York: Silhouette, 1997; *Meant to Be Married.* New York: Silhouette, 1998; *For Christmas, Forever.* New York: Silhouette, 1998; *Rio Grande Wedding.* New York: Silhouette, 1999; *Beautiful Stranger.* New York: Silhouette, 2000; *In the Midnight Rain.* New York: Silhouette, 2000; *Born Brave.* New York: Silhouette, 2001; *Countdown.* New York: Silhouette, 2005; *The Diamond Secret.* New York: Silhouette, 2006.

JOHN CHARLES AND JOANNE HAMILTON-SELWAY

ALICIA SCOTT. *See* Lisa Gardner

REGINA SCOTT

Regina Scott. Courtesy of Regina Scott.

Regina Scott formally began her writing career in the third grade when she completed her first story, "Mummies at the Lake," a dark horror tale that perfectly reflected her own reading tastes at the time. As Scott fondly recalls, "Thankfully for literature as we know it, that story was never published." Even at that young age Scott knew that she wanted to be a writer. The problem was that as Scott grew up, she was introduced to the idea that most writers ended up starving away in a garret somewhere. Since Scott had become somewhat attached to the concept of eating, she wisely, but somewhat sadly, put away her childhood hopes of one day writing for a living and instead sought more financially rewarding types of jobs. Even though Scott explored several different careers, she still kept writing at night and eventually chose to try to fulfill her dream of becoming a published author.

Scott, the pseudonym for Regina Lundgren, was born in Tacoma, Washington, in 1959. Her father was with the Washington Air National Guard for many years as a quality control technician, and he later worked for Boeing in a similar capacity. Her mother was a schoolteacher who pioneered the first kindergarten at a Catholic school in Tacoma. Scott grew up in the Seattle and Tacoma area, later attending Pierce College in Steilacoom, Washington, where she received an associate of arts degree in early childhood education.

---

also writing as Regan Allen

Before she began writing, Scott had many other jobs. She worked as a preschool teacher and then as a day-care professional, where she achieved the position of director of the largest before- and after-school program in Tacoma. After continuing her own education at the University of Washington, where she earned a bachelor's degree in scientific and technical communication, Scott took a job serving as a communications specialist for a leading not-for-profit research and development organization. Ten years later, Scott moved into the public relations side of that company but found she missed working with the scientists and engineers to help communicate environmental, safety, and health risks to lay audiences. Scott's experiences working with the scientific community led her to write a book on the subject of risk communication, and she was subsequently promoted to a scientific position within the company, which she held for three years.

While Scott had believed that trying to earn a living as a novelist was the equivalent of living in a garret, she discovered that even after becoming a scientist, she and her husband still needed two jobs to support their family. Then one day, Scott and her husband were having a discussion about how they each defined themselves. "That's easy," Scott remembers replying smugly, "I am a writer." Frowning, Scott's husband replied, "You're not a writer. You never write."

"You would have thought there'd be a divorce that day, I was so angry," Scott recalls. But later on, Scott realized her husband was right. If she truly did want to call herself a writer, she had to start producing something and making an effort to get it published. Scott says the following about how she decided what to write: "I had dozens of stories I'd played around with over the years, everything from horror to children's stories to romance and fantasy. In college, however, I'd fallen in love with traditional Regency romances. Researching the writing field, I learned they were in constant demand at the time and difficult to write because of the short length, dedication to historical accuracy, and need for a period voice. I could write short novels, knew the period, and had learned as a technical writer to modify my voice to fit the requirements of a particular situation. Regencies, I thought, would be the perfect place for me to break in to writing. And I was right."

Scott stumbled across the Romance Writers of America, and then the Beau Monde, their special interest chapter for writers of Regency romances. One of the Beau Monde's newsletters noted that Kensington had suddenly found itself with a hole in its publication schedule and was desperate for traditional Regency manuscripts. Scott sent off a synopsis and the first three chapters of the book she was working on and within a week got back a request for the full manuscript. As Scott later remembers, "Surely they'd expect me to provide the book just as quickly, so I scrambled to finish the book, and got it back to them within a week." A few weeks later, Scott got a call from John Scognamiglio at Kensington, making an offer for her book, *The Unflappable Miss Fairchild,* and requesting that Scott write their Christmas book for 1998 (which would become *The Twelve Days of Christmas*).

With *The Unflappable Miss Fairchild,* published in 1998, Scott quickly earned a reputation with Regency readers for her lively, laughter-laced love stories and her wonderfully appealing characters. With her next book, *The Twelve Days of Christmas,* Scott continued to demonstrate her gift for clever humor. She used the classic holiday song as a source of inspiration for her tale of a wealthy, charming nobleman who bets a poor but lovely lady that he can give to her all of the items mentioned in the song without spending a penny. More expertly crafted traditional Regencies followed as Scott matched up a wealthy, intellectual heiress with a handsome fortune hunter (*The Bluestocking on His Knee,* 1999); a chaperone who can't quite believe an extremely eligible viscount actually prefers her over her "diamond of the first water" cousin (*The Incomparable Miss Compton,* 2001); and a wonderfully "managing" heroine, who while trying to play matchmaker for her stepsister somehow manages to find herself the object of her target's interest (*Lord Borin's Secret Love,* 2002).

Scott's 2002 book, *Utterly Devoted,* is yet another example of her keen sense of wit. Scott delivers a wonderfully clever tale of Eloise Watkin, who first appeared as a secondary character in *The Irredeemable Miss Renfield* (2001). When infamous rake Jareth Darby approaches Eloise and asks her to forgive him as part of his campaign to reform his public image and gain an estate from his brother, Eloise sees the perfect opportunity to exact revenge on Jareth, the man who once rejected her. While Eloise is determined that Jareth must suffer for the emotional pain he caused her, she soon discovers her feelings for him keep getting in the way of her plan to pay him back. Beautifully written with just the right blend of humor and emotional depth, *Utterly Devoted* is one of Scott's best traditional Regencies.

In 2003, Scott made the transition from writing traditional Regency romances to longer Regency historicals with the publication of *Starstruck* (2003) and *Perfection* (2003). While both books have the wonderful sense of period that flavored Scott's traditional Regency romances, the longer word count for these two books allowed Scott greater possibilities for character and plot developments, which she used to great advantage in both books. *Starstruck* is a particularly fascinating tale of an unconventional Regency heroine, astronomer Cassie Bentbrooke, who meets her match in the form of charming, sexy Frenchman Devon Sebastien, who moves into her neighborhood. Scott deftly sprinkles real historical details about a comet that was visible in England in 1811–1812 into the plot of *Starstruck* as Cassie fights to record her observations of the astronomical event while trying to elude Devon, a French privateer who believes the Bentebrooke family papers hold the key to a fortune in stolen jewels. Actually, *Starstruck* was the first Regency romance Scott wrote, but because of its length and complex plot, it did not fit neatly into the traditional Regency mold. So she set her manuscript aside until the market for longer Regency historicals developed.

After the publication of *Perfection,* Scott adopted a new pseudonym, Regan Allen, partly at the suggestion of her publisher. In addition, says Scott, "[I] was changing the type of book I was writing, and I wanted to send a clear signal to my fans." Under the name of Allen, Scott continued to write the same kind of longer Regency historicals as *Perfection* and *Starstruck,* but with a hint of magic. Scott's first work published as Allen was, appropriately enough, the novella "A Touch of Magic," which appeared in the anthology *How to Marry a Duke* (2005). In "A Touch of Magic," the hero, Stephen Anthony, the Duke of Langford, isn't sure what to think when a mysterious woman, Tess Dewood, shows up at his estate claiming to be a faery queen whom Stephen is fated to wed. Allen does a superb job keeping both Stephen, and the reader, guessing as to whether or not Tess really is a faery queen or just a local lass pretending to be something she is not in order the marry the man of her dreams.

Scott's first novel writing as Allen was *The Pleasure Garden,* which was also published in 2005. In it, the author once again playfully teases readers with a hint of magic. The book's heroine, penniless governess Angelica Pruitt, agrees to help entertain a group of antique collectors at a party being held at Vauxhall Gardens, thinking it would at least give her the chance to have a decent meal. When Angelica meets notorious treasure hunter Jason Kitterage at the party, she finds herself becoming mixed up not only with him but also his recent discovery: the legendary mask of Aphrodite. Since the ancient mask reputedly has the power to cast a love spell over any man, Angelica wonders whether Jason loves her for herself. Allen spices this bewitching Regency novel with some fascinating tidbits of Greek myths and history, as she skillfully creates a simmering sense of chemistry between her hero and heroine—a chemistry that leaves little doubt in the reader's mind that the love between Angelica and Jason is real and not magic.

Scott says about the romance genre, "It's all about happy endings. So few people feel like they get happy endings on a day-to-day basis—we need that infusion of hope." Whether she is dreaming up traditional Regency romances or Regency historicals, using the name Scott or Allen, she has found her own "happily ever after" ending as a writer, which is fortunate not only for herself but also for her many devoted readers.

BIBLIOGRAPHY

Writing as Regina Scott

Books: *The Unflappable Miss Fairchild.* New York: Zebra, 1998; *Twelve Days of Christmas.* New York: Zebra, 1998; *The Bluestocking on His Knee.* New York: Zebra, 1999; *Dangerous Dalliance.* New York: Zebra, 2000; *The Marquis' Kiss.* New York: Zebra, 2000; *The Incomparable Miss Compton.* New York: Zebra, 2001; *The Irredeemable Miss Renfield.* New York: Zebra, 2001; *Lord Borin's Secret Love.* New York: Zebra, 2002; *Utterly Devoted.* New York: Zebra, 2002; *Starstruck.* New York: Zebra, 2003; *Perfection.* New York: Zebra, 2003.

Novellas: "Sweeter than Candy" in *A Match for Mother.* New York: Zebra, 1999; "A Place by the Fire" in *Mistletoe Kittens.* New York: Zebra, 1999; "The June Bride Conspiracy" in *His Blushing Bride.* New York: Zebra, 2001.

Writing as Regan Allen

Book: *The Pleasure Garden.* New York: Zebra, 2005.
Novella: "A Touch of Magic" in *How to Marry a Duke.* New York: Zebra, 2005.

JOHN CHARLES

JOHN SHARPE. *See* Alice Duncan

KATHRYN SHAY

Kathryn Shay. Photo by DigiQuick Portrait Studios. Courtesy of Kathryn Shay.

When Kathryn Shay began planning her writing career at the tender age of 15, she decided she should also pursue a degree in teaching so that she would have an occupation "to fall back on," in case the writing thing didn't work out. Her original intent was to become a journalist, but once she began reading romances, the thought occurred to her, "I can do that." Since then, Shay has written over twenty-five novels, including three Holt Medallion winners and five *Romantic Times* awards. She now muses, "As it turns out, I could."

Born and raised in Corning, New York, by parents Geraldine and Benjamin Ruocco, Shay is the fourth of five children. Her father, an Italian immigrant, was a foreman for the Corning Glass Works, and her mother was a career homemaker. As planned, Shay completed her teaching education with a bachelor's degree in English at Nazareth College of Rochester and a master's degree in education from State University of New York at Brockport. She married her husband, Jerry, and had two children, April and Ben.

Shay discovered that she truly loved teaching. Rather than having to choose between the two careers, Shay spent the next 33 years happily engaged in both writing and teaching. Although she now writes full-time, Shay comments, "Someday, I'm going to give a talk about having a day job being good for your writing career. It makes you disciplined and grateful for the time you do have to write." In fact, Shay believes the reason she was never troubled by writer's block is because juggling her teaching and writing careers forced her to maximize her time.

Shay describes her writing style as "character driven, realistic and emotion-filled." Her readers often call her books "heart wrenching." Shay says her books' heroes are "usually tortured men," who find themselves in love relationships to which they cannot commit. Her heroines often suffer similar commitment dilemmas, but occasionally, some are optimistic and positive. Shay often expresses her own philosophies, values, and views through her characters. One such example is her 2002 novel, *Promises to Keep,* in which, according to Shay, "the government intervenes and handles school violence as I think it should be handled." Joe Stonehouse, a Secret Service agent, has always protected people. However, while he's away on an assignment, his beloved niece is shot and killed by another student at her high school. His guilt and grief are palpable. Joe, whose degree is in clinical psychology, becomes a member of the special School Threat Assessment Team. He goes undercover as a school counselor at New York's Fairholm High School, with another agent, Luke Ludzecky, who masquerades as his defiant nephew. When principal Suzanna Quinn discovers that her new staff member is really a Secret Service agent, she becomes enraged ... until a suicide note left by a student warns that there are plans for violent acts at the school. Even though Suzanna resents Joe's presence and its effect on her "open school with lots of trust" philosophy, she eventually sees the need for them to work together cooperatively. As they do, she begins to respect him. School violence is a difficult subject at best, but Shay balances harsh reality with hope for a solution. Her characters have incredibly realistic reactions to the situation, and Shay uncannily mirrors the feelings of the reader to such an extent that this powerful, compelling story doesn't even seem like fiction.

For Shay, story inspiration is found in everyday living: "I was a teacher and wrote several books about teachers; I love firefighters and did a lot of research for books about them." One of her novels is set in a charity soup kitchen, which happens to be an activity for which Shay frequently volunteers.

Plot and character ideas seem to occur simultaneously for Shay, with the hero and the scenario emerging together. She prefers to use contemporary settings in upstate New York and New York City, places she knows very well. Shay frequently uses a recurring theme of redemption. She explains, "You can be flawed, make mistakes, and make up for them; or your background can be really dysfunctional, but you can overcome it and live a good life."

Most fascinating for Shay is the way the writing process takes on a life of its own, with scenes frequently veering off in delightfully unintended directions. The romance genre is particularly appealing to her because of the way it empowers women. Bailey O'Neil of *Someone to Believe In* (2005) is one example of Shay's strong heroines. She and Clay Wainwright have been enemies for years. When Clay was New York City's uncompromising district attorney, he sent Bailey, a social activist and antigang advocate known as the "Street Angel," to jail for harboring a criminal. Clay, now a conservative senator from New York, continues to antagonize Bailey by denying funding for her cause. In an ironic twist of fate, Clay and Bailey end up on the same gang-violence task force, and they decide, for the good of the city, to call a truce. Much to their amazement, they discover that in spite of their differences, they are physically attracted to each other. Since Bailey's incarceration, her family and friends hate Clay. Likewise, Clay's conservative law-enforcement friends despise Bailey and her methods. Clay's mother has someone far more politically and socially suitable in mind to be her daughter-in-law. This starkly realistic, conflict-ridden story of gang members and the people involved in prevention and intervention programs is brutally honest. Even the secondary characters—notorious gang member Taz; Clay's son, the liberal environmentalist; Bailey's overprotective, hovering brothers—are multilayered and three-dimensional. Evocative, moving, and riveting, this book showcases Shay's powerful writing style.

Of her novels, Shay names two that were harder to write than the others. Her 2003 novel *Trust in Me* (2003) has scenes of intense spousal abuse that were very difficult for her to put into words. Nevertheless, this novel is also one of her favorites. In *Trust in Me*, the Outlaws, a gang of teenage hoodlums, kept the police of Glen Oaks busy. Inseparable as youths, their lives become connected again as adults. Ironically, Linc, their former leader, has become a minister; but he never stopped loving his high-school sweetheart, Margo, who is, unfortunately, an atheist. Linc's sister, Beth, the widow of race car driver Danny, is raising a troubled teenage boy on her own. Tucker Quaid, the driver most people feel is responsible for Danny's death, has been asked by the town council to use his fame as a racing celebrity to woo NASCAR to Glen Oaks. Linc's former best friend, Joe, who has been divorced by his wife, Annie, because of his physical and mental abuse, is back in town—rehabilitated but filled with guilt. Annie, however, refuses to forgive him. This is a book about all aspects of human emotion, and it's done so well that the reader experiences the longing, guilt, joy, and despair of each character. Linc's never-ending inner battle between his deep religious faith and his lifelong love for a woman who doesn't believe in God gives him a special vulnerability as he reaches into the depths of his soul for strength and refuses to consummate their relationship. Shay expertly and sensitively shares the power of love and friendship in this unforgettable, emotion-packed story.

In 2005's *Nothing More to Lose,* a passionately dedicated firefighter suffers a career-ending injury on 9/11. Shay admits, "I cried writing most of that book." Ian Woodward, one of the firefighter heroes of the 9/11 terrorist attack, has been crippled both physically and emotionally since that terrible incident. His brother-in-law, Noah Callahan (*On the Line,* 2004), talks Ian into teaching at the Hidden Cove Fire Academy. Having become a so-called poster child for self-pity, Ian ends his relationship with Broadway actress Lisel Loring. After having a nervous breakdown, she returns to Hidden Cove, where she is still stalked by a relentlessly obsessed fan. Lisel hires ex-cop Rick Ruscio to protect her, ignoring the fact that he has left the force in disgrace. Rick can't devote himself full-time to Lisel's welfare—he has to do community service at a preschool, where he meets teacher Faith McPherson. Like Ian, Rick has also lost his belief in himself, and Faith tries to restore his self-confidence. Self-acceptance is a long journey away for these men, but the redemptive power of love puts them back on the right track. Shay's insightful treatment of this subject is a realistic adaptation of the fallout that infamous event had on people's lives.

Shay says her easiest novel to write, and also one of her favorites, is 1998's *Cop of the Year,* because she "knew so much about the topic." High school English teacher Cassie Smith is devoted to helping her at-risk students. After all, she had been one herself, and if it hadn't been for the dedication of a very special teacher, Cassie's life might have taken a different and self-destructive turn. Mitch Lansing, a police officer, also does work in the classes for at-risk students. Both Cassie and Mitch are concerned about the increasing influence of gang members in the school. Unfortunately, their philosophies and approaches to the problem collide—he's a cop who goes strictly by the rules, and she's a teacher who believes that it's alright to bend them. Shay's extensive experience as a teacher comes into play in this gripping story about committed educators who tackle a very real issue in today's classrooms.

Some people are keen observers of the human condition. Some people are outstanding writers. Shay's compelling oeuvre is a sterling example of what happens when both talents reside in the same person.

BIBLIOGRAPHY

Books: *The Father Factor.* Toronto: Harlequin, 1995; *A Suitable Bodyguard.* Toronto: Harlequin, 1996; *Just One Night.* Toronto: Harlequin, 1997; *Michael's Family.* Toronto: Harlequin, 1997; *Because It's Christmas.* Toronto: Harlequin, 1998; *Cop of the Year.* Toronto: Harlequin, 1998; *The Man Who Loved Christmas.* Toronto: Harlequin, 1999; *Feel the Heat.* Toronto: Harlequin, 1999; *A Christmas Legacy.* Toronto: Harlequin, 2000; *Finally a Family.* Toronto: Harlequin, 2000; *Code of Honor.* Toronto: Harlequin, 2000; *The Fire Within.* Toronto: Harlequin, 2001; *Count on Me.* Toronto: Harlequin, 2001; *Practice Makes Perfect.* Toronto: Harlequin, 2002; *Promises to Keep.* New York: Berkley, 2002; *A Place to Belong.* Toronto: Harlequin, 2002; *After the Fire.* New York: Berkley, 2003; *Against the Odds.* Toronto: Harlequin, 2003; *Trust in Me.* New York: Berkley, 2003; *On the Line.* New York: Berkley, 2004; *The Unknown Twin.* Toronto: Harlequin, 2004; *Nothing More to Lose.* New York: Berkley, 2005; *Our Two Sons.* Toronto: Harlequin, 2005; *A Time to Give.* Toronto: Harlequin, 2005; *Someone to Believe In.* New York: Berkley, 2005; *Tell Me No Lies.* Toronto: Harlequin, 2006; *Ties That Bind.* New York: Berkley, 2006.
Novellas: "Men at Work" in *Lipstick Chronicles.* New York: Penguin, 2003; "Taking Care of Business" in *More Lipstick Chronicles.* New York: Berkley, 2004.

SHELLEY MOSLEY AND SANDRA VAN WINKLE

CHRISTINA SKYE

Christina Skye. Courtesy of Christina Skye.

Christina Skye never intended on becoming a best-selling romance author, but then again, she never thought she would some day eat snake meat in Shanghai or dine on armadillo in Canton. Somehow and somewhere, Skye's original plans to enter the world of academia and teach at the university level changed, leaving romance readers delighted they did.

Skye was born Roberta Kaye Helmer in Dayton, Ohio, in 1950. Her father was a teacher, and her mother a textile designer. She grew up in Dayton, eventually attending boarding school in Lake Forest. In 1972, she graduated cum laude from the University of Pennsylvania with distinction in her major of Chinese studies and married Christopher Stallberg. Skye continued her education at Ohio State University, where she received a master's degree and then a PhD in Chinese language and literature.

Just as she was poised to enter the working world, Skye discovered the limited job market for someone with her special skills. With only three career choices available—working for the CIA, working for the State Department, or teaching at a small women's college in Kansas—Skye instead choose to set off for Peking to work as a translator for an international petroleum consortium.

Her otherwise dull experience as a technical translator did have some memorable moments. It was in China that Skye sampled foods she never would have found in any small college cafeteria. There was also the time her boss issued an ultimatum for her to help him smuggle two ladies of so-called dubious virtue into the highly guarded State Guest House. Despite her best efforts to convince the armed People's Liberation Army soldiers that the ladies were secretarial help to assist in the drafting of a trade document, Skye found that even her experienced translating skills were not going to sell this piece of creative fiction. Hoping to avoid any personal experience with the Chinese penal system, she decided it would be a good time for another career change.

Returning to the United States, Skye picked up a contract to finish a book on Chinese arts and crafts. After that, she went on to complete four books on classical Chinese culture and several articles for academic journals. When a group of classically trained Chinese puppeteers came to America for the first time in 1980, Skye became their tour manager and translator.

It was in 1989 that Skye turned to writing fiction. She had always loved Regency romances, so the genre seemed to be an obvious choice for her first romance. However, from the very beginning she chose to bend the conventions of the historical Regency sub-genre, usually by adding Asian elements to her stories. In 1990, her first romance, *Defiant Captive,* was published; it was followed by *The Black Rose* in 1991.

Like *Defiant Captive,* Skye's other early historicals strongly reflect her deep interest in Asian culture. The exotically intriguing Ceylon with its tea-growing culture becomes one of the settings in *The Ruby* (1992), as Barrett Winslow finds romance in the arms of Deveril Pagan, the Tiger Sahib. Chessy Cameron, the martial arts expert and heroine of *East of Forever* (1993), needs the help of Tony Morland to locate a fabulously jeweled, erotic Chinese pillow book.

Come the Night (1994) is the first in a two-book set by Skye featuring the Delamere family whose "wealth was beyond measuring and their eccentricities beyond numbering." In this passionate tale of romance and danger, Silver St. Clair's search for her family's secret formula for a rare lavender-based perfume called Millefleurs puts her in the path of England's most notorious highwayman, "Luc" Delamere.

Skye then used Luc's sister, India Delamere, as the heroine of *Come the Dawn* (1995). Devlyn Carlisle, the man India had secretly married, was believed to have died in battle, and India is crushed. But when her missing war-hero husband returns a year later, claiming he has no knowledge of their past relationship, the stubborn English beauty must find a way to restore his memories or lose the only man she can ever love.

Skye's next book represented a significant change for an author who was quickly gaining a reputation for her compelling, richly adventurous, and exotic historical romances. *Hour of the Rose* (1994) introduced readers to Draycott Abbey and became the first in Skye's much-beloved series set at the magical, haunted stately home that is guarded by the ghostly Adrian and his magical cat-companion, Gideon.

Hour of the Rose would be followed by six more Draycott Abbey romances and one novella set in the haunted abbey. Rare wines, legendary relics, roses, time travel, a priceless Whistler painting, a hint of humor, and a generous measure of danger all show up in one or another of the Draycott books. Juggling such a diverse array of elements was not easy, and Skye found *Christmas Knight* (1998), one of the Draycott romances, to be a particularly challenging book to write. The heroine, Hope O'Hara, is about to lose the thirteenth-century Scottish home she has lovingly restored and turned into a bed-and-breakfast, when the hero, medieval knight Ronan MacLeod, is sent forward 700 years in time to save her. Balancing the contemporary voice of Hope with the historical voice of Ronan, as well as writing a romance from such different points of view, wasn't easy; but Skye did a superior job with this poignant, beautifully written time-travel romance.

With *2000 Kisses* (1999), Skye's writing turned toward contemporary romantic suspense as she became inspired by the predictions of just what a new millennium would do to the nation's computers. In *2000 Kisses,* public relations expert Tess O'Mara discovers that a million dollars has been added to her bank account. Believing the money to be a bonus from her wealthy client, she proceeds to spend the money until she discovers something odd—and possibly dangerous—about the deposit. Soon she is sent into hiding in the small town of Almost, Arizona, and tangles with the local sheriff, T. J. McCall; but she finally realizes that she's going to need serious help when the men who put the money into her account come looking for it.

More sexy, humorous contemporary romantic suspense novels followed with *Going Overboard* (2001), *My Spy* (2002), and *Hot Pursuit* (2003)—all of which feature Navy SEAL heroes. *Hot Pursuit* gave Skye the opportunity to show just what the life of a writer is really like, as the heroine, best-selling mystery author Taylor O'Toole, finds herself mixed up in the search for a traitor.

Whether it's adventurous historical romances set in exotic locations; a story about a mystical, magical English Abbey that brings together star-crossed lovers; or sexy romantic suspense lightened with an edge of humor, Christina Skye has taken on a multitude of formats with success. She has proved that with a good education, an obsession for research, and a talent for writing, the possibilities for creating entertaining stories are limited only by an author's imagination.

BIBLIOGRAPHY

Books: *Defiant Captive.* New York: Dell, 1990; *The Black Rose.* New York: Dell, 1991; *The Ruby.* New York: Dell, 1992; *East of Forever.* New York: Dell, 1993; *Come the Night.* New York: Dell, 1994; *Hour of the Rose.* New York: Avon, 1994; *Come the Dawn.* New York: Dell, 1995; *Bridge of Dreams.* New York: Avon, 1995; *Bride of the Mist.* New York: Avon, 1996; *Key to Forever.* New York: Avon, 1997; *Season of Wishes.* New York: Avon, 1997; *Christmas Knight.* New York: Avon, 1998; *The Perfect Gift.* New York: Avon, 1999; *2000 Kisses.* New York: Dell, 1999; *Going Overboard.* New York: Dell, 2001; *My Spy.* New York: Dell, 2002; *Hot Pursuit.* New York: Dell, 2003; *Code Name: Nanny.* New York: Dell, 2004; *Code Name: Princess.* New York: Dell, 2004; *Code Name: Baby.* Toronto: Harlequin, 2005; *Code Name: Blondie.* Toronto: Harlequin, 2006.

Novellas: "Enchantment" in *Avon Books Presents: Haunting Love Stories.* New York: Avon, 1991; "What Dreams May Come" in *Avon Books Presents: Bewitching Love Stories.* New York: Avon, 1992.

JOHN CHARLES AND JOANNE HAMILTON-SELWAY

BERTRICE SMALL

The sobriquet of "Lust's Leading Lady," while often applied to Bertrice Small by both critics and fans, does a disservice to the emotionally fulfilling romances written by the legendary author. Small's novels of beautiful heroines of intelligence and courage and the men who love them bring sixteenth- and seventeenth-century history alive with the sights, sounds, smells and colors of England, Scotland, and other more exotic settings. To read the first book in the Skye O'Malley series is to enter a world populated by fascinating, powerful characters—a world that continues through myriad books. Skye's family—children and siblings, cousins and in-laws—grows until the O'Malley family tree becomes as familiar as the reader's own (and a lot more exciting).

Born Bertrice Williams in Manhattan in 1937, Small was the daughter of two broadcasters. She graduated from St. Mary's School in Peekskill, New York, and attended Western College for Women in Oxford, Ohio, and the Katherine Gibbs Secretarial School. Her marriage to George Sumner Small IV, a photographer and designer, produced one son, Thomas. She worked as a secretary at Young and Rubican Advertising in New York and also as a sales assistant for Weed Radio and Television and Edward Petry and Company, both radio/television representatives. She became a freelance writer in 1969.

Small's romance-writing career began with her first book, *The Kadin,* published in 1977. *The Kadin* tells the story of the beautiful Lady Janet Leslie, who is abducted from her homeland and sold into slavery to the Sultan Selim. There, she assumes a new identity as Cyra Hafise, mistress to a sultan. Small's brilliance in evoking the historical locations of sixteenth-century Scotland and Turkey, and the depth of her characters, created a multitude of fans. Luckily, they didn't have to wait long for Small's next book, *Love Wild and Fair* (1978), which continued the story of the Leslie family with Cyra's beautiful great-granddaughter, Cat. The themes of these books—an independent woman struggling to escape the lust of a powerful ruler and her ability to survive and thrive through intrigue, danger, and a whole host of hazards—are echoed in the other books that followed.

Small launched her well-known and much-loved O'Malley series in 1980, with *Skye O'Malley,* featuring the beautiful and feisty title character. Skye, born in Ireland in 1540, finds happiness with four different men, is a rival to Queen Elizabeth I, and manages to survive the political intrigues of Elizabethan England. Considered a classic romance by many reviewers and readers, the book is filled with real historical characters; smoldering, sensual love scenes; and vivid descriptions of exciting locales. Skye is a lively and compelling character whose adventures and progeny would keep readers enthralled through 12 books. Small has said that she didn't intend to write a series, because "series were not, with one or two exceptions, particularly marketable. But Skye was a phenom." And fans agreed.

The last book with a connection to Skye O'Malley was published in 2003 as the final chapter of Small's O'Malley series. *Vixens* introduces readers to the great-great-granddaughters of the legendary Skye and details their entrance into the glittering world of Restoration England. Divided into three parts, the book features the romantic escapades of three beautiful, young cousins. Tragic widow Frances Devers, nicknamed "Fancy," catches the attention of the king, lusty Charles II, while Fancy's cousin Diana "Siren" Stuart must choose between identical twins. Cynara "Sin" Stuart falls in love with a cynical earl and must pursue him and convince him to love her. When Small informed her fans that this book would be the last one in the O'Malley series, they were bereft. The fans couldn't get enough of the O'Malley clan, whose five generations had absorbed 12 books and spanned 130 years of history.

In 1999, Kensington launched its Brava imprint with an anthology dedicated to erotic romance. Small was a natural choice for the first collection, *Captivated,* which proved to be so popular with readers that Kensington issued three more—*Fascinated* (2000), *Delighted* (2002), and *I Love Rogues* (2003)—with Small as a contributor to each.

In 2002, Small began another series, The Friarsgate Inheritance, with *Rosamund* as the first book. Rosamund Bolton is the heiress to the magnificent estate on the border between England and Scotland, known as Friarsgate. Her scheming uncle wants the estate and plans to wed the twice-widowed Rosamund to his son. Rosamund's quick thinking, as well as the patronage of King Henry VII, rescues her from this fate. Sharing similar traits with Skye O'Malley, Rosamund Bolton is a worthy heroine to carry Small's new series.

With more than thirty historical romances, several erotic novellas, and a loyal following to her credit, Small took a creative risk by branching out into the contemporary romance subgenre. Her first and only contemporary novel, *Private Pleasures,* published in 2004, is an erotic tale of revenge. It tells the story of devoted housewife Nora Buckley, who turns to her women friends for comfort when she learns her husband is trading her in for a younger model. Their consolation includes a secret that unleashes her wildest, wickedest fantasies; but everything has a price, as the reader discovers.

It has been said that Bertrice Small puts the sense in sensuality, as she involves all of the senses in her writing. Her descriptions of the rich fabrics of the costumes, the scents and flavors of the food and drink, and the vividly erotic love scenes boldly bring history and her characters to life, delighting her legions of fans and winning her new readers with each book she writes.

BIBLIOGRAPHY

Books: *The Kadin.* New York: HarperCollins, 1977; *Love Wild and Fair.* New York: HarperCollins, 1978; *Adora.* New York: Random House, 1980; *Skye O'Malley.* New York: Random House, 1980; *Unconquered.* New York: Random House, 1982; *Beloved.* New York: Random House, 1983; *All* *the Sweet Tomorrows.* New York: Random House, 1984; *This Heart of Mine.* New York: Random House, 1985; *A Love for All Time.* New York: Penguin, 1986; *Enchantress Mine.* New York: Penguin, 1987; *Blaze Wyndham.* New York: Penguin, 1988; *Lost Love Found.* New York: Random House, 1989; *The Spitfire.* New York: Random House, 1990; *A Moment in Time.* New York: Random House, 1991; *Wild Jasmine.* New York: Random House, 1992; *To Love Again.* New York: Random House, 1993; *Love Remember Me.* New York: Random House, 1994; *The Love Slave.* New York: Random House, 1995; *Hellion.* New York: Random House, 1995; *Betrayed.* New York: Random House, 1997; *Deceived.* New York: Kensington, 1998; *Darling Jasmine.* New York: Kensington, 1998; *Bedazzled.* New York: Kensington, 1999; *The Innocent.* New York: Random House, 1999; *A Memory of Love.* New York: Random House, 2000; *Besieged.* New York: Kensington, 2000; *Intrigued.* New York: Kensington, 2001; *The Duchess.* New York: Random House, 2001; *Just Beyond Tomorrow.* New York: Kensington, 2002; *Rosamund.* New York: Penguin, 2002; *Vixens.* New York: Kensington, 2003; *Until You.* New York: Penguin, 2003; *The Dragon Lord's Daughters.* New York: Kensington, 2004; *Private Pleasures.* New York: Penguin, 2004; *Philippa.* New York: Penguin, 2004; *The Last Heiress.* New York: Penguin, 2005; *Lara.* Toronto: Harlequin, 2005; *A Distant Tomorrow.* Toronto: Harlequin, 2006.

Novellas: "Ecstasy" in *Captivated.* New York: Kensington, 1999; "Mastering Lady Lucinda" in *Fascinated.* New York: Kensington, 2000; "The Awakening" in *Delighted.* New York: Kensington, 2002; "Zuleika and the Barbarian" in *I Love Rogues.* New York: Kensington, 2003.

JOANNE HAMILTON-SELWAY

JENNIFER SMITH. *See* Jennifer Crusie

JENNIFER CRUSIE SMITH. *See* Jennifer Crusie

SHARON STEWART. *See* Sharon Swan

LAEL ST. JAMES. *See* Linda Lael Miller

TINA ST. JOHN

True love does conquer all in Tina St. John's vividly detailed and richly emotional medieval romances, but St. John is also interested in exploring the theme of a person finding their true place in the world. Fortunately for St. John's heroes and heroines, that place is next to the person each loves.

The eldest of three siblings, St. John was born in 1966 in Hastings, Michigan. Her father's family came from New England, and included among their ancestors is Mayflower passenger William Bradford, governor of Plymouth Colony. After serving in the Army, St. John's father relocated to Michigan, where he met St. John's mother, a recent immigrant from Germany. St. John grew up in Michigan, moving around the state whenever her father was transferred. After attending public schools in Michigan, St. John went on to college and expected to become a psychologist; but a part-time summer job working for a large auto manufacturer led St. John to postpone college in favor of entering the workforce full-time.

St. John held a variety of jobs before becoming a writer, including receptionist, secretary, executive assistant to the president of a multimillion-dollar corporation, technical writer, and others. All these jobs "prepared me for the business side of being an author—and their endless monotony inspired me to entertain myself with some of the stories I am currently working to put down on paper," she says.

Since her two favorite things were reading and writing, St. John had always dreamed of one day being a writer, but St. John never thought her dream job could actually become a real career. She says, "The odds of that happening seemed enormous—how could I, a small-town college dropout, ever make it past the door of a New York City publisher?" For St. John, the push to become a writer came from her very own real-life hero, her husband. The two have been inseparable since they first met, 18 years ago; after they had known each other for 8 years, they were married. St. John's husband knew how important her dream of becoming a writer was, and he offered to support her so that she could quit her corporate job and devote herself full-time to writing.

While St. John was an avid reader, she didn't always read romances: "I read one when I was sixteen, and although I loved the high emotion and titillating sensuality of that book, my tastes at that time ran more toward supernatural thrillers. It wasn't until I began toying with ideas of my own that I realized how great the pull was for me toward relationships and strong alpha-male heroes. It seemed like all my ideas had a very powerful romantic thread to them, so I began exploring the genre, buying tons of romances, and discovering all the great books and authors I'd been missing."

Her first attempt at writing was a Civil War–era romance, but after three chapters, St. John realized her true love was medieval romances. So she switched gears and spent the next two years writing what would become *Lord of Vengeance,* which she sold to Ballantine in 1998. St. John found her first book to be the most difficult for her to write. It was a learning experience, she says, "mainly because I had never written a complete novel before, and I wasn't sure that I could do it." St. John's first historical is a wonderful variation on the classic captor/captive romance. The hero, Gunnar Rutledge, seeks vengeance against Lord D'Bussy, the man he holds responsible for his parents' deaths. When Gunnar takes D'Bussy's daughter, Raina, hostage, he never expects to fall in love with the daughter of his enemy.

Published in 2002, St. John's fourth medieval historical romance was *Black Lion's Bride,* which, she says, "started out as a cross between *La Femme Nikita* and the *Arabian Nights.*" The book's heroine, veiled beauty Zahirah bint Sinan, is a medieval assassin who meets her match in Sebastian of Montborne, "the Black Lion," who is a secondary character from St. John's *White Lion's Lady* (2001), who is off on Crusades with his king. St John's research for *Black Lion's Bride* led her to information about a group called the Assassins, a radical Isma'ili sect, and its leader, Rashid al-Din Sinan, known as the "Old Man of the Mountains." After discovering this, St. John began wondering, what if there had been a female assassin in this sect? Thus came the idea of her heroine. St. John found *Black Lion's Bride* to be the easiest of her books to write. She says, "The conflict between the two main characters was so complex and layered—both the external and internal conflicts stemming from who these people were and what they represented to each other—the book had built-in momentum."

St. John believes the one trait that must be found in any romantic hero is honor.

> I certainly strive to endow each of my heroes with that trait. Not all of them are upstanding members of society; in fact, at first glance they are generally the least approachable, least compassionate characters in the book. They are gruff, tough men of action—often loners at heart, even if they are surround by admirers and people dependent on their numerous skills. But at their core, each of these men has a deep sense of honor—a code they will not compromise. It is this inner resolve that intrigues their respective heroines, making [the heroines] dig a little deeper [and] push past their womanly fears in an effort to understand these enigmatic, compelling men.

A perfect example of this is Braedon le Chasseur from St. John's *Heart of the Hunter* (2004). A dangerous, ruthless man with a past he would like to forget, Braedon somehow still finds himself helping the book's heroine, Lady Ariana of Clairmont, in her mission to deliver the ransom needed to free her kidnapped brother. Even when presented with several opportunities to abandon Ariana, Braedon's own personal code of honor ensures that he sees her safely to the end of her journey.

In contrast, St. John characterizes her heroines as follows: "A good heroine must possess two key traits: courage and compassion. She must be stalwart enough to face the difficult, often frightening man who will become her hero, and she must be sympathetic enough to want to understand him. She is the only woman who can break through his defenses, and that always takes an enormous amount of strength and, often, forgiveness." Ariana is an excellent illustration of this as she struggles to understand Braedon, and it is her love for him that ultimately redeems Braedon.

The Middle Ages is clearly a time period that intrigues St. John. She says, " It's such a distant mirror—far enough behind us that we can imagine it as a wild, untamed time, yet paradoxically, a time when honor and chivalry were held in highest regard. The medieval era is magical to me, and a rich source of ideas for characters and stories." St. John has taken this magic and shared it with her readers.

BIBLIOGRAPHY

Books: *Lord of Vengeance*. New York: Ballantine, 1999; *Lady of Valor*. New York: Ballantine, 2000; *White Lion's Lady*. New York: Ballantine, 2001; *Black Lion's Bride*. New York: Ballantine, 2002; *Heart of the Hunter*. New York: Ballantine, 2004.

JOHN CHARLES

DEB STOVER

Deb Stover. Courtesy of Deb Stover.

Deb Stover says she prefers to "write into a mist with as little planning as possible." As a 10-time *Romantic Times* award nominee, plus the winner of a 2005 *Romantic Times* Career Achievement Award, her technique appears to be working.

Growing up in Wichita, Kansas, Stover always wanted to be a writer. After high school, she attended college intermittently in pursuit of a journalism degree, while also raising a family, acting as an advocate for students with disabilities, and working at a local newspaper.

She has been writing full-time since 1993 and sold her first romance, *Shades of Rose,* in 1995. In this time-travel novel, pediatrician Dylan Marshall stands to inherit his grandfather's property in Serenity Springs, as long as he moves into the old family cabin as stipulated in the will and lives there for 30 days. No sooner does Dylan arrive than he meets a beautiful ghost, Rose, who is rumored to haunt the cabin. He recognizes her as the lover who has been tantalizing him in his dreams. Dylan suddenly finds himself in a time warp, drawn back into the past where he has the opportunity to apply his skills as a doctor, changing his own future by changing history. In doing so, Dylan is able to bring the woman out of his dreams and into his life.

Stover enjoys the freedom that writing offers as well as being able to create stories and characters uniquely her own that she can share with her readers. She likes the romance genre's emphasis on rich character development. She comments, "I think romance novels delve into character much more deeply than any other fiction genre." Stover's writing encompasses a variety of settings and styles, including romantic fantasies, mysteries, historicals, contemporary romances, and time-travel stories. She finds story ideas everywhere.

The historicals written by Stover are usually set in Victorian America, after the Civil War but before the twentieth century. These titles include *Stolen Wishes* (1999), and *No Place for a Lady* (2001).

Stover's contemporary romances include *Mulligan Stew* (2002) and *Mulligan Magic* (2003), which are set in Ireland. Elements such as a mysterious haunted castle, Caislean Dubh, and its fabled curse add texture to the stories. In *Mulligan Stew*, bad things happen in threes for Bridget Mulligan. She learns that her grandmother, Granny Frye, has died penniless, and that their trailer home is in foreclosure. Bridget then learns that her husband, Culley, whom she thought had abandoned her the day after their wedding, is actually dead. Their marriage had been so brief that his personal effects were sent to his next of kin in Ireland, whom Bridget has never met. Nevertheless, they invite Bridget and her son, Jacob, to stay with them. Kiley Mulligan, Culley's brother, has his suspicions about Bridget and her intentions for the family's wealth and intends to prove that she's an imposter. Still, there's no denying the strong family resemblance in her son. Before long, Kiley begins to see Bridget through kinder eyes, and the two fall in love. This tale has many conflicts—mistrust versus faith, a family curse versus a hopeful future, and self-loathing versus the redemptive power of love—which Stover seamlessly weaves together, along with their resolutions, to make a happy ending.

Mulligan Magic is the story of Maureen Fazzini, the widowed matriarch of the Fazzini crime family, who seeks the assistance of former police officer Nick Desmond in staging her death. Maureen wishes to escape to Ireland with her granddaughter, Erin, to raise her away from the mob lifestyle. In exchange, Maureen will provide Nick with evidence that will clear his name, restore his badge, avenge his father's death, and destroy the Fazzini family syndicate. Maureen hires Nick to be her bodyguard under the guise of a nephew as she and Erin settle in Ballybrounagh, Ireland. Meanwhile, Maggie Mulligan has also moved to Ballybrounagh, in search of a teaching position; but depressed local economic conditions threaten cutbacks that would include closing the local school. When Maggie meets the irresistibly handsome Nick, things start looking up. However, while the attraction between them grows, eerie things are happening in Ballybrounagh, such as when the two begin to hear whispers that seem to travel on the wind. The atmosphere of the book is one in which Stover deftly contrasts the other-worldly Irish countryside and the harsh realities of a village in trouble.

Another Dawn (1999), also a paranormal story, was inspired by some old political science notes and articles Stover discovered while cleaning out a file cabinet. They told of a young man who had survived the electric chair, only to be taken back again for execution. The story intrigued her and became the premise for her fifth, and favorite, book. After 11 years in prison, Luke Nolan faces execution in the electric chair for a crime he didn't commit. An equipment malfunction causes an explosion that sends Luke hurtling back in time, to the aptly named town of Redemption, Colorado, in the year 1891. Accompanying him is the beautiful young woman who had been tearfully witnessing his near-execution. Recovering from the explosion, Luke takes the identity of a priest who was killed in the blast, and he suspects that the woman lying unconscious, whose bracelet identifies her only as Sophie, is the deathwatch doctor. As Sophie regains consciousness, she can't remember anything prior to the explosion and doesn't recognize Luke as the man from the electric chair. Luke and Sophie discover that their arrival in Redemption couldn't be more timely. The town is in the middle of a smallpox epidemic, where Sophie's medical skills are desperately needed. As she and Luke work closely together providing comfort and aid to the sick and dying, Sophie develops a strong attraction to the impostor priest, and despite her terrible misgivings, is unable to stop the love that grows between them. Love transcends time in Stover's touching novel about a man given a second chance.

Stover describes her heroes as men who exhibit "honor above self," and her heroines as "earthy and sassy." No glitz or glamour here. While her books aren't written with a recurrent theme, one of Stover's readers noted that her novels often deal with justice and retribution—something Stover hadn't intended but with which she is inclined to agree. She concedes, "They do, at least on some level."

The writing method used by Stover involves creating a synopsis and characters for her agent to market; the story writing follows. She avoids overplotting the story, which she feels diminishes the magic of writing. Stover says most of her stories begin with "an inciting event" involving one or more characters, which forms the basis of the plot. The rest of the story unfolds from there. Her cure for writer's block is to write ahead, starting a new scene a few chapters later; she then returns to the problem area to close the gap in the action.

Of all her books, Stover chooses the time-travel story *Some Like It Hotter* (1997), often described as Dirty Harry meets Scarlet O'Hara, as the most difficult to write because of its darkness and intensity. Officer Mike Faricy strikes a deal with the devil to avenge the death of his partner and finds himself transported into the post–Civil War era, where he will be able to kill the murderer's forefather. Mike lands unconscious in the home of Abigail Kingsley, whose life has been ravaged by the war. Mike offers to help Abigail get back on her feet in exchange for room and board, while he secretly plots the demise of his adversary. Mike knows that as soon as he completes his mission, Satan will take his soul. The only hope for Mike is if the love he feels for Abigail is strong enough to dissuade him from his vendetta and ultimately save his life.

Stover's easiest book to write was 2000's *A Moment in Time*. It was written on a short three-month deadline, but despite the time crunch, Stover says that "the words flowed easily." Stover describes the end result as "an outrageous romp, and not a story to be taken seriously." While hiking back to town after her date deserts her during a disastrous weekend in the mountains, sassy hairdresser Jackie Clarke takes a wrong turn into a ghost town, where she becomes transported back in time to the year 1891. Jackie finds herself in Devil's Gulch, Colorado, where she is mistaken for a famous saloon singer, Lolita Belle. Unable and unwilling to play the part, Jackie escapes; but the saloon keeper hires Cole Morrison, a gold miner and single father, to retrieve her. Cole is offered a sizable reward that he could certainly use to supplement his meager mining income and help provide for his son, Todd. When Cole locates the lovely "Lolita," he kidnaps her and heads back to Devil's Gulch to claim his reward. Along the trail, their passions flare, and Cole realizes that the love of this priceless beauty is worth more to him than any ransom.

Stover has taken the paranormal genre and demonstrated a remarkable sense of versatility and refreshing willingness to explore the many subgenres of romance. Even though as an author, Stover likes to "fly into a mist," she invariably makes her writing journey so fascinating that her readers don't care where she takes them; they're just delighted to be along for the ride.

BIBLIOGRAPHY

Books: *Shades of Rose.* New York: Kensington, 1995; *A Willing Spirit.* New York: Kensington, 1996; *Some Like It Hotter.* New York: Kensington, 1997; *Almost an Angel.* New York: Kensington, 1997;

Another Dawn. New York: Kensington, 1999; *Stolen Wishes.* New York: Kensington, 1999; *A Matter of Trust.* New York: Kensington, 2000; *A Moment in Time.* New York: Kensington, 2000; *No Place for a Lady.* New York: Kensington, 2001; *Mulligan Stew.* New York: Jove, 2002; *Mulligan Magic.* New York: Jove, 2003; *The Gift.* New York: Dorchester, forthcoming.

Novellas: "The Enchanted Garden" in *A Dangerous Magic.* New York: DAW, 1999; "Citizen Daisy" in *Some Enchanted Evening.* New York: Kensington, 2002; "Punkinella" in *Vengeance Fantastic.* New York: DAW, 2002; "Skin Deep" in *Irresistible Forces.* New York: New American Library, 2004; "Keeper of the Well" in *Murder Most Romantic.* New York: Gramercy, 2004.

SANDRA VAN WINKLE

DIANA STUART. *See* Jane Toombs

OLIVIA SUMNER. *See* Jane Toombs

SHARON SWAN

Sharon Swan. Courtesy of Sharon Swan.

A chance meeting with Hollywood sex symbol Pierce Brosnan at a Phoenix, Arizona, shopping mall gave Sharon Swan a close-up look at a living, breathing romance legend and inspired her to begin writing love stories. Her resulting first novel, *Daring Dreams,* was never published, but it ignited a passion for writing that led to the books that followed.

Sharon Swan was born Sharon Amelia Swearengen to an all-American, blue-collar Chicago family in 1942. Her father was a truck driver, and her mother an office worker. She grew up on the colorfully storied South Side of Chicago and, like many young girls, dreamed of becoming a dancer. Swan graduated from Kelly High School and attended DePaul University, where she took classes in psychology and history.

The award-winning Swan credits her success as a writer to her mother, who would often read to her and who encouraged Swan to develop her own love of books. She makes a point to write every day, even if it's only one sentence. According to Swan, her favorite part of the writing process is watching the characters develop before her eyes. She is fascinated by the way they practically come to life and control the direction of the plot to its eventual happy ending. Swan's heroes are take-charge, alpha guys, and her heroines possess an abiding inner strength, not unlike her own. Wimpy damsels in distress need not apply.

---

also writing as Sharon Stewart

Swan says she finds inspiration for her stories from everyday life and by imagining, "What if …" Fellow authors who inspire her writing include Susan Elizabeth Phillips, Nora Roberts, and Jayne Ann Krentz. Having spent much of her life in large cities, Swan prefers to write about the ambience and intimacy of small towns in her stories. Her preferred setting is the American Southwest, often Arizona. A frequent theme in Swan's books is family and the importance of family ties.

Using the pseudonym Sharon Stewart, Swan began her writing career with the publication of *Love for Sale,* written for Harlequin's Love and Laughter line in 1997. Her sense of humor shines in this book about Matthew Kent, a decidedly nonromantic fellow who finds himself the half owner of a store devoted to all things romantic. On the other hand, Rachel McCarthy, Matthew's partner, is a firm believer in love and all of its trappings. The delightful ending finds Matthew a changed man and a hopeless romantic himself.

The nom de plume Sharon Swan first appeared in 2002 with the book *Cowboys and Cradles,* Swan's first title with the Harlequin American line. This is the novel she says was the easiest to write since "everything just fell into place." Once again, Swan's humor enlivens the pages as ranch foreman Ryder Quinn comes to grips with new owner Eve Terry's plan to turn the spread into a day-care center.

Swan's most difficult novel, and her sentimental favorite, is *Husbands, Husbands … Everywhere* (2002), because of its proximity to the tragic events of Sept. 11. She recalls that she was near the midpoint of this novel when the event occurred, and it was difficult to continue writing about hope and happy endings; but when she did, she wrote with far greater emotion. In this book, Abby Prentiss has a fiancé and is the guardian of an orphaned baby when she finds out that her former husband, Ryan Larabee, is at her aunt's bed-and-breakfast. Ryan, who is suffering from amnesia, has no idea who Abby is. The characters are multilayered and have realistic emotions, while the humor in this book is apparent but more subtle than in her previous novels.

Home-Grown Husband (2002) begins Swan's Welcome to Harmony series, which is set in the small town of Harmony, Arizona. This book features widow Tess Cameron, mother of 10-year-old Ali. Tess hasn't had a date for three years. Since Ali is spending the summer with her grandparents, Tess feels that she has the freedom to start dating again. Former border patrol agent Jordan Trask is trying to figure out what he wants to do with his life. Tess lacks self-confidence, especially where her looks are concerned, and Jordan doesn't want to race to commitment. Swan deftly balances their angst with humor by staging a poorly timed, unexpected visit from Ali and her grandmother.

Despite Swan's ready sense of humor, she also skillfully deals with more serious themes. *Husband in Harmony* (2004), for example, tackles the theme of divorced fathers and their relationships with their children. The importance of family ties is also the theme of *Four-Karat Fiancée* (2003), where businesswoman Amanda Bradley discovers that she has four younger half siblings and that they need a home. A solution appears when her business rival, Dev Devlin, suggests they marry and provide a family for the children.

In 2003's *Her Necessary Husband,* Ross Hayward decides to run for mayor. However, he realizes that if the public finds that his beautiful housekeeper, Jenna Lorenzo, lives in his home, the perception of scandal might cost him the election. Coincidentally, Ross has two young daughters who need a mother, so he does the logical, politically correct thing and proposes marriage to Jenna. Once again, Swan's theme is family.

Swan's favorite pastime is reading, and she encourages aspiring writers to do the same. Her advice is to "write what you love to read." She echoes writer and theorist Joseph Campbell's mantra, "Follow your bliss," which is exactly what she's done.

BIBLIOGRAPHY

Writing as Sharon Swan

Books: *Cowboys and Cradles.* Toronto: Harlequin, 2002; *Home-Grown Husband.* Toronto: Harlequin, 2002; *Husbands, Husbands ... Everywhere.* Toronto: Harlequin, 2002; *Four-Karat Fiancée.* Toronto: Harlequin, 2003; *Her Necessary Husband.* Toronto: Harlequin, 2003; *Husband in Harmony.* Toronto: Harlequin, 2004.

Writing as Sharon Stewart

Book: *Love for Sale.* Toronto: Harlequin, 1997.

SANDRA VAN WINKLE AND SHELLEY MOSLEY

JAYNE TAYLOR. *See* Jayne Ann Krentz

VICKI LEWIS THOMPSON

Vicki Lewis Thompson. Photo by Rembrandt Photography. Courtesy of Vicki Lewis Thompson.

S exy love scenes, strongly defined characters, and a nicely handled sense of humor are all hallmarks of Vicki Lewis Thompson's impressive list of romances. Thompson's engaging and clever heroines and rugged, classic heroes have made her stories popular reads in both series and single-title forms.

Vicki Lewis Thompson was born in Willimantic, Connecticut, in 1944. Her father was a psychologist, and her mother an English teacher, which Thompson says "explains nearly everything about her." Thompson grew up all over the United States as her family followed her father's career teaching at different colleges around the country.

Thompson attended the University of Arizona where she graduated with a master's degree in English literature. Thompson had wanted to be a writer ever since she was eight, but the only jobs she thought writers could earn a living at were teaching and journalism—so naturally she tried both. Thompson didn't like being in a classroom anymore than kids do, so she eventually left the teaching profession. She then spent three years writing for the *Territorial,* a weekly newspaper published in Tucson. While Thompson enjoyed writing for a newspaper, she found some of her editor's ideas for potential stories a bit scary in terms of the amount of research and time involved.

---

also writing as Cory Kenyon

Thompson's husband was responsible for getting her started writing romances. He happened to notice an article in the *Territorial* about the formation of a local chapter of the Romance Writers of America in Tucson. Because of a scheduling conflict, Thompson could not attend the first meeting, so her husband went in her place. He also bought Thompson her first Harlequin romances to read, and after reading these contemporary romances, she discovered how much she had been missing. These romances helped reacquaint her with just how fun reading could be, and she says they changed her previous "snobby English major misperceptions" of the romance genre. Thompson interviewed the Tucson chapter's founder, Mary Tate Engels, for the newspaper and was so impressed by her that she joined the chapter and decided to try writing a romance herself.

Even though Thompson had a background in literature and experience as a journalist, writing her first romance was not easy. In fact, she found the process of writing that romance so intimidating that she says she "used a reporter's notebook and pretended she was taking dictation." Thompson's first romance never did sell, but her second one found a publisher in 1983. Harlequin wanted the book for their new line called Project 229, which eventually became the series line known as Harlequin Temptation.

When Harlequin rejected the third book she submitted, Thompson, being a new and somewhat naïve author, was certain her career as a romance writer was over. When she voiced her concerns to Mary Tate Engels, Engels convinced Thompson to coauthor a romance for the romance line she had been writing for, Dell Ecstasy. Engels and Thompson would go on to write a total of five romances as Cory Kenyon for Dell before the publisher closed its Ecstasy line. They sold one coauthored book to Harlequin, but found that their style did not quite fit the tone of the Temptation line at the time.

Meanwhile, Thompson discovered that Harlequin liked her writing as she continued to sell on her own to a variety of different lines, including Harlequin Superromances and Harlequin Love and Laughter. Most of Thompson's books were published as novels in the Harlequin Temptation line since her sexy, humorous contemporary romances were a natural fit for this line.

Not only did Thompson's publisher and readers like her writing, but fellow writers also recognized her talent. Her 1984 title *Promise Me Sunshine,* became her first book to be nominated for the Romance Writers of America's RITA award. Then in 1986, *When Angels Dance* (1985) was nominated for a RITA, too. The following year, *Butterflies in the Sun* (1986) became her third romance to be nominated for a RITA. By 2002, eight of Thompson's romances had been nominated for the prestigious RITA award.

When Harlequin introduced their Blaze line of contemporary romances in 2001, Thompson was asked to launch the line with her sexy romance *Notorious.* Rancher Noah Garfield, who meets up with Keely Branscom, the so-called bad girl of his youth, mistakes her profession based on his past impressions of her. The story is the perfect example of Thompson's type of romance with its skillful writing, smoldering love scenes, strong characters, and deft use of humor.

In May of 2003, *Nerd in Shining Armor,* the first of Thompson's single-title romances, was published. A droll, playful romp that features a geeky hero stranded on a deserted island with a provocative, sexy heroine, *Nerd in Shining Armor* brought Thompson to the attention of a new and wider audience of romance readers—especially once it was chosen by popular daytime talk-show host Kelly Ripa as one of her book club picks in June 2003. With the wild success of this book, four other Nerd books followed (*The Nerd Who Loved Me,* 2004; *Nerd Gone Wild,* 2005; *Gone with the Nerd,* 2005; *Talk Nerdy to Me,* 2006), each with its own rich cast of unforgettable secondary characters, such as the retired Vegas showgirls in *The Nerd Who Loved Me.* Whether it is one of her old series titles or her new single-title romances, readers can be certain that Thompson will continue to provide them with the sexy, humorous books they crave.

BIBLIOGRAPHY

Writing as Vicki Lewis Thompson

Books: *Mingled Hearts.* Toronto: Harlequin, 1984; *Promise Me Sunshine.* Toronto: Harlequin, 1984; *When Angels Dance.* Toronto: Harlequin, 1985; *An Impractical Passion.* Toronto: Harlequin, 1985; *Butterflies in the Sun.* Toronto: Harlequin, 1986; *The Fix-It Man.* Toronto: Harlequin, 1986; *As Time Goes By.* Toronto: Harlequin, 1986; *Golden Girl.* Toronto: Harlequin, 1987; *Cupid's Caper.* Toronto: Harlequin, 1987; *Spark.* Toronto: Harlequin, 1988; *The Flip Side.* Toronto: Harlequin, 1988; *Impulse.* Toronto: Harlequin, 1988; *Connections.* Toronto: Harlequin, 1989; *Be Mine, Valentine.* Toronto: Harlequin, 1989; *Full Coverage.* Toronto: Harlequin, 1989; *'Tis the Season.* Toronto: Harlequin, 1989; *Forever Mine, Valentine.* Toronto: Harlequin, 1990; *Your Place or Mine?* Toronto: Harlequin, 1991; *It Happened One Weekend.* Toronto: Harlequin, 1991; *Anything Goes.* Toronto: Harlequin, 1992; *Ask Dr. Kate.* Toronto: Harlequin, 1992; *Critical Moves.* Toronto: Harlequin, 1992; *Only in the Moonlight.* Toronto: Harlequin, 1993; *Fools Rush In.* Toronto: Harlequin, 1993; *Loverboy.* Toronto: Harlequin, 1994; *Wedding Song.* Toronto: Harlequin, 1994; *The Bounty Hunter.* Toronto: Harlequin, 1994; *Adam Then and Now.* Toronto: Harlequin, 1995; *The Trailblazer.* Toronto: Harlequin, 1995; *The Drifter.* Toronto: Harlequin, 1995; *The Lawman.* Toronto: Harlequin, 1995; *Holding Out for a Hero.* Toronto: Harlequin, 1996; *Hero in Disguise.* Toronto: Harlequin, 1996; *Stuck with You.* Toronto: Harlequin, 1996; *One Mom Too Many.* Toronto: Harlequin, 1997; *Going Overboard.* Toronto: Harlequin, 1997; *Mr. Valentine.* Toronto: Harlequin, 1997; *The Heartbreaker.* Toronto: Harlequin, 1997; *Santa in a Stetson.* Toronto: Harlequin, 1997; *Operation Gigolo.* Toronto: Harlequin, 1998; *Manhunting in Montana.* Toronto: Harlequin, 1998; *Single in the Saddle.* Toronto: Harlequin, 1998; *Single Sexy … and Sold!* Toronto: Harlequin, 1999; *Pure Temptation.* Toronto: Harlequin, 1999; *With a Stetson and a Smile.* Toronto: Harlequin, 1999; *Bachelor Father.* Toronto: Harlequin, 1999; *Bringing Up Baby New Year.* Toronto: Harlequin, 1999; *Colorado Kid.* Toronto: Harlequin, 2000; *Two in the Saddle.* Toronto: Harlequin, 2000; *Boone's Bounty.* Toronto: Harlequin, 2000; *That's My Baby.* Toronto: Harlequin, 2000; *Her Best Friend's Baby.* Toronto: Harlequin, 2001; *Notorious.* Toronto: Harlequin, 2001; *Every Woman's Fantasy.* Toronto: Harlequin, 2001; *The Nights Before Christmas.* Toronto: Harlequin, 2001; *Acting on Impulse.* Toronto: Harlequin, 2002; *Truly, Madly, Deeply.* Toronto: Harlequin, 2002; *Double Exposure.* Toronto: Harlequin, 2002; *Drive Me Wild.* Toronto: Harlequin, 2003; *After Hours.* Toronto: Harlequin, 2003; *Nerd in Shining Armor.* Toronto: Harlequin, 2003; *Old Enough to Know Better.* Toronto: Harlequin, 2004; *Killer Cowboy Charm.* Toronto: Harlequin, 2004; *The Nerd Who Loved Me.* Toronto: Harlequin, 2004; *Nerd Gone Wild.* Toronto: Harlequin, 2005; *Gone with the Nerd.* Toronto: Harlequin, 2005; *Talk about Sex ….* Toronto: Harlequin, 2005; *Forever Mine, Valentine.* Toronto: Harlequin, 2006; *Talk Nerdy to Me.* Toronto: Harlequin, 2006.

Novellas: "Valentine Mischief" in *My Valentine.* Toronto: Harlequin, 1992; "Once Upon a Mattress" in *My Secret Admirer.* Toronto: Harlequin, 1999; "Mystery Lover" in *Midnight Fantasies.* Toronto: Harlequin, 2001; "Heaven Scent" in *Behind the Red Doors.* Toronto: Harlequin, 2003; "Illicit Dreams" in *Invitations to Seductions.* Toronto: Harlequin, 2003; "Fooling Around" in *Fool for Love.* Toronto: Harlequin, 2004.

Writing with Mary Engels as Cory Kenyon

Books: *Sheer Delight.* New York: Dell, 1986; *Fortune Hunter.* New York: Dell, 1986; *Ruffled Feathers.* New York: Dell, 1986; *The Quintessential Woman.* New York: Dell, 1987; *Fancy Footwork.* New York: Dell, 1987; *The Nesting Instinct.* Toronto: Harlequin, 1988.

JOANNE HAMILTON-SELWAY

JANE TOOMBS

Although Jane Toombs isn't using a nom de plume now, there was a time when editors thought Toombs wasn't the best name for a romance author, and so she had many pseudonyms. Toombs was born in Los Angeles, California, in 1926. When she was nine months old, her parents, James K. Jamison and Frances Jamison, both teachers, took her to Michigan's upper peninsula, where she grew up. Her father, who became a state representative and deputy auditor general for Michigan, was also an author of nonfiction, primarily history. Toombs became a registered nurse in 1949, with the equivalent of three years of college. She divorced her first husband, and her second husband died. In "Gift of the Century: Jane and Elmer's True Story" in *Millennial Milestones: A Celebration of Change* (2000), published by DiskUs Publishing, Toombs expounds on the present man in her life. She has a blended family of seven children, seven grandchildren, and two great-grandchildren.

Toombs always wanted to be a writer but kept her day job as a registered nurse for many years, even after she began selling her work. Now, she writes full-time. Since she creates her books with a computer, Toombs edits as she goes along and then does one more beginning-to-end edit before finishing the story. However, her goal of 10 single-spaced pages a day quite often ends up as only 5.

What appeals to Toombs most about writing romance is the eternal truth of love. Although she puts male-female relationships her books, they aren't always romances, and those outside the romance genre may not have the requisite "happily ever after" ending. Her heroes solve problems, and the heroines do their best to save themselves.

---

also writing as Olivia Sumner
also writing as Diana Stuart
also writing as Lee David Willoughby
also writing as Rebecca Drury
also writing as Jane Anderson
also writing as Ellen Jamison

Toombs prefers to write about areas where she's lived, which includes New York state, various areas of California, northern Nevada, and Michigan's upper peninsula. She's also written about many places she's never visited, stating that "research is a wonderful tool." For Toombs, any time period makes a good setting, whether it's past, present, or future.

Plot usually comes first in Toombs's writing, although on occasion characters have inspired her. A theme that often runs through her books is the following: "To be happy with another, one must learn to compromise without destroying one's own beliefs." Toombs claims that she's not sure how much of herself appears in her books, but she did include one of her favorite foods, pasties, in *Racing with the Moon* (2003). The pastie recipe appears in *Winging It in the Kitchen* (2003), a cookbook published by Wings ePress.

Since Toombs rarely watches television, her characters don't watch it either. However, they do all sorts of things she's never even tried, such as riding on camels or entering the Iditarod. Her book *Leader of the Pack* (1985) came out the same year a woman won the dogsled race in Alaska. Toombs's heroine could have won but chose to save the hero's life instead.

Besides romances, Toombs has written a nonfiction how-to-write book, *Becoming Your Own Critique Partner* (2006), which she coauthored with Janet Lane Walters; thirteen-plus short stories or novellas; and a novelization of *Knot's Landing* (a popular TV series that ran from 1979 to 1993). An early believer in the potential of the evolving e-book, Jane continues to expand into that market. As for genres, besides contemporary and historical romances, including Regency stories, she writes horror, fantasy, paranormal stories, mystery, and suspense. Over the years, Toombs has won many awards, including two RITA nominations—for *Arapaho Spirit* (1984) and *The Scots* (1984). Toombs often weaves Native American lore into her books and usually puts a touch of the paranormal into almost every book she writes. Her six books for Silhouette's Shadows series were paranormal romances, as was her Moonrunner Trilogy (*Under the Shadow,* 1992; *Gathering Darkness,* 1993; and *Dark Sunrise,* 1997).

Even when Toombs takes on down-to-earth, familiar story subjects, such as babies, she gives each tale a new twist. In *Designated Daddy* (1999), Steve Henderson, a government agent, takes on the responsibility of his ex-wife's child, because she told everyone at the hospital that the baby was his before she died. In *Detective Daddy* (2004), Dan Sorenson not only helps a pregnant woman during a blizzard, but also ends up delivering her baby girl. In *Nobody's Baby* (1997), Zed Adams is accused of being a baby's father, despite the fact he has never met the mother. Of course, no one believes him when his DNA proves positive for paternity.

Toombs's first book, *Tule Witch,* (1973), was the easiest for her to write. It pits an African American nurse against a deranged doctor and a warlock. The nurse is in dire peril until the man she loves comes to her rescue. Of all Toombs's works, her favorite is *The Scots* (1984). This story is about two families who immigrate to the United States in the 1800s; it follows their successes and failures and what happens when a man from each family falls in love with the same woman. It follows the traumatic effect this has on future generations, until at last the breech is healed.

Toombs gets her inspiration everywhere and doesn't suffer from writer's block. If she's having trouble writing, she says it's because she's "not sure what happens next." A day or two away from the computer always solves the problem—Toombs believes in letting her subconscious work on this kind of thing.

With her amazing versatility and willingness to try new formats and venues, Toombs continues to produce outstanding love stories. What she likes best about writing is getting the idea and then finishing the book; it's the in-between part that is work.

BIBLIOGRAPHY

Writing as Jane Toombs

Books: *Tule Witch.* New York: Avon, 1973; *Point of Lost Souls.* New York: Avon, 1975; *A Topaz for My Lady Fair.* New York: Ballantine, 1975; *The Star-Fire Prophecy.* New York: Berkley, 1976; *The Fog Maiden.* New York: Ballantine, 1976; *Chippewa Daughter.* New York: Dell, 1982; *Arapaho Spirit.* New York: Dell, 1983; *Restless Obsession.* Toronto: Harlequin, 1984; *Shadowed Hearts.* Kingston, Ontario: Blue Heron Press, 1984; *The Scots.* New York: Dell, 1984; *Heart of Winter.* New York: Walker Books, 1985; *Creole Betrayal.* New York: Kensington, 1988; *Sunset Temptation.* New York: Kensington, 1989; *Midnight Whispers.* New York: Kensington, 1989; *Doctors and Lovers.* New York: New York: Kensington, 1989; *Riverboat Rogue.* New York: Kensington, 1990; *Rebel's Tender Caress.* New York: Kensington, 1991; *The Emerald Shadows of Seacliff House.* New York: Kensington, 1991; *Dead Silent.* New York: Kensington, 1992; *Traitor's Kiss.* New York: Kensington, 1992; *Under the Shadow.* New York: Silhouette, 1992; *Return to Bloodstone House.* New York: Silhouette, 1993; *Dark Enchantment.* New York: Silhouette, 1993; *Gathering Darkness.* New York: Silhouette, 1993; *What Waits Below.* New York: Silhouette, 1993; *Jewels of the Heart.* New York: Kensington, 1993; *The Volan Curse.* New York: Silhouette, 1994; *Passion's Melody.* New York: Kensington, 1994; *Love's Desire.* New York: Kensington, 1995; *The Woman in White.* New York: Silhouette, 1995; *The Abandoned Bride.* New York: Silhouette, 1995; *Lover's Moon.* New York: Kensington, 1997; *Nobody's Baby.* New York: Silhouette, 1997; *Dark Sunrise.* New York: Silhouette, 1997; *Birds of War.* Jupiter, FL: Kappa Books, 1997; *Golden Chances.* Lake Park, GA: New Concepts Publishing, 1998; *Baby of Mine.* New York: Silhouette, 1998; *Harte's Gold.* England: Robinson Scarlet, 1998; *Accidental Parents.* New York: Silhouette, 1999; *Designated Daddy.* New York: Silhouette, 1999; *Secret Dilemma.* Lake Park, GA: New Concepts Publishing, 1999; *Quoth the Raven.* Lake Park, GA: New Concepts Publishing, 1999; *Wild Mustang.* New York: Silhouette, 2000; *Her Mysterious Houseguest.* New York: Silhouette, 2001; *The Missing Heir.* New York: Silhouette, 2001; *Nightingale Man.* Amherst Junction, WI: Hardshell Word Factory, 2002; *Racing with the Moon.* Richmond, KY: Wings ePress, 2003; *Vigil House.* Lake Park, GA: New Concepts Publishing, 2004; *Detective Daddy.* New York: Silhouette, 2004; *Temple of Time: Forsaken.* Lake Park, GA: New Concepts Publishing, 2004; *Temple of Time: Forbidden.* Lake Park, GA: New Concepts Publishing, 2004; *Night of the Owl.* Richmond, KY: Wings ePress, 2004; *Out of the Blue.* Goose Creek, SC: Vintage Romance Publishing, 2004; *A Beguiling Intrigue.* Wisconsin Rapids, WI: Amber Quill Press, 2005; *The Only One of Its Kind.* Calgary, Alberta: Champagne Books, 2005; *High Risk.* Calgary, Alberta: Champagne Books, 2005; *Dangerous Medicine.* Wisconsin Rapids, WI: Amber Quill Press, 2006; *Tower of Shadows.* Calgary, Alberta: Champagne Books, 2007.

Novellas: "Daughter of the Green Mountain" in *Daughters of the Land.* Bend, OR: Maverick Press, 1988; "The Tarnished Angel" in *Mistletoe Marriages.* Albany, IN: DiskUs Publishing, 1999; "Ghost of Love" in *Millennium Magic: Magical Tales for a New Century.* Amherst Junction, WI: Hardshell Word Factory, 1999; "Gift of the Century: Jane and Elmer's True Story" in *Millennial Milestones: A Celebration of Change.* Albany, NY: DiskUs, 2000; "The Loveland Curse" in *Alien Encounters.* Lake Park, GA: New Concepts Publishing, 2003; "Midnight's Door" in *Shifters.* Lake Park, GA: New Concepts Publishing, 2003; "The Turquoise Mask" in *Tales from the Treasure Trove, Vol. 1.* Casper, WY: Whiskey Creek Press, 2004; "Up the Airy Mountain." (e-story). Lake Park, GA: New Concepts Publishing, 2004; "Winter Enchantment" in *Jewels of the Quill Christmas Anthology.* Casper, WY: Whiskey Creek Press, 2004; "Early Falls the Dew." (e-story). Albany, IN: DiskUs Publishing, 2004; "Gambling Trouble" in *The Trouble with Romance.* Sierra Vista, AZ: Treble Heart Books, 2005; "Beltane Fire." (e-novella). Lake Park, GA: New Concepts Publishing, 2005; "The Turquoise Talisman" in *Tales from the Treasure Trove, Vol. 2.,* Casper, WY: Whiskey Creek Press, 2006; "Return to Deville's Crossing." (e-story). Wisconsin: Chippewa Publishing, 2006.

Novelization: *Moment of Truth* for *Knots Landing,* 1987.

Writing as Olivia Sumner

Books: *A Daring Masquerade.* New York: Kensington,1991; *A Trifling Affair.* New York: Kensington,1992; *An Improper Alliance.* New York: Kensington, 1992; *A Most Unsuitable Bride.* New York: Kensington, 1993; *A Beguiling Intrigue.* New York: Kensington, 1994; *Lord Devlin's Dilemma.* New York: Kensington, 1995; *A Deceptive Bequest.* New York: Kensington, 1996.

Novellas: "The Mischievous Matchmaker" in *In a Mother's Heart.* New York: Kensington, 1992; "Winter Enchantment" in *In a Christmas to Cherish.* New York: Kensington, 1992; "Music of the Heart" in *In a Valentine Embrace.* New York: Kensington, 1995.

Writing as Diana Stuart

Books: *Destiny's Bride.* New York: Berkley, 1978; *Cry for Paradise.* New York: Pocket, 1981; *Prime Specimen.* New York: Silhouette, 1984; *Leader of the Pack.* New York: Silhouette, 1985; *The Shadow Between.* New York: Silhouette, 1986; *Out of a Dream.* New York: Silhouette, 1986; *The Moon Pool.* New York: Silhouette, 1991.

Writing as Lee Davis Willoughby

Books: *The Creoles.* New York: Dell, 1982; *The Outlaws.* New York: Dell, 1984.

Writing as Rebecca Drury

Books: *Blue Glory.* New York: Dell, 1982; *Savage Beauty.* New York: Dell, 1982.

Writing as Jane Anderson

Books: *Deception's Bride.* New York: Kensington, 1998; *Loveland.* New York: Kensington, 1998.

Writing as Ellen Jamison

Books: *And Then Came the Darkness.* New York: Kensington, 1992; *Stone Dead.* New York: Kensington, 1993.

MARION EKHOLM

PAT WARREN

With a literary career spanning nearly twenty years, Pat Warren knows a good romantic story when she writes one, particularly if it is one with a healthy dose of her white-knuckle suspense. Warren had always aspired to become a writer and says she has an early collection of "very bad stories" written longhand in notebooks to prove it. Warren confesses that she's saving them for their "comedic value."

Warren was born and raised in Akron, Ohio, "back when dinosaurs ruled the earth." Her father, Thomas Cox, was a commercial artist, and her mother a homemaker. Following high school, she attended community college in Michigan for a couple of years, taking a variety of evening courses. Before becoming a full-time professional writer, she worked as an executive secretary to the vice president of a bank. She worked for United Airlines and her husband's travel agency for a few years, while also raising four children. In addition to novels, Warren wrote a humorous column in the *Detroit News* for three years. She says prefers the writing life: being able to work comfortably at home, setting her own hours "in my own office with my things around me and my dog, Sammy, sleeping by my desk."

Warren's initial interest was in writing mysteries, until she discovered the appeal of the romance genre. Now, Warren captures the best of both in her romantic suspense novels, which have been inspired by newspapers, television, movies, and even song titles. Her story ideas begin with characters that pop into her mind, and she crafts a plot around them. Once the plot is underway, it drives the action as the romance and suspense build into a single, well-crafted, and exhilarating conclusion.

Warren uses trust as a recurrent theme in her contemporary novels. She says, "If you don't have trust in a relationship, you have nothing." Warren's locales are the places she knows best: Arizona, Michigan, and Florida. She believes that using familiar places makes the writing process easier and that the level of detail makes the story more realistic.

---

also writing as Patricia Cox

For example, *Beholden* (1996) is set in her hometown of Phoenix, where Warren and her husband, Frank, live. In *Beholden,* Warren cites actual street names, locations, and even the name of the local newspaper, which adds a feeling of authenticity to the story.

The ever-popular staples of category romances—cowboys and ranches and secret babies—have also turned up in Warren's books, but she always manages to put her own distinctive spin on them. In *Her Kind of Cowboy* (2004), 20-year-old Abby falls in love with sexy cowboy Jesse. Unfortunately, their young love couldn't survive a terrible accident, and Jesse leaves. Six years later, Jesse returns to Abby and wants to pick up where they left off. Abby now has a daughter, and she's not as sure about getting back together. Warren explores the possibilities of mending a broken relationship and includes scenes from Abby and Jesse's youth to help the reader understand the feelings they had for each other then.

Warren says her heroes are honorable men—not too tough, but not "wimpy" either—and they're often "drop dead gorgeous." In *Forbidden* (1995), Liz Townsend and Senator Adam MacKenzie are reunited after years of separation that began when he chose his political career over their young love. Now that Adam is the front-runner for the vice presidency, their paths cross again, reigniting the flames that still linger between them. Liz is widowed with a daughter, but Adam is caught in a loveless marriage, and his ambitious wife, Diane, isn't about to give him up easily. Diane can sense the longing between Adam and Liz and will do whatever is necessary to stop Adam from leaving when he finds out that Liz's daughter, Sara, is his child.

Warren's heroines are strong women, self-reliant and intelligent, who are secure in their independence but open to love. Terry Ryan, the heroine of *Beholden* (1996), is a political cartoonist who witnesses the murder of a newspaper reporter, and she recognizes the gunman's accomplice as a top-ranking police official. Terrified and knowing she can't report the incident to the authorities, she runs for her life. Within hours, she is traveling with her cousin, Lynn, to a mountain hideaway where she can drop out of sight for a while. En route, the brakes fail on Terry's car, and they are involved in a fiery accident in which Terry is disfigured and Lynn is killed. When the body is mistakenly identified as Terry's, Luke Tanner, a U.S. Marshal sent to protect Terry, uses the opportunity to place her in the Witness Protection Program. However, before long, they're both on the run from a determined killer, and the danger and desperation they experience drives them into the comfort of each other's arms.

Warren has also written characters who have impairments and physical problems not often found in romances. "All kinds of people can be romantic," Warren observes. For instance, in *Bright Hopes* (1992), one of the two books Warren wrote for Harlequin's popular Tyler series, Pam Casals, the heroine, has been named the football coach for Tyler High School. Former all-star Patrick Kelsey is definitely not in favor of having a female coach, even if she is an Olympic gold medalist. However, Pam is an excellent, enthusiastic coach, and not only does Patrick change his opinion—he falls in love with her. No one, not even Patrick, knows that Pam has multiple sclerosis. Pam is afraid that if she shares her terrible secret, she'll lose both her position at the school and the man she loves. Warren's poignant portrayal of a once-healthy young woman now faced with a debilitating condition is written with great sensitivity, and yet Warren's writing is so strong that the reader cheers for the heroine instead of feeling pity for her plight.

Warren feels it's inevitable that a writer's own personality and beliefs are conveyed in his or her characters. "No matter how you try to keep it out, your feelings and thoughts and convictions come out in the people you write about," she says.

Warren's most difficult novel to write was *Til Death Do Us Part* (1992). She says that's because maintaining the proper balance of suspense and romance. "giving each one enough attention and having both come out right in the end," was a challenge. In this story, the heroine is living a dream, happily married to a successful husband and residing in a beautiful home in an exclusive Detroit suburb. But her idyllic life suddenly turns into a frightening reality when her husband becomes her worst nightmare—a relentless killer, who will stop at nothing to eliminate her.

The easiest novel for Warren to write was *My First Love, My Last* (1990) because it reminded her of her own romance. The novel seemingly wrote itself. "I'm drawn to the concept that a first love is the strongest, best love, maybe because it happened to me," she says. Nora Maddox's son, Bobby, has been kidnapped by her dangerously disturbed ex-husband and taken into the rugged Oregon wilderness. Desperate for her son's safe return, Nora is joined in the manhunt by Rafe Sloan, the first and only true love of her life, whom Nora had jilted years before when she suddenly married her now ex-husband. Despite this, Nora senses that the chemistry between Rafe and herself is as strong as ever. Alone deep in the woodlands of Oregon, they must confront their past and consider their future when Rafe learns the truth about Bobby.

Of all her books, Warren's favorite is *No Regrets* (1997). She feels that even though the plot involves a serial killer, the story still has a happy ending. Maggie Spencer is devastated when she learns that her father, a construction company owner, has been killed in a tragic fall; but she doubts that it was simply an accident. The insurance investigator assigned to the case, Ben Whalen, finds himself attracted to Maggie. And together, while their feelings for each other intensify, they uncover the 30-year-old secret that led to the old man's death.

Warren's only experience with writer's block was when she took an editor's rejection to heart. She became filled with self-doubt and dissatisfaction with her writing, which took several months to overcome. With the help of her agent, she was able to understand that her brooding was self-defeating. "Every writer I know remembers the negative comments much longer than the praise," says Warren. This best-selling author's advice to aspiring writers is something she learned early in her own career: "If a person settles on a writing career, they'd better be a self-motivator; well read, especially in the genre they choose; strong enough to handle the rejections that inevitably come their way; and then, smart enough to not allow the praise to go to their head."

BIBLIOGRAPHY

Writing as Pat Warren

Books: *With This Ring.* New York: Silhouette, 1987; *Final Verdict.* New York: Silhouette, 1987; *Season of the Heart.* New York: Silhouette, 1988; *Look Homeward Love.* New York: Silhouette, 1988; *Summer Shadows.* New York: Silhouette, 1988; *The Evolution of Adam.* New York: Silhouette, 1988; *Build Me a Dream.* New York: Silhouette, 1989; *Perfect Strangers.* New York: Silhouette, 1989; *Long Road Home.* New York: Silhouette, 1989; *The Lyon and the Lamb.* New York: Silhouette, 1990; *My First Love, My Last.* New York: Silhouette, 1990; *Winter Wishes.* New York: Silhouette, 1990; *Till I Loved You.* New York: Silhouette, 1991; *An Uncommon Love.* New York: Silhouette, 1991; *Til Death Do Us Part.* New York: Kensington, 1992; *Under Sunny Skies.* New York: Silhouette, 1992; *Bright Hopes.* New York: Silhouette, 1992; *Sunshine.* New York: Silhouette, 1992; *That Hathaway Woman.* New York: Silhouette, 1992; *Simply Unforgettable.* New York: Silhouette, 1993; *Nowhere to Run.* New York: Kensington, 1993; *This I Ask of You.* New York: Silhouette, 1993; *On Her Own.* New York: Silhouette, 1993; *Murder Under the Tree.* New York: Kensington, 1993; *Only the Lonely.* New York: Silhouette, 1994; *A Bride for*

Hunter. New York: Silhouette, 1994; *Outlaw Lovers.* New York: Silhouette, 1995; *Forbidden.* New York: Warner, 1995; *Shattered Vows.* New York: Kensington, 1995; *Nobody's Child.* New York: Silhouette, 1995; *Beholden.* New York: Warner, 1996; *A Home for Hannah.* New York: Silhouette, 1996; *Michael's House.* New York: Silhouette, 1996; *Keeping Kate.* New York: Silhouette, 1996; *No Regrets.* New York: Warner, 1997; *Daddy's Home.* New York: Silhouette, 1998; *Come Morning.* New York: Warner, 1998; *Stand-in Father.* New York: Silhouette, 1998; *Stranded on the Ranch.* New York: Silhouette, 1998; *Daddy by Surprise.* New York: Silhouette, 2000; *The Doctor and the Debutante.* New York: Silhouette, 2000; *The Lawman and the Lady.* New York: Silhouette, 2000; *The Baby Quest.* New York: Silhouette, 2000; *The Way We Wed.* New York: Silhouette, 2001; *Outlaw Lovers.* New York: Silhouette, 2001; *My Very Own Millionaire.* New York: Silhouette, 2002; *A Mother's Secret.* New York: Silhouette, 2003; *Her Kind of Cowboy.* New York: Silhouette, 2004; *The Road Back Home.* New York: Silhouette, forthcoming.

Writing as Patricia Cox

Books: *Forever Friends.* Toronto: Harlequin, 1987; *The Forever Choice.* Toronto: Harlequin, 1989; *Daye and Knight.* Toronto: Harlequin, 1992.

Sandra Van Winkle

SHERI WHITEFEATHER

Sheri WhiteFeather. Courtesy of Sheri WhiteFeather.

S heri WhiteFeather's contemporary novels are deeply rooted in the culture and tradition of the Native American people. Her writing is not only influenced by her husband's Oklahoma Muscogee Creek Indian Nation heritage, but she also researches and writes about many other nations as well, including Cherokee and Comanche. Members of the Native American community have expressed their approval of WhiteFeather's novels, which reaffirm their pride in their heritage. "To me, that's one of the highest compliments I can receive," she comments.

Born in Pennsylvania in 1958, WhiteFeather and her family moved two years later to Southern California, where she grew up in Los Angeles and Orange County. Her father, Frank, a retired truck driver lives, in Laughlin, Nevada. Her mother, Lee, and stepfather, Rick, worked in property management for 25 years. Now in retirement, Rick restores vintage cars, and Lee assists WhiteFeather with her writing research. WhiteFeather met her husband, Dru, while living in Hollywood. An accomplished silversmith and leather craft artisan, he is also an avid wildlife advocate. Many of his interests and activities appear in WhiteFeather's novels.

Before becoming a writer, WhiteFeather worked as a retail manager and a video makeup artist. She also did freelance artwork for Fender Guitars Custom Shop, painting guitar straps and accessories for their Waylon Jennings tribute guitars.

As early as elementary school, WhiteFeather's talent for writing was apparent, but she didn't pursue it until she was in her thirties. As an avid romance reader herself, it seemed the natural writing genre for her with its emphasis on love, family, and lifelong commitments. "It just felt right," she says. WhiteFeather also writes in the romantic suspense genre, with stories that focus on action but that have romantic subplots.

Depending on the characters and plot, WhiteFeather writes in several voices. Some of her novels are dark and serious, and others light and humorous. She often uses California as her location but enjoys researching other places as well. WhiteFeather's settings are contemporary, weaving Native American cultural elements into modern-day plots. She says she finds inspiration for story ideas by "watching the world and analyzing the people in it. " She finds that in sharing their feelings, she is able to develop realism in her characters.

For WhiteFeather, the best part of the writing process is the sense of becoming totally engrossed in it, or as she describes, "losing myself in my work." Writing six to seven days each week, and sometimes 10 to12 hours a day, WhiteFeather takes full-time writing to a new level. The euphoria of creative accomplishment is exhilarating, and it motivates her to continue raising the bar on her writing career. "It makes me appreciate my craft and what I've worked so hard to attain," she says.

Character development precedes plotting in WhiteFeather's writing. Once she can hear the characters' voices, see their faces, and get to know them, she is able to mold the plot around them. WhiteFeather says she writes a bit of her own personality into each of her characters: "My heart is inside them. They're like my children."

WhiteFeather describes her heroes as "strong, yet kind; tough, yet caring." They have a genuine respect for women and know how to treat them right. The title character of *Skyler Hawk: Lone Brave* (2000) is a good example of this. Even though a heroic act has left him with amnesia, Skyler Reed, a rodeo rider, becomes roommates with teacher Windy Hall, who has been the victim of vandals and who needs another person in her home to discourage that from happening again. Windy sees the goodness in Skyler and falls in love with him, ignoring the fact that he doesn't remember who he really is and that he's only supposed to stay for three months. Skyler loves Windy, too; however, he won't make a commitment until his memory has returned, since he fears what he's going to remember. WhiteFeather uses Native American symbolism to play an important part in Skyler's road to self-discovery.

Another such hero is Michael Elk from *Cherokee Dad* (2003), whose missing girlfriend, Heather Richmond, turns up at his doorstep unexpectedly, baby in tow. Having disappeared 18 months earlier, Heather has been on the run with her brother, who is turning state's evidence against the Mafia. She tells Michael that the baby belongs to her brother and his terminally ill girlfriend. However, Michael believes that the baby is really his and Heather's. No matter whom the baby belongs to, Michael has a generous nature—he takes the little boy into his home, and into his heart, never guessing that Heather had miscarried their child. WhiteFeather's theme of family and its importance is beautifully reflected throughout this novel.

WhiteFeather's romance heroines are strong-willed women who long for the "happily ever after" of love, marriage, and family. When she's writing in the suspense genre, her heroines take on a femme fatale quality. She describes them as "beautifully lethal." *Always Look Twice,* a book written for Silhouette's Bombshell line in 2005, features Olivia Whirlwind, a psychic who assists the police in their investigations. The police force wants her to help find the serial killer of Native American women. Her instant attraction to Ian West, the FBI agent assigned to her case, puts her in danger in more ways than one. WhiteFeather brews a perfect blend of multiculturalism, suspense, and, of course, romance in this fast-paced thriller.

Another of WhiteFeather's brave female protagonists is Kelly Baxter, from *Night Wind's Woman* (2000), who has to deal with the birth of her child alone since her boyfriend abandoned her. She retreats to her late grandfather's cabin to think about her future, goes into labor, and is helped through her delivery by neighbor Shane Nightwind, who is half Comanche. Shane has feelings for Kelly and her baby but resists them, believing that the father will come to his senses and return for them. This quietly poignant story is augmented by three-dimensional characterizations and realistic emotions.

No single novel was more difficult for WhiteFeather to write than her others. In general, she considers the beginnings and endings of her books to be the hardest to write. Once the plot is well underway, she finds the middle is easy. She is also reluctant to choose a favorite novel. Each of her books has personal and emotion significance, and WhiteFeather likes them all for different reasons.

The award-winning WhiteFeather is very open and candid about her life. She and her husband overcame drug additions in the 1980s and have survived times of turbulence over the years, growing together and remaining strongly committed as a family. She intends one day to return to college and earn a degree in American Indian studies. The WhiteFeathers have two grown children, a son, Nikki, and a daughter, Brenna.

As so many writers continue to perpetuate the myth of the so-called noble savage and other stereotypical images of Native Americans, WhiteFeather is one of the few who portrays them as real people with real strengths and real weaknesses. She not only entertains with her wonderful stories, but also breaks down stereotypes with each book she writes.

BIBLIOGRAPHY

Books: *Warrior's Baby.* New York: Silhouette, 1999; *Skyler Hawk: Lone Brave.* New York: Silhouette, 2000; *Jesse Hawk: Brave Father.* New York: Silhouette, 2000; *Cheyenne Dad.* New York: Silhouette, 2000; *Night Wind's Woman.* New York: Silhouette, 2000; *Tycoon Warrior.* New York: Silhouette, 2001; *Cherokee.* New York: Silhouette, 2001; *Comanche Vow.* New York: Silhouette, 2001; *Cherokee Marriage Dare.* New York: Silhouette, 2002; *Sleeping with Her Rival.* New York: Silhouette, 2003; *Lone Wolf.* New York: Silhouette, 2003; *Cherokee Baby.* New York: Silhouette, 2003; *Cherokee Dad.* New York: Silhouette, 2003; *The Heart of a Stranger.* New York: Silhouette, 2003; *Cherokee Stranger.* New York: Silhouette, 2004; *A Kept Woman.* New York: Silhouette, 2004; *Steamy Savannah Nights.* New York: Silhouette, 2004; *Always Look Twice.* New York: Silhouette, 2005; *Betrayed Birthright.* New York: Silhouette, 2005; *Apache Nights.* New York: Silhouette, 2005; *Once a Rebel.* New York: Silhouette, 2006; *Never Look Back.* New York: Silhouette, 2006; *Expecting Thunder's Baby.* New York: Silhouette, 2006.
Novellas: "The Dare Affair" in *Summer in Savannah.* New York: Silhouette, 2004.

SANDRA VAN WINKLE AND SHELLEY MOSLEY

SUSAN WIGGS

Susan Wiggs. Courtesy of Susan Wiggs.

All the world's a stage, and two-time RITA winner Susan Wiggs has called a lot of it home. Wiggs was born in 1958 in Olean, New York, to Nick Klist, an engineer, and his wife, Lou, a teacher. The family traveled widely when Wiggs was a child, and she spent her youth in western New York State; Brussels, Belgium; and Versailles, France.

While Wiggs attended public schools when living in the States, she went to private schools during her stints overseas. She received her bachelor's degree in education from Stephen F. Austin State University in Texas and her master's degree from Harvard. In 1980, she married Jay Wiggs, a high school English teacher, and the couple has one daughter, Elizabeth. Before becoming a full-time writer, Wiggs was a math teacher.

Wiggs always wanted to be a writer. She even scribbled stories before she learned how to write. Her favorite book is still *A Book about Some Bad Kids,* based on her and her siblings' misadventures, which she penned at age eight. Wiggs says that was her first "real book." Her first published book, *Texas Wildflower,* a historical romance set against the Machiavellian machinations involved in the fight for Texas statehood, came out 21 years later, in 1987.

Wiggs didn't set out to be a romance writer but says that romance is where she found her voice. She says that the "delicious drama of meeting and falling in love as well as the hopefulness of the final commitment between the hero and heroine" are aspects that drew her to the genre. The common themes that run through her books are the importance of relationships and the healing power of love, though she says this is not deliberate on her part. A new theme has emerged in her later books, which tend to be women's fiction: the complexities of family relationships.

Unlike most authors, Wiggs writes the first draft in longhand. From that, she types a draft that goes through, in her words, "many, many edits." The writing process itself appeals to Wiggs because she gets to create a story out of thin air. For that reason, she finds writing the first draft the most exciting.

Wiggs begins each book with a character, which quickly leads to the plot. An example of this is her heroine, Pippa Trueblood, a fearless street urchin who spends the first scene in *Dancing on Air* (1996) taunting crowds with clever jokes and insults and juggling anything for money, just to stay alive. Pippa's mysterious past becomes the lynchpin for the plot, and the Irish hero, Aidan, The O'Donoghue, Lord of Castleross, finds that it's part of all the intrigue and conspiracy that permeate the court of Elizabeth I.

Each character that Wiggs creates has a little bit of her own personality. With the exception of *Lord of the Night* (1993), which won a RITA award, her heroes usually don't have a lot of darkness in them, and their personalities run the gamut. The heroines in Wiggs's novels are usually realistically flawed or see themselves as flawed, but they are very brave and eventually find their own special strengths. *Halfway to Heaven* (2001), a RITA finalist, features heroine Abigail Cabot, who is a brilliant astronomer with a crippled foot. Mistress Lark in *Vows Made in Wine* (1995) faces great danger as a person rescuing those condemned to death by Queen Mary I, "Bloody Mary." RITA finalist *Circle in the Water* (1994) features a gypsy horse thief, Juliana Romanov. When she interrupts King Henry VIII's royal hunt, the ruler gives arrogant nobleman Stephen de Lacey, Baron of Wimberleigh, a mandate: marry her, or watch her hang. As an outspoken feminist, Wiggs delights in creating heroines who are almost always the smartest character in the book.

Another recurrent theme in Wiggs's novels is fire. Her compelling Great Chicago Fire trilogy explores the effect of the conflagration on the following characters: an heiress kidnapped by a stranger who is hell-bent on revenge (*The Hostage,* 2000); a poor Irish girl and a con artist, who are both at a society party, pretending to be rich (RITA winner *The Mistress,* 2000); and a suffragist who raises a baby that she saved from a burning building only to face a heart-wrenching dilemma years later when she discovers the child's real father is still alive (*The Firebrand,* 2001). In *Miranda* (1996), a historical romance set in Regency London, a woman survives a fiery explosion but has amnesia and finds herself with two suitors—one who wants to marry her and one who wants to murder her. Later, in *The Ocean Between Us* (2004), a contemporary novel featuring a naval officer's family, Wiggs uses a similar device to open the book; but this time, it's on a Navy carrier.

Wiggs is known for her strong openings, having mastered the ability to hook readers from the very first sentence. The following excerpts are just a few examples:

She wore long sleeves to cover the bruises. (*Enchanted Afternoon,* 2002)

Sandro Cavalli's day took a turn for the worse when he walked into the airy, sunlit studio and encountered a naked woman. (*Lord of the Night,* 1993)

Oliver de Lacey had died badly. (*Vows Made in Wine,* 1995)

While Wiggs's openings immediately captivate the reader, the strength of each book in its entirety is what makes her a nationally best-selling author.

For Wiggs, there is no favorite locale or time period. Her books are set anywhere on earth. Likewise, she has written about all sorts of time periods—contemporary, medieval, Tudor,

America's Gilded Age, Regency, Victorian, colonial America. Likewise, Wiggs's varied interests—reading, skiing, travel, knitting, and photography—often show up in her books. Although cooking isn't one of her hobbies, she wrote a book in which the heroine owns a restaurant. Her life as a Christmas tree farmer hasn't appeared in any of her books yet.

The easiest book for Wiggs to write was *The Charm School* (1999), which was named one of Romance Writers of America's Top Ten Favorite Books of the Year. She found two primary sources that laid out all the research for her—a memoir of a sea captain's wife who sailed with her husband; and *House and Street,* a book about Rio de Janeiro in the nineteenth century. From this, she penned a quirky Pygmalion tale about a band of pirates who train a young woman to be a real lady. The Pygmalion theme also shows up in *Halfway to Heaven,* where Jamie Calhoun plays Professor Higgins to Abigail Cabot's Eliza Doolittle.

Wiggs says that the hardest book she's written is *The Ocean Between Us,* which is about a Navy family who has more secrets than the perfect military family they appear to be. According to Wiggs, the intricacies of the military culture were hard to nail. With its focus on the many relationships in a woman's life, this 2004 title leans more toward women's fiction than romance, as do many of her more recent novels. Whether writing romances or women's fiction, Wiggs continues to create books that ensure her a spot among the top writers of the genre.

BIBLIOGRAPHY

Books: *Texas Wildflower.* New York: Kensington, 1987; *Briar Rose.* New York: Avon, 1987; *Moonshadow.* New York: Avon, 1989; *October Wind.* New York: Tor, 1991; *The Raven and the Rose.* New York: Harper, 1991; *The Lily and the Leopard.* New York: Severn House, 1992; *The Mist and the Magic.* New York: Harper, 1993; *Jewel of the Sea.* New York: Tor, 1993; *Lord of the Night.* New York: Harper, 1993; *Kingdom of Gold.* New York: Tor, 1994; *Circle in the Water.* New York: Harper, 1994; *Vows Made in Wine.* New York: Harper, 1995; *Dancing on Air.* New York: Harper, 1996; *Miranda.* New York: Harper, 1996; *The Lightkeeper.* Toronto: Harlequin, 1997; *The Drifter.* Toronto: Harlequin, 1998; *The Charm School.* Toronto: Harlequin, 1999; *Husband for Hire.* Toronto: Harlequin, 1999; *The Horsemaster's Daughter.* Toronto: Harlequin, 1999; *The Hostage.* Toronto: Harlequin, 2000; *The Mistress.* Toronto: Harlequin, 2000; *The You I Never Knew.* New York: Warner, 2001; *The Firebrand.* Toronto: Harlequin, 2001; *Halfway to Heaven.* Toronto: MIRA, 2001; *Passing Through Paradise.* New York: Warner, 2002; *Enchanted Afternoon.* Toronto: MIRA, 2002; *A Summer Affair.* Toronto: MIRA, 2003; *Home Before Dark.* Toronto: MIRA, 2003; *The Ocean Between Us.* Toronto: MIRA, 2004; *Summer by the Sea.* Toronto: MIRA, 2004; *Table for Five.* Toronto: MIRA, 2005; *Lakeside Cottage.* Toronto: MIRA, 2005.
Novellas: "The Trysting Hour" in *Irish Magic.* New York: Kensington, 1995; "Belling the Cat" in *A Purrfect Romance.* New York: Harper, 1995; "The Borrowed Bride" in *This Time … Marriage.* Toronto: Harlequin, 1996; "Cinderfella" in *Merry Christmas, Baby.* Toronto: Harlequin, 1996; "The Changeling" in *Irish Magic II.* New York: Kensington, 1997; "Island Time" in *That Summer Place.* Toronto: MIRA, 1998; "Bridge of Dreams" in *In Our Dreams.* New York: Kensington, 1998; "The St. James Affair" in *It Happened One Christmas.* Toronto: Harlequin, 2003.

SHELLEY MOSLEY

LEE DAVID WILLOUGHBY. *See* Jane Toombs

RACHEL WILSON. *See* Alice Duncan

RUTH WIND. *See* Barbara Samuel

KARYN WITMER. *See* Elizabeth Grayson

REBECCA YORK

Rebecca York. Courtesy of Rebecca York.

For many readers, Rebecca York *is* suspense. York's novels from the 43 Light Street series, written for Harlequin's Intrigue line, provide readers with exactly the kind of compelling blend of passion and danger that romantic suspense fans crave. Even when writing for Harlequin's Blaze line or paranormal romances for Berkley, York finds a way to incorporate a strong measure of suspense into her love stories, so it is no surprise that she has received *The Romantic Times* Career Achievement Award for both Series Romantic Suspense and Series Romantic Mystery.

Rebecca York, a pseudonym for Ruth Glick, was born in Lexington, Kentucky, and grew up in Washington, D.C. Her father was a psychiatrist, and her mother a junior high school science teacher. She recalls having a difficult time in school because she suffered from dyslexia and struggled with reading and spelling. In time, she managed to overcome these difficulties, graduating from Woodrow Wilson High School in Washington, D.C., and earning a bachelor's degree

also writing as Alyssa Howard
also writing as Alexis Hill
also writing as Alexis Hill Jordan
also writing as Amanda Lee
also writing as Samantha Chase
also writing as Tess Marlowe

in American thought and civilization from George Washington University. She went on to earn a master's degree in American studies at the University of Maryland.

York's reading interests had always been science fiction, fantasy, mystery, and adventure. When a friend introduced her to romance novels, she was captivated by the relationships involving only one man and one woman, something she had always looked for in other stories. "I do love to write about a man and a woman falling in love and forging a relationship against a background of suspense and danger," she says. To York, the attraction of the romance genre lies both in the way the entire plot develops around a romantic relationship and the unfailingly happy endings.

Early in her writing career, York wrote under several different pseudonyms, including Alexis Hill, Alexis Hill Jordan, and Amanda Lee, and with several different writing partners. It was in 1986, when York teamed up with Eileen Buckholtz to write together under the name Rebecca York, that she found romantic suspense. Under the pen name Rebecca York, the two authors wrote the 1986 three-book Peregrine Connection series (*Talons of the Falcon, Flight of the Raven, In Search of the Dove*) and then began their 43 Light Street series with *Life Line,* which was published in 1990. The book introduced readers to the now-famous fictional building located at 43 Light Street, where the various offices include the Light Street Detective Agency and the Light Street Foundation. York would continue to write romantic suspense with Buckholtz until 1997, when the partners split to pursue different interests. York now writes under the Rebecca York pseudonym by herself.

York's romantic plots are written in a tense, suspenseful style, and many, such as *Prince of Time* (1995) and *Out of Nowhere* (2004), contain paranormal elements. In *Prince of Time,* the 12th book in the 43 Light Street series, travel agent and State Department operative Cassandra Devereaux meets a man who truly is out of this world when she finds him held captive in a secret underground installation, deep in the Alaskan mountains. *Out of Nowhere,* which is also a 43 Light Street book, features private detective Max Dakota, whose investigation into a smuggling ring in Florida is interrupted by an amnesiac woman who falls off a bridge. Max is forced to choose between rescuing her from drowning and risking that he might blow his cover.

"My main goal is to make sure my readers feel the emotions of my characters," explains York. Her plots usually begin with a story idea that involves characters in dire circumstances who have serious problems to overcome. York says her heroines tend to be "sweet" women, the kind of people her readers would like and respect. She believes they are an idealized version of herself and the kind of person she would like to be. Most of her heroes carry emotional scars from failed relationships in their past. Having been wounded, they're unwilling to trust again, and they steel themselves against new relationships until the healing power of love intervenes. "I put my characters through hell; then I reward them with a long, happy life together," says York.

York's novels are contemporary and are set in places she has visited or with which she is familiar. She says, "I want to get the details right. I usually set the book in the season during which I visited an area so I will know which flowers and plants are blooming." Maryland is a frequent locale, with many of her novels set in Baltimore as well as the small towns and rural areas of Maryland's eastern shore. She has also used settings in southern Georgia's Okefenokee Swamp and her husband's hometown of Santa Barbara, California. York usually has more than one book project going at once, so she doesn't experience writer's block. If she begins having trouble with one book, she simply switches to another. She admits, however, "I dread the blank page." She tries to write her first drafts quickly and devotes considerable time to editing, polishing, and perfecting scenes.

York believes the most difficult book for her to write was *Phantom Lover,* published in 2003 and also part of her 43 Light Street series, in which the hero may (or may not) be a ghost. In *Phantom Lover,* private detective Bree Brennan arrives at Ravencrest, an estate in California, to look into the possible disappearance of Troy London, who hasn't left his rooms in months but is rumored to wander the estate at night. When Bree begins receiving visits from a ghostly lover at night, both she and the reader are never really sure if her phantom lover is a ghost or Troy. Wonderfully atmospheric and spookily suspenseful, *Phantom Lover* is an excellent example of York's gift for mingling suspense with a touch of the supernatural.

While York is best known for the romantic suspense novels she has written for Harlequin's Intrigue line, she has also written for other Harlequin lines, including Blaze. The challenge for York in writing for the Blaze line was to find a way to meld the type of suspense-focused plot she loves with the sexy, push-the-sensual-envelope tone for which Blaze books were created. With *Body Contact* (2002), York pairs an ex-CIA agent with a security expert searching for her employer's missing daughter. With *Bedroom Therapy* (2004), a sex-advice columnist needs the help of a private investigator to keep her safe from a killer. Both books have plenty of the steamy sensuality for which the Blaze books are known, but they also have the strong, suspenseful plots that York's readers have come to expect.

In 2003, York was invited by Berkley to help launch their new imprint, Berkley Sensation, which draws from all romance genres. York wrote a trilogy of werewolf romances for Berkley, including *Witching Moon* (2003), *Killing Moon* (2003), and *Edge of the Moon* (2003). Each book in the trilogy features a strong measure of danger, desire, and the darker side of the paranormal romance subgenre. York's intense, passionate, and genre-blurring Moon books proved to be so popular with readers that the trilogy was continued with another book in 2005, *Crimson Moon,* her 100th book. Her next Berkley novel, *Beyond Control* (2005), introduced telepaths whose powers do not develop until they link sexually with another of their kind.

York and her husband, Norman, have been together for more than forty years, and they have two children, daughter Elissa and son Ethan. They live in Maryland, where York is busy plotting her next enthralling blend of romance and suspense.

BIBLIOGRAPHY

Writing as Rebecca York

Books: *Talons of the Falcon,* New York: Dell, 1986; *Flight of the Raven.* New York: Dell, 1986; *In Search of the Dove.* New York: Dell, 1986; *Life Line.* Toronto: Harlequin, 1990; *Shattered Vows.* Toronto: Harlequin, 1991; *Whispers in the Night.* Toronto: Harlequin, 1991; *Trial by Fire.* Toronto: Harlequin, 1992; *Only Skin Deep.* Toronto: Harlequin, 1992; *Bayou Moon.* Toronto: Harlequin, 1992; *Hopscotch.* Toronto: Harlequin, 1993; *What Child Is This?* Toronto: Harlequin, 1993; *Cradle and All.* Toronto: Harlequin, 1993; *Flight of the Raven.* Toronto: Harlequin Books, 1994; *Midnight Kiss.* Toronto: Harlequin Books, 1994; *Talons of the Falcon.* Toronto: Harlequin, 1994; *Tangled Vows.* Toronto: Harlequin, 1994; *Prince of Time.* Toronto Harlequin, 1995; *In Search of the Dove.* Toronto: Harlequin, 1995; *Till Death Us Do Part.* Toronto: Harlequin, 1995; *Face to Face.* Toronto: Harlequin, 1996; *Father and Child.* Toronto: Harlequin, 1997; *For Your Eyes Only.* Toronto: Harlequin, 1997; *Nowhere Man,* Toronto: Harlequin, 1998; *Shattered Lullaby.* Toronto: Harlequin, 1999; *Midnight Caller.* Toronto: Harlequin, 1999; *Amanda's Child.* Toronto: Harlequin, 2000; *Never Too Late.* Toronto: Harlequin, 2000; *The Man from Texas.* Toronto: Harlequin, 2001; *Lassiter's Law.* Toronto: Harlequin, 2001; *Never Alone.* Toronto: Harlequin, 2001; *Body Contact.* Toronto: Harlequin, 2002; *Gypsy Magic.* Toronto: Harlequin, 2002; *Dark Secrets.* Toronto:

Harlequin, 2002; *From the Shadows*. Toronto: Harlequin, 2002; *Witching Moon*. New York: Berkley, 2003; *Killing Moon*. New York: Berkley, 2003; *Edge of the Moon*. New York: Berkley, 2003; *Intimate Strangers*. Toronto: Harlequin, 2003; *Phantom Lover*. Toronto: Harlequin, 2003; *Out of Nowhere*. Toronto: Harlequin, 2004; *Bedroom Therapy*. Toronto: Harlequin, 2004; *Undercover Encounter*. Toronto: Harlequin, 2004; *Crimson Moon,* New York: Berkley, 2005; *Spellbound*. Toronto: Harlequin, 2005; *Beyond Control*. New York: Berkley, 2005; *Riley's Retribution*. Toronto: Harlequin, 2005; *Life Force*. New York: Berkley, 2006; *Shadow of the Moon*. New York: Berkley, 2006; *Night Terrors*. Toronto: Harlequin, 2006; *Secret Night*. Toronto: Harlequin, 2006; *Full Moon*. New York: Penguin, 2006.

Novellas: "Remington and Juliet" in *Key to My Heart*. Toronto: Harlequin, 1998; "Counterfeit Wife" in *After Dark*. Toronto: Harlequin, 1999; "Tyler" in *Bayou Blood Brothers*. Toronto: Harlequin, 2001; "Wyatt" in *Gypsy Magic*. Toronto: Harlequin, 2002; "Bayou Reunion" in *Witchcraft*. Toronto: Harlequin, 2003; "Jordan" in *Boys in Blue*. Toronto: Harlequin, 2003; "Burning Moon" in *Cravings*. New York: Jove, 2004; "Dangerous Seduction" in *Silk and Magic, Book One*. Cannon City, CO: ImaJinn Books, 2004; "Night Ecstasy" in *Immortal Bad Boys*. New York: Kensington, 2004; "Luke's Story" in *Desert Sons*. Toronto: Harlequin, 2005; "Shattered Dreams" in *What Dreams May Come*. New York: Berkley, 2005; "Second Chance" in *Midnight Magic*. New York: Tor, 2006.

Writing as Alyssa Howard

Books: *Love Is Elected*. New York: Silhouette, 1982; *Southern Persuasion*. New York: Silhouette, 1983.

Writing as Alexis Hill

Book: *In the Arms of Love*. New York: Dell, 1983.

Writing as Alexis Hill Jordan

Books: *Brian's Captive*. New York: Dell, 1983; *Reluctant Merger*. New York: Dell, 1983; *Summer Wine*. New York: Dell, 1984; *Beginner's Luck*. New York: Dell, 1984; *Mistaken Image*. New York: Dell, 1985; *Hopelessly Devoted*. New York: Dell, 1985; *Summer Stars*. New York: Dell, 1985; *Stolen Passions*. New York: Dell, 1985.

Writing as Amanda Lee

Books: *End of Illusion*. New York: Silhouette, 1984; *More Than Promises*. New York: Silhouette, 1985; *Logical Choice*. New York: Silhouette, 1986; *Great Expectations*. New York: Silhouette, 1987; *A Place in Your Heart*. New York: Silhouette, 1988; *Silver Creek Challenge*. New York: Silhouette, 1989.

Writing as Samantha Chase

Book: *Postmark*. New York: Tudor, 1988; *Needlepoint*. New York: Tudor, 1989.

Writing as Tess Marlowe

Book: *Indiscreet*. New York: Silhouette, 1988.

SANDRA VAN WINKLE

ADDITIONAL RESOURCES

BOOKS

Beard, Julie. *The Complete Idiot's Guide to Getting Your Romance Published.* Indianapolis, IN: Alpha Books, 2000.

Borcherding, David H., ed. *Romance Writer's Sourcebook: Where to Sell Your Manuscripts.* Cincinnati, OH: Writer's Digest Books, 1996.

Bouricius, Ann. *The Romance Readers' Advisory: The Librarians' Guide to Love in the Stacks.* Chicago: American Library Association, 2000.

Buck, Gayle. *How to Write and Market the Regency Romance.* Cleveland, OH: Regency Press, 1991.

Estrada, Rita Clay, and Rita Gallagher. *You Can Write a Romance.* Cincinnati, OH: Writer's Digest Books, 1999.

Falk, Kathryn. *How to Write a Romance and Get It Published.* New York: Signet, 1990.

Falk, Kathryn. *How to Write a Romance for the New Markets … and Get Published.* Columbus, MS: Genesis Press Inc., 1999.

Fallon, Eileen. *Words of Love: A Complete Guide to Romance Fiction.* New York: Garland Publishing Inc., 1984.

Gallagher, Rita, and Rita Clay Estrada. *Writing Romances: A Handbook by the Romance Writers of America.* Cincinnati, OH: Writer's Digest Books, 1997.

Grant, Vanessa. *Writing Romance: Create a Bestseller.* Rev. ed. Vancouver, BC: Self-Counsel Press Inc., 2001.

Guiley, Rosemary. *Love Lines: A Romance Reader's Guide to Printed Pleasures.* New York: Facts on File, 1983.

Jaegly, Peggy J. *Romantic Hearts: A Personal Reference for Romance Readers.* 3rd ed. Lanham, MD: Rowman & Littlefield Publishers Inc., 1997.

Krentz, Jayne Ann, ed. *Dangerous Men and Adventurous Women: Romance Writers on the Appeal of the Romance.* Philadelphia: University of Pennsylvania Press, 1992.

Lee, Linda. *How to Write and Sell Romance Novels: A Step-by-Step Guide.* Edmonds, WA: Heartsong Press, 1988.

Little, Denise, and Laura Hayden, eds. *The Official Nora Roberts Companion.* New York: Berkley Books, 2003.

Michaels, Leigh. *Writing the Romance Novel.* Sydney: Publishing and Broadcasting Ltd., 2003.

Mussell, Kay, and Johanna Tunon, eds. *North American Romance Writers.* Lanham, MD: Scarecrow Press, 1999.

Parv, Valerie. *The Art of Romance Writing: Practical Advice from an Internationally Bestselling Romance Writer.* Rev. ed. St. Leonards, Australia: Allen & Unwin, Pty. Ltd., 2005.

Pianka, Phyllis Taylor. *How to Write Romances.* Rev. ed. Cincinnati, OH: F & W Publications, 1998.

Ramsdell, Kristin. *Happily Ever After: A Guide to Reading Interests in Romance Fiction.* Littleton, CO: Libraries Unlimited, 1987.

Ramsdell, Kristin. *Romance Fiction: A Guide to the Genre.* Englewood, CO: Libraries Unlimited, 1999.

Regis, Pamela. *A Natural History of the Romance Novel.* Philadelphia: University of Pennsylvania Press, 2003.

Saricks, Joyce. *The Readers' Advisory Guide to Genre Fiction.* Chicago: American Library Association, 2001.

Vasudevan, Aruna, Lesley Henderson, and Alison Light, eds. *Twentieth Century Romance and Historical Writers.* 3rd ed. Detroit, MI: St. James Press, 1994.

Vinyard, Rebecca. *The Romance Writer's Handbook: How to Write Romantic Fiction and Get It Published.* Waukesha, WI: Writer Incorporated, 2004.

Wainger, Leslie. *Writing a Romance Novel for Dummies.* Hoboken, NJ: John Wiley & Sons, 2004.

Walker, Kate. *Kate Walker's 12-Point Guide to Writing Romance.* London: Studymates Ltd., 2004.

WEB SITES

Romance Writers of America. http://www.rwanational.org.

Romantic Times. http://www.romantictimes.com.

INDEX

ABOUT THE EDITORS AND CONTRIBUTORS

JOHN CHARLES and SHELLEY MOSLEY have both received the Romance Writers of America's Librarian of the Year award (2001 and 2002, respectively) for their work in promoting romance fiction in libraries. Both are two-time recipients of RWA's Veritas Award (1995, 2000) for their journalistic contributions about the genre. In addition, both Mosley and Charles have been reviewing romance fiction for more than seven years for *Booklist* and have been contributing to the romance section of Gale's *What Do I Read Next?* since 1999. Their work has appeared in such journals as *Library Journal, Wilson Library Bulletin,* and *VOYA* (*Voice of Youth Advocates*). Charles writes for *Novelist* and the *Chicago Tribune Book Review.* Mosley and Charles have recently completed a reference book, *The Suffragists in Literature for Youth: The Fight for the Vote* (2006). With Joanna Morrison and Candace Clark, Charles has also written *The Mystery Readers' Advisory: The Librarian's Clues to Murder and Mayhem* (2002). Writing with Deborah Mazoyer as Deborah Shelley, Mosley is a five-time published romance author. Their first novel, *Talk about Love,* was a Holt Medallion finalist. Mosley, now an adjunct reference librarian at Glendale Community College in Arizona, worked at the Glendale Public Library for 24 years, retiring as a branch manager. Charles has been a reference librarian at the Scottsdale Public Library in Arizona for 15 years. Both Charles and Mosley received their master of library science degrees from the University of Arizona.

JOANNE HAMILTON-SELWAY has been a librarian at the Scottsdale Public Library in Arizona for almost 25 years. Named RWA's 2005 Librarian of the Year, Hamilton-Selway has also reviewed books and interviewed authors for more than 10 years as host of the City of Scottsdale's award-winning cable television show *@yourlibrary.* For the past decade, Hamilton-Selway has been in demand for her presentations on both reader's advisory and collection development. Hamilton-Selway received her master's degree in library science from the University of Arizona.

SANDRA VAN WINKLE is a freelance writer who began writing seriously as a bibliographer 20 years ago. She has designed pamphlets for public education. Van Winkle specializes in technical writing and is an experienced grant writer. She has also begun her first novel. Van Winkle received her bachelor of arts degree in public administration from Ottawa University.

MARION EKHOLM, a freelance writer, has published more than a dozen short stories. She has finished three romance novels and edited and written for both academic and religious periodicals. Ekholm, who gives workshops on the technical aspects of writing, received her degree in fine art from the prestigious Rhode Island School of Design.

SHANNON PRESCOTT, a freelance writer, earned her bachelor's degree in creative writing and her master's degree in corporate communications from the University of Arizona.

KRISTIN RAMSDELL is librarian emerita at California State University, East Bay; Romance Writers of America's Librarian of the Year, 1996; romance fiction columnist for *Library Journal*; editor of the romance section Gale's *What Do I Read Next?*; and author of *Romance Fiction: A Guide to the Genre* and *Happily Ever After: A Guide to Reading Interests in Romance Fiction*.